T0235943

Lecture Notes in Computer Science 12695

More information about this subseries at http://www.springer.com/series/7409

Pedro Henriques Abreu ·
Pedro Pereira Rodrigues ·
Alberto Fernández · João Gama (Eds.)

Advances in Intelligent Data Analysis XIX

19th International Symposium on Intelligent Data Analysis, IDA 2021
Porto, Portugal, April 26–28, 2021
Proceedings

 Springer

Editors
Pedro Henriques Abreu 🆔
University of Coimbra
Coimbra, Portugal

Alberto Fernández
University of Granada
Granada, Spain

Pedro Pereira Rodrigues 🆔
University of Porto
Porto, Portugal

João Gama 🆔
University of Porto
Porto, Portugal

ISSN 0302-9743 ISSN 1611-3349 (electronic)
Lecture Notes in Computer Science
ISBN 978-3-030-74250-8 ISBN 978-3-030-74251-5 (eBook)
https://doi.org/10.1007/978-3-030-74251-5

LNCS Sublibrary: SL3 – Information Systems and Applications, incl. Internet/Web, and HCI

This Springer imprint is published by the registered company Springer Nature Switzerland AG
The registered company address is: Gewerbestrasse 11, 6330 Cham, Switzerland

Preface

We are delighted to introduce the proceedings of the 19th International Symposium on Intelligent Data Analysis (IDA 2021). Ten years after its last visit to Porto, Portugal, IDA was back in town for a worldwide scientific event that aimed at exploiting new ideas of and applications for intelligent data analysis. Although it ended up being held completely online, we were delighted that the community chose to have IDA 2021 in Portugal, in a year filled with a wealth of other very important scientific events that were being organized in the country. IDA traditionally limits the presentation to a single-tier meeting, allowing a fruitful discussion without parallel spreading of researchers, but with a research-oriented program which aims at being a forum for high-quality, novel research in intelligent data analysis; this year was not different. The research program also included three invited speakers, namely, Preslav Nakov, Golnoosh Farnadi, and Rebecca Krauthamer, one PhD track, and the well-renowned Frontier Prize.

The event received 113 paper submissions, of which 35 (31%) were accepted for inclusion in the symposium after a round of single blind review, where we managed to collect at least three highly qualified independent reviews per paper. Papers were evaluated on the basis of novelty, technical quality, and scholarship more than significance of contribution in order to allow for breakthrough ideas this volume contains the full papers accepted for presentation at the symposium. The scientific program resulted from continuous collaboration among the General Chairs and Program Chairs, with invaluable overview of the Advisory Chairs, Allan Tucker, Francisco Herrera, and Matthijs van Leeuwen, whom we thank for kindly sharing their experience. We would also like to acknowledge the help of Nathalie Japkowicz in organizing the Horizon Talks and Rita Ribeiro and Sara C. Madeira for managing the PhD track, as well as Eyke Hüllermeier for hosting the Frontier Prize. Throughout we had the unfaltering support of the Local Chairs, Ana Rebelo and Luís Paulo Reis, the Publicity Chairs, José Pedro Amorim and Miriam Seoane Santos, and the Web Chair Ricardo, Cardoso Pereira, who, along with Daniela Ferreira Santos, stepped up to help in the (by then virtual) local organization of the event. The quality of IDA 2021 was only possible due to the tremendous efforts of the Program Committee; we extend our sincere thanks for all the great work and patience which made these proceedings possible. Last but not least, we would like to sincerely thank all the authors who submitted their work to the symposium.

We deeply believe this volume of proceedings will allow you to remember the fruitful and everlasting event that was held in Porto!

April 2021

Pedro Henriques Abreu
Pedro Pereira Rodrigues
Alberto Fernández
João Gama

Organization

General Chairs

João Gama   University of Porto, Portugal
Pedro Henriques Abreu   University of Coimbra, Portugal

Program Chairs

Alberto Fernández   University of Granada, Spain
Pedro Pereira Rodrigues   University of Porto, Portugal

Advisory Chairs

Allan Tucker   Brunel University London, UK
Francisco Herrera   University of Granada, Spain
Matthijs van Leeuwen   University of Leiden, Netherlands

Horizon Talks Chair

Nathalie Japkowicz   American University, USA

PhD Track Chairs

Rita Ribeiro   University of Porto, Portugal
Sara C. Madeira   University of Lisbon, Portugal

Frontier Prize Chair

Eyke Hüllermeier   University of Paderborn, Germany

Local Chairs

Ana Rebelo   Portucalense University, Portugal
Luís Paulo Reis   University of Porto, Portugal

Publicity and Web Chairs

José Pedro Amorim   University of Coimbra, Portugal
Miriam Seoane Santos   University of Coimbra, Portugal
Ricardo Cardoso Pereira   University of Coimbra, Portugal

IDA Council

Matthijs van Leeuwen	Leiden University, Netherlands
Jaakko Hollmen	Aalto University, Finland
Joost Kok	University of Twente, Netherlands
Elizabeth Bradley	University of Colorado, USA
Tijl De Bie	Ghent University, Belgium
Elisa Fromont	University of Rennes 1, France
Frank Höppner	Ostfalia University of Applied Sciences, Germany
Arno Siebes	Utrecht University, Netherlands
Allan Tucker	Brunel University London, UK
Michael Berthold	Konstanz University, Germany
Xiaohui Liu	Brunel University London, UK

IDA Advisory Board

Niall Adams	Imperial College London, UK
Michael Berthold	Konstanz University, Germany
Hendrik Blockeel	KU Leuven, Belgium
Henrik Boström	Stockholm University, Sweden
Jean-Francois Boulicaut	INSA Lyon, France
Elizabeth Bradley	University of Colorado, USA
Paul Cohen	University of Arizona, USA
Tijl De Bie	Ghent University, Belgium
Wouter Duivesteijn	Eindhoven University of Technology, Netherlands
Fazel Famili	University of Ottawa, Canada
Ad Feelders	Utrecht University, Netherlands
Douglas Fisher	Vanderbilt University, USA
Elisa Fromont	University of Saint-Etienne, France
David Hand	Imperial College London, UK
Jaakko Hollmen	Aalto University, Finland
Frank Höppner	Ostfalia University of Applied Sciences, Germany
João Gama	University of Porto, Portugal
Frank Klawonn	Ostfalia University of Applied Sciences, Germany
Arno Knobbe	Leiden University, Netherlands
Joost Kok	University of Twente, Netherlands
Georg Krempl	Utrecht University, Netherlands
Nada Lavrac	Jožef Stefan Institute, Slovenia
Hans-Joachim Lenz	Freie Universität Berlin, Germany
Xiaohui Liu	Brunel University London, UK
Panagiotis Papapetrou	Stockholm University, Sweden
José María Pena	Universidad Politécnica de Madrid, Spain
John Shawe-Taylor	University College London, UK
Arno Siebes	Utrecht University, Netherlands
Carlos Soares	University of Porto, Porto
Stephen Swift	Brunel University London, UK

Allan Tucker   Brunel University London, UK
Antti Ukkonen   University of Helsinki, Finland
Matthijs van Leeuwen   Leiden University, Netherlands
Veronica Vinciotti   Brunel University London, UK
David Weston   Birckbeck, University of London, UK

Program Committee Advisors

Ana Carolina Lorena   Technological Institute of Aeronautics, Brazil
Arno Siebes   Utrecht University, Netherlands
Frank Klawonn   Ostfalia University of Applied Sciences, Germany
Jaakko Hollmén   Aalto University School of Science, Finland
Jerzy Stefanowski   Poznan University of Technology, Poland
Michael Berthold   University of Konstanz, Germany
Mykola Pechenizkiy   Eindhoven University of Technology, Netherlands
Nada Lavrac   Jožef Stefan Institute, Slovenia
Panagiotis Papapetrou   Stockholm University, Sweden
Xiaohui Liu   Brunel University London, UK

Program Committee

Ad Feelders   Utrecht University, Netherlands
Albrecht Zimmermann   Caen-Normandy University, France
Alicia Troncoso   Pablo de Olavide University, Spain
Alina Miron   Brunel University London, UK
Alípio Jorge   University of Porto, Portugal
Ana Nogueira   INESC TEC, Portugal
Andreas Nuernberger   Otto von Guericke University, Germany
Antonio Barata   Leiden University, Netherlands
Arno Siebes   Utrecht University, Netherlands
Baptiste Jeudy   Jean Monnet University, France
Barbara Hammer   Bielefeld University, Germany
Bartosz Krawczyk   Virginia Commonwealth University, USA
Brais Cancela   University of A Coruña, Spain
Brígida Mónica Faria   Polytechnic of Porto, Portugal
Bruno Cremilleux   University of Caen, France
Bruno Veloso   INESC TEC, Portugal
Carlos Ferreira   INESC TEC, Portugal
Carlos Soares   University of Porto, Portugal
Catherine Blake   University of Illinois at Urbana-Champaign, USA
Cèsar Ferri   Polytechnic University of Valencia, Spain
César Teixeira   University of Coimbra, Portugal
Christin Seifert   University of Twente, Netherlands
Cláudia Camila Dias   University of Porto, Portugal
Cor Veenman   Leiden University, Netherlands
Daniel Castro Silva   University of Porto, Portugal

Peter van der Putten — Leiden University, Netherlands
Ricardo Cardoso Pereira — University of Coimbra, Portugal
Ricardo Cerri — Federal University of São Carlos, Brazil
Rita P. Ribeiro — University of Porto, Portugal
Roberta Siciliano — University of Naples Federico II, Italy
Rodrigo Barros — Pontifical Catholic University of Rio Grande do Sul, Brazil
Ronaldo Prati — Federal University of ABC, Brazil
Ruggero G. Pensa — University of Torino, Italy
Rui Camacho — University of Porto, Portugal
Rui Gomes — University of Coimbra, Portugal
Salvador García — University of Granada, Spain
Sara Madeira — University of Lisbon, Portugal
Saso Dzeroski — Jožef Stefan Institute, Slovenia
Shazia Tabassum — University of Porto, Portugal
Solange Rezende — University of São Paulo, Brazil
Sónia Teixeira — INESC TEC, Portugal
Szymon Wilk — Poznan University of Technology, Poland
Thiago Andrade — INESC TEC, Portugal
Tomas Horvath — Eötvös Loránd University, Hungary
Vera Migueis — University of Porto, Portugal

Local Team

José Pedro Amorim — University of Coimbra, Portugal
Miriam Seoane Santos — University of Coimbra, Portugal
Ricardo Cardoso Pereira — University of Coimbra, Portugal
Daniela Ferreira Santos — University of Porto, Portugal

Contents

Modeling Language and Graphs

Modeling with Neural Networks

Hyperspherical Weight Uncertainty in Neural Networks

Biraja Ghoshal$^{(\boxtimes)}$ and Allan Tucker

Brunel University London, Uxbridge UB8 3PH, UK
biraja.ghoshal@brunel.ac.uk
https://www.brunel.ac.uk/computer-science

Abstract. Bayesian neural networks learn a posterior probability distribution over the weights of the network to estimate the uncertainty in predictions. Parameterization of prior and posterior distribution as Gaussian in Monte Carlo Dropout, Bayes-by-Backprop (BBB) often fails in latent hyperspherical structure [1,15]. In this paper, we address an enhanced approach for selecting weights of a neural network [2] corresponding to each layer with a uniform distribution on the Hypersphere to efficiently approximate the posterior distribution, called *Hypersphere Bayes by Backprop*. We show that this Hyperspherical Weight Uncertainty in Neural Networks is able to model a richer variational distribution than previous methods and obtain well-calibrated predictive uncertainty in deep learning in non-linear regression, image classification and high dimensional active learning. We then demonstrate how this uncertainty in the weights can be used to improve generalisation in Variational Auto-Encoder (VAE) problem.

Keywords: Bayesian neural networks · Hyperspherical Weight Uncertainty · Uncertainty estimation

1 Introduction

In Bayesian neural networks, weights are assigned a probability distribution instead of a single value or point estimate like standard neural networks. These probability distributions describe the uncertainty in weights and can be used to estimate uncertainty in predictions. Training a Bayesian neural network via variational inference learns the parameters of these distributions instead of the weights directly. Recently there has been increasing work on scalable approaches to Bayesian deep learning such as:

- Variational Inference: Here, the posterior is approximated over the weights of neural networks through a simple form, for example, independent Gaussians [7]. This technique was generalized by Kingma et al. [10] and is based on a reparameterisation trick for training deep latent variable models, whose parameters are estimated by optimising the expected lower bound on the

© Springer Nature Switzerland AG 2021
P. H. Abreu et al. (Eds.): IDA 2021, LNCS 12695, pp. 3–11, 2021.
https://doi.org/10.1007/978-3-030-74251-5_1

marginal likelihood. On the other hand, training with gradient noise approximates samples from the posterior is proposed by Stochastic gradient Langevian dynamics [16]. Mean-field variational inference methods learn approximate posteriors with full support over the weight-space, which assumes independent weight distributions [8]. Blundell et al. [2] specified variational distribution approximates to the posterior as product of normal distribution using reparameterisation trick with normality assumption. Though the mean field approximation with normal distributions makes the problem scalable, however, normality assumption doubles the number of parameters due to mean and variance, which makes optimization more challenging.

– Regularized Bayesian Approximation: A stochastic regularisation technique (e.g.: Dropout based VI), reinterpreted approximate Bayesian inference in deep Gaussian processes in Bayesian neural networks [5,6], suffers from several issues such as improper use of prior distributions and singular approximating posterior distribution [9].

Bayesian Neural Networks provide a principled approach to estimate the uncertainty of a model [5]. However, Bayesian inference in Neural Networks involves marginalizing over all possible assignments of weights, which is extremely computationally demanding and intractable without approximations. Question is: How do we learn a posterior distribution on network weights (w)? The formulation involves placing a prior distribution over all the parameters of the network, and obtaining the posterior given the input data (D). The distribution of predictions provided by a trained model helps to capture the model's uncertainty. We approximate the true posterior $P(w|D)$ with a variational approximation $q(w|\theta)$ and then optimising θ to minimise the expected lower bound $L(D, \theta)$, the loss function (the sum of a prior-dependent part, called the complexity cost, and a data-dependent part, called the likelihood cost), the Kullback-Leibler (KL) divergence with the true posterior. However, in existing approaches, an approximate Gaussian posterior distribution is practically indistinguishable from uniform distributions on the unit sphere in high dimensions [3], which limits their general applicability in modern deep learning.

2   Background: On Gaussian Distributions

It is known that standard Gaussian distribution in high dimensional space have mass around a Hypersphere far away from the mean like a "soap-bubble" [3] and practically indistinguishable from uniform distribution on the surface of a Hypersphere. An uniform prior over the entire Hypersphere space would only stimulate the variance of the posterior without forcing its mean towards the center. So Bayesian deep learning does not capture the full posterior distribution of the data and the probability assigned to almost all possible weights is exactly zero, leading to sub-optimal learning.

A well-known property of normal distribution is that, it is a centred and normalised random vector, uniformly distributed on an unit sphere [15]. Suppose Hypersphere space $\mathbb{R}^m$, where the dimension m is large. Let I be the m-dimensional identity matrix and consider a normal random vector:

$$\mathbf{X} \equiv (X_1, ..., X_m) \sim \mathrm{N}(\mathbf{0}, \sigma^2 \boldsymbol{I}) \tag{1}$$

Let $\mathcal{S}_r^m \equiv \{\mathbf{x} \in \mathbb{R}^m \mid \sum x_i^2 = r^2\}$ denote the m-dimensional sphere with radius r, then we have:

$$\frac{\mathbf{X}}{||\mathbf{X}||} \sim \mathrm{U}(\mathcal{S}_1^m) \tag{2}$$

It is also well-known that the distribution of the scaled-norm of the random vector is:

$$\frac{||\mathbf{X}||}{\sigma\sqrt{m}} \sim \frac{\chi_m}{\sqrt{m}} \tag{3}$$

Taking $m \to \infty$, the right-hand-side convergences in probability to one. Thus, for large m we have:

$$\mathbf{X} \overset{\mathrm{Approx}}{\sim} \mathrm{U}(\mathcal{S}_{\sigma\sqrt{m}}^m) \tag{4}$$

This shows that when m becomes large, the points from this normal random vector are approximately distributed on the surface of a Hypersphere with radius $\sigma\sqrt{m}$.

3   Hypersphere Bayesian Neural Networks

In high dimensions, Gaussian distributions are practically indistinguishable from uniform distributions on the unit sphere. From an epistemic uncertainty perspective, assigning zero posterior probability almost everywhere is an unreasonable overconfidence. This should be considered as a significant shortcomings in estimating uncertainty in Bayesian Deep Learning.

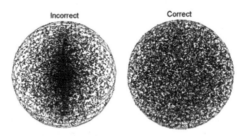

Fig. 1. Comparison of the most common mistake and correct method for learning a probability distribution on the weights of a neural network within the sphere [1]

Blundell, et al. [2] introduced Bayes by Backprop algorithm and used local reparameterisation trick [10] to learn a probability distribution on the weights of a neural network [11, 12]. This means, that the posterior sample of the weights $w \sim q_\theta(w)$ is reparameterised through variational posterior parameters and an auxiliary noise variable. For a Gaussian model, we define weights w_i that the mean μ and add ϵ, multiply it with the standard deviation, as a sample of a standard Gaussian distribution σ. This looks as follows:

$$w_i = t(\theta_i, \epsilon_i) = \mu_i + \sigma_i \epsilon_i \tag{5}$$

where t is the deterministic function with variational posterior parameters $\theta_i = \{\mu_i, \sigma_i^2\}$; as a result, posterior sample of the weights w_i is normally distributed with mean μ_i and standard deviation σ_i^2.

Lemma 1. For $q(w|\theta)$ a Gaussian distribution parameterised by $\theta = (\mu; \sigma)$ such that $w = \mu + \sigma\epsilon$ where $\epsilon \approx N(0, I)$, we have that $q(\epsilon)d\epsilon = q(w|\theta)dw$, where the $q(.)$ are probability density functions and $(.)$ is pointwise multiplication of matrices.

Proof: Firstly, from the definition of $w = \mu + \sigma\epsilon$, we have that $\frac{dw}{d\epsilon} = \sigma$. Secondly, from the definition of the Gaussian probability density function:

$$q(w|\theta) = \frac{1}{\sigma\sqrt{2\pi}} e^{-(w-\mu)^2/2\sigma^2} \tag{6}$$

$$= \frac{1}{\sigma\sqrt{2\pi}} e^{-(\epsilon)^2/2} \tag{7}$$

$$q(\epsilon) = \frac{1}{\sqrt{2\pi}} e^{-(\epsilon)^2/2} \tag{8}$$

Therefore, $\frac{q(\epsilon)}{q(w|\theta)} = \sigma$.

The Algorithm (1) then proceeds by sampling from the variational posterior (possibly several times), computing a forward pass, and backpropagating the loss through the model parameters.

Following [2,4,14], we approximate posterior distribution as follows:

$$w_i = t(\theta_i, \epsilon_i) = \mu_i + \sigma_i \cdot \frac{\epsilon_i}{\|\epsilon_i\|} \tag{9}$$

The distribution is now uniform over the surface of an n-dimensional sphere S^{n-1}. Sample of the weights w from the hyperspace variational posterior can be obtained by:

On line 5, we compute $q(\mathbf{w})$ and $P(w)$ by simply plugging the sample of w back into $q(.)$ and into the prior density function, respectively. $P(w|D)$ is the likelihood of the data given the model, which we compute (as in a typical neural network) by doing a forward pass, for all the training data, and accumulating the total loss according to the loss function. This illustrates the remarkable simplicity of learning a distribution over weights.

In implementation, we have used symmetric sampling technique (i.e.: sampling paired Gaussian noise which differ only by a negative sign) to reduce variance and learning converges faster.

Algorithm 1. Hypersphere Bayes by Backprop

1: **for** all epochs **do**
2:     $\mathcal{F} \leftarrow 0$
3:     **for** $i = 1, 2, \ldots, N$ **do**
4:         Sample $\epsilon \sim \mathcal{N}(0, I)$
5:         Set network parameters to $\mu_i + \sigma_i \cdot \frac{\epsilon_i}{\|\epsilon_i\|}$
6:         Compute $f = \log q(w|\theta) - \log P(w) - \log P(D|w)$
7:         $\mathcal{F} \leftarrow \mathcal{F} + f$
8:     **end for**
9:     $\mathcal{F} \leftarrow \mathcal{F}/N$
10:     Backpropagate $\mathcal{F}$ through the model parameters w
11: **end for**

---

4 Results

4.1 Non-linear Regression

We present some empirical evaluation of the methods on a non-linear regression task in Fig. 2 and Fig. 3. We were curious to explore the ability of Hypersphere weight uncertainty to help in settings where the labelled data is expensive. Finally, we explored the use of our technique in an active learning framework.

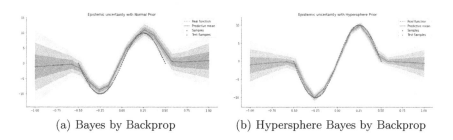

(a) Bayes by Backprop   (b) Hypersphere Bayes by Backprop

Fig. 2. We can clearly see that epistemic uncertainty using Hypersphere prior is lower in regions of training data than it is in region of no training data compared than normal prior

4.2 Image Classification

We examine the effects of replacing the variational posterior on some of the weights with a constant, to determine the level of redundancy in the network, similar to regularised networks using dropout. We took a trained network with two layers of 1200 units and ordered the weights by their signal-to-noise ratio. We removed the weights with the lowest signal to noise ratio. As seen in Fig. 4, the error in Hypershpere Bayes by Backprop network stays almost 50% less compared Bayes by Backprop network even when half of the weights have been removed. However, there is a drop in performance at the same error rate like Bayes by Backprop network once 80% of the weights have been removed.

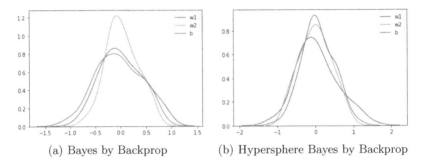

(a) Bayes by Backprop   (b) Hypersphere Bayes by Backprop

Fig. 3. Histogram of the trained weights of the neural network, for Bayes by Backprop [2] and samples from Hypersphere Bayes by Backprop. We can observe that Symmetric sampling technique lower variance gradient estimates.

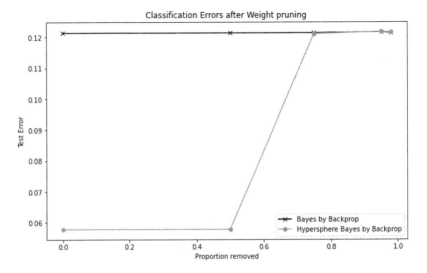

Fig. 4. MNIST classification errors after weight pruning

4.3   Measuring Uncertainty

The Fig. 5(a) shows the histogram of each sample's individual prediction to visualize model's uncertainty on the following five entries from the FMNIST test dataset [13].

The graphs show that Hypersphere Bayes by Backprop (Orange) is highly confident in its overall correct predictions (sampling 100 times from the model), whereas the graph below (Blue) of Bayes by Backprop model was confused i.e.: shows slight uncertainty for the boot and the shirt, as a sneaker is very similar to a boot, and a top is the very similar to a shirt.

The mean weights are also the median and mode weights, because of the choice of a Gaussian distribution for our variational posterior. We can see from

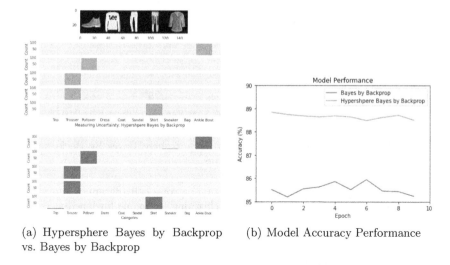

(a) Hypersphere Bayes by Backprop
vs. Bayes by Backprop

(b) Model Accuracy Performance

Fig. 5. Weight uncertainty in FMNIST classification

Fig. 5(b), combining the outputs of samples of Hypersphere Bayes by Backprop (in Orange) model provides a better test accuracy than Bayes by Backprop (in Blue). We have also observed that combining the outputs of samples, Hypersphere Bayes by Backprop model provides 88.76% a better ensemble accuracy than any individual sample (including that from the mean weights), whereas for Bayes by Backprop model ensemble accuracy was 87.84%.

4.4 Active Learning Using Uncertainty Quantification

We have explored the ability of Hypersphere weight uncertainty (i.e.: Algorithm 1) in active learning (AL), where the labelling of data is expensive. In Fig. 6, we found that the use of uncertainty from Hypersphere Bayes by Backprop in active learning shows better performance, which could indicate that Hypersphere Bayes by Backprop was able to request labels with the highest value of information i.e. more certain than Bayes by Backprop.

4.5 Variational Auto-encoders

We have shown the utility of replacing the Gaussian distribution with the Hyperspherical posterior distribution for generating latent representations in Variational Auto-Encoders. Hypersphere Bayes By Backprop outperform normal VAEs with the Gaussian variational posterior in recovering a hyperspherical latent structure. Note that in Fig. 7(a) all mass is concentrated around the center, since the prior mean is zero. Conversely, in Fig. 7(b) all available space is evenly covered due to the uniform prior, resulting in more separable clusters in hyperplane. In high dimensional spaces posterior becomes more expressive due

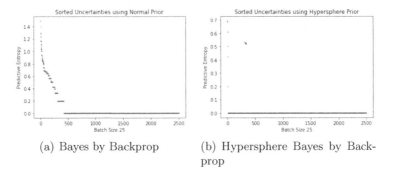

(a) Bayes by Backprop

(b) Hypersphere Bayes by Back-prop

Fig. 6. Ordering MNIST examples by information entropy - Histogram of information entropy of the 2500 samples selected by active learning technique for labelling

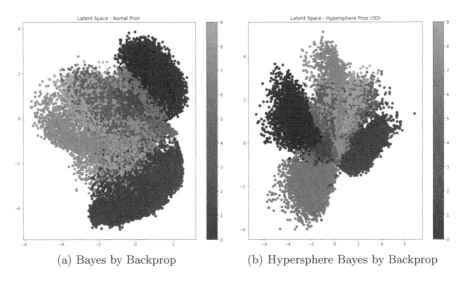

(a) Bayes by Backprop

(b) Hypersphere Bayes by Backprop

Fig. 7. Latent space visualization of the 10 MNIST digits in 2 dimensions of both for Bayes by Backprop VAE [2] and samples from Hypersphere Bayes by Backprop VAE

to the higher number of variance parameters and the Gaussian's density starts to approximate in the outer shell of its Hypersphere.

5   Conclusion

We have addressed the shortcomings and assumptions on variational inference posterior distribution of learning neural networks with uncertainty on the weights called Hypersphere Bayes by Backprop. It optimises an objective function to learn a posterior distribution on the weights of a neural network in high dimensions. We have demonstrated on a simple non-linear regression problem that the uncertainty introduced allows the network to make more reasonable predictions about unseen data. Finally, in active learning, we showed how Hypersphere Bayes by Backprop can automatically request the labels of data with the highest entropy. We demonstrated that estimated uncertainty from Hypersphere Bayes by Backprop have better uncertainty properties - show signs of knowing what model know, and when model does not in higher dimensions.

References

1. Arthur, M.K.: Point picking and distributing on the disc and sphere. Tech. rep, Army Research Laboratory (2015)
2. Blundell, C., Cornebise, J., Kavukcuoglu, K., Wierstra, D.: Weight uncertainty in neural networks. In: Proceedings of the 32nd International Conference on Machine Learning, pp. 1613–1622 (2015)
3. Davidson, T.R., Falorsi, L., De Cao, N., Kipf, T., Tomczak, J.M.: Hyperspherical variational auto-encoders. arXiv preprint arXiv:1804.00891 (2018)
4. Farquhar, S., Osborne, M., Gal, Y.: Radial bayesian neural networks: robust variational inference in big models. arXiv preprint arXiv:1907.00865 (2019)
5. Gal, Y.: Uncertainty in deep learning. Ph.D. thesis, University of Cambridge (2016)
6. Ghoshal, B., Tucker, A., Sanghera, B., Lup Wong, W.: Estimating uncertainty in deep learning for reporting confidence to clinicians in medical image segmentation and diseases detection. Comput. Intell. (2019)
7. Graves, A.: Practical variational inference for neural networks. In: Advances in Neural Information Processing Systems, pp. 2348–2356 (2011)
8. Hinton, G.E., Van Camp, D.: Keeping the neural networks simple by minimizing the description length of the weights. In: Proceedings of the Sixth Annual Conference on Computational Learning Theory, pp. 5–13 (1993)
9. Hron, J., Matthews, A.G.D.G., Ghahramani, Z.: Variational bayesian dropout: pitfalls and fixes. arXiv preprint arXiv:1807.01969 (2018)
10. Kingma, D.P., Welling, M.: Auto-encoding variational bayes. arXiv preprint arXiv:1312.6114 (2013)
11. MacKay, D.J.: A practical bayesian framework for backpropagation networks. Neural Comput. 4(3), 448–472 (1992)
12. Neal, R.M.: Bayesian learning via stochastic dynamics. In: Advances in Neural Information Processing Systems, pp. 475–482 (1993)
13. Nitarshan, R.: Weight uncertainty in neural networks. https://www.nitarshan.com/bayes-by-backprop/ (2018)
14. Oh, C., Gavves, E., Welling, M.: Bock: Bayesian optimization with cylindrical kernels. arXiv preprint arXiv:1806.01619 (2018)
15. Weisstein, E.W.: Hypersphere. https://mathworld.wolfram.com/ (2002)
16. Welling, M., Teh, Y.W.: Bayesian learning via stochastic gradient langevin dynamics. In: Proceedings of the 28th International Conference on Machine Learning (ICML-11), pp. 681–688 (2011)

Partially Monotonic Learning for Neural Networks

Joana Trindade[1]([✉]) [iD], João Vinagre[1,2] [iD], Kelwin Fernandes[3] [iD], Nuno Paiva[4],
and Alípio Jorge[1,2] [iD]

[1] Faculdade de Ciências, Universidade do Porto, Porto, Portugal
amjorge@fc.up.pt
[2] LIAAD - INESC TEC, Porto, Portugal
jnsilva@inesctec.pt
[3] NILG.AI, Porto, Portugal
kelwin@nilg.ai
[4] NOS Comunicações, S.A., Porto, Portugal
nuno.paiva@nos.pt

Abstract. In the past decade, we have witnessed the widespread adoption of Deep Neural Networks (DNNs) in several Machine Learning tasks. However, in many critical domains, such as healthcare, finance, or law enforcement, transparency is crucial. In particular, the lack of ability to conform with prior knowledge greatly affects the trustworthiness of predictive models. This paper contributes to the trustworthiness of DNNs by promoting monotonicity. We develop a multi-layer learning architecture that handles a subset of features in a dataset that, according to prior knowledge, have a monotonic relation with the response variable. We use two alternative approaches: (i) imposing constraints on the model's parameters, and (ii) applying an additional component to the loss function that penalises non-monotonic gradients. Our method is evaluated on classification and regression tasks using two datasets. Our model is able to conform to known monotonic relations, improving trustworthiness in decision making, while simultaneously maintaining small and controllable degradation in predictive ability.

Keywords: Interpretability · Deep Neural Networks · Monotonicity

1 Introduction

In the past few years, the Artificial Intelligence (AI) research community has identified the problem of trustworthiness in Machine Learning (ML) models. Black-box models, such as Deep Neural Networks (DNN) and ensemble models, can achieve high predictive performance, but the complexity of their structure and internal computations are hard to interpret and explain. As a response to this problem, multiple lines of research on interpretability, mostly under the explainable AI (XAI) has become central. One obvious way to boost trustworthiness is to use intrinsically more interpretable models, such as rule- or tree-based

P. H. Abreu et al. (Eds.): IDA 2021, LNCS 12695, pp. 12–23, 2021.
https://doi.org/10.1007/978-3-030-74251-5_2

models. However, black-box models consistently outperform simpler methods in several tasks (e.g., computer vision, language models, and many standard tabular datasets). Besides, simpler models are limited in some level of interpretation and it is not guaranteed that these models always improve interpretability [7].

There are two paths to improve the interpretability of ML models [4]: incorporating prior knowledge in the learning process, also known as *in-model* methods; or using *post-hoc* methods that aim to provide intuitive explanations based on the output generated by the model. The post-hoc approach is the most common for interpreting black-box models. However, according to Rudin [11], the use of post-hoc methods perpetuates a bad practice, which can cause damage to society in high-risk scenarios and, therefore, the in-model approach is more adequate to ensure trustworthy AI [14]. The in-model approach imposes constraints based on domain knowledge, using different types of reasoning: rules, cases, sparsity, or monotonicity. The best technique, or combination of techniques, depends on the application and all of them have some form of trade-off with predictive ability.

In this work, we address interpretability in DNNs by promoting monotonicity, while minimising degradation of predictive ability. We know that monotonic relations (i.e., only vary in one direction) between independent variables and a learned objective function exist in many ML problems, particularly in business contexts. For example, we know that increasing the price of some product or service, without any other change, will very likely reduce sales. Doctors know that higher bad cholesterol levels increase the risk of stroke. However, ML algorithms tend to create non-linear, non-monotonic, and even non-continuous functions to approximate the relations between variables. Even if ML models that do not consider monotonic properties are accurate in most predictions, often provide others that are quite obviously wrong. In critical applications, the consequences can be disastrous. By imposing monotonicity, we can leverage knowledge to obtains more accurate, robust, and trustworthy ML models of the data considered [3].

Our main contributions are the following:

- We propose a generally applicable learning framework to train semi-monotonic neural networks with a loss function that induces monotonicity;
- We conduct an evaluation of existing approaches to monotonic neural networks on two distinct problems: classification and regression.

The remainder of the paper is structured as follows: Sect. 2 presents related work. Section 3 focuses on fundamental concepts and Sect. 4 describes the proposed approach. Section 5 provides details about the datasets, our experimental methodology, the obtained results, and discusses these results. Finally, Sect. 6 concludes this work and addresses future research directions.

2 Related Work

According to [3], one of the taxonomies for monotonic algorithms is based on the generation of predictive models satisfying the monotonic constraints partially or totally. There are several families of predictors depending on the type of model they build, for instance, decision trees or rule-based models, ensembles, support vector machines, and DNN. In the latter, we can find two approaches in the literature to impose monotonicity: (1) by imposing hard constraints on the model's structure and/or parameters, or (2) by applying soft constraints in the training process, e.g. by penalising non-monotonic behaviour. Structural modification in DNNs was first proposed by Archer and Wang [1], who used positive weight constraints. Sill [12] introduced these constraints into a three-layer neural network, performing maximum and minimum operations on groups of hyperplanes. The signals of the hyperplane weights are limited to simulate total monotonicity. Daniels and Velikova [5] extended some results obtained on MIN-MAX networks [12], using partially monotonic functions in low-dimension spaces. Zhu et al. [16] proposed a generalisation of extreme learning machines for monotonic classification. The proposal involves a quadratic programming problem. You et al. [15] focused on the challenge of learning partially monotonic flexible functions. For this, they developed Deep Lattice Networks, that alternate between three types of layers: linear embeddings, calibrators, and lattice ensembles. Silva et al. [13] developed an interpretable DNN able to generate explanations in different styles and granularities, according to the preferences of the decision-maker. Recently, Nguyen et al. [9] developed a DNN architecture called MonoNet. It learns high-level arbitrary features that are monotonically related to the target variable. For each feature, MonoNet learns a score of importance obtained by exploiting "local explainability". Márquez-Neila et al. [8] compare soft with hard constraints and argue that soft constraints perform better. Pathak et al. [10] formulate the loss function to optimise convolutional networks with arbitrary linear constraints on the structured output space of image pixel labels. Gupta et al. [6] introduce a gradient-based point-wise loss function to impose partial monotonicity on any DNN without changing the network architecture.

Our approach combines the model architecture similar to [13] to promote partial monotonicity, and a learning method to train semi-monotonic neural networks, based on [6]. We further develop this approach for dealing with arbitrary scales when choosing the desired trade-off. We also compare hard and soft constraints in real-world datasets with partially monotonic feature spaces.

3   Monotonicity

As in [9], we assume that f is a predictor that operates on vectors $\mathbf{x} \in \mathbb{R}^n$ of $\mathbf{x} = \{x_1, x_2, ..., x_n\}$ features in the dataset such that $\mathbf{y} = f(\mathbf{x})$. The monotonicity analysis for a given independent feature x_i is easily performed: we generate a new vector $\mathbf{x}'$ by introducing a disturbance x_i', where $x_i' = x_i + \Delta$ and $\Delta \geq 0$, in the independent feature's domain, and fixing the remaining independent features. We observe its behaviour with the target feature.

Definition 1. *A function* $f : \mathbb{R}^n \to \mathbb{R}$ *is called* **monotonically increasing** *w.r.t.* x_i *if* $x_i \leq x_i'$ *implies* $f(\boldsymbol{x}) \leq f(\boldsymbol{x}')$). *Equivalently, if* $x_i \leq x_i'$, *it is required to check, for all* $i = \{1, ..., n\}$, *the (univariate) constraint* $f|_i : x_i \mapsto y$:

$$f(x_1, x_2, ..., x_i, ..., x_n) \leq f(x_1, x_2, ..., x_i', ..., x_n) \, . \tag{1}$$

by fixing all the components except the x_i, in the usual sense of monotonicity for univariate functions.

The definition is similar for *monotonically decreasing functions*. If the function does not respect the conditions, then it is called *non-monotonic function*. According to [2], there are two main classes to distinguish monotonic problems. The contrast is based on the set of independent features on which the function f depends monotonically. Thus, monotonicity can be classified as *total* or *partial*.

Total Monotonicity. *The function f depends monotonically on all independent features of the dataset. We assume that y in the dataset is generated by:*

$$\mathbf{y} = f(\mathbf{x}) + \epsilon, \tag{2}$$

where f is a monotonic function and ϵ is a random error.

The total monotonicity constraint of f on $\mathbf{x}$ is defined according to Definition 1, for all independent features x_i, for any i.

Partial Monotonicity. *The function f depends monotonically on a subset of features of the dataset. In partially monotonic problems, the total set of features $\boldsymbol{x}$ is separated into $\mathbf{x}^m$ and $\mathbf{x}^n$ subsets to represent, respectively, the monotonic and non-monotonic feature subsets. Therefore, the dataset $\mathcal{D} = (\mathbf{x}^m, \mathbf{x}^n, \mathbf{y})$, where $\mathbf{x} = (\mathbf{x}^m, \mathbf{x}^n)$. We assume that the target $\boldsymbol{y}$ in the dataset is generated by:*

$$\mathbf{y} = f(\mathbf{x}^m, \mathbf{x}^n) + \epsilon, \tag{3}$$

where f is a monotonic function in $\mathbf{x}^m$ and ϵ is a random error.

The partial monotonicity constraint of f on $\mathbf{x}$ is defined according to Definition 1, for independent features in $\mathbf{x}^m$. Note that although f is monotonic, the data generated by Eq. (2) and (3) are not necessarily monotonic due to the random effect of ϵ.

4   Partially Monotonic Learning

In most real-world datasets, the target feature depends monotonically on a subset of features, but not on all of them. However, fully monotonic models cannot model non-monotonic features. To enable partial monotonicity, we build an architecture based on the proposal by [13]. This architecture consists of two independent neuronal subnets that process separately the monotonic and non-monotonic features. The monotonicity constraints are applied on the monotonic stream in which, without loss of generality, we assume that the probability of observing the positive class increases with the value of the monotonic features. The sign of the input monotonic features that have a monotonically decreasing behaviour is inverted to admit monotonically increasing relations. Then, both subnets are concatenated and processed again by a sequence dense layers with monotonicity constraints (Fig. 1). The unconstrained subnet maps its feature space into a latent monotonic space, requiring additional parameters to learn complex patterns.

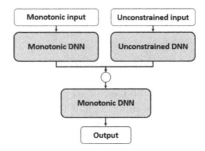

Fig. 1. Proposed architecture. Schema based on [13].

4.1   Loss Function

Using the architecture in Fig. 1, we can easily model monotonicity using hard constraints. Our proposal is an approach that uses this architecture with soft-constraints, using a modified loss function that penalises non-monotonic behaviour.

As in [6], we assume the general configuration of a supervised learning problem with a training set with k instances composed by $\mathcal{D} = (\mathbf{x}, \mathbf{y})$, where $\mathbf{x} = (\mathbf{x}^n, \mathbf{x}^m)$. The label could either be real-valued, $\mathbf{y} \in \mathbb{R}$, or binary, $\mathbf{y} \in \{0, 1\}$. The objective is to determine an estimator function f which is differentiable and monotonic w.r.t. $\mathbf{x}^m = \mathbf{x}[M]$, where M is a subset of monotonic features defined by $M \subseteq \mathcal{D}$ in $\mathbf{x} \in \mathbb{R}^{\mathcal{D}}$. We only consider increasing monotonicity. Thus, the objective function $\mathcal{L}$ combines a monotonic loss component, $\mathcal{L}_{mono}$, and a standard empirical loss component, $\mathcal{L}_{NN}$. Computed on each monotonic feature x_i^m, for $i = \{1, ..., k\}$, Eq. (4) describes a objective function through the sum of these components in the following form:

$$\mathcal{L} = p \cdot s \cdot \left(\underbrace{\sum_{i=1}^{k} max\left(0, -\nabla \cdot_M f(x_i^m; \theta)\right)}_{\mathcal{L}_{mono}} \right) + (1-p) \cdot \mathcal{L}_{NN} \ . \tag{4}$$

The hyperparameter p is a monotonicity weight, s is a scale adjustment factor, $\nabla \cdot_M$ is divergence w.r.t feature set $\mathbf{x}[M]$ i.e., $\sum_j \frac{\partial f(x_i^m; \theta)}{\partial x[M]_i^j} \forall j \in M$, θ are trainable parameters and $\mathcal{L}_{NN}$ refers to the empirical risk minimisation (ERM) for neural networks.

During each gradient descent step, the maximum of monotonic component penalises only trends of monotonically decreasing gradients. In this case, the minus sign of a negative partial derivative of $f(x_i^m; \theta)$ w.r.t. the monotonic features of $\mathbf{x}[M]$ results in a positive value, indicating that the maximum between zero and that value, results a gradient penalty. As for gradients that obey monotonicity, the maximum in the first component is zero and, hence, there are no penalties on gradients.

Hyperparameter p is a simple weight factor to control the relative contribution of each of the loss components. With $p = 1$, the model adjusts for monotonicity only, whereas with $p = 0$, the model does not care about monotonic relations at all.

The scale adjustment factor s aims to balance between the scales of the two optimisation components. A dominant loss component induces its dominance through gradients with large magnitudes, which prevent the harmonisation of the training stage, making the definition of p harder. We propose multiplying the magnitude order of the majority component by the minority component. To do this, we calculate the quotient r between the averages of the loss components $\mathcal{L}_{NN}$ and $\mathcal{L}_{mono}$ in each epoch. The result r denotes the amount of necessary adjustment to balance the components. To prevent both tasks from making exactly equal contributions – that would artificially flatten differences through successive epochs –, we assume the quotient magnitude order r as a re-scaling factor s. We calculate s using 10 to the power of $\lfloor \log_{10}(r) \rfloor$. All the necessary quantities above are calculated according to (5).

$$m_{NN} = \overline{\mathcal{L}_{NN}} \qquad m_{mono} = \overline{\mathcal{L}_{mono}} \qquad r = \frac{m_{NN}}{m_{mono}} \qquad s = 10^{\lfloor \log_{10}(r) \rfloor} . \qquad (5)$$

5   Evaluation

To evaluate our proposal, we assess the effect of monotonic component on the predictive ability of classification and regression problems. The first problem arises from the recommendation of service upgrades to customers of a large telecom service provider. The problem consists of predicting whether a specific customer will accept or refuse a personalised upgrade offer. We refer to this dataset as *Dataset 1*. The second problem consists of predicting the price sales of used cars. We refer to this dataset as *Dataset 2*.

In both problems, monotonic features are previously known. In the classification case, we know, for instance, that between two offers A and B with the exact same conditions, but where the price of A is higher than the price of B, it is very unlikely that the customer will prefer A over B. The same applies to other not so obvious features, such as internet speed or call limits. In the car price prediction task, features such as mileage and cylinders are also likely to follow a monotonic relation with the target feature (i.e., sale price).

5.1   Datasets

Table 1 summarises the details of the two datasets.

For the first task, we use a proprietary dataset, collected between January 8th and November 30th, 2018, which contains the history of offers made to customers, as well as whether the customer accepted the offer. Each transaction contains the features of the current subscription, as well as the features of the offered upgrade, plus some previously engineered features. For the second task

Table 1. Characteristics of each dataset.

Characteristics	Dataset 1	Dataset 2
N° of instances	>574 000	401 204
N° of features	328	17
N° of monotonic features	28	6
Data accessibility	Proprietary	Public
Data Context	Telecom operator	Car sales
Task	Classification	Regression

– used car price prediction –, we use the available dataset from Kaggle[1]. It contains information about the condition of use, manufacturer and model, year of manufacture, odometer, and other categories.

5.2 Methodology

We randomly split both datasets into 80%–20% for training and testing, respectively. The training set is further divided into 80%–20% for training and validation. Dataset 1 is ready to use, however, Dataset 2 requires some pre-processing tasks. First, several categorical features, such as links to web pages, manufacturer and model are ignored, and some other categorical features (e.g. size, condition) are transformed into numerical features. For features with missing values, we apply the iterative imputation strategy[2]. Some noisy instances are also manually removed, e.g., data whose year of manufacture is greater than 2020 or fictitious prices below 100 and over 300,000 dollars. The `year` feature – the manufacturing year – requires special attention, given that the monotonicity signal of the feature is inverted once a car becomes a "classic". We assume that a vehicle becomes a classic when it turns 25 years from its manufacturing year. We translate `year` into two new features to reflect this: `classic_years` and `modern_years`, which means, respectively, the number of years after becoming a classic and the vehicle's age until it reaches 25 years. The reference year is 2020. Thus, the `classic_years` and `modern_years` features are monotonically increasing and decreasing with the sale price, respectively.

For weight initialisation, we consider a uniform distribution, whose lower limit takes non-negative values. The activation function for intermediate layers is LeakyReLU, to avoid the "Dying ReLU" problem. The loss function for the regression problem is Mean Squared Logarithmic Error (MSLE), defined as $\mathcal{L}_{NN}(y, \hat{y}) = \frac{1}{N} \sum_{i=0}^{N} \left(log(y_i + 1) - log(\hat{y}_i + 1)\right)^2$. Unlike MSE and MAE, MSLE minimises the penalising effect of high differences in the predicted values. To improve and stabilise the training of the models, we use regularisation with

---

[1] https://kaggle.com/austinreese/craigslist-carstrucks-data.

[2] https://scikit-learn.org/stable/modules/generated/sklearn.impute.IterativeImputer. html.

dropout and batch normalisation (BN) layers. The BN layers are fundamental for the hard constraints model because it allows to soften the constraints and guarantee the power of representation of the objective function. The optimal set of hyperparameters for the network architecture were obtained using Grid Search.

5.3   Monotonic Features Extraction

In Dataset 1, we define as monotonic features those referring to the recommended service. As for Dataset 2, we select the subset of features that keep a monotonic relation with the sales price. The features for monotonicity analysis are grouped as follows[3]:

- Monotonically increasing features: condition, size, classic_years and cylinders.
- Monotonically decreasing features: modern_years and odometer.
- Without monotonic constraints: remaining features in the dataset.

5.4   Models

We simulate the two approaches to enforce monotonicity presented in Sect. 1. For the first approach, we rely on Silva et al. [13] to implement the model's parameter constraints. The second approach is based on Gupta et al. [6] to change the learning process. Both models are compared against an baseline *Unconstrained Model* (UM), whose model architecture is described by Fig. 1. The monotonic models are, respectively:

- *Monotonic Model* (MM) with two input layers with constraints on the network weights.
- *Partial Monotonic Model* (PMM) with two input layers with an adapted loss function.

5.5   Monotonicity Analysis

This section presents the results of three experiments: monotonicity evaluation, predictive performance evaluation and impact of hyperparameter p.

Monotonicity Evaluation. To evaluate features monotonicity, we present a comparative analysis between Models UM and PMM in Figs. 2–5. Recall that the only difference between these two models is the modified loss function. For each dataset, we chose a feature from the monotonic subset to perform the monotonicity analysis of the models: rsp_tens feature represents the difference in ten units in the RSP (retail selling price) for Dataset 1; and classic_years for Dataset 2.

---

[3] In most real-world problems, including the ones illustrated in this paper, domain expertise is essential to distinguish between true and spurious monotonic relations.

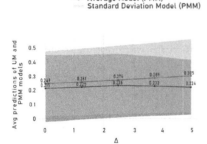
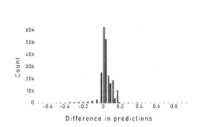

Fig. 2. Relation of Δ in average and SD predictions of feature `rsp_tens` (Dataset 1).

Fig. 3. Distribution of average predictions of feature `rsp_tens` (Dataset 1).

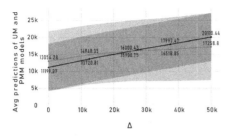
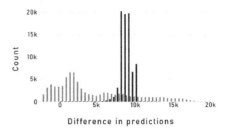

Fig. 4. Relation of Δ in average and SD predictions of `classic_years` (Dataset 2).

Fig. 5. Distribution of average predictions of `classic_years` (Dataset 2).

Figures 2 and 4 show the average and standard deviation (SD) of the predictions of each model, after adding a Δ value. It allows checking which direction the target feature takes as a gradual increase in the values of a given feature occurs. Figures 3 and 5 indicate the predictions distribution of each model, after adding a Δ value. In Model PMM, `rsp_tens` has an increasing monotonic function with propensity (see Fig. 2). It means that propensity tends to increase when offer's RSP is discounted one or more tens. By contrast, we can see an inflexion point ($\Delta = 2.5$) in curve of Model UM. Thus, this model cannot recognise a monotonic function with propensity. Model UM contains around 43.6% of non-monotonic cases, while Model PMM includes only 0.02% (Fig. 3). In Dataset 2, both models learn that `classic_years` and sales price relation is a monotonically increasing function (Fig. 4). This means that the older a classic car is, the more the car is valued. Model UM records 19% of non-monotonic examples, while Model PMM does not cover any non-monotonic example (Fig. 5).

Predictive Performance Evaluation. The evaluation metrics for the classification problem are AUC-ROC (Area Under the ROC Curve), AUC-PR (Area Under the Precision-Recall Curve) and global lift (value obtained in the first decile) – higher values are better. For regression problem, the evaluation metrics are MSE (Mean Squared Error) and MAE (Mean Absolute Error) – lower values are better. For Model PMM, we assumed a monotonicity weight equal to 10%. Table @reftab:modelosspsABCDspsnos shows the results of the predictive performance obtained for each model, regarding Datasets 1 and 2, described in Sect. 5.1.

Table 2. Summary of the values obtained from used evaluation metrics to each model.

	Dataset 1 (classification)			Dataset 2 (Regression)	
	AUC-ROC	Global lift	AUC-PR	MAE	MSE
UM	**0.849**	**3.70**	**0.689**	4802	7.68×10^7
MM	0.834	3.468	0.651	**4462**	**6.95×10^7**
PMM ($p = 10\%$)	0.837	3.430	0.653	4853	7.85×10^7

In Dataset 1, Model UM has the best performance but, in Dataset 2, it is second worse. In contrast, Model MM has the best predictive performance values achieved in Dataset 2. However, in Dataset 1, it is the worst performing model in AUC-ROC and AUC-PR. Model PMM is the worst performing model according to all metrics, but nevertheless with relatively small degradation. In the classification task, Models MM and PMM have very similar results, while with the regression task, Model PMM is closer to Model UM.

Impact of Hyperparameter p. Hyperparameter p controls the relative importance of the empirical and monotonic loss components in Model PMM. We observe that imposing monotonicity causes a performance degradation (see comparison between Models UM and PMM in Table @reftab:modelosspsABCDspsnos). Thus, we study the influence of p weight on model's predictive ability, in Dataset 1. Figure 6 describes the results of the global lift metric, assuming a set of monotonicity weights with spaced values of 10%. Figure 7 shows, for a subset of features, the proportion of instances that do not respect the monotonicity constraints with increasing p.

In general, the increase in the weight of the monotonicity component leads to a degradation of global lift (see Fig. 6). When p reaches 100%, the empirical loss minimisation is cancelled, and we are basically training a random model with rigid monotonic constraints. All features indicate that very few instances have non-monotonic cases when $p \geq 10\%$ (see Fig. 7). We also note that $p = 10\%$ already allows to obtain, simultaneously, accurate and monotonic results.

Discussion. The trade-off between monotonicity and predictive performance depends essentially on hyperparameter p. In Fig. 6, we see that p can influence the learning curve $\mathcal{L}_{NN}$ and hence, the learning curve $\mathcal{L}$. The higher the weighting

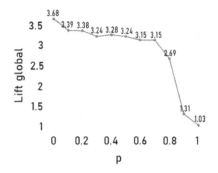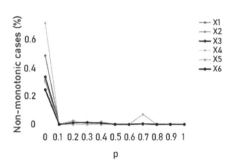

Fig. 6. Relation between monotonicity weight and global lift in Model PMM (Dataset 1).

Fig. 7. Relation between monotonicity weight and proportion of non-monotonic cases in Model PMM (Dataset 1).

of the monotonicity component, the more evident this relation becomes, showing that there is an obvious trade-off between the loss components.

Results in Sect. 5.5 confirm that isolating the monotonic features from the others to enforce monotonicity are not enough to limit the model learning (see Fig. 2 and 4). Although the usage of monotonicity constraints confirms a substantial refinement in the integration of domain knowledge in black-box models. Besides, we found that the imposition of these constraints does not considerably deteriorate the predictive performance.

6   Conclusion and Future Work

In this work, we present a ML model architecture that integrates an additional penalty for learning monotonic relations from a predefined subset of features. The results show that monotonicity can promote or ensure, in the best case, the monotonic function of relevant features to the predictions, without considerably hurting predictive ability. Thus, the application of monotonicity constraints is a solution to connect domain knowledge in the learning process. Steps for future work include: testing for more use-cases, especially on smaller datasets; the research of scale adjustment techniques for a more robust balance between loss components; and the addition of non-compensatory decision-making strategy to our method.

Acknowledgements. This work is partially developed within project AIDA - Adaptive, Intelligent and Distributed Assurance Platform (reference POCI-01-0247-FEDER-045907) co-financed by the ERDF - European Regional Development Fund through the Operational Programme for Competitiveness and Internationalisation – COMPETE 2020 and by the Portuguese Foundation for Science and Technology – FCT, under CMU Portugal.

References

1. Archer, N.P., Wang, S.: Application of the back propagation neural network algorithm with monotonicity constraints for two-group classification problems. Decis. Sci. **24**(1), 60–75 (1993)
2. Bartolj, T.: Testing monotonicity of variables. Master's thesis, Faculty of Economics and Business Administration, Tilburg University (2010)
3. Cano, J.R., Gutiérrez, P.A., Krawczyk, B., Woźniak, M., García, S.: Monotonic classification: an overview on algorithms, performance measures and data sets. Neurocomputing **341**, 168–182 (2019)
4. Carvalho, D.V., Pereira, E.M., Cardoso, J.S.: Machine learning interpretability: a survey on methods and metrics. Electronics **8**(8), 832 (2019)
5. Daniels, H., Velikova, M.: Monotone and partially monotone neural networks. IEEE Trans. Neural Netw. **21**(6), 906–917 (2010)
6. Gupta, A., Shukla, N., Marla, L., Kolbeinsson, A., Yellepeddi, K.: How to incorporate monotonicity in deep networks while preserving flexibility? arXiv preprint arXiv:1909.10662 (2019)
7. Lipton, Z.C.: The mythos of model interpretability: in machine learning, the concept of interpretability is both important and slippery. Queue **16**(3), 31–57 (2018)
8. Márquez-Neila, P., Salzmann, M., Fua, P.: Imposing hard constraints on deep networks: promises and limitations. arXiv preprint arXiv:1706.02025 (2017)
9. Nguyen, A.P., Martínez, M.R.: Mononet: towards interpretable models by learning monotonic features. arXiv preprint arXiv:1909.13611 (2019)
10. Pathak, D., Krahenbuhl, P., Darrell, T.: Constrained convolutional neural networks for weakly supervised segmentation. In: Proceedings of the IEEE International Conference on Computer Vision, pp. 1796–1804 (2015)
11. Rudin, C.: Stop explaining black box machine learning models for high stakes decisions and use interpretable models instead. Nature Mach. Intell. **1**(5), 206–215 (2019)
12. Sill, J.: Monotonic networks. Adv. Neural Inf. Process. Syst. **10**, 661–667 (1997)
13. Silva, W., Fernandes, K., Cardoso, M.J., Cardoso, J.S.: Towards complementary explanations using deep neural networks. In: Stoyanov, D., et al. (eds.) MLCN/DLF/IMIMIC -2018. LNCS, vol. 11038, pp. 133–140. Springer, Cham (2018). https://doi.org/10.1007/978-3-030-02628-8_15
14. Toreini, E., Aitken, M., Coopamootoo, K., Elliott, K., Zelaya, C.G., van Moorsel, A.: The relationship between trust in AI and trustworthy machine learning technologies. In: Proceedings of the 2020 Conference on Fairness, Accountability, and Transparency, pp. 272–283 (2020)
15. You, S., Ding, D., Canini, K., Pfeifer, J., Gupta, M.: Deep lattice networks and partial monotonic functions. In: Advances in Neural Information Processing Systems, pp. 2981–2989 (2017)
16. Zhu, H., Tsang, E.C., Wang, X.Z., Ashfaq, R.A.R.: Monotonic classification extreme learning machine. Neurocomputing **225**, 205–213 (2017)

Multiple-manifold Generation with an Ensemble GAN and Learned Noise Prior

Matthew Amodio[1] and Smita Krishnaswamy[1,2(✉)]

[1] Department of Computer Science, Yale University, New Haven, USA
smita.krishnaswamy@yale.edu
[2] Department of Genetics, Yale University, New Haven, USA

Abstract. Generative adversarial networks (GANs) learn to map samples from a noise distribution to a chosen data distribution. Recent work has demonstrated that GANs are consequently sensitive to, and limited by, the shape of the noise distribution. For example, for a single generator to map continuous noise (e.g. a uniform distribution) to discontinuous output (e.g. separate Gaussians), it must generate off-manifold points in the discontinuous region with nonzero probability. While existing applications generally ignore these outliers, they nevertheless represent a hindrance to accurate modeling in current frameworks. We address this problem by learning to generate from multiple networks such that the generator's output is an ensemble of distinct sub-generators. We contribute a novel formulation of multi-generator models where we learn a prior over the generators conditioned on the noise, parameterized by another neural network. Thus, this network not only learns the optimal rate to sample from each generator but also optimally shapes the noise received by each generator. The resulting Noise Prior GAN (NPGAN) achieves flexibility that surpasses both single generator models and previous multi-generator models even when the total number of parameters in the ensemble is the same as the single-generator models.

1 Introduction

Learning generative models of high-dimensional data is of perpetual interest to the machine learning community, as its wide suite of applications include synthesizing conversations, creating artwork, or designing biological agents [21]. Deep models, especially generative adversarial networks (GANs), have significantly improved the state of the art at modeling these complex distributions, thus encouraging further research.

Whether implicitly or explicitly, works that use GANs make a crucial modeling decision known as the *manifold assumption* by way of the starting noise distribution [23]. This is the assumption that high-dimensional data lies on a (a) single (b) low-dimensional manifold which (c) smoothly varies and where (d) local Euclidean distances in the low-dimensional space correspond to complex transformations in the high-dimensional space. While generally true in many applications, this assumption does not always hold [11].

P. H. Abreu et al. (Eds.): IDA 2021, LNCS 12695, pp. 24–36, 2021.
https://doi.org/10.1007/978-3-030-74251-5_3

For example, recent work has emphasized situations where the data lies not on one single manifold, but on multiple, disconnected manifolds [7,9,11]. In this case, GANs must attempt to learn a continuous cover of the multiple manifolds, which inevitably leads to the generation of off-manifold points which lie in between with nonzero probability [10].

These points, which are far from any training point, are interpolations between *disconnected* manifolds. It is problematic when the real underlying data distribution is disconnected, but our GAN still produces points that are "interpolated" into the disconnected region. We interchangeably refer to these generated points as *off-manifold points* and *outliers*.

The generator tries to minimize the number of these off-manifold points and make its continuous cover match the disjoint target distribution as best as is possible. Thus, the off-manifold points are generally just a small fraction of the total generated distribution. As such, they barely affect the typical coarse-grain GAN evaluation measures (like Inception and FID scores for images), which measure the average quality of the generated distribution across all points.

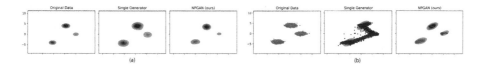

Fig. 1. (a) A typical visualization of GANs trying to model disconnected data, which shows only the KDE. When viewed this way, a single generator appears to have modeled the disconnected data perfectly adequately. (b) When shown with a scatter plot of ten thousand points, though, it becomes clear that the single generator generates points off the support. Only our ensemble method NPGAN can model the disconnected data without producing any points in between the data regions (the generator in the ensemble that generated each point is indicated by its color). (Color figure online)

Moreover, a common practice is to either use a scatter plot where off-manifold outliers are present but not mentioned [1,4], or more usually a KDE plot is used to avoid visualizing the problem [6,16,20,22]. An illustration of this on our own disconnected data is shown by comparing parts (a) and (b) in Fig. 1.

Thus, this problem is usually ignored, as other aspects of the generation are prioritized. Nonetheless, previously published work has sought remedies to this problem, both to enhance understanding of the implications of modeling an arbitrary distribution with a GAN, and because it is important to be able to address this flaw when necessary [7,9,11].

The unavoidable nature of these off-manifold points when a single generator is used with a continuous latent space has theoretical implications for proofs of GAN convergence [15]. Works that address this problem of disconnected manifolds simultaneously train multiple generators and use established regularizations [3] to coax them into dividing up the space and learning separate manifolds.

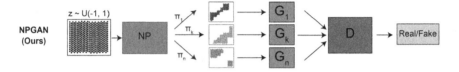

Fig. 2. The Noise-Prior GAN (NPGAN) architecture. Unlike previous work, the NP network learns a prior over the generators conditioned on the noise distribution z. This allows it to both control the sampling frequency of the generators and shape the input appropriate to each one, in an end-to-end differentiable framework.

Beyond theoretical problems, these outliers can be catastrophic in some applications: more catastrophic in fact than slight imperfections in modeling the most dense regions of the space (Fig. 2).

For example, consider the goal of deciding whether one is talking on the phone to an automated, artificial agent or a real human: a version of the famous Turing Test. If the voice on the other line incorrectly uses a particularly common sentence structure that was in its training data 60% of the time instead of 40% of the time, it will not be noticeable. However, generating a *single* gibberish sentence will give away its identity as an robot. In this application, improving the quality of the worst generated point is paramount.

As another example, consider safety in the field of autonomous vehicles. Avoiding the generation of even a single erroneous, unpredictable action can prevent collisions and save lives.

We are not the first method to tackle this problem of disconnected data with an ensemble of generators. Previous methods can be divided into two categories: (i) imposing information theoretic losses to encourage output from different generators to be distinguishable [9,11] (ii) changing the initial noise distribution to be disconnected [7]. Our approach falls into the second category. Previous efforts to change the noise distribution to handle disconnectedness has exclusively taken the form of sampling from a mixture of Gaussians rather than the typical single Gaussian (with sampling fixed and uniform over the mixture), which requires knowing the exact number of components ahead-of-time.

Our approach differs significantly from those previously. We use multiple generators as before, but instead of dividing up the noise space into factorized Gaussians and sending one to each generator, we let an additional neural network determine how best to divide up the noise space and dispatch it to each generator. This network learns a prior over the generators, conditioned on the noise space. Thus, we call our additional third network a noise-prior (NP) network. We incorporate this rich neural network prior into a framework that is entirely differentiable, allowing us to optimize the NP network along with the generators during training.

We note that with this strategy, we significantly increase the expressivity of each generator over the previous disconnected manifold models. Imagine a 2D uniform latent space: by dividing up this space into four vertical rectangles, and sending the 1st and 3rd rectangle to one generator and the 2nd and 4th rectangle to the other generator, we can generate four disconnected manifolds with just two generators (since the 1st and 3rd rectangle are disconnected input to the first generator). Previous work would have to devote precisely four generators to this task, with degradation in performance if fewer or more generators are chosen for the hyperparameter. Here, the prior network learns to divide the noise space appropriately for whatever number of generators is chosen, and is thus more expressive as well as more robust than previous models.

Moreover, much existing work has exclusively framed the problem as, and tailored solutions for, the disconnected manifold problem. Our approach is more generalized, addressing any mis-specification between noise distribution and the target distribution. This means that our approach does not become redundant or unnecessary in the case of single complex manifolds, for example.

Our contributions can be summarized as:

1. We introduce the first multi-generator ensemble to learn a prior over the noise space, using a novel soft, differentiable loss formulation.
2. We present a multi-generator method that can learn to sample generators in proportion to the relative density of multiple manifolds.

2 Related Work

Several previous works have included multiple generators, mixing and matching a few commonly used features. Some use completely distinct generators [2,11], while others tie some or all of their weights [7,9]. Most use a single parametric noise source (e.g. a single Gaussian) [9,11] while one uses a mixture of Gaussians [7]. Most sample the generators randomly with equal probability, but one attempts to find (in a non-differentiable way) a sampling scheme to not sample from redundant generators [11]. [5] encourages diversity among generator outputs by introducing a classifier that tries to identify the generator a data point came from, or whether it is a real data point (reminiscent of an auxiliary classifier [17] or the mutual information loss of [3]). A more theoretical analysis of convergence and equilibrium existence in the loss landscape motivated a multiple-generator, multiple-discriminator mixture in [2]. We discuss in detail the works with the most resemblance to our approach here:

DeLiGAN. The DeLiGAN [7] was designed to handle diverse datasets with a limited amount of datapoints. It used a single generator and a Gaussian mixture model latent space. To train, a single random $Gaussian_i$ out of the mixture is chosen, and then they added μ_i to the $Normal(0, 1)$ noise and multiplied it by σ_i, with both μ_i and σ_i as learnable parameters. This differs from our work because while the noise is separated into different components, the probability of selecting each component is cut off from the gradient information in the model and is not differentiable (each Gaussian is selected with an equal probability, and this never changes). Also, every component of the noise is parameterized as a Gaussian. Finally, only one component of the noise is trained at a time (a single μ_i and σ_i is randomly selected for each training batch), while our model learns to model the data over the full collection of generators in each minibatch.

MGAN. The MGAN [9] focused on the problem of mode collapse and addressed it by using multiple generators which are really the same network except for the first linear projection layer. They introduced a new loss term into the traditional GAN training: to encourage the generators to learn different parts of the data space, a lower bound on mutual information between the generated images and the generator they came from was maximized. This is helpful because the generators share almost weights between them and otherwise may redundantly use multiple generators to cover the same part of the space. Unlike in our work, they use a single noise source and let the single first layer of the generators learn to project it to different parts of the space before going through the same convolutions. In our work, this transformation of the noise before going to each generator is done with a separate network which gets gradient information through the generator, but is not optimized jointly with the generator weights. Moreover, like the DeLiGAN, the probability over the multiple generators was assumed to be fixed and uniform.

DMWGANPL. The DMWGANPL [11] exclusively viewed multi-generator models as a solution for disconnected manifolds. Each generator is given the same single noise sample, and the same mutual information criteria (termed $Q(G_i|x)$, the probability that x came from generator G_i) as the MGAN was used to ensure each generator learned a different part of the space. Unlike the previous works, they do not assume an equal probability of selecting each generator. Instead, they sample each generator G_i with probability r_i. After each step of the generator and discriminator during training, the r_i's are updated to maximize mutual information between their distribution and $Q(G_i|x)$. This has the primary effect of not sampling redundant generators whose output is hard to distinguish from another generator's output, and is completely disassociated from the minimax GAN game. Each generator gets the same noise sample that takes a single parametric form $(Normal(0, 1))$, and the effect this has on the minimax game and the quality of generated images is only indirect and tangential to the objective being minimized.

3   Model

Motivated by the success of ensemble models [8], our NPGAN represents the generating function G with multiple distinct generators of the same architecture. We use the NP network as a teacher network, to select a generator G_i based on a prior conditioned on the particular input it sees. By learning a probabilistic mixture of the generators for any particular noise sample, this NP network delegates each input point to the appropriate generator that is optimally prepared to handle it. Its output is then a weighted sum of the distinct generators, which as a soft formulation assures differentiability of the whole framework.

Formally, consider the standard GAN setup as follows. Let $X \sim P_X, x_i \in \mathbb{R}^d, i = 1...N_x$ be a sample of N_x points from a d-dimensional distribution P_X. We seek a generator G that learns to mimic P_X by mapping from a noise distribution

$Z \sim P_Z$. To do this, we train a discriminator D and pit them against each other in the standard GAN framework:

$$\min_G \max_D L_{GAN} = \mathbb{E}_{x \sim P_x}[log(D(x))]$$
$$+ \mathbb{E}_{z \sim P_z}[log(1 - D(G(z)))]$$

where G tries to minimize and D tries to maximize this objective.

When traditionally training a GAN, the generator and discriminator alternate gradient descent steps, allowing gradient information to flow through the other network while keeping it fixed and only optimizing with respect to the given network's parameters. We extend this to our third noise prior network NP, allowing gradient information to flow through the fixed generators G_i and discriminator D while optimizing the GAN loss with respect to the parameters of NP. During training, we let both the NP network and the generators use a soft version of the GAN loss, weighting each generator output by the learned probabilities $NP(G_i|z)$. Then, during inference, the choice of G_i is sampled from this learned prior. Our total generator ensemble G can be decomposed into:

$$G(z) = \Sigma_i NP(G_i|z) \cdot G_i(z)$$

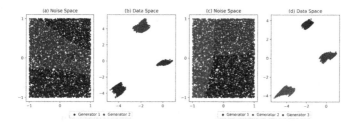

Fig. 3. We investigate the NP network by using two-dimensional uniform noise and plotting the learned prior over the generators. The three unequally sampled Gaussians in the data can have their density matched with three generators (c–d) or by creating a discontinuity with two generators (a–b).

The NP network looks at the random sample of points from Z and determines how best to assign them to the generators to achieve the goal of modeling P_X. In the special case where P_X is disconnected, NP can dispatch Z in multiple ways such as giving each generator a continuous area of Z, or giving some generators multiple disconnected areas of Z (as we demonstrate later in the experiments). Nothing in our model formulation is specifically designed to model disconnectedness or any other specific property in P_X, however, so NP can learn to divide the sample from Z in whatever way is most appropriate for the given shape of P_X.

Thus, we model a distribution over our generators rather than simply sampling them uniformly and concatenating their output. Moreover, we learn this distribution over the generators with another network which is conditioned on the input noise, allowing it to choose the shape of input each generator receives. This network does not optimize a separate loss that is a heuristic indirectly related to the GAN framework, but directly participates in the GAN minimax game. To summarize, we fully and flexibly incorporate the multiple-generator framework into a GAN such that the model can learn for itself how best to use the generators. This is achieved by modeling a prior over the generators that is conditioned on the noise input and optimizing it with respect to the GAN loss directly.

4   Experiments

4.1   Disconnected Manifolds

Our first experimental dataset consists of a mixture of samples from 2-D Gaussians such that the three Gaussians are not sampled with equal probability (7000, 5000, and 3000 points, respectively). We compare our NPGAN's ability to model this distribution to a single generator model, MGAN [9], DMW-GANPL [11], and DeLiGAN [7]. The noise distribution for each model was a 100-dimensional $Uniform(-1, 1)$ except the DeLiGAN, which requires samples from $Normal(0, 1)$. The generators in each case share the same architecture of three layers with 200-100-20 neurons per layer and Leaky ReLU activations. The discriminator in all cases had three layers of 1000-200-100 neurons and used minibatch discrimination [19]. All models were run on a single GPU and written in Tensorflow.

To investigate how the NPGAN models this data, we first use 2-D noise distribution of $Z \sim Uniform(-1, 1) \in \mathbb{R}^2$, so that we can plot the noise in two dimensions. In Fig. 3a and 3c, we see the noise space for two and three generators, respectively. Notably, in both cases there are three partitions, no matter the number of generators. By learning to give one generator disconnected input, the NP network effectively models a third manifold without having a dedicated generator responsible for it. Viewing the latent space also informs us how the NPGAN can easily model non-equally sampled manifolds, as well, as the size of each partition of the noise space expands or contracts to match the underlying data distribution.

Moving to the comparison to other models (Fig. 4), we first see that a single generator cannot model this distribution without generating trailing points that connect the manifolds. By looking at the underlying density plots, we see that *most* of the generated data lies on the manifolds, in terms of proportions of points. However, when densely sampling the noise distribution, these few off-support outliers still arise. We note that this is true across many different architectures and loss functions: these off-manifold points get generated even when adding depth, adding neurons, using a WGAN loss, changing activation functions, or adding regularizations.

Next, we evaluate all of the multi-generator models with three generators, which we know to be the true underlying number of disconnected manifolds in this synthetic situation. The MGAN and DeLiGAN fail to model each manifold with a distinct generator and thus cover multiple manifolds with one of their generators and produce a trail of points in between. This failure stems from their sampling the generators with a fixed, equal probability. Since the disconnected manifolds do not have exactly the sample probability, their model formulations cannot effectively manage this situation. The DMWGANPL does learn a prior over the generators, but this prior only learned to eliminate redundant generators. Thus, it does learn an unequal sampling of the generators and each generator produces points that are distinct from the other generators, but does so without accurately modeling the data. The NPGAN, however, assigns each manifold to an individual generator and matches the data distribution without generating any off-manifold points. This is confirmed quantitatively in Table 1, where we measure the percentage of points each model generates that are off the manifold, which we define to be any point farther from the center of any Gaussian than the largest distance of any of the true points. There we see that the NPGAN generates no points off the manifold, while the other models are all forced to generate a trail of points connecting two of the Gaussians.

We next demonstrate the improved flexibility of the NPGAN over previous models by choosing two generators, imagining ourselves in the realistic case of not knowing the true underlying number of disconnected manifolds in a particular dataset (Fig. 5). In this case, all of the other models must inevitably cover two manifolds with a single generator. Since each generator receives a continuous, unaltered noise distribution, this means they produce points off the manifold (Table 1). The NPGAN alone learns to model three disconnected manifolds with two generators without generating off-manifold points in between.

Table 1. Scores for each model on each artificial dataset and the number of generators used (2Gen or 3Gen). For the Gaussian data, the score is the percentage of generated points off the manifold. For the parabolas, the score represents the percentage of real points without any generated point in its neighborhood.

	2 Gen Gaussian	3 Gen Gaussian	2 Gen Parabolas	3 Gen Parabolas
NPGAN	**0.000**	**0.000**	**0.003**	**0.007**
MGAN	0.031	0.162	0.088	0.083
DMWGANPL	0.037	0.026	0.076	0.082
DeLiGAN	0.134	0.055	0.196	0.320

4.2   CelebA+Photo

To test the NPGAN's ability to model disconnected, unevenly sampled manifolds on real images, we combine two distinct datasets. We take 1500 images randomly from the CelebA [14] dataset and combine them with the 6000 photographs dataset from [24]. To effectively match this data distribution with two generators,

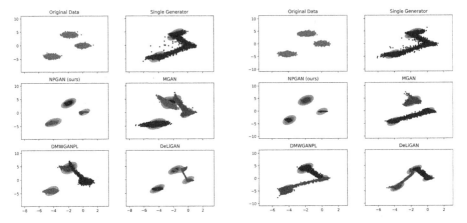

Fig. 4. When shown with a scatter plot of ten thousand points, though, it becomes clear that the single generator generates points off the support. Only our NPGAN samples the generators in proportion to the data (the generator is indicated by the point's color). (Color figure online)

Fig. 5. Only our NPGAN learns to create a discontinuity in the support of one generator and capture three manifolds with just two generators (the generator indicated by point color). The KDE underneath shows the off-manifold points are a small proportion but nonetheless exist as inaccuracies. (Color figure online)

the models will have to either learn to sample generators at a differential rate, or have one generator cover a discontinuity (or both).

The images were resized to 32 × 32, and all models use a DCGAN architecture [18], with three convolutional transpose layers in the generators and three convolutional layers in the discriminator. Each convolution used stride length two, kernel size three, batch normalization on all layers except the first layer of the discriminator, and ReLU activations in the generator with Leaky ReLU activations in the discriminator. Training was performed on minibatches of 32 with an Adam optimizer [12] with learning rate 0.0001.

In the MGAN and DeLiGAN, the generators are all the same network except for the initial linear projection of the noise (or the adding of the generator-specific mean and the multiplying of the generator-specific standard deviation in the DeLiGAN). In our NPGAN and the DMWGANPL, the generators do not share weights. To compensate for the increased capacity that this would otherwise provide, we decrease the number of filters per generator learned to keep the total number of parameters across all models (within 1%).

Figure 6 shows randomly selected images from each model, and there we can see the consequences of the MGAN and DeLiGAN sampling generators at a fixed rate and giving each generator the same continuous noise. In each case, one of the generators effectively generates photos, but the other generator gets caught in between generating photos and CelebA images, producing many blurry images. The DMWGANPL samples generators at a different rate, but again did so ineffectively: one generator makes photos, but the other generator makes both CelebA images and some photos that are not being made by the other generator.

Even though it is an imperfect measure of capturing outliers, the FID scores reported in Table 2 show that the imbalance affects their ability to model the underlying dataset, too. We add a comparison to a standard WGAN-GP model on this dataset as a baseline. To add an uncertainty measure to this score, we average the last three model checkpoints and report the mean and standard deviation. In Fig. 6, we see the NPGAN learns to sample more from the generator that exclusively makes photos, while also using its ability to create discontinuity in its input to allow the other generator to make both CelebA images and a few realistic photos.

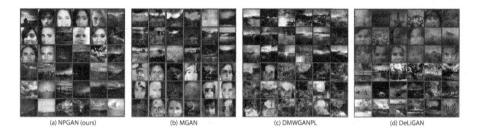

(a) NPGAN (ours)   (b) MGAN   (c) DMWGANPL   (d) DeLiGAN

Fig. 6. Randomly selected images from each model trained on the CelebA+Photo dataset. Only our NPGAN avoids generating any images that are a blurry point halfway in between a face and a landscape photo.

4.3   Complex-But-Connected Image Dataset

In this section, we explore how connectedness affects the results of the models for image datasets. The previous works on multiple generators have emphasized disconnectedness, but we show here that the NPGAN outperforms the alternatives even without disconnected data. The effects of other properties, like class/mode imbalance, dominate the results. We test this notion by modifying the dataset from the previous section to create a connection between the Face and Photo images. To do this, we randomly choose images in each dataset and perform linear interpolation between them with a mixing coefficient α chosen from a $Uniform(0,1)$ distribution. We add these interpolations to the Face+Photo dataset to make a ConnectedFace+Photo dataset. Conceptually, ConnectedFace+Photo takes the shape of a "barbell" with a narrow trail connecting two areas of density in data space (Table 3).

We then repeat the experiment of the previous section and report the results. Notably, the quantitative results remain the same. As in the artificial cases, the other models have difficulty dealing with density imbalances, and this difficulty dominates the effects of whether the data is disconnected or not.

Table 2. FID scores.

	Face-photo	Connected Face-photo
NPGAN	58.9 ± 2.4	51.7 ± 4.1
MGAN	65.5 ± 1.5	63.1 ± 3.4
DeLiGAN	64.1 ± 3.1	68.6 ± 2.6
DMWGANPL	81.0 ± 6.2	83.4 ± 5.5
WGAN-GP	66.5 ± 4.9	69.3 ± 5.9

Table 3. Outlier distance scores.

	FaceBed	CIFAR
NPGAN	$\mathbf{16.3 \pm 0.2}$	$\mathbf{18.9 \pm 0.3}$
WGAN-GP	17.8 ± 0.1	20.7 ± 0.2
DMWGANPL	17.5 ± 0.1	19.6 ± 0.3
DeLiGAN	17.6 ± 0.3	19.6 ± 0.1
MGAN	17.4 ± 0.2	19.5 ± 0.2

4.4   CIFAR

Next, we explore the NPGAN on the canonical CIFAR10 dataset [13]. For a quantitative assessment, we introduce a new measure of how bad a model's worst samples are: outlier manifold distance. As previously discussed, we need this measure because FID is not a good measure of whether a model produced outliers or not, since generating 1% bad samples off the manifold will be unnoticed in FID score if coupled with a slight improvement of sample quality on the other 99% of the samples. Unlike FID, our outlier manifold distance is sensitive to a model generating outliers, irrespective of how good its best samples are. We calculate this distance by finding the average distance of the 1% furthest generated points from the real data manifold, as measured by the distance to the closest real point in the last feature map of the Inception network for each generated point. The outlier manifold distance for each model is then the average of the 1% largest distances (the 1% "most anomalous" points). In Table 3, we see that NPGAN has the best outlier manifold distance of all models. As a sanity check, we also calculate it on the previous FaceBed data, and show that it confirms quantitatively what we saw qualitatively and with FID score, that other models produce outliers that are worse than NGPAN's worst samples.

5   Discussion

In order to generate data points accurately in complex data spaces, such as those consisting of disconnected manifolds, intersections of manifolds or layered data, we introduce a novel GAN framework that we call NPGAN (Noise Prior GAN) which includes multiple generators and a teacher Noise Prior network that chooses a probabilistic mixture of generators to generate from any particular noise sample. We imagine the most important direction of future work along these lines would focus on improved computational efficiency. The model we proposed needs to calculate the output of each network in order to backpropagate, even though only one network's output is sampled. This inefficiency could be even more problematic with dramatically more networks in the ensemble, and thus would be very beneficial to develop moving forward.

References

1. Arjovsky, M., Chintala, S., Bottou, L.: Wasserstein GAN. arXiv preprint arXiv:1701.07875 (2017)
2. Arora, S., Ge, R., Liang, Y., Ma, T., Zhang, Y.: Generalization and equilibrium in generative adversarial nets (GANs). arXiv preprint arXiv:1703.00573 (2017)
3. Chen, X., Duan, Y., Houthooft, R., Schulman, J., Sutskever, I., Abbeel, P.: Info-GAN: interpretable representation learning by information maximizing generative adversarial nets. In: Advances in Neural Information Processing Systems, pp. 2172–2180 (2016)
4. Dumoulin, V., et al.: Adversarially learned inference. arXiv preprint arXiv:1606.00704 (2016)
5. Ghosh, A., Kulharia, V., Namboodiri, V.P., Torr, P.H., Dokania, P.K.: Multi-agent diverse generative adversarial networks. In: Proceedings of the IEEE Conference on Computer Vision and Pattern Recognition, pp. 8513–8521 (2018)
6. Gulrajani, I., Ahmed, F., Arjovsky, M., Dumoulin, V., Courville, A.C.: Improved training of wasserstein GANs. In: Advances in Neural Information Processing Systems, pp. 5767–5777 (2017)
7. Gurumurthy, S., Kiran Sarvadevabhatla, R., Venkatesh Babu, R.: DeLiGAN: generative adversarial networks for diverse and limited data. In: Proceedings of the IEEE Conference on Computer Vision and Pattern Recognition, pp. 166–174 (2017)
8. Hinton, G., Vinyals, O., Dean, J.: Distilling the knowledge in a neural network. arXiv preprint arXiv:1503.02531 (2015)
9. Hoang, Q., Nguyen, T.D., Le, T., Phung, D.: MGAN: training generative adversarial nets with multiple generators (2018)
10. Kelley, J.L.: General Topology. Courier Dover Publications, New York (2017)
11. Khayatkhoei, M., Singh, M., Elgammal, A.: Disconnected manifold learning for generative adversarial networks. arXiv preprint arXiv:1806.00880 (2018)
12. Kingma, D.P., Ba, J.: Adam: a method for stochastic optimization. arXiv preprint arXiv:1412.6980 (2014)
13. Krizhevsky, A., Nair, V., Hinton, G.: The CIFAR-10 dataset, p. 4 (2014). http://www.cs.toronto.edu/kriz/cifar.html
14. Liu, Z., Luo, P., Wang, X., Tang, X.: Deep learning face attributes in the wild. In: Proceedings of International Conference on Computer Vision (ICCV) (2015)
15. Mescheder, L., Geiger, A., Nowozin, S.: Which training methods for GANs do actually converge? arXiv preprint arXiv:1801.04406 (2018)
16. Metz, L., Poole, B., Pfau, D., Sohl-Dickstein, J.: Unrolled generative adversarial networks. arXiv preprint arXiv:1611.02163 (2016)
17. Odena, A., Olah, C., Shlens, J.: Conditional image synthesis with auxiliary classifier GANs. In: Proceedings of the 34th International Conference on Machine Learning, vol. 70, pp. 2642–2651. JMLR.org (2017)
18. Radford, A., Metz, L., Chintala, S.: Unsupervised representation learning with deep convolutional generative adversarial networks. arXiv preprint arXiv:1511.06434 (2015)
19. Salimans, T., Goodfellow, I., Zaremba, W., Cheung, V., Radford, A., Chen, X.: Improved techniques for training GANs. In: Advances in Neural Information Processing Systems, pp. 2234–2242 (2016)
20. Srivastava, A., Valkov, L., Russell, C., Gutmann, M.U., Sutton, C.: VEEGAN: reducing mode collapse in GANs using implicit variational learning. In: Advances in Neural Information Processing Systems, pp. 3308–3318 (2017)

21. Tan, W.R., Chan, C.S., Aguirre, H.E., Tanaka, K.: ArtGAN: artwork synthesis with conditional categorical GANs. In: 2017 IEEE International Conference on Image Processing (ICIP), pp. 3760–3764. IEEE (2017)
22. Wang, C., Xu, C., Yao, X., Tao, D.: Evolutionary generative adversarial networks. IEEE Trans. Evol. Comput. **23**(6), 921–934 (2019)
23. Zhu, J.-Y., Krähenbühl, P., Shechtman, E., Efros, A.A.: Generative visual manipulation on the natural image manifold. In: Leibe, B., Matas, J., Sebe, N., Welling, M. (eds.) ECCV 2016. LNCS, vol. 9909, pp. 597–613. Springer, Cham (2016). https://doi.org/10.1007/978-3-319-46454-1_36
24. Zhu, J.Y., Park, T., Isola, P., Efros, A.A.: Unpaired image-to-image translation using cycle-consistent adversarial networks. In: Proceedings of the IEEE International Conference on Computer Vision, pp. 2223–2232 (2017)

Simple, Efficient and Convenient Decentralized Multi-task Learning for Neural Networks

Amaury Bouchra Pilet[1,2,3,4(✉)], Davide Frey[1,2,3,4], and Francois Taïani[1,2,3,4]

[1] Univ Rennes, Rennes, France
[2] Inria, Rennes, France
[3] CNRS, Rennes, France
[4] IRISA, Rennes, France
`Amaury.Bouchra-Pilet@IRISA.fr`

Abstract. Machine learning, and in particular neural networks, require large amounts of data, which is increasingly highly distributed (e.g. over user devices, or independent storage systems). Aggregating this data at one site for learning can be unpractical due to network costs, legal constraints, or privacy concerns. Decentralized machine learning holds the potential to address these concerns, but unfortunately, most of the approaches proposed so far for distributed learning with neural networks are mono-task, and do not transfer easily to multi-task problems. In this paper, we propose a novel learning method for neural networks that is *decentralized, multi-task,* and that keeps users' data *local.* Our approach works with different learning algorithms, on various types of neural networks. We formally analyze the convergence of our method, and we evaluate its efficiency in a range of neural networks and learning algorithms, demonstrating its benefits in terms of learning quality and convergence.

1 Introduction

A critical requirement for machine learning is training data. In some cases, a great amount of data is available from different distributed sources, but aggregating this data for training is not always practical. The data might for instance be large and costly to transfer, or may contain sensitive information users wish to keep private (e.g. browsing histories, health records) [7].

To address these issues, several works have proposed to share model-related information (gradients, model coefficients) rather than raw data [4,17,25]. These approaches are however typically mono-task: all users are assumed to be solving the same ML task. Unfortunately, this is not necessarily true in a distributed setting. Consider the example of speech recognition on mobile devices: users differ in their individual voices, but these differences are further colored by regional and national differences (e.g. French speakers from Canada or France), implying noticeable differences between tasks. A decentralized or federated learning (a concept supported by industry leaders such as Google [3] and Facebook [20]) platform should therefore accommodate for both types of differences between tasks: at the level of single users and at the level of groups of users.

© Springer Nature Switzerland AG 2021
P. H. Abreu et al. (Eds.): IDA 2021, LNCS 12695, pp. 37–49, 2021.
https://doi.org/10.1007/978-3-030-74251-5_4

Although distributed multitask learning approaches exist, they are typically limited to either linear [22] or convex [2] optimization problems, and are typically not applicable to neural networks, in spite of their general success in solving a broad range of machine-learning problems. Some recent preprints have explored approaches multitask federated learning with neural networks, but they suffer from significant limitations (no effective parallelism, client-sever model) [8,15].

In this paper, we introduce a novel effective solution for *decentralized multitask learning with neural networks*, usable in decentralized or federated setups. Its novelty is twofold. First, to the best of our knowledge, it is the first to combine decentralization, the ability to address multiple tasks, and support for general neural networks. Second, it does not require any input regarding task similarities, yet can still benefit from such knowledge when available, as our experimental evaluation suggests.

At its core, our approach exploits model averaging (like other mono-task federated learning techniques [4]), but makes this averaging *partial* along two key dimensions. First, averaging can be limited to some specific subsets of model parameters. Second, the averaging of these subsets can be limited to peers sharing similar tasks when this knowledge is available. Experimental results show that partial averaging outperforms both local learning and global averaging.

2   The Method

We consider a federated/peer-to peer-setup where each local device (peer), p, has an individual dataset, and a neural-network N^p. Each peer wants to learn a specific task. All tasks are similar but not exactly the same (e.g. recognizing speech from different speakers).

2.1   Intuition

We reuse the mechanism of model averaging proposed for federated learning [4]. Each peer performs a sequence of local learning (e.g. using Stochastic Gradient Descent -SGD-) followed by an averaging step and this is repeated until some convergence criterion (e.g. no change greater than some ϵ) is met. In our system though, unlike in classical federated learning, we use partial averaging to enable multi-task learning. Our intuition is that the models of similar but different tasks can be divided into different portions (*partial models*) that represent different levels of "specialization" of each task. As a simple example, the model of each task might be divided into a global portion (*global model*, a partial model shared over all peers), and a local portion (*local model*, a partial model associated with only one peer), specific to the peer's task. Such a split would be similar to transfer learning [24], albeit applied to a multi-task decentralized set-up.

Moreover, our approach goes beyond a global/local split. To account for task similarities within subgroups of peers, some portions of a peer's neural network might be averaged with only a subset of other peers (*semi-local model*, a model that is partially averaged over several but not all peers).

2.2 Description

Each neuron, N_i^p, of N^p consists of an activation function, a weight vector, $\mathbf{w}$, and a vector of activation-function parameters, $\mathbf{q}$; both vectors are real-valued, $N_i^p = (f, \mathbf{w}, \mathbf{q}) \in (\mathbb{R} \times \mathbb{R}^k \to \mathbb{R}) \times \mathbb{R}^j \times \mathbb{R}^k$, and may be learned by any training method. Neurons take an input vector, $\mathbf{i} \in \mathbb{R}^k$, and return a real value, $f(\mathbf{i} \cdot \mathbf{w}, \mathbf{q})$.

Concretely, we implement partial models by partitioning the set of neurons of each peer into *slices* ($N^p = \biguplus_i S^{p,i}$, where $S^{p,i}$ is a slice and $\biguplus$ is disjoint union). Each slice of a peer is associated with one of the partial models this peer implements. All slices associated with a single partial model have the same structure, in terms of neurons and of the interconnections between them.

The recurring averaging among peers implementing the same partial model causes the parameter values associated with the corresponding slices across the different peers to converge to the same values. The averaging process proceeds on a by-neuron basis. For each neuron, it averages the activation-function parameter vectors, $\mathbf{q}$, and only the input weights ($\mathbf{w}$ vectors) that are internal to the slice (i.e. that connect neurons in the same slice, Fig. 1a). For inter-slice (inter-model) input weights, i.e. weights that connect different slices, we leverage a notion of *dependency* that may exist between partial models (slices). Specifically, a slice (model) A *depends* on slice (model) B, if the presence of (a slice implementing) A on a peer implies the presence (a slice implementing) B on this peer. For example a partial model that recognizes Québécois French may depend on a model that recognizes generic French. In our averaging process, for a neuron in slice A, we average an associated inter-slice weight only if it connects the neuron with another neuron in a slice B on which A depends, regardless of whether this is an input or an output connection. For example, in Fig. 1b, Model m_2 in red depends on model m_1 in blue. As a result, all peers implementing m_2 average inter model weights between the two models (the red edges between m_1 and m_2). If no such hierarchical relationship exists (since dependency is a partial order), we do not average inter-slice weights (Fig. 1c). Relying on this dependency ensures that inter-model weights have the same meaning for all the peers that implement a given model, making their averaging possible. Figure 2 shows an example of 3 peers with 5 partial models and dependencies.

The slices of each peer's neural network, and their grouping across peers, can be arbitrary. They are not restricted to the network's last few layers?, as common in centralized transfer learning. This partitioning/grouping process can be informed by prior knowledge about the similarities between individual tasks for further optimization, but it does not need to. Similarly, dependencies do not constrain the network structure but constitute an engineering choice that can optimize the learning process (by averaging more weights).

3 Theoretical Analysis

Due to the high level of generality of our system (not limited to one specific kind of neural network or learning rule), we provide an analysis of our system's behavior compared to local learning, which can be used to adapt existing convergence proofs to our model. More precisely, we show that in the case of loss-based

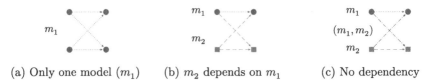

(a) Only one model (m_1)   (b) m_2 depends on m_1 (c) No dependency

Fig. 1. Averaging inter-model weights with different dependencies. A neuron's color and shape indicates the model associated with the neuron; an edge color and style indicates for which model this edge weight will be averaged. We represent two models: blue circles and dotted lines versus red squares and dashed lines. Purple edges refers to weights that are not averaged in either model (Color figure online).

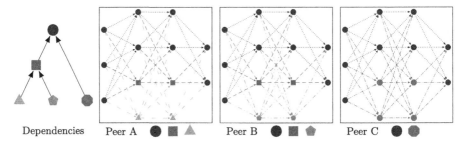

Fig. 2. A dependency graph between 5 models (left-most graph, X → Y means that X depends on Y), and the neural networks of 3 peers using these models (Blue global; Red semi-local; Green, Cyan & Purple local). Links (weights) connecting two neurons from different models belong to the dependent model (if any) for averaging purposes (Color figure online).

learning (e.g. SGD), our decentralized system is essentially equivalent to a single model that comprises the whole set of partial models on a single system.

Each peer p has a parameter vector depending on time t (discrete, $\in \mathbb{N}$) $x_p(t) \in \mathbb{R}^{n_p}$ and a loss function $l_p \in \mathbb{R}^{n_p} \to \mathbb{R}$. The notation $p \Vdash m$ means that peer p implements model m. Since all peers' parameters are associated with a partial model (which can be local, for the parameters that are not averaged), we define a global parameter vector. To this end, we just take all partial models used, $m_0(t) \in \mathbb{R}^{r_0}, m_1(t) \in \mathbb{R}^{r_1}, ..., m_q(t) \in \mathbb{R}^{r_q}$ and concatenate them: $M(t) = m_0(t)m_1(t)...m_q(t) \in \mathbb{R}^u$ ($u = \sum_i r_i$). If a peer p implements models 1, 3 and 5, then, after averaging, we have $x_p(t) = m_1(t)m_3(t)m_5(t)$.

For the analysis, we need to define a global loss function $L \in \mathbb{R}^u \to \mathbb{R}$ for our problem. To this end, we first define a set of functions $h_p \in \mathbb{R}^u \to \mathbb{R}$ with $h_p(v) = l_p(v')$ where v' restricts v to the models implemented by peer p. For example, if $v = w_0w_1w_2w_3w_4$ and peer p implements models 1, 2 and 4, then $h_p(v) = l_p(w_1w_2w_4)$. Since the values of parameters associated with models not implemented by peer p have no direct influence on the output of p's neural network, it is logical that they have no influence on p's loss. Now we can simply define our global loss function as the sum of all h's: $L(y) = \sum_p h_p(y)$.

Let $v_{\llcorner k \lrcorner}$ correspond to the coordinates of vector v associated with model k. We assume that each peer uses a learning rule satisfying the following property $\mathbb{E}[x_p(t+1) - x_p(t)] = -\lambda_p(t) \circ \nabla l_p(x_p(t))$ (where $\lambda_p(t)$ is the vector of the learning rates of peer p at time t for all parameters, and $z \circ z'$ is the element-wise product of vectors z and z'), which holds true for common variants of SGD. To distinguish peers' models before and after averaging, we use $x_p(t)$ for the value before averaging and $x'_p(t)$ for the value after averaging $(x'_p(t)_{\llcorner k \lrcorner} = m_k(t))$ and the version of the previous formula that we apply is $\mathbb{E}[x_p(t+1) - x'_p(t)] = -\lambda_p(t) \circ \nabla l_p(x'_p(t))$.

Now, for each model m_i we have:

$$m_k(t+1) - m_k(t) = \frac{\sum_{p|p\Vdash m_k} x_p(t+1)_{\llcorner k \lrcorner}}{\#\{p \mid p \Vdash m_k\}} - m_k(t)$$

From which we can derive:

$$\mathbb{E}[m_k(t+1) - m_k(t)] = -\frac{\sum_{p|p\Vdash m_k} \lambda_p(t)_{\llcorner k \lrcorner} \circ \nabla l_p(x'_p(t))_{\llcorner k \lrcorner}}{\#\{p \mid p \Vdash m_k\}}$$

We now add the assertion that all peers implementing a model use the same learning rate for the parameters part of this model $\forall_{k,p,p'|p\Vdash m_k \wedge p'\Vdash m_k} \lambda_p(t)_{\llcorner k \lrcorner} = \lambda_{p'}(t)_{\llcorner k \lrcorner} = \Lambda_k(t)$.

$$\mathbb{E}[m_k(t+1) - m_k(t)] = -\frac{\sum_{p|p\Vdash m_k} \Lambda_k(t) \circ \nabla l_p(x'_p(t))_{\llcorner k \lrcorner}}{\#\{p \mid p \Vdash m_k\}}$$

If the learning rate is supposed to be variable and not depending only on t, it is possible to compute a single learning rate for all peers implementing a model or to compute an optimal learning rate locally for each peer, average all value and use this averaged value. Now we can write $\lambda_k(t) = \frac{\Lambda_k(t)}{\#\{p|p\Vdash m_k\}}$ and $\Lambda(t) = \lambda_0(t)\lambda_1(t)...\lambda_q(t)$, from which we can derive:

$$\mathbb{E}[m_k(t+1) - m_k(t)] = -\lambda_k(t) \circ \nabla L(M(t))_{\llcorner k \lrcorner}$$

Which, when we consider all models at the same time, gives us:

$$\mathbb{E}[M(t+1) - M(t)] = -\Lambda(t) \circ \nabla L(M(t))$$

This property for the global learning rule is the same as for the local ones, except that the loss function is the sum of the local losses and the learning rate of each parameter is divided by the number of peers using this parameter in their model.

This requires some discussion. Is having the learning rates divided by the number of peers implementing the corresponding model bad? Remember that the global loss function is a sum. If we consider the simple case where all peers have the same loss function, the values and the gradient of the global loss function will be equal to those of local learning multiplied by the number of peers.

The reduced learning rate compensates for the increased gradient and makes federated learning equivalent to local learning with an unchanged learning rate, as it should be.

We can summarize this analysis the following way: for a loss-based learning algorithm (typically SGD), our decentralized system is equivalent to training the whole set of partial models at once (on a single system) with a loss function that is the sum of peers local loss functions and a learning rate that is, for each partial model, divided by the number of peers implementing the model.

4   Experiments

We evaluate our approach on two types of neural networks (multi-layer perceptrons, and associative networks), and four datasets (FEMNIST, MNIST, and vehicular signatures)[1]. Additional results and details are available in our tech report (https://hal.archives-ouvertes.fr/hal-02373338).

4.1   Setting

Neural Networks. We focus on the Multi-Layer Perceptron, because it is a well-known, simple and efficient kind of neural network that is easy to train (with gradient descent). We also conduct additional experiments with a second kind of neural network, a custom neural network relying on associative learning, to show that our method is not limited to MLP and SGD.

Multi-layer Perceptron. We use an MLP [12] with similar layouts to those proposed in the original MNIST paper [19], their simple design being well suited for testing. For the same reason, we train our models using classical Stochastic Gradient Descent with Back Propagation [27], with a learning rate of 0.1 and a sigmoid activation function $f(x) = \frac{1}{1+e^{-x}}$. While improvements to SGD or the addition of convolutional layers [18] may give better performance, we stick to the most classical case to keep our results clean from potential side effects of more complex designs. We consider symbol-recognition tasks with "Accuracy" simply representing the proportion of recognized symbols. A symbol is considered recognized if the most active neuron in the last layer corresponds to it.

We define the "averaging level" as the proportion of neurons in each hidden layer that are in the global model (i.e. shared by all peers). An averaging level of 0 is equivalent to local learning, while 100 is equivalent to training a single global model (with averaging), similar to federated averaging. This approach of partial averaging of layers, rather than averaging specific layers, has proved its superiority in preliminary experiments.

---

[1] Code at https://gitlab.inria.fr/abouchra/distributed_neural_networks.

Associative Neural Network. We designed a custom kind of neural network using an associative learning rule. It is a proof of concept to show how our method performs on a network that differs significantly from the MLP and that uses a learning algorithm different from gradient descent.

We took elements from Hopfield Networks [14] for the neurons themselves and Restricted Boltzmann Machines [28] for the structure of the network. Our network is divided into a visible and a hidden layer, forming a complete (directed) bipartite graph. The activation functions are fixed thresholds (output is either 1 or 0) and the network is used for completion tasks: a partial vector (with 0 instead of 1 for some of its coordinates) is given as input and the network must return the complete vector as its output.

The visible layer's neurons' outputs are set to the values of the input vector, the outputs of the hidden-layer neurons are computed from the values of the visible layer, and finally, the values of the visible layer's neurons are updated, based on the hidden layer's values. If the weighted sum of the inputs of a neuron is $\geqslant$ some threshold (hyperparameter), the output is 1, 0 otherwise.

The training process takes a complete vector as input to the visible layer, then it computes the hidden layer's values and updates the weights of both neuron layers. If two neurons are active together, the weight of the link between them is increased, if one is active and not the other, this weight is decreased. Increment values depend on a fixed learning rate (half of the distance from the extreme value times the learning rate) and weights are in the interval $[-1; 1]$.

Partial averaging is done by averaging only a specific portion of neurons from the hidden layer.

Datasets

FEMNIST (Multi-layer Perceptron). The FEMNIST dataset [5] targets the recognition of 62 classes of handwritten characters (uppercase and lowercase letters, plus digits). FEMNIST is derived from the NIST Special Database 19 [21], as is the well-known MNIST [19] dataset. Compared to MNIST, FEMNIST adds non-digit characters and groups characters by writer. To use FEMNIST as a federated multi-task dataset, we exploit the fact that different writers do not have the same handwriting. We first partition data by writer and assign exactly one writer to each peer, then we limit all peers' (writers') sets of samples to the same size. We divide the dataset of each peer in a training and a testing section.

Modified MNIST (Multi-layer Perceptron). The well-known MNIST [19] dataset also targets handwritten recognition but only on digits. To generate different but related learning tasks for each peer, we permute digits. Compared to FEMNIST, this more artificial testing allows us to perform a more precise evaluation, by providing better control on the respective tasks of peers. To obtain different training sets for different peers, we divide the MNIST training set in successive sequences. We introduce differences between peers by permuting digits.

VSN (Multi-layer Perceptron). We also test the MLP on a significantly different task: vehicle recognition from sensors. We use a dataset from [10] containing data from sensors (notably seismic and acoustic sensors) produced while some (military) vehicle passes near the sensor. The task consists in recognizing the class of vehicle (*assault amphibious* or *dragon wagon*) from each sensor's data (binary classification). To allow an MLP to perform this task, the data from each set of sensors (node) is first transformed into 50 seismic and 50 acoustic features (100 total inputs). This process (based on Fast Fourier Transform) is described in the original paper [10].

For our distributed multi-task setup, we consider each node as a peer. The tasks are similar, as all peers classify the same kinds of vehicles from the same kind of data, but different due to the location of sensors influencing their output.

Binary Vector Completion (Associative Neural Network). To test binary-vector completion on associated neural networks, we generate binary vectors of size n ($\in \{0,1\}^n$) with $2m$ 1's (and $n - 2m$ 0's). For training, we give the network the full vectors as input; for testing, we give the network a partial input with only m 1's and observe the output. To complicate the task, we add noise to the vectors by flipping a fixed number z of random bits (1 becomes 0 and 0 becomes 1) in all vectors (training and testing) before feeding them to the network.

We consider the task successful if the number of matching 1's between the expected output and the actual output is greater than or equal to the number of non-matching 1's. More formally (**c** is expected output, **a** is actual output), a test is considered successful if and only if $\mathbf{c} \wedge \mathbf{a}$ contains at least as many 1's as $\mathbf{c} \oplus \mathbf{a}$. To generate differences between peers, we simply change, for some peers, half of the 1's that are not in the testing input.

4.2   Results

We present our results as median values over 10 runs for (FE)MNIST and VSN (20 for MNIST in Fig. 4c), and 100 runs for Associative. The error bars corresponds to the second and third quintiles. Figure 3 summarizes our results. We see that our approach systematically outperforms both local training and global training (non-multi-task federated averaging). In the following we detail a subset of our experiments.

Partial Averaging ((FE)MNIST). Figure 4a shows accuracy as a function of the averaging level on FEMNIST (results are similar on MNIST). Each line corresponds to a different number of mini-batches. We can conclude that, regardless of the number of mini batches, partial averaging always achieves the best performance, in general using an averaging level of 80. This validates our partial-averaging concept.

Figure 4b provides a different perspective by showing accuracy as a function of the number of peers that average their parameters together on FEMNIST. In each case, we have the same fixed number of peers (64) but we vary the size of the

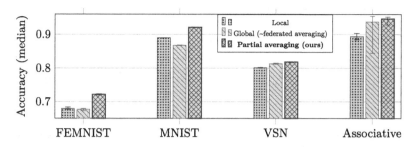

Fig. 3. Accuracy obtained by our partial averaging vs. 2 baselines (4 datasets). Partial averaging level is 80% for all datasets but Associative (for which it is 70%)

averaging groups. Each line corresponds to a different averaging level. Obviously, the line for a 0 averaging level is flat, since the number of peers has no influence in this case. It clearly appears that full averaging (100) rapidly loses efficiency when the number of peers increases, specifically at the beginning. This is due to increased number of different tasks, an averaging level of 100 being unable to perform multi-task learning. For an averaging level of 80, we observe, however, that our multi-task learning system seems to allow effective gains, especially with numerous peers.

With MNIST, we observed significant gains with an increased number of peers for high averaging levels, while no difference was visible with local learning. The difference was stronger for higher averaging levels. 80 partial averaging was leading in all cases.

Semi-local Averaging (MNIST). Here, we evaluate how a combination of global, semi-local and local models performs. We perform this test only with MNIST as this particular dataset and the way we modify it allow for a pertinent benchmark of semi-local models. We test the following schemes: (i) no averaging (local), (ii) complete averaging of all peers' neural networks (global), (iii) complete averaging limited to peers with identical permutations (per class), (iv) averaging with an 80 level of all peers' neural networks (partial avg), (v) averaging with a 70 level of all peers' neural networks combined with averaging with a 30 level for peers 0 and 1 and averaging with a 15 level for peers 2 and 3 (semi-local). For the last scheme, we test two variants: in the first case, no model is declared dependent of another one (nodep), which means that no inter-model weight is averaged, in the second case, the semi-local models are declared dependent on the global model (dep), allowing inter-model weights between global and semi-local models to be averaged at the same time as the semi-local models' internal weights. Figure 4c presents the results. Each line corresponds to one of the mentioned averaging schemes. On this test, due to the important differences between peers, global averaging is clearly inferior to all other schemes, including no averaging (local). Partial averaging performs better than local, but still worse than averaging per class with big enough mini-batches. Semi-local performs best and declaring dependencies provides further performance gains.

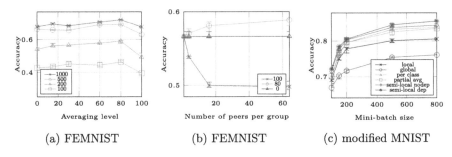

Fig. 4. Accuracy on FEMNIST (a,b) and modified MNIST (c) based on (a): averaging level for various mini batch sizes; (b): number of peers per group for various averaging levels; (c): mini-batch size for various averaging schemes including semi-local models

General Analysis of Results. Our experiments show that our method effectively enables multi-task learning with neural networks. Partial model averaging yields better results than no averaging or complete averaging on different tasks, synthetic and real, with a variety of parameters, different kinds of neural networks and learning algorithms. Among the considered problem instances, a high level of averaging (60–80%) usually turns out to be the best solution, but this may not hold true for all problem instances. Semi-local averaging and the associated dependency system further improve performance when groups of peers share more similar functions than the whole system. Multi-task learning with the MLP benefits, at least in some tasks, from the possibility to share portions of layers rather than just complete layers.

5   Related Work

Transfer learning was introduced in [24]. While the term "transfer learning" is often used to refer to a particular case of multi-task learning with neural networks, involving reusing pretrained generic first layers with task-specific final layers, transfer learning is actually a much more generic notion. Transfer learning refers to any kind of utilization of knowledge from a certain learning process for another. This is not limited to neural networks and the whole multi-task learning field is actually a subfield of transfer learning [23].

A number of researchers have addressed the problem of distributed [25], decentralized [2] or federated learning [17] focusing on single tasks. Most of these works consider SGD, even if some approaches, like federated model averaging [4], can in principle be applied to other learning algorithms. In the context of model averaging, a recent contribution [16] suggests that changing the frequency of (model) synchronization depending on the obtained accuracy can reduce communication overhead. We plan to consider this possibility as future work.

The majority of solutions for multi-task learning focus on a local setup, rather than a distributed one [26], but some decentralized solutions exist. The first, to the best of our knowledge, such contribution [22] proposes a decentralized multi-task learning algorithm limited to linear models, while a recent theoretical paper [6] proposes the use of kernel methods to learn non-linear models in federated learning. Some researchers have instead proposed a form of decentralized multi-task learning, in which each peer needs to learn a personalized convex model influenced by neighborhood relationships in a collaboration graph [2]. In a more recent paper, they also presented an algorithm to jointly learn both the personalized convex models and the collaboration graph itself [29]. In this paper, we do not use a collaboration graph; rather, we express similarities between learning tasks by defining sub-models that are shared with the entire networks (global models) or with a group of peers (semi-local models). Moreover, unlike the above solutions, our approach can optimize non-convex loss functions.

More recently, several preprints have proposed methods for federated multi-task/personalized learning with neural networks. But, none of these works considers a decentralized setup, semi-local models, or flexible layouts like ours. The method for federated multi-task learning proposed in [8] relies on a client-server model in which clients operate sequentially, performing their updates one after the other. This negates any speed gains that may result from distribution and results in very poor scalability making this method unsuitable for most practical applications. A better approach, closer to ours, is proposed in [15], with effective parallelism but still no decentralization or semi-local models. After our own initial preprint publication, in November 2019, other approaches were proposed. An approach that can be considered as a significantly more limited version of our own work, only allowing specific layers to be local (as we show in experiments, this is not always the optimal solution) is proposed in [1]. Approaches similar to [15] are presented in [11] and [9].

6 Conclusion

In this work, we introduced an effective solution for distributed multi-task learning with neural networks, applicable with different kinds of learning algorithms and not requiring mandatory prior knowledge about the nature, nor magnitude, of the differences between tasks, while still being able to benefit from such knowledge when available. The simplicity, range of application, and flexibility of our method significantly distinguishes it from existing works.

This work also opens several new directions in different fields. First, in the context of machine learning, we plan to design an algorithm that allows models to be automatically assigned to peers. Second, it would be interesting to reduce communication overhead similarly to [16]. Third, it would be interesting to apply our method to other kinds of neural networks, like LSTMs [13]. In the context of game theory, it would be interesting to study what rational peers gain by participating in the system.

Acknowledgements. We are grateful to Marc Tommasi and Aurelien Bellet our useful discussions and for their comments on earlier versions of this paper. This work was partially funded by the Pamela ANR grant (ANR-16-CE23-0016) and by the O'Browser ANR grant (ANR-16-CE25-0005).

References

1. Arivazhagan, M.G., Aggarwal, V., Singh, A.K., Choudhary, S.: Federated learning with personalization layers. arXiv preprint arXiv:1912.00818 (2019)
2. Bellet, A., Guerraoui, R., Taziki, M., Tommasi, M.: Personalized and private peer-to-peer machine learning. In: AISTATS 2018 (2018)
3. Bonawitz, K., et al.: Towards federated learning at scale: system design. In: MLSys2019 (2019)
4. Brendan McMahan, H., Moore, E., Ramage, D., Hampson, S., Agüera y Arcas, B.: Communication-efficient learning of deep networks from decentralized data. In: AISTATS2017 (2017)
5. Caldas, S., et al.: Leaf: a benchmark for federated settings. arXiv preprint arXiv:1812.01097 (2019)
6. Caldas, S., Smith, V., Talwalkar, A.: Federated kernelized multi-task learning. In: SysML2018 (2018)
7. Chen, M., Hao, Y., Hwang, K., Wang, L., Wang, L.: Disease prediction by machine learning over big data from healthcare communities. IEEE Access **5**, 8869–8879 (2017)
8. Corinzia, L., Buhmann, J.M.: Variational federated multi-task learning. arXiv preprint arXiv:1906.06268 (2019)
9. Deng, Y., Kamani, M.M., Mahdavi, M.: Adaptive personalized federated learning. arXiv preprint arXiv:2003.13461 (2020)
10. Duarte, M.F., Hen, H.Y.: Vehicle classification in distributed sensor networks. J. Parallel Distrib. Comput. **64**(7), 826–838 (2004)
11. Fallah, A., Mokhtari, A., Ozdaglar, A.: Personalized federated learning: a meta-learning approach. arXiv preprint arXiv:2002.07948 (2020)
12. Goodfellow, I., Bengio, Y., Courville, A.: Deep Learning. Cambridge, MIT press (2016)
13. Hochreiter, S., Schmidhuber, J.: Long short-term memory. Neural Comput. **9**(8), 1735–1780 (1997)
14. Hopfield, J.J.: Neural networks and physical systems with emergent collective computational abilities. PNAS **79**(8), 2554–2558 (1982)
15. Jiang, Y., Konečný, J., Rush, K., Kannan, S.: Improving federated learning personalization via model agnostic meta learning. arXiv preprint arXiv:1909.12488 (2019)
16. Kamp, M., et al.: Efficient decentralized deep learning by dynamic model averaging. In: ECMLPKDD2018 (2018)
17. Konečný, J., Brendan McMahan, H., Ramage, D., Richtarik, P.: Federated optimization: distributed machine learning for on-device intelligence. arXiv preprint arXiv:1610.02527 (2016)
18. LeCun, Y., Bengio, Y.: Convolutional networks for images, speech, and time-series. In: The handbook of brain theory and neural networks (1995)
19. LeCun, Y., Bottou, L., Bengio, Y., Haffner, P.: Gradient-based learning applied to document recognition. Proc. of the IEEE **86**(11), 2278–2324 (1998)

20. Li, T., Sanjabi, M., Beirami, A., Smith, V.: Fair resource allocation in federated learning. In: ICLR2020 (2020)
21. National Institute of Standards and Technology, U.G.: Nist special database 19 (2016)
22. Ormándi, R., Hegedűs, I., Jelasity, M.: Gossip learning with linear models on fully distributed data. Concurrency Comput. Pract. Experience **25**(4), 556–571 (2012)
23. Pan, S.J., Yang, Q.: A survey on transfer learning. In: TKDE2009 (2009)
24. Pratt, L.Y., Mostow, J., Kamm, C.A.: Direct transfer of learned information among neural networks. In: AAAI1991 (1991)
25. Recht, B., Ré, C., Wright, S.J., Niu, F.: Hogwild: a lock-free approach to parallelizing stochastic gradient descent. In: NIPS'11 (2011)
26. Ruder, S.: An overview of multi-task learning in deep neural networks. arXiv preprint arXiv:1706.05098 (2017)
27. Rumelhart, D.E., Hinton, G.E., Williams, R.J.: Learning internal representations by error propagation. In: Parallel Distributed Processing: Explorations in the Microstructure of Cognition (1986)
28. Smolensky, P.: Information processing in dynamical systems: foundations of harmony theory. In: Parallel Distributed Processing: Explorations in the Microstructure of Cognition (1986)
29. Zantedeschi, V., Bellet, A., Tommasi, M.: Fully decentralized joint learning of personalized models and collaboration graphs. arXiv preprint arXiv:1901.08460 (2019)

Deep Hybrid Neural Networks with Improved Weighted Word Embeddings for Sentiment Analysis

Rania Othman[1(✉)], Rim Faiz[2], Youcef Abdelsadek[3], Kamel Chelghoum[3], and Imed Kacem[3]

[1] LARODEC, Institut Supérieur de Gestion de Tunis,
Université de Tunis, Tunis, Tunisia
rania.othman@gmx.com
[2] LARODEC, Institut des Hautes Études Commerciales de Carthage,
Université de Carthage, Tunis, Tunisia
rim.faiz@ihec.rnu.tn
[3] LCOMS, Université de Lorraine, Metz, France
{youcef.abdelsadek,kamel.chelghoum,imed.kacem}@univ-lorraine.fr

Abstract. Deep learning models such as Convolutional Neural Network (CNN) and Long Short-Term Memory (LSTM) models have recently emerged as effective solutions to various NLP tasks with comparatively remarkable results. The CNN model efficiently extracts higher level features using convolutional layers and max-pooling layers while the LSTM model allows capturing long-term dependencies between word sequences. In this paper, we propose a hybrid CNN-LSTM model taking advantage of both models to overcome the sentiment analysis problem on Twitter data. We employ a multi-channel CNN that extracts local n-gram features in different sizes using several filters of different lengths. We also employ a weighted average word embeddings method which incorporates sentiment information in the continuous representation of words based on an adapted version of the delta TFIDF measure. These word representations will be the input for the CNN-LSTM model. Experiment results substantiate our intuition by reaching good macro average recall and accuracy scores beating several existing models as well as our same model using individual CNN and LSTM.

Keywords: Sentiment analysis · Neural networks · Weighted word embeddings · Word2Vec · Natural Language Processing

1 Introduction

As the volume of data from social network services increases, there has been a burgeoning interest in an exciting Natural Language Processing (NLP) related area namely, sentiment analysis (SA), which allows to distill knowledge from this huge and opinion-rich resource.

© Springer Nature Switzerland AG 2021
P. H. Abreu et al. (Eds.): IDA 2021, LNCS 12695, pp. 50–62, 2021.
https://doi.org/10.1007/978-3-030-74251-5_5

SA, can be defined as the field of study that analyzes people's opinions, sentiments, evaluations, appraisals, attitudes, and emotions towards entities such as products, services, individuals, and their attributes [8]. The potential gains of an efficient SA system are many. For instance, this helps companies keep track and have general overview on their customer opinions about the brand.

Several works have been addressed to tackle the problem of sentiment analysis involving supervised and unsupervised approaches. Supervised approaches [1,17] rely typically on bag-of-words (BoW) model which suffers from high dimensionality and sparsity and cannot sufficiently capture the complex linguistic characteristics of words while ignoring context, grammar and even word order. More recent works [4] tend to employ dense word embeddings, which encode meanings of words to low dimensional vector spaces.

Although existing word embedding learning algorithms such as Word2Vec [10] and GloVe [18] have been shown to be effective in general classification task, sentiment is not properly encoded in those vectors. This is problematic for sentiment analysis as words with similar syntactic context but opposite sentiment polarity, such as 'best' and 'worst', can be mapped to close word vectors.

In this paper, we propose a weighted average word embeddings method which encodes sentiment information in the continuous representation of words based on an adapted version of the delta TFIDF measure [9]. To the best of our knowledge, this is the first research weighting word embeddings vectors by the Delta TFIDF measure.

These word representations will be the input for our hybrid CNN-LSTM model to determine the sentiment polarity. In fact, Long Short-Term Memory (LSTM) and Convolutional Neural Network (CNN) models have been widely employed in several NLP tasks achieving effective results. The CNN model extracts local features using convolutional layers while the LSTM model allows to efficiently capture long distance dependencies across word sequences. We assume that combining the two deep neural networks allows to take advantage of both models.

The rest of the paper is organized as follows: Sect. 2 reviews the related work on both sentiment analysis and vector representation. Our hybrid model for sentiment analysis is described in Sect. 3. The experimental protocol as well as the obtained results are presented in Sect. 4. Finally, Sect. 5 outlines the main conclusions and future work.

2   Related Work

2.1   Sentiment Analysis

Existing works addressed to mine opinions from unstructured reviews can be very broadly divided into two main categories supervised and unsupervised. On the one hand, the supervised learning approaches are based on a machine-learning model that is trained on manually labeled data to extract and classify the feature set in the reviews. Although these techniques provide good results for the sentiment analysis task, they require extensive manual work for the training set preparation, they are also time consuming, and sometimes domain dependent. The most common techniques employed in supervised approaches are decision tree, support vector machine (SVM), K-nearest neighbor (KNN), Naïve Bayesian classifier and neural network [1,17]. On the other hand, unsupervised approaches which calculate the sum of the sentiment orientation of each word or phrase in the text to determine the contextual polarity according to the pre-labeled positive and negative words in the lexicons. Several studies have already been published in this direction. Kamps et al. [6] determined semantic polarity of adjectives using a distance metric on WordNet. Othman et al. [15] employed the lexicon SentiWordnet created by Baccianella et al. [2] to compute tweet polarities for sentiment summarization in public conversations.

More recently, several researchers attempt to employ deep learning algorithms. Baziotis et al. [3] built a framework with a 2-layer Bidirectional LSTM, equipped with two kinds of mechanisms. In [14], the authors also presented a deep learning-based approach to sentiment analysis on product reviews from tweets. The presented architecture combines TF-IDF weighted Glove word embedding with CNN-LSTM architecture. In our work, we also combine the two neural networks with a novel strategy of weighting vector representation of words.

2.2 Vector Representation

Most existing supervised approaches for sentiment analysis follow Pang et al. [17] who employed BoW representation, representing each word as a one-hot vector. Although this method has shown to be effective, it suffers from high dimensionality and sparsity and cannot sufficiently capture the complex linguistic characteristics of words.

An effective feature learning method to capture both the syntactic structure and contextual information is to compose continuous embeddings of words. Bespalov et al. [4] initialized the word embedding by Latent Semantic Analysis and represented each document as the linear weighted of n-gram vectors.

The biggest issue is that most studies employing word embeddings for sentiment analysis, usually only model the syntactic context of words so that they cannot distinguish words with similar context and opposite sentiment polarity. To tackle this problem, recent studies have suggested learning sentiment embeddings [12,20]. These works employ positive and negative polarity labels provided by the training instances and apply an objective function to optimize word vectors.

Tang et al. [20] developed sentiment-specific word embeddings (SSWE) composed by Min, Max and Avg unordered composition functions and learned within a simple neural model. The learned embedding vectors were, then, fed to classical supervised classifiers. For their part, Mulki et al. [12] presented syntax-ignorant, sentiment-specific n-gram embeddings for sentiment analysis of several Arabic dialects. In their proposed model, the sentiment was expressed by embeddings, composed via the unordered additive composition function and learned within a shallow neural architecture. In this paper, we adopt another strategy to learn sentiment embeddings where an adapted version of the delta TFIDF measure is employed as the weight of each word.

3   Proposed Model

Our model combines convolutional and recurrent neural networks notably, CNN and LSTM, on Twitter data, and is composed of six types of layers: embedding, convolution, max-pooling, LSTM, dense, and softmax. The intuition behind our model is that the convolution layer will extract local features while the LSTM layer will be able to employ the ordering of extracted features to learn about the input's text ordering. Below, we detail each of the subcomponents of our model in turn.

3.1   Embedding Layer

The embedding layer represents the initial layer of the model. The layer allows for the initialization of vocabulary words vectors through the pre-trained word vectors matrix. Every tweet is regarded as a sequence of numerical word tokens t_1, t_2, ..., t_N, where t_N is a number representing a real word and N represents the length of the token vector. The output of the embedding layer is a matrix $T \in \Re^{N \times d}$ where d is the dimension of each word vector.

We adopt our novel word embedding weighting scheme, in which we weight each word embedding vector by the add-one smoothing Delta Term Frequency-Inverse Document Frequency (Delta TFIDF) of the word it represents. We present in the following the different phases of learning sentiment-specific word embedding.

Word Embeddings
We use the pre-trained word embeddings, generated with the Word2Vec [10] which comes in two models, the Continuous Bag-of-Words (CBOW) and the Skip-Gram model. In this work, we consider the CBOW model to learn word embeddings, since it is more efficient and performs better with frequent words and sizeable data than Skipgram.

The CBOW model predicts the center word given the representation of its surrounding words using continuous distributed bag-of-words representation of the context [10].

A softmax function is applied over the vocabulary V to predict the center word w_0 while the context vector is got by averaging the embeddings of each contextual word. More formally, let d be the word embedding dimension, the output matrix $O \in \Re^{|V| \times d}$ maps the context vector c into a $| V |$ dimensional vector representing the center word, and maximizes the following probability:

$$P(v_0 \mid w_{[-b,b]}) = \frac{\exp v_0^T O_c}{\sum_{v \epsilon V} \exp v^T O_c} \tag{1}$$

where b is a hyperparameter defining the window of context words, O_c represents the projection of the context vector c into the vocabulary V and v is a one-hot representation.

We instantiated the training algorithm using the set of tweets in which each tweet is represented by a set of sentences of tokenized words. We use the publicly available pr-trained word2vec vectors trained on part of Google News dataset, which is composed of approximately 100 billion words[1].

Delta TFIDF Weighted Word Embeddings

We adopt a word embedding weighting approach, in which we weight each word embedding vector by the Delta Term Frequency-Inverse Document Frequency (Delta TFIDF) of the word it represents. Delta TFIDF is a supervised weighting measure representing the difference of a term's idf values in the positive and negative training documents [9]. Unlike TFIDF which does not consider the relevance of a feature toward each category, this measure term frequency provides a clean linear division between positive and negative sentiment features. Delta TFIDF boosts the importance of words that are unevenly distributed between the positive and negative classes and discounting evenly distributed words. Martineau and Finin [9] show that this term frequency produces better results than the traditional tf or binary weighting scheme in a sentiment classification task. Delta TFIDF of a word w in a tweet t is given by the following Equation:

$$V_{w,t} = C_{w,t} \times \log_2(\frac{|N| \, P_w}{N_w \, |P|}) \tag{2}$$

Where $C_{w,t}$ is the number of times word w occurs in tweet t, $|N|$ and $|P|$ represent the number of tweets in the negatively and positively labeled training sets respectively, N_w and P_w represent the number of tweets in the negatively and positively labeled training sets respectively with word w.

A problem with Delta TFIDF is that it is susceptible to the errors caused by the case of $N_w = 0$ or $P_w = 0$. To deal with this problem, we employ a smoothing parameter $\alpha = 0.5$ [16], the Delta TFIDF is then defined as:

$$V_{w,t} = C_{w,t} \times \log_2(\frac{|N| \, P_w + \alpha}{|P| \, N_w + \alpha}) \tag{3}$$

On analysis, we observed that, the add-one smoothing leads to unreasonably large weight for both high and low frequency singular terms. To illustrate this, let's take a real example. We extract 3 terms where t_1 with $P_w = 100$ and $N_w = 0$, term t_2 with $P_w = 2$ and $N_w = 0$ and term t_3 with $P_w = 100$ and $N_w = 1$. Having our test set involving $N^+ = 2,375$ and $N^- = 3,972$, the obtained global weight of t_1, t_2 and t_3 is $g_1 = 18.85$, $g_2 = 13.21$ and $g_3 = 9.22$ respectively.

This result violates our intuition of having the weight of t_1 and t_3 relatively higher than t_2. Another illogical observation is that the weight of t_1 is too large compared to t_3, while their frequency and distribution are close to each other. To resolve this problem, we employ a novel add-one smoothing which is given by the following Equation:

$$V_{w,t} = C_{w,t} \times \log_2(\frac{|N| \, (P_w + \alpha)}{|P| \, (N_w + \alpha)}) \tag{4}$$

---

[1] https://code.google.com/p/word2vec/.

Using the novel add-one smoothing, the weights of t_1, t_2 and t_3 become $g_1 =$ 6.90, $g_2 = 1.57$ and $g_3 = 5.32$ respectively. These results seem more reasonable while the weights of t_1 and t_3 are close and relatively large and the weight of t_2 is small compared to t_1 and t_3.

Calculating Tweet Vectors

In order to get the sentence vectors, we calculate the average weighted embedding vector V_t of all the words involved in each tweet as follows:

$$V_t = \frac{\sum_{i=1}^{|V|} (v_{w_i} \times wgt(w_i, t))}{\sum_{i=1}^{|V|} wgt(w_i, t)} \tag{5}$$

where v_{w_i} is the embedding vector of the word w_i generated by word2vec, $wgt(w_i, t)$ is the weight of the word w_i in a given tweet t and $|V|$ is the number of word vectors in t.

3.2   Convolution Layer

In a convolutional layer, m filters are applied to a sliding window of width w over the matrix of previous embedding layer to extract new local w-gram features. The structure of convolution employed for sentence classification is shown in Fig. 1 [7]. Let $F \in \Re^{w \times d}$ be a filter matrix. The result of each filter F will be a feature map denoted f, where the i-th element of f is learnt as follows:

$$f_i = fct(T_{i:i+w-1} \circ F + b) \tag{6}$$

Where fct denotes a nonlinear activation function, we employ ReLU function [13] for faster calculation, $\circ$ represents a convolution operation, $T_{i:i+w-1}$ denotes the token vectors t_i, t_{i+1}, ..., $t_{i:i+w-1}$ (if $k > N$, $t_k = 0$), and $b \in \Re$ is a bias term.

We apply multi-channel CNN by using multiple convolving filters in order to extract active local n-gram features in different sizes. Token vectors are padded before convolution in order to keep identical size for outputs of different filters.

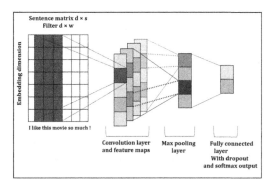

Fig. 1. Convolutional neural networks for sentence classification

3.3   Max-Pooling and Dropout Layer

We apply pairwise max pooling operation over the feature map to down-sample and consolidate the features learned in the convolutional layer by taking the maximum of the result of each filter. We employ max rather than mean pooling because the salient feature represents the most distinguishing trait of a tweet. Max-pooling allows also to reduce the computation for upper layers by eliminating non-maximal values. The obtained region vectors are fed thereafter to an LSTM layer. We apply a dropout layer after both a convolution and max-pooling layer to prevent overfitting.

3.4   LSTM Layer

Unlike traditional Recurrent Neural Network RNN unit, LSTM unit keeps the existing memory c_t at time t. The input at time t is input vector x_t, hidden state h_{t-1}, cell state c_{t-1} , the output is h_t, c_t. They can be updated using three different gates by the following equations:

$$i_t = sigmoid(W_i x_t + U_i h_{t-1} + b_i) \tag{7}$$

$$f_t = sigmoid(W_f x_t + U_f h_{t-1} + b_f) \tag{8}$$

$$\tilde{c}_t = tanh(W_c x_t + U_c h_{t-1} + b_c) \tag{9}$$

$$c_t = i_t \odot \tilde{c}_t + f_t \odot c_{t-1} \tag{10}$$

$$o_t = sigmoid(W_o x_t + U_0 h_{t-1} + b_0) \tag{11}$$

$$h_t = o_t \odot \tanh(c_t) \tag{12}$$

where i_t, f_t, o_t are input, forget, and output gates at time t, respectively. W_k, U_k represent LSTM parameterized weight matrices, b_k is the bias vector for each k in $\{i, f, c, o\}$ and ($\odot$) denotes an element-wise vector product, known as the Hadamard product which is simply an entrywise multiplication. Figure 2 [11] illustrates the inner architecture of a standard LSTM module.

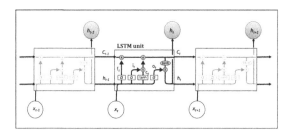

Fig. 2. The inner architecture of a standard LSTM module

3.5 Fully-Connected Layer

The fully connected layer multiplies results from the previous layer with a weight matrix and adds a bias vector. The ReLU activation function is also applied. The result vectors are finally input to the output layer.

3.6 Output Layer

The output layer is a fully connected layer using softmax as an activation function to output the final classification result. Softmax function is calculated by the following equation:

$$p(y = j \mid x) = \frac{\exp^{x^T w_j}}{\sum_{s=1}^{S} \exp^{x_s^T w_j}} \tag{13}$$

where x is the input vector, w is the weight vector, and S is the number of sentiment classes. The final classification result $\hat{y}$ will be then given as follows:

$$\hat{y} = argmax_j P(y = j \mid x) \tag{14}$$

4 Experiments and Results

4.1 Dataset Description

We employ the training and test datasets provided by the SemEval- 2017 competition for task 4 Subtask A. The dataset is among the largest manually-annotated corpus, labeled on CrowdFlower. A summary of the datasets is given in Table 1. As shown in the table, the dataset involves 62,617 tweets labeled in three classes positive, negative and neutral.

Table 1. Statistics about the SemEval-2017 training and testing datasets for task 4 subtask A

Dataset	Positive	Neutral	Negative	Total
Train	19,902	22,591	7,840	50,333
Test	2,375	5,937	3,972	12,284

4.2 Parameters

The experiments were developed by using Scikit-learn machine learning library [2] and Keras deep learning library [3] with TensorFlow backend [4]. The best parameters for our models were initially selected based on previous implementations of CNNs and LSTMs, and further fine-tunned by manual testing. Different employed parameters are summarized in Table 2.

---

[2] https://scikit-learn.org/stable/.
[3] https://keras.io/.
[4] https://www.tensorflow.org/.

Table 2. Parameters selected for our CNN-LSTM model

Embedding Dimension	32
Batch Size	128
Epochs	6
Filters	32
Kernel size	3
Pool Size	2
Dropout	0.5

4.3 Evaluation Metrics

To evaluate our system performance, we employ the macro-averaged recall (AvgRec) and accuracy since they are the most popular measures used in the sentiment analysis task, they are also the official two evaluation metrics employed in SemEval 2017 Task 4, subtask A. AvgRec is calculated among three classes (i.e., positive, negative and neutral) as follows:

$$R_{macro} = \frac{R_{Pos} + R_{Neg} + R_{Neu}}{3} \tag{15}$$

where the recall for each polarity is computed using the following formula:

$$Recall = \frac{TP}{TP + FN} \tag{16}$$

The accuracy is given as follows:

$$Accuracy = \frac{TP + TN}{TP + TN + FP + FN} \tag{17}$$

While TP, TN, FP, FN denote respectively the number of relevant identified features, the number of relevant non identified features, the number of irrelevant identified features and the number of irrelevant non-identified features.

4.4 Results and Discussion

Fig. 3 and 4 show the model's accuracy and loss graphs through epochs respectively. From Fig. 4, we can see that there is no significance difference between the training and validation loss. The training loss continues to decrease after each epoch which means that the model is learning to recognize the specific patterns. Similarly, the validation loss continues to decrease to reach 0.33. On the other hand, the plot in Fig. 3 shows that the model has comparable consistent accuracy on both train and validation sets. Both curves continue to increase without a sudden decrease of the validation accuracy, indicating a good fit and reaching an accuracy score of 0.659.

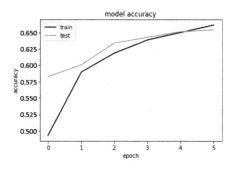

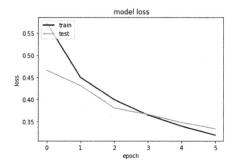

Fig. 3. Accuracy vs epochs for our deep hybrid model

Fig. 4. Loss vs epochs for our deep hybrid model

Furthermore, we compare the performance of our system with the top three ranking teams participated to Subtask A of SemEval sentiment classification task on the same dataset. BB_twtr [5] used an ensemble of LSTMs and CNNs with multiple convolution operations, while DataStories [3] employed deep LSTM networks with an attention mechanism. From their part, LIA team [19] proposes an ensemble of Deep Neural Network (DNN) models involving Convolutional Neural Network (CNN) and Recurrent Neural Network Long Short-Term Memory (RNN-LSTM).

Table 3 lists the AvgRec and the accuracy of the top SemEval ranking systems as well different variants of our system. Datastories, BB_twtr and LIA reach 0.681, 0.681, and 0.676 in AvgRec while achieving 0.651, 0.658 and 0.661 accuracy scores respectively. We reach 0.723 macro-recall score and 0.659 accuracy score by using our deep hybrid model with Delta TFIDF weighted embeddings as input. The results indicate that our system is competitive providing higher macro-averaged recall and close accuracy score.

Table 3. Performance of different variants of our system and the top ranked systems.

System	R_{macro}	Acc
Our system	0.723	0.659
DataStories	$0.681_{(1)}$	$0.651_{(5)}$
BB_twtr	$0.681_{(1)}$	$0.658_{(3)}$
LIA	$0.676_{(3)}$	$0.661_{(2)}$
CNN	0.602	0.581
LSTM	0.664	0.612
Unweighted WE	0.511	0.492
TFIDF WE	0.540	0.532

Moreover, we compare our obtained results with the results generated by our system using unweighted and TFIDF weighted embeddings generated by word2vec denoted "Unweighted WE" and "TFIDF WE" respectively as well as individual CNN and LSTM.

From Table 2, we can see that the performance of unweighted and TFIDF weighted embeddings are obviously lower than all the systems. TFIDF weighted embeddings outperforms unweighted word embeddings by exploiting more contextual information in the sentiment classification while Delta TFIDF produces significantly better weights than TFIDF. Indeed, the TFIDF boosts the value of terms that occur many times in a given document while occurring rarely in other documents. Since our datasets are composed of opinionated documents, sentimental words tend to be very frequent in the documents giving poor IDF scores which can lead to a biased sentiment word discrimination.

On the other hand, TFIDF weighted embeddings do not explicitly exploit the sentiment information of the text, as a result, words with similar context but opposite polarity such as good and bad are mapped to close word vectors. Our sentiment weighted word embeddings effectively distinguish words with opposite sentiment polarity and perform better results compared with TFIDF weighted embeddings.

Furthermore, we can see that employing individual CNN reveals lower results than individual LSTM with 0.602 AvgRec and 0.581 accuracy against 0.664 and 0.612 AvgRec and accuracy respectively obtained by LSTM. Our model gives a better performance than LSTM and CNN which proves the efficiency of our approach which takes the advantages of both models. The results proves the validity of our idea.

5   Conclusion

In this paper, we have presented our model that aims to combine two powerful neural networks notably CNN and LSTM to achieve better performance on sentiment analysis. We also employ a weighted average word embeddings method which incorporates sentiment information in the continuous representation of words based on an adapted version of the delta TFIDF measure. The experimental results demonstrate that our model is promising by reaching good macro average recall and accuracy scores beating several existing models as well as individual CNN and LSTM. In the future, we attempt to adapt our system to be multi-lingual system in order to support tweets from other languages, such as Arabic.

References

1. Agarwal, A., Xie, B., Vovsha, I., Rambow, O., Passonneau, R.: Sentiment analysis of twitter data. In: Proceedings of the Workshop on Languages in Social Media. Association for Computational Linguistics, pp. 30–38 (2011)
2. Baccianella, S., Esuli, A., Sebastiani, F.: Sentiwordnet 3.0: an enhanced lexical resource for sentiment analysis and opinion mining. In: Proceedings of the Seventh International Conference on Language Resources and Evaluation (LREC2010), vol. 10, pp. 2200–2204 (2010)
3. Baziotis, C., Pelekis, N., Doulkeridis, C.: Datastories at semeval-2017 task 4: deep lstm with attention for message-level and topic-based sentiment analysis. In: Proceedings of the 11th international workshop on semantic evaluation (SemEval-2017), pp. 747–754 (2017)
4. Bengio, Y., Courville, A., Vincent, P.: Representation learning: a review and new perspectives. IEEE Trans. Pattern Anal. Mach. Intell. **35**(8), 1798–1828 (2013)
5. Cliche, M.: Bb_twtr at semeval-2017 task 4: twitter sentiment analysis with CNNS and LSTMS. arXiv preprint arXiv:1704.06125 (2017)
6. Kamps, J., et al.: Using wordnet to measure semantic orientations of adjectives. In: LREC, vol. 4, pp. 1115–1118. Citeseer (2004)
7. Kim, Y.: Convolutional neural networks for sentence classification. arXiv preprint arXiv:1408.5882 (2014)
8. Liu, B.: Sentiment analysis and opinion mining. Synth. Lect. Hum. Lang. Technol. **5**(1), 1–167 (2012)
9. Martineau, J.C., Finin, T.: Delta TFIDF: an improved feature space for sentiment analysis. In: Third international AAAI conference on weblogs and social media (2009)
10. Mikolov, T., Chen, K., Corrado, G., Dean, J.: Efficient estimation of word representations in vector space. arXiv preprint arXiv:1301.3781 (2013)
11. Minaee, S., Azimi, E., Abdolrashidi, A.: Deep-sentiment: sentiment analysis using ensemble of cnn and bi-lstm models. arXiv preprint arXiv:1904.04206 (2019)
12. Mulki, H., Haddad, H., Gridach, M., Babaoglu, I.: Syntax-ignorant n-gram embeddings for dialectal arabic sentiment analysis. Nat. Lang. Eng. **1**, 24 (2019)
13. Nair, V., Hinton, G.E.: Rectified linear units improve restricted boltzmann machines. In: Proceedings of the 27th international conference on machine learning (ICML-10), pp. 807–814 (2010)
14. Onan, A.: Sentiment analysis on product reviews based on weighted word embeddings and deep neural networks. Concurrency Comput. Pract. Experience p. e5909 (2020)
15. Othman, R., Belkaroui, R., Faiz, R.: Customer opinion summarization based on twitter conversations. In: Proceedings of the 6th International Conference on Web Intelligence, Mining and Semantics, p. 4. ACM (2016)
16. Paltoglou, G., Thelwall, M.: A study of information retrieval weighting schemes for sentiment analysis. In: Proceedings of the 48th Annual Meeting of the Association for Computational Linguistics, pp. 1386–1395. Association for Computational Linguistics (2010)
17. Pang, B., Lee, L., Vaithyanathan, S.: Thumbs up?: sentiment classification using machine learning techniques. In: Proceedings of the ACL-02 Conference on Empirical Methods in Natural Language Processing, Vol. 10, pp. 79–86. Association for Computational Linguistics (2002)

18. Pennington, J., Socher, R., Manning, C.: Glove: global vectors for word representation. In: Proceedings of the 2014 Conference on Empirical Methods in Natural Language Processing (EMNLP), pp. 1532–1543 (2014)
19. Rouvier, M.: Lia at semeval-2017 task 4: an ensemble of neural networks for sentiment classification. In: Proceedings of the 11th International Workshop on Semantic Evaluation (SemEval-2017), pp. 760–765 (2017)
20. Tang, D., Wei, F., Yang, N., Zhou, M., Liu, T., Qin, B.: Learning sentiment-specific word embedding for twitter sentiment classification. In: Proceedings of the 52nd Annual Meeting of the Association for Computational Linguistics (Volume 1: Long Papers), vol. 1, pp. 1555–1565 (2014)

Explaining Neural Networks by Decoding Layer Activations

Johannes Schneider[1]([✉]) and Michalis Vlachos[2]

[1] Institute of Information Systems, University of Liechtenstein, Vaduz, Liechtenstein
`johannes.schneider@uni.li`
[2] Department of Information Systems, HEC, University of Lausanne, Lausanne, Switzerland

Abstract. We present a 'CLAssifier-DECoder' architecture (*ClaDec*) which facilitates the comprehension of the output of an arbitrary layer in a neural network (NN). It uses a decoder to transform the non-interpretable representation of the given layer to a representation that is more similar to the domain a human is familiar with. In an image recognition problem, one can recognize what information is represented by a layer by contrasting reconstructed images of *ClaDec* with those of a conventional autoencoder(AE) serving as reference. We also extend *ClaDec* to allow the trade-off between human interpretability and fidelity. We evaluate our approach for image classification using Convolutional NNs. We show that reconstructed visualizations using encodings from a classifier capture more relevant information for classification than conventional AEs. Relevant code is available at https://github.com/JohnTailor/ClaDec.

1 Introduction

Understanding a NN is a multi-faceted problem, ranging from understanding single decisions, single neurons and single layers, up to explaining complete models. In this work, we are interested in better understanding the decision of a NN with respect to one or several user-defined layers that originate from a complex feature hierarchy, as commonly found in deep learning models. In a layered model, each layer corresponds to a transformed representation of the original input. Thus, the NN succinctly transforms the input into representations that are more useful for the task at hand, such as classification. From this point of view, we seek to answer the question: *"Given an input X, what does the representation $L(X)$ produced in a layer L tell us about the decision and about the network?"*. To address this question, we propose a classifier-decoder architecture called *ClaDec*. It uses a decoder to transform the representation $L(X)$ produced by a layer L of the classifier, with the goal to explain that layer via a human understandable representation, i.e., one that is similar to the input domain. The layer in question provides the "code" that is fed into a decoder. The motivation for this architecture stems from the observation that AE architectures are good at (re)constructing high-dimensional data from a low-dimensional representation. The idea behind this, stems from the observation that the classifier to be

P. H. Abreu et al. (Eds.): IDA 2021, LNCS 12695, pp. 63–75, 2021.
https://doi.org/10.1007/978-3-030-74251-5_6

explained is expected to encode faithfully aspects relevant to the classification and ignore input information that does not impact decisions. Therefore, use of a decoder can lead to accurate reconstruction of parts and attributes of the input that are essential for classification. In contrast, inputs that have little or no influence to the classification will be reconstructed at lower fidelity. Attributes of an input might refer to basic properties such as color, shape, sharpness but also more abstract, higher-level concepts. That is, reconstructions of higher-level constructs might be altered to be more similar to prototypical instances.

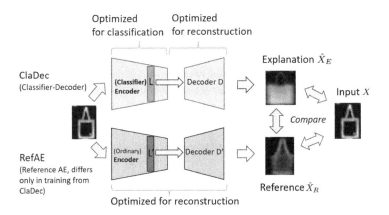

Fig. 1. Basic architecture of *ClaDec* and *RefAE* and explanation process

Explanations should fulfill many partially conflicting objectives. We are interested in the trade-off between fidelity (How accurately does the explanation express the model behavior?) and interpretability (How easy is it to make sense of the explanation?). While these properties of explanations are well-known, existing methods typically do not accommodate adjusting this trade-off. In contrast, we propose an extension of our base architecture *ClaDec* by adding a classification loss. It allows to balance between producing reconstructions that are similar to the inputs, i.e., training data that a user is probably more familiar with (easier interpretation), and reconstructions that are strongly influenced by the model to explain (higher fidelity) but may deviate more from what the user knows or has seen. Our approach relies on an auxiliary model, a decoder, to provide explanations. Similar to other methods that use auxiliary or proxy models, e.g., to synthesize inputs [10] or approximate model behavior [11], we face the problem that explanation fidelity may be negatively impacted by a poor auxiliary model. That is, reconstructions produced by AEs (or GANs) might suffer from artifacts. For example, AEs are known to produce images that might appear more blurry than real images. People have noticed that GANs can produce clearer images but they may suffer from other artifacts as shown in [10]. Neglecting that the explainability method might introduce artifacts can have an adverse impact on understandability and even lead to wrong conclusions on model behavior. When looking at the reconstruction, a person not familiar with such artifacts might not attribute the distortion to the auxiliary model being used but she might believe that it is due to the model to be explained. While evaluation of explainability methods has many known open questions [19], this is the first work that has made this observation.

To avoid any wrongful perceptions with respect to artifacts in reconstruction, we suggest to compare outcomes of auxiliary models to a reference architecture. We employ an auto-encoder *RefAE* with the exact same architecture as *ClaDec* to generate outputs for comparison as shown in Fig. 1. The encoder of *RefAE* is not trained for classification, but the *RefAE* model optimizes the reconstruction loss of the original inputs as any conventional AE. Therefore, only the differences visible in the reconstructions of *RefAE* and *ClaDec* can be attributed to the model to be explained. The proposed comparison to a reference model can also be perceived as a rudimentary sanity check, i.e., if there are no differences then either the explainability method is of little value or the objective of the model to be explained is similar to that of the reference AE, as we shall elaborate more in our theoretical motivation. We believe that such sanity checks are urgently needed, since multiple explanation methods have been scrutinized for failing "sanity" checks and simple robustness properties [1,5,8]. For that reason, we also introduce a sanity check that formalizes the idea that inputs plus explanations should lead to better performance on downstream tasks than inputs alone. In our context, we even show that auxiliary classifiers trained on either reconstructions from *RefAE* or *ClaDec* perform better on the latter, although the reference AE leads to reconstructions that are closer to the original inputs. Thus, the reconstructions of *ClaDec* are more amendable for the task to be solved. Overall, we make the following **contributions**:

i) We present a novel method to understand layers of NNs. It uses a decoder to translate non-interpretable layer outputs into a human understandable representation. It allows to trade interpretability and fidelity.

ii) We introduce a method dealing with artifacts created by auxiliary models (or proxies) through comparisons with adequate references. This includes evaluation of methods.

2   Method and Architecture

The *ClaDec* architecture is shown on the top portion of Fig. 1. It consists of an encoder and a decoder reconstructing the input. The encoder is made of all layers of a classifier up to a user-specified layer L. The entire classifier has been trained beforehand to optimize classification loss. Its parameters remain unchanged during the explanation process. To explain layer L of the classifier for an input X, we use the activations of layer $L(X)$. The activations $L(X)$ are provided to the decoder. The decoder is trained to optimize the reconstruction loss with respect to the original inputs X. The *RefAE* architecture is identical to *ClaDec*. It differs only in the training process and the objective. For the reference AE, the encoder and decoder are trained jointly to optimize the reconstruction loss of inputs X.

In contrast, the encoder is treated as fixed in *ClaDec*. Once the training of all components is completed, explanations can be generated without further need for optimization. That is, for an input X, *ClaDec* computes the reconstruction $\hat{X}_E$ serving together with the original input and the reconstruction from *RefAE* as the explanation.

However, comparing the reconstruction $\hat{X}_E$ to the input X may be difficult and even misleading, since the decoder can introduce distortions. Image reconstruction in general by AEs or GANs is not perfect. Therefore, it is unclear, whether the differences between the input and the reconstruction originate from the encoding of the classifier or the inherent limitations of the decoder. This problem exists in other methods as well, e.g. [10], but it has been ignored. Thus, we propose to use both the *RefAE* (capturing unavoidable limitations of the model or data) and *ClaDec* (capturing model behavior). The evaluation proceeds by comparing the reconstructed "reference" from *RefAE*, the explanation from *ClaDec* and the input. Only differences between the input and the reconstruction of *ClaDec* that do not occur in the reconstruction of the reference can be attributed to the classifier. Figure 2 shows an extension of the base architecture of *ClaDec* (Fig. 1) using a second loss term for the decoder training. It is motivated by the fact that *ClaDec* seems to yield reconstructions that capture more aspects of the input domain than of the classifier. That is, reconstructions might be easy to interpret, but in some cases it might be preferable to allow for explanations that are more fidel, i.e. capturing more aspects of the model that should be explained.

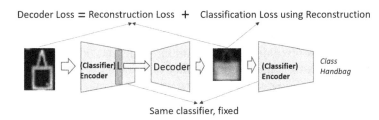

Fig. 2. Extension of the *ClaDec* architecture. The decoder is optimized for reconstruction and classification loss

More formally, for an input X, a classifier C (to be explained) and a layer L to explain, let $L(X)$ be the activations of layer L for input X, and $Loss(CL(X), Y)$ the classification loss of X depending on the true classes Y. The decoder D transforms the representation $L(X)$ into the reconstruction $\hat{X}$. For *ClaDec* the decoder loss is:

$$Loss(X) := (1 - \alpha) \cdot \sum_i (X_i - \hat{X}_{E,i})^2 + \alpha \cdot Loss(CL(\hat{X}_E), Y) \tag{1}$$

$$\text{with } \hat{X}_E := D(L(X)) \text{ and } \alpha \in [0, 1]$$

The trade-off parameter α allows to control whether reconstructions $\hat{X}_E$ are more similar to inputs with which the domain expert is more familiar, or reconstructions that are more shaped by the classifier and, thus, they might look more different than training data a domain expert is familiar with. For reconstructions $X_{R,i}$ of *RefAE* the loss is only the reconstruction loss $\sum_i (X_i - \hat{X}_{R,i})^2$.

3   Theoretical Motivation of *ClaDec*

We provide rational for reconstructing explanations using a decoder from a layer of a classifier that should be explained, and comparing it to the output of a conventional AE, i.e. *RefAE* (see Fig. 1). AEs perform a transformation of inputs to a latent space and then back to the original space. This comes with information loss on the original inputs because reconstructions are typically not identical to inputs. To provide intuition, we focus on a simple architecture with a linear encoder (consisting of a linear model that should be explained), a single hidden unit and a linear decoder as depicted in Fig. 3. An AE, i.e. the reference AE *RefAE*, aims to find an encoding vector E and a reconstruction vector R, so that the reconstruction $\hat{x} = R \cdot y$ of the encoding $y = E \cdot x$ is minimal using the L2-loss, i.e. $\min_{R,E} ||x - R \cdot E \cdot x||^2$. The optimal solution which minimizes the reconstruction loss stems from projecting onto the eigenvector space (as given by a Principal Component Analysis) [3]. That is, given there is just a single latent variable, the optimal solution for $W = R \cdot E$ is the first eigenvector u_1. This is illustrated in Fig. 3 in the upper part with $y = u_1 \cdot x$. For *ClaDec* the goal is to explain a linear regression model $y = E \cdot x$. The vector E is found by solving a regression problem. We fit the decoder R to minimize the reconstruction loss on the original inputs given the encoding, i.e. $\min_R ||x - R \cdot y||^2$ with $y = E \cdot x$. The more similar the regression problem is to the encoding problem of an AE, the more similar are the reconstructions. Put differently, the closer E is to u_1 the lower the reconstruction loss and the more similar are the optimal reconstructions for the reference AE and *ClaDec*. Assume that E differs strongly from u_1, i.e. say that the optimal solution to the regression problem is

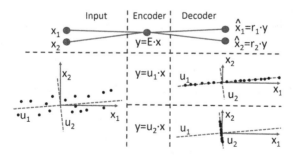

Fig. 3. An AE with optimal encoder $y = u_1 \cdot x$ (and decoder) captures more information than any other encoder. But a regression/classification model serving as encoder, e.g. $y = u_2 \cdot x$, combined with an optimized decoder, might capture some input attributes more accurately, e.g. x_2.

the second eigenvector $y = u_2 \cdot x$. This is shown in the lower part of Fig. 3. When comparing the optimal reconstruction of the *RefAE*, i.e. using $y = u_1 x$, and the illustrated reconstruction of *ClaDec*, i.e. using $y = u_2 x$, it becomes apparent that for the optimal encoding $y = u_1 x$ the reconstructions of both coordinates x_1 and x_2 are fairly accurate on average. In contrast, using $y = u_2 x$, coordinate x_2 is reconstructed more accurately (on average), whereas the reconstruction of x_1 is mostly very poor.

Generally, this suggests that a representation obtained from a model (trained for some task) captures less information than an encoder optimized towards reconstructing inputs. But aspects of inputs relevant to the task should be captured relatively in more detail than those that are irrelevant. Reconstructions from *ClaDec* should show more similarity to original inputs for attributes relevant to classification and less similarity for irrelevant attributes. But, overall reconstructions from the classifier will show less similarity to inputs than those of an AE.

4   Assessing Interpretability and Fidelity

Fidelity is the degree to which an explanation captures model behavior. That is, a "fidel" explanation captures the decision process of the model accurately. The proposed evaluation (also serving as sanity check) uses the rational that fidel explanations for decisions of a well-performing model should be helpful in performing the task the model addresses. Concretely, training a new classifier C_{eval}^E on explanations and, possibly, inputs should yield a better performing classifier than relying on inputs only. That is, we train a baseline classifier $C_{eval}^R(\hat{X}_R)$ on the reconstructions of the *RefAE* and a second classifier with identical architecture $C_{eval}^E(\hat{X}_E)$ on explanations from *ClaDec*. The latter classifier should achieve higher accuracy. This is a much stronger requirement than the common sanity check demanding that explanations must be valuable to perform a task better than a "guessing" baseline. One must be careful that explanations do not contain additional external knowledge (not present in the inputs or training data) that help in performing the task. For most methods, including ours, this holds true. Therefore, it is not obvious that training on explanations allows to improve on classification performance compared to training on inputs that are more accurate reconstructions of the original inputs. Improvements seem only possible if an explanation is a more adequate representation to solve the problem. Formally, we measure the similarity between the reconstructions $\hat{X}_R$ (using *RefAE*) and $\hat{X}_E$ (of *ClaDec*) with the original inputs X. We show that explanations (from *ClaDec*) bear less similarity with original inputs than reconstructions from *RefAE*. Still, training on explanations $\hat{X}_E$ yields classifiers with better performance than training on the more informative outputs $\hat{X}_R$ from *RefAE*.

Interpretability is the degree to which the explanation is human understandable. We build upon the intuitive assumption that a human can better and more easily interpret explanations made of concepts that she is more familiar with. We argue that a user is more familiar with real-world phenomena and concepts as captured in the training data than possibly unknown concepts captured in representations of a NN. This implies that explanations that are more similar to the training data are more interpretable than those with strong deviation from the training data. Therefore, we quantify interpretability by measuring the distance to the original input, i.e. the reconstruction loss. If explanations show concepts that are highly fidelitous, but non-intuitive for a user (high reconstruction loss) a user can experience difficulties in making sense of the explanation. In contrast, a trivial explanation (showing the unmodified input) is easy to understand but it will not reveal any insights into the model behavior, i.e., it lacks fidelity.

5   Evaluation

In our qualitative and quantitative evaluation we focus on image classification using CNNs and the following experiments: (i) Explaining different layers for correct and incorrect classifications, (ii) Varying the fidelity and interpretability tradeoff. Our decoder follows a standard design, i.e. using 5×5 deconvolutional layers. For the classifier (and encoder) we used the same architecture, i.e. a VGG-5 and ResNet-10. For ResNet-10 we reconstructed after each block. Both architectures behaved similarly, thus we only report for VGG-5. Note, that the same classifier architecture (but trained with different input data) serves as encoder in *RefAE*, classifier in *ClaDec* and for classifiers used for evaluation of reconstructions, i.e. classifier C_{Eval}^{E} (for assessing *ClaDec*) and C_{Eval}^{R} (for *RefAE*). The evaluation setup is shown in the right panel of Fig. 4 for *ClaDec*. Thus, we denote by "Acc Enc *ClaDec*" the validation accuracy of the encoder, i.e. classifier, of the *ClaDec* architecture and by "Acc Eval *RefAE*" the validation accuracy of the classifier C_{Eval}^{R} used for evaluation as shown in Fig. 4 trained on reconstructions from the reference AE. Other combinations are analogous.

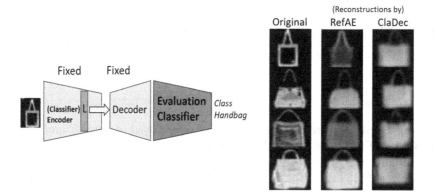

Fig. 4. Left panel: Evaluation setup using a dedicated evaluation classifier. Right panel: Comparison of original inputs and reconstructions using the FC layer of the encoder for handbags. Comparing *RefAE* and *ClaDec* shows that both do not reconstruct detailed textures. The classifier does not rely on graytones, which are captured by *RefAE*. It uses prototypical shapes.

Note that the decoder architecture varies depending on which layer is to be explained. The original architecture allows to either obtain reconstructions from the last convolutional layer or the fully connected layer. For a lower layer, the highest deconvolutional layers from the decoder have to be removed, so that the reconstructed image $\hat{X}$ has the same width and height as the original input X. We employed three datasets namely Fashion-MNIST, MNIST and TinyImageNet. Since all datasets behaved similarly, we focus on Fashion-MNIST consisting of 70000 28 × 28 images of clothing stemming from 10 classes that we scaled to 32 × 32. 10000 samples are used for testing. We train all models using the Adam optimizer for 64 epochs. That is, the *refAE*, the decoder of *ClaDec*, the classifier serving as encoder in *ClaDec* as well as the classifiers used for evaluation. We conducted 5 runs for each reported number. We show both averages and standard deviations.

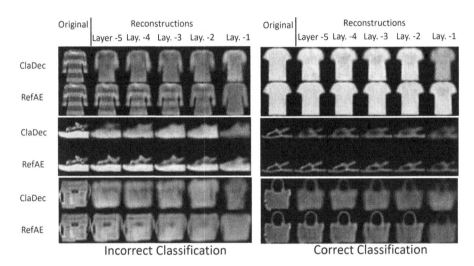

Fig. 5. Comparison of original inputs and reconstructions using multiple layers of the encoder. For incorrect samples it shows a gradual transformation into another class. Differences between *RefAE* and *ClaDec* increase with each layer

5.1 Qualitative Evaluation

Varying Explanation Layers: Reconstructions based on *RefAE* and *ClaDec* are shown in Figs. 4 and 5. For the last layer, i.e. the fully connected (FC) layer, there is only one value per class, implying a representation of 10 dimensions for Fashion-MNIST. For the handbags depicted in Fig. 4 and explained in the caption, comparing the original inputs and the reconstructions by *RefAE* and *ClaDec* shows clear differences in reconstructions. Some conclusions are knowledge of precise graytones is not used to classify these objects. Reconstructions from *ClaDec* resemble more prototypical, abstract features of handbags. Figure 5 shows reconstructions across layers. For all samples one can observe a gradual abstraction resulting in change of shape and graytones as well as loss of details. The degree of abstraction varies significantly among samples, e.g. modest for T-Shirt and strong for handbags in the right panel. Reconstructions from *ClaDec* are more blurry than for *RefAE*. Blurriness indicates that the representation of the layer does not contain information needed to recover the details. However, the reason is not (primarily) distortions inherent in the decoder architecture, since *RefAE* produces significantly sharper images, but rather the abstraction process of the classifier. This is most apparent for incorrectly classified samples (left panel). One can observe a gradual modification of the sample into another class. This helps in understanding, how the network changed input features and at which layer. For example, the sandal (second row) appears like a sneaker at layer -3, whereas the reconstruction from *RefAE* still maintains the look of a sandal. The black "holes" in the sandals have vanished at layer -3 for the incorrectly classified sandal, whereas for the correctly classified sandal (right panel, same row), these holes remain. The bag (third row) only shows signs of a T-shirt in the second layer, where stumps of arms appear.

$\alpha = .999$

$\alpha = .9$

Fig. 6. Adding classification loss ($\alpha > 0$) yields worse reconstructions for the last conv. layer. Using classification loss only, reconstructions are not human recognizable.

Fidelity and Interpretability Trade-off: Figure 6 shows for the last conv. layer (second to last overall) the impact of adding a classification loss (Fig. 2) to modulate how much the model impacts reconstructions. Neglecting reconstruction loss, i.e. $\alpha = 1$, yields non-surprisingly non-interpretable reconstructions (not shown in Figure). Already modest reconstruction loss leads to well-recognizable shapes. The quality of reconstructions in terms of sharpness and amount of captured detail constantly improves the more emphasis is put on reconstruction loss. It also becomes evident that the NN learns "prototypical" samples (or features) towards which reconstructed samples are being optimized. For example, the shape of handbag handles shows much more diversity for values of α close to 0, it is fairly uniform for relatively large values of α. Thus, the parameter α provides a means to reconstruct a compromise between the sample that yields minimal classification loss and a sample that is true to the input. It suggests that areas of the reconstruction of *ClaDec* that are similar to the original input are also similar to a "prototype" that minimizes classification loss.

That is, the network can recognize them well, whereas areas that are strongly modified, resemble parts that seem non-aligned with "the prototype" encoded in the network.

5.2 Quantitative Evaluation

Varying Explanation Layers: Results in Table 1 contain two key messages: First, the reconstruction loss is lower for *RefAE* than for *ClaDec*. This is expected since *RefAE* is optimized entirely towards minimal reconstruction loss of the original inputs. Second, the classification (evaluation) accuracy is higher, when training the evaluation classifier C_{Eval} using reconstructions from *ClaDec* than from *RefAE*. This behavior is not obvious, since the reconstructions from *ClaDec* are poorer according to the reconstruction loss. That is, they contain less information about the original input than those from *RefAE*. However, it seems that the "right" information is encoded using a better suited representation. Aside from these two key observations there are a set of other noteworthy behaviors: As expected the reconstruction loss increases the more encoder layers, i.e. the more transformations of the input, are used. The impact is significantly stronger for *ClaDec*. The difference between *RefAE* and *ClaDec* increases the closer the layer to explain is to the output. This is not surprising, since lower layers are known to be fairly general, i.e. in transfer learning lower layers are the most applicable to work well for varying input data. There is a strong increase for the last layer, this is also no surprise, since the last layer consists of fairly fewer dimensions, i.e. 10 dimensions (one per class) compared to more than 100 for the second last layer. The classification accuracy for the evaluation classifier somewhat improves the more layers are used as encoder, i.e. of the classifier that should be explained. The opposite holds for *RefAE*. This confirms that *RefAE* focuses on the wrong

Table 1. Explaining layers: *ClaDec* has larger reconstruction loss but the evaluation classifier has higher accuracy on *ClaDec*'s reconstructions

Layer	Rec Loss *ClaDec*	Rec Loss *RefAE*	Δ	Acc Eval *ClaDec*	Acc Eval *RefAE*	Δ
-1	$28.6_{\pm 0.6851}$	$8.48_{\pm 0.3799}$	20.2	$0.89_{\pm 0.0031}$	$0.83_{\pm 0.0105}$	0.06
-3	$4.56_{\pm 0.0921}$	$3.63_{\pm 0.0729}$	0.93	$0.877_{\pm 0.0074}$	$0.863_{\pm 0.0093}$	0.014
-5	$1.93_{\pm 0.1743}$	$1.87_{\pm 0.0933}$	0.06	$0.878_{\pm 0.0073}$	$0.875_{\pm 0.0048}$	0.003

Table 2. Adding classification loss $\alpha > 0$ (Eq. 1) yields worse reconstructions, but higher evaluation accuracy

α	Total Loss *ClaDec*	Rec Loss	Classifier Loss	Acc Eval *ClaDec*
.0	$0.01_{\pm 0.0033}$	$285.5_{\pm 52.01}$	$0.0_{\pm 0.0}$	$0.9028_{\pm 0.0035}$
.001	$0.03_{\pm 0.0023}$	$25.4_{\pm 0.9292}$	$0.03_{\pm 0.0009}$	$0.9033_{\pm 0.0022}$
.1	$0.84_{\pm 0.0132}$	$8.35_{\pm 0.1195}$	$0.75_{\pm 0.0106}$	$0.9011_{\pm 0.0026}$
1.0	$7.49_{\pm 0.1119}$	$7.49_{\pm 0.1119}$	$4.4_{\pm 0.254}$	$0.8824_{\pm 0.0042}$

information, whereas the classifier trained towards the task focuses on the right information and encodes it well.

Fidelity and Interpretability Tradeoff: Table 2 shows that evaluation accuracy increases when adding a classification loss, i.e. $\alpha > 0$ yields an accuracy above 90% whereas $\alpha = 0$ gives about 88%. Reconstructions that are stronger influenced by the model to explain (larger α) are more truthful to the model, but they exhibit larger differences from the original inputs. Choosing α slightly above the minimum, i.e. larger than 0, already has a strong impact.

6   Related Work

We categorize explainability methods [13] into methods that synthesize inputs (like ours and [10,20]) and methods that rely on saliency maps [18] based on perturbation [11,21] or gradients [2,16]. Saliency maps show feature importance of inputs, whereas synthesized inputs often show higher level representations encoded in the network. Perturbation-based methods include occlusion of parts of the inputs [21] and investigating the impact on output probabilities of specific classes. Linear proxy models such as LIME [11] perform local approximations of a black-box model using simple linear models by also assessing modified inputs. Saliency maps [18] highlight parts of the inputs that contributed to the decision. Many explainability methods have been under scrutiny for failing sanity checks [1] and being sensitive to factors not contributing to model predictions [8] or adversarial perturbations [5]. We anticipate that our work is less sensitive to targeted, hard to notice perturbations [5] as well as translations or factors not impacting decisions [8], since we rely on encodings of the classifier. Thus, explanations only change if these encodings change, which they should. The idea to evaluate explanations on downstream tasks is not new, however a comparison to a "close" baseline like our *RefAE* is. Our "evaluation classifier" using only explanations (without inputs) is more suitable than methods like [14] that use explanations together with inputs in a more complex, non-standard classification process. Using inputs and explanations for the evaluation classifier is diminishing differences in evaluation outcomes for any compared methods since a network might take missing information in the explanation from the input. So far, inputs have only been synthesized to understand individual neurons through activation maximization in an optimization procedure [10]. The idea is to identify inputs that maximize the activation of a given neuron. This is similar to the idea to identify samples in the input that maximize neuron activation. [10] uses a (pre-trained) GAN on natural images relevant to the classification problem. It identifies through optimization the latent code that when fed into the GAN results in a more or less realistic looking image that maximally activates a neuron [20] uses regularized optimization as well, yielding artistically more interesting but less recognizable images. Regularized optimization has also been employed in other forms of explanations of images, e.g. to make human understand how they can alter visual inputs such as handwriting for better recognizability by a CNN [12]. [6,7] allow to investigate high level concepts that are relevant to a specific decision. DeepLift [17] compares activations to a reference and propagates them backwards. Defining the reference is non-trivial and domain specific. [9] estimates the impact of individual training samples. [4] uses a variational AE for contrastive explanations. They use distances in latent space to identify samples which are closest to a sample X of class Y but actually classified as Y'.

7   Conclusions

Our explanation method synthesizes human understandable inputs based on layer activations. It takes into account distortions originating from the reconstruction process. It is verified using novel sanity checks. In the future, we plan to investigate differences among networks, e.g. a result of model fine-tuning as in personalization [15] or to look at subsets of layer activations.

References

1. Adebayo, J., Gilmer, J., Muelly, M., Goodfellow, I., Hardt, M., Kim, B.: Sanity checks for saliency maps. In: Neural Information Processing Systems (2018)
2. Bach, S., Binder, A., Montavon, G., Klauschen, F., Müller, K.R., Samek, W.: On pixel-wise explanations for non-linear classifier decisions by layer-wise relevance propagation. PloS one **10**(7), e0130140 (2015)
3. Baldi, P., Hornik, K.: Neural networks and principal component analysis: Learning from examples without local minima. Neural Netw. **2**(1), 53–58 (1989)
4. van Doorenmalen, J., Menkovski, V.: Evaluation of CNN performance in semantically relevant latent spaces. In: Berthold, M.R., Feelders, A., Krempl, G. (eds.) IDA 2020. LNCS, vol. 12080, pp. 145–157. Springer, Cham (2020). https://doi.org/10.1007/978-3-030-44584-3_12
5. Ghorbani, A., Abid, A., Zou, J.: Interpretation of neural networks is fragile. In: AAAI Conference on Artificial Intelligence (2019)
6. Ghorbani, A., Wexler, J., Zou, J.Y., Kim, B.: Towards automatic concept-based explanations. In: Advances in Neural Information Processing Systems (2019)
7. Kim, B., et al.: Interpretability beyond feature attribution: Quantitative testing with concept activation vectors (TCAV). arXiv preprint arXiv:1711.11279 (2017)
8. Kindermans, P.J., et al.: The (un) reliability of saliency methods. In: Explainable AI: Interpreting, Explaining and Visualizing Deep Learning (2019)
9. Koh, P.W., Liang, P.: Understanding black-box predictions via influence functions. In: Proceedings of International Conference on Machine Learning, pp. 1885–1894 (2017)
10. Nguyen, A., Dosovitskiy, A., Yosinski, J., Brox, T., Clune, J.: Synthesizing the preferred inputs for neurons in neural networks via deep generator networks. In: Advances in Neural Information Processing Systems, pp. 3387–3395 (2016)
11. Ribeiro, M.T., Singh, S., Guestrin, C.: Why should i trust you?: explaining the predictions of any classifier. In: SIGKDD (2016)
12. Schneider, J.: Human-to-AI coach: improving human inputs to AI systems. In: International Symposium on Intelligent Data Analysis (2020)
13. Schneider, J., Handali, J.P.: Personalized explanation for machine learning: a conceptualization. In: European Conference on Information Systems (ECIS) (2019)

14. Schneider, J., Vlachos, M.: Reflective-net: learning from explanations. In: arxiv: 2011.13986 (2020)
15. Schneider, J., Vlachos, M.: Personalization of Deep Learning. Data Science – Analytics and Applications, pp. 89–96. Springer, Wiesbaden (2021). https://doi.org/10.1007/978-3-658-32182-6_14
16. Selvaraju, R.R., Cogswell, M., Das, A., Vedantam, R., Parikh, D., Batra, D.: Gradcam: visual explanations from deep networks via gradient-based localization. In: IEEE International Conference on Computer Vision (ICCV), pp. 618–626 (2017)
17. Shrikumar, A., Greenside, P., Kundaje, A.: Learning important features through propagating activation differences. In: International Conference on Machine Learning, pp. 3145–3153 (2017)
18. Simonyan, K., Vedaldi, A., Zisserman, A.: Deep inside convolutional networks: visualising image classification models and saliency maps. arXiv preprint arXiv: 1312.6034 (2013)
19. Yang, F., Du, M., Hu, X.: Evaluating explanation without ground truth in interpretable machine learning. arXiv preprint arXiv:1907.06831 (2019)
20. Yosinski, J., Clune, J., Nguyen, A., Fuchs, T., Lipson, H.: Understanding neural networks through deep visualization. arXiv preprint arXiv:1506.06579 (2015)
21. Zeiler, M.D., Fergus, R.: Visualizing and understanding convolutional networks. In: Fleet, D., Pajdla, T., Schiele, B., Tuytelaars, T. (eds.) ECCV 2014. LNCS, vol. 8689, pp. 818–833. Springer, Cham (2014). https://doi.org/10.1007/978-3-319-10590-1_53

Analogical Embedding for Analogy-Based Learning to Rank

Mohsen Ahmadi Fahandar[1(✉)] and Eyke Hüllermeier[2]

[1] Department of Computer Science, Paderborn University, Paderborn, Germany
ahmadim@mail.upb.de
[2] Institute of Informatics, LMU Munich, Munich, Germany
eyke@upb.de

Abstract. Learning to rank based on principles of analogical reasoning has recently been proposed as a novel approach to preference learning. The approach essentially builds on a regularity assumption of the following kind: Given objects A B, C, D, if A relates to B as C relates to D, and A is preferred to B, then C is presumably preferred to D. This assumption is formalized in terms of so-called analogical proportions, which operate on a feature representation of the objects. A suitable representation is therefore essential for the success of analogy-based learning to rank. Therefore, we propose a method for analogical embedding, i.e., for embedding the data in a target space such that, in this space, the aforementioned analogy assumption is as valid and strongly pronounced as possible. This is accomplished by means of a neural network with a quadruple Siamese structure, which is trained on a suitably designed set of examples in the form of quadruples of objects. By conducting experiments on several real-world data sets, we provide evidence for the usefulness of analogical embedding and its potential to improve the performance of analogy-based learning to rank.

Keywords: Preference learning · Analogical reasoning · Embedding · Neural networks

1 Introduction

In machine learning, principles of analogical reasoning have recently been applied to tackle preference learning tasks, such as learning to rank [1,5,6]. The basic idea is to invoke an inference pattern of the following kind, suggesting an analogical relationship to hold between pairwise preferences: If object A relates to B as C relates to D, and A is preferred to B, then C is presumably preferred to D. Corresponding methods have shown competitive performance in terms of predictive accuracy, and, moreover, exhibit other appealing properties, for example regarding interpretability [12].

An illustration is shown in Fig. 1, where objects are represented as points in $\mathbb{R}^2$. In the right panel, the relationship between A and B is roughly the same

© Springer Nature Switzerland AG 2021
P. H. Abreu et al. (Eds.): IDA 2021, LNCS 12695, pp. 76–88, 2021.
https://doi.org/10.1007/978-3-030-74251-5_7

as the relationship between C and D, if "relationship" is understood in the (geometric) sense of "relative location". Therefore, if A is known to be preferred to B, one may suspect that C is preferred to D (suggesting that decreasing the value of x_1 and increasing the value of y_1 has a positive influence on preference).

Needless to say, preferences will not always satisfy this form of analogical relationship. Nevertheless, even if the relationship holds only approximately, or the number of quadruples (A, B, C, D) violating it remains sufficiently small, good overall predictions may still be produced. In any case, as already suggested by Fig. 1, the feature representation of objects will have a major influence on how well the analogy assumption applies. In this paper, we therefore propose a method for analogical embedding, i.e., for embedding the data in a target space such that, in this space, the aforementioned analogy assumption is as valid and strongly pronounced as possible. This is accomplished by means of a neural network with a quadruple Siamese structure, which is trained on a suitably designed set of examples in the form of quadruples of objects.

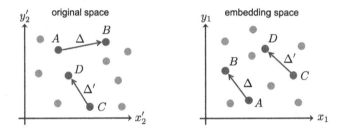

Fig. 1. Geometric illustration of analogical relationships: In the embedding space (right), the four objects are in analogical relationship, because the "delta" between A and B is roughly the same as between C and D. In the original space (left), this is not the case.

This work is a follow up on our previous work on feature selection for analogy-based learning to rank [2], since feature selection can be seen as a specific type of embedding (in a lower-dimensional space). Although this approach led to a reduction of complexity, in the sense that objects could be represented by less features, no significant improvements in terms of predictive performance could be achieved. This motivates the use of more flexible, nonlinear embedding techniques as put forward in this paper.

The remainder of the paper is organized as follows. In the next section, we recall the approach to analogy-based learning to rank as put forward in [1], followed by an overview of related work on analogical embedding in Sect. 3. Our own embedding method is then introduced in Sect. 4, and evaluation empirically in Sect. 5.

2   Analogy-Based Learning to Rank

Consider a reference set of objects $\mathcal{O}$, where each object $o \in \mathcal{O}$ is a q-dimensional real-valued feature vector, i.e., $o \in \mathbb{R}^q$. The *object ranking* problem aims at learning a ranking function that accepts any (query) subset $Q = \{o_1, \ldots, o_n\} \subseteq \mathcal{O}$ of objects, and outputs a ranking π, represented by a bijection $\{1, \ldots, n\} \rightarrow \{1, \ldots, n\}$, such that $\pi(k)$ is the position of the kth object in Q. The training data are given in the form $\mathcal{D} = \{(Q_1, \pi_1), \ldots, (Q_M, \pi_M)\}$, where each ranking π_ℓ is a linear order of the objects in Q_ℓ.

A new approach to object ranking was recently put forward on the basis of analogical reasoning [1]. This approach does not follow the common scheme of inductive inference. Instead, it is transductive (and lazy) in the sense that it constructs a (hypothetical) ranking $\hat{\pi}_0$ of the objects in a query set Q_0, assuming the data $\mathcal{D}$ as well as Q_0 to be given. This is accomplished by transferring information from $\mathcal{D}$ (the source) to the new set of objects (the target), invoking an inference pattern of the following kind: Assume source object a relates to source object b as target object c relates to target object d. Then, on the basis of this relationship, the preference $a \succ b$ on the first pair (i.e., a is preferred to b) is hypothetically transferred to the second pair, suggesting that $c \succ d$.

This principle is formalized using the notion of analogical proportion [17]. Consider four values a, b, c, d from an attribute domain. Then, the analogical proportion for the quadruple (a, b, c, d) is denoted by $a : b :: c : d$, which reads as "a relates to b as c relates to d". Specifically, analogy is considered as a matter of degree, i.e., the quadruple $(a, b, c, d) \in [0, 1]^4$ can be in analogy to some degree [11], denoted by $v(a, b, c, d) \in [0, 1]$. An example is the arithmetic proportion defined as follows:

$$v(a, b, c, d) = 1 - |(a - b) - (c - d)|, \tag{1}$$

if $(a - b)(c - d) > 0$ or $(a - b) = (c - d) = 0$, and 0 otherwise. The analogy degree of individual values can be extended to feature vectors, i.e., $v(a, b, c, d)$, by *averaging* the individual degrees $v(a_i, b_i, c_i, d_i)$, amongst other options.

Provided with a measure of analogy, the object ranking task is tackled as follows: Take any pair of query objects $o_i, o_j \in Q_0$. Having searched for the k highest analogy degrees $v(z_i, z_j, o_i, o_j)$ for any z_i, z_j in the training data (for which the preference is known), the preference $z_i \succ z_j$ provides evidence in favor of $o_i \succ o_j$. By collecting all pieces of evidence of that kind, either in favor of $o_i \succ o_j$ or $o_j \succ o_i$, an overall preference measure $\hat{p}_{i,j}$ can be derived for this pair of objects. Once the preference matrix $\hat{P} = (\hat{p}_{i,j})_{1 \le i, j \le n}$ is obtained for all pairs of objects in the query set Q_0, these measures are combined into an overall consensus ranking using an appropriate aggregation technique; see e.g., [3]. We refer to [1] for a detailed description of this method, which is called *able2rank* (analogy-based learning to rank).

3   Related Work

Although, to the best of our knowledge, we are the first to apply such techniques in the context of preference learning, analogical embedding has been studied by other authors before. In this section, we give a brief overview of the contributions most closely related to ours.

The idea of embeddings data so as to achieve analogies is very popular in natural language processing (NLP). In word embedding, for example, the data objects to be embedded are words, and the goal is to construct analogical structures such as $man : woman :: king : queen$ [15,18,19]. In knowledge graph embedding, i.e., the problem of learning the latent representations in the graph containing factual information in the form of subject-relation-object triplets, a framework that explicitly encodes analogical structures in the embedding is proposed in [16].

The work of [13] utilizes analogy structures for the task of visual object categorization. They propose to take advantage of analogy structures among (image) categories in order to enrich the generalization, and thereby manage to improve object categorization. It is argued that imposing analogy constraints in the embedding space can facilitate a form of transfer from class pairs (images) that are more distinguishable (in the original space) to those pairs that are not, among other advantages mentioned in the paper. To this end, the existing Large Margin Embedding [21] (a "distance-only" approach) is equipped with an analogy regularizer, so that not only the data points in the semantic embedding space are close to their semantic category embedding, but the category embeddings form a parallelogram as well, to reflect their analogy-based relationships. That is, those class labels that are assumed to be in analogy are regularized to form a parallelogram in terms of the length of the opposite sides, as much as possible.

Later on, the use of analogical reasoning for visual analogy questions of the form "image A is to image B as image C is to *what*" was proposed in [20]. This task is boiled down to discovering the mapping that takes image A to B, and then applying the same mapping on image C and searching for image D such that the analogy between the four images holds. For this purpose, a Convolutional Neural Network (CNN) with a quadruple Siamese architecture is used to find an embedding that encourages pairs of analogous images with similar transformations to be close to each other, and pushing dissimilar transformations apart. In particular, the network is trained using image quadruples in the form of correct (i.e., analogous image pairs with similar transformation) and incorrect (i.e., analogous image pairs with different transformation) analogies. The goal is to map similar transformations to a similar location and push dissimilar transformations outside a margin. To this end, contrastive loss is used, and the error is back-propagated through SGD to adjust the parameters.

In a more recent line of work, analogical embedding is used for the problem of answer selection in query-answering systems, namely finding the correct answer for a given question from a set of candidate (potentially correct) answers [9]. Analogy quadruples are defined in the form of $q_p : a_p :: q_i : a_{ij}$, where q_p and a_p denote a question and its correct answer (so-called "prototypes"), and q_i, a_{ij} are the ith question and its jth candidate answer. To tackle the problem, the authors utilize a BiGRU network [7] with a quadruple Siamese architecture that takes four sentences as input, and projects each sentence onto a vector representation. The network is trained by minimizing a contrastive loss on positive (i.e., a_{ij} is correct) and negative (i.e., a_{ij} is incorrect) quadruples as training data. In order to enforce the analogy relationship, the error with respect to the cosine similarity between the vector shifts of each pair is back-propagated to the network, which encourages the resulting vectors to form a parallelogram in the embedding space.

4   Analogical Embedding

Let $E(o)$ be the embedding of the object $o \in \mathbb{R}^q$, where $E : \mathbb{R}^q \to \mathbb{R}^q$ is a differentiable network parameterized by θ. The data seen by the network comprise positive and negative examples. We define the analogy quadruple (a, b, c, d) as a positive example if the preferences on both sides are coherent, i.e., either $a \succ b$ and $c \succ d$, or $b \succ a$ and $d \succ c$; otherwise, it is a negative example. The goal is then to learn an embedding that leads to high degrees of analogy for positive examples and low degrees for negative ones.

Note that the analogical proportion defined in (1), as a function $\mathbb{R}^4 \to \mathbb{R}$, is discontinuous (and hence not differentiable everywhere). Therefore, we propose to replace it by the well-known cosine similarity as a proxy, or, equivalently, the cosine distance (between the vector shifts of analogous pairs) as a *surrogate loss* for training the network:

$$\mathsf{dis}(a, b, c, d) = \frac{1}{2}\left(1 - \frac{\sum_{i=1}^{q}(a_i - b_i)(c_i - d_i)}{\sqrt{\sum_{i=1}^{q}(a_i - b_i)^2}\sqrt{\sum_{i=1}^{q}(c_i - d_i)^2}}\right). \tag{2}$$

As can be seen, the larger the number of tuples $a_i - b_i$ and $c_i - d_i$ with the same sign, the lower the cosine distance, which is in line with the idea of analogical proportions.

4.1   Training the Embedding Network

The goal of the embedding network E is to make (2) low (close to 0) for positive examples (a, b, c, d) and high (close to 1) for negative examples. More specifically, we train the network by using a double-margin contrastive loss [8], so that, by adapting the network parameters θ, the cosine distance is decreased for positive examples and increased for negative examples. Given an input quadruple (a, b, c, d), the contrastive loss is defined as

$$\mathcal{L}(y, \hat{y}) = y\left[\hat{y} - m_1\right]_+ + (1 - y)\left[m_2 - \hat{y}\right]_+, \tag{3}$$

where $[h]_+ = \max(0, h)$, y is the target label (1 for positive and 0 for negative quadruples), and $\hat{y} = \mathsf{dis}\big(E(a), E(b), E(c), E(d)\big)$. The two margins m_1 and m_2 relax the goal to realize the ideal distances of 0 for positive and 1 for negative quadruples, respectively: For the former, a distance $\leq m_1$ is enough to achieve a loss of 0, and similarly, a distance $\geq m_2$ is considered large enough for negative examples. For each training example, the loss (3) is back-propagated to the network using SGD to adjust the parameters $\boldsymbol{\theta}$ accordingly; see Fig. 2 for a pictorial representation of the network. The question of how to construct training examples from the original preference data will be addressed next.

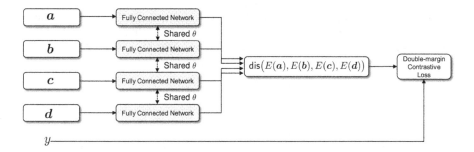

Fig. 2. The schematic of the used quadruple Siamese network.

4.2   Constructing Training Examples

Recall that training data for preference learning comes in the form (Q, π), where $Q = \{\boldsymbol{o}_1, \ldots, \boldsymbol{o}_n\}$ is a set of objects and π a ranking (permutation). In the following, we assume a single ranking of that kind to be given. Based on this information, a training example for the embedding network can be constructed for each subset of 4 distinct objects $\{\boldsymbol{a}, \boldsymbol{b}, \boldsymbol{c}, \boldsymbol{d}\} \subseteq Q$, i.e., for the set of quadruples

$$\mathbb{S} = \mathbb{S}(Q) = \left\{ (\boldsymbol{o}_i, \boldsymbol{o}_j, \boldsymbol{o}_k, \boldsymbol{o}_l) \,\middle|\, 1 \leq i < j < k < l \leq n \right\}.$$

We partition $\mathbb{S}$ into the subset of positive examples $\mathbb{S}^+$ and negative examples $\mathbb{S}^-$, for which $(\pi(i) - \pi(j))(\pi(k) - \pi(l))$ is positive and negative, respectively. Obviously, $\mathbb{S}$ as defined may quickly grow in size, making training of the embedding network inefficient. Besides, it is clear that not all examples are equally useful for finding a good embedding. Therefore, we propose to reduce the set of potential training examples. To this end, we consider two strategies.

– **NN-Selection** (Nearest-Neighbor-based): Our first selection method is inspired by the principle proposed in [22] in the context of metric learning, which consists of including, for each training example, its k nearest neighbors from the same class and k nearest neighbors from the opposite class. The intuition is that these neighbors are maximally relevant for this example, and will remain relevant provided the embedding maintains the topological structure of the training data to some extent. Concretely, for each tuple $(\boldsymbol{a}, \boldsymbol{b})$ that occurs as part of any quadruple in $\mathbb{S}^+$, the (at most) k nearest neighbors are selected, i.e., those quadruples $(\boldsymbol{c}, \boldsymbol{d}, \boldsymbol{a}, \boldsymbol{b})$ or $(\boldsymbol{a}, \boldsymbol{b}, \boldsymbol{c}, \boldsymbol{d})$ in $\mathbb{S}$ for which the degree of analogical proportion is highest among all quadruples of that kind. Examples from $\mathbb{S}^-$ are selected in the same way.

– **Top-Selection**: The second technique selects 5% of the entire set of quadruples in $\mathbb{S}^+$ and 5% in $\mathbb{S}^-$, namely those with the overall highest degrees of analogy. Consequently, the network is trained on only 10% of the potentially possible examples in $\mathbb{S}$.

5   Experiments

Our experiments are designed for two purposes. First, we assess the effectiveness of our instance selection approaches by evaluating the quality of the embedding space by means of appropriate metrics. Second, we show how the embedding can improve the performance of the *able2rank* method.

5.1   Data and Experimental Setup

We use real-world data collected from various domains (e.g., sports, education, tourism, etc.) and comprising different types of feature (e.g., numeric, binary, ordinal). All data sets together with a detailed description are publicly available[1], as well as the Python implementation used for conducting the experiments.

For *able2rank*, an important pre-processing step involves normalizing the features of the objects $o \in \mathbb{R}^q$. We apply min-max normalization, so that $o \in [0, 1]^q$. This transformation is applied to the combination of source and target data, unless the two data sets differ in terms of their distribution. Therefore, we first conduct a Kolmogorov-Smirnov test [14] to examine whether the two parts of the data are drawn from the same distribution. In case the null hypothesis is rejected (at a significance level of $\alpha = 0.05$), normalization is done on the two data sets separately.

For training the network, we randomly split the original training data of the form (Q, π) into two disjoint parts: One part for training, and the other part for validation. We subsequently generate quadruples as explained in Sect. 4.2. After computing the degree of analogy for each quadruple, we refine the set of generated instances using any of the techniques discussed above. We set the margins in the contrastive loss as $m_1 = 0.1$ and $m_2 = 0.5$, which deemed to be plausible given that the used cosine distance takes values in $[0, 1]$. We also fix the maximum number of epochs to 500, and apply early-stopping during training, i.e., the training process stops once the loss does not improve (to 10^{-4} precision) for five consecutive epochs. The fully connected embedding network is set to have a single hidden layer with the number of neurons equivalent to the dimension of the input vectors. Thus, we end up with an embedding space having the same dimension as the original space. As we use the sigmoid activation function, the instances remain in $[0, 1]$ in the embedding space.

In each of the following case studies, the network is trained with parameters set as explained. As the batch size is an important hyper-parameter for training the network (i.e., the back-propagation happens for every batch size), we try

---

[1] github.com/mahmadif.

different batch sizes in $\{2^5, 2^6, 2^7, \ldots\}$ until it exceeds the number of training samples. For the first case study, we report the average of the performances for different batch sizes. In the second case study, we choose the batch size that leads to an embedding space that is well-suited for analogy-based learning to rank.

5.2   Case Study 1: Analysing the Embedding Space

In this experiment, we train the network once with training instances refined according to the NN-Selection principle, and once based on the Top-Selection approach.

Recall our motivation for analogical embedding, namely to find a latent space in which the analogy assumption holds better than in the original data space. In light of this, we compare the degree of analogy (on the unseen validation data) for all generated quadruples (as outlined in Sect. 4.2) before and after embedding: With $o' = E(o)$ denoting the object o in the embedding space, we expect to see $v(a', b', c', d') > v(a, b, c, d)$ for $(a, b, c, d) \in \mathbb{S}^+$, and $v(a', b', d', c') < v(a, b, d, c)$ for $(a, b, d, c) \in \mathbb{S}^-$. Therefore, we determine the proportion of positive quadruples whose analogy degrees are improved in the embedding space:

$$\frac{1}{|\mathbb{S}^+|} \sum_{(a,b,c,d) \in \mathbb{S}^+} [\![v(a', b', c', d') > v(a, b, c, d)]\!] \, , \tag{4}$$

where $[\![.]\!]$ is the indicator function. Similarly, for negative quadruples, we determine

$$\frac{1}{|\mathbb{S}^-|} \sum_{(a,b,d,c) \in \mathbb{S}^-} [\![v(a', b', d', c') < v(a, b, d, c)]\!] \, . \tag{5}$$

We also inspect the degree of analogy for positive quadruples compared to the respective negative ones within each feature space separately. That is, we explore the extent of support for $v(a, b, c, d) > v(a, b, d, c)$ in the original space, and for $v(a', b', c', d') > v(a', b', d', c')$ in the embedding space:

$$\frac{1}{|\mathbb{S}^+|} \sum_{(a,b,c,d) \in \mathbb{S}^+} [\![v(a', b', c', d') > v(a', b', d', c')]\!] \, . \tag{6}$$

NN-Selection: For this method, we report the results for $k = 10$, which was empirically found to perform best among the candidate values $k \in \{10, 20, 50\}$. Figure 3 presents the results in terms of the average and standard deviation of different batch sizes, from which one can make the following observations:

1) In terms of metric (4), more than 85% of the positive quadruples have seen improvement (compared to their analogy degree in the original space) through analogical embedding in all use-cases (except for the FB2 case) as witnessed by the left plot.

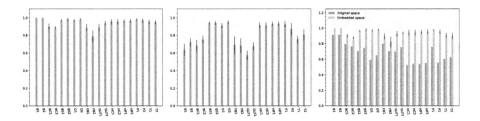

Fig. 3. From left to right, average and standard deviation of the performance in terms of the metrics (4), (5), and (6) for the network trained with NN-Selection on real-world data.

2) Likewise, the improvements are also visible with respect to metric (5) (i.e., in the case of negative quadruples) in the middle plot.
3) In line with our motivation, namely having $v(a', b', c', d') > v(a', b', d', c')$, the improvements, in terms of metric (6), are also considerable as shown in the right plot.

Overall, the results clearly confirm that the learned embedding space meets our goals and confirms our expectations of analogical embedding.

Top-Selection: We next evaluate the quality of the embedding space learned by a network that is trained with quadruples selected based on the Top-Selection principle. Figure 4 reports the results in terms of the average and standard deviation of different batch sizes. By looking at the figures, one can make the same observations as in the previous case, and conclude that analogical embedding is successful.

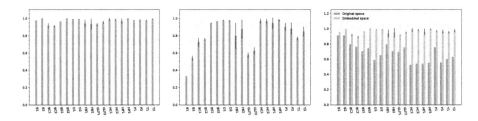

Fig. 4. From left to right, average and standard deviation of the performance in terms of the metrics (4), (5), and (6) for the network trained with Top-Selection on real-world data.

5.3   Case Study 2: Performance of *able2rank*

Here, we investigate how analogical embedding influences the performance of *able2rank*, a learning-to-rank algorithm based on analogical reasoning. The performance of the ranking $\hat{\pi}$ produced as a prediction by *able2rank* is evaluated using a suitable metric, typically the *ranking loss* d_{RL}:

Table 1. Results for accuracy (acc) and ranking loss (d_{RL}) on the target data, i.e., d_{RL} and acc in the original space compared to d'_{RL} and acc' in the embedding space.

$\mathcal{D}_{train} \rightarrow \mathcal{D}_{test}$	acc	acc'	d_{RL}	d'_{RL}
B1 $\rightarrow$ B2	0.922	**0.935**	0.092	**0.065**
B2 $\rightarrow$ B1	0.941	**0.961**	0.033	**0.030**
BC1 $\rightarrow$ BC2	0.939	**0.951**	0.038	0.045
BC2 $\rightarrow$ BC1	0.942	**0.952**	0.038	**0.035**
BS1 $\rightarrow$ BS2	0.891	**0.985**	0.043	**0.011**
BS2 $\rightarrow$ BS1	0.909	**0.989**	0.024	**0.011**
D1 $\rightarrow$ D2	0.817	**0.971**	0.056	**0.029**
D2 $\rightarrow$ D1	0.785	**0.966**	0.099	**0.033**
FB1 $\rightarrow$ FB2	0.933	**0.989**	0.074	**0.010**
FB2 $\rightarrow$ FB1	0.933	**0.984**	0.052	**0.014**
GLF1 $\rightarrow$ GLF2	0.938	**0.968**	0.036	**0.032**
GLF2 $\rightarrow$ GLF1	0.953	**0.982**	0.025	**0.011**
HC1 $\rightarrow$ HC2	0.717	**0.888**	0.131	**0.112**
HC2 $\rightarrow$ HC1	0.679	**0.879**	0.225	**0.121**
HP1 $\rightarrow$ HP2	0.707	**0.959**	0.181	**0.040**
HP2 $\rightarrow$ HP1	0.707	**0.962**	0.173	**0.038**
P1 $\rightarrow$ P2	0.885	**0.976**	0.054	**0.024**
P2 $\rightarrow$ P1	0.909	**0.986**	0.045	**0.012**
T1 $\rightarrow$ T2	0.839	**0.933**	0.062	0.067
T2 $\rightarrow$ T1	0.779	**0.936**	0.154	**0.062**

$$d_{RL}(\pi, \hat{\pi}) = \frac{\sum_{1 \leq i,j \leq n} [\![\pi(i) < \pi(j)]\!][\![\hat{\pi}(i) > \hat{\pi}(j)]\!]}{n(n-1)/2}.$$

Since the algorithm derives a preference degree $\hat{p}_{i,j}$ for any pair of objects o_i, o_j in the target data (prior to generating the full ranking), we additionally inspect this matrix in terms of predicting the true preference between any pair of objects. In particular, we define an overall accuracy measure as follows:

$$acc(\pi, \hat{P}) = \frac{\sum_{1 \leq i,j \leq n} [\![\pi(i) < \pi(j)]\!][\![\hat{p}_{i,j} > \hat{p}_{j,i}]\!]}{n(n-1)/2}.$$

Results: In our experiments, within each domain, predictions are produced for target data $\mathcal{D}_{test}$ using another data set $\mathcal{D}_{train}$ as a source; such experiment is denoted by $\mathcal{D}_{train} \rightarrow \mathcal{D}_{test}$ in Table 1. After training the network with different batch sizes, we choose the network configuration for which the metric defined in (6) is maximized on the (unseen) validation data. That network configuration gives us the feature space into which both source and target data can be embedded. We next run *able2rank* once using the original data and once using the embedded data. To turn the generated preference matrix $\hat{P}$ into an overall ranking in the second step of *able2rank*, we use Borda's method [4], which is a scoring rule that sorts objects according to the sum of weighted preferences or "votes" in favor of each object, i.e., $\hat{\pi} = \arg\mathrm{sort}\{s_1, s_2, \ldots, s_n\}$, where $s_i = \sum_{i=1}^{n} \hat{p}_{i,j}$.

Table 1 reports the results of the conducted experiments, where d_{RL} and acc are the evaluation measures in the original space, and d'_{RL} and acc' denote the same measures in the embedding space. As can be seen, analogical embedding leads to clear and very consistent improvements (highlighted in bold font) for both measures.

6   Conclusion

This paper elaborates on the problem of analogical embedding for analogy-based learning to rank. To address this problem, we utilized neural networks with a quadruple Siamese structure, which is trained on a set of suitably constructed examples of (sought) analogical relationships between quadruples of objects. We analysed the quality of the embedding space and showed that the basic assumption of analogical relationships between preferences is more pronounced in the embedding than in the original space. Finally, we studied the performance of the learning-to-rank algorithm *able2rank* when analogical embedding is applied as a pre-processing step, and again observed clear improvements compared to the original version.

As future work, we plan to elaborate on the dimensionality of the embedding space, which, for simplicity, was taken to be the same as the dimensionality of the original space in this work. Furthermore, the idea of heterogeneous domain adaptation [10] appears to be interesting, i.e., the idea of embedding objects with different feature representations into a common space. This may provide a means for realizing transfer learning, where the source objects a, b and target objects c, d are of different nature.

References

1. Ahmadi Fahandar, M., Hüllermeier, E.: Learning to rank based on analogical reasoning. In: Proceedings of the AAAI 2018, 32th AAAI Conference on Artificial Intelligence, New Orleans, Louisiana, USA, pp. 2951–2958 (2018)
2. Ahmadi Fahandar, M., Hüllermeier, E.: Feature selection for analogy-based learning to rank. In: Kralj Novak, P., Šmuc, T., Džeroski, S. (eds.) DS 2019. LNCS (LNAI), vol. 11828, pp. 279–289. Springer, Cham (2019). https://doi.org/10.1007/978-3-030-33778-0_22
3. Ahmadi Fahandar, M., Hüllermeier, E., Couso, I.: Statistical inference for incomplete ranking data: the case of rank-dependent coarsening. In: Proceedings of the ICML 2017, 34th International Conference on Machine Learning (2017)
4. Borda, J.: Mémoire sur les élections au scrutin. Histoire de l'Académie Royale des Sciences (1781)

5. Bounhas, M., Pirlot, M., Prade, H.: Predicting preferences by means of analogical proportions. In: Cox, M.T., Funk, P., Begum, S. (eds.) ICCBR 2018. LNCS (LNAI), vol. 11156, pp. 515–531. Springer, Cham (2018). https://doi.org/10.1007/978-3-030-01081-2_34

6. Bounhas, M., Pirlot, M., Prade, H., Sobrie, O.: Comparison of analogy-based methods for predicting preferences. In: Ben Amor, N., Quost, B., Theobald, M. (eds.) SUM 2019. LNCS (LNAI), vol. 11940, pp. 339–354. Springer, Cham (2019). https://doi.org/10.1007/978-3-030-35514-2_25

7. Cho, K., van Merrienboer, B., Bahdanau, D., Bengio, Y.: On the properties of neural machine translation: encoder-decoder approaches. In: Proceedings of the SSST 2014, 8th Workshop on Syntax, Semantics and Structure in Statistical Translation (2014)

8. Chopra, S., Hadsell, R., LeCun, Y.: Learning a similarity metric discriminatively, with application to face verification. In: Proceedings of the CVPR 2005, IEEE Conference on Computer Vision and Pattern Recognition, pp. 539–546 (2005)

9. Diallo, A., Zopf, M., Fürnkranz, J.: Learning analogy-preserving sentence embeddings for answer selection. In: Proceedings of the CoNLL 2019, 23th Conference on Computational Natural Language Learning, Hong Kong, China, pp. 910–919 (2019)

10. Duan, L., Xu, D., Tsang, I.W.: Learning with augmented features for heterogeneous domain adaptation. In: Proceedings of the ICML 2012, 29th International Conference on Machine Learning, Madison, WI, USA, pp. 667–674 (2012)

11. Dubois, D., Prade, H., Richard, G.: Multiple-valued extensions of analogical proportions. Fuzzy Sets Syst. **292**, 193–202 (2016)

12. Hüllermeier, E.: Towards analogy-based explanations in machine learning. In: Torra, V., Narukawa, Y., Nin, J., Agell, N. (eds.) MDAI 2020. LNCS (LNAI), vol. 12256, pp. 205–217. Springer, Cham (2020). https://doi.org/10.1007/978-3-030-57524-3_17

13. Hwang, S.J., Grauman, K., Sha, F.: Analogy-preserving semantic embedding for visual object categorization. In: Proceedings of the ICML 2013, 30th International Conference on Machine Learning, Atlanta, Georgia, USA, vol. 28, pp. 639–647 (2013)

14. Kolmogorov, A.: Sulla determinazione empirica di una legge di distribuzione. Giornale dell'Istituto Italiano degli Attuari **4**, 83–91 (1933)

15. Levy, O., Goldberg, Y.: Neural word embedding as implicit matrix factorization. In: Proceedings of the NeurIPS 2014, 27th International Conference on Neural Information Processing Systems, Cambridge, MA, USA, pp. 2177–2185 (2014)

16. Liu, H., Wu, Y., Yang, Y.: Analogical inference for multi-relational embeddings. In: Proceedings of the ICML 2017, 34th International Conference on Machine Learning (2017)

17. Miclet, L., Prade, H.: Handling analogical proportions in classical logic and fuzzy logics settings. In: Sossai, C., Chemello, G. (eds.) ECSQARU 2009. LNCS (LNAI), vol. 5590, pp. 638–650. Springer, Heidelberg (2009). https://doi.org/10.1007/978-3-642-02906-6_55

18. Mikolov, T., Sutskever, I., Chen, K., Corrado, G.S., Dean, J.: Distributed representations of words and phrases and their compositionality. In: Proceedings of the NeurIPS 2013, 26th International Conference on Neural Information Processing Systems, pp. 3111–3119 (2013)

19. Mikolov, T., Yih, W.t., Zweig, G.: Linguistic regularities in continuous space word representations. In: Proceedings of the NAACL 2013, the 2013 Conference of the North American Chapter of the Association for Computational Linguistics: Human Language Technologies, Atlanta, Georgia, pp. 746–751 (2013)
20. Sadeghi, F., Zitnick, C.L., Farhadi, A.: Visalogy: answering visual analogy questions. In: Proceedings of the NeurIPS 2015, 28th Conference on Neural Information Processing Systems, pp. 1882–1890 (2015)
21. Weinberger, K.Q., Chapelle, O.: Large margin taxonomy embedding for document categorization. In: Proceedings of the NeurIPS 2009, 21st Conference on Neural Information Processing Systems, pp. 1737–1744 (2009)
22. Weinberger, K.Q., Saul, L.K.: Distance metric learning for large margin nearest neighbor classification. J. Mach. Learn. Res. **10**, 207–244 (2009)

HORUS-NER: A Multimodal Named Entity Recognition Framework for Noisy Data

Diego Esteves[1,3(✉)], José Marcelino[1], Piyush Chawla[2], Asja Fischer[4], and Jens Lehmann[3]

[1] Farfetch.com, London, UK
{diego.esteves,jose.marcelino}@farfetch.com
[2] The Ohio State University, Columbus 43210, USA
[3] SDA Research Group, Bonn, Germany
[4] Faculty of Mathematics, Ruhr-Universität Bochum, 44801 Bochum, Germany

Abstract. Recent work based on Deep Learning presents state-of-the-art (SOTA) performance in the named entity recognition (NER) task. However, such models still have the performance drastically reduced in noisy data (e.g., social media, search engines), when compared to the formal domain (e.g., newswire). Thus, designing and exploring new methods and architectures is highly necessary to overcome current challenges. In this paper, we shift the focus of existing solutions to an entirely different perspective. We investigate the potential of embedding word-level features extracted from images and news. We performed a very comprehensive study in order to validate the hypothesis that images and news (obtained from an external source) may boost the task on noisy data, revealing very interesting findings. When our proposed architecture is used: (1) We beat SOTA in *precision* with simple CRFs models (2) The overall performance of decision trees-based models can be drastically improved. (3) Our approach overcomes off-the-shelf models for this task. (4) Images and text consistently increased *recall* over different datasets for SOTA, but at cost of *precision*. All experiment configurations, data and models are publicly available to the research community at horus-ner.org

Keywords: Named entity recognition · WNUT · Noisy text · Information retrieval · Images · Text · Multi-modal

1 Introduction

In this paper, we address the problem of recognizing named-entity (NE) types in noisy data. While NER on formal domain (e.g. CoNLL) has been shown to be reasonably accurate – achieving average F_1 measure up to 90% [34] – most of the approaches for noisy data designed in the past years still heavily rely on carefully constructed orthographic features and language-specific resources, such as *gazetteers*. To bridge this gap, more recent work have proposed architectures based on LSTM networks. Although this not necessarily introduces SOTA

© Springer Nature Switzerland AG 2021
P. H. Abreu et al. (Eds.): IDA 2021, LNCS 12695, pp. 89–100, 2021.
https://doi.org/10.1007/978-3-030-74251-5_8

performance [16,19], the trained networks achieved very similar performance on a popular *newswire* corpora (respectively 88.83% and 90.94% on CoNLL-2003 test set). Besides supporting different languages with low effort, the great advantage of such (end-to-end) approaches lies in the fact that specific knowledge resources are not required (excepting for specific *embeddings*, which are - usually - language dependent), alleviating the dependency on manually annotated data and encoded rules. However, unlike *newswire*, *microblogs* often deal with more informal languages, which do not have such implicit linguistic formalism [14,22,29]. With respect to that–not surprisingly–the performance of SOTA degrades significantly in the noisy data domain, evidencing the sensibility of the proposed models when dealing with noisy and out-of-domain text. In recent work [5,20,21,29], F_1 ranging from 0.19 to 0.52 have been reported in the noisy domain. Hence, devising models to deal with linguistically complex scenarios such as *twitter* remains an open and very challenging problem to tackle, regardless of the architecture's design. In this paper, we extend previous work [12] to face this challenge through a novel perspective: we develop a framework that learns latent features from images and textual information to detect named entities, without requiring further engineering effort. This is obtained by extracting related information from an external source, given an input query string (e.g., a token). In this work we use the Web and DBPedia as external sources. We argue that images and text associated to a given token may contain missing information required to improve performance of NER on noisy data. Our main contribution is a framework that implements an enhanced methodology to extract, pre-process and generate feature vectors based on images and text - associated to each single token of a sentence. These vectors are then concatenated and used throughout several different NER architectures. Furthermore, a great advantage of our proposed model is that challenging (pre-processing) tasks, such as *text normalization* [1], is bypassed. To the best of our knowledge, this is the first *comprehensive* study in an attempt to derive and explore features based on images and news to improve NER on noisy data. The proposed methodology does not rely on *gazetteers*, *lookups* and *normalization* and also does not implement any encoded rules. Due to the nature of the generated feature vectors, we argue the outcomes of this work are of high relevance not only for NER on social media, but also to related (e.g., *entity linking* [27]) and also other downstream tasks [13]. Our experiments show that this has a direct positive impact in CRF and Decision Trees-based models, and the potential to improve overall B-LSTMs performance when more training data is available. As a contribution to the community we also released all metadata. The result is a word-level feature database for based on image and text. This database contains approx. 3 millions data features for more than 72.000 distinct English tokens and has been explored over 5.904 experiments in several different configurations. As consequence, we built an open-source framework dubbed HORUS, which we detail in the following sections. The data, metadata and code is released open-source and available at the project website: horus-ner.org.

2   Methodology and Features

First, one needs to note, that for each category of interest (i.e., a named entity class) one can identify a certain set of representative contents or objects, which have a high chance of being present in images belonging to nouns of this category. For instance, a name of a person has a high correlation to images containing *faces* whereas a name of a country has a high correlation to images containing *maps* or *landscapes*. Thus, named entities can be classified as belonging to a certain category by detecting these representative objects in the related images. Therefore, for each token $t \in$ a sentence S we extract a set of image and text feature vectors $\mathcal{F} = (\mathcal{F}_1, \ldots, \mathcal{F}_n)$ that serve as input features to a NER classifier. Following the foundations of our previous work [12], we use the Web to obtain (top 10) images and websites associated to a given token t. In this paper, we have extended and explored this methodology in a variety of ways: (1) We explored other clustering-based features (*Brown Clusters*); (2) We proposed and extended new visual features; (3) we performed *several* new experiments, obtaining further (valuable) insights; (4) we extended and included SOTA neural mechanisms in the underlying framework: (4.1) Topic Modeling + Convolution Neural Networks (CNN) for text classification [37] (4.2) CNN for object detection [32] (4.3) Topic Modeling over Word2vec [26] top v tokens (4.4) Cross-similarity measure over top v tokens and (4.5) Basic NN prediction statistics (5) We benchmark different NER classifiers in different gold-standard datasets.

Baseline Methodology: In our previous work [12] we perform the following steps: for each defined named entity category $c \in \mathcal{C}$ a set of text-based or image-based classifiers $\xi_m^c, m = 1, \ldots, M$ and $\Phi_l^c, l = 1, \ldots, L$, respectively, are applied. Given an element from $d \in \mathcal{D}_t$ (or $i \in \mathcal{I}_t$) each binary classifier outputs a prediction if the text (or image) belongs to a certain category c or not, i.e. $\Phi_l^c(i), \xi_m^c(d) \in \{-1, 1\}$. The text-based and image-based models produce the following feature sets: $\mathcal{TX}$ and $\mathcal{CV}$, respectively. These scores (feature vectors) $R_{\mathcal{D}_t}^c$ and $R_{\mathcal{I}_t}^c$ for all $c \in \mathcal{C}$ can now be used to construct the features $F(t)$ for the final classifier.

Improved Methodology: In the following we detail each additional feature implemented in our Framework. **1. Brown Clusters ($\mathcal{B}$)**: *Brown hierarchical word clustering* algorithm uses distributional information to group similar words [4]. It takes a *corpus* and outputs K clusters of word types in a hard-fashion, i.e., each token only appears in one cluster k. Essentially, it derives a tree graph with two kinds of information – the cluster of a word and the hierarchy between classes. Since the default number of clusters $K = 1000$ may not often yield optimal results (although widely considered as default value) [8], we performed some exploratory experiments to obtain the better hyper-parameter based on Derczynski et al. findings. The features are extracted by truncating the patches at $[1: \text{bits} - 2]$, e.g., the cluster path 1100101 yields features $\{1, 11, 110, 1100, 11001\}$. **2. Standard Features ($\mathcal{S}$)**: Besides *lexicon-based* such as Part-of-speech (POS) and *stop words*, *character-based* features, such as: "is numeric?", "initial capital?", "special character?" are also part of the classical features we study. For example the token "P@rty" would lead to vector similar to $[0, 1, 1, \ldots]$ **3. Topic**

Modeling + CNNs ($\mathcal{TX}_{nn}$): Originally designed for computer vision, Convolutional Neural Networks (CNNs) have subsequently been shown to be effective for NLP, achieving excellent results in diverse tasks, including sentence classification [17]. We trained a convolution neural networks with Topic Modeling [35] for text-classification due to its state of the art performance, which presents excellent results even with low hyper-parameter tuning [18]. The main idea is to classify each document (website) linked to a given token into a pre-defined number of "topics" (in this case, the labels PER, LOC and ORG), similarly to the $\mathcal{TX}$ module. Likewise, we used DBPedia to collect data for training the model. In practice, for each returned website w_i, we return a confidence score for w_i being labelled as one of the pre-defined classes. As result, we have a vector similar to: $[(0, 0.40170625), (1, 0.06669136), (2, 0.39819494), (3, 0.06670282), (4, 0.066704586)]$ where each key represents a certain topic (PER, LOC, ORG and OTHERS). **4. Seeds x Word2Vec ($\mathcal{TX}_{emb}$):** This model extracts the correlation between a pre-defined number of tokens (seeds) related to a certain class and nearest tokens to a given token t. We compute the distance in the intersection of the top 5 most similar words ($\mathcal{W}_{top}^t = s_1^t \ldots s_5^t$) to a given t with a set of *seeds* $\mathcal{E}$ defined by common-sense: $\mathcal{TX}_{emb}^c = \mathcal{W}_{top}^t \cap \mathcal{E}^c$. For instance, if - hypothetically - the token $t = Berlin$ has the following (5) nearest words $\mathcal{W}_5 = [Munich, Hamburg, Frankfurt, Germany, Dusseldorf]$. For each, we compute the average distance from each $e \in \mathcal{E}$. For e.g. LOC, we set the following vector = ["city", "country", "place", "beach", "mountain", "forest", "location"]. **5. Keyword Extraction ($\mathcal{TX}_{stats}$)** Similar to Sect. 2, this model outputs the likelihood of a certain token t belonging to a certain class c based on word distance. We extract the most frequent tokens from the set of documents $\mathcal{D}$ (websites) and cross-compute the distance from terms in $\mathcal{E}$. **6. Convolutional Neural Nets ($\mathcal{CV}_{nn}$)** As mentioned, CNNs is a state of the art technique for image recognition (e.g., detecting people or objects in a given image). For instance, the Inception model [33] achieves state of the art position, reaching 5.6% top-5 error rate on the ILSVR [30] classification challenge. Also, Places365 [38] performs state of the art in several datasets for place recognition. Another major advantage is that CNNs require little pre-processing when compared to standard approaches, such as SIFT [24] and SURF [2]. We re-trained this architecture to detect a list of pre-defined objects associated to each class c (as proposed in our previous work [12]). The classifier ϕ returns the probability distribution of a given image contain one of the desired classes.

3 Experimental Setup

We benchmark our approach in four different gold-standard datasets ($\mathcal{DS}$) for NER in social media. The Ritter dataset and three datasets from the most famous Workshop on Noisy User-generated Text: WNUT-15, WNUT-16 and WNUT-17. Figure 1 depicts the pipeline that 1) performs the mapping of 3-MUC entities for all datasets. 2) enhances each of them with POS annotations. 3) Finally we get images and news associated with each of potential entity candidate.

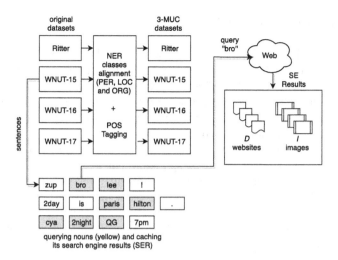

Fig. 1. Pre-processing step for the benchmark setup: adding POS tagger and filtering NNs. In the sequence, searching the Web to obtain images and websites for each filtered noun candidate and its compounds.

4) As a last step, we run the feature extraction modules (Sect. 2 - *Improved Methodology*) to generate the feature vectors associated to each token t. Then we have training data for our NER task. Following this last step, we implemented different weak and strong NER baselines, as follows:

(1) *Off-the-shelf NER* As a sanity check for defining baselines, we also briefly reported the performance of some off the shelf frameworks that claim state-of-the-art performance on NER: NLTK, Spacy, MITIE [1], OSU Twitter NLP, Stanford CoreNLP.

(2) *Weak NER Baselines* Two standard algorithms were used as weak baseline. A classical solution for sequence-to-sequence problems (CRF) and a Decision Tree-based method.

(3) *Strong NER Baselines* LSTMs represent cutting-edge architectures for NER both in *formal domains* [16,19] but also in *noisy data* [10] (despite performance drop when compared to *formal domains*). We implemented different SOTA LSTM-based models (B-LSTM+CRF [16], B-LSTM+CNN+CRF [25], Char+B-LSTM+CRF [19]).

In order to fully assess the impact of the proposed features and have a fair and proper comparison study, we performed a comprehensive benchmark on several *local* and *global* features. The full set of input features that we feed in our final classifier is given by the concatenation of two or more possible feature sets $\mathcal{F} = (\mathcal{TX} \cup \mathcal{CV} \cup \mathcal{TX}_{cnn} \cup \mathcal{CV}_{cnn} \cup \mathcal{TX}_{emb} \cup \mathcal{TX}_{stats} \cup \mathcal{B} \cup \mathcal{S})$. We grouped these features into several *experiment configurations* (cfg01 to cfg41) (Table 1).

---

[1] https://github.com/mit-nlp/MITIE.

4   Results and Discussion

We first evaluate the performance of off the shelf tools on the selected datasets. As expected, results indicate that these solutions underperform when confronted with noisy data (AVG F1 from 0.2961 to 0.4878). This also confirms findings by Derczynski et al. [9]. Therefore, as the average F1-measures are below current SOTA for the task on noisy data [12] and corroborating with past studies, we do not move on experiments for these frameworks[2].

In order to have a comprehensive and fair environment to benchmark different weak and SOTA NER algorithms, we split different feature configurations. The complete benchmark configuration has the following dimensions: $cfg \times (\mathcal{DS}_{train} + (\mathcal{DS}_{train} \times \mathcal{DS}_{test})) \times \mathcal{A}$; where cfg is the total of feature sets (i.e., distinct configurations), $\mathcal{D}_{train}$ is the total of training sets, $\mathcal{D}_{test}$ is the total of test sets and finally $\mathcal{A}$ is the total number of algorithms. This leads to the following number of experiments: $41 \times (4 + (4 \times 3)) \times 9 = 5.904^3$. Table 1 summarizes the groups of experiments performed, i.e., different experiment dimensions. It helps to understand the impact of images and textual features. It is worth mentioning that experiment configurations from 30 to 41 include the best Brown cluster in theirs respective pairs (e.g., `cfg30` represents `cfg18` including the best brown cluster). Therefore, they are let out of this table to improve readability.

Figure 2 shows the performance of CRF in different datasets/feature sets. The x-axis represents the different feature sets, while y-axis average of F1-measure[4]. To highlight the impact of the different groups of features, we categorize F1's in four ascending scales, from worse to the best: *red, yellow, gray* and *green*. Some patterns w.r.t. the addition of images and text as input features are clearly observable. First, standard textual features ($\mathcal{TX}$) have often a much worse performance when compared to standard image features ($\mathcal{CV}$) as well as in the combination of both, as observed in the following sets `cfg02`×`cfg03`×`cfg04`, `cfg06`×`cfg07`×`cfg08` and `cfg15`×`cfg16`×`cfg17`. This is at some extend expected since the adopted committee strategy [12] to classify *news* data is not a straightforward task. In this sense, a better solution might be taking into account probabilities instead of binary values. Moreover, we notice our improvement in the $\mathcal{TX}$ component (`cfg19`, `cfg20` and `cfg21`) outperform the similar features proposed by [12]. Among those, it is worth noting that the *text correlation* ($\mathcal{TX}_{stats}$, Sect. 2) has a greater impact than any other textual feature. This is due to the higher level of abstraction when computing word embedding distances across *seeds* in a distance supervision fashion. Regarding the image detection component, introducing state-of-the-art computer vision algorithms ($\mathcal{CV}_{cnn}$) has also been beneficial to beat previous strategy ($\mathcal{CV}$), although without bringing major improvements as in the $\mathcal{TX}$. This is due to

---

[2] For the sake of fair comparison, 3-MUC is also the base for experiments.

[3] 41 experiment configurations, 4 training sets (`Ritter`, `WNUT-15`, `WNUT-16` and `WNUT-17`), 3 test sets (`WNUT-15`, `WNUT-16` and `WNUT-17`) and 9 NER architectures (DT, RF, CRF, CRF-PA, LSTM, B-LSTM+CRF, Char+B-LSTM+CRF and B-LSTM+CNN+CRF).

[4] 3-fold cross-validation.

Table 1. The impact of images and textual features grouped by different experiment configurations. More detailed information for each configuration omitted due to page limit, but available on the project website horus-ner.org.

	Description	Configurations	Note
1	Standard	cfg01, cfg05, cfg09-14	Usual features
2	Brown Clusters	cfg09-14	Usual features + Brown
3	Images	cfg03, cfg07, cfg15 cfg18, cfg26	Computer vision (only)
4	Text	cfg02, cfg06, cfg16 cfg19-23	Text mining (only)
5	Images	cfg03, cfg07, cfg15	Inspired by [12]
6	Text	cfg02, cfg06, cfg16	Inspired by [12]
7	Images and Text	cfg04, cfg08, cfg17	Inspired by [12]
8	Images	cfg18	This paper (Sect. 2)
9	Text	cfg19-23	This paper (Sect. 2)
10	Images and Text	cfg24, cfg08, cfg17	This paper (Sect. 2)

the *common-sense* rules proposed by [12] in this layer. Finally, the inclusion of tuned Brown clusters[5] along with proposed features shows to be beneficial to the performance. Overall, the best results were obtained from the concatenation of the previous and proposed features in conjunction with Brown clusters (cfg41).

Table 2 presents detailed results for each NER model. To recap, for each model, the first column (cfg10) in Table 2 represents the classic NER features (e.g. *lexical*); The configuration cfg04 representing standard image and text features (proposed in [12]); Finally, in cfg41 we see results for the image and text features proposed in this work. As expected, CRFs and SOTA NNs architectures performed best and overall images and news (cfg04 and cfg41) have a great impact in CRFs, helping to overcome SOTA (LSTMs) w.r.t. *precision*. The comparison shed light on the impact of our proposed features (best configuration, cfg41) when compared to the broadly implemented (standard) NER features (cfg10) and the features proposed in our previous work [12] (cfg04). We can see that overall the additional features introduced in this work clearly improves the performance of the majority of the NER models - both weak and strong baselines - (DT, RF, CRF, B-LSTM+CRF) in all data sets. CRF-PA slightly overperformed the standard CRF, confirming findings presented by Derczynski et al. [7]. However, it is worth noticing the ability of NNs to improve recall, the major challenging in noisy-data [1].

The results confirm that the proposed features consistently boost the performance of the models in the majority of the experiments. It is worth noting the substantial impact in the CRF-based model. Our proposed features (cfg41) improves *Lexical + Brown Cluster* and [12] in more than 90% of the cases (and

---

[5] $\mathcal{B}_{best}$, cfg30-41.

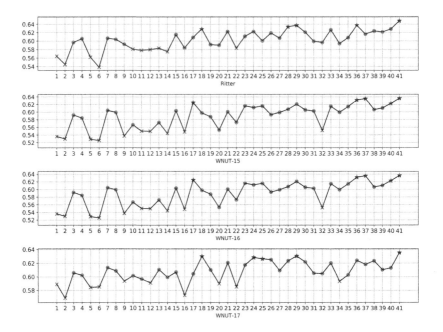

Fig. 2. The CRF performance (`cfgXX` × F1) over different feature sets. Each subgraph representing one dataset. Performances of configurations using our methodology are positively impacted.

at least similar in 100% of the cases). Moreover, we notice that a basic CRF architecture with the best feature configuration (`cfg41`) outperforms a state-of-the-art B-LSTM architecture w.r.t. *precision*. The same feature set also positively impacted *recall* of B-LSTM in all experiments. Finally, we trained a B-LSTM+CRF architecture with an expanded set created merging all data sets. We removed duplication from the union of the respective *training*, *dev* and *test* sets, i.e., occurrences of overlap sentences. The SOTA B-LSTM+CRF F1-measure has achieved 0.5217. Integrating our methodology has increased the results to ↑0.5352 (`cfg04`) and ↑0.5352 (`cfg41`). Despite modest results, this benchmark indicates that images and news are definitely a great asset to improve both precision and overall performance of NER architectures in noisy contexts.

5   Related Work

Named Entity Recognition is a sub task of information extraction which seeks to identify entities in textual content. Over the past few years, the problem of recognizing named entities in noisy data has been addressed by different approaches that have emerged specifically designed to better perform on short and noisy texts, such as `T-NER` [29] and `TwiterIE` [3]. The first performs tokenization, POS tagging and noun-phrase chunking before using topic models to find named entities whereas the second – an extension of GATE ANNIE [6] – implements an

Table 2. The performance measure's improvements (*green*) and decreases (*red*) in different datasets, feature sets (`cfg`) and NER models. Results are represented in a color gradient of 5 points interval. 0% represents a tiny improvement i ($0.1\% \leq i \leq 0.99\%$), which is not representative, although technically not zero. The percentage variation both in 04 and 41 columns are according to the baseline performance for each NER architecture (column 10).

NER Benchmark on Noisy Data																		
			Weak Baselines									Strong Baselines						
Dataset			Decision Trees			Random Forest			CRF			B-LSTM [16] CRF			B-LSTM [19] C+CRF			B-LSTM [25] C+CRF+CNN		
cfg →			10	04	41	10	04	41	10	04	41	10	04	41	10	04	41	10	04	41
Ritter	P		0.48	+2%	+4%	0.51	+1%	+24%	0.73	+5%	+7%	0.77	+1%	−3%	0.81	−5%	−1%	0.81	−5%	−5%
	R		0.49	+1%	+3%	0.48	−1%	−2%	0.58	−8%	−2%	0.63	+5%	+5%	0.59	+5%	+4%	0.62	+3%	+5%
	F		0.49	+1%	+3%	0.49	+4%	+7%	0.58	+2%	+7%	0.68	+1%	+1%	0.67	+1%	+1%	0.69	−1%	+1%
WNUT-15	P		0.49	+2%	+5%	0.52	+7%	+25%	0.72	+7%	+9%	0.72	−4%	−2%	0.77	−3%	−4%	0.78	−4%	−5%
	R		0.50	+0%	+5%	0.49	+0%	+1%	0.48	−1%	+6%	0.69	+1%	+1%	0.65	+2%	+2%	0.66	+2%	+2%
	F		0.50	+0%	+5%	0.50	+5%	+9%	0.56	+2%	+8%	0.68	+0%	+0%	0.69	+0%	−1%	0.71	−1%	−2%
WNUT-16	P		0.49	+1%	+6%	0.52	+14%	+23%	0.72	+7%	+9%	0.72	−4%	−2%	0.77	−3%	−3%	0.78	−4%	−6%
	R		0.50	+1%	+6%	0.48	+0%	+2%	0.48	−1%	+6%	0.69	+0%	+1%	0.65	+2%	+2%	0.66	+2%	+2%
	F		0.49	+1%	+6%	0.50	+5%	+10%	0.56	+2%	+8%	0.69	−1%	+0%	0.69	+0%	+0%	0.71	−1%	−2%
WNUT-17	P		0.44	+3%	+7%	0.47	+13%	+24%	0.76	+2%	+1%	0.76	−2%	−2%	0.76	+0%	−2%	0.77	−3%	−3%
	R		0.45	+4%	+6%	0.44	+3%	+4%	0.50	+0%	+5%	0.63	+1%	+1%	0.64	+0%	+1%	0.62	+1%	+1%
	F		0.44	+4%	+6%	0.45	+6%	+12%	0.60	+0%	+4%	0.67	+0%	+0%	0.69	+0%	−1%	0.67	+0%	−1%

NLP pipeline customized to microblog texts at every stage (including Twitter-specific data import and metadata handling). Liu et al. [22] propose a gradient-descent graph-based method for text normalization and recognition. Likewise, these approaches are highly dependent on hand-crafted rules. Most recently, approaches followed Lample et al. [19] architecture based on BiLSTMs. Limsopatham and Collier [20] proposed a neural architecture for NER on *microblogs*, which combines a bidirectional LSTM with an CRF achieving a F_1 measure of 52.41 for *English* text. Models supporting other languages were proposed, however, similar performances (min-max F_1 measure) have also been observed across different languages other than English, such as French, Portuguese and Chinese, for instance ([23] - $21.28 - 58.59$, [28] - $24.40 - 52.78$ and [15] - $44.29 - 54.50$, respectively). Esteves et al. [12] proposed a methodology to encode image and news features into NER architectures, showing promising preliminary results. [36] followed the same idea to detect entities in Twitter, but just analyzing existing images associated to a given tweet, which drastically restricts the approach. In the three years the NER in social media benchmarking workshop W-NUT ran, in social media[6], modest results have been reported by a vast number of different NER architectures: $16.47 - 56.41$, $19.26 - 52.41$ and $39.98 - 41.86$ (min-max F_1 in WNUT 2015, 2016, 2017, respectively) [1,11,31]. Therefore, although neural architectures pose a good choice to outperform standard architectures (e.g. CRFs), the task is still far from being solved in noisy contexts.

---

[6] http://noisy-text.github.io.

6   Conclusion

In this paper, we benchmark and extend a novel multilevel NER approach in different ways. We integrate features which rely on state-of-the-art computer vision and text mining techniques. We show that its major advantage is the fact that it does not rely on hand-crafted features and domain-specific knowledge. In order to support this claim, we conducted a massive number of experiments in the same computational environment with different feature sets and over different gold-standard data. In traditional NER architectures (e.g. CRF), the proposed features have proved feasible to notably improve its overall model performance (i.e. $F1$) and, when compared to SOTA, beat in *precision*. SOTA had improved in *recall*, but at expense of *precision*. However, when benchmarking the models across different training-test sets (which is often not tested in most research publications) the images and news also proved to be beneficial for the task. We also confirmed that this solution performs better than existing off-the-shelf frameworks on the noisy context, as expected. The main issue w.r.t. SOTA neural networks for this domain seems to be the size of the available training data sets (WNUT). As future work we plan to explore the combination of the models given their probability distributions, extending also the analysis to more named entity classes. Also, since it shows to be language-agnostic, we would like to explore new languages other than English. Finally, we plan to integrate this architecture into Named Entity Disambiguation and Linking frameworks.

References

1. Baldwin, T., de Marneffe, M.C., Han, B., Kim, Y.B., Ritter, A., Xu, W.: Shared tasks of the 2015 workshop on noisy user-generated text: twitter lexical normalization and named entity recognition. In: Proceedings of the Workshop on Noisy User-generated Text, pp. 126–135 (2015)
2. Bay, H., Ess, A., Tuytelaars, T., Van Gool, L.: Speeded-up robust features (surf). Comput. Vis. Image Underst. **110**(3), 346–359 (2008). https://doi.org/10.1016/j.cviu.2007.09.014
3. Bontcheva, K., Derczynski, L., Funk, A., Greenwood, M.A., Maynard, D., Aswani, N.: Twitie: an open-source information extraction pipeline for microblog text. In: RANLP, pp. 83–90 (2013)
4. Brown, P.F., Desouza, P.V., Mercer, R.L., Pietra, V.J.D., Lai, J.C.: Class-based n-gram models of natural language. Comput. Linguist. **18**(4), 467–479 (1992)
5. Chang, Y.S., Sung, Y.H.: Applying name entity recognition to informal text. Recall **1**(1) (2005)
6. Cunningham, H., et al.: Text Processing with GATE (Version 6). University of Sheffield Department of Computer Science 15 (2011)
7. Derczynski, L., Bontcheva, K.: Passive-aggressive sequence labeling with discriminative post-editing for recognising person entities in tweets. In: Proceedings of the 14th Conference of the European Chapter of the Association for Computational Linguistics, volume 2: Short Papers, pp. 69–73 (2014)
8. Derczynski, L., Chester, S., Bøgh, K.S.: Tune your brown clustering, please. In: International Conference Recent Advances in Natural Language Processing, RANLP. Association for Computational Linguistics, vol. 2015, pp. 110–117 (2015)

9. Derczynski, L., et al.: Analysis of named entity recognition and linking for tweets. Inf. Process. Manage. **51**(2), 32–49 (2015)

10. Derczynski, L., Nichols, E., van Erp, M., Limsopatham, N.: Results of the wnut2017 shared task on novel and emerging entity recognition. In: Proceedings of the 3rd Workshop on Noisy User-generated Text. Association for Computational Linguistics, pp. 140–147 (2017). https://doi.org/10.18653/v1/W17-4418

11. Derczynski, L., Nichols, E., van Erp, M., Limsopatham, N.: Results of the wnut2017 shared task on novel and emerging entity recognition. In: Proceedings of the 3rd Workshop on Noisy User-generated Text, pp. 140–147 (2017)

12. Esteves, D., Peres, R., Lehmann, J., Napolitano, G.: Named entity recognition in twitter using images and text. In: Garrigós, I., Wimmer, M. (eds.) ICWE 2017. LNCS, vol. 10544, pp. 191–199. Springer, Cham (2018). https://doi.org/10.1007/978-3-319-74433-9_17

13. Esteves, D., Reddy, A.J., Chawla, P., Lehmann, J.: Belittling the source: trustworthiness indicators to obfuscate fake news on the web. In: Proceedings of the First Workshop on Fact Extraction and VERification (FEVER), pp. 50–59 (2018)

14. Gattani, A., et al.: Entity extraction, linking, classification, and tagging for social media: a wikipedia-based approach. Proc. VLDB Endow. **6**(11), 1126–1137 (2013). https://doi.org/10.14778/2536222.2536237

15. He, H., Sun, X.: A unified model for cross-domain and semi-supervised named entity recognition in Chinese social media. In: AAAI, pp. 3216–3222 (2017)

16. Huang, Z., Xu, W., Yu, K.: Bidirectional LSTM-CRF models for sequence tagging. arXiv preprint arXiv:1508.01991 (2015)

17. Kim, Y.: Convolutional neural networks for sentence classification. arXiv preprint arXiv:1408.5882 (2014)

18. Kim, Y.: Convolutional neural networks for sentence classification. In: Proceedings of the 2014 Conference on Empirical Methods in Natural Language Processing (EMNLP). Association for Computational Linguistics, pp. 1746–1751 (2014). https://doi.org/10.3115/v1/D14-1181

19. Lample, G., Ballesteros, M., Subramanian, S., Kawakami, K., Dyer, C.: Neural architectures for named entity recognition. arXiv preprint arXiv:1603.01360 (2016)

20. Limsopatham, N., Collier, N.: Bidirectional LSTM for named entity recognition in twitter messages. WNUT **2016**, 145 (2016)

21. Liu, X., Zhang, S., Wei, F., Zhou, M.: Recognizing named entities in tweets. In: Proceedings of the 49th Annual Meeting of the Association for Computational Linguistics: Human Language Technologies. Association for Computational Linguistics, Vol. 1, pp. 359–367 (2011)

22. Liu, X., Zhou, M., Wei, F., Fu, Z., Zhou, X.: Joint inference of named entity recognition and normalization for tweets. In: Proceedings of the 50th Annual Meeting of the Association for Computational Linguistics: Long Papers-Vol. 1, pp. 526–535. Association for Computational Linguistics (2012)

23. Lopez, C., et al.: Cap 2017 challenge: twitter named entity recognition. arXiv preprint arXiv:1707.07568 (2017)

24. Lowe, D.G.: Object recognition from local scale-invariant features. In: Proceedings of the seventh IEEE international Conference on Computer Vision, Vol. 2, pp. 1150–1157. IEEE (1999)

25. Ma, X., Hovy, E.: End-to-end sequence labeling via bi-directional LSTM-CNNS-CRF. arXiv preprint arXiv:1603.01354 (2016)

26. Mikolov, T., Chen, K., Corrado, G., Dean, J.: Efficient estimation of word representations in vector space. arXiv preprint arXiv:1301.3781 (2013)

27. Moussallem, D., Usbeck, R., Röder, M., Ngonga Ngomo, A.C.: MAG: a multilingual, knowledge-base agnostic and deterministic entity linking approach. In: Proceedings of the Knowledge Capture Conference, K-CAP 2017, p. 8. ACM (2017)

28. Peres, R., Esteves, D., Maheshwari, G.: Bidirectional LSTM with a context input window for named entity recognition in tweets. In: Proceedings of the Knowledge Capture Conference, p. 42. ACM (2017)

29. Ritter, A., et al.: Named entity recognition in tweets: an experimental study. In: Proceedings of the Conference on Empirical Methods in Natural Language Processing, Association for Computational Linguistics, pp. 1524–1534 (2011)

30. Russakovsky, O., et al.: ImageNet large scale visual recognition challenge. Int. J. Comput. Vis. **115**(3), 211–252 (2015). https://doi.org/10.1007/s11263-015-0816-y

31. Strauss, B., Toma, B., Ritter, A., de Marneffe, M.C., Xu, W.: Results of the wnut16 named entity recognition shared task. In: Proceedings of the 2nd Workshop on Noisy User-generated Text (WNUT), pp. 138–144 (2016)

32. Szegedy, C., et al.: Going deeper with convolutions. In: Proceedings of the IEEE Conference on Computer Vision and pattern Recognition, CVPR, pp. 1–9 (2015)

33. Szegedy, C., et al.: Going deeper with convolutions. In: CVPR, pp. 1–9. IEEE (2015)

34. Tkachenko, M., Simanovsky, A.: Named entity recognition: exploring features. In: KONVENS, pp. 118–127 (2012)

35. Wallach, H.M.: Topic modeling: beyond bag-of-words. In: Proceedings of the 23rd International Conference on Machine Learning, pp. 977–984. ACM (2006)

36. Zhang, Q., Fu, J., Liu, X., Huang, X.: Adaptive co-attention network for named entity recognition in tweets. In: AAAI (2018)

37. Zhang, X., Zhao, J., LeCun, Y.: Character-level convolutional networks for text classification. In: Advances in Neural Information Processing Systems, pp. 649–657 (2015)

38. Zhou, B., Lapedriza, A., Khosla, A., Oliva, A., Torralba, A.: Places: a 10 million image database for scene recognition. IEEE Trans. Pattern Anal. Mach. Intell. **40**(6), 1452–1464 (2017)

Modeling with Statistical Learning

Incremental Search Space Construction for Machine Learning Pipeline Synthesis

Marc-André Zöller[1]([✉]), Tien-Dung Nguyen[2], and Marco F. Huber[3,4]

[1] USU Software AG, Rüppurrer Street 1, Karlsruhe, Germany
marc.zoeller@usu.com
[2] University of Technology Sydney, Sydney, Australia
TienDung.Nguyen-2@student.uts.edu.au
[3] Institute of Industrial Manufacturing and Management IFF,
University of Stuttgart, Stuttgart, Germany
marco.huber@ieee.org
[4] Center for Cyber Cognitive Intelligence CCI, Fraunhofer IPA,
Nobelstr. 12, Stuttgart, Germany

Abstract. Automated machine learning (AutoML) aims for constructing machine learning (ML) pipelines automatically. Many studies have investigated efficient methods for algorithm selection and hyperparameter optimization. However, methods for ML pipeline synthesis and optimization considering the impact of complex pipeline structures containing multiple preprocessing and classification algorithms have not been studied thoroughly. In this paper, we propose a data-centric approach based on meta-features for pipeline construction and hyperparameter optimization inspired by human behavior. By expanding the pipeline search space incrementally in combination with meta-features of intermediate data sets, we are able to prune the pipeline structure search space efficiently. Consequently, flexible and data set specific ML pipelines can be constructed. We prove the effectiveness and competitiveness of our approach on 28 data sets used in well-established AutoML benchmarks in comparison with state-of-the-art AutoML frameworks.

Keywords: Pipeline structure search · Meta-learning · AutoML

1 Introduction

AutoML promises to automate the synthesis of ML pipelines, handling hyperparameter optimization (HPO), algorithm selection and pipeline structure search. Many publications have proven the superiority of Bayesian optimization for HPO and algorithm selection, formulated as combined algorithm selection and hyperparameter optimization (CASH), over classic approaches like grid or random search [2,10]. More recently, methods for composing complete ML pipelines from a set of algorithms have been proposed. Those methods have a holistic view on pipeline synthesis: pipeline structure search is considered as an

© Springer Nature Switzerland AG 2021
P. H. Abreu et al. (Eds.): IDA 2021, LNCS 12695, pp. 103–115, 2021.
https://doi.org/10.1007/978-3-030-74251-5_9

extension of CASH where, instead of a single algorithm, a combination of multiple algorithms is selected and optimized simultaneously. Due to the exponential growth in complexity, the pipeline structure space is usually not evaluated thoroughly.

In contrast to current AutoML approaches, data scientists often create an ML pipeline in several small distinct steps. Starting from an empty pipeline, data scientists add algorithms to an ML pipeline incrementally by taking a detailed look at how the data set evolves in a pipeline in combination with their profound experience. Only if a pipeline structure performs well enough, a fine-tuning via hyperparameters is performed.

In this paper, we propose an alternative data-centric view on pipeline structure synthesis inspired by human behavior that allows an adaption of a pipeline to a specific data set. Through extensive use of meta-learning, we are able to dynamically prune the pipeline structure search space depending on meta-features of intermediate data sets. Intermediate data sets are the outputs of the execution of each individual step in a pipeline. Furthermore, the HPO of a pipeline candidate is boosted via knowledge-sharing between different pipelines. The main contributions of this paper are as follows:

- We reformulate the CASH and pipeline synthesis problem to enable efficient measures to reduce the pipeline search space and warm-starting CASH.
- We present a data-centric approach for incremental pipeline synthesis and hyperparameter optimization without expert knowledge inspired by human behavior called DSWIZARD.
- To ensure reproducibility of the results, we publish our meta-learning base consisting of 13.5 million unique ML pipelines on 28 data sets.

In Sect. 2 related work regarding pipeline structure synthesis and meta-learning in AutoML is discussed. Section 3 describes how we model the pipeline synthesis and the creation of the meta-learning base. The effectiveness of this approach is evaluated in Sect. 4 followed by a short conclusion in Sect. 5.

2   Preliminary and Related Work

Let a classification task—containing a data set $D = \{(\vec{x}_1, y_1), \ldots, (\vec{x}_m, y_m)\}$ with $\vec{x}_i \in \mathbb{X}^d$ being the input domain and $y \in \mathbb{Y} \subset \mathbb{N}$ the target domain and a loss function $\mathcal{L} : \mathbb{Y}^2 \to \mathbb{R}$—be given. Furthermore, let a fixed set of algorithms be given as $\mathcal{A} = \{A^{(1)}, A^{(2)}, \ldots, A^{(n)}\}$. Each algorithm $A^{(i)}$ is a transformation $\phi : \mathbb{Z} \to \mathbb{Z}'$ between two arbitrary domains. In case of $\mathbb{Z}' = \mathbb{Y}$ we denote the algorithm as a *classifier*, otherwise as a *preprocessor*. Usually $A^{(i)}$ is configured by hyperparameters $\vec{\lambda}^{(i)}$ from a domain $\Lambda_{A^{(i)}}$. $A^{(i)}$ transforming a data set D being configured by $\vec{\lambda}$ is denoted as $\phi_{\vec{\lambda}}^{(i)}(D)$. An ML pipeline $\mathcal{P}$ is a sequential combination of algorithms mapping data from an input domain to a target domain $f_{\mathcal{P}} : \mathbb{X}^d \to \mathbb{Y}$. It consists of a pipeline structure g—usually modeled as a directed acyclic graph (DAG)—with length $|g|$, algorithms $\vec{A} =$

$[A_1, \ldots, A_{|g|}]$ and the according hyperparameters $\vec{\lambda} = [\Lambda_1, \ldots, \Lambda_{|g|}]$. AutoML aims at generating a pipeline $\mathcal{P}$ that optimizes

$$(g, \vec{A}, \vec{\lambda})^* \in \underset{g \in G, \vec{A} \in \mathcal{A}^{|g|}, \vec{\lambda} \in \Lambda_{A_1} \times \cdots \times \Lambda_{A_{|g|}}}{\arg \min} \pi\left(g, \vec{A}, \vec{\lambda}, D\right)$$

with

$$\pi\left(g, \vec{A}, \vec{\lambda}, D\right) = \frac{1}{m} \sum_{i=1}^{m} \mathcal{L}(\hat{y}_i, y_i) \tag{1}$$

with $\hat{y}_i$ being the predicted output on the sample $\vec{x}_i$. We refer to this extension of the CASH problem as pipeline synthesis and optimization (PSO) problem.

The CASH notation, as originally introduced by [20], extends HPO by introducing an additional categorical meta-hyperparameter that represents an algorithm choice. This approach does not scale well as the search space grows exponentially with the length of the pipeline [12]. To counter this problem, many frameworks use a fixed pipeline structure based on best-practices reducing PSO to CASH, e.g. [13,19]. AUTOSKLEARN [7] allows the omission of single steps in a fixed pipeline, effectively replacing a fixed pipeline structure with a small set of pipeline candidates. Similarly, P4ML [9] uses a set of hand-crafted, best-practice pipelines for a wide variety of task instances. Appropriate pipeline candidates are selected based on data set meta-features followed by a fine-tuning via HPO. Yet, even when selecting from a set of fixed structures, the pipeline structure cannot be freely adapted to a specific problem instance.

TPOT [17] uses genetic programming to solve the PSO problem. RECEIPE [18] extends TPOT by incorporating a context-free grammar to guide the construction of pipeline structures. Even though this approach is able to build flexible tree-shaped pipelines, experiments have shown that genetic programming approaches tend to build pipelines using only one or two algorithms [22].

Multiple approaches that use a Monte Carlo tree search (MCTS) [5] for pipeline synthesis have been proposed. ML-PLAN [15] traverses a hierarchical task network with a MCTS to perform PSO. By design, the structure is determined first followed by the HPO. To assess the score of incomplete pipelines, random path completion is used, which does not scale well to high dimensions [11]. Similarly, ALPHAD3M [6] uses a combination of MCTS and neural networks to build pipeline structures based on a grammar while ignoring HPO completely. These approaches are more flexible in comparison to semi-fixed pipelines but still enforce specific pipeline patterns.

Many AutoML approaches use meta-learning to warm-start CASH or find promising pairs of preprocessors and classifiers [11]. ALPHAD3M uses meta-features and the algorithms in the current pipeline to predict the performance of a possible pipeline candidate. However, all those approaches only calculate meta-features of the initial data set.

3   DSWIZARD Methodology

Our approach, dubbed DSWIZARD, is inspired by the behavior of a human data scientist creating an ML pipeline. Starting from a very basic pipeline with default hyperparameters, the pipeline structure is extended gradually based on the characteristics of the intermediate data sets and the experience from previous tasks. After obtaining a combination of algorithms, a fine-tuning of the hyperparameters is performed. Figure 1 contains an overview of our proposed approach.

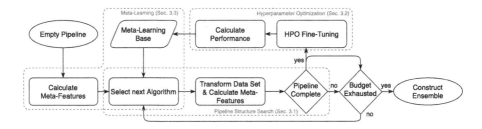

Fig. 1. General pipeline synthesis procedure in DSWIZARD.

Starting from an empty pipeline and a given data set, at first the meta-features of the data set are extracted. Based on these meta-features, a suited algorithm is selected using information from a pre-computed meta-learning base. Next, the data set is transformed using the selected algorithm and its default hyperparameters. Whenever the pipeline ends in a classifier, a fine tuning via HPO is performed to obtain a performance measure. This procedure is repeated until a predefined time budget is exhausted. Finally, ensemble selection [4] is used to create an ensemble of the best performing pipelines.

More formally, we reformulate the pipeline synthesis and optimization problem as a bilevel optimization problem:

$$(g, \vec{A}, \vec{\lambda}^*)^* \in \underset{g \in G, \vec{A} \in \mathcal{A}^{|g|}}{\arg\min} \quad \pi\left(g, \vec{A}, \vec{\lambda}^*, D\right)$$

$$\text{s.t.} \quad \vec{\lambda}^* \in \underset{\vec{\lambda} \in \Lambda_{A_1} \times \cdots \times \Lambda_{A_{|g|}}}{\arg\min} \quad \pi\left(g, \vec{A}, \vec{\lambda}, D\right).$$

The outer optimization problem is used for pipeline structure search and algorithm selection. The inner optimization problem performs the HPO of the selected algorithms. The implementation is publicly available on GitHub.[1]

3.1   Incremental Pipeline Structure Search

As each pipeline has to have a finite length and the set of algorithms $\mathcal{A}$ is finite, it is possible to enumerate the complete pipeline search space up to a

---

[1] See https://github.com/Ennosigaeon/dswizard.

depth d. The resulting search space can be interpreted as a layered DAG. Each node/state s_t represents a pipeline candidate g_{s_t}, i.e., a list of algorithms with hyperparameters, and a vector of meta-features of the intermediate data set D_{s_t} obtained by applying the (incomplete) pipeline candidate to the input data set; each edge/action corresponds to an algorithm $A_t \in \mathcal{A}$. All nodes of a layer have pipeline candidates with identical lengths. We use an adapted MCTS [5] to efficiently traverse the search graph. In contrast to the state-of-the-art, we explicitly calculate the meta-features of each intermediate data set and not only of the initial data set. The policy for MCTS's *selection* and *expansion* phase—inspired by *polynomial upper confidence trees* [1]—is

$$A_t \in \underset{A \in \mathcal{A}}{\arg \max} \; o(s_t) \cdot \left(Q(s_t, A) + c(\tau) \cdot U(s_t, A) \right)$$

balancing the exploitation Q and exploration U by a function c for a given state s_t. Additionally, the expected reward is weighted by an overfitting function $o(s_t)$. Exploitation of an action $A \in \mathcal{A}$ is defined as

$$Q(s_t, A) = \frac{P(s_t, A)}{1 + N(s_t, A)} \sum_{s' \in s_t(A)} \pi(s') \qquad (2)$$

with $P(s_t, A)$ being a prior performance estimate (see Sect. 3.3), $N(s_t, A)$ being the number of times action A was selected in state s_t, $s_t(A)$ the state obtained after applying action A and $\pi(s')$ a previously observed performance measure in state s'. Exploration, defined as

$$U(s_t, A) = \frac{\sqrt{\sum_{b \in \mathcal{A}} N(s_t, b)}}{1 + N(s_t, A)},$$

calculates the multiplicative inverse of the relative number of selections of A, giving a higher weight to less frequently selected actions. To account for overfitting we introduce an additional exponential term

$$o(s_t) = 1 - \frac{c^{|g_{s_t}|}}{c^{l_{\max}}}$$

that reduces the node reward depending on the current pipeline length $|g_{s_t}|$ and a predefined maximum pipeline length $l_{\max}$ and scaling constant $c > 1$.

The MCTS procedure is adapted such that selection can be aborted if the current node has a higher reward than all child nodes. Similarly, expansion can be skipped. During each expansion step the data set in s_t is transformed by A_t and stored yielding s_{t+1}. Usually, MCTS uses a *simulation* to calculate the reward of s_t. However, a few random simulations do not scale well in high dimensional search spaces and many simulations are prohibitively expensive [11]. Instead, expansion is repeated recursively until the pipeline candidate ends in a classifier. After e consecutive expansions the selection of a classifier is enforced. Conceptually, this is similar to a random simulation. However, as we immediately know the meta-features of each intermediate data set, the simulation can be guided by the meta-learning base explained in Sect. 3.3. This approach explicitly does not restrict the pipeline structure via a grammar or similar measures.

The performance measure $\pi(s_{t+1})$ is not directly obtained during the MCTS. Instead it is computed via the HPO procedure described in Sect. 3.2. Therefore, pipeline structure search and HPO can be solved independently of each other while still being tightly coupled.

Finally, it remains to decide how many HPO samples are drawn to determine the reward of a state. To discard unpromising structures quickly, we wrap the complete structure search procedure in a multi-fidelity approach similar to HYPERBAND [14]. Yet, instead of deterministically calculated budgets—the number of HPO iterations—we adapt the greediness of the policy depending on the passed optimization time τ and

$$c(\tau) = w \cdot \left(\exp\left(\frac{\tau_{\max} - \tau}{\tau_{\max}} \right) - 1 \right),$$

with $\tau_{\max}$ being the total optimization time and w a non-negative weighting constant. For each pipeline candidate a small fixed number of HPO iterations is performed leading to more HPO iterations on well-performing candidates.

Using this procedure, the pipeline structure search space is incrementally expanded whenever a new layer of the graph is visited. Simultaneously, ineffective—the algorithm does not modify the data set—, incompatible or bad performing transformations can be identified quickly. Consequently, the search graph is pruned efficiently, often even without any HPO.

3.2   Hyperparameter Optimization

After fixing the pipeline structure, its actual performance has to be assessed. In general, this step is computationally equally expensive as optimizing the hyperparameter for a fixed pipeline. Consequently, an efficient HPO procedure is key to evaluating various pipeline structures.

Traditional CASH procedures model the problem for a fixed structure g with—for simplicity—only one algorithm by

$$\vec{\lambda}^* \in \underset{A^{(i)} \in \mathcal{A}, \vec{\lambda} \in \Lambda_{A^{(i)}}}{\arg\min} \pi_g\left(A^{(i)}, \vec{\lambda}, D \right).$$

selecting the actual algorithm and its hyperparameters simultaneously, configuring all algorithms accordingly and finally evaluating the performance on the input data set. This approach has three major drawbacks: 1. The transformation of the data set being processed is not considered. 2. The algorithms in a pipeline may be incompatible with each other due to implicit requirements of the used algorithms on the input data. Selecting and fitting all algorithms at once may lead to wasted optimization time as incompatibilities are only detected during fitting [16]. 3. Sharing knowledge about well performing configurations between different pipeline structures using the same subset of algorithms is not possible. Instead we propose, to use a distinct optimization instance

$$\vec{\lambda}_i^* \in \underset{\vec{\lambda} \in \Lambda_{A^{(i)}}}{\arg\min} \; \pi \left(A^{(i)}, \vec{\lambda}, D \right)$$

for each algorithm only considering HPO. To prevent an improper impact of previous algorithms and their hyperparameter on the optimization, we additionally require that all meta-features of the transient data set D have to be similar. Otherwise, a new HPO instance is created. This allows sharing knowledge about well-performing hyperparameters between identical algorithms in different pipeline candidates, given that the pipeline prefixes yielded similar data sets.

The hyperparameters of each algorithm can be selected "on-the-fly" in the order of appearance of the algorithms. After selecting the hyperparameters for each algorithm, the final performance is back-propagated to update each optimizer leading to a formulation compatible with current CASH formulations

$$\vec{\lambda}^* \in \underset{\vec{\lambda}_1 \in \Lambda_1, \ldots, \vec{\lambda}_{|g|} \in \Lambda_{|g|}}{\arg\min} \; \pi \left(A_{|g|}, \vec{\lambda}_{|g|}, \phi_{\vec{\lambda}_{|g|}}^{(|g|)} \left(\phi_{\vec{\lambda}_{|g-1|}}^{(|g-1|)} \left(\ldots \phi_{\vec{\lambda}_1}^{(1)}(D) \right) \right) \right)$$

with $\vec{A}$ and g being provided via the previously described structure search and $\vec{\lambda}^* = \vec{\lambda}_1 \cup \cdots \cup \vec{\lambda}_{|g|}$. Consequently, the hyperparameter search space for a single algorithm is significantly smaller than the complete CASH search space. This imposes two major benefits: 1. Bayesian optimization methods have been proven to be more powerful for low dimensional search spaces [12]. 2. The small search space improves the applicability of warm-starting. Based on the meta-features of the intermediate data set, samples for warm-starting can be extracted from previously evaluated configurations on different pipeline structure candidates. Each individual optimization problem can be solved via standard procedures like SMAC or HYPEROPT. In the context of this work tree Parzen estimators [2] are used. Each instance of this procedure yields a hyperparameter candidate $\vec{\lambda}$ allowing the computation of the performance $\pi(s_{t+1})$ according to Eq. (1) to be used in the MCTS procedure in Eq. (2).

3.3 Meta-Learning

Traditional MCTS uses *simulations* to determine the score of an unvisited node. As extensive simulations are prohibitively expensive in the context of ML, current AutoML tools use a small number of random completions, potentially restricted by a grammar, to estimate the reward of a state, e.g. [15]. We propose to guide the random completions by considering intermediate meta-features.

To get a diverse foundation for the meta-learning base, we collected 30 unique data sets from OPENML [21]. Starting from the input data set, each available algorithm is applied using its default hyperparameters. The transformed data set is added to the meta-learning base—in case of a classifier, the transformed data set consists of the input data set with the prediction added as a new feature.

This procedure is repeated exhaustively until the maximum pipeline length of five algorithms is reached. For each data set in the meta learning base, 40 meta-features are extracted. As the meta-feature extraction has to be applied in each stage of the MCTS, a fast calculation of the meta-features is important, which limits the available meta-features to general, statistical, information-theoretical and simple model-based meta-features.[2]

If the applied algorithm comprises a classifier, the current performance is evaluated. For preprocessing algorithms the performance is estimated using all subsequent classification algorithms. Using this approach, we extracted the performance of over 13.5 million unique pipelines on 30 diverse data sets.

To account for the stochastic environment, the performance prediction of an algorithm for a given state is modeled by a normal distribution

$$P(s_t, A) \sim \mathcal{N}\left(RF_\mu(s_t, A), RF_\sigma(s_t, A)\right)$$

with RF_μ and RF_σ being two random forest regression models trained on the mean and standard deviation of the performance, respectively. The complete meta-learning base, namely the raw data and trained models, is publicly available alongside the source code but we also plan to publish all pipelines on OPENML.

4   Experiments

To prove the effectiveness and efficiency of our approach, DSWIZARD is compared with the two best established AutoML tools: AUTOSKLEARN and TPOT. As a baseline, an untuned random forest is added. We perform an ablation study testing DSWIZARD without meta-learning, dubbed DSWIZARD*, to get an impression of the impact of meta-learning during structure synthesis on the performance.

4.1   Experiment Setup

To ensure fair and comparable results, the existing OPENML AutoML benchmark framework [8] is used for all experiments. We reuse the predefined constraints of a 60 min optimization timeout per fold. Experiments are conducted on *e2-standard-4* virtual machines on Google Cloud Platform equipped with Intel Xeon E5 processors with 4 cores and 16 GB memory.

All frameworks are evaluated on 28 publicly available binary and multiclass classification data sets from established and curated AutoML benchmark suits [3, 8]. More specifically, OPENML tasks are used for each data set. A task provides information about a data set, for example how train-test splits have to be done or which loss function to use, to enable comparable results. The performance of each final configuration is computed using a hold-out validation data set. For binary and multiclass tasks *AUC* and *logloss* are used as metric, respectively.

---

[2] The complete list of all data sets, algorithms and used meta-features is available in the online Appendix alongside the source code at https://git.io/JIOaJ.

To eliminate the impact of different search spaces on the final performance, the existing TPOT and AUTOSKLEARN adapters are adopted to use the same search space as DSWIZARD. This includes the available algorithms, hyperparameters per algorithm as well as search ranges.[3] The complete search space consists of 35 algorithms with 38 categorical and 62 numerical hyperparameters. A short summary of the configuration space is provided in the online Appendix.

To prevent a leaking of information via meta-learning in DSWIZARD, we construct an individual meta-learning base for each data set excluding the data set under evaluation. The OPENML AutoML benchmark's AUTOSKLEARN adapter always performs label encoding before passing the data to the optimization routine. Similarly, the TPOT adapter always performs label encoding and an imputation of missing data. As these algorithms are not obtained via an optimization procedure, they are not further considered.

4.2   Experiment Results

Table 1 and 2 contain the final test performances of all evaluations. For each data set, the mean performance and standard deviation over 10 folds is reported. Bold face represents the best mean value for each data set. Results not significantly worse than the best result, according to a two-sided Wilcoxon signed-rank test with $p = 0.05$, are underlined. If a framework consistently failed to yield results for at least three folds, the performance for that data set is not recorded.

On average, DSWIZARD outperforms the other frameworks. However, absolute performance differences are small and, especially for *logloss*, often not significant. TPOT and DSWIZARD/DSWIZARD* struggled with some data sets. For TPOT, single configuration evaluations often exceeded the global timeout leading to an aborted evaluation. In contrast, DSWIZARD/DSWIZARD* exceeded the available memory leading to a crash. The results for DSWIZARD* show that meta-learning is able to significantly boost the results of DSWIZARD for 10 of 28 data sets. In contrast, DSWIZARD* yields only insignificant improvements on 3 data sets. Yet, even without meta-learning the more thoroughly evaluation of the pipeline search space yielded configurations outperforming either TPOT or AUTOSKLEARN on 13 data sets. The RF baseline is basically always outperformed significantly.

Figure 2 shows the structure of the final pipelines aggregated over all data sets and folds. For better readability we substituted each used algorithm by an abstract algorithm class, namely *balancing, classifier, decomposition, discretization, encoding, filtering, generation, imputation, scaling* and *selection*. The assignment of algorithm to algorithm class is available in the online Appendix. Additionally, we treat ensembles of pipelines as sets of individual pipelines. Possible pipeline starts are indicated by rounded corners. The frequency of node and edge visits is encoded using a color scheme. Darker colors represent a more frequent usage. For better readability, edges and nodes that appear in less than 1% of all pipelines are excluded.

---

[3]   At least if supported by the frameworks. For example, TPOT can only handle discretized continuous hyperparameters.

Table 1. Final test performance for all tested binary classification data sets using AUC as metric. Larger values are better.

Data set	RF	AUTOSKLEARN	TPOT	DSWIZARD	DSWIZARD*
Australian	0.937 ± 0.021	0.934 ± 0.019	0.938 ± 0.018	$\mathbf{0.966 \pm 0.013}$	0.946 ± 0.022
ada_agnostic	0.891 ± 0.015	0.905 ± 0.016	0.903 ± 0.014	$\mathbf{0.914 \pm 0.014}$	0.912 ± 0.017
adult	0.909 ± 0.004	$\mathbf{0.928 \pm 0.005}$	—	0.893 ± 0.012	0.892 ± 0.010
bank-marketi	0.931 ± 0.007	$\mathbf{0.935 \pm 0.007}$	—	0.917 ± 0.030	0.909 ± 0.013
blood-transfu	0.687 ± 0.064	0.729 ± 0.054	0.760 ± 0.066	$\mathbf{0.788 \pm 0.065}$	0.731 ± 0.063
credit-g	0.796 ± 0.035	0.772 ± 0.032	0.773 ± 0.052	$\mathbf{0.853 \pm 0.026}$	0.805 ± 0.031
eeg-eye-state	0.986 ± 0.003	$\mathbf{0.991 \pm 0.003}$	—	0.990 ± 0.004	—
higgs	0.803 ± 0.006	$\mathbf{0.808 \pm 0.006}$	0.790 ± 0.012	0.726 ± 0.084	0.767 ± 0.035
jasmine	0.889 ± 0.015	0.881 ± 0.017	0.888 ± 0.017	$\mathbf{0.907 \pm 0.018}$	0.898 ± 0.021
kc2	0.821 ± 0.102	0.816 ± 0.093	0.825 ± 0.160	$\mathbf{0.891 \pm 0.045}$	0.787 ± 0.052
kr-vs-kp	0.999 ± 0.001	0.999 ± 0.001	0.997 ± 0.005	$\mathbf{1.000 \pm 0.001}$	0.998 ± 0.006
nomao	0.995 ± 0.001	$\mathbf{0.996 \pm 0.001}$	0.994 ± 0.004	0.994 ± 0.001	0.994 ± 0.002
numerai28.6	0.519 ± 0.005	0.529 ± 0.005	0.527 ± 0.004	$\mathbf{0.531 \pm 0.012}$	0.529 ± 0.008
phoneme	0.965 ± 0.009	0.963 ± 0.010	0.966 ± 0.008	$\mathbf{0.966 \pm 0.009}$	0.964 ± 0.009
sa-heart	0.718 ± 0.058	0.759 ± 0.049	0.755 ± 0.120	0.797 ± 0.107	$\mathbf{0.832 \pm 0.065}$
sylvine	0.983 ± 0.004	0.990 ± 0.004	0.986 ± 0.008	$\mathbf{0.990 \pm 0.003}$	0.986 ± 0.004

Table 2. Final test performance for all tested multiclass classification data sets using *logloss* as metric. Smaller values are better.

Data set	RF	AUTOSKLEARN	TPOT	DSWIZARD	DSWIZARD*
Helena	—	$\mathbf{3.009 \pm 0.115}$	—	3.023 ± 0.083	3.228 ± 0.220
Jannis	0.729 ± 0.005	$\mathbf{0.702 \pm 0.024}$	0.730 ± 0.042	0.758 ± 0.052	0.786 ± 0.086
Shuttle	0.001 ± 0.000	$\mathbf{0.001 \pm 0.000}$	3.600 ± 1.265	0.001 ± 0.001	—
analcatdata_a	0.162 ± 0.014	0.069 ± 0.129	0.012 ± 0.021	0.018 ± 0.038	$\mathbf{0.007 \pm 0.009}$
analcatdata_d	3.503 ± 0.573	1.752 ± 0.023	—	$\mathbf{1.715 \pm 0.029}$	1.750 ± 0.068
car	0.143 ± 0.009	0.005 ± 0.007	$\mathbf{0.003 \pm 0.004}$	0.012 ± 0.030	0.045 ± 0.103
connect-4	0.494 ± 0.003	$\mathbf{0.418 \pm 0.069}$	—	0.683 ± 0.111	0.699 ± 0.074
jungle_chess	0.439 ± 0.010	$\mathbf{0.179 \pm 0.035}$	0.239 ± 0.011	—	—
mfeat-factors	0.235 ± 0.021	0.106 ± 0.039	0.116 ± 0.049	$\mathbf{0.062 \pm 0.039}$	0.112 ± 0.053
mfeat-morph	0.889 ± 0.296	0.618 ± 0.069	0.656 ± 0.103	$\mathbf{0.560 \pm 0.078}$	0.592 ± 0.082
segment	0.084 ± 0.019	0.074 ± 0.069	0.060 ± 0.038	$\mathbf{0.051 \pm 0.029}$	0.070 ± 0.036
vehicle	0.498 ± 0.034	0.452 ± 0.050	0.441 ± 0.090	$\mathbf{0.389 \pm 0.058}$	0.433 ± 0.038

In Fig. 2a it is clearly visible that AUTOSKLEARN uses a semi-fixed pipeline structure where single steps can be omitted. A strict order of algorithms exists, from the top left of the graph to the bottom. *Imputation, balancing* and *classifier* are present in each pipeline and the remaining algorithms are roughly selected with identical frequencies. On average, each pipeline contains 5.48

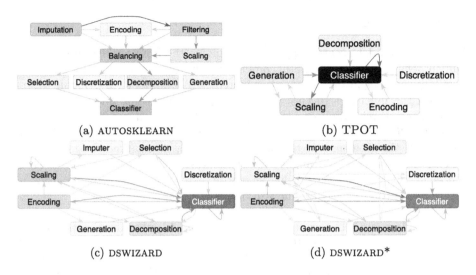

Fig. 2. Schematic representation of final structures

algorithms. Due to the semi-fixed structure of AUTOSKLEARN, often ineffective algorithms are present in pipelines, e.g. imputation even though the data set does not contain missing values. TPOT is able to construct pipelines with highly vary-ing shapes. However, each pipeline, on average, only contains 1.66 algorithms, mostly classifiers. Even though more complex pipelines are constructed, those complex pipelines represent less than 15% of all pipelines leading to the heavily pruned graph depicted in Fig. 2b. DSWIZARD constructs more diverse pipelines in terms of selected algorithms and transitions between algorithms. Without meta-learning (compare Fig. 2c and 2d), structure search is less guided leading to longer pipelines (2.85 vs. 3.07 algorithms) and a more uniform distribution of the selected algorithms. Yet, as DSWIZARD* performs worse than DSWIZARD, the guidance seems to be helpful to find well performing pipeline structures.

Finally, we take a more detailed look at *credit-g* and *higgs*, two data sets where DSWIZARD performs especially well and badly, respectively. For *credit-g* 71% of the pipelines in the final ensemble have a long complex structure that can not be created by AUTOSKLEARN. Most pipelines combine stacked classifiers with multiple preprocessors. For *higgs* the meta-learning directs the structure search in a wrong direction leading to many ineffective transformations. As a result, only very basic pipelines containing combinations of the same four algorithms are constructed. Even with HPO, these simple pipelines do not perform well.

In summary, DSWIZARD significantly outperforms either AUTOSKLEARN or TPOT on 42% of the data sets. Moreover, it has a similar performance to the state-of-the-art on 32% of the data sets.

5   Conclusion

We presented a data-centric approach for solving the PSO problem inspired by human behaviour using MCTS in combination with Bayesian optimization. The possibility to expand the search space incrementally allows for a dynamic adaptation of the pipeline structure to a specific data set. Unpromising regions of the pipeline search graph can be identified and discarded quickly—often even without HPO—through the extensive use of meta-features allowing an efficient traversal of the growing search space. Furthermore, sharing knowledge between pipeline structures is implemented for warm-starting HPO. This allows a more thorough exploration of the pipeline structure search space with a dynamic adaptation to a specific data set while still obtaining competitive results.

Acknowledgement. This work was partially supported by the Ministry of Economic Affairs of the state Baden-Württemberg within the KI-Fortschrittszentrum "Lernende Systeme" under Grant No. 036-170017 and the German Federal Ministry for Economic Affairs and Energy in the project FabOS (project no. 01MK20010N).

References

1. Auger, D., Couëtoux, A., Teytaud, O.: Continuous upper confidence trees with polynomial exploration – consistency. In: Blockeel, H., Kersting, K., Nijssen, S., Železný, F. (eds.) ECML PKDD 2013. LNCS (LNAI), vol. 8188, pp. 194–209. Springer, Heidelberg (2013). https://doi.org/10.1007/978-3-642-40988-2_13
2. Bergstra, J., Yamins, D., Cox, D.D.: Hyperopt: a Python library for optimizing the hyperparameters of machine learning algorithms. In: Python in Science Conference, pp. 13–20 (2013)
3. Bischl, B., et al.: OpenML benchmarking suites and the OpenML100. arXiv preprint arXiv:1708.03731v1 (2017)
4. Caruana, R., Niculescu-Mizil, A., Crew, G., Ksikes, A.: Ensemble selection from libraries of models. In: ICML, p. 18 (2004)
5. Coulom, R.: Efficient selectivity and backup operators in Monte-Carlo tree search. In: 5th International Conference on Computer and Games (2006)
6. Drori, I., et al.: Automatic machine learning by pipeline synthesis using model-based reinforcement learning and a grammar. In: ICML (2019)
7. Feurer, M., Klein, A., Eggensperger, K., Springenber, J.T., Blum, M., Hutter, F.: Efficient and robust automated machine learning. In: NeurIPS, pp. 2755–2763 (2015)
8. Gijsbers, P., LeDell, E., Thomas, J., Poirier, S., Bischl, B., Vanschoren, J.: An open source AutoML benchmark. In: ICML (2019)
9. Gil, Y., et al.: P4ML: a phased performance-based pipeline planner for automated machine learning. In: ICML, pp. 1–8 (2018)
10. Hutter, F., Hoos, H.H., Leyton-Brown, K.: Sequential model-based optimization for general algorithm configuration. In: Coello, C.A.C. (ed.) LION 2011. LNCS, vol. 6683, pp. 507–523. Springer, Heidelberg (2011). https://doi.org/10.1007/978-3-642-25566-3_40
11. Hutter, F., Kotthoff, L., Vanschoren, J.: Automated Machine Learning: Methods, Systems, Challenges. Springer, Cham (2018). https://doi.org/10.1007/978-3-030-05318-5

12. Kandasamy, K., Schneider, J., Póczos, B.: High dimensional Bayesian optimisation and bandits via additive models. In: ICML, pp. 295–304 (2015)
13. Komer, B., Bergstra, J., Eliasmith, C.: Hyperopt-Sklearn: automatic hyperparameter configuration for Scikit-learn. In: ICML, pp. 2825–2830 (2014)
14. Li, L., Jamieson, K.G., DeSalvo, G., Rostamizadeh, A., Talwalkar, A.: Hyperband: a novel bandit-based approach to hyperparameter optimization. JMLR **18**, 1–52 (2018)
15. Mohr, F., Wever, M., Hüllermeier, E.: ML-Plan: automated machine learning via hierarchical planning. Mach. Learn. **107**(8), 1495–1515 (2018). https://doi.org/10.1007/s10994-018-5735-z
16. Nguyen, T.D., Maszczyk, T., Musial, K., Zöller, M.A., Gabrys, B.: AVATAR - machine learning pipeline evaluation using surrogate model. In: IDA, pp. 352–365 (2020)
17. Olson, R.S., Moore, J.H.: TPOT: a tree-based pipeline optimization tool for automating machine learning. In: ICML, pp. 66–74 (2016)
18. de Sá, A.G.C., Pinto, W.J.G.S., Oliveira, L.O.V.B., Pappa, G.L.: RECIPE: a grammar-based framework for automatically evolving classification pipelines. In: McDermott, J., Castelli, M., Sekanina, L., Haasdijk, E., García-Sánchez, P. (eds.) EuroGP 2017. LNCS, vol. 10196, pp. 246–261. Springer, Cham (2017). https://doi.org/10.1007/978-3-319-55696-3_16
19. Swearingen, T., Drevo, W., Cyphers, B., Cuesta-Infante, A., Ross, A., Veeramachaneni, K.: ATM: a distributed, collaborative, scalable system for automated machine learning. In: IEEE BigData, pp. 151–162 (2017)
20. Thornton, C., Hutter, F., Hoos, H.H., Leyton-Brown, K.: Auto-WEKA: combined selection and hyperparameter optimization of classification algorithms. In: ACM SIGKDD, pp. 847–855 (2013)
21. Vanschoren, J., van Rijn, J.N., Bischl, B., Torgo, L.: OpenML: networked science in machine learning. ACM SIGKDD **15**(2), 49–60 (2014)
22. Zöller, M.A., Huber, M.F.: Benchmark and survey of automated machine learning frameworks. JAIR **70**, 409–472 (2021)

Adversarial Vulnerability of Active Transfer Learning

Nicolas M. Müller[✉] and Konstantin Böttinger

Fraunhofer AISEC, Garching near Munich, Germany
nicolas.mueller@aisec.fraunhofer.de

Abstract. Two widely used techniques for training supervised machine learning models on small datasets are Active Learning and Transfer Learning. The former helps to optimally use a limited budget to label new data. The latter uses large pre-trained models as feature extractors and enables the design of complex, non-linear models even on tiny datasets. Combining these two approaches is an effective, state-of-the-art method when dealing with small datasets.

In this paper, we share an intriguing observation: Namely, that the combination of these techniques is particularly susceptible to a new kind of data poisoning attack: By adding small adversarial noise on the input, it is possible to create a collision in the output space of the transfer learner. As a result, Active Learning algorithms no longer select the optimal instances, but almost exclusively the ones injected by the attacker. This allows an attacker to manipulate the active learner to select and include arbitrary images into the data set, even against an overwhelming majority of unpoisoned samples. We show that a model trained on such a poisoned dataset has a significantly deteriorated performance, dropping from 86% to 34% test accuracy. We evaluate this attack on both audio and image datasets and support our findings empirically. To the best of our knowledge, this weakness has not been described before in literature.

1 Introduction

Training supervised machine learning algorithms such as neural networks requires large amounts of labeled training data. In order to solve problems for which there is no or little training data, previous work has developed techniques such as Transfer Learning and Active Learning.

Transfer Learning (TL) applies knowledge gained from one problem to a second problem. For example, consider the problem of training a Neural Network on a very small image dataset (say $N = 500$). Training directly on the dataset will yield poor generalization due to the limited number of training examples. A better approach is to use a second, already-existing network trained on a different task to extract high-level semantic features from the training data, and train one's network on these features instead of the raw images themselves. For images, this is commonly employed practice and easily accessible via the *tensorflow* library. For audio data, similar feature extractors are also easily accessible [13].

P. H. Abreu et al. (Eds.): IDA 2021, LNCS 12695, pp. 116–127, 2021.
https://doi.org/10.1007/978-3-030-74251-5_10

Active Learning (AL) on the other hand is a process where a learning algorithm can query a user. AL is helpful when creating or expanding labeled datasets. Instead of randomly selecting instances to present to a human annotator, the model can query for specific instances. The model ranks the unlabeled instances by certainty of prediction. Those instances for which it is most uncertain are the ones where a label is queried from the human annotator. Model uncertainty can be understood as the distance to the decision surface (SVM), or entropy of the class predictions (*uncertainty sampling* for Neural Networks). In summary, Active Learning can help in finding the optimal set of instances to label in order to optimally use a given budget [15].

Since these approaches are complementary, they can be combined straightforwardly: One designs a *transfer active learning* system by combining an untrained network with a pre-trained feature extractor and then allows this combined model to query a human expert. Previous work has examined this in detail and finds that it can accelerate the learning process significantly [8,18,19].

In this work, we are the first to observe that this combination of AL with TL is highly susceptible to data poisoning. Our contribution is to present this novel weakness, which

- allows an attacker to reliably control the samples queried by the active learner (94.8 % success rate even when the poisoned samples are outnumbered 1:50 by clean training data),
- considerably deteriorates the test performance of the learner (by more than 50% in absolute test accuracy),
- is hard to detect for a human annotator.

We evaluate the attack on both audio and image datasets and report the results in Sect. 4. To the best of our knowledge, this attack has not been described in literature before whatsoever.

2   Related Work

In this section, we discuss related work on transfer active learning. We first present work on combining transfer and active learning and then discuss related data poisoning attacks for each approach. We observe that there is no prior work on data poisoning for the combined method of transfer active learning.

Active Learning with Transfer Learning. Kale et al. [8] present a transfer active learning framework which "leverages pre-existing labeled data from related tasks to improve the performance of an active learner". They take large, well-known datasets such as *Twenty Newsgroup*, and evaluate the number of queries required in order to reach an error of 0.2 or less. They can reduce the number of queries by as much as 50% by combining transfer learning with active learning. The authors of [19] perform similar experiments, and find that "the number of labeled examples required for learning with transfer is often significantly smaller than that required for learning each target independently". They also evaluate combining active learning and transfer learning, and find that the "combined active transfer learning algorithm [...] achieve[s] better prediction performance than alternative methods".

Chan et al. [5] examine the problem of training a word sense disambiguation (WSD) system on one domain and then applying it to another domain, thus 'transferring' knowledge from one domain to another domain. They show that active learning approaches can be used to help in this transfer learning task. The authors of [17] examine how to borrow information from one domain in order to label data in another domain. Their goal is to label samples in the current domain (in-domain) using a model trained on samples from the other domain (out-of-domain). The model then predicts the labels of the in-domain data. Where the prediction confidence of the model is low, a human annotator is asked to provide the label, otherwise, the model's prediction is used to label the data. The authors report that their approach significantly improves test accuracy.

Related Data Poisoning Attacks. Data poisoning is an attack on machine learning systems where malicious data is introduced into the training set. When the model trains on the resulting poisoned training dataset, this induces undesirable behavior at test time. Biggio et al. [4] were one of the first to examine the effects of data poisoning on Support Vector Classifiers. The branch of data poisoning most related to our work is *clean poison* attacks. These introduce minimally perturbed instances with the 'correct' label into the data set. For example, the authors of [16] present an attack on transfer learners which uses *clean poison* samples to introduce a back-door into the model. The resulting model misclassifies the targeted instance, while model accuracy for other samples remains unchanged. To give an example, these *clean poison* samples may be manipulated pictures of dogs that, when trained on by a transfer learner, will at test time cause a *specific* instance of a cat to be classified as a dog. Other samples than the targeted 'cat' instance will not be affected. Such *clean label* attacks have also been explored in a black-box scenario [20].

Data Poisoning not only affects classification models but also regression learners. Jagielski et al. [7] present attacks and defenses on regression models that cause a denial of service: By injecting a small number of malicious data into the training set, the authors induce a significant change in the prediction error.

Poisoning Active Learning. Poisoning active learners requires the attacker to craft samples which, in addition to adversely affecting the model, have to be selected by the active learner for labeling and insertion into the dataset. This attack aims at both increasing overall classification error during test time as well as increasing the cost for labeling. In this sense, poisoning active learning is harder than poisoning conventional learners, since two objectives have to be satisfied simultaneously. Miller et al. [12] present such an attack: They poison linear classifiers and manage to satisfy both previously mentioned objectives (albeit with some constraints): Poisoned instances are selected by the active learner with high probability, and the model trained on the poisoned instances induces significant deterioration in prediction accuracy.

Adversarial Collisions. There exists some related work on adversarial collisions, albeit with a different focus from ours: Li et al. [11] observe that neural networks can be insensitive to adversarial noise of large magnitude. This results in 'two very different examples sharing the same feature activation' and results in a feature collision. However, this constitutes an attack at test time (evasion attack), whereas we present an attack at training time (poison attack).

3   Attacking Active Transfer Learning

In this section, we introduce the proposed attack. We first present the threat model and then detail the attack itself. In Sect. 4, we evaluate the effectiveness of our attack empirically.

3.1   Threat Model

In this work, we assume that an attacker has the following capabilities:

- The attacker may introduce a small number of adversarially perturbed instances into the active learning pool. These instances are unlabeled. They are screened by the active learning algorithm and may, along with the benign instances, be presented to the human annotator for labeling.
- The attacker cannot compromise the output of the human annotator, i.e. they cannot falsify the labels assigned to either the benign or poison instances.
- The attacker knows the feature extractor used. This could, for example, be a popular open-source model such as *resnet50* [6] or *YAMNet* [14]. These models are readily available and widely used [1].
- The attacker has no knowledge about, or access to the model trained on top of the feature extractor.
- The attacker does not know the active learning algorithm.

3.2   Feature Collision Attack

Since transfer active learning is designed to use found data, i.e. data from untrusted sources, it is highly susceptible to data poisoning attacks. In this section, we present such an attack and show how it completely breaks the learned model.

Let X, Y be a set of unpoisoned data, where the data X and targets Y consist of N instances. An instance pertains to one of M different classes (e.g. 'dog' or 'cat'). Let f be the pretrained feature extractor, which maps a sample $x_i \in X$ to a d_ζ dimensional feature vector (i.e. $f(x_i) = \zeta_i$). Let g be the dense model head, which maps a feature vector ζ_i to some prediction $y_{pred} \in [0,1]^M$, where y_{pred} is a one-hot vector, i.e. $\sum_{m=0}^{M-1} y_{pred}^m = 1$. Thus, an image is classified by the subsequent application of the feature extractor f and the dense model head g:

$$y = \arg\max_i g(f(x_i)) \tag{1}$$

For a set of instances $\{x_i\}$, a set of adversarial examples $\{x_i + \delta_i\}$ can be found by minimizing, for each x_i separately:

$$\delta_i = \arg\min_\delta \left\| f(x_i + \delta) - \mu \right\|_2 + \beta\|\delta\|_2 \tag{2}$$

where $\beta \in \mathbb{R}^+$ and μ is a fixed vector of size d_ζ. Solving Eq. 2 will find adversarial examples that 1) are selected by the active learner 2) break the model, and 3) are imperceptible to the human annotator:

1. **Examples are queried.** A set of thusly found adversarial examples $\{x_i+\delta_i\}$ will all be mapped to the same output μ, i.e. $f(x_i + \delta_i) = \mu$ for all i. This will 'confuse' the active learner, since all adversarial examples share the same feature vector, but have different class labels. Thus, the active learner will incur high uncertainty for instances mapped to this *collision vector* μ, and thus will query almost exclusively these (we verify this experimentally in Sect. 4.2).
2. **Examples are harmful.** These examples will break any model head trained on the extracted features ζ_i, since all adversarial examples share identical features, but different labels.
3. **Examples are undetected by a human annotator.** Once queried, the adversarial examples $x_i + \delta_i$ will be reviewed by a human annotator and labeled accordingly. The second part of Eq. 2 ensures that the adversarial noise is small enough in magnitude to remain undetected by human experts. The adversarial example will thus be assigned the label of x_i, but not raise suspicion of the human annotator. The scalar β is a hyperparameter controlling the strength of this regularisation.

Choice of Collision Vector. The *Collision Vector* μ is chosen as the zero vector $\mu = 0^{d_\zeta}$ because of two reasons: First, we find that it helps numerical convergence of Eq. 2 when training with Gradient Descent. Second, a zero-vector of features is highly uncommon with unpoisoned data. Thus, it induces high uncertainty with the active learner, which in turn helps to promote the adversarial poison samples for labeling and inclusion in the training dataset from the beginning. It is possible to chose a different μ, for example the one-vector $\mu = 1^{d_\zeta}$, or the mean of the feature values $\mu = \overline{\zeta_i}$. However, we find that the zero-vector works best, most likely due to the reasons detailed above.

Improving Attack Efficiency. We propose two improvements over the baseline attack. First, when choosing the base instances from the test set to poison and to include in the train set, it is advisable to select those where

$$\|f(x) - \mu\|_2 \tag{3}$$

is smallest. Intuitively, this pre-screens the samples for those where the optimization step (Eq. 2) requires the least work. Second, maintaining class balance within the poison samples improves effectiveness. This helps in maximally confusing the active learner since a greater diversity of different labels for the same feature vector μ increases the learner's uncertainty with respect to future samples that map to μ. In all the following analysis, we evaluate the attack with these improvements in place.

4   Implementation and Results

In this section, we first describe our transfer active learning setup and the data sets used for evaluation. We then implement our attack and demonstrate its effectiveness (c.f. Sect. 4.2).

4.1   Active Transfer Learner Setup

This section describes the data we use and our choice of transfer learner.

For our experiments, we use image and audio data. This is because Active Learning requires a human oracle to annotate instances, and humans are very good at annotating both image and audio data, but rather inefficient in processing purely numerical data. This motivates the choice of the active learner, namely a neural network, which in recent times has been shown to provide state-of-the-art performance on image and audio data.

Thus, we create the transfer learner as follows: We use a large, pre-trained model to perform feature extraction on the audio and image data. For image data, we use a pre-trained *resnet50* model [6], which comes with the current release of the python *tensorflow* library. For audio data, we build a feature extractor from the *YAMNet* model, a deep convolutional audio classification network [14]. Both of these feature extractors map the raw input data to a vector of features. For example, *resnet50* maps images with $32 * 32 * 3 = 3072$ input dimensions to a vector of 2048 higher-level features. A dense neural network (*dense head*) is then used to classify these feature vectors. Our Active Learner uses Entropy Sampling [15] to compute the uncertainty

$$\text{uncertainty}(x_i) = H(g(f(x_i))) \tag{4}$$

$$= - \sum_{m \in M} g(f(x_i))^m \log g(f(x_i))^m \tag{5}$$

for all unlabeled x_i. The scalar value $g(f(x_i))^m$ indicates softmax-probability of the m-th class for of the network's output. The active learner computes the uncertainty for all unlabeled instances x_i and selects the one with the highest uncertainty to be labeled.

Prevention of Overfitting. As detailed in Sect. 1, we use active transfer learning in order to learn from very small datasets. Accordingly, we use at most $N = 500$ instances per dataset in our experiments. In this scenario, overfitting can easily occur. Thus, we take the following countermeasures: First, we keep the number of trainable parameters low and use a dense head with at most two layers and a small number of hidden neurons. Second, we use high Dropout (up to 50%) and employ early stopping during training. Third, we refrain from training the weights of the Transfer Learner (this is commonly referred to as *fine-tuning*). This is motivated by the observation that the *resnet50* architecture has more than 25 Million trainable weights, which makes it prone to overfitting, especially on very small datasets.

Datasets. We use three datasets to demonstrate our attack.

– *Google AudioSet* [3], a large classification dataset comprising several hundred different sounds. We use only a subset of ten basic commands (*right, yes, left,* etc.).
– *Cifar10* [9], a popular image recognition dataset with 32×32 pixel images of cars, ships, airplanes, etc.
– *STL10* [2], a semi-labeled dataset, comprising several thousand labeled 96×96 pixel images in addition to tens of thousand unlabeled images, divided into ten classes. In this supervised scenario, we use only the labeled subset.

Each dataset is split into a *train* set and two test sets, *test1* and *test2* using an 80, 10 and 10% split. Following previous work [16], we train on the *train* set, use the *test1* set to craft the adversarial examples, and evaluate the test accuracy on the *test2* set. Thus, the adversarial examples base instances originate from the same distribution as the train images, but the two sets remain separate.

4.2 Feature Collision Results

We now verify empirically that the created instances look inconspicuous and are hard to distinguish from real, benign instances. Consider Fig. 1. It shows four randomly selected poison instances of the *STL10* dataset. Observe that the poisoned images are hardly distinguishable from the originals. We also provide the complete set of audio samples for the Google Audio Set[1], both poisoned and original .wav files.

We now proceed to visually illustrate the results of the feature collision. Consider Fig. 2: For the poisoned and benign training data in the *AudioSet10* dataset, it shows the corresponding feature vectors after PCA-projection in two dimensions. Thus, it shows what the dense model head 'sees' when looking at the poisoned data set. Note that while the unpoisoned data has a large variety along the first two principal components (as is expected, since the individual instances pertain to different classes), the poison data's features collide in a single point

---

[1] https://drive.google.com/file/d/1JtXUu6degxnQ84Kggav8rgm9ktMhyAq0/view.

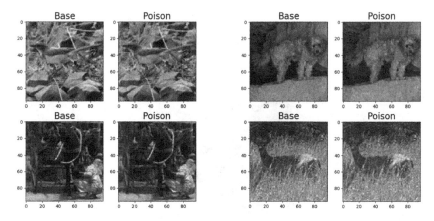

Fig. 1. Images with index 155 (bird), 308 (horse), 614 (dog) and 3964 (deer) from the STL dataset. The left image of each pair shows the base instance, i.e. the unpoisoned image. The right image shows the poisoned image which causes the collision in the transfer learner's output space.

(red dot) - even though they also pertain to different classes. Thus, we observe a 'feature collision' of the poison samples to a single point in feature space, which, in combination with the different labels, will cause maximum 'confusion' in the active learner.

4.3   Impact on the Model

In this section, we evaluate the impact on the classification accuracy of transfer active learners when exposed to the poison samples. For each of the three datasets, we create 500 poison samples and include them into the training set. We then create a transfer active learner (a neural network with one/two layers), train it on 20 unpoisoned samples, and simulate human annotation by letting the active learner query for 500 new instances from the training set (which contains a majority of benign data plus the injected poison samples). We find that the active learner

- almost exclusively selects poisoned samples, and
- test performance is degraded severely (by up to 50% absolute).

Table 1 details our results.

For example, consider the first row, which evaluates a one-layer neural network (NN1) on the STL-dataset. In an unpoisoned scenario, after having queried 500 images, the active learner has a test-accuracy of 86%. When introducing 500 poison instances, we observe the following: First, even though the poison instances are outnumbered 1:8, the active learner chooses 500 out of 500 possible poison instances for manual annotation - a success rate of 100%. In comparison, if the adversarial instances would be queried with the same probability as unpoisoned samples, only 12.6% of them would be chosen (random success

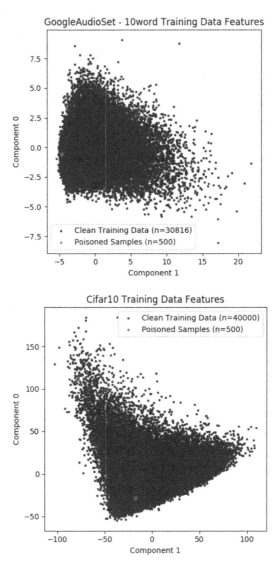

Fig. 2. Visualisation of the transfer learner's feature space. The top image shows the first two principal components of the *Google AudioSet 10* dataset's features when using the YAMNet feature extractor. The bottom image shows the same visualization of the *Cifar10* dataset, using the *imagenet50* feature extractor. The blue dots represent the unpoisoned training data. The red dots represent poison data found via Eq. 2, chosen equally per class (50 instances for each of the ten classes). Observe the large diversity of the unpoisoned training data compared to the adversarial poison data, which is projected onto a single point, thus creating a 'feature collision' which massively deteriorates the active learner's performance. (Color figure online)

Table 1. Results of the feature collision poisoning on three data sets: Cifar10, STL and Google Audio Set. The Head of the Active Learner has one (NN1) or two (NN2) dense layers. The success rate provides the ratio with poison samples are selected by the active learner.

Dataset	Model	Accuracy (clean)	Accuracy (poisoned)	Loss (adv.)	Loss (initital)	N	Success rate (poison)	Success rate (random)	Time (s)
STL	NN1	0.862	0.347	107.729	66450.624	500	1.0	0.126	113.08
Cifar10	NN1	0.432	0.267	39.746	5016.588	500	1.0	0.013	93.425
Audio Set 10	NN1	0.252	0.143	0.488	24.59	500	1.0	0.016	73.083
STL	NN2	0.844	0.7	107.729	66450.624	500	0.86	0.126	113.08
Cifar10	NN2	0.428	0.341	39.746	5016.588	500	0.832	0.013	93.425
Audio Set 10	NN2	0.263	0.141	0.488	24.59	500	0.998	0.016	73.083

rate). Secondly, observe that test accuracy is degraded significantly from 86% to 34%. This is because the model can not learn on data that, due to the feature collision attack, looks identical to one another for the dense head.

4.4 Hyper Parameters and Runtime

Table 1 details the run time to find a single adversarial example on an Intel Core i7-6600 CPU (no GPU), which ranges from one to two minutes. We used the following hyperparameters to find the adversarial samples: For the audio samples, we used $\beta = 0.3$ and 2000 iterations with early stopping and adaptive learning rate. For the image samples, we used $\beta = 1e - 5$ and 500 iterations. The difference in β between image and audio data is due to the difference in input feature scale, which ranges from ± 127 for images to $\pm 2^{15}$ for audio data.[2]

4.5 Adversarial Retraining Defense

We find that there exists a trivial defense against our proposed attack: Unfreezing, i.e. training of the feature extractor f. When f is trained in conjunction with g, training on the poison samples actually serves as 'adversarial retraining', which boosts model robustness [10]. In our experiments, we find that restraining completely negates the effects of the poisoning attack. However, it is not a suitable defense due to the following concerns.

- **Lack of labeled samples.** In order to unfreeze the weights of the feature extractor f, a large number of labeled samples is required. These are not available at the start of the active learning cycle. Thus, retraining can only occur during later stages. Until then, however, the adversary has free reign to introduce their poison samples into the dataset.
- **High computational overhead.** Retraining the feature extractor f incurs high computational overhead in comparison to training only the dense head g.

---

[2] 16bit audio has a feature range of $\pm[0, ..., 2^{15} - 1]$, where one bit is reserved for the sign.

– **Overfitting**. Training f, especially on a small dataset, may result in overfitting, as described in Sect. 4.1.

In summary, while unfreezing and adversarial retraining does mitigate the attack, this strategy may be hard to apply due to several practical concerns. Thus, a better defense strategy is required, which we leave for future work.

5   Conclusion and Future Work

In this work, we point out an intriguing weakness of the combination of active and transfer learning: By crafting feature collisions, we manage to introduce attacker-chosen adversarial samples into the dataset with a success rate of up to 100%. Additionally, we decreased the model's test accuracy by a significant margin (from 86 to 36%). This attack can effectively break a model, wastes resources of the human oracle, and is very hard to detect for a human when reviewing the poisoned instances. To the best of our knowledge, this particular weakness of transfer active learning has not been observed before.

References

1. ResNet and ResNetV2. https://keras.io/api/applications/resnet/. Accessed on 26 Nov 2020
2. STL-10 dataset (2011). http://ai.stanford.edu/~acoates/stl10/. Accessed 26 Nov 2020
3. Google audio set (2017). https://research.google.com/audioset/. Accessed 26 Nov 2020
4. Biggio, B., Nelson, B., Laskov, P.: Poisoning attacks against support vector machines. arXiv preprint arXiv:1206.6389 (2012)
5. Chan, Y.S., Ng, H.T.: Domain adaptation with active learning for word sense disambiguation. In: Proceedings of the 45th Annual Meeting of the Association of Computational Linguistics, Prague, Czech Republic, pp. 49–56. Association for Computational Linguistics, June 2007
6. He, K., Zhang, X., Ren, S., Sun, J.: Deep residual learning for image recognition. In: Proceedings of the IEEE Conference on Computer Vision and Pattern Recognition, pp. 770–778 (2016)
7. Jagielski, M., Oprea, A., Biggio, B., Liu, C., Nita-Rotaru, C., Li, B.: Manipulating machine learning: poisoning attacks and countermeasures for regression learning. In: 2018 IEEE Symposium on Security and Privacy (SP), pp. 19–35. IEEE (2018)
8. Kale, D., Liu, Y.: Accelerating active learning with transfer learning. In: 2013 IEEE 13th International Conference on Data Mining, pp. 1085–1090, December 2013
9. Krizhevsky, A., Hinton, G., et al.: Learning multiple layers of features from tiny images. Citeseer (2009)
10. Li, B., Vorobeychik, Y., Chen, X.: A general retraining framework for scalable adversarial classification. arXiv preprint arXiv:1604.02606 (2016)
11. Li, K., Zhang, T., Malik, J.: Approximate feature collisions in neural nets. In: Advances in Neural Information Processing Systems, pp. 15842–15850 (2019)
12. Miller, B., et al.: Adversarial active learning. In: Proceedings of the 2014 Workshop on Artificial Intelligent and Security Workshop, pp. 3–14 (2014)

13. Pan, S.J., Yang, Q.: A survey on transfer learning. IEEE Trans. Knowl. Data Eng. **22**(10), 1345–1359 (2009)
14. Plakal, M., Ellis, D.: YAMNet. github.com/tensorflow/models/tree/master/research/audioset/yamnet
15. Settles, B.: Active learning literature survey. Technical report, Department of Computer Sciences, University of Wisconsin-Madison (2009)
16. Shafahi, A., et al.: Poison frogs! Targeted clean-label poisoning attacks on neural networks. In: Advances in Neural Information Processing Systems, pp. 6103–6113 (2018)
17. Shi, X., Fan, W., Ren, J.: Actively transfer domain knowledge. In: Daelemans, W., Goethals, B., Morik, K. (eds.) ECML PKDD 2008, Part II. LNCS (LNAI), vol. 5212, pp. 342–357. Springer, Heidelberg (2008). https://doi.org/10.1007/978-3-540-87481-2_23
18. Wang, X., Huang, T.-K., Schneider, J.: Active transfer learning under model shift. In: Xing, E.P., Jebara, T. (eds.) Proceedings of the 31st International Conference on Machine Learning, Bejing, China. Proceedings of Machine Learning Research, vol. 32, pp. 1305–1313. PMLR, 22–24 Jun 2014
19. Yang, L., Hanneke, S., Carbonell, J.: A theory of transfer learning with applications to active learning. Mach. Learn. **90**(02), 161–189 (2013). https://doi.org/10.1007/s10994-012-5310-y
20. Zhu, C., et al.: Transferable clean-label poisoning attacks on deep neural nets. arXiv preprint arXiv:1905.05897 (2019)

Revisiting Non-specific Syndromic Surveillance

Moritz Kulessa[1]([envelope]) [iD], Eneldo Loza Mencía[1] [iD], and Johannes Fürnkranz[2] [iD]

[1] Technische Universität Darmstadt, Darmstadt, Germany
mkulessa@ke.tu-darmstadt.de, research@eneldo.net
[2] Johannes Kepler Universität Linz, Linz, Austria
juffi@faw.jku.at

Abstract. Infectious disease surveillance is of great importance for the prevention of major outbreaks. Syndromic surveillance aims at developing algorithms which can detect outbreaks as early as possible by monitoring data sources which allow to capture the occurrences of a certain disease. Recent research mainly focuses on the surveillance of specific, known diseases, putting the focus on the definition of the disease pattern under surveillance. Until now, only little effort has been devoted to what we call *non-specific* syndromic surveillance, i.e., the use of all available data for detecting any kind of outbreaks, including infectious diseases which are unknown beforehand. In this work, we revisit published approaches for non-specific syndromic surveillance and present a set of simple statistical modeling techniques which can serve as benchmarks for more elaborate machine learning approaches. Our experimental comparison on established synthetic data and real data in which we injected synthetic outbreaks shows that these benchmarks already achieve very competitive results and often outperform more elaborate algorithms.

Keywords: Syndromic surveillance · Outbreak detection · Anomaly detection

1 Introduction

The spread of infectious disease outbreaks could be diminished tremendously by applying control measures as early as possible, which indeed can save lives and reduce suffering. For that purpose, *syndromic surveillance* has been introduced which aims to identify illness clusters before diagnoses are confirmed and reported to public health agencies [6]. The fundamental concept of syndromic surveillance is to define indicators for a particular infectious disease on the given data, also referred to as *syndromes*, which are monitored over time to be able to detect unexpectedly high numbers of infections which might indicate an outbreak of that disease. Syndromic data can be obtained from *clinical* data sources (e.g., diagnosis in an emergency department), which allow to directly measure the symptoms of individuals, as well as *alternative* data sources (e.g., internet-based health inquiries), which indirectly capture the presence of a disease [6].

© Springer Nature Switzerland AG 2021
P. H. Abreu et al. (Eds.): IDA 2021, LNCS 12695, pp. 128–140, 2021.
https://doi.org/10.1007/978-3-030-74251-5_11

In general, the definition of syndromes is a challenging task since symptoms are often shared by different diseases and a particular disease can have different disease patterns in the early phase of an infection. Moreover, this kind of filtering is a highly handcrafted approach and only allows to monitor known infectious diseases. Rather than developing highly specialized algorithms which are based on a specific disease and assume particular characteristics of outbreak shapes [8], we argue that the task of outbreak detection should be viewed as a general anomaly detection problem where an outbreak alarm is triggered if the distribution of the incoming data changes in an unforeseen and unexpected way. Therefore, we distinguish between *specific* syndromic surveillance, where factors related to a specific disease are monitored, and *non-specific* syndromic surveillance, where general, universal characteristics of the stream of data are monitored for anomalies. While specific syndromic surveillance is a well-studied research area, we found that only little research has been devoted to non-specific syndromic surveillance with only very few algorithms available. In particular, the close relation to anomaly detection motivated us to investigate the problem of non-specific syndromic surveillance from a machine learning perspective and to make the task more approachable for the anomaly detection community.

In this paper, we revisit algorithms for non-specific syndromic surveillance and compare them to a broad range of anomaly detection algorithms. Due to little effort on implementing baselines in previous works on non-specific syndromic surveillance, we propose a set of benchmarks relying on simple statistical assumptions which nonetheless have been widely used before in specific syndromic surveillance. We experimentally compare the methods on an established synthetic dataset [3,11] and real data from a German emergency department in which we injected synthetic outbreaks. Our results demonstrate that the simple statistical approaches, which have not been considered in previous works, are quite effective and often can outperform more elaborate machine learning algorithms.

2   Non-specific Syndromic Surveillance

2.1   Problem Definition

Syndromic data can be seen as a constant stream of instances of a population $\mathcal{C}$. Each instance $\mathbf{c} \in \mathcal{C}$ is represented by a set of attributes $\mathcal{A} = \{A_1, A_2, \ldots, A_m\}$ where each attribute can be either categorical (e.g., *gender*), continuous (e.g., *age*) or text (e.g., *chief complaint*). Following the notation of Wong et al. [11], we refer to these attributes as *response attributes*. To be able to detect changes over time, instances are grouped together according to pre-specified time slots (e.g., all patients arriving at the emergency department in one day). Hence, the instances for a specific time slot t are denoted as $\mathcal{C}(t) \subset \mathcal{C}$.

In addition, each group $\mathcal{C}(t)$ is associated with an environmental setting $\mathbf{e}(t) \in E_1 \times E_2 \times \ldots \times E_k$ where $\mathcal{E} = \{E_1, E_2, \ldots, E_k\}$ is a set of *environmental attributes*. Environmental attributes are independent of the response attributes and represent external factors which might have an influence on the distribution of instances $\mathcal{C}(t)$ (e.g., during the winter flu-like symptoms are more frequent). In particular, a specific characteristic of syndromic data is *seasonality*, in machine learning also known as *cyclic drift* [10]. Environmental variables can help the algorithm to adapt to this kind of concept drift. Thus, the information available for time slot t can be represented by the tuple $(\mathcal{C}(t), \mathbf{e}(t))$ and the information about prior time slots can be denoted as $\mathcal{H} = ((\mathcal{C}(1), \mathbf{e}(1)), \ldots, (\mathcal{C}(t-1), \mathbf{e}(t-1)))$.

The main goal of non-specific syndromic surveillance is to detect anomalies in the set $\mathcal{C}(t)$ of the current time slot t w.r.t. the previous time slots $\mathcal{H}$ as potential indicators of an infectious disease outbreak. Therefore, the history $\mathcal{H}$ is used to fit a model $f_{\mathcal{H}}(\mathbf{e}(t), \mathcal{C}(t))$ which is able to generate a score for time slot t, representing the likelihood of being in an outbreak.

Viewed from the perspective of specific syndromic surveillance, the non-specific setting can be seen as the monitoring of all possible syndromes at the same time. The set of all possible syndromes can be defined as

$$\mathcal{S} = \left\{ \prod_{i \in \mathcal{I}} A_i \mid A_i \in \mathcal{A} \wedge \mathcal{I} \subseteq \{1, 2, \ldots, m\} \wedge |\mathcal{I}| \geq 1 \right\}$$

where $\prod_{i \in \mathcal{I}} A_i$ for $|\mathcal{I}| = 1$ is defined as $\{\{a\} \mid a \in A \wedge A \in \mathcal{A}\}$. In addition, we denote $\mathcal{S}_{\leq n} = \{s \mid s \in \mathcal{S} \wedge |s| \leq 2\}$ as the set of all possible syndromes having a maximum of n conditions and $\mathcal{H}_s = (s(1), s(2), \ldots, s(t-1))$ as the time series of counts for a particular syndrome $s \in \mathcal{S}$.

2.2   Evaluation

To evaluate a data stream it is split into two parts, namely a *training part*, containing the first time slots which are only used for training, and a *test part*, which contains the remaining time slots of the data stream. The evaluation is performed on the test part incrementally which means that for evaluating each time slot t the model will be newly fitted on the complete set of previously observed data points $\mathcal{H} = ((\mathcal{C}(1), \mathbf{e}(1)), \ldots, (\mathcal{C}(t-1), \mathbf{e}(t-1)))$. Alarms raised during an outbreak are considered as true positives while all other raised alarms are considered as false positives.

For measuring the performance, we rely on the *activity monitor operating characteristic (AMOC)* [4]. AMOC can be seen as an adaptation of the *receiver operating characteristic* in which the true positive rate is replaced by the *detection delay*, i.e., the number of time points until an outbreak has been first detected by the algorithm. In case the algorithm does not raise an alarm during the period of an outbreak, the detection delay is equal to the length of the outbreak. Moreover, for syndromic surveillance we are interested in a very low false alarm rate for the algorithms and therefore only report the partial area under AMOC-curve for a false alarm rate less than 5%, to which we refer to as $AAUC_{5\%}$. Note that contrary to conventional AUC values in this case lower values represent better results. Since one data stream does normally not contain enough outbreaks to draw conclusions, the evaluation is usually performed on a set of data streams. To obtain a final score for the set, we take the average over the computed $AAUC_{5\%}$ results which are computed on each data stream.

3   Machine Learning Algorithms

In a survey of the relevant literature we have identified only a few algorithms which relate to non-specific syndromic surveillance, described in Sects. 3.1, 3.2 and 3.3. In Sect. 3.4 we introduce a way how common anomaly detection algorithms can be applied in the setting of non-specific syndromic surveillance.

3.1   Data Mining Surveillance System (DMSS)

One of the first algorithms able to identify new and interesting patterns in syndromic data was proposed by Brossette et al. [1] who adopted the idea of association rule mining [12] to the field of public health surveillance. In order to detect an outbreak for time slot t, an association rule mining algorithm needs to be run on $\mathcal{C}(t)$ and a reference set of patients $\mathcal{R} \subset \mathcal{C}$ is created by merging the instances of a selected set of previous time slots. For each association rule the confidence of the rule on $\mathcal{C}(t)$ is compared to the confidence of the rule computed on $\mathcal{R}$ using a χ^2 or a Fisher's test. If the confidence has significantly increased on $\mathcal{C}(t)$, the finding is reported as an unexpected event. In order to reduce the complexity, the authors propose to focus only on mining high-support association rules. An aggregation of the observations for one time slot is not performed and environmental attributes are not considered by this approach.

3.2   What Is Strange About Recent Events? (WSARE)

The family of *WSARE* algorithms has been proposed by Wong et al. [11]. All algorithms share the same underlying concept, namely to monitor all possible syndromes having a maximum of two conditions $\mathcal{S}_{\leq 2}$ simultaneously. The three WSARE algorithms only differ in the way how the reference set of patients $\mathcal{R}$ is created on which the expected proportion for each syndrome is estimated. Each expected proportion is compared to the proportion of the respective syndrome observed on the set $\mathcal{C}(t)$ using the χ^2 or Fisher's exact test. In order to aggregate the p-values of the statistical tests for one time slot, a *permutation test* with 1,000 repetitions is performed. The following three versions have been considered:

WSARE 2.0 merges the instances of a selected set of prior time slots together for the reference set $\mathcal{R}$. Since their evaluation was based on single-day time slots, they combined the instances of the previous time slots 35, 42, 49 and 56 to consider only instances of the same weekday.

WSARE 2.5 merges the instances of all prior time slots together which share the same environmental setting as for the current day $\mathbf{e}(t)$. This has the advantage that the expected proportions are conditioned on the environmental setting $\mathbf{e}(t)$ and that potentially more instances are contained in the reference set $\mathcal{R}$, allowing to have more precise expectations.

WSARE 3.0 learns a Bayesian network over all recent data $\mathcal{H}$ from which 10,000 instances for the reference set $\mathcal{R}$ are sampled given the environmental attributes $\mathbf{e}(t)$ as evidence.

3.3   Eigenevent

The key idea of the *Eigenevent* algorithm proposed by Fanaee-T and Gama [3] is to track changes in the data correlation structure using eigenspace techniques. Instead of monitoring all possible syndromes, only overall changes and dimension-level changes are observed by the algorithm. Therefore, a dynamic baseline tensor is created using the information of prior time slots $\mathcal{H}$ which share the same environmental setting $\mathbf{e}(t)$. In the next step, information of the instances $\mathcal{C}(t)$ and the baseline tensor are decomposed to a lower-rank subspace in which the eigenvectors and eigenvalues are compared to each other, respectively. Any significant changes in the eigenvectors and eigenvalues between the baseline tensor and the information of instances $\mathcal{C}(t)$ indicate an outbreak.

3.4   Anomaly Detection Algorithms

A direct application of point anomaly detection is in general not suitable for syndromic surveillance [11] because these methods aim to identify single instances $\mathbf{c} \in \mathcal{C}$ as outliers and could thus, e.g., be triggered by a patient who is over a hundred years old. In order to still apply point anomaly detectors to discover outbreaks, we form a dataset $\mathcal{D}$ using the syndromes $s \in \mathcal{S}$ as features and the respective syndrome counts $\mathcal{H}_s$ as values. Hence, each instance represents the occurrence counts of all syndromes for one particular time slot and the dataset contains $t-1$ instances in total. This dataset can be used to fit an anomaly detector which can be then applied to the instance of syndrome counts for time slot t. Hence, an outbreak could be identified by an unusual combination of syndrome counts. In this work, we consider the following anomaly detection algorithms. Due to space restrictions, we refer to Chandola et al. [2] and Zhao et al. [13] and the references therein for a comprehensive review of the methods.

One-Class SVM extends the support vector machine algorithm to perform outlier detection by separating instances $\mathcal{D}$ from the complement of $\mathcal{D}$.

Local Outlier Factor computes the outlier score for an instance based on how isolated the instance is with respect to the surrounding neighborhood.

Gaussian Mixture Models approximate the distribution of the dataset $\mathcal{D}$ using a mixture of Gaussian distributions. The outlier score is based on how dense the region of the evaluated instance is.

Copula-Based Outlier Detection (COPOD) creates an empirical copula for the multi-variate distribution of $\mathcal{D}$ on which tail probabilities for an instance can be predicted to estimate the outlier score.

Isolation Forest constructs an ensemble of randomly generated decision trees in which anomalies can be identified by counting the number of splittings required to isolate an instance.

Autoencoder learns an identity function of the data through a network of multiple hidden layers. Instances which have a high reconstruction error are considered to be anomalous.

Multiple-Objective Generative Adversarial Active Learning (GAAL) constructs multiple generators having different objectives to generate outliers for learning a discriminator which can assign outlier scores to new instances.

4   Basic Statistical Approaches

In addition to the machine learning models introduced in Sect. 3, we also include statistical techniques, which are commonly used for specific syndromic surveillance, into our comparison and adapt them to a non-specific syndromic surveillance setting. The key idea of these adaptations is to monitor all possible syndromes S simultaneously. For the purpose of monitoring syndromes, a parametric distribution $P_s(x)$ is fitted for each single syndrome $s \in S$ using the empirical mean μ and the empirical variance σ^2 computed over $\mathcal{H}_s$:

$$\mu = \frac{1}{|\mathcal{H}_s|} \sum_{i=0}^{|\mathcal{H}_s|} s(i) \qquad \sigma^2 = \frac{1}{|\mathcal{H}_s| - 1} \sum_{i=0}^{|\mathcal{H}_s|} (s(i) - \mu)^2$$

On the fitted distribution $P_s(x)$, a one-tailed significance test is performed in order to identify a suspicious increase of cases. For a particular observed count $s(t)$, the p-value is computed as the probability $\int_{s(t)}^{\infty} P_s(x)dx$ of observing $s(t)$ or higher counts. Thus, for evaluating a single time slot t, we obtain $|S|$ p-values which need to be aggregated under consideration of the multiple-testing problem. Following Roure et al. [7], we only report the minimum p-value for each time slot t because the Bonferroni correction can be regarded as a form of aggregation of p-values based on the minimum function. In particular, note that scale-free anomaly scores are sufficient for the purpose of identifying the most suspicious time slots. The complement of the selected p-value represents the anomaly score reported for time slot t. For our benchmarks we have considered the following distributions:

Gaussian. Not tailored for count data but often used in syndromic surveillance is the Gaussian distribution $N(\mu, \sigma^2)$. This distribution will serve as reference for the other distributions which are specifically designed for count data.
Poisson. The Poisson distribution $Pois(\lambda)$ is directly designed for count data. For estimating the parameter λ, we use the maximum likelihood estimate which is the mean μ.
Negative Binomial. To be able to adapt to overdispersion, we include the negative binomial distribution $NB(r, p)$. We have estimated the parameters with $r = \frac{\mu^2}{\sigma^2 - \mu}$ and $p = \frac{r}{r + \mu}$.

Our preliminary experiments showed that statistical tests on rare syndromes are often too sensitive to changes, causing many false alarms. In addition, outbreaks are usually associated with a high number of infections. Therefore, we set the standard deviation σ^2 to a minimum of one before fitting the Gaussian distribution and for the Poisson and the negative binomial distribution we set the mean μ to a minimum of one. We leave the standard deviation untouched for the negative binomial distribution since manipulating the overdispersion can lead to extreme distortions in the estimation.

Table 1. Synthetic data.

Attribute	Type	#values
Age	Response	3
Gender	Response	2
Action	Response	3
Symptom	Response	4
Drug	Response	4
Location	Response	9
Flu level	Environmental	4
Day of week	Environmental	3
Weather	Environmental	2
Season	Environmental	4

Table 2. Real data.

Attribute	Type	#values
Age	Response	3
Gender	Response	2
mts	Response	28
Fever	Response	2
Pulse	Response	3
Respiration	Response	3
Oxygen saturation	Response	2
Blood pressure	Response	2
Day of week	Environmental	7
Season	Environmental	4

5   Experiments and Results

The goal of the experimental evaluation reported in this section is to provide an overview of the performance of non-specific syndromic surveillance methods in general, and in particular, to re-evaluate the established methods in context of the proposed base statistical approaches and the anomaly detection algorithms. We conducted experiments on synthetic data, which already have been used for the evaluation of the algorithms Eigenevent and WSARE [3,11], and on real data of a German emergency department (cf. Sect. 5.3). As the emergency department data do not contain any information about real outbreaks, we decided to inject synthetic outbreaks which is common practice in the area of syndromic surveillance, allowing us to evaluate and compare the algorithms in a controlled environment.

5.1   Evaluation Setup

Synthetic Data. The synthetic data consists of 100 data streams, generated with the synthetic data generator proposed by Wong et al. [11]. The data generator is based on a Bayesian network and simulates a population of people living in a city of whom only a subset are reported to the data stream at each simulated time slot. Detailed information about the attributes in the data stream is given in Table 1. Each data stream captures the information about the people on a daily basis over a time period of two years, i.e., each time slot $\mathcal{C}(t)$ contains the patients of one day. In average 34 instances are reported per time slot and 270 possible syndromes are contained in the set $\mathcal{S}_{\leq 2}$. The first year is used for the training part while the second year serves as the test part. Exactly one outbreak is simulated in the test part which starts at a randomly chosen day and always lasts for 14 days. During the outbreak period, the simulated people have a higher chance of catching a particular disease.

Table 3. Results for the $AAUC_{5\%}$ measure on the synthetic data.

Name	Rerun	Min. p-value	Permutation test	Imported p-values
Eigenevent	4.993	–	–	4.391
WSARE 2.0	–	2.963	3.805	4.925
WSARE 2.5	–	1.321	1.614	1.931
WSARE 3.0	–	0.899	1.325	1.610

Real Data. We rely on routinely collected, fully anonymized patient data of a German emergency department, captured on a daily basis over a time period of two years. We have extracted a set of response attributes and added two environmental attributes (cf. Table 2). Continuous attributes, such as *respiration*, have been discretized with the help of a physician into meaningful categories. In addition, we include the Manchester-Triage-System (MTS) [5] initial assessment which is filled out for every patient on arrival. To reduce the number of values for the attribute MTS, we group classifications which do not relate to any infectious disease, such as various kinds of injuries, into a single value. In average 165 patients are reported per day and in total 574 syndromes can be formed for the set $|\mathcal{S}_{\leq 2}|$. In preparation for the injection of simulated outbreaks, we replicated the data stream 100 times. For each data stream, we used the first year as the training part and the second year as the test part in which we injected exactly one outbreak. In order to simulate an outbreak, we first uniformly sampled a syndrome from $\mathcal{S}_{\leq 2}$. In a second step, we sampled the size of the outbreak from a Poisson distribution with mean equal to the standard deviation of the daily patient visits and randomly selected the corresponding number of patients from all patients that exhibit the sampled syndrome. To avoid over-representing outbreaks on rare syndromes, only 20 data streams contain outbreaks with syndromes that have a lower frequency than one per day. In total, 29 outbreaks are based on syndromes with one condition and 71 with two.

Additional Benchmarks. We also include the *control chart*, the *moving average* and the *linear regression* algorithms into our analysis. Compared to our *syndrome-based* statistical benchmarks, these *global* statistical benchmarks only monitor the total number of instances per time slot and therefore can only give a very broad assessment of outbreak detection performance. For a detailed explanation of these algorithms, we refer to Wong et al. [11].

Implementation and Parameterization. For the Eigenevent algorithm we rely on the code provided by the authors.[1] All other algorithms are implemented in Python.[2] Parameters for the DMSS and the anomaly detection algorithms have been tuned in a grid search using 1000 iterations of *Bootstrap Bias Corrected*

---

[1] https://github.com/fanaee/EigenEvent.
[2] Our code is publicly available at https://github.com/MoritzKulessa/NSS.

Cross-Validation [9] which allows to integrate hyperparameter tuning and reliable performance estimation into a single evaluation loop. The evaluated parameter combinations can be found in our repository. The WSARE, the Eigenevent, the COPOD and the statistical algorithms do not contain any parameters which need to be tuned.

5.2 Preliminary Evaluation

In a first experiment, we replicated the experiments on the synthetic data of [3]. More specifically, we imported and re-evaluated the outlier scores for the synthetic data from the Eigenevent repository (*imported p-values*) and compare these to our own results with rerunning the Eigenevent algorithm (*rerun*) and to our implementation of the WSARE algorithms. For the latter, we additionally evaluate the results of just reporting the minimal p-value for each time slot (*min. p-value*, cf. Sect. 4) instead of performing an originally proposed permutation test with 1000 repetitions (*permutation test*). The results are shown in Table 3.

Our rerun of the Eigenevent algorithm returned slightly worse results than the imported p-values, which could be caused by the random initialization. For the WSARE algorithms, we can observe that our implementation achieves better results than the imported p-values, probably due to the different Bayesian network used. In particular, the results for the minimal p-value were better than those for the more expensive permutation test. Thus, we chose to only report the minimal p-value for the WSARE algorithms in the following experiments.

5.3 Results

The results on the synthetic and real data are both shown in Table 4. For syndrome-based algorithms, the results for monitoring $S_{\leq 1}$ and $S_{\leq 2}$ are reported in the respective columns while results for the other methods are reported in the columns *none*. Note that the worst possible result on the synthetic data is 14 while for the real data the worst result is 1. In the first paragraphs, we will discuss the results without specifically considering the size of the syndrome sets unless needed. The effect of using $S_{\leq 1}$ or $S_{\leq 2}$ is discussed in the last paragraph.

Comparison Between Non-specific Syndromic Surveillance Algorithms. Firstly, we analyze the results of the non-specific syndromic surveillance approaches which have been presented in Sects. 3.1, 3.2 and 3.3. In general, the WSARE algorithms outperform the other algorithms in the group. In particular, the results of the modified versions WSARE 2.5 and WSARE 3.0 on the synthetic data show that the use of environmental attributes can be beneficial. However, the results on the real data indicate the opposite. We further investigated this finding by rerunning WSARE 3.0 on the real data without the use of environmental variables and observed a substantial improvement of the results to 0.613 for $S_{\leq 1}$ and 0.570 for $S_{\leq 2}$, respectively. Therefore, we conclude that the modelling of the environmental factors should be done with care since it can easily lead to worse estimates if the real distribution does not follow the categorization imposed by defined attributes.

Table 4. Results for the $AAUC_{5\%}$ measure on the synthetic and real data.

Category	Algorithm name	Synthetic data			Real data		
		None	$S_{\leq 1}$	$S_{\leq 2}$	None	$S_{\leq 1}$	$S_{\leq 2}$
Non-specific syndromic surveillance	WSARE 2.0	–	3.028	2.963	–	0.661	0.590
	WSARE 2.5	–	1.099	1.321	–	0.917	0.867
	WSARE 3.0	–	0.803	0.899	–	0.882	0.847
	DMSS	2.430	–	–	0.953	–	–
	Eigenevent	4.993	–	–	0.878	–	–
Anomaly detectors	One-class SVM	–	1.043	1.262	–	0.468	0.495
	Local outlier factor	–	2.000	2.260	–	0.642	0.610
	Gaussian mixture model	–	1.117	3.547	–	0.444	0.791
	Isolation forest	–	4.576	4.948	–	0.873	0.835
	COPOD	–	5.216	5.032	–	0.816	0.800
	Autoencoder	–	1.521	1.643	–	0.550	0.576
	GAAL	–	7.024	6.766	–	0.792	0.866
Global benchmarks	Control chart	5.086	–	–	0.891	–	–
	Moving average	7.012	–	–	0.910	–	–
	Linear regression	3.279	–	–	0.819	–	–
Syndrome-based benchmarks	Gaussian	–	0.806	0.941	–	0.328	0.267
	Poisson	–	1.294	1.347	–	0.598	0.486
	Negative binomial	–	0.895	0.958	–	0.299	0.216

The results of the DMSS algorithm suggest that monitoring association rules is not as effective as monitoring syndromes. In particular, the space of possible association rules is much greater than the space of possible syndromes S which worsens the problem of multiple testing. Especially on the real data this results in a bad performance since the high number of instances per time slot yields too many rules. Conversely, by monitoring only rules with very high support most of the outbreaks remain undetected since the disease pattern could not be captured anymore. In contrast to the results reported by Fanaee-T and Gama [3], the Eigenevent algorithm performs poorly compared to the WSARE algorithms. A closer analysis reveals that the difference in these results can be explained by the used evaluation measure. Fanaee-T and Gama [3] consider only p-values in the range $[0.02, 0.25]$ to create the AMOC-curve. However, exactly the omitted low p-values are particularly important when precise predictions with low false positive rates are required which is why we explicitly included this range into the computation of the AMOC-curve.

Comparison to the Anomaly Detection Algorithms. Regarding the synthetic data, which was specifically created in order to evaluate the WSARE algorithms, we can observe that no anomaly detection algorithm can reach competitive $AAUC_{5\%}$ scores to WSARE 3.0. Considering the gap to WSARE 2.0, which in comparison to 3.0 does not distinguish between environmental settings, one reason could be that the anomaly detection algorithms are not able to take the environmental variables into account. Another reason could be the low number of training instances (one for each day) which might have caused problems, especially for the neural networks. Only the SVM, which is known to work well with only few instances, and the Gaussian mixture model are able to achieve acceptable results. These two approaches are in fact able to outperform the WSARE variants on the real data for which we already found evidence that the environmental information might not be useful.

Comparison to the Benchmarks. In the following, we will put the previously discussed results in relation to the benchmarks. For the global benchmarks, we can observe that monitoring the total number of cases per time slot is not sufficient to adequately detect most of the outbreaks. Notably, many of the machine learning approaches do in fact not perform considerably better than these simple benchmarks. The comparison to our proposed statistical benchmarks applied on each possible syndrome separately allow further important insights. Our main observation is that, despite its simplicity, they outperform most of the previously discussed, more sophisticated approaches. In fact, in the case of the real data the Gaussian and the negative binomial benchmarks achieve the best scores. On the synthetic data they are able to achieve results that are competitive to WSARE 3.0 even though the benchmarks do not take the environmental attributes into account.

Comparison Between $S_{\leq 1}$ and $S_{\leq 2}$. We can make two basic observations regarding the complexity of the monitored syndromes: Firstly, the outbreaks in the synthetic data are better detected by the algorithms and benchmarks for nonspecific syndromic surveillance when monitoring single condition syndromes $S_{\leq 1}$ while for the real data we benefit from pair patterns $S_{\leq 2}$. Secondly, almost no anomaly detector is able to profit from the explicit counts for $S_{\leq 2}$ regardless of the dataset. For understanding the first effect, we take a closer look at the results of our proposed benchmarks. These approaches can only take cooccurrences between conditions into account if explicitly given or if the $S \setminus S_{\leq 1}$ patterns greatly affect the counts for the composing conditions. Hence, monitoring a larger set of syndromes increases the sensitivity of detecting outbreaks with complex disease patterns. However, it comes at the cost of a higher false alarm rate due to multiple testing. For the real dataset, for which we know that it contains more outbreaks based on two than on one condition, the higher sensitivity is able to outweigh the increased false alarm rate. On the other hand, the results on the synthetic dataset suggests that most of the outbreaks in the synthetic data are lead by single indicators, resulting in more false alarms when monitoring $S_{\leq 2}$.

In contrast to the non-specific syndromic surveillance approaches, only some anomaly detectors benefit and only slightly from the explicit counts for $\mathcal{S}_{\leq 2}$, such as the local outlier factor algorithm and the isolation forests. This indicates that the remaining approaches, such as SVM and neural networks, already adequately consider correlations between attributes. Especially remarkable is the case of Gaussian mixture models, which achieves the best results in the group when monitoring $\mathcal{S}_{\leq 1}$ but is strongly affected by the $\mathcal{S}_{\leq 2}$ patterns.

6   Conclusion

In this work, we presented non-specific syndromic surveillance from the perspective of machine learning and gave an overview of the few approaches addressing this task. Furthermore, we introduced a way of how anomaly detection algorithms can be applied on this problem and a set of simple statistical algorithms which we believe should serve as reference points for future experimental comparisons. In an experimental evaluation, we revisited the non-specific syndromic surveillance approaches in face of the previously not considered statistical benchmarks and a variety of anomaly detectors. Eventually, we found that these benchmarks outperform most of the more sophisticated techniques and are competitive to the best approaches in the field.

Acknowledgments. We thank our project partners the *Health Protection Authority of Frankfurt*, the *Hesse State Health Office and Centre for Health Protection*, the *Hesse Ministry of Social Affairs and Integration*, the *Robert Koch-Institut*, the *Epias GmbH* and especially the *Sana Klinikum Offenbach GmbH* who provided data and expertise that greatly assisted the research. This work was funded by the *Innovation Committee of the Federal Joint Committee* (G-BA) [ESEG project, grant number 01VSF17034].

References

1. Brossette, S., Sprague, A., Hardin, J., Waites, K., Jones, W., Moser, S.: Association rules and data mining in hospital infection control and public health surveillance. J. Am. Med. Inform. Assoc. **5**, 373–381 (1998)
2. Chandola, V., Banerjee, A., Kumar, V.: Anomaly detection: a survey. ACM Comput. Surv. **41**(3), 1–58 (2009)
3. Fanaee-T, H., Gama, J.: Eigenevent: an algorithm for event detection from complex data streams in syndromic surveillance. Intell. Data Anal. **19**, 597–616 (2015)
4. Fawcett, T., Provost, F.: Activity monitoring: noticing interesting changes in behavior. In: Proceedings of the 5th ACM SIGKDD International Conference on Knowledge Discovery and Data Mining, pp. 53–62 (1999)
5. Gräff, I., et al.: The German version of the manchester triage system and its quality criteria-first assessment of validity and reliability. PLoS ONE **9**(2), e88995 (2014)
6. Henning, K.J.: What is syndromic surveillance? Morb. Mortal. Wkly Rep.: Suppl. **53**, 7–11 (2004)
7. Roure, J., Dubrawski, A., Schneider, J.: A study into detection of bio-events in multiple streams of surveillance data. In: Zeng, D., et al. (eds.) BioSurveillance 2007. LNCS, vol. 4506, pp. 124–133. Springer, Heidelberg (2007). https://doi.org/10.1007/978-3-540-72608-1_12

8. Shmueli, G., Burkom, H.: Statistical challenges facing early outbreak detection in biosurveillance. Technometrics **52**(1), 39–51 (2010)
9. Tsamardinos, I., Greasidou, E., Borboudakis, G.: Bootstrapping the out-of-sample predictions for efficient and accurate cross-validation. Mach. Learn. **107**(12), 1895–1922 (2018). https://doi.org/10.1007/s10994-018-5714-4
10. Webb, G.I., Hyde, R., Cao, H., Nguyen, H.L., Petitjean, F.: Characterizing concept drift. Data Min. Knowl. Disc. **30**(4), 964–994 (2016). https://doi.org/10.1007/s10618-015-0448-4
11. Wong, W., Moore, A., Cooper, G., Wagner, M.: What's strange about recent events (WSARE): an algorithm for the early detection of disease outbreaks. J. Mach. Learn. Res. **6**, 1961–1998 (2005)
12. Zhang, C., Zhang, S.: Association Rule Mining: Models and Algorithms. Springer, Heidelberg (2002)
13. Zhao, Y., Nasrullah, Z., Li, Z.: PyOD: a Python toolbox for scalable outlier detection. J. Mach. Learn. Res. **20**(96), 1–7 (2019)

Gradient Ascent for Best Response Regression

Victoria Racher[1,3(✉)] and Christian Borgelt[1,2]

[1] Department of Mathematics, University of Salzburg, Salzburg, Austria
[2] Department of Computer Sciences, University of Salzburg, Salzburg, Austria
[3] Paracelsus Medical University, Salzburg, Austria
victoria.racher@pmu.ac.at

Abstract. Although regression is among the oldest areas of statistics, new approaches may still be found. One recent suggestion is Best Response Regression, where one tries to find a regression function that provides, for as many instances as possible, a better prediction than some reference regression function. In this paper we propose a new method for Best Response Regression that is based on gradient ascent rather than mixed integer programming. We evaluate our approach for a variety of noise (or error) distributions, showing that especially for heavy-tailed distributions best response regression outperforms, on unseen data, ordinary least squares regression, both w.r.t. the sum of squared errors as well as the number of instances for which better predictions are provided.

Keywords: Best response regression · Objective function smoothing · Gradient ascent · Resilient backpropagation · Newton–Raphson method

1 Introduction

Prediction is central to both Statistics and Machine Learning. Given a set of instances, described by one or more explanatory (or input) variables, along with a response (or output) value for each instance, a predictor has to identify the response for a new (unseen) instance as accurately as possible. Usually, if the response value is categorical, the prediction task is called classification, if it is metric, it is called regression. Many approaches to such problems are well known. For instance, in the case of regression, we commonly aim to minimize the sum of squared errors, often for a simple linear prediction function. Admittedly, linear regression is one of the simplest models to understand in terms of regression. Nevertheless, this does not mean that the classical statistical approaches are the best or even only ones. On the contrary, the combination of different subfields of Mathematics and Computer Science allows new and interesting perspectives. We follow the recent idea by Ben-Porat and Tennenholtz, which is called Best Response Regression [2]. The essential theory behind Best Response Regression is the combination of concepts from game theory and statistical learning.

© Springer Nature Switzerland AG 2021
P. H. Abreu et al. (Eds.): IDA 2021, LNCS 12695, pp. 141–154, 2021.
https://doi.org/10.1007/978-3-030-74251-5_12

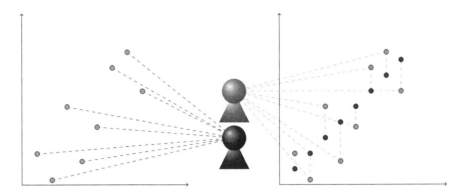

Fig. 1. Illustration of the main idea of Best Response Regression. An expert (blue) sees instances along with their true response values to make predictions, an agent (green) sees also the discrepancies between the expert's predictions and the true values. (Color figure online)

This paper list organized as follows: In Sect. 2 we review Best Response Regression and point out some shortcomings of the original approach. In Sect. 4 we derive our own gradient ascent based approach drawing on a relaxation (or "smoothing") of the original objective function. In Sect. 5 we report experimental results, focusing on exploring different noise (or error) distributions. Finally, in Sect. 6 we draw conclusions from our discussion.

2   Best Response Regression

In 2017, Ben-Porat and Tennenholtz [2] proposed a completely new way of interpreting (linear) regression tasks based on machine learning techniques, which they called Best Response Regression. They interpreted the prediction task as a game that two players, an agent and an expert, play against each other. The expert uses a number of historical instances along with their response values to make predictions for a new (unseen) instance. The agent also sees the historical instances and their true response values, but gets as additional information the discrepancies between the expert's predictions and the true values. The main idea is illustrated in Fig. 1. The fundamental difference to classical approaches is that Best Response Regression is no longer trying to minimize the discrepancy between predicted and observed values, but focuses on maximizing the probability to predict better than an expert (represented, e.g., by a reference prediction function). For more details and a game theoretical justification, we refer to [2].

2.1   Shortcomings of the Approach by Ben-Porat and Tennenholtz

To find a best response regression function, Ben-Porat and Tennenholtz formulated a Mixed Integer Linear Problem, where the optimization step relied on the Simplex Algorithm. Unfortunately, as the number of explanatory variables increases, the runtime of the Simplex Algorithm increases exponentially. This problem is handled by setting timeouts, that is, the implementation outputs the best solution that could be found before the timeout. However, one does know neither whether this is the final optimal solution nor whether the solution is unique. Therefore, we considered a new approach using gradient ascent on "smoothed" versions of the objective function. Even though such an approach also cannot guarantee that an optimal solution is found, it is computationally much more efficient and, in principle, applicable to arbitrary regression functions and arbitrary numbers of explanatory (or independent) variables.

3   Notation

Let a data set $(\mathbf{X}, \boldsymbol{y})$ be given, where $\mathbf{X} = (\boldsymbol{x}_1, \ldots, \boldsymbol{x}_n)$ is a tuple of input vectors with $\boldsymbol{x}_i = (x_{i1}, \ldots, x_{im}) \in \mathbb{R}^m$ and $\boldsymbol{y} = (y_1, \ldots, y_n) \in \mathbb{R}^n$ is a vector of output values. Let $f_\circ(\boldsymbol{x})$ be a reference regression function and $f_*(\boldsymbol{x}; \boldsymbol{a})$ a best response regression function with parameters $\boldsymbol{a}$. To simplify notation, we define

$$g_\pm(\boldsymbol{a}; \boldsymbol{x}_i, y_i, \varepsilon) = f_*(\boldsymbol{x}_i; \boldsymbol{a}) - (y_i \pm (1 - \varepsilon) \cdot |f_\circ(\boldsymbol{x}_i) - y_i|),$$

where ε, $0 < \varepsilon \ll 1$, is a required minimum prediction improvement. With this notation, the objective function of best response regression can be written as

$$F_H(\boldsymbol{a}; \mathbf{X}, \boldsymbol{y}) = \sum_{i=1}^{n} \Big(H\big(g_-(\boldsymbol{a}; \boldsymbol{x}_i, y_i, \varepsilon)\big) - H\big(g_+(\boldsymbol{a}; \boldsymbol{x}_i, y_i, \varepsilon)\big) \Big),$$

where H is the Heaviside function (or unit step function)

$$H : \quad \mathbb{R} \to \{0, 1\}, \quad z \mapsto \begin{cases} 1, & \text{if } z \geq 0, \\ 0, & \text{otherwise.} \end{cases}$$

The objective function F_H is to be maximized by choosing $\boldsymbol{a}$. Note that this optimization problem may not have a unique solution, since the objective function is essentially counting for how many data points the best response regression function yields a better prediction than the reference regression function and the same count may be obtained for different best response regression functions.

4   Gradient Ascent Approach

We propose to relax the optimization problem by using a "smoothed" Heaviside function, for which the (scaled) logistic function is a natural (first) choice:

$$L_\beta(z) = \frac{1}{1 + e^{-\beta z}} = \left(1 + e^{-\beta z}\right)^{-1}.$$

Here β is a steepness parameter: the greater β, the steeper (and thus the less "smooth") the function $L_\beta(z)$ is. For $\beta \to \infty$ we get $L_\beta(z) \to H(z)$. This leads to a "smoothed" objective function (on which a gradient ascent becomes possible)

$$F_{L_\beta}(\boldsymbol{a}; \mathbf{X}, \boldsymbol{y}) = \sum_{i=1}^{n} \Big(L_\beta\big(g_-(\boldsymbol{a}; \boldsymbol{x}_i, y_i, \varepsilon)\big) - L_\beta\big(g_+(\boldsymbol{a}; \boldsymbol{x}_i, y_i, \varepsilon)\big) \Big),$$

which is again to be maximized by choosing $\boldsymbol{a}$. Figure 2 provides an illustration of one term of the original and the smoothed objective function.

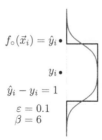

Fig. 2. The value y_i is the true output for input vector $\boldsymbol{x}_i$, while $\hat{y}_i$ is the output produced by the reference regression function, that is, $\hat{y}_i = f_\circ(\boldsymbol{x}_i)$. The black and red lines show the ith term of the original objective function $F_H(\boldsymbol{a}; \mathbf{X}, \boldsymbol{y})$ and the "smoothed" version $F_{L_\beta}(\boldsymbol{a}; \mathbf{X}, \boldsymbol{y})$, respectively. The shape of the red curve relative to the black curve depends on the value of β and on the distance between $\hat{y}_i$ and y_i (which is set to 1 here for illustrative purposes). (Color figure online)

Clearly, a best response regression function has to pass through the region, in which the depicted ith term of $F_H(\boldsymbol{a}; \mathbf{X}, \boldsymbol{y})$ (black line) is one, in order to "win" the ith data point. The core idea of our approach is to relax this condition by asking for a value as high as possible for the ith term of $F_{L_\beta}(\boldsymbol{a}; \mathbf{X}, \boldsymbol{y})$ (red line). Note that by letting the parameter β grow in the course of the optimization, we can always approach the original function $F_H(\boldsymbol{a}; \mathbf{X}, \boldsymbol{y})$ as closely as desired.

In order to find a maximum of the objective function $F_{L_\beta}(\boldsymbol{a}; \mathbf{X}, \boldsymbol{y})$ we consider, in a first approach, a gradient ascent scheme. That is, we start from an initial guess $\boldsymbol{a}^{(0)}$ of the parameters $\boldsymbol{a}$ and update them iteratively according to

$$\boldsymbol{a}^{(i+1)} = \boldsymbol{a}^{(i)} + \eta \cdot \nabla_{\boldsymbol{a}} \, F_{L_\beta}(\boldsymbol{a}; \mathbf{X}, \boldsymbol{y})\big|_{\boldsymbol{a}^{(i)}} = \boldsymbol{a}^{(i)} + \eta \cdot \big(\nabla_{\boldsymbol{a}} \, F_{L_\beta}(\boldsymbol{a}; \mathbf{X}, \boldsymbol{y})\big)\big(\boldsymbol{a}^{(i)}\big),$$

where η is a step width parameter that has to be chosen by a user. In order to be able to evaluate this expression, we first compute

$$L_\beta'(z) \;\; = \;\; \frac{\mathrm{d}}{\mathrm{d}z} L_\beta(z) \;\; = \;\; \frac{\mathrm{d}}{\mathrm{d}z}\big(1 + e^{-\beta z}\big)^{-1} \;\; = \;\; \beta \cdot L_\beta(z) \cdot (1 - L_\beta(z)),$$

the well-known expression for the derivative of the logistic function, as well as

$$\nabla_{\boldsymbol{a}} \, g_\pm(\boldsymbol{a}; \boldsymbol{x}_i, y_i, \pm\varepsilon) = \nabla_{\boldsymbol{a}} \, (f_*(\boldsymbol{x}_i; \boldsymbol{a}) - (y_i \pm (1-\varepsilon) \cdot |f_\circ(\boldsymbol{x}_i) - y_i|)) = \nabla_{\boldsymbol{a}} f_*(\boldsymbol{x}_i; \boldsymbol{a}).$$

This leads to the following gradient of the objective function

$$\nabla_a F_{L_\beta}(a; \mathbf{X}, y) = \nabla_a \sum_{i=1}^{n} \left(L_\beta\big(g_-(a; x_i, y_i, \varepsilon)\big) - L_\beta\big(g_+(a; x_i, y_i, \varepsilon)\big) \right)$$

$$= \sum_{i=1}^{n} \left(\nabla_a \, L_\beta\big(g_-(a; x_i, y_i, \varepsilon)\big) - \nabla_a \, L_\beta\big(g_+(a; x_i, y_i, \varepsilon)\big) \right)$$

$$= \sum_{i=1}^{n} \left(L'_\beta\big(g_-(a; x_i, y_i, \varepsilon)\big) - L'_\beta\big(g_+(a; x_i, y_i, \varepsilon)\big) \right) \cdot \nabla_a f_*(x_i; a).$$

If we consider the special case $f_*(x, a) = a^\top x^*$, where it is $a = (a_0, a_1, \ldots, a_m)$ and $x^* = (1, x_1, \ldots, x_m)$ for $x = (x_1, \ldots, x_m)$, that is, a linear function, we get

$$\nabla_a \, f_*(x; a) = \nabla_a \, a^\top x^* = x^* \qquad \text{and therefore}$$

$$\nabla_a \, F_{L_\beta}(a; \mathbf{X}, y) = \sum_{i=1}^{n} \left(L'_\beta\big(g_-(a; x_i, y_i, \varepsilon)\big) - L'_\beta\big(g_+(a; x_i, y_i, \varepsilon)\big) \right) \cdot x_i^*.$$

As a second approach we may draw on gradient method improvements as they have been developed, for example, in artificial neural networks, There is a large variety of such approaches like the introduction of a momentum term [11], Nesterov's accelerated gradient [10], self-adaptive error backpropagation [15], resilient error backpropagation [12,13], quick backpropagation [6], AdaGrad [5], RMSProp [14], AdaDelta [16], Adam and AdaMax [9], and NAdam [4]. For simplicity, we choose one of them, namely resilient backpropagation, which uses the signs of the current and the previous gradient to adapt a parameter step width, one for each parameter. That is, the general update scheme is $a_k^{(i+1)} = a_k^{(i)} + \Delta a_k^{(i)}$ and the step width $\Delta a_k^{(i)}$ (which is specific to parameter a_k) is computed as

$$\Delta a_k^{(i)} = \begin{cases} c^- \cdot \Delta a_k^{(i-1)}, & \text{if } (\nabla_{a_k} F_{L_\beta})|_{a_k^{(i)}} \cdot (\nabla_{a_k} F_{L_\beta})|_{a_k^{(i-1)}} < 0, \\ c^+ \cdot \Delta a_k^{(i-1)}, & \text{if } (\nabla_{a_k} F_{L_\beta})|_{a_k^{(i)}} \cdot (\nabla_{a_k} F_{L_\beta})|_{a_k^{(i-1)}} < 0 \\ & \land (\nabla_{a_k} F_{L_\beta})|_{a_k^{(i-1)}} \cdot (\nabla_{a_k} F_{L_\beta})|_{a_k^{(i-2)}} \geq 0, \\ \Delta a_k^{(i-1)}, & \text{otherwise.} \end{cases}$$

That is, the step width is increased if the current and the previous gradient point in the same direction, and it is decreased if they point in opposite directions, thus indicating that an optimum was leaped over. We chose the growth factor $c^+ = 1.2$ and the shrink factor $c^- = 0.5$, which is a typical choice.

As a third approach one may carry out a root search on the gradient, for example, by applying the Newton–Raphson method to the gradient. In this case the parameter update rule is generally (note: no step width parameter η)

$$a^{(i+1)} = a^{(i)} - \left(\nabla_a^2 \, F_{L_\beta}(a; \mathbf{X}, y)|_{a^{(i)}} \right)^{-1} \cdot \left(\nabla_a \, F_{L_\beta}(a; \mathbf{X}, y)|_{a^{(i)}} \right).$$

For this we first compute the second derivative of the logistic function:

$$L''_\beta(z) = \frac{d}{dz} L'_\beta(z) = \frac{d}{dz} \left(\beta \cdot L_\beta(z) \cdot (1 - L_\beta(z)) \right)$$

$$= \beta^2 \cdot L_\beta(z) \cdot (1 - L_\beta(z)) \cdot (1 - 2L_\beta(z)),$$

With this result we compute the second derivative of the objective function as

$$\nabla_a^2 \, F_{L_\beta}(a; \mathbf{X}, \mathbf{y})$$

$$= \nabla_a \left(\sum_{i=1}^{n} \left(L_\beta'\big(g_-(a; x_i, y_i, \varepsilon)\big) - L_\beta'\big(g_+(a; x_i, y_i, \varepsilon)\big) \right) \cdot \nabla_a f_*(x_i; a) \right)$$

$$= \sum_{i=1}^{n} \Bigg(\left(L_\beta'\big(g_-(a; x_i, y_i, \varepsilon)\big) - L_\beta'\big(g_+(a; x_i, y_i, \varepsilon)\big) \right) \cdot \nabla_a^2 f_*(x_i; a)$$

$$+ \nabla_a \left(L_\beta'\big(g_-(a; x_i, y_i, \varepsilon)\big) - L_\beta'\big(g_+(a; x_i, y_i, \varepsilon)\big) \right) \cdot \big(\nabla_a f_*(x_i; a)\big)^\top \Bigg)$$

$$= \sum_{i=1}^{n} \Bigg(\left(L_\beta'\big(g_-(a; x_i, y_i, \varepsilon)\big) - L_\beta'\big(g_+(a; x_i, y_i, \varepsilon)\big) \right) \cdot \nabla_a^2 f_*(x_i; a)$$

$$+ \left(L_\beta''\big(g_-(a; x_i, y_i, \varepsilon)\big) - L_\beta''\big(g_+(a; x_i, y_i, \varepsilon)\big) \right) \cdot \nabla_a f_*(x_i; a) \cdot \big(\nabla_a f_*(x_i; a)\big)^\top \Bigg).$$

If we consider the special case $f_*(x, a) = a^\top x^*$, where it is $a = (a_0, a_1, \ldots, a_m)$ and $x^* = (1, x_1, \ldots, x_m)$ for $x = (x_1, \ldots, x_m)$, that is, a linear function, we get

$$\nabla_a^2 \, F_{L_\beta}(a; \mathbf{X}, \mathbf{y}) = \sum_{i=1}^{n} \left(L_\beta''\big(g_-(a; x_i, y_i, \varepsilon)\big) - L_\beta''\big(g_+(a; x_i, y_i, \varepsilon)\big) \right) \cdot x_i^* x_i^{*\top},$$

since $\nabla_a^2 \, a^\top x^* = \mathbf{0}$ where $\mathbf{0}$ is the null matrix. That is, the update rule reads

$$a^{(i+1)} = a^{(i)} - \left(\sum_{i=1}^{n} \left(L_\beta''\big(g_-(a; x_i, y_i, \varepsilon)\big) - L_\beta''\big(g_+(a; x_i, y_i, \varepsilon)\big) \right) \cdot x_i^* x_i^{*\top} \right)^{-1}$$

$$\cdot \left(\sum_{i=1}^{n} \left(L_\beta'\big(g_-(a; x_i, y_i, \varepsilon)\big) - L_\beta'\big(g_+(a; x_i, y_i, \varepsilon)\big) \right) \cdot x_i^* \right).$$

An alternative way of "smoothing" the Heaviside function is

$$R_\beta^\gamma(z) = \begin{cases} \frac{1}{2} e^{\beta z}, & \text{if } z < 0, \\ 1 - \frac{1}{2} e^{-\gamma z}, & \text{if } z \geq 0. \end{cases}$$

Here the flank of the Heaviside function is replaced by two exponential functions, where β and γ are steepness parameters. For $\beta, \gamma \to \infty$ we get $R_\beta^\gamma(z) \to H(z)$. The difference to $L_\beta(z)$ is that for $\beta \neq \gamma$ this function is not continuously differentiable at $z = 0$. However, as this is only a single point, this appears to be acceptable and seems to work in practice (see experiments below).

The underlying idea is to have a stronger gradient outside the "win region", and a smaller one inside it (except close to the boundaries), so that an improvement inside the "win region" (pushing the prediction closer to the center) for one point cannot easily compensate another point not being inside this region.

This alternative smoothing approach leads to the objective function

$$F_{R_\beta^\gamma}(a; \mathbf{X}, \mathbf{y}) = \sum_{i=1}^{n} \left(R_\beta^\gamma\big(g_-(a; x_i, y_i, \varepsilon)\big) + R_\beta^\gamma\big(-g_+(a; x_i, y_i, \varepsilon)\big) - 1 \right),$$

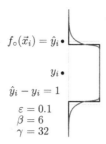

$$f_o(\vec{x}_i) = \hat{y}_i \bullet$$

$$y_i \bullet$$

$$\hat{y}_i - y_i = 1$$

$$\varepsilon = 0.1$$
$$\beta = 6$$
$$\gamma = 32$$

Fig. 3. The value y_i is the true output for input vector $\boldsymbol{x}_i$, while $\hat{y}_i$ is the output produced by the reference regression function, that is, $\hat{y}_i = f_o(\boldsymbol{x}_i)$. The black and red lines show the ith term of the original objective function $F_H(\boldsymbol{a}; \mathbf{X}, \boldsymbol{y})$ and the "smoothed" version $F_{R_\beta^\gamma}(\boldsymbol{a}; \mathbf{X}, \boldsymbol{y})$, respectively. The shape of the red curve relative to the black curve depends on the value of β, but *not* on the distance between $\hat{y}_i$ and y_i (which is set to 1 here for illustrative purposes). (Color figure online)

which is again to be maximized by choosing $\boldsymbol{a}$. Figure 3 provides an illustration of one term of the original and the smoothed objective function.

In order to conduct the optimization, we need the derivative of $R_\beta^\gamma(z)$, i.e.

$$R_\beta^{\gamma\prime}(z) = \frac{\mathrm{d}}{\mathrm{d}z} R_\beta^\gamma(z) = \begin{cases} \frac{\mathrm{d}}{\mathrm{d}z} \frac{1}{2} e^{\beta z} = \beta \frac{1}{2} e^{\beta z} = \beta R_\beta(z), & \text{if } z < 0, \\ \frac{\mathrm{d}}{\mathrm{d}z}(1 - \frac{1}{2} e^{-\gamma z}) = \gamma \frac{1}{2} e^{-\gamma z} = \gamma(1 - R_\beta^\gamma(z)), & \text{if } z \geq 0, \end{cases}$$

if we use the right hand derivative ($\neq$ left hand derivative) at $z = 0$. We obtain

$$\boldsymbol{\nabla}_{\boldsymbol{a}} F_{R_\beta^\gamma}(\boldsymbol{a}; \mathbf{X}, \boldsymbol{y})$$

$$= \boldsymbol{\nabla}_{\boldsymbol{a}} \sum_{i=1}^n \left(R_\beta^\gamma(g_-(\boldsymbol{a}; \boldsymbol{x}_i, y_i, \varepsilon)) + R_\beta^\gamma(-g_+(\boldsymbol{a}; \boldsymbol{x}_i, y_i, \varepsilon)) - 1 \right)$$

$$= \sum_{i=1}^n \left(\boldsymbol{\nabla}_{\boldsymbol{a}} R_\beta^\gamma(g_-(\boldsymbol{a}; \boldsymbol{x}_i, y_i, \varepsilon)) + \boldsymbol{\nabla}_{\boldsymbol{a}} R_\beta^\gamma(-g_+(\boldsymbol{a}; \boldsymbol{x}_i, y_i, \varepsilon)) - \boldsymbol{\nabla}_{\boldsymbol{a}} 1 \right)$$

$$= \sum_{i=1}^n \left(R_\beta^{\gamma\prime}(g_-(\boldsymbol{a}; \boldsymbol{x}_i, y_i, \varepsilon)) - R_\beta^{\gamma\prime}(-g_+(\boldsymbol{a}; \boldsymbol{x}_i, y_i, \varepsilon)) \right) \cdot \boldsymbol{\nabla}_{\boldsymbol{a}} f_*(\boldsymbol{x}_i; \boldsymbol{a}).$$

For a Newton-Raphson approach we also need the second derivative of $R_\beta(z)$:

$$R_\beta^{\gamma\prime\prime}(z) = \frac{\mathrm{d}}{\mathrm{d}z} R_\beta^{\gamma\prime}(z) = \begin{cases} \frac{\mathrm{d}}{\mathrm{d}z} \beta \frac{1}{2} e^{\beta z} = \beta^2 \frac{1}{2} e^{\beta z} = \beta^2 R_\beta(z), & \text{if } z < 0, \\ \frac{\mathrm{d}}{\mathrm{d}z} \gamma \frac{1}{2} e^{-\gamma z} = -\gamma^2 \frac{1}{2} e^{-\gamma z}, = \gamma^2(R_\beta^\gamma(z) - 1), & \text{if } z \geq 0. \end{cases}$$

Again we use the right hand side derivative at $z = 0$, where the derivative $R'_\beta(z)$ itself is not even continuous. For the objective function this leads to

$$
\nabla_a^2 F_{R_\beta}(\boldsymbol{a}; \mathbf{X}, \boldsymbol{y})
$$

$$
= \nabla_a \left(\sum_{i=1}^{n} \left(R'_\beta\big(g_-(\boldsymbol{a}; \boldsymbol{x}_i, y_i, \varepsilon)\big) - R'_\beta\big(-g_+(\boldsymbol{a}; \boldsymbol{x}_i, y_i, \varepsilon)\big) \right) \cdot \nabla_a f_*(\boldsymbol{x}_i; \boldsymbol{a}) \right)
$$

$$
= \sum_{i=1}^{n} \left(\quad \left(R'_\beta\big(g_-(\boldsymbol{a}; \boldsymbol{x}_i, y_i, \varepsilon)\big) - R'_\beta\big(-g_+(\boldsymbol{a}; \boldsymbol{x}_i, y_i, \varepsilon)\big) \right) \cdot \nabla_a^2 f_*(\boldsymbol{x}_i; \boldsymbol{a}) \right.
$$

$$
\left. + \nabla_a \left(R'_\beta\big(g_-(\boldsymbol{a}; \boldsymbol{x}_i, y_i, \varepsilon)\big) - R'_\beta\big(-g_+(\boldsymbol{a}; \boldsymbol{x}_i, y_i, \varepsilon)\big) \right) \cdot \big(\nabla_a f_*(\boldsymbol{x}_i; \boldsymbol{a})\big)^\top \right)
$$

$$
= \sum_{i=1}^{n} \left(\left(R'_\beta\big(g_-(\boldsymbol{a}; \boldsymbol{x}_i, y_i, \varepsilon)\big) - R'_\beta\big(-g_+(\boldsymbol{a}; \boldsymbol{x}_i, y_i, \varepsilon)\big) \right) \cdot \nabla_a^2 f_*(\boldsymbol{x}_i; \boldsymbol{a}) \right.
$$

$$
\left. + \left(R''_\beta\big(g_-(\boldsymbol{a}; \boldsymbol{x}_i, y_i, \varepsilon)\big) + R''_\beta\big(-g_+(\boldsymbol{a}; \boldsymbol{x}_i, y_i, \varepsilon)\big) \right) \cdot \nabla_a f_*(\boldsymbol{x}_i; \boldsymbol{a}) \cdot \big(\nabla_a f_*(\boldsymbol{x}_i; \boldsymbol{a})\big)^\top \right).
$$

If we consider the special case $f_*(\boldsymbol{x}, \boldsymbol{a}) = \boldsymbol{a}^\top \boldsymbol{x}^*$, where it is $\boldsymbol{a} = (a_0, a_1, \ldots, a_m)$ and $\boldsymbol{x}^* = (1, x_1, \ldots, x_m)$ for $\boldsymbol{x} = (x_1, \ldots, x_m)$, that is, a linear function, we get

$$
\nabla_a^2 F_{R_\beta}(\boldsymbol{a}; \mathbf{X}, \boldsymbol{y}) = \sum_{i=1}^{n} \left(R''_\beta\big(g_-(\boldsymbol{a}; \boldsymbol{x}_i, y_i, \varepsilon)\big) + R''_\beta\big(-g_+(\boldsymbol{a}; \boldsymbol{x}_i, y_i, \varepsilon)\big) \right) \cdot \boldsymbol{x}_i^* \boldsymbol{x}_i^{*\top},
$$

since $\nabla_a^2 \, \boldsymbol{a}^\top \boldsymbol{x}^* = \mathbf{0}$ where $\mathbf{0}$ is the null matrix.

5   Experiments

We implemented our gradient ascent approach in both Python and C, but used only the C implementation for the experiments (due to its much shorter execution time).[1] We implemented both "smoothed" versions of the objective function that are described in the preceding section, using a minimum prediction improvements $\varepsilon \in \{0.001, 0.01, 0.1\}$ and steepnesses $\beta \in \{1, 3, 6, 10\}$ and $\gamma = 32$.

We confined ourselves to a very simple univariate linear regression with the model $y = x + \epsilon$, where ϵ is a noise (or error) term. Although our approach is, in principle, applicable to multivariate and non-linear regression, our focus was more on understanding how different types of noise (or error) distributions affect the regression performance, for which univariate linear regression appears sufficient. Note that in [2] no systematic investigation is conducted with the help of simulated data. Hence that paper does not provide any information about the influence of different types of noise (or error) distributions.

We drew the x-values of all data samples (with $n \in \{20, 50, 100\}$ data points) from either a uniform or a normal distribution (Fig. 4 top left; both have a standard deviation of 2) and the noise ϵ from either a uniform, a normal, a Laplace, or a Cauchy distribution, or computed it as a product of two or three samples from a normal distribution (Fig. 4 bottom). All distributions were parameterized

---

[1] These implementations are publicly available at www.borgelt.net/brreg.html.

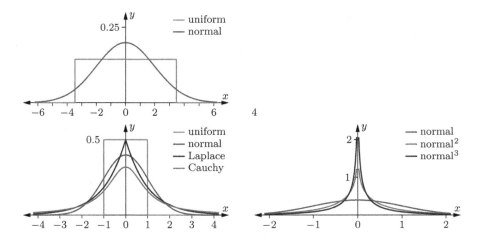

Fig. 4. The distributions from which the x-values were sampled (left diagram) and the distributions from which the error ϵ was sampled (bottom diagrams). The distributions normal^2 and normal^3 are obtained by multiplying two or three samples, resp., from a normal distribution.

with a dispersion parameter of 1. Note that a Cauchy distribution has no finite variance (its dispersion parameter is half the interquartile range), which is why it is often used to model extremal events [3].

Since we use a simple linear model as the ground truth to sample from, it is natural to use ordinary least squares (OLS) linear regression as the reference. As a baseline for comparisons we chose robust linear regression based on M-estimators [7,8] using Tukey's bisquare (or biweights) function [1] for the error weights, since it is geared towards providing better parameter estimates for heavy-tailed noise distributions, which is what we wanted to investigate.

As a baseline for the optimization, we used a bootstrap sampling scheme, in which 1000 bootstrap samples were drawn from the given data, an OLS regression computed for each, and the one that "won" the most data points compared to OLS regression on all data points chosen as the result. The advantage of such a scheme is that it can also be applied for the original (non-smoothed) objective function F_H. Furthermore we used standard gradient ascent and resilient backpropagation with a(n initial) step with of $\eta = 0.001$, growth factor $c^+ = 1.2$ and shrink factor $c^- = 0.5$; and the Newton-Raphson method. All optimization methods were executed for 200 iterations and final parameters returned.

A selection of experimental results is shown in Figs. 5 to 7, all of which are computed from 10 000 runs. For a comparison of the different objective functions and optimization approaches, we chose data with 20 data points, x-values drawn from a uniform distribution and noise computed as the product of two samples from a uniform distribution. Figures 5 and 6 show the win rate, that is, the percentage of sets of unseen data on which the objective function/method pair indicated at the top right of each diagram performed better than OLS regression,

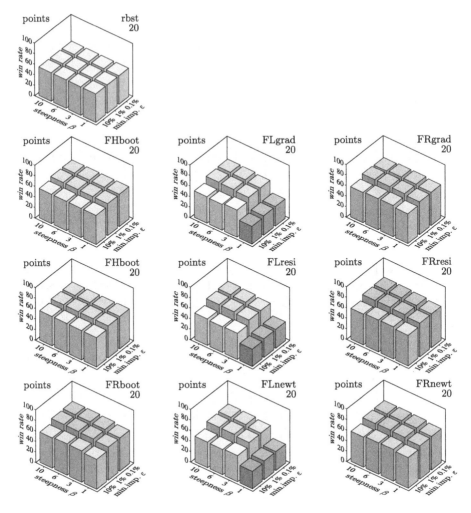

Fig. 5. Better prediction win rate on test data relative to ordinary least squares regression for 20 data points (x-values drawn from a uniform distribution, error is the product of two samples from a normal distribution). Left: classical robust regression, below: our approaches to best response regression ("FH", "FL", "FR": objective function; "boot", "grad", "resi", "newt": optimization method).

that is, won more points in Fig. 5 or provided a lower sum of squared errors (SSE) in Fig. 6. Note that in the diagram at the top left (robust regression) all bars have the same height (for easier comparison) as the parameters have no influence. Note that Best Response Regression, at least with proper parameters, outperforms robust regression, especially with objective function F_R. Objective function F_L works slightly less well and requires a large steepness β.

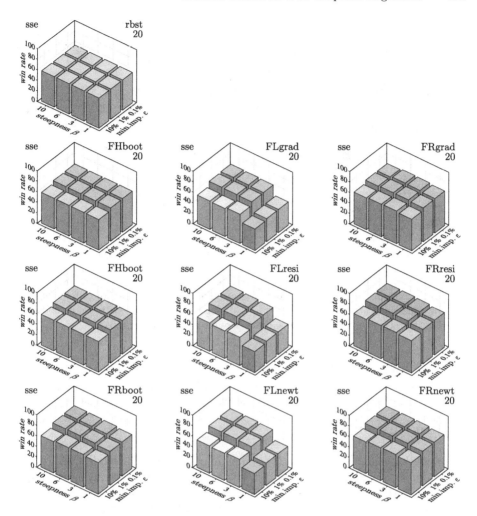

Fig. 6. Sum of squared errors win rate on test data relative to ordinary least squares regression for 20 data points (x-values drawn from a uniform distribution, error is the product of two samples from a normal distribution). Left: classical robust regression, below: our approaches to best response regression ("FH", "FL", "FR": objective function; "boot", "grad", "resi", "newt": optimization method).

Figure 7 shows the performance of best response regression for different noise distributions. For uniform noise and normally distributed noise, ordinary least squares (OLS) is clearly superior to best response regression, but for Laplace-distributed noise it can just edge out OLS (provided the required minimum prediction improvement ε is small). However, for noise computed as a product of two or three samples from a normal distribution and particularly for Cauchy-distributed noise, Best Response Regression clearly has the upper hand. As the

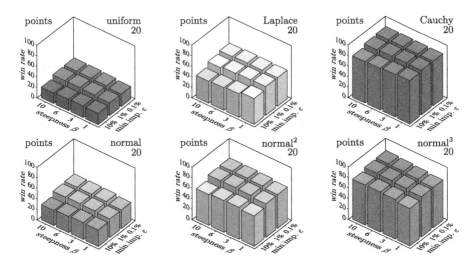

Fig. 7. Better prediction win rate on test data relative to ordinary least squares regression for 20 data points (x-values drawn from a uniform distribution) for different error distributions (indicated on top right, "normal²" and "normal³" refer to an error computed as a product of two or three samples from a normal distribution).

full result diagrams[2] show, Best Response Regression can, for these distributions, usually also beat robust regression, although not always by a wide margin.

6 Conclusions

In our work we limited experiments and simulations to linear models. However, our gradient ascent approach for best response regression contains no assumptions about the regression function. In principle, our approach also works for, e.g., polynomial or logistic regression functions, which is an improvement over [2]. Our simulations show that best response regression is a very promising approach to optimize classical regression models. Moreover, our gradient ascent approach does not require any distribution assumptions for the error terms or the explanatory variables and therefore, our approach is less restrictive than classical regression models. Obviously, if there is a very strong linear dependence between the explanatory and target variables, it is very difficult for the best response regression to beat the "expert" (classical regression model, reference function). The other way round, if the "expert" performs badly, best response regression has far more potential to maximize the probability to predict better than the expert. In addition, best response regression has a clear advantage on small sample size data sets. Our experiments showed as a rule of thumb $n < 50$. With larger sample sizes, classical statistical methods have a greater advantage

---

[2] All result diagrams are available at www.borgelt.net/docs/brreg.pdf.

due to the underlying asymptotic results. Nevertheless, we would like to emphasize that with this work we could show that well known regression tasks, such as linear regression, can be reinterpreted. Ben-Porat and Tennenholtz motivated Best Response Regression as a game between an expert and an agent. In some way, we can interpret our new approach as optimizing linear regression predictions.

Acknowledgments. The second author gratefully acknowledges the financial support from Land Salzburg within the WISS 2025 project IDA-Lab (20102-F1901166-KZP and 20204-WISS/225/197-2019).

References

1. Beaton, A.E., Tukey, J.W.: The fitting of power series, meaning polynomials, illustrated on band-spectroscopic data. Technometrics **16**, 147–185. American Society for Quality and the American Statistical Association, Milwaukee, WI and Boston, MA, USA (1974)
2. Ben-Porat, O., Tennenholtz, M.: Best response regression. In: Advances in Neural Information Processing Systems 30 (NIPS 2017, Long Beach, CA), Curran Associates, Red Hook, NY, USA pp. 1499–1508 (2017)
3. Embrechts, P., Klüppelberg, C., Mikosch, T.: Modelling Extremal Events: For Insurance and Finance. Springer Science & Business Media, Berlin, Germany (2013)
4. Dozat, T.: Incorporating nesterov momentum into adam. In: Proceedings International Conference on Learning Representations (ICLR Workshop 2016, San Juan, Puerto Rico). openreview.net (2016)
5. Duchi, J., Hazan, E., Singer, Y.: Adaptive subgradient methods for online learning and stochastic optimization. J. Mach. Learn. Res. **12**, 2121–2159. Microtome Publishing, Brookline, MA, USA (2011)
6. Fahlman, S.E.: An Empirical Study of Learning Speed in Backpropagation Networks. Proceedings of the Connectionist Models Summer School (Carnegie Mellon University). Morgan Kaufman, San Mateo, CA, USA (1988)
7. Huber, P.J.: Robust estimation of a location parameter. In: Kotz, S., Johnson, N.L. (eds.) Breakthroughs in Statistics. Springer Series in Statistics (Perspectives in Statistics). Springer, New York, NY (1992). https://doi.org/10.1007/978-1-4612-4380-9_35
8. Huber, P.J.: Robust Statistics. J. Wiley & Sons, New York, NY, USA (1981)
9. D.P. Kingma and J. Ba. Adam: A method for stochastic optimization. In: Proceedings International Conference on Learning Representations (ICLR 2015, San Diego, CA). openreview.net (2015)
10. Nesterov, Y.E.: A method of solving a convex programming problem with convergence rate $O(1/k^2)$. Soviet Math. Doklady **27**(2), 372–376 (1983)
11. Polyak, B.T.: Some methods of speeding up the convergence of iteration methods. USSR Comput. Math. Math. Phys. **4**(5), 1–17 (1964)
12. Riedmiller, M., Braun, H.: Rprop-a fast adaptive learning algorithm. Technical Report, University of Karlsruhe, Karlsruhe, Germany (1992)
13. Riedmiller, M., Braun, H.: A direct adaptive method for faster backpropagation learning: the RPROP algorithm. In: International Conference on Neural Networks (ICNN-93, San Francisco, CA), pp. 586–591. IEEE (1993)

14. Tieleman, T., Hinton, G.: Lecture 6.5-RMSPROP: divide the gradient by a running average of its recent magnitude. COURSERA: Neural Netw. Mach. Learn. **4**(2), 26–31 (2012)
15. Tollenaere, T.: SuperSAB: Fast adaptive back propagation with good scaling properties. Neural Netw. **3**(5), 561–573 (1990)
16. Zeiler, M.D.: AdaDelta: an adaptive learning rate method. arXiv:1212.5701 (2012)

Intelligent Structural Damage Detection: A Federated Learning Approach

Ali Anaissi[1][⊠] , Basem Suleiman[1] , and Mohamad Naji[2]

[1] School of Computer Science, The University of Sydney, Sydney, Australia
ali.anaissi@sydney.edu.au
[2] School of Computer Science, University of Technology Sydney, Ultimo, Australia

Abstract. Data-driven machine learning models, compared to numerical models, shown promising improvements in detecting damage in Structural Health Monitoring (SHM) applications. In data-driven approaches, sensors' data are used to train a model either in a centralized server or locally inside each sensor unit node (decentralized model similar to edge computing). The centralize learning model suffers from issues including wireless transmission costs and data sensitive data vulnerability. The decentralized model also poses different challenges such as feature correlations and relationships loss in decentralized learning. To handle the shortcomings of both models, we proposes a new Federated Learning model augmented with tensor data fusion to detect damage in SHM. Our approach enables the central machine learning model to gain experience from diverse datasets located at different sensor locations. It also trains a shared centralized machine learning model using datasets stored and distributed across multiple sensor nodes. Our experimental results on real structural datasets demonstrate promising damage detection accuracy without the need to transmit the actual data to the centralized learning model. It also shows that the data correlations and relationship from all participating sensors are preserved.

Keywords: Federated learning · Stochastic gradient descent · Structural Health Monitoring · Damage detection · Tensor · Data fusion

1 Introduction

There has been an exponential growth of data generated from sensors and computing devices connected to the Internet known as the Internet of Things (IoT). The IoT has penetrated pervasively into most aspects of human life everywhere such as civil infrastructures, health-care centres, transportation, etc., wherein smart services are utilized to continuously monitor every activity at all times and in real-time. In the field of civil infrastructures, IoT has provided flexibility and added value to Structural Health Monitoring (SHM) applications to generate actionable insights.

© Springer Nature Switzerland AG 2021
P. H. Abreu et al. (Eds.): IDA 2021, LNCS 12695, pp. 155–170, 2021.
https://doi.org/10.1007/978-3-030-74251-5_13

The aim of SHM applications is to provide an automated process for damage detection in complex structures such as bridges using sensing data collected through multiple networked sensors attached to it [9]. This data is then utilized to gain insight into the health of a structure and make timely and economic decisions about its maintenance. One of the traditional approaches for structural damage detection is known as model-driven which constructs a numerical model for the structure based on finite element analysis [8]. However, a numerical model can be impractical as it cannot always sensibly capture the behavior of the real structure. On the other hand, a modern technique known as the data-driven approach has been successfully adopted in SHM and its applications. The data-driven approach uses machine learning algorithms to construct a model from measured data and then makes predictions for new measured responses to detect structural damage. This approach has brought a concrete aspect to IoT in SHM and enabled IoT smart applications. In fact, bridges are critical to our society as they connect various separated locations to allow the flows of people and goods within cities. Bridges are influenced by several factors such as environmental conditions (wind, ambient temperature change,.. etc.) and various loads (constant and temporary loads), which makes them prone to damage and potential failures. Any problem with such a structure from small damage to catastrophic failures would result in significant economic and life losses. Most of the structural maintenance approaches are time-based, visual inspections are carried out at a predefined regular schedule which can be either too early or too late to detect damage. However, SHM is a condition-based approach; it uses data sensed continuously to provide real-time monitoring so that necessary maintenance actions can be taken once damage, or abnormal change in the structure behaviour, occur.

There are two data-driven mechanisms that have been commonly known for damage detection in complex structures. The first mechanism relies on a centralized machine learning model which requires transmitting the generated sensing data from the deployed sensors to a central processing unit to assess the structural condition. The data then is either aggregated or fused in one data structure to capture the correlation and relations between the measured variables from all sensors, and to learn the different aspects of the data (temporal, spatial, and feature) at the same time [1, 2]. This mechanism allows capturing the underlying structural aspects using multi-way sensing data which has made it successful as it achieved good accuracy in terms of damage detection. However, the use of such a centralized model has its drawbacks, especially for SHM. It is not practical in the context of real-time monitoring and resource-constrained environment since sensors collect vibration measurements using accelerometers at high frequency during a time period, thus, contain a sequence of thousands of data points to be transmitted very frequently to the central model. Moreover, wireless transmission costs more energy than local processing, thus poses several challenges for battery-powered wireless nodes.

The alternative mechanism to handle the centralized model restrictions is to perform the learning from the sensed data in a distributed environment similar to the promising edge or distributed computing paradigms [18]. The distributed learning approach has a number of benefits including reducing the intensive data transmission over the network, conserving the energy of sensor nodes and, reducing the workload overhead on the central server on which data processing (learning) occurs. One challenge that emerges with the distributed learning approach is that the measured data in SHM are often multi-way and highly redundant and correlated, i.e., many sensors at different locations simultaneously collect data over time. Therefore, a single sensor node analysis cannot capture all of these correlations and relationships together in a distributed learning model. In contrast, the centralized learning analysis allows learning from such data in multiple modes at the same time. The work proposed by Mehri *et al.*[18] has thoroughly investigated and compared the performance of the centralized prediction models versus a single sensor node model (decentralized) prediction. Their experimental results show that the centralized model was able to successfully detect the presence of very small damage in a structure and to monitor its progress over time. On the other hand, the distributed learning models which were constructed for each sensor not only reduced the sensitivity of the models but also failed to monitor the progress of damage in the monitored structure.

Therefore, developing an effective and efficient damage detection model for SHM applications requires information derived from many spatially-distributed locations throughout large infrastructure covering various points in the monitored structure. However, consolidating this data in a centralized learning model can often be computationally complex and costly. This motivates for developing a more advanced model that utilizes the centralized learning model but without the need to transmit the frequently measured data to a single processing unit. In this study, we propose a novel approach to overcome the above-discussed challenges of centralized and decentralized learning mechanisms in SHM. Our approach is developed based on Federated Learning augmented with Tensor Data Fusion for damage detection in complex structures such as bridges. Our approach is derived from an auto-encoder neural network (ANN) as a damage detection model and employs tensor data analysis to perform data fusion for a wired connected sensor in SHM applications to reduce the communications in the FL network. The emerging Federated Learning (FL) concept was initially proposed by Google for improving security and preventing data leakages in distributed environments [16]. FL allows the central machine learning model to build its learning from a broad range of data sets located at different locations. It aims to train a shared centralized machine learning model using datasets stored and distributed across multiple devices or sensors. In the context of our study, we devise an FL-approach that enables multiple IoT devices (sensors) to collaborate on the development of a central learning model, but without needing to directly share or pool all data measured from several sensors with each other. Our approach can work efficiently and effectively by sharing the model coefficients of each client model only rather than the whole data collected by all participating sensors at each period of time. The effectiveness of the model learning continues to improve over the course of several training iterations during which the shared models get exposed to a significantly wider range of data than what any single sensor node possesses in-house.

2   Background

2.1   Autoencoder Deep Neural Network

Autoencoder neural network (ANN) is an unsupervised learning process which has the ability to learn from one class data. It is an extension of the traditional neural network which basically designed for supervised learning when the class labels are given with the training examples. The rational idea of an autoencoder is to force the network to learn a lower dimensional space for the input features, and then try to reconstruct the original feature space. In other words it sits the target values to be approximately equal to its original inputs. In this sense, the main objective of autoencoders is to learn reproducing input vectors $\{x_1, x_2, x_3, \ldots, x_v\}$ as outputs $\{\hat{x}_1, \hat{x}_2, \hat{x}_3, \ldots, \hat{x}_v\}$. The architecture of ANN is made up of L layers ($L = 3$ for simplification) denoted by input, hidden and output layers. Each layer consists from a set of nodes. Layer l_1 is the input layer represents features which encoded into the hidden layer l_2, and then decoded into the output layer l_3. The learning process of ANN starts by successively computing the output of each node in the network. For a node i in layer l it calculates the output value $z_i^{(l)}$ by computing the total weighted sum of the input values which also includes the bias term using the following equation:

$$z_i^{(l)} = \sum_{j=1}^{n} w_{ij}^{(l-1)} a_j^{(l-1)} \tag{1}$$

where w is the coefficient weight written as w_{ij} when associated with the connection between node j in layer $l - 1$, and node i in layer l, and $a_j^{(l-1)}$ is the output value of node j in layer $l - 1$. The resultant output is then processed through an activation function denoted by $a_i^{(l)}$, and it is defined as follows:

$$a_i^{(l)} = f(z_i^{(l)}) \tag{2}$$

where $f()$ is the activation functions. The most common activation functions in the hidden layers are sigmoid and hyperbolic tangent. However, in autoencoder settings a linear function is used in the output layer since we don't scale the output of the network to a specific interval.

The autoencoder uses back propagation algorithm to learn the parameters $h_w(x) \approx x$. In each iteration of the training process, we calculate the cost error $\mathcal{L}(w_{ij}^{(l)}; x)$ using Eq. 3 and then propagate it backward to the network layer.

$$\mathcal{L}(w_{ij}^{(l)}; x) = \frac{1}{v} \sum_{i=1}^{v} \left(\frac{1}{2} \|x^i - \hat{x}^i\|^2 \right) \tag{3}$$

In this setting, we perform a stochastic gradient descent step to update the learning parameters $w_{ij}^{(l)}$. This is done by computing the partial derivative of the cost function $\mathcal{L}(w_{ij}^{(l)}; x)$ (defined in Eq. 3) as follows:

$$w_{ij}^{(l)} := w_{ij}^{(l)} - \alpha \frac{\partial}{\partial w_{ij}^{(l)}} \mathcal{L}(w_{ij}^{(l)}; x) \tag{4}$$

The complete steps are summarized in Algorithm 1.

Algorithm 1. Autoencoder training algorithm

Require: A set of n positive samples $X = \{x^{(i)}\}_{i=1}^{n}$
Ensure: Initialize w_{ij}^{l} to a small random value $\mathcal{N}(0, \epsilon^2)$
   while not converged **do**
      for $i \leftarrow 1$ to n **do**
         Perform a feedforward pass to compute all nodes activations using Eqs. 1 and 2.
         Compute the cost function $\mathcal{L}(w_{ij}^{l}; x_i)$ using Eq. 3
         Update w_{ij}^{l} using Eq. 4
      end for
   end while
   return w_{ij}^{l}

Once we successfully trained the autoencoder, the network will be able to reconstruct an new incoming positive data, while it fails with anomalous data. This will be judged based on the reconstruction error (RE) which is measured by applying the Euclidean norm to the difference between the input and output nodes as shown in Eq. 5.

$$RE(x) = \|x^i - \hat{x}^i\|^2 \tag{5}$$

The measured value of RE is used as anomaly score for a given new sample. Intuitively, examples from the similar distribution to the training data should have low reconstruction error, whereas anomalies should have high anomaly score.

3   Federated Learning Augmented with Tensor Data Fusion for SHM

3.1   Data Structure

Consider a set of n sensor nodes mounted on different locations of a bridge to measure and transmit sensing data related to a structural event. Each sensor node $\mathcal{S}$ can perform computation on sensed acceleration data to detect the damage in their vicinity. The data points collected concerning to the vibration responses are assumed to be a vector as $X_i = [x_1, x_2, \ldots, x_k]$; where $i = 1, \ldots, s$ are the sensor nodes, and k is the total number of data points sensed by a sensor node S over a time duration. Due to the lack of available data from the damaged state of the structure in most cases, the acceleration measurements we collect from a bridge is often corresponding to the healthy condition of the bridge. This data covers various environmental and ambient conditions as well as operational conditions, such as traffic loading. Therefore, in the training phase, we construct a one-class model by extracting the statistical features from raw acceleration data in the healthy condition of the bridge. The trained model will be used later to classify the raw acceleration measurement from unknown conditions of the bridge as either healthy or damaged. Each healthy training sample $\{x_i\}_{i=1}^k \in \{X_i\}_{i=1}^n$ is an m-dimensional feature vector $V^v = v^1, v^2, \ldots, v^j$, where $v = 1, \ldots, j$ are the statistical features extracted from sensed acceleration data in healthy condition of the bridge. The total number of features j depends on the sampling frequency and sampling window, and the total number of data points (k) in X_i depends on the number of events. In our approach, we use an auto-encoder neural network as an anomaly detection method to fit a one-class model using healthy data. However, we need now to formulate this model in a FL setting with the help of tensor data analysis.

3.2   Problem Formulation in Federated Learning

In FL setting, a set of S clients (sensors) each of which has access to its local data, but they are connected to a central server to solve the following problem:

$$\min_{w \in \mathbb{R}^d} f(w) := \frac{1}{n} \sum_{i=1}^n f_i(w) \tag{6}$$

where f_i is the loss function corresponding to a sensor node client S which defined as follows:

$$f(w) := \mathbb{E}\mathcal{L}_i(w; x_i)] \tag{7}$$

where $\mathcal{L}_i(w; x_i)$ measures the error of model w given the input x_i defined in Eq. 3.

The stochastic gradient descent (SGD) method solves the above problem defined in Eq. 7 by repeatedly updates w to minimize $\mathcal{L}(w; x_i)$. It starts with some initial value of $w^{(t)}$ and then repeatedly performs the update as follows:

$$w^{(t+1)} := w^{(t)} + \eta \frac{\partial \mathcal{L}}{\partial w}(x_i^{(t)}, w^{(t)}) \tag{8}$$

In FL, each client performs a number of E epochs at each round to compute the gradient of the loss over its local data and send the model parameters w_i^{t+1} to the server. The central sever aggregates these gradients and applies the global model parameters update by taking the average of the resulting models parameters as follows:

$$w^{(t+1)} := \frac{1}{n} \sum_{i=1}^{n} w_i^{(t+1)};$$ (9)

3.3   Tensor Data Fusion

Our proposed approach also incorporates a data fusion step which merges data from a set of connected sensor nodes $\mathcal{S}$ into one client node. A naive approach would simply concatenate the features obtained from different connected clients. However, unfolding the multi-way data and analyzing them using two-way methods may result in information loss and misinterpretation since it breaks the modular structure inherent in the data. Therefore, we present a method for data fusion using a tensor data structure which arranges the data from a set of connected sensor nodes as one single client node $\mathcal{T}$ we call it a tensor node. This tensor node $\mathcal{T}$ has data in a form of a three-way tensor $\mathcal{X} \in \mathbb{R}^{I \times J \times K}$ where I represents the number of connected clients, J represents the number of features in each client, and K is the total number of data points sensed by a sensor node $\mathcal{S}$. The structure of this tensor is shown in Fig. 1 Once we arrange the data in a tensor form, we apply a tensor decomposition to extract latent information in each dimension of tensor $\mathcal{X}$. This work adopts the CP decomposition (CANDE-COMP/PARAFAC decomposition) method for tensor decomposition due to its ease of interpretation compared with the Tucker method [15].

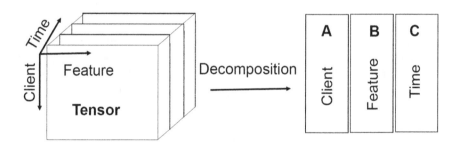

Fig. 1. Connected clients fused in a tensor.

CP decomposes $\mathcal{X} \in \mathbb{R}^{I \times J \times K}$ into three matrices $A \in \mathbb{R}^{I \times R}$, $B \in \Re^{J \times R}$ and $C \in \Re^{K \times R}$ where R is the latent factors. Each matrix represents latent information for each mode or dimension. It can be written as follows:

$$\mathcal{X}_{(ijk)} \approx \sum_{r=1}^{R} A_{ir} \circ B_{jr} \circ C_{kr}$$ (10)

where "$\circ$" is a vector outer product.

We formulate the problem as follows:

$$\min_{A,B,C} \left\| \mathcal{X} - \sum_{r=1}^{R} \lambda_r \ A_r \circ B_r \circ C_r \right\|_f^2, \tag{11}$$

where $\|\mathcal{X}\|_f^2$ is the norm value which is the sum squares of all elements of $\mathcal{X}$, and the subscript f denotes the Frobenius norm. A_r, B_r and C_r are r-th columns of component matrices $A \in \mathbb{R}^{I \times R}$, $B \in \mathbb{R}^{J \times R}$ and $C \in \mathbb{R}^{K \times R}$.

We applied the alternating least square (ALS) technique to solve the CP decomposition problem. It iteratively solves each factor matrix by fixing the other two matrices using a least-square technique until it meets a convergence criterion [3]. The ALS technique is described in Algorithm 2. Once the conver-

---

Algorithm 2. CP Decomposition Using Alternating Least Squares

Require: : Tensor $\mathcal{X} \in \mathbb{R}^{I \times J \times K}$, latent factors R
Ensure: : Initialize A, B, C
   repeat
      $A \leftarrow \arg\min_{A} \frac{1}{2} \|X_{(1)} - A(C \odot B)^T\|^2$
      $B \leftarrow \arg\min_{B} \frac{1}{2} \|X_{(2)} - B(C \odot A)^T\|^2$
      $C \leftarrow \arg\min_{C} \frac{1}{2} \|X_{(3)} - C(B \odot A)^T\|^2$
      $\rightarrow \odot$ *is the Khatri-Rao product and* $X_{(i)}$ *is an unfolding matrix of*
   $\mathcal{X}$ *in mode i*
   until convergence criterion is met
   return Matrices $A \in \mathbb{R}^{I \times R}$, $B \in \mathbb{R}^{J \times R}$, and $C \in \mathbb{R}^{K \times R}$

---

gence criteria are met, the ALS algorithm returns the three matrices A, B and C. As mentioned before, the matrix $C \in \Re^{K \times R}$, which is associated with the time mode, will be used later for constructing the central model. This matrix has K rows, each of which represents a data instance aggregated from all the clients given in a tensor node $\mathcal{T}$ at a specific time.

3.4   The Client-Server Learning Phase

Based on the FL problem formulation and tensor data fusion described above, we present our structural damage detection approach. Our method uses the FL approach which is augmented with a tensor data fusion method, and an auto-encoder neural network model for structural damage detection. Each tensor node $\mathcal{T}$ on the client-side will initially fuse the sensors data in a tensor $\mathcal{X}$ and apply CP algorithm using ALS to decompose $\mathcal{X}$ into three matrices A, B, and C. The matrix C, which represents the time mode, will be then used in the learning process. Our auto-encoder neural network uses the stochastic gradient descent algorithm to learn reconstructions $\hat{C}$ that is close to its original input C. At each round, each client $\mathcal{T}$ performs a number of E epochs to update the model

---

Algorithm 3. Client Side Learning

Require: I, E, η, R and $X_{i=1}^I \in \mathbb{R}^{K \times J}$
Ensure: Initialize A, B, C and $\mathcal{X} \in \mathbb{R}^{I \times J \times K}$
    for $i \leftarrow 1$ to I **do**
        Append $X_i \in \mathbb{R}^{K \times J}$ to $\mathcal{X} \in \mathbb{R}^{I \times J \times K}$
    end for
    Compute A, B, and C using Algorithm 2
    for $i \leftarrow 1$ to E **do**
        Compute $\hat{C}$ using Equations 1 and 2.

$$\mathcal{L}(w_{ij}^{(l)}; x) = \frac{1}{v} \sum_{i=1}^v \left(\frac{1}{2} \| x^i - \hat{x}^i \|^2 \right)$$

$$w^{(t+1)} := w^{(t)} + \eta \frac{\partial \mathcal{L}}{\partial w} (x_i^{(t)}, w^{(t)})$$

    end for
    return $w^{(t+1)}$

---

parameters and report them to the central server. Algorithm 3 explains the learning phase at given a tensor node $\mathcal{T}$.

Each client with a tensor node $\mathcal{T}$ will report the model parameters $w^{(t+1)}$ back to the central server. Once the updates are received, the central server will aggregate them using Eq. 9 and send them back to all client tensor nodes $\mathcal{T}$. Algorithm 4 explains the learning phase at the central server.

Algorithm 4. Server side learning

Require: K number of client nodes $\mathcal{T}$
Ensure: Initialize w
    while not converged **do**
        for $i \leftarrow 1$ to K **in parallel do**
            Compute $w_i^{(t+1)}$ using Algorithm 3
        end for
        $w^{(t+1)} := \frac{1}{n} \sum_{i=1}^n w_i^{(t+1)}$;
    end while
    return w

---

4 Related Work

Federated learning has earned a lot of interests in recent years and has attracted many researchers working in the area of machine learning [13,22]. Numerous practical application has been found to be well suited to the FL setting where data needs to be decentralized and privacy to be preserved. However, few applications have been reported in the literature found to employ the FL approach in constructing a global model. For instance, Bonawitz et al. [12] follow the FL setting to develop a system to solve the problem of next-word-prediction in mobile devices. On the other hand, several papers are still addressing the challenges of training a central model that will work well for all local data especially when the distribution of data across clients is highly non-IID (independent and identically distributed). In fact, Hanzely et al. [11] claim that a central model is still too far mature from the typical usage of a client. Similarly, Kairouz *et al.* [13] discuss the broad challenges and open problems in the field of FL. In this sense, McMahan *et al.* [19] propose the first FL algorithm named FedAvg. It uses the local SGD updates to build a global model by taking average model coefficients from a subset of clients with non-IID data. Subsequently, Guha *et al.* [10] propose a new method to learn a global model in one single round of communication between the client and the central model. Other related work in [7,20] address the limitations on communications in a FL setting by performing periodic averaging, partial device participation, and quantized message-passing, while [17,21,23] suggest multiple local optimization rounds before reporting to the server. In this paper, we address the limitations of communications by using tensor as a data fusion method for wired connected clients in SHM applications. Tensor analysis has been successfully applied in many application domains such as civil engineer, social network analysis, and computer vision [4,5,14], and produced promising results. To the best of our knowledge, there are still few works in which researchers try to apply FL methods to practical application domain such as SHM which deal with multi-way datasets.

5   Experimental Results

5.1   Data Collection

We conducted experiments on two case studies using structural vibration based datasets acquired from a network of accelerometers mounted on two bridges in Australia, Cable-Stayed Bridge and Arch Bridge. For all experiments, three hidden layers were used in our ANN and the accuracy values were obtained using the F-Score (FS), defined as $F\text{-}score = 2 \cdot \dfrac{\text{Precision} \times \text{Recall}}{\text{Precision} + \text{Recall}}$ where $\text{Precision} = \dfrac{\text{TP}}{\text{TP} + \text{FP}}$ and $\text{Recall} = \dfrac{\text{TP}}{\text{TP} + \text{FN}}$ (the number of true positive, false positive and false negative are abbreviated by TP, FP and FN, respectively). The core consistency diagnostic technique (CORCONDIA) technique described in [6] was used to determine the number of rank-one tensors R when it decomposed using CP-ALS method described in 2. The CORCONDIA suggests $R = 2$ for all experimented data sets.

The Cable-Stayed Bridge. We instrumented the Cable-Stayed Bridge by 24 uniaxial accelerometers and 28 strain gauges. However, we only used accelerations data collected from sensors Ai with $i \in [1; 24]$. Figure 2 shows the locations of these 24 sensors on the bridge deck. Each set of sensors on the bridge along on one line (e.g. A1: A4) is connected to one client node and fused in a tensor

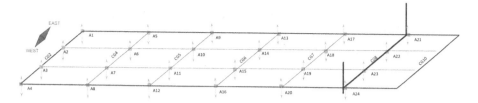

Fig. 2. The locations on the bridge's deck of the 24 Ai accelerometers used in this study. The cross girder j of the bridge is displayed as CGj [2].

node $\mathcal{T}$ to representing one client in our FL network. It results with six tensor nodes $\mathcal{T}$.

For the sake of experiments, we emulated two different types of damage on this bridge by placing a large static load (vehicle) at different locations of a structure. Thus, three scenarios have been considered which includes: no vehicle is placed on the bridge (healthy state), a light vehicle with the approximate mass of 3 t is placed on the bridge close to location A10 ("Car-Damage") and a bus with the approximate mass of 12.5 t is located on the bridge at location A14 ("Bus-Damage"). This emulates slight and severe damage cases which were used in our evaluation Sect. 5.2.

This experiment generates 262 samples (a.k.a events) each consists of acceleration data for a period of 2 s at a sampling rate 600 Hz. We separated the 262 data instances into two groups, 125 samples related to the healthy state and 137 samples for the damage state. The 137 damage examples were further divided into two different damaged cases: the "Car-Damage" samples (107) generated when a stationary car was placed on the bridge, and the "Bus-Damage" samples (30) emulated by the stationary bus.

The Arch Bridge. The Arch bridge is mounted with many accelerometer sensors to measure the vibration responses. Each joint underside the deck is instrumented by three tri-axial accelerometers mounted on the left, middle and right side of the joint, as shown in Fig. 3. The data collected from the three sensors are fused in one tensor node $\mathcal{T}$ which represents one client node in our FL network. This study uses six joints (named 1 to 6) where only one joint (number four) was known as a cracked joint. The data used in this study contains 36952 events as shown in Table 1 which were collected over a period of three months. Each event is recorded by a sensor node for a period of 1.6 s at a sampling rate 375 Hz resulting with a feature vector of 600 attributes in the time domain. All the events in the datasets (1, 2, 3, 5, and 6) are labelled positive (healthy events), where all the events in dataset 4 (joint 4) are labelled negative (damaged events).

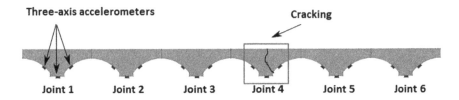

Fig. 3. Evaluated joints on the Arch Bridge.

5.2 Results and Discussions

This section presents the classification performance of the constructed models in our FL network for each of the datasets.

Table 1. Number of samples in each joint of the Arch Bridge dataset.

Dataset	Number of samples	Training	Test
Joint 1	6329	4430	1899
Joint 2	7237	5065	2172
Joint 3	4984	3488	1496
Joint 4	6886	0	6886
Joint 5	6715	4700	2015
Joint 6	4801	3360	1441

The Cable-Stayed Bridge. For each reading of the uni-axial accelerometer, we normalized its magnitude to have a zero mean and one standard variation. The fast Fourier transform (FFT) is then used to represent the generated data in the frequency domain. Each event now has a feature vector of 600 attributes representing its frequencies. The resultant data at each sensor node T has a structure of 4 sensors × 600 features × 262 events. We separated the 262 data instances into two groups, 125 samples related to the healthy state and 137 samples for the damage state. The 137 damage examples were further divided into two different damaged cases: the "Car-Damage" samples (107) generated when a stationary car was placed on the bridge, and the "Bus-Damage" samples (30) emulated by the stationary bus.

We randomly selected eighty percent of the healthy events (100 samples) from each tensor node T to form training multi-way of $\mathcal{X} \in \mathbb{R}^{4 \times 600 \times 100}$ (i.e. *training* set). The 137 examples related to the two damage cases were added to the remaining 20% of the healthy data to form a *testing* set, which was later used for the model evaluation.

At each client node $\mathcal{T}$, we initially applied Algorithm 2 to decompose the tensor $\mathcal{X}$ into three matrices A, B, and C which was used to construct learn the ANN model at each client as well as the central model using Algorithms 3 and 4. Although no data from damaged state has been employed to construct the central model, each local client model was able to identify the damage events related to "Car-Damage" and "Bus-Damage" with an average F-score accuracy of 0.87 ± 0.02. We compared the results of our FL network with tensor (FL-tensor) to FL without tensor (FedAvg). Table 2 shows the resultant FP, TP and F-score accuracies. As can be seen, FL-tensor produced better results than FedAvg especially in FR rate. Furthermore, the central model was also able to separate the two damage cases ("Car-Damage" and "Bus-Damage") where the reconstruction error values were further increased for the samples related to the more severe damage cases related to "Bus-Damage". This is what we anticipated discovering from tensor which has the ability to extract damage sensitive features. Moreover, it reduces the time communication by reducing the number of clients in our FL network.

The Arch Bridge. For each reading of the tri-axial accelerometer (x,y,z), we calculated the magnitude of the three vectors and then the data of each event is normalized to have a zero mean and one standard variation. Since the accelerometer data is represented in the time domain, it is noteworthy to represent the generated data in the frequency domain using Fourier transform. The resultant six datasets (using the middle sensor of each joint) have 300 features that represent the frequencies of each event. For each dataset, we randomly selected 80% of the positive events for training and 20% for testing in addition to the unhealthy events in dataset 4.

At each client/joint $\mathcal{T}$, we fused data from the three sensors in a multi-way tensor of $\mathcal{X} \in \mathbb{R}^{3 \times 300 \times n}$ where n represents number of the training samples defined in Table 1. Similar to the last case study, we applied the three Algorithms 2, 3 and 4 to decompose the tensor $\mathcal{X}$ and to learn the ANN model at each client as well as central model, respectively. Each client model was able to identify its local healthy samples with an average F-score equal to 0.81 ± 0.03. The model at client/joint 4 was also able to identify 0.83 of the damage samples. These results demonstrate that FL approach using centralize model without data sharing is still able to identify damage events even-though these events were not involved in the training process. There is no doubt that this work also demonstrates that learning from massively decentralized data is still challenging and needs improvement especially in the prediction accuracy of damage events at joint 4. Table 2 shows the resultant FP, TP and F-score accuracies of FL-tensor compared FedAvg. Similarly, FL-tensor outperformed FedAvg in damage prediction accuracy with less false alarm rates.

Table 2. Comparison of the TP, the FP, and the *F-score* between our FL-Tensor and FL-FedAvg.

		FL-Tensor	FL-FedAvg
Cable	TP	**0.91±0.02**	0.86±0.04
	FP	**0.16±0.02**	0.29±0.04
	F-score	**0.87±0.02**	0.78±0.04
Arch	TP	**0.82±0.03**	0.79±0.06
	FP	**0.21±0.03**	0.24±0.06
	F-score	**0.81±0.03**	0.77±0.06

6 Conclusions

In this paper, we present a new damage detection method in SHM applications based on federated learning and tensor data fusion techniques. Our approach employs the FL technique to support learning the data collected from several sensors attached to a complex structure continuously locally without the need to share the data into a centralized learning model. Instead, our approach captures the correlations and relationships among the various sensor node and share the learning to a central model. Our experimental evaluation on two real bridge structure datasets showed promising damage detection accuracy by considering different damage scenarios. In the "Cable-Stayed Bridge" dataset, our method achieved an accuracy of 94–97%. Our centralized model based on shared models learning also showed that we were able to monitor the progress of damage in the structure by providing increasing reconstruction error values for the samples related to "Bus-damage" events. In "Arch Bridge dataset, our method achieved 86% damage detection accuracy. The experimental results of these case studies demonstrated the ability of our FL damage detection approach with the incorporation of tensor data fusion method to improve damage detection accuracy and avoid the problems of transmitting sensed data over the network (network traffic, the low energy consumption of the sensor nodes and vulnerability of the data). Our future work aims to improve our prediction accuracy by employing the personalized federated learning approach in our FL network.

Acknowledgements. The authors wish to thank the Roads and Maritime Services (RMS) in New South Wales, New South Wales Government in Australia and Data61 (CSIRO) for provision of the support and testing facilities for this research work. Thanks are also extended to Western Sydney University for facilitating the experiments on the cable-stayed bridge.

References

1. Anaissi, A., Lee, Y., Naji, M.: Regularized tensor learning with adaptive one-class support vector machines. In: Cheng, L., Leung, A.C.S., Ozawa, S. (eds.) ICONIP 2018. LNCS, vol. 11303, pp. 612–624. Springer, Cham (2018). https://doi.org/10. 1007/978-3-030-04182-3_54
2. Anaissi, A., Makki Alamdari, M., Rakotoarivelo, T., Khoa, N.: A tensor-based structural damage identification and severity assessment. Sensors **18**(1), 111 (2018)
3. Anaissi, A., Suleiman, B., Zandavi, S.M.: Necpd: an online tensor decomposition with optimal stochastic gradient descent. arXiv preprint arXiv:2003.08844 (2020)
4. Anaissi, A., Suleiman, B., Zandavi, S.M.: Online tensor decomposition with optimized stochastic gradient descent: an application in structural damage identification. In: IEEE Symposium Series on Computational Intelligence (SSCI), pp. 1257–1264. IEEE (2020)
5. Bader, B.W., Harshman, R.A., Kolda, T.G.: Temporal analysis of semantic graphs using ASALSAN. In Seventh IEEE international conference on data mining (ICDM 2007), pp. 33–42. IEEE (2007)
6. Bro, R., Kiers, H.A.: A new efficient method for determining the number of components in PARAFAC models. J. Chemometr. **17**(5), 274–286 (2003)
7. Dai, X., et al.: Hyper-sphere quantization: communication-efficient SQD for federated learning. arXiv preprint arXiv:1911.04655 (2019)
8. Doebling, S.W., Farrar, C.R., Prime, M.B., Shevitz, D.W.: Damage identification and health monitoring of structural and mechanical systems from changes in their vibration characteristics: a literature review. Tech. rep, Los Alamos National Laboratory, NM, USA (1996)
9. Farrar, C.R., Worden, K.: Structural Health Monitoring: A Machine Learning Perspective. John Wiley & Sons (2012)
10. Guha, N., Talwalkar, A., Smith, V.: One-shot federated learning. arXiv preprint arXiv:1902.11175 (2019)
11. Hanzely, F., Richtárik, P.: Federated learning of a mixture of global and local models. arXiv preprint arXiv:2002.05516 (2020)
12. Hard, A., et al.: Federated learning for mobile keyboard prediction. arXiv preprint arXiv:1811.03604 (2018)
13. Kairouz, P., et al.: Advances and open problems in federated learning. arXiv preprint arXiv:1912.04977 (2019)
14. Khoa, N.L.D., Anaissi, A., Wang, Y.: Smart infrastructure maintenance using incremental tensor analysis. In: Proceedings of the 2017 ACM on Conference on Information and Knowledge Management, pp. 959–967. ACM (2017)
15. Kolda, T.G., Bader, B.W.: Tensor decompositions and applications. SIAM review **51**(3), 455–500 (2009)
16. Konečný, J., McMahan, H.B., Yu, F.X., Richtárik, P., Suresh, A.T., Bacon, D.: Federated learning: strategies for improving communication efficiency. arXiv preprint arXiv:1610.05492 (2016)
17. Lin, T., Stich, S.U., Patel, K.K., Jaggi, M.: Don't use large mini-batches, use local sgd. arXiv preprint arXiv:1808.07217 (2018)
18. Makki Alamdari, M., Anaissi, A., Khoa, N.L., Mustapha, S.: Frequency domain decomposition-based multisensor data fusion for assessment of progressive damage in structures. Struct. Control Health Monit. **26**(2), e2299 (2019)
19. McMahan, B., Moore, E., Ramage, D., Hampson, S., y Arcas, B.A.: Communication-efficient learning of deep networks from decentralized data. In: Artificial Intelligence and Statistics, pp. 1273–1282. PMLR (2017)

20. Reisizadeh, A., Mokhtari, A., Hassani, H., Jadbabaie, A., Pedarsani, R.: FEDPAQ: a communication-efficient federated learning method with periodic averaging and quantization. In: International Conference on Artificial Intelligence and Statistics, pp. 2021–2031 (2020)
21. Stich, S.U.: Local SGD converges fast and communicates little. arXiv preprint arXiv:1805.09767 (2018)
22. Dinh, C.T., Tran, N., Nguyen, T.D.: Personalized federated learning with moreau envelopes. In: Advances in Neural Information Processing Systems, p. 33 (2020)
23. Wang, J., Joshi, G.: Cooperative SGD: a unified framework for the design and analysis of communication-efficient SGD algorithms. arXiv preprint arXiv:1808.07576 (2018)

Composite Surrogate for Likelihood-Free Bayesian Optimisation in High-Dimensional Settings of Activity-Based Transportation Models

Vladimir Kuzmanovski[1,2,4]([⊠])[iD] and Jaakko Hollmén[1,3]

[1] Department of Computer Science, Aalto University, Espoo, Finland
{vladimir.kuzmanovski,jaakko.hollmen}@aalto.fi
[2] Department of Knowledge Technologies, Jožef Stefan Institute, Ljubljana, Slovenia
vladimir.kuzmanovski@ijs.si
[3] Department of Computer and Systems Sciences,
Stockholm University, Stockholm, Sweden
jaakko.hollmen@dsv.su.se
[4] Smart City Center of Excellence, TalTech, Estonia

Abstract. Activity-based transportation models simulate demand and supply as a complex system and therefore large set of parameters need to be adjusted. One such model is Preday activity-based model that requires adjusting a large set of parameters for its calibration on new urban environments. Hence, the calibration process is time demanding, and due to costly simulations, various optimisation methods with dimensionality reduction and stochastic approximation are adopted. This study adopts Bayesian Optimisation for Likelihood-free Inference (BOLFI) method for calibrating the Preday activity-based model to a new urban area. Unlike the traditional variant of the method that uses Gaussian Process as a surrogate model for approximating the likelihood function through modelling discrepancy, we apply a composite surrogate model that encompasses Random Forest surrogate model for modelling the discrepancy and Gaussian Mixture Model for estimating the its density. The results show that the proposed method benefits the extension and improves the general applicability to high-dimensional settings without losing the efficiency of the Bayesian Optimisation in sampling new samples towards the global optima.

Keywords: Transportation model · High-dimensional data · Bayesian optimisation · Likelihood-free inference · Random forest

This work has been supported by the European Commission through the H2020 project Finest Twins (grant No. 856602).

© Springer Nature Switzerland AG 2021
P. H. Abreu et al. (Eds.): IDA 2021, LNCS 12695, pp. 171–183, 2021.
https://doi.org/10.1007/978-3-030-74251-5_14

1   Introduction

Activity-based transportation models (ABM) are designed to simulate the transportation demand and supply as a self-organising agent-based complex system [11]. Such models simulate activities per agent or individual, resulting in a costly execution in terms of computational time. In addition, the transportation-related activities of individuals rely on complex decisions, modelling of which require a large set of parameter adjustments. One such model is Preday ABM, which motivates this study, and plays an important role in a simulation toolset on transportation - SimMobility [1].

Application of the Preday ABM in simulating various environments requires systematic adjustments or calibration of a large set of parameters (further referred to as ABM parameters), in order to align the associated outputs more closely to the observed values or true output statistics. For that purpose, various optimisation methods are adopted, including primarily gradient-free metaheuristics [28,29,31]. However, Bayesian inference with the recent developments provides a valuable analytical approach for the calibration process [35,36], a great advantage of which is the elimination of necessity to simulate a large sample set in finding the global optima [14,18,20,36].

The Bayesian Optimisation for Likelihood-free Inference (BOLFI) [14] is a method for inferring parameters of simulation-based models by modelling the discrepancy between observed and simulated output statistics. Its state-of-the-art performance are achieved with nonparametric approximation of the likelihood function with regression by Gaussian Processes (GPs) [3], applied in various domains, such as population genetics [18], spreading of pathogens [22], atomic structure of materials [40], as well as cosmology [20].

The BOLFI facilitates likelihood-free inference of the response function that maps the parameters' values with the discrepancy in the output statistics, by combining probabilistic (Bayesian) inference and iterative search (optimisation). The former inherits the theory of approximate Bayesian computation (ABC) [22,24] to support the likelihood-free inference. The iterative search is used for acquiring new samples (parameters' values) that have great potential to direct the search towards global optima (minimum discrepancy), by utilising identified and evaluated optimal points from previous iterations.

However, the ABC methods have limited applicability in settings of high-dimensional data and costly simulations [16,27,32], constituting a bottleneck for their broader adoption in settings of complex simulation models. Therefore, applicability of the BOLFI method for calibrating the Preday ABM to a new urban environment is limited, and neither of the proposed solutions, such as dimensionality reduction [7,35], or introduction of synthetic parametric/nonparametric likelihoods [2,30,32,37,42], circumvent the obstacle. Namely, the former requires increased number of simulations, while the latter are applicable to problems with low number of parameters.

The aim of this study is to overcome the aforementioned bottleneck, for which we propose an improvement of the BOLFI method with so called Composite Surrogate Model (BOLFIw/CSM) as a robust surrogate model that handles the high-dimensional data and takes advantage of the BOLFI method to limit the number of costly simulations. Namely, the BOLFI method, as specified in [9,14], uses a Gaussian Process (GP) as a surrogate model for modelling the response, i.e., discrepancy, which limits the applicability on high-dimensional data. On the other hand, if the GP is replaced with more robust surrogate regression model (e.g., Random Forest as in [15]), then the non-probabilistic point estimates of the posterior affect the acquisition of new samples (through an acquisition function) to efficiently identify the regions of interest in the parameter space, i.e. the exploitation-exploration trade-off [17]. Therefore, the proposed BOLFIw/CSM method adopt the Random Forest [8] as a surrogate model and combines it with a Gaussian Mixture Model [33] as conditional density estimator for semi-parametric estimation of the posterior distribution.

The rest of the manuscript is organised as follows. In Sect. 2 we introduce the Preday ABM and the BOLFI method, followed by a formalisation of the proposed extension to the BOLFI method, in Sect. 3. Section 4 introduces the experimental design and discusses the achieved results. Finally, the work and conclusions are summarized in Sect. 5.

2   Materials and Methods

2.1   Preday ABM

The Preday ABM model is a fundamental part of a comprehensive simulation tool SimMobility and it is used to simulate the mid-term demand of a transportation network in a given urban area [1]. The demand is formulated as daily travel activities of households and individuals, and the simulation is based on population characteristics of the simulated urban area.

The model consists of 22 discrete choice sub-models, with total of 817 parameters. The daily activity schedule of agents are modelled with application of hierarchical discrete choice models using a Monte-Carlo simulation, over pre-defined set of activities per agent by using the random utility theory [5,23].

Overall, the daily simulated activities are categorized in accordance to the activity type (*work*, *education*, *shopping*, and *others*) and transportation modes (*MRT, Bus, Private Bus, Car-drive alone, Shared car-drive with 2 passengers, Shared car-drive with 3 passengers, Motorcycle, Taxi*, and *Walk*). These categorizations are used for statistical comparison of the simulated data with the observed data, where the output statistics is expressed as a number of activities per different combination of activity type and transportation mode (e.g., number of bus rides for work-based commuting).

Calibration of Preday ABM has been performed in several studies, whereby parameters are estimated by Simultaneous perturbation stochastic approximation (SPSA) method with its variants [28,29,31]. However, all studies considered reduction of the dimensionality of the parameter space either by sensitivity analysis (SA) [34] or principal component analysis (PCA) [19].

2.2   Bayesian Optimisation for Likelihood-Free Inference

Likelihood-free inference approach is a method for inferring a posterior distribution of parameters of a simulation-based model [14]. The simulation-based model is defined as a generative process that under certain parameter values generates data similar to observations of an underlying phenomenon. Often the simulation-based models are of black-box nature or unknown analytical form, hence their likelihood function is intractable.

From the Bayesian perspective, the inference task corresponds to a statistical inference of a finite number of parameters $\theta \in \mathbb{R}^d$ of the simulation-based model from a set of observations Y_o:

$$p(\theta|Y_o) = \frac{p(Y_o|\theta) \cdot p(\theta)}{p(Y_o)}, \tag{1}$$

where $p(\theta)$ encodes our prior beliefs on the distribution of parameter values and $p(Y_o|\theta)$ represents the likelihood of the observations, given the parameters, derived from the known function $\mathcal{L}(\theta)$. Since the analytical form of $\mathcal{L}(\theta)$ is unknown in the underlying challenge, we use the notation $L(\theta)$ that need to be approximated over a set of N samples - $\tilde{L}^N(\theta)$. The notation is simplified if the marginal distribution $p(Y_o)$ is omitted because it does not depend on θ:

$$p(\theta|Y_o) \propto L(\theta) \cdot p(\theta), \tag{2}$$

where the $L(\theta)$ is approximated over finite sample set ($\tilde{L}^N(\theta)$) and it is reconstructed as the number of samples increases:

$$\lim_{N \to \infty} \tilde{L}^N(\theta) = L(\theta) \tag{3}$$

The approximation ($\tilde{L}^N(\theta)$) of the likelihood function ($L(\theta)$) can be performed in parametric or non-parametric manner. The former assumes that the likelihood belongs to a certain parametric family, and hence it is called synthetic likelihood [42]. The latter, alternatively, approximate the likelihood function by a kernel density estimation [12] or surrogate regression [14].

The Bayesian Optimisation for Likelihood-free Inference (BOLFI), as an iterative process, approximates the likelihood function from the posterior distribution of the response function, i.e., modelled discrepancy with surrogate regression model, which is updated at each iteration following the Bayes's theorem [14]. The iterative update of the posterior distribution triggers acquiring new evidence from the parameter space with a highest potential to progress towards global optima. So, an *acquisition function* $A(\theta)$ is introduced, whereby $s \in \mathbb{R}$ generated samples are credited with an utility. The iterative process continues by enriching the evidence with simulated $k \leq s$ samples with the highest utility.

In [9,17] several acquisition functions are defined, but for the purpose of this study, we adopt the *expected improvement* (EI) [26], defined as follows:

$$EI(\theta) = \sigma(\theta)[z\Phi(z) + \phi(z)], \tag{4}$$

$$z = \frac{f^* - \mu(\theta)}{\sigma(\theta)}, \tag{5}$$

where $\sigma(\theta)$ and $\mu(\theta)$ are statistics of the inferred posterior distribution, f^* is the most optimal output, i.e., minimal discrepancy discovered, and Φ and ϕ are probability density and cumulative distribution function in terms of the standard normal distribution, respectively. The expected improvement $EI(\theta) = 0$ if $\sigma(\theta) = 0$. The analogy behind (4) reveals the exploration-exploitation trade-off that favours larger uncertainty proximal to the known optimal region(s).

2.3   Limitations of BOLFI for Calibrating Preday ABM

The Preday ABM can be seen as a black-box model with costly executions, parameters of which need to be adjusted so that the simulated output corresponds to the observed quantities. Therefore, for minimizing the discrepancy in the output with limited number of simulations, the BOLFI method fits naturally. However, its applicability is limited to settings with up to 10-dimensional parametric space [17,38], which clearly does not suffice the requirement of Preday ABM model with total of 817 ABM parameters.

To overcome the limitation of likelihood-free inference over high-dimensional spaces when applied with Bayesian optimisation, earlier attempts propose sequential investigation of effective sub-spaces [10,41] or discovery of active subspaces [35]. Both require larger set of simulations and yet have been proven to work for up to 400 features. Recent attempts opt for employment of Deep Gaussian Processes (DGPs) [3] and combination of GPs [39] for splitting the discrepancies in accordance to a latent variable, and dimensions of the parameter space, respectively. Both reported successful application over couple of domains, albeit with much lower order of magnitude in terms of dimensionality, than the underlying problem of calibrating the Preday ABM. Other approaches consider replacement of the regression surrogate model, in particular with Random Forest [15,32], but on use-cases defined over 76- and 2-dimensional parameter space.

3   BOLFI with Composite Surrogate Model

The proposed extension of the BOLFI method adds on the previous works that consider the Random Forests (RF) [8] as a surrogate model for likelihood approximation through modelling the discrepancy, extended with a Gaussian Mixture model [13,33] as a density estimator conditioned on the approximated likelihoods. The novelty of the proposed method lies in the density estimation of predictions from a robust surrogate model, which can be utilised by existing acquisition functions that depend on probabilistic inputs. The combination of both components is referred to as a composite surrogate model and the overall proposed method abbreviated as BOLFIw/CSM.

Random Forest. [8] is an ensemble method composed of C regression trees. Regression trees follows the concept of a decision tree, with structure made of decision binary nodes, built iteratively in top-down fashion. Each regression tree is built over a sub-space of the parameter space, which is designed by random subsets of both the features (dimensions) and bootstrap samples. Therefore, each regression tree predicts the target, given a dataset, for a specific region in the defined space. Ensemble prediction, on the other hand, is an aggregation (average) of the outcomes of all C tree components:

$$\mathcal{RF}(\theta|\Theta_o, Y_o) = \frac{1}{C} \sum_{i=1}^{C} \tau_i(\theta|\Theta_{s_i}, Y_{s_i}), \qquad (6)$$

where C is the number of tree components, Θ_{s_i} and Y_{s_i} are training dataset of i-th regression tree τ_i, while Θ_o and Y_o global training dataset.

The RF regression method has relatively small number of hyper-parameters that can significantly influence the outcome. Commonly adjusted are: the number of tree components C; the minimum number of samples in a terminating node that controls the structure growth and overfitting settings of the individual tree components; and number of features to design a sub-space or partition.

Gaussian Mixture Model (GMM). [13,33] is a semiparametric density function composed of weighted sum of M components, where each component is a Gaussian distribution (function). In this study we are considering one-dimensional model over a vector of values $x \in \mathbb{R}^C$, defined as follows:

$$p(x) = \sum_{i=1}^{M} w_i \, \mathcal{N}(x|\mu_i, \sigma_i); \ \sum_{i=1}^{M} w_i = 1, \ w_i > 0. \qquad (7)$$

$$\mathcal{N}(x|\mu_i, \sigma_i) = \frac{1}{\sigma_i \sqrt{2\pi}} exp(-\frac{1}{2\sigma_i^2}(x - \mu_i)^2), \qquad (8)$$

Composite surrogate model (CSM) extends the RF surrogate model with a GMM density estimator. The proposed method takes advantage of the RF as a robust regression method in terms of the high-dimensional data, and compensates its limitations regarding the expected parametric posterior estimates for likelihood approximation. Namely, the RF model is: (i) unable to predict a value outside of the observed range; and (ii) is characterised with the non-probabilistic nature of the predicted outcome. Thus, as a standalone surrogate the RF greatly affects the efficiency of the selected acquisition function $A(\theta)$, i.e., EI, in acquiring new promising samples. Consequently, the GMM extension to the base surrogate model compensate the limitations and estimates the posterior in a semiparametric form from the predicted outcomes. As such, the overall composite nature of the discrepancy surrogate model is considered being semiparametric, as well.

In previous studies where RF surrogate model is used, [15] consider empirical or simple average as posterior point estimates, which retain the limitations, while the study of [32] uses quantile-based estimation of the posterior cumulative distribution by Quantile RF [25]. The latter introduces a probabilistic outcome, but limited to quantile-based representation only, whereby a potential multi-modality of the probability function remains a challenge.

The CSM approximates the likelihood of a given set of parameter values θ as linear combination of component-wise approximated likelihood functions through predicted discrepancies (T) from individual regression trees in a RF:

$$L^N(\theta) = \sum_{i=1}^{M} w_i \, A(\mathcal{N}(T|\mu_i, \sigma_i)) \tag{9}$$

$$T = \{ \, \tau_i \mid \tau_i = \tau_i(\theta|\Theta_{s_i}, Y_{s_i}), \ i = 1, ..., C \, \}. \tag{10}$$

The abstraction behind the proposed method compartmentalises the high-dimensional parameter space into regions examined individually in terms of their exploration-exploitation trade-off. The regions that over the aggregated exploitation points show possibility to improve the exploration will further be favoured.

4 Results

Performances of the proposed method are empirically evaluated through an experimental setup, as described hereafter.

The algorithm of BOLFIw/CSM is described in Algorithm 1. It is initialised with four input parameters: initial and iteration sample size, maximum number of iterations, and random variation rate of new samples. While the rest of the algorithm is covered with previously formalised elements or they are self-sufficiently named, the last parameter and sampling function are to be clarified.

The sampling function is used at the initial phase, when n_i samples are generated and in the iterative process, for generating new n_t samples for evaluation. In case of the former, the function generates random samples (ABM parameter

---

Algorithm 1: BOLFIw/CSM

Input:
$n_i/n_t \leftarrow$ initial/iteration sample size;
$max_t \leftarrow$ maximum number of iterations;
$\rho \leftarrow$ variation rate for random variation of new samples;
Result: Θ, S_Θ
$\Theta \leftarrow$ generateInitialSample(n_i);
$S_\Theta \leftarrow$ simulate(Θ);
$\Theta_{best} \leftarrow$ pullOptimalTheta(Θ,S_Θ);
while ! terminate(max$_t$) **do**
  $\quad \Theta_t \leftarrow$ generateSample(n_t,ρ) ;
  $\quad T \leftarrow$ fitRandomForest(Θ,S_Θ) ;
  $\quad \Lambda_t \leftarrow$ estimateDensity(T,Θ_t) ;
  $\quad EI_t^* \leftarrow$ acquisition(Λ_t) ;
  $\quad \Theta_t^* \leftarrow$ pullOptimalEstimatedTheta(EI_t^*);
  $\quad S_{\Theta_t^*} \leftarrow$ simulate(Θ_t^*);
  $\quad \Theta, S_\Theta \leftarrow$ updateParameterSet(Θ_t^*,$S_{\Theta_t^*}$) ;
end

Table 1. Summary of BOLFIw/CSM and BOLFIw/RF hyper-parameters.

Parameter	BOLFIw/CSM	BOLFIw/RF
Density estimator	GMM [6]	Empirical mean/variance
Variation rate (ρ)	0.3; 0.5; 0.8; 1.0	0.3; 0.5; 0.8; 1.0
Iteration sample size (n_t)	100	100

values) from a uniform distribution across all dimensions. For the latter, the sampling function follows the currently optimal set of ABM parameter values and assign new values to a random portion ρ (variation rate) of the dimensions. The newly assigned values are randomly sampled from a Gaussian distribution with unit variance and mean - the value observed in the currently optimal sample, for the corresponding dimensions. Analogously, newly sampled sets of ABM parameter values are generated from the neighbourhood of the optimal ABM parameters. The underlying implementation encompasses RF and GMM algorithms implemented in R and described in [21] and [6], respectively[1].

The data used for empirical evaluation of the proposed method include statistical, economic and demographic description of population of a virtual city, provided along the SimMobility simulation toolbox. The virtual city is designed so that reflects characteristics of the urban area in Singapore, encapsulating population data, built environment, and transportation network description [4]. It is designed with population of 351 518 individuals, 100 000 households, and six modes of transportation (MRT, bus, car, motorcycle, taxi, and walk). In addition, the provided virtual city is specified with calibrated ABM parameter values, which are considered as a ground truth in the discussion of the achieved results within this study.

Due to the time constraints and computationally-demanding simulations, we sampled 10% of the population given in the database. The sampling is performed in stratified manner, according to the features registered in the database.

For comparing purposes, the simulated daily activities are summarised to a set of summary statistics, including: number of tours, number of stops, and number of trips. Furthermore, the summary statistics are calculated in regards to three different categories: (i) per person, (ii) per person and tour type (purpose of travel), and (iii) per person and transportation mode. Therefore, the final simulated results are summarised through total of 9 summary statistics. Finally, the discrepancy between simulations are defined as a Euclidean distance between corresponding vectors of the summary statistics.

The proposed BOLFIw/SCM method is applied for calibrating the Preday ABM to fit the observed daily activities in the virtual city - provided as a supplementary material on the SimMobility transportation simulation toolset. The application is based on predefined set of input parameters of the algorithm, with the variation rate being changed and its effects examined. In addition, for

---

[1] Code available at: https://version.aalto.fi/gitlab/kuzmanv1/bolfiwcsm-preday.

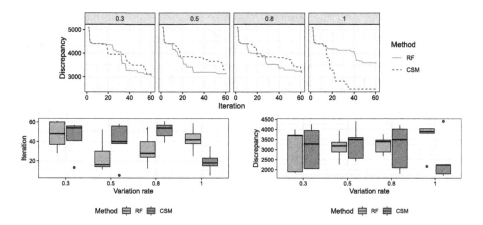

Fig. 1. Average discrepancy reached across all iterations (upper). Variation rates in sampling new parameters compared to the iteration at which the optimal result were first achieved (lower-left) and the discrepancy for both methods (lower-right).

performance evaluating purposes, the experimental setup includes application of the BOLFI method with Random Forest (BOLFIw/RF) as a surrogate model - a method proposed in [15]. Complete set of input parameters concerning the application of both methods are summarised in Table 1. Each run of the both methods with varying variation rate (random portion of the parameters that are changed at each sampling) starts with the same initial set of 10 simulated samples and terminated after the 50-th iteration. The Random forest method is applied with default hyper-parameter values (500 regression trees, and minimum number of instances in a leaf is 5. The results are summarised over 5 repeated runs with different random seed (Fig. 1).

The results, as shown in Fig. 1 (upper figure), distinguish the dominance of the BOLFIw/CSM method, when applied with variation rate of 1.0, which means that sampled parameter values differ completely from the most optimal set at the given iteration. The dominance is observed in terms of pace, at which the final or best score is achieved. Namely, the BOLFIw/CSM method with $\rho = 1.0$ needs approximately 20 iterations on average, for achieving the final results of the other methods (after 50 iterations).

The Fig. 1 (lower figures) shows the performance in terms of the iterations when the final optimal result was first achieved, as well as the achieved discrepancy at the end of the iterative processes. The former address the issue of early achievement of the minimum discrepancy, while the latter, the overall optima attained in terms of the discrepancy. In both analyses, when $\rho = 1.0$, the BOLFIw/CSM shows significantly better results with as twice as better performance than the its counterpart. However, aforementioned performances are not attained with lower variation rates, where the progress towards the global minimum is on average similar for both methods, with exception when $\rho = 0.5$.

The analogy behind the observed outcome suggests that the methods with the lower variation rates ($\rho < 1.0$) tend to generate less spread samples in the high-dimensional space, and hence, the density function of the predicted values by the RF surrogate model tends to be more uniformly shaped, without distinct Gaussian components. Therefore, the convergence of the GMM density estimator is affected, resulting in non-reliable density estimates. In such cases, it is apparent that the empirical average over the predicted values is more informative. On the other hand, the benefit of the GMM density estimator is significant when the sampling function is able to produce scattered new samples, triggering significant progress towards the global optimum.

The calibration of the Preday ABM with the overall lowest discrepancies is achieved by BOLFIw/CSM with variation rate of 1.0, where the distance between the summary statistics derived from simulated and observed data is 1713.26. The best record of its counterpart is 2163.98. Both, however, lags behind the ground truth, whereby the sampled 10% of the population from the virtual city simulates daily activity schedules with discrepancy of 193.89.

5   Summary and Conclusions

This study addresses the issue of calibrating Preday activity-based simulation model from the SimMobility toolset with a limited number of simulations. It corresponds to the task of parameter inference of a simulation-based model with intractable likelihood function over high-dimensional parameter space. For such class of problems, Bayesian Optimisation for Likelihood-free Inference (BOLFI) [14] is of great importance. However, the number of ABM parameters in the Preday ABM is greater than models of previous adoption of the BOLFI method.

Therefore, we aimed at improving the surrogate model to approximate the likelihood through modelling discrepancy. The improved model would be able to encapsulate the knowledge from high-dimensional data with limited sample size, and to tailor the acquisition function to efficiently identify the regions of interest. Consequently, we propose the BOLFI approach with Composite Surrogate Model (BOLFIw/CSM), whereby the posterior distribution for approximating the intractable likelihood function is composed by a density estimates over the regression model. The surrogate model is set to be Random Forest (RF), non-aggregated output of which is fed into a Gaussian Mixture model (GMM) density estimator. The mixture of Gaussians is then used for acquiring new evidence that guides efficiently the search towards the global optima. The proposed method inherits the robust characteristics of the RF models in terms of limited overfit to the small sample size in high-dimensional settings. Moreover, the GMM density estimator adapts the output so that the existing acquisition function can be used without loss of its efficiency in the context of the Bayesian Optimisation.

The BOLFIw/CSM method shows promising results for calibrating the Preday ABM on a new city environment, with data provided as demo data along the SimMobility toolset. The method is compared to the BOLFI approach applied with the RF for approximation of the likelihood, following empirical mean and variance. The BOLFIw/CSM shows great performance with sampling function that generates scattered new samples. Otherwise, as new samples get proximal to the latest most optimal point, the surrogate model tends to predict more uniformly distributed values, which limits the convergence of the density estimator.

In further work, the BOLFIw/CSM method is to be examined in more extensive experimental setup regarding the applicable domains, method's parameters, and confronting with a larger set of comparative methods. Finally, the calibration of the Preday ABM is to be extended to a real-world urban environment and compared with the non-Bayesian approaches.

References

1. Adnan, M., et al.: Simmobility: a multi-scale integrated agent-based simulation platform. In: 95th Annual Meeting of the Transportation Research Record (2016)
2. An, Z., Nott, D.J., Drovandi, C.: Robust bayesian synthetic likelihood via a semi-parametric approach. Stat. Comput. **30**(3), 543–557 (2020)
3. Aushev, A., Pesonen, H., Heinonen, M., Corander, J., Kaski, S.: Likelihood-free inference with deep gaussian processes. arXiv preprint arXiv:2006.10571 (2020)
4. Basak, K.: SimMobility demo data (2019). https://github.com/smart-fm/simmobility-prod/wiki/Demo-Data. Accessed 1 Aug 2020
5. Ben-Akiva, M., Lerman, S.R.: Discrete Choice Analysis: Theory and Application to Travel Demand. Transportation Studies (2018)
6. Benaglia, T., Chauveau, D., Hunter, D., Young, D.: mixtools: an R package for analyzing finite mixture models. J. Stat. Softw. **32**(6), 1–29 (2009)
7. Blum, M., et al.: Comparative review of dimension reduction methods in approximate bayesian computation. Stat. Sci. **28**(2), 189–208 (2013)
8. Breiman, L.: Random forests. Mach. Learn. **45**(1), 5–32 (2001)
9. Brochu, E., Cora, V.M., De Freitas, N.: A tutorial on bayesian optimization of expensive cost functions, with application to active user modeling and hierarchical reinforcement learning. arXiv preprint arXiv:1012.2599 (2010)
10. Chen, B., Castro, R., Krause, A.: Joint optimization and variable selection of high-dimensional gaussian processes. arXiv preprint arXiv:1206.6396 (2012)
11. Chu, Z., Cheng, L., Chen, H.: A review of activity-based travel demand modeling. In: CICTP 2012: Multimodal Transportation Systems, pp. 48–59 (2012)
12. Davis, R.A., Lii, K.-S., Politis, D.N.: Remarks on some nonparametric estimates of a density function. Selected Works of Murray Rosenblatt. SWPS, pp. 95–100. Springer, New York (2011). https://doi.org/10.1007/978-1-4419-8339-8_13
13. Day, N.: Estimating the components of a mixture of normal components. Biometrika **56**(3), 463–474 (1969)
14. Gutmann, M.U., Corander, J.: Bayesian optimization for likelihood-free inference of simulator-based statistical models. J. Mach. Learn. Res. **17**(1) (2016)
15. Hutter, F., Hoos, H.H., Leyton-Brown, K.: Sequential model-based optimization for general algorithm configuration. In: Coello, C.A.C. (ed.) LION 2011. LNCS, vol. 6683, pp. 507–523. Springer, Heidelberg (2011). https://doi.org/10.1007/978-3-642-25566-3_40
16. Izbicki, R., Lee, A.B., Pospisil, T.: ABC-CDE: Toward approximate bayesian computation with complex high-dimensional data and limited simulations. J. Comput. Graph. Stat. **28**(3), 481–492 (2019)

17. Järvenpää, M., Gutmann, M.U., Pleska, A., Vehtari, A., Marttinen, P., et al.: Efficient acquisition rules for model-based approximate bayesian computation. Bayesian Anal. **14**(2), 595–622 (2019)
18. Järvenpää, M., Gutmann, M.U., Vehtari, A., Marttinen, P., et al.: Gaussian process modelling in approximate bayesian computation to estimate horizontal gene transfer in bacteria. Ann. Appl. Stat. **12**(4), 2228–2251 (2018)
19. Jolliffe, I.T., Cadima, J.: Principal component analysis: a review and recent developments. Philos. Trans. R. Soc. A Math. Phys. Eng. Sci. **374**(2065), 20150202 (2016)
20. Leclercq, F.: Bayesian optimization for likelihood-free cosmological inference. Phys. Rev. D **98**(6), 063511 (2018)
21. Liaw, A., et al.: Classification and regression by random forest. R. news **2**(3), 18–22 (2002)
22. Lintusaari, J., Gutmann, M., Dutta, R., Kaski, S., Corander, J.: Fundamentals and recent developments in approximate Bayesian computation. Syst. Biol. **66**, e66–e82 (2017)
23. Lu, Y., et al.: Simmobility mid-term simulator: a state of the art integrated agent based demand and supply model. In: 94th Annual Meeting of the Transportation Research Board (2015)
24. Marin, J.M., Pudlo, P., Robert, C.P., Ryder, R.J.: Approximate Bayesian computational methods. Stat. Comput. **22**(6), 1167–1180 (2012)
25. Meinshausen, N.: Quantile regression forests. JMLR **7**, 983–999 (2006)
26. Močkus, J.: On Bayesian methods for seeking the extremum. In: Marchuk, G.I. (ed.) Optimization Techniques 1974. LNCS, vol. 27, pp. 400–404. Springer, Heidelberg (1975). https://doi.org/10.1007/3-540-07165-2_55
27. Nott, D., Fan, Y., Marshall, L., Sisson, S.: Approximate Bayesian computation and bayes' linear analysis: toward high-dimensional ABC. J. Comput. Graph. Stat. **23**(1), 65–86 (2014)
28. Oh, S., Seshadri, R., Azevedo, C., Ben-Akiva, M.E.: Demand calibration of multimodal microscopic traffic simulation using weighted discrete SPSA. Trans. Res. Rec. **2673**(5), 503–514 (2019)
29. Petrik, O., Adnan, M., Basak, K., Ben-Akiva, M.: Uncertainty analysis of an activity-based microsimulation model for Singapore. Future Gener. Compt. Syst. (2018)
30. Price, L.F., Drovandi, C.C., Lee, A., Nott, D.J.: Bayesian synthetic likelihood. J. Comput. Graph. Stat. **27**(1), 1–11 (2018)
31. Qurashi, M., Maa, T., Chaniotakis, E., Antoniou, C.: PC-SPSA: employing dimensionality reduction to limit SPSA noise in DTA model calibration. In: 2nd Symposium on Management of Future motorway and Urban Traffic Systems (2018)
32. Raynal, L., Marin, J., Pudlo, P., Ribatet, M., Robert, C., Estoup, A.: ABC random forests for bayesian parameter inference. Bioinformatics **35**(10), 1720–1728 (2019)
33. Reynolds, D.A.: Gaussian mixture models. Encycl. Biometrics **741**, 659–663 (2009)
34. Saltelli, A., Tarantola, S., Campolongo, F., Ratto, M.: Sensitivity Analysis in Practice: A Guide to Assessing Scientific Models. vol. 1. Wiley Online Library (2004)
35. Schultz, L., Sokolov, V.: Bayesian optimization for transportation simulators. Procedia Comput. Sci. **130**, 973–978 (2018)
36. Sha, D., Ozbay, K., Ding, Y.: Applying Bayesian optimization for calibration of transportation simulation models. Transp. Res. Record **2674**(10), 215–228 (2020)
37. Sisson, S.A., Fan, Y., Beaumont, M.: Handbook of Approximate Bayesian Computation. CRC Press (2018)

38. Snoek, J., Larochelle, H., Adams, R.: Practical Bayesian optimization of machine learning algorithms. In: NIPS, pp. 2951–2959 (2012)
39. Thomas, O., Pesonen, H., Sá-Leão, R., de Lencastre, H., Kaski, S., Corander, J.: Split-BOLFI for for misspecification-robust likelihood free inference in high dimensions. arXiv preprint arXiv:2002.09377 (2020)
40. Todorović, M., Gutmann, M., Corander, J., Rinke, P.: Bayesian inference of atomistic structure in functional materials. NPJ Comput. Mater. **5**(1), 1–7 (2019)
41. Wang, Z., et al.: Bayesian optimization in high dimensions via random embeddings. In: IJCAI, pp. 1778–1784 (2013)
42. Wood, S.N.: Statistical inference for noisy nonlinear ecological dynamic systems. Nature **466**(7310), 1102–1104 (2010)

Active Selection of Classification Features

Thomas T. Kok[1,2]([✉])[iD], Rachel M. Brouwer[3], Rene M. Mandl[3], Hugo G. Schnack[3][iD], and Georg Krempl[2][iD]

[1] IDLab, Ghent University - imec, Ghent, Belgium
thomas.kok@ugent.be
[2] Department of Information and Computing Sciences, Utrecht University, Utrecht, The Netherlands
g.m.krempl@uu.nl
[3] Department of Psychiatry, UMCU Brain Center, University Medical Center Utrecht, Utrecht University, Utrecht, The Netherlands

Abstract. Some data analysis applications comprise datasets, where explanatory variables are expensive or tedious to acquire, but auxiliary data are readily available and might help to construct an insightful training set. An example is neuroimaging research on mental disorders, specifically learning a diagnosis/prognosis model based on variables derived from expensive Magnetic Resonance Imaging (MRI) scans, which often requires large sample sizes. Auxiliary data, such as demographics, might help in selecting a smaller sample that comprises the individuals with the most informative MRI scans. In active learning literature, this problem has not yet been studied, despite promising results in related problem settings that concern the selection of instances or instance-feature pairs.

Therefore, we formulate this complementary problem of Active Selection of Classification Features (ASCF): Given a primary task, which requires to learn a model $f : x \rightarrow y$ to explain/predict the relationship between an expensive-to-acquire set of variables x and a class label y. Then, the ASCF-task is to use a set of readily available selection variables z to select these instances, that will improve the primary task's performance most when acquiring their expensive features x and including them to the primary training set.

We propose two utility-based approaches for this problem, and evaluate their performance on three public real-world benchmark datasets. In addition, we illustrate the use of these approaches to efficiently acquire MRI scans in the context of neuroimaging research on mental disorders, based on a simulated study design with real MRI data.

Keywords: Classification · Active learning · Semi-supervised learning · Active feature selection · Active feature acquisition · Active class selection

1 Introduction

In data analysis, the acquisition of data and inductive modelling are traditionally performed in distinct phases. However, combining them offers the possible

© Springer Nature Switzerland AG 2021
P. H. Abreu et al. (Eds.): IDA 2021, LNCS 12695, pp. 184–195, 2021.
https://doi.org/10.1007/978-3-030-74251-5_15

advantage to focus acquisition efforts on the most insightful data, in particular when data are expensive or tedious to obtain. This has been acknowledged by a rich literature on selective sampling and active learning of *labels* [19]. In contrast, the active selection of data concerning *features* has received little attention yet [1,4,12]. In particular, there are data analysis applications where data on some features are not readily available and expensive to obtain, while data on other features are cheap. An example is neuroimaging research on mental disorders: Here, often large sample sizes are required, specifically when predicting diagnosis or prognosis. In current classification studies based on Magnetic Resonance Imaging (MRI), sample sizes required are several hundreds of subjects. MRI being a complex and expensive measurement tool, these numbers are hard to acquire. Given the heterogeneity in diagnoses and brain morphology, not all subjects are informative for answering the interdisciplinary research question: some subjects are 'redundant' and others are very informative. However, prior to acquiring expensive MRI data, other data might readily be available on each individual, such as their demographics or questionnaire answers. Such 'auxiliary' data might help in selecting those individuals, whose brain scans are expected to be (the most) informative. Unfortunately, there is currently no method to identify these individuals. This motivates the novel active learning problem of **Actively Selecting Classification Features** (ASCF) addressed in this paper: *Given a primary task, which is to learn a model* $f : x \rightarrow y$, *wherein a set of expensive, yet-to-be-acquired* classification *features* x *is used to explain/predict a class label* y, *the ASCF task consists of using a set of readily available, cheap* selection *features* z *to construct the training set for the primary task. Thus, the aim is to use* z *to select these instances, for which acquiring* x *and adding them to the training set improves the primary task's model* $f : x \rightarrow y$ *the most. In the unsupervised variant of this problem, the labels* y *are unknown during selection, while in the supervised variant they are readily available*

As we will show when reviewing the literature in Sect. 2, this problem complements existing research in active learning, in particular on the related problems of instance completion, active feature acquisition, and active class selection. Ultimately, our aim is an ASCF-approach that guides researchers to compose the primary task's training sample in the most efficient way, thereby hopefully leading to significant reductions in sample size and costs. For this purpose, we present one supervised and one unsupervised utility-based ASCF-approach in Sect. 3[1]. Following a benchmark evaluation on three real-world datasets in Sect. 4, we will conclude with a case study in Sect. 4.2, where we will apply our approach in a supervised setting to simulate the efficient 'acquisition' of MRI brain scans from a large in-house database and evaluate the resulting predictive model's performance.

---

[1] The code of their implementations is available as open source here: https://github.com/thomastkok/active-selection-of-classification-features.

2   Related Work

The active selection and acquisition of data during data modelling has been studied under the umbrella terms of active learning and selective sampling [13,19]. The predominantly considered problem in this literature is the active selection of instances for labelling. That is, given a pool or stream of instances with only their feature values known, the aim is to select instances to acquire their label. Some research has also been dedicated to problems related to the acquisition of features. These problems are *Active Feature Acquisition* (AFA), *Active Feature Selection* (AFS) and *Active Class Selection* (ACS). These are closely related to the problem of Actively Selecting Classification Features considered here. However, in contrast to ASCF, they don't consider a separate set of selection features but rather consider all features for selection (of features/instances) as well as for classification. Thus, they are not directly applicable when the classification features (x) differ from the features (z) that are available during selection, as in the case of ASCF. Nevertheless, the following review of these approaches will serve as a starting point for deriving our ASCF-approaches in Sect. 3.

In Active Feature Acquisition [15,16,18,20,21], the aim is to select and query the missing classification feature-value pairs in a dataset, which are deemed to be the most useful to improve the prediction model. That is, for which instances to acquire values of x. Two alternative problem formulations exist, which differ by the number of instance values that are queried simultaneously: The most common one is *active feature-value acquisition* [18], where each feature-value pair is queried individually, and *instance completion* [21], where the missing features of an instance are queried all at once.

In active feature-value acquisition, as defined in [18], missing feature-value pairs are queried, given an incomplete feature matrix F, a complete label set and a cost matrix C corresponding to the feature matrix. The aim is to construct the best-performing classifier, given that a query $F_{i,j}$ for the value of the i-th feature of the j-th training instance can be placed at cost $C_{i,j}$. The cost matrix C is optional, with a matrix of ones as default (equal costs). Of particular relevance for our work are the approaches based on *Sampled Expected Utility* proposed in [15,16]. These approaches first compute a score for each potential query, which indicates the (expected) increase in performance of the classifier given the corresponding feature value is acquired. Then, they select the query with the highest score, acquire the corresponding feature-values, and repeat the process after updating the classifier. Specifically, as defined in [16], for a discrete feature x_i with $k = 1, 2, \ldots K$ possible feature values, the expected utility score is

$$score(x_{i,j}) = \sum_{k=1}^{K} P(F_{i,j} = V_k) \cdot U(F_{i,j} = V_k) \tag{1}$$

where $P(F_{i,j} = V_k)$ is the probability of the i-th feature in the j-th instance having the k-th feature value, and $U(F_{i,j} = V_k)$ is the utility of acquiring that feature value. The latter is calculated as difference in classification performance before and after incorporating the feature value in the training set, and divided by the cost of this query. While the idea of estimating the expected utility from selecting a feature-value pair, and subsequently selecting the feature-value pair with the maximum expected utility, is at the core of most active feature-value acquisition approaches, they differ in the way they estimate the utility and the expected value distribution of the missing features.

Instance Completion, the other variant of the Active Feature Acquisition problem, was introduction by [21]. Here, all unknown features of an instance are queried at once. It is assumed that the labels are available, while missing features occur in some instances. The goal is to build a classifier using a subset of K instances with all available features, and to improve the performance when compared to using only features available in all N instances. The approaches proposed by [20] also follow the estimation of values and utility framework. Two main approaches were proposed: Acquisition based on the Variance of Imputed Data (*AVID*) and Goal Oriented Data Acquisition (*GODA*). As their names indicate, the former estimates the utility on the variance of the predicted value, while the latter estimates the utility based on the change in performance measure with the predicted values.

In Active Feature Selection [3], the problem is to select individual features, whose values are subsequently acquired for all instances at once. Thus, it complements the previously discussed instance completion, where all missing features were acquired simultaneously for one instance.

Active Class Selection [14] 'inverts' the role of features and labels as selection target from the conventional active learning setting: Instead of using features to select an instance among a set of candidate instances, and subsequently querying its label, the selection specifies a label, for which then a novel instance with corresponding label and complete feature vector is queried. Five different active class selection approaches were proposed in [14], the best performing one being *redistricting*. In each iteration, this approach selects instances from the most volatile class. This is the class that comprises the most instances that were classified differently in the previous iteration. More recently, approaches based on probabilistic active learning have been proposed for this problem in [12] and [4], which were shown to yield superior performance in comparison to redistricting.

Further similar approaches based on reinforcement learning and budgeted learning exist, but generally focus on an integrated training and test phase, or still have feature-related costs during the test phase [5,10,11].

3   Utility-Based Active Selection of Classification Features

Given are a set $\mathcal{C}$ of candidate instances, each with known selection feature vector z and (possibly already known) class label y, but unknown classification feature vector x, i.e., $\mathcal{C} = \{(z,y), \cdots\}$, and a set $\mathcal{A}$ of instances with already acquired classification features, i.e., $\mathcal{A} = \{(z,x,y), \cdots\}$, which might be initially empty. We propose two approaches for the active selection of classification features, i.e., for selecting instances from $\mathcal{C}$ for acquiring their classification feature x and moving them to $\mathcal{A}$. Both follow the utility-principle in [18], by estimating the utility of acquiring the classification feature vector x of an instance. To this end, we first formulate an auxiliary (potentially multiple multivariate) linear regression problem $h : z \rightarrow x$, which we use to predict the most likely classification feature vector x of each candidate instance in $\mathcal{C}$. Based on this auxiliary model, we propose two approaches in the next subsections. Both differ in their data requirements and the utility measure they use: The first addresses a potentially *unsupervised* case, i.e., it does not require the class labels y to be known during selection, and uses the *variance in the imputation of the missing data* as measure for utility. The second one is designed for *supervised* settings, where the class labels are already known during selection, as it is the case in our case study. This latter approach uses the *probability of misclassification* as measure for utility.

3.1 Unsupervised, Imputation Variance-Based Variant (U-ASCF)

Designed for cases, where the class label might not be available during instance selection, this first variant uses an ensemble of B estimators $h_b : z_b \rightarrow x_b$, which are obtained by bootstrapping from the already acquired data $\mathcal{A}$. The variance in the imputations of these bootstrapped estimators is used as an indicator of the resulting utility: The greater the variance, the higher is the imputation uncertainty and the resulting utility of acquiring the classification features of that instance. In analogy to [21], we define this utility as follows:

$$U(z, \Theta) = \frac{1}{D} \cdot \sum_{d=1}^{D} var(\{\forall \theta \in \Theta : h_\theta(z)_d\}) \tag{2}$$

where $h_\theta(z)_d$ is the estimate for the d-th dependent variable (i.e., the d-th classification feature) by a regression model trained on a bootstrapped version θ of $\mathcal{A} = (z, x)$, and Θ is the set of B imputation models. Thus, as utility we use the average over the variances in the B bootstrapped estimates of the individual classification features. As shown in the pseudocode in Algorithm 1, we first train the ensemble of bootstrap estimators, use them to compute this utility for all candidate instances in $\mathcal{C}$, and then acquire the classification features of the instance with the highest utility.

3.2 Supervised, Probabilistic Selection Variant (S-ASCF)

For cases where the class labels are already available during selection, and probabilistic classifiers are used in the primary classification task $f : x \rightarrow y$, their class' posterior estimates allow to adapt the probability-based utility measure discussed in [6] to our problem setting. In [6], for a given instance with unknown feature x this measure is defined as

$$score_x = \frac{p(1-p)}{(-2b+1)p + b^2} \tag{3}$$

where p corresponds to the probability of misclassification, and $b \in [0,1]$ is an asymmetry parameter with default value $0.5 + \frac{1}{2 \cdot |\mathcal{A}|}$ for $|\mathcal{A}|$ corresponding to

---

Algorithm 1. Unsupervised, Imputation-Variance Based Approach

procedure U-ASCF($\mathcal{A} = \{(z_{acq\_1}, x_{acq\_1}), \cdots\}, \mathcal{C} = \{(z_{cand\_1}), \cdots\}, B$)
   $\Theta \leftarrow []$
   for $\theta \leftarrow 1, 2, \cdots B$ **do**
     $\mathcal{A}_\theta \leftarrow$ sample($\mathcal{A}$)
     $\Theta \leftarrow \Theta \cup \{h_\theta \leftarrow \text{trainregressor}(\mathcal{A}_\theta)\}$ ▷ Train $h_\theta : z \rightarrow x$
   end for
   for each unacquired instance $j \in \mathcal{C}$ **do**
     feature_estimates$_j \leftarrow \forall \theta \in \Theta : h_\theta(z_j)$
     $U_j \leftarrow avg(var(\text{feature\_estimates}_j))$ ▷ Use Eq. 2
   end for
   $j^* = \text{argmax}_j U_j$ ▷ Select instance j^*
   $x_{j^*} \leftarrow acquire(j^*)$ ▷ Acquire class. feat.
   return $\mathcal{A}' = \mathcal{A} \cup \{z_{j^*}, x_{j^*}\}, \mathcal{C}' = \mathcal{C} \setminus \{z_{j^*}\}$
end procedure

---

the number of already previously queried and completed instances, such that b converges towards 0.5 as the number of queried instances increases.

As shown in the pseudocode in Algorithm 2, we first train the primary classifier $f : x \rightarrow y$ and the auxiliary regressor $h : z \rightarrow x$ on the set of already acquired instances $\mathcal{A}$. For the candidate instances in $\mathcal{C}$, we then use their selection features z and the auxiliary regression model to obtain estimates for their classification features $\hat{x} = h(z)$, on which we deploy the primary classifier to get posterior estimates $f(x)_{prob}$ of their most likely class. This is then used in a supervised probability-based utility measure adopted to the ASCF-task:

$$U(f, h, z, y) = \frac{P(f(h(z)) \neq y) \cdot (1 - P(f(h(z)) \neq y))}{(-2b + 1) \cdot P(f(h(z)) \neq y) + b^2} \qquad (4)$$

Algorithm 2. Supervised, Probability-Based ASCF

procedure S-ASCF($\mathcal{A} = \{(z_{acq\_1}, x_{acq\_1}, y_{acq\_1}), \cdots\}, \mathcal{C} = \{(z_{cand\_1}, y_{cand\_1}), \cdots\}$)
   $f \leftarrow$ trainprobclassifier($\mathcal{A}$)   ▷ train $f : x \rightarrow y$
   $h \leftarrow$ trainregressor($\mathcal{A}$)   ▷ train $h : z \rightarrow x$
   $b \leftarrow \frac{1}{2} + \frac{1}{2*|\mathcal{A}|}$ ▷ Estimate metaparameter
   for each unacquired instance $j \in \mathcal{C}$ **do**
     $x_j \leftarrow h(z_j)$
     $p \leftarrow 1 - f(x_j)_{prob}$
     $U_j \leftarrow \frac{p(1-p)}{(-2b+1)p+b^2}$ ▷ Use Eq. 4
   end for
   $j^* = \text{argmax}_j U_j$ ▷ Select instance j^*
   $x_{j^*} \leftarrow acquire(j^*)$ ▷ Acquire class. feat.
   return $\mathcal{A}' = \mathcal{A} \cup \{z_{j^*}, x_{j^*}, y_{j^*}\}, \mathcal{C}' = \mathcal{C} \setminus \{z_{j^*}, y_{j^*}\}$
end procedure

---

4   Experimental Results

We have designed a series of experiments, which simulate a real-world deployment of each ACFS-approach (U-ASCF, S-ASCF, and random selection as baseline). Therein, all selection feature values z as well as the class labels y are readily available[2] for each instance of the training set (which corresponds to $\mathcal{C}$), while all classification feature values x are initially concealed (and have to be acquired by the selection approach, thus $\mathcal{A} = \emptyset$ initially). The primary classifier is trained on the selected subset of the training set by the relevant approach, and tested on the classification feature values and corresponding class labels of the test set. The predictions of this primary classifier are then compared to the true class labels, and evaluated.

All approaches use the same splits into training and test sets, obtained via repeating 5-fold cross-validation 10 times, and the same classifier technique with a priori tuned hyperparameters. For the experiments, B is set to 10. As classifier, *logistic regression* [2] with $C = 1.0$ and $L2$ regularization is used[3]. For each selection step, the next instance to acquire is selected, and the training set and primary classifier are updated, and its resulting performance on the test set is evaluated and plotted in a comparison with that of its competitors.

Real-World Benchmark Datasets. For reproducibility of the comparative evaluation, three benchmark datasets from the public UCI Machine Learning Repository [7] are used. The datasets should be binary classification datasets, with a relatively large number of numerical features. Since these datasets do not provide distinguished selection and classification features, we manually split the features in these datasets into two groups, such that the simpler and easier obtainable ones were assigned to the selection set. The active selection of instances for the training set does *not* alter instances that are in the hold out test set. We have used the following datasets and selection features (all remaining features are classification features):

1. *Breast Cancer Coimbra* with Age and BMI as selection features
2. *Heart Disease* with Age, Sex and Chest Pain Type as selection features
3. *Wine* with Alcohol, Color intensity and Hue as selection features

4.1   Comparative Results

The results in terms of the F1-score, shown on ordinate, defined as harmonic mean of precision and recall, for both proposed approaches and a random baseline are shown in Fig. 1. The learning steps shown on the abscissa range from 0 to all instances having been acquired for their classification feature. The 10th and 90th percentile are displayed as error bars on the learning curves, slightly

---

[2] The unsupervised approach U-ASCF does not use these labels during selection.

[3] Experiments with SVMs were also performed with similar results, see our website.

spread out for each approach as to not overlap. The objective is fast convergence to high F1 scores, while with an increasing number of queried instances -and thus converging training sets- all approaches should converge to the same performance.

Using a one-sided Wilcoxon signed-ranked test with $\alpha = 0.1$, for each step of the learning curve and each approach, we test the statistical significance in the F1-score difference compared to the random selection baseline. All steps with such a significant difference in performance compared to random sampling are then highlighted with a outlines in black.

The results are differing, depending on the dataset (but independent of the classifier model). For the Heart Disease dataset, the *unsupervised ASCF* method performed consistently better than the random sampling baseline, both at the early segment of the learning curve as well as near the later stages. Its average performance is better at all stages of the learning curve, but differs not significantly at most points in the middle segment. For the Breast Cancer and Wine datasets, the relative performance varies with the learning stage: On both datasets, there is a steep learning curve initially, followed by a subsequent loss in relative comparison. On the Breast Cancer dataset, this loss is significant between 5–30 acquisitions, while U-ASCF and random are en par afterwards. For the Wine dataset, U-ASCF yields significant improvement until 25 acquisitions, but falls significantly below random later on. The *supervised, probability-based ASCF* method provides initially better performance then random. On the Wine dataset, its performance remains significantly better. On the Heart Disease dataset, the initially significantly better performance later declines to a significantly lower performance after 60 acquisitions. On the Breast Cancer dataset, this happens already after about 17 acquisitions. Overall, for both approaches the results vary between datasets and learning step. They are promising in early learning stages, but their relative performance does not remain consistently superior in later stages. In conclusion, if learning with a very limited budget is the objective and performance with few acquisition matters, they showed in all but the Breast Cancer dataset an improvement over random sampling.

4.2 Case Study

For this problem setting, we considered the real-world problem of the prediction of the schizophrenia diagnosis based on MRI brain scans. Using the database of processed MRI brain images ($N > 1000$) at the Department of Psychiatry, UMC Utrecht, Netherlands, we simulated a study to answer the following neuroimaging research question: Can we classify schizophrenia patients and healthy subjects, based on their MRI brain scans? It has been previously shown that this can be done with reasonable accuracy, using several hundreds of subjects [17].

Using the FreeSurfer processing software [8], the following brain features were extracted: thickness, surface area and volume of 68 cortical regions of interest, and volumes of the subcortical structures. These features were used to train diagnostic classification models. After selecting subjects with available 'cheap' selection features (age, sex, IQ), the sample available for our experiment included

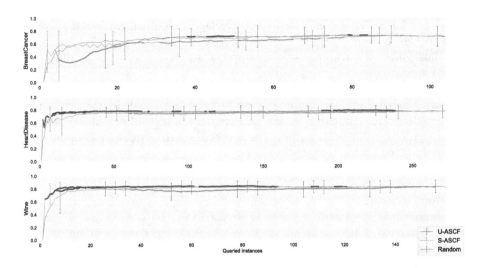

Fig. 1. Comparison of the F1-score of the two utility methods and the random baseline, on the UCI datasets. Error bars denote the 10th and 90th percentile of the results. Black outlines denote statistically significant difference compared to random selection, with $\alpha = 0.1$.

633 (age, sex and IQ) or 814 (age and sex) subjects, labeled as schizophrenia patient or healthy control subject.

The MRI database forms 'the population' (sociodemographic and clinical data are available). The default approach to answer this neuroimaging research question is to include a large number (N = several hundreds) of scans from 'the population', on which a classification model is learned passively. The results of this approach serve as a reference. The alternative approach is to acquire a significantly smaller number of scans by searching and selecting subjects from 'the training population'. Whether or not a new subject will be selected to obtain an MRI scan will be based on the selection features. The performance of the active learning approach were performed in terms of classification accuracy and reduction of sample size needed to obtain this result.

For the simulated case study, we used recursive feature elimination [9] to reduce the number of features and improve performance. It aims to reduce the number of features used recursively, using cross-validation and the logistic regression classifier model to select the least relevant features. When performing this feature elimination process, we noted the optimal number of features to used for both instantiations of the dataset: 33 for the instances with IQ score, and 9 for all instances.

As our goal for this case study is to reduce the number of instances needed with similar performance, we will evaluate primarily using the learning curve as seen in Fig. 2 with a focus on the mid-to-latter part of the curve. In both configurations of the dataset, the approach using the probability-based utility method provided a consistent improvement over the random baseline. This sug-

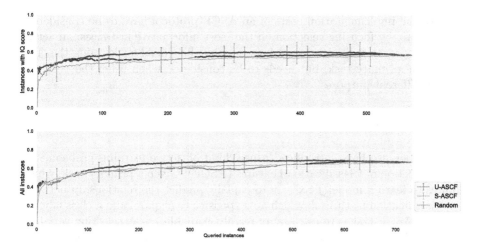

Fig. 2. Comparison of the F1-score of the two utility methods and the random baseline, on the two configurations of the case study dataset. Error bars denote the 10th and 90th percentile of the results. Black outlines denote statistically significant difference compared to random selection, with $\alpha = 0.1$.

gests that if these approaches would have been used in the real-world scenario, either (a) the number of needed instances could have been reduced, or (b) for the same number of instances a better performance could have been obtained. This is especially supported by looking at the end of the learning curve. In the case of the learning curve of the random baseline, it consistently increases until it reaches its best performance score at the end—as makes sense, as more information is obtained. However, for our approach, the learning curve is able to reach its best performance much earlier, and even decreases near the end (where the approach is forced to acquire also the uninformative instances). This means that these approaches are able to *filter out the instances with negative usefulness.* These are instances that do not make sense with the rest of the dataset or the model, and thus we can say that these approaches are able to select instances in a useful manner.

The unsupervised ASCF method is able to improve upon the random baseline in one configuration with statistical significance for a majority of the learning curve, and for the other configuration is able to statistically significantly improve upon this baseline given a higher number of sampled instances.

The supervised ASCF method provides even better results, providing a statistically significant improvement on the F1-scored over the random baseline at almost every point of the experiment for both datasets.

All in all, we can consider these approaches to be very useful in this experimentation setting, if we are to consider the F1-score performance measure. This allows for consistent and significant improvement upon the random sampling baseline. The most consistent seem to be the supervised, probability-based ASCF approach. In practice, the implications of the improved F1-scoring in comparison with the implementation costs of an ASCF-protocol have to be considered. Furthermore, by focusing selection on the most informative instances, an active learning approach will introduce a bias, which is beneficial for learning the classifier in the primary task, but needs to be considered when using the obtained data for different purposes.

5   Conclusion

In this paper, we have introduced a new kind of active learning problem, the Active Selection of Classification Features (ASCF): Given a primary task, which requires to learn a model $f : x \rightarrow y$ to explain/predict the relationship between a set classification features x, which are expensive to acquire, and a class label y. Then, the ASCF-task is to use a set of readily available, cheap selection variables z to select these instances, that will improve the primary task's performance most when acquiring their expensive features x and including them to the primary training set.

For this problem, we have proposed two utility-based approaches: First, an unsupervised approach that does not require labels during selection and uses the variance within data imputations as indicator of utility. Second, a supervised approach, which uses a measure adopted from probability-based active feature acquisition to select when labels in addition to selection features are available. Evaluation on three public benchmark datasets shows promising performance in initial learning stages, but also the need to improve robustness in later learning stages. A case study in the context of neuroimaging research on mental disorders indicates that the approaches are capable of reducing the number of MRI scans, that need to be acquired for reaching the same predictive performance, in comparison to random-based selection.

Acknowledgements. We would like to thank Ad Feelders for valuable discussions on this topic. Furthermore, we would like to thank the SIG Applied Data Science at UU/UMCU for funding the research project "Using active learning to reduce the costs of population-based neuroimaging studies".

References

1. Attenberg, J., Melville, P., Provost, F., Saar-Tsechansky, M.: Selective data acquisition for machine learning. In: Krishnapuram, B., Yu, S., Bharat Rao, R., (eds.), Cost-Sensitive Machine Learning. CRC Press (2011)
2. Berkson, J.: Application of the logistic function to bio-assay. J. Am. Stat. Assoc. **39**(227), 357–365 (1944)
3. Bilgic, M., Getoor, L.: VOILA: efficient feature-value acquisition for classification. In: Proceedings of the National Conference on Artificial Intelligence, vol. 22, pp. 1225–1230. MIT Press (2007)
4. Bunse, M., Morik, K.: What can we expect from active class selection? In: Proceedings of Lernen, Wissen, Daten, Analysen (LWDA) 2019, vol. 2454, pp. 79–83 (2019)

5. Contardo, G., Denoyer, L., Artières, T.: Sequential cost-sensitive feature acquisition. In: Boström, H., Knobbe, A., Soares, C., Papapetrou, P. (eds.) IDA 2016. LNCS, vol. 9897, pp. 284–294. Springer, Cham (2016). https://doi.org/10.1007/978-3-319-46349-0_25
6. Dhurandhar, A., Sankaranarayanan, K.: Improving classification performance through selective instance completion. Mach. Learn. **100**(2–3), 425–447 (2015)
7. Dua, D., Graff, C.: UCI machine learning repository (2017)
8. Fischl, B., et al.: Sequence-independent segmentation of magnetic resonance images. Neuroimage **23**(Suppl. 1), S69–S84 (2004)
9. Guyon, I., Weston, J., Barnhill, S., Vapnik, V.: Gene selection for cancer classification using support vector machines. Mach. Learn. **46**, 389–422 (2002)
10. He, H., Daumé III, H., Eisner, J.: Cost-sensitive dynamic feature selection. In: ICML Inferning Workshop (2012)
11. Kachuee, M., Goldstein, O., Kärkkäinen, K., Sarrafzadeh, M.: Opportunistic learning: budgeted cost-sensitive learning from data streams. In: International Conference on Learning Representation (2019)
12. Kottke, D., et al.: Probabilistic active learning for active class selection. In: Proceedings of the NIPS Workshop on the Future of Interactive Learning Machines (2016)
13. Kumar, P., Gupta, A.: Active learning query strategies for classification, regression, and clustering: a survey. J. Comput. Sci. Technol. **35**(4), 913–945 (2020)
14. Lomasky, R., Brodley, C.E., Aernecke, M., Walt, D., Friedl, M.: Active class selection. In: Kok, J.N., Koronacki, J., Mantaras, R.L., Matwin, S., Mladenič, D., Skowron, A. (eds.) ECML 2007. LNCS (LNAI), vol. 4701, pp. 640–647. Springer, Heidelberg (2007). https://doi.org/10.1007/978-3-540-74958-5_63
15. Melville, P., Saar-Tsechansky, M., Provost, F., Mooney, R.: Active feature-value acquisition for classifier induction. In: Fourth IEEE International Conference on Data Mining (ICDM 2004), pp. 483–486 (2004)
16. Melville, P., Saar-Tsechansky, M., Provost, F., Mooney, R.: An expected utility approach to active feature-value acquisition. In: Proceedings of the 5th International Conference on Data Mining (ICDM 2005). IEEE (2005)
17. Nieuwenhuis, M., van Haren, N.E.M., Pol, H.E.H., Cahn, W., Kahn, R.S., Schnack, H.G.: Classification of schizophrenia patients and healthy controls from structural MRI scans in two large independent samples. Neuroimage **61**(3), 606–612 (2012)
18. Saar-Tsechansky, M., Melville, P., Provost, F.: Active feature-value acquisition. Manag. Sci. **55**(4), 664–684 (2009)
19. Settles, B.: Active Learning. Number 18 in Synthesis Lectures on Artificial Intelligence and Machine Learning. Morgan and Claypool Publishers, San Rafael (2012)
20. Zheng, Z., Padmanabhan, B.: Selectively acquiring customer information: a new data acquisition problem and an active learning-based solution. Manag. Sci. **52**, 697–712 (2006)
21. Zheng, Z., Padmanabhan, B.: On active learning for data acquisition. In: Proceedings of the 2002 IEEE International Conference on Data Mining, pp. 562–569 (2002)

Feature Selection for Hierarchical Multi-label Classification

Luan V. M. da Silva and Ricardo Cerri$^{(\boxtimes)}$ (iD)

Department of Computer Science,
Federal University of São Carlos, São Carlos, SP, Brazil
luan@estudante.ufscar.br, cerri@ufscar.br

Abstract. In this work we study how conventional feature selection methods can be applied to Hierarchical Multi-label Classification Problems. In Hierarchical Multi-label Classification, instances can belong to two or more classes (labels) simultaneously, where such classes are hierarchically structured. Feature selection plays an important role in Machine Learning classification tasks, once it can effectively reduce the dataset dimensionality by removing irrelevant and/or redundant features, improving classification accuracy. Although many relevant real-world problems are from the hierarchical and multi-label domains, the majority of the related researches address the feature selection task focusing on single-label problems. In many works, even when the proposal deals with multi-label problems, the classes are not associated with a hierarchical structure. Therefore, in this work we study how feature selection can be applied in the Hierarchical Multi-label Classification context. For this, we propose four hierarchical strategies combining the Binary Relevance (BR) and Label Powerset (LP) multi-label transformations with the attribute evaluators ReliefF (RF) and Information Gain (IG). We tested our strategies on 10 real-world datasets from the functional genomic field, commonly used in Hierarchical Multi-label Classification works. As main results, three of the four proposed strategies produced some relevant subsets of features, while keeping predictive performances in comparison to the use of the complete set of features.

Keywords: Feature selection · Hierarchical Multi-label Classification · Machine Learning

1 Introduction

In the majority of the classification tasks found in the literature, a single class is assigned to a given instance, and the classes of the problem assume a flat (non-hierarchical) structure [2]. However, in several real-world problems, the classes are organized in superclasses and subclasses, forming a hierarchical taxonomy. As an example, a protein complex or organelle can be categorized in a class taxonomy associated with its cellular localization in the Gene Ontology [4]. Other examples can be found in Botanic and Zoology, where classification structures

© Springer Nature Switzerland AG 2021
P. H. Abreu et al. (Eds.): IDA 2021, LNCS 12695, pp. 196–208, 2021.
https://doi.org/10.1007/978-3-030-74251-5_16

of living beings are hierarchically organized, or in the musical field, where songs can be assigned to many genres and sub-genres.

These kind of classification problems are known in the Machine Learning (ML) literature as Hierarchical Multi-label Classification (HMC), a special case of Hierarchical Classification (HC), due to the fact that an instance can be assigned to two or more paths in the hierarchy simultaneously. According to the problem domain, a hierarchical structure can be represented as a Tree or as a Directed Acyclic Graph (DAG).

In hierarchical problems where the taxonomy is a tree-shaped structure (Fig. 1a), each class node has only one parent node, which means that each class has a single depth value (number of edges between the root node and a given node). Hence, there is just one possible path between the root and any other node. On the other hand, in DAG-shaped structures (Fig. 1b), a given class node can have more than one parent node, which means a class can have multiple depth values, since there may be several paths between the root node and another hierarchical node. These hierarchical characteristics should be considered in the development and evaluation of hierarchical classifiers.

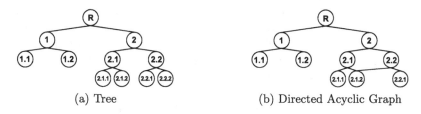

(a) Tree

(b) Directed Acyclic Graph

Fig. 1. Hierarchical structures. Adapted from [14].

Definition: Considering $\mathbf{X}$ the space of instances, the HMC problem consists of finding a function (classifier) f to map each instance $\mathbf{x}_i \in \mathbf{X}$ to a set of classes $C_i \in C$, with C the set of all classes in the problem. The function f must respect the constraints of the hierarchy, and optimize a quality criterion [2].

The hierarchy constraint states that when a class is predict, all its super-classes should also be predicted. As an example, in Fig. 1a, an instance classified in class 2.1.1 should also be classified in classes 2.1 and 2.

In classification problems, Feature Selection (FS) plays an important role, since it can effectively reduce the dimensionality of data by removing irrelevant and/or redundant features, improving classification performance. Although there are many real-world problems that are hierarchical and multi-label, the majority of the FS methods in the literature deal only with single-label problems. In addition, although there are works proposing FS methods for multi-label problems, they focus on non-hierarchical scenarios. Thus, we investigate here how FS can be applied to Hierarchical Multi-label Classification, focusing on tree-shaped hierarchies. We rely on the work of Spolaôr et al. [17] to propose strategies combining the Binary Relevance (BR) and Label Powerset (LP) multi-label transformations with the attribute evaluators ReliefF (RF) and Information Gain (IG).

The remainder of this paper is organized as follow. Section 2 defines the general Feature Selection task and presents the methods used in this work; Sect. 3 presents an overview of the related works in the literature, while Sect. 4 describes our proposed strategies for FS in HMC problems; Sect. 5 details our methodology, with the datasets and evaluation measures used; in Sect. 6 the experiments are presented and discussed; finally, in Sect. 7 we present our conclusions and future research directions.

2   Feature Selection

Feature Selection (FS) aims at finding a minimum number of attributes which describe a dataset as well as the original feature space. It is a pre-processing step, performing an important role in Machine Learning classification problems, once it reduces the feature space by removing redundant or irrelevant attributes, reducing training time while increasing or keeping predictive performance [10,21].

In general, there are three basic FS approaches: Filter, Wrapper and Embedded. While the Embedded approach performs the FS within the training process of a specific algorithm [8], the Wrapper approach requires a specific learning algorithm to evaluate and determine which features to select. This approach tends to find features better suited for the specific learning algorithm. However it has a high computational cost.

Filter-based FS methods are widely used due to their efficiency and low complexity. This method scores the attributes using some criterion and discards those who weren't selected. Different from Wrappers, they do not require the use of a learning algorithm to evaluate the features.

Among the different criteria used in the Filter approach to evaluate the importance of an attribute, ReliefF and Information Gain are very popular for single-label classification. Since we used them in our proposal, they are briefly described in the next sections.

2.1   ReliefF

The original Relief attribute estimator is limited to deal with two class problems. Its key idea is to estimate the quality of an attribute according to how well its values distinguish between instances that are near to each other. The ReliefF (RF) algorithm overcomes this limitation, being more robust and dealing with incomplete and noisy data. For that purpose, given a randomly selected instance R_i, RF searches for its k nearest neighbors from the same class, called nearest hits (H_j), and also the k nearest neighbors from each of the different classes, called nearest misses $M_j(C)$. It updates the quality estimation $W[A]$ for all attributes A depending on their values for R_i, H_j and misses $M_j(C)$. The contribution for each class of the misses is weighted with the prior probability of that class $P(C)$

(estimated from the training set) [13]. The parameter k for hits and misses is the basic difference from the original Relief, and ensures greater robustness of the algorithm concerning noise. The whole process is repeated m times, where m is a user-defined parameter. For more details on ReliefF, please refer to the work of Robnik-Šikonja and Kononenko [13].

2.2   Information Gain

Information Gain (IG) is a measure based on the concept of entropy. It measures the dependency between each feature of a space of instances and a single class label. It ranks features (a_j) based on their amount of information; the higher is the IG value for a feature a_j, the stronger is the relationship between that feature a_j and the label. The Information Gain measure is calculated by the difference between the entropy of a dataset D and the weighted sum of each subset $D_v \subseteq D$, where D_v consists of the set of instances where a_j has the value v. Therefore, if a_j has 10 distinct values in D, the sum would be applied to 10 different D_v datasets. For details please refer to Spolaôr et al. [18].

3   Related Work

Although scarce in the hierarchical multi-label scenarios, multi-label feature selection has gained attention from the machine learning, statistical computing and related communities. This section briefly describes some related works proposed for multi-label classification in non-hierarchical and hierarchical scenarios.

In the work of Amazal et al. [1], the authors address the multi-label feature selection task proposing a weighted Chi-square feature selection approach called Distributed Category Term Frequency Based on Chi-square (CTF-CHI), and used a Multinominal Naive Bayes (MNB) classifier to evaluate the efficiency of a selected subset of features. The authors performed feature selection by transforming the original problem into a single-label one.

Gao et al. [6] proposed a multi-label feature selection method named Feature Redundancy Maximization (FRM) to deal with the problem of overestimating the redundancy of some candidate features, entailed by traditional multi-label feature selection methods which employ the cumulative summation strategy.

Petkovic et al. [12] investigated two groups of feature ranking for multi-target regression (MTR) tasks, by studying the feature ranking scores (Symbolic, Genie3, and Random Forest scores) based on ensembles (bagging, random forest, extra trees) of predictive clustering trees, and a score derived of the RReliefF method. MTR problems consist of multiple continuous target variables, where the goal is to learn a model for predicting all of them simultaneously.

Slavkov et al. [15] address feature ranking in the context of HMC problem by focusing in the ReliefF feature importance estimator, a continuation of author's previous work [16]. The authors tested their propose on five datasets from the biology and image fields, and obtained better results when compared with a feature ranking algorithm based on BR.

Still in feature ranking, Petkovic et al. [11] extended his work on Multi-target regression [12] for HMC. They applied a group of feature ranking approaches based on the Symbolic, Genie3 and Random Forest scoring functions, coupled with Bagging, Random Forest and Extra Trees ensembles of PCTs. The authors evaluated their approaches on 30 HMC benchmark datasets by using a kNN model that considers feature importance scores in the distance function. The results obtained outperformed the HMC-Relief feature ranking method, and demonstrated that Symbolic and Genie3 yield relevant feature rankings.

4   Applying Feature Selection in HMC

In this section we introduce our proposal for applying FS in HMC problems. We first briefly introduce the Binary Relevance (BR) and Label-Powerset (LP) multi-label transformations, which are used in our proposal.

4.1   Binary Relevance

Binary Relevance (BR) consists in learning a different classifier for each class of the problem. The original multi-label problem is transformed into $|C|$ binary problems, where C is the set of classes from the original problem. The i-th $(i = 1 \ldots |C|)$ classifier decides if an instance belongs to the i-th class [5]. A final multi-label classification is then obtained combining the single-label predictions.

4.2   Label Powerset

Label Powerset (LP) considers each subset of classes from C as a new and unique class, forming a single-label multi-class problem. One multi-class classifier is trained for the new problem. Given a new instance, the classifier predicts its most probable class, which represents a set of classes. Unlike BR, LP considers the correlation among labels, but since the transformation increases the number of classes, these can end having very few positive instances [7].

4.3   Our Proposal

We use the work of Spolaôr et al. [17], which combines the BR and LP transformations with ReliefF (RF) and Information Gain (IG), resulting in four non-hierarchical multi-label feature selection methods:

- **RF-BR:** ReliefF based on the BR transformation;
- **RF-LP:** ReliefF based on the LP transformation;
- **IG-BR:** Information Gain based on the BR transformation;
- **IG-LP:** Information Gain based on the LP transformation.

We focus on HMC problems with hierarchies structured as trees. Since each hierarchical level can be considered a multi-label non-hierarchical problem (see Fig. 1a), we apply the four above methods in each level. The selected features for each level are then combined to form a new hierarchical dataset. This results in four different strategies for FS in HMC.

Let $\mathbf{D}$ be a Hierarchical Multi-label Dataset, with $\mathbf{X}$ denoting the space of instances, $\mathbf{Y}$ denoting the space of classes, $\mathbf{A}$ denoting the space of attributes, and n denoting the number of levels of the hierarchy.

We first apply a pre-processing in the tree structure level by level, transforming a HMC dataset in n non-Hierarchical (flat) Multi-label (nHMC) datasets. We thus have a new flat multi-label dataset for each of the n levels of the hierarchy. We name each of these n flat datasets as datalevels. Each datalevel inherits the original feature space $\mathbf{A}$ of the problem. The i-th datalevel, with $i = \{1, \ldots, n\}$, contains the instances which are classified in the classes located in the i-th level of the original dataset $\mathbf{D}$. To deal with the hierarchy constraint (mentioned in Sect. 1), the instances classified in classes located in the i-th level are also assigned to their superclasses. Thus, if an instance is in datalevel i, it is also in all the previous $i - 1$ datalevels. As an example, in Fig. 1a, we would have three datalevels, and the instances belonging to the third datalevel (level 3) would also belong to the second (level 2) and first (level 1) datalevels simultaneously.

In a second step, we apply one the FS methods (RF-BR, RF-LP, IG-BR, IG-LP) to all datalevels. These methods return, for each feature, a score representing the importance of that feature. Thus, the features of a datalevel are sorted in a descending order according to the values of their scores. We have now to apply a score threshold in order to select a given number of features.

The choice of an optimal threshold for each datalevel is not trivial, since each datalevel has specific characteristics, such as different numbers of attributes from different domains and contexts. Low threshold values may lead to the selection of many no relevant or redundant features. In the other hand, high threshold values may leave behind relevant attributes by selecting a very small set.

Since we are not interested in selecting specific features, but instead we want to evaluate the ability of our proposal in selecting features, we adopt a different strategy to choose thresholds. We use a boxplot to analyze the position, dispersion, and symmetry regarding the attributes after obtaining their scores for each FS method applied to each datalevel. We consider features with a score above 0.

By putting all scores in a boxplot, we can analyze different numbers of selected features without having to directly apply a threshold. We select 100% of the features (corresponding to the interval between the worst and the best score), the features in the interval between the first quartile and the best score, the features in the interval between the median and the best score, and finally the features in the interval between the third quartile and the best score.

After selecting features for each level independently, a third step generates a new HMC dataset, where the new feature space $\mathbf{A'}$ is the union of all the features selected in all datalevels. We execute the previous steps for each of the FS methods RF-BR, RF-LP, IG-BR and IG-LP.

Finally, we induce a Hierarchical Multi-Label classifier in the new hierarchical dataset having the reduced number of features. In our experiments, we employed Clus-HMC [19], one of the state-of-the-art HMC methods in the literature. Figure 2 illustrates all steps of our proposal.

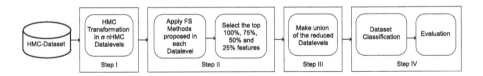

Fig. 2. Illustration of all the steps of our proposal.

5   Methodology

This section presents the datasets used in our experiments, the base classifier used to validate our proposal, and the evaluation measures employed.

5.1   Datasets

We used ten HMC protein function datasets modeled as a tree. They are commonly used to evaluate hierarchical multi-label classifiers [9], and are freely available[1]. They come with already prepared training, validation and test partitions, which have been used by many works in the literature. Table 1 presents the main characteristics of the used datasets.

Many methods in the literature, such as Clare [3], Vens et al. [19], Cerri et al. [2], and Wehrmann et al. [20] have presented the results of their proposals on these datasets, training their models on 2/3 of each dataset and testing on the remaining 1/3. Here we use exactly the same schema, by putting together the training and validation sets, and testing on the remaining test set.

5.2   Base Classifier

Clus-HMC [19] is an algorithm which builds decision tree classifiers. It is based on Predictive Clustering Trees (PCTs), where the root node corresponds to a cluster containing all training data, which is recursively partitioned in minor clusters while going down to the leaf nodes. PCTs are built in such a way that each division aims to maximize the variance reduction within each cluster.

To apply PCTs to the HMC task, first, the instance labels are represented as binary vectors: the i-th vector component is assigned 1 if the instance belongs to class c_i, and 0 otherwise. To analyze the variance in the HMC context, Clus-HMC considers the similarity in higher hierarchical levels as more important than

---

[1] FunCat2018 - https://itec.kuleuven-kulak.be/?page_id=5236.

Table 1. Datasets: #attributes ($|A|$); #classes per level ($|C|$); #instances ($|X|$); attribute type (Type): numerical (Quanti), qualitative (Quali) or both (Mixed).

No.	Dataset	$|A|$	$|C|$	Type	$|X|$		
					Training	Validation	Testing
D1	Cellcycle	77	20/86/210/171/92/6	Quanti	1628	848	1281
D2	Church	27	20/86/210/171/92/6	Mixed	1630	844	1281
D3	Derisi	63	20/86/210/171/92/6	Quanti	1608	842	1275
D4	Eisen	79	19/84/201/159/83/6	Quanti	1058	529	837
D5	Expr	551	20/86/210/171/92/6	Mixed	1639	849	1291
D6	Gasch1	173	20/86/210/171/92/6	Quanti	1634	846	1284
D7	Gasch2	52	20/86/210/171/92/6	Quanti	1639	849	1291
D8	Pheno	69	20/86/198/156/83/5	Quali	656	353	582
D9	Seq	478	20/86/210/171/93/6	Mixed	1701	879	1339
D10	Spo	80	20/86/210/171/92/6	Mixed	1600	837	1266

similarity in low levels. This is performed weighting classes for the calculation of the Euclidean distance between the binary vectors. Here we used the Clus-HMC implementation provided within the Clus framework, which is freely available[2]. For more details on Clus-HMC, please refer to Vens et al. [19].

5.3   Evaluation Measures

We used Precision-Recall (PR) curves to evaluate our results. Since Clus-HMC outputs a probability of an instance to belong to each class, we can use different threshold values in the range [0.0, 1.0] in order to produce many PR points, generating a curve plotting the precision of a model as a function of its recall. In this work, we used two PR-curve variations, defined below.

- **Weighted Average of the Areas Under the individual PR curves** ($\overline{AUPRC}_w$): average the areas under individual PR-curves, weighting classes by their frequencies $w_i = v_i / \sum_j v_j$, with v_i the frequency of class c_i. It gives more importance to more frequent classes. $\overline{AUPRC}_w$ is given by Eq. 1.
- **Average Area Under the PR Curves** ($\overline{AUPRC}$): an instantiation of the previous $\overline{AUPRC}_w$, where all weights are set to $1/|C|$, with C the set of classes, $\overline{AUPRC}$ is given by Eq. 2.

$$\overline{AUPRC}_w = \sum_i w_i \times AUPRC_i \quad (1) \qquad \overline{AUPRC} = \frac{1}{|C|} \times \sum_i AUPRC_i \quad (2)$$

---

[2] https://dtai.cs.kuleuven.be/clus/.

6   Experiments and Discussion

Figures 3 and 4 present our results with different numbers of selected features, as described in our boxplot strategy. We executed Clus-HMC with its best hyper-parameter values as suggested by Vens et al. [19][3]. We also compare our proposal with a version of PCA able to deal with both numeric and categorical features (PCAMix). Since PCA is an unsupervised method, it was applied to the whole feature set just once, without separating the original dataset in many datalevels. The figures use the following notation.

- Min: 100% of the selected features with score higher than 0, corresponding to the interval between the worst and the best score;
- 1st Quartile: the features between the first quartile and the best score;
- Median: the features between the median and the best score;
- 3rd Quartile: the features between the third quartile and the best score;
- Reference: Clus-HMC in the hierarchical dataset without feature selection;
- PCAMix: PCA applied to the hierarchical dataset without separating it in non-hierarchical datasets;

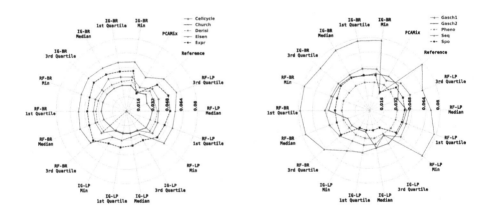

Fig. 3. Results for $\overline{AUPRC}$.

Although there is no strategy that led to predictive enhancements in all cases, three out of the four proposed FS strategies have selected relevant features in at least 6/10 cases in some boxplot partitions. The results belonging to the Min boxplot partition, which represents 100% of the features selected (score higher than 0), did not lead to predictive changes considering IG-BR, RF-BR and RF-LP. The Eisen and Seq datasets were the only ones with a predictive loss in the 1st quartile for BR in both evaluation measures. For all the strategies proposed,

---

[3] https://dtai.cs.kuleuven.be/clus/hmcdatasets/ftests.txt.

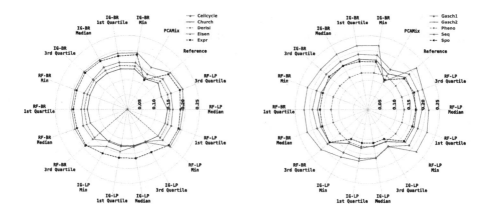

Fig. 4. Results for $\overline{AUPRC}_w$.

the Median boxplot partition was the one that led to the best results, with IG-BR producing discrete predictive gains in 8/10 datasets considering $\overline{AUPRC}_w$, such as 4% in Spo, 1% in Gasch2, 2% in Expr, 2% in Derisi, and less than 1% in the remaining datasets. The exceptions were Eisen and Seq. Still in the Median partition, BR-RF led to gains in 7/10 datasets in both evaluation measures, such as 4% in Derisi, 3% in Eisen, 5% in Gasch1, 4% in Gasch2 and about 1% in the remaining datasets. The exceptions were Cellcycle, Church and Seq. Finally, RF-LP in the Median boxplot partition led to gains in 6/10 datasets in $\overline{AUPRC}$, with the exception of Cellcycle, Gasch1, Gasch2 and Seq.

The IG-LP strategy, although selecting extremely few features, produced the worst predictive performance at all. This result is visible in Figs. 3 and 4, where the curves decay sharply in all subdivisions of quartiles referring to IG-LP. It is also possible to see that in the Derisi dataset, no features have been selected.

Although PCA considerably reduced the feature space (23.8% of the original space in Derisi and 64.2% of the original space in Seq), the evaluation measures show that the principal components actually contributed negatively to the predictive performances. In comparison to the reference value, the performances after applying PCA were 45,8% lower in the Church dataset, 38.5% lower in Derisi, and 50,5% lower in Expr. Predictive gains were obtained in Pheno, with 3.4% and 4.5% higher performances in $\overline{AUPRC}$ and $\overline{AUPRC}_w$, respectively.

Figure 5 shows the percentage of features selected by each strategy, relative to the total number of features. The figure also shows the number of principal components as a percentage of the number of original features. We show the principal components which explain 90% or more of the data variation. Note that it is possible to see a common pattern in our FS strategies. In most of them, many attributes are selected near to the first boxplot quartile, while fewer attributes are selected near to the third quartile. As an example, taking RF-BR, we see almost no features selected near to the first quartile, while 62% of the original features are selected near to the third quartile. Another observation is that, as the Min partition corresponds to the 100% selected features with scores higher than 0, some datasets may have the Min below the 100% line, since some attributes didn't have a score. Thus, the Min partitions in the radar plots may differ from the baseline, such as the dataset Spo with IG-BR.

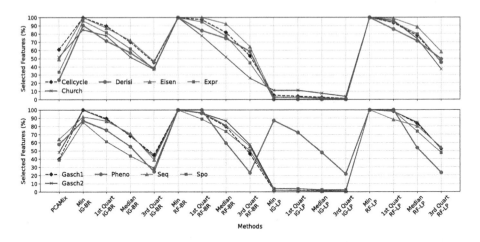

Fig. 5. Percentage of selected features according to each strategy.

7   Conclusion and Future Work

In this work we proposed strategies to apply feature selection methods in hierarchical multi-label datasets. Our proposal divides the original hierarchy in many non-hierarchical (flat) multi-label datasets, applies feature selection strategies combined with multi-label transformations in each flat dataset, and then combines the features selected forming a hierarchy with a new reduced feature space.

From our experiments, we can conclude that three (IG-BR, RF-BR e RF-LP) out of the four proposed FS strategies have selected relevant subsets of features. While reducing the feature space, these three methods improved or maintained predictive performances, with the exception of some few dataset. It is also possible to conclude that PCA is not a good choice for feature space reduction when related to hierarchical structures.

As can be seen from our work, feature selection focusing on hierarchical problems still has a large space for improvements. Other FS methods could be applied using our proposal, and new specific methods still need to be developed. As future works, we would like to study how feature selection methods can be applied in HMC problems with hierarchies structured as Directed Acyclic Graphs. Since in these structures the depth of a class is dependent on the different paths between it and the root class, our proposal is not directly applicable.

References

1. Amazal, H., Ramdani, M., Kissi, M.: Towards a feature selection for multi-label text classification in Big Data. In: Hamlich, M., Bellatreche, L., Mondal, A., Ordonez, C. (eds.) SADASC 2020. CCIS, vol. 1207, pp. 187–199. Springer, Cham (2020). https://doi.org/10.1007/978-3-030-45183-7_14
2. Cerri, R., Barros, R.C., de Carvalho, A.C., Jin, Y.: Reduction strategies for hierarchical multi-label classification in protein function prediction. BMC Bioinformatics **17**(1), 373 (2016)
3. Clare, A.: Machine learning and data mining for yeast functional genomics. Doctor of Philosophy, Aberystwyth, The University of Wales (2003)
4. Gene Ontology Consortium: The Gene Ontology (GO) database and informatics resource. Nucleic Acids Res. **32**(suppl–1), D258–D261 (2004)
5. Doquire, G., Verleysen, M.: Feature selection for multi-label classification problems. In: Cabestany, J., Rojas, I., Joya, G. (eds.) IWANN 2011. LNCS, vol. 6691, pp. 9–16. Springer, Heidelberg (2011). https://doi.org/10.1007/978-3-642-21501-8_2
6. Gao, W., Hu, J., Li, Y., Zhang, P.: Feature redundancy based on interaction information for multi-label feature selection. IEEE Access **8**, 146050–146064 (2020)
7. Kashef, S., Nezamabadi-pour, H., Nikpour, B.: Multilabel feature selection: a comprehensive review and guiding experiments. Wiley Interdiscip. Rev: Data Min. Knowl. Discov. **8**(2), e1240 (2018)
8. Liu, C., Ma, Q., Xu, J.: Multi-label feature selection method combining unbiased Hilbert-Schmidt independence criterion with controlled genetic algorithm. In: Cheng, L., Leung, A.C.S., Ozawa, S. (eds.) ICONIP 2018. LNCS, vol. 11304, pp. 3–14. Springer, Cham (2018). https://doi.org/10.1007/978-3-030-04212-7_1
9. Nakano, F.K., Lietaert, M., Vens, C.: Machine learning for discovering missing or wrong protein function annotations. BMC Bioinformatics **20**(1), 485 (2019)
10. Peralta, D., Triguero, I., García, S., Saeys, Y., Benitez, J.M., Herrera, F.: Distributed incremental fingerprint identification with reduced database penetration rate using a hierarchical classification based on feature fusion and selection. Knowl-Based Syst. **126**, 91–103 (2017)
11. Petkovic, M., Dzeroski, S., Kocev, D.: Feature ranking for hierarchical multi-label classification with tree ensemble methods. Acta Polytechnica Hungarica **17**(10), 129–148 (2020)
12. Petković, M., Kocev, D., Džeroski, S.: Feature ranking for multi-target regression. Mach. Learn. **109**(6), 1179–1204 (2020). https://doi.org/10.1007/s10994-019-05829-8
13. Robnik-Šikonja, M., Kononenko, I.: Theoretical and empirical analysis of ReliefF and RReliefF. Mach. Learn. **53**(1–2), 23–69 (2003). https://doi.org/10.1023/A:1025667309714
14. Silla, C.N., Freitas, A.A.: A survey of hierarchical classification across different application domains. Data Min. Knowl. Disc. **22**(1–2), 31–72 (2011). https://doi.org/10.1007/s10618-010-0175-9
15. Slavkov, I., Karcheska, J., Kocev, D., Džeroski, S.: HMC-ReliefF: feature ranking for hierarchical multi-label classification. Comput. Sci. Inf. Syst. **15**(1), 187–209 (2018)
16. Slavkov, I., Karcheska, J., Kocev, D., Kalajdziski, S., Džeroski, S.: ReliefF for hierarchical multi-label classification. In: Appice, A., Ceci, M., Loglisci, C., Manco, G., Masciari, E., Ras, Z.W. (eds.) NFMCP 2013. LNCS (LNAI), vol. 8399, pp. 148–161. Springer, Cham (2014). https://doi.org/10.1007/978-3-319-08407-7_10

17. SpolaôR, N., Cherman, E.A., Monard, M.C., Lee, H.D.: A comparison of multi-label feature selection methods using the problem transformation approach. Electron. Notes Theor. Comput. Sci. **292**, 135–151 (2013)
18. Spolaôr, N., Monard, M.C., Tsoumakas, G., Lee, H.D.: A systematic review of multi-label feature selection and a new method based on label construction. Neurocomputing **180**, 3–15 (2016)
19. Vens, C., Struyf, J., Schietgat, L., Džeroski, S., Blockeel, H.: Decision trees for hierarchical multi-label classification. Mach. Learn. **73**(2), 185–214 (2008). https://doi.org/10.1007/s10994-008-5077-3
20. Wehrmann, J., Cerri, R., Barros, R.: Hierarchical multi-label classification networks. In: Proceedings of Machine Learning Research, vol. 80, pp. 5075–5084 (2018)
21. Wei, L., Wan, S., Guo, J., Wong, K.K.: A novel hierarchical selective ensemble classifier with bioinformatics application. Artif. Intell. Med. **83**, 82–90 (2017)

Bandit Algorithm for both Unknown Best Position and Best Item Display on Web Pages

Camille-Sovanneary Gauthier[1,3(✉)], Romaric Gaudel[2], and Elisa Fromont[3]

[1] Louis Vuitton, Paris, France
camille-sovanneary.gauthier@louisvuitton.com
[2] Univ. Rennes, Ensai, CNRS, CREST, Rennes, France
romaric.gaudel@ensai.fr
[3] Univ. Rennes, IUF, Inria, IRISA, Rennes, France
elisa.fromont@irisa.fr

Abstract. Multiple-play bandits aim at displaying relevant items at relevant positions on a web page. We introduce a new bandit-based algorithm, PB-MHB, for online recommender systems which uses the Thompson sampling framework with Metropolis-Hastings approximation. This algorithm handles a display setting governed by the position-based model. Our sampling method does not require as input the probability of a user to look at a given position in the web page which is difficult to obtain in some applications. Experiments on simulated and real datasets show that our method, with fewer prior information, delivers better recommendations than state-of-the-art algorithms.

Keywords: Multi-armed bandit · Position-Based Model · Thomson Sampling · Metropolis-Hasting

1 Introduction

An online recommender systems (ORS) chooses an item to recommend to a user among a list of N potential items. The relevance of the item is measured by the users' feedback: clicks, time spent looking at the item, rating, etc. Since a feedback is only available when an item is presented to a user, the ORS needs to present both attractive items (a.k.a. *exploit*) to please the current user, and some items with an uncertain relevance (a.k.a. *explore*) to reduce this uncertainty and perform better recommendations to future users. It faces the *exploration-exploitation dilemma* expressed by the *multi-armed bandit setting* [3].

On websites, online recommender systems select L items per time-stamp, corresponding to L specific positions in which to display an item. Typical examples of such systems are (i) a list of news, visible one by one by scrolling; (ii) a list of products, arranged by rows; or (iii) advertisements spread in a web page. To be selected (clicked) by a user in such context, an item needs to be relevant

P. H. Abreu et al. (Eds.): IDA 2021, LNCS 12695, pp. 209–221, 2021.
https://doi.org/10.1007/978-3-030-74251-5_17

by itself, but also to be displayed at the right position. Several models express the way a user behaves while facing such a list of items [9,23] and they have been transposed to the bandit framework [14,15].

Retailers often spread their commercials over a web page or display their items on several rows all at once. Thus, in this paper, we will focus on the *Position-Based Model* (PBM) [23]. This model assumes that the probability to click on an item i in position ℓ results only from the combined impact of this item and its position: items displayed at other positions do not impact the probability to consider the item at position ℓ. PBM also gives a user the opportunity to give more than one feedback: she may click on all the items relevant for her. It means we are facing the so-called *multiple-play* (semi-)bandit setting [5]. PBM setting is particularly interesting when the display is dynamic, as often on modern web pages, and may depend on the reading direction of the user (which varies from one country to another) and on the ever-changing layout of the page.

Contribution. We introduce PB-MHB (Position Based Metropolis-Hastings Bandit), a bandit algorithm designed to handle PBM with a Thompson sampling framework. This algorithm does not require the knowledge of the probability of a user to look at a given position: it learns this probability from past recommendations/feedback. This is a strong improvement w.r.t. previous attempts in this research line [13,17] as it allows the use of PB-MHB in contexts where this information is not obvious. This improvement results from the use of the Metropolis-Hastings framework [22] to sample parameters given their true *a posteriori* distribution, even thought it is not a usual distribution. While Markov Chain Monte Carlo methods are well-known and extensively used in Bayesian statistics, they were rarely used for Thomson Sampling [10,12,21,24] and it is the first time that the Metropolis-Hastings framework is used in the PBM setting. Besides this specificity, we also experimentally show that PB-MHB suffers a smaller regret than its competitors.

The paper is organized as follows: Sect. 2 presents the related work and Sect. 3 precisely defines our setting. PB-MHB is introduced in Sect. 4 and is experimentally compared to state-of-the-art algorithms in Sect. 5. We conclude in Sect. 6.

2   Related Work

PBM [9,23] relies on two vectors of parameters: $\boldsymbol{\theta} \in [0,1]^N$ and $\boldsymbol{\kappa} \in [0,1]^L$, where $\boldsymbol{\theta}_i$ is the probability for the user to click on item i when she observes that item, and $\boldsymbol{\kappa}_\ell$ is the probability for the user to observe the position ℓ. These parameters are unknown, but they may be inferred from user behavior data: we need to first record the user feedback (click vs. no-click per position) for each set of displayed items, then we may apply an *expectation-maximization* framework to compute the maximum a posteriori values for $(\boldsymbol{\theta}, \boldsymbol{\kappa})$ given these data [7].

PBM is transposed to the bandit framework in [13,14,17]. [13] and [17] propose two approaches based on a Thompson sampling (TS) framework, with two different sampling strategies. [17] also introduce several approaches based on the *optimism in face of uncertainty* principle [3]. However, the approaches in [13,17] assume $\boldsymbol{\kappa}$ known beforehand. [14] proposes the only approach learning both $\boldsymbol{\theta}$ and $\boldsymbol{\kappa}$ while recommending but it still requires the $\boldsymbol{\kappa}_\ell$ values to be organized in decreasing order, which we do not require. Note also that the corresponding approach is not based, as ours, on Thompson sampling.

While more theoretical results are obtained when applying the *optimism in face of uncertainty* principle to the bandit setting, approaches based on TS are known to deliver more accurate recommendations [1,4,6,12]. The limitation of TS is its requirement to draw from 'exotic' distributions when dealing with complex models. By limiting themselves to a setting where $\boldsymbol{\kappa}$ is known, [13] and [17] face simpler distributions than the one which arises from $\boldsymbol{\kappa}$ being unknown. In the following, we propose to use Metropolis-Hastings framework to handle this harder distribution. [10,24] investigate a large range of distribution approximation strategies to apply TS framework to the distributions arising from the *contextual bandit* setting, and [12,21] apply approximate sampling to other settings. Overall, these articles handle a pure bandit setting while we are in a semi-bandits setting: for each recommendation we receive as reward a list of 1 or 0 (click or not). As most of commercial website can track precisely on which product each client clicks, we aim at exploiting that fine-grain information.

The *cascading model* (CM) [9] is another popular model of user behavior. It assumes that the positions are observed in a known order and that the user leaves the website as soon as she clicks on an item[1]. More specifically, if she clicks on the item in position ℓ, she will not look at the following positions: $\ell+1, \ldots, L$. This setting has been extensively studied within the bandit framework [6,8,11, 15,16,20,27]. However, the assumption of CM regarding the order of observation is irrelevant when considering items spread in a page or on a grid (especially as reading direction of the user may varies from one country to another).

A few approaches simultaneously handle CM and PBM [18,19,26]. Their genericity is their strength and their weakness: they do not require the knowledge of the behavioral model, but they cannot use that model to speed-up the process of learning the user preferences. Moreover, these algorithms assume that the best recommendation consists in ordering the items from the more attractive to the less attractive ones. In the context of PBM, this is equivalent to assuming $\boldsymbol{\kappa}$ to be sorted in decreasing order. Our algorithm does not make such assumption. Anyhow, we also compare PB-MHB to TopRank [18] in Sect. 5 in order to ensure that our model benefits from the knowledge of the click model.

3   Recommendation Setting

The proposed approach handles the following online recommendations setting: at each time-stamp t, the ORS chooses a list $\boldsymbol{i}(t) = (\boldsymbol{i}_1(t), \ldots, \boldsymbol{i}_L(t))$ of L distinct items among a set of N items. The user observes each position ℓ with a probability $\boldsymbol{\kappa}_\ell$, and if the position is observed, the user clicks on the item $\boldsymbol{i}_\ell$ with a probability $\boldsymbol{\theta}_{\boldsymbol{i}_\ell}$. We denote $\boldsymbol{r}_\ell(t) \in \{0,1\}$ the reward in position ℓ obtained

---

[1] Some refined models assume a probability to leave. With these models, the user may click on several items.

by proposing i at time t, namely 1 if the user did observe the position ℓ and clicked on item $i_\ell(t)$, and 0 otherwise. We assume that each draw is independent, meaning $r_\ell(t) \mid i_\ell(t) \overset{iid.}{\sim}$ Bernoulli $(\theta_{i_\ell}\kappa_\ell)$, or in other words

$$\begin{cases} \mathbb{P}\left(r_\ell(t) = 1 \mid i_\ell(t)\right) = \theta_{i_\ell}\kappa_\ell, \\ \mathbb{P}\left(r_\ell(t) = 0 \mid i_\ell(t)\right) = 1 - \theta_{i_\ell}\kappa_\ell. \end{cases}$$

The ORS aims at maximizing the *cumulative reward*, namely the total number of clicks gathered from time-stamp 1 to time-stamp T: $\sum_{t=1}^{T}\sum_{\ell=1}^{L} r_\ell(t)$.

Without loss of generality, we assume that $\max_\ell \kappa_\ell = 1$.[2] To keep the notations simple, we also assume that $\theta_1 > \theta_2 > \cdots > \theta_N$, and $\kappa_1 = 1 > \kappa_2 > \cdots > \kappa_L$.[3] The best recommendation is then $i^* = (1, 2, \ldots, L)$, which leads to the expected instantaneous reward $\mu^* = \sum_{\ell=1}^{L} \theta_\ell \kappa_\ell$.

The pair (θ, κ) is unknown from the ORS. It has to infer the best recommendation from the recommendations and the rewards gathered at previous time-stamps, denoted $D(t) = \{(i(1), r(1)), \ldots, (i(t-1), r(t-1))\}$. This corresponds to the *bandit setting* where it is usual to consider the *(cumulative pseudo-)regret*

$$R_T \overset{def}{=} \sum_{t=1}^{T}\sum_{\ell=1}^{L} \mathbb{E}\left[r_\ell \mid i_\ell^*\right] - \sum_{t=1}^{T}\sum_{\ell=1}^{L} \mathbb{E}\left[r_\ell(t) \mid i_\ell(t)\right] = T\mu^* - \sum_{t=1}^{T}\sum_{\ell=1}^{L} \theta_{i_\ell(t)}\kappa_\ell. \quad (1)$$

The regret R_T denotes the cumulative expected loss of the ORS w.r.t. the oracle recommending the best items at each time-stamp. Hereafter we aim at an algorithm which minimizes the expectation of R_T w.r.t. its choices.

4   PB-MHB Algorithm

We handle the setting presented in the previous section with the online recommender system depicted by Algorithm 1 and referred to as PB-MHB (for Position Based Metropolis-Hastings Bandit). This algorithm is based on the Thompson sampling framework [2,25]. First, we look at rewards with a fully Bayesian point of view: we assume that they follow the statistical model depicted in Sect. 3, and we choose a uniform prior on the parameters θ and κ. Therefore the posterior probability for these parameters given the previous observations $D(t)$ is

$$\mathbb{P}\left(\theta, \kappa \mid D(t)\right) \propto \prod_{i=1}^{N}\prod_{\ell=1}^{L} (\theta_i \kappa_\ell)^{S_{i,\ell}(t)} (1 - \theta_i \kappa_\ell)^{F_{i,\ell}(t)}, \quad (2)$$

where $S_{i,\ell}(t) = \sum_{s=1}^{t-1} \mathbb{1}_{i_\ell(s)=i} \mathbb{1}_{r_\ell(s)=1}$ denotes the number of times the item i has been clicked while being displayed in position ℓ from time-stamp 1 to $t-1$, and $F_{i,\ell}(t) = \sum_{s=1}^{t-1} \mathbb{1}_{i_\ell(s)=i} \mathbb{1}_{r_\ell(s)=0}$ denotes the number of times the item i has not been clicked while being displayed in position ℓ from time-stamp 1 to $t-1$.

---

[2] As stated in [14], we may replace (θ, κ) by $(\theta. \max_\ell \kappa_\ell, \kappa/\max_\ell \kappa_\ell)$.

[3] Our algorithm and the experiments only assume $\kappa_1 = 1$.

Algorithm 1. PB-MHB, Metropolis-Hastings based bandit for Position-Based Model

---

$D(1) \leftarrow \{\}$
for $t = 1, \ldots$ **do**
    draw $(\tilde{\boldsymbol{\theta}}, \tilde{\boldsymbol{\kappa}}) \sim \mathbb{P}(\boldsymbol{\theta}, \boldsymbol{\kappa}|D(t))$ using Algorithm 2
    display the L items with greatest value in $\tilde{\boldsymbol{\theta}}$, ordered by decreasing values of $\tilde{\boldsymbol{\kappa}}$
    get rewards $\boldsymbol{r}(t)$
    $D(t+1) \leftarrow D(t) \cup (\boldsymbol{i}(t), \boldsymbol{r}(t))$
end for

Second, we choose the recommendation $\boldsymbol{i}(t)$ at time-stamp t according to its posterior probability of being the best arm. To do so, we denote $(\tilde{\boldsymbol{\theta}}, \tilde{\boldsymbol{\kappa}})$ a sample of parameters $(\boldsymbol{\theta}, \boldsymbol{\kappa})$ according to their posterior probability, we keep the best items given $\tilde{\boldsymbol{\theta}}$, and we display them in the right order given $\tilde{\boldsymbol{\kappa}}$.

4.1 Sampling w.r.t. the Posterior Distribution

The posterior probability (2) does not correspond to a well-known distribution. [13,17] tackle this problem by considering that $\boldsymbol{\kappa}$ is known in order to manipulate N independent simpler distributions $\mathbb{P}_i(\boldsymbol{\theta}_i|\boldsymbol{\theta}_{-i}, \boldsymbol{\kappa}, D(t))$. By having $\boldsymbol{\kappa}$ and $\boldsymbol{\theta}$ both unknown, we have to handle a law for which the components $\boldsymbol{\theta}_1, \ldots, \boldsymbol{\theta}_N$ and $\boldsymbol{\kappa}_1, \ldots, \boldsymbol{\kappa}_L$ are correlated (see Eq. 2). We handle it thanks to a carefully designed Metropolis-Hastings algorithm [22] (cf. Algorithm 2). This algorithm consists in building a sequence of m samples $(\boldsymbol{\theta}^{(1)}, \boldsymbol{\kappa}^{(1)}), \ldots, (\boldsymbol{\theta}^{(m)}, \boldsymbol{\kappa}^{(m)})$ such that $(\boldsymbol{\theta}^{(m)}, \boldsymbol{\kappa}^{(m)})$ follows a good approximation of the targeted distribution. It is based on a Markov chain on parameters $(\boldsymbol{\theta}, \boldsymbol{\kappa})$ which admits the targeted probability distribution as its unique stationary distribution.

At iteration s, the sample $(\boldsymbol{\theta}^{(s)}, \boldsymbol{\kappa}^{(s)})$ moves toward sample $(\boldsymbol{\theta}^{(s+1)}, \boldsymbol{\kappa}^{(s+1)})$ by applying $(N + L - 1)$ transitions: one per item and one per position except for $\boldsymbol{\kappa}_1$. Let's start by focusing on the transition regarding item i (Lines 5–9) and denote $(\boldsymbol{\theta}, \boldsymbol{\kappa})$ the sample before the transition.

The algorithm aims at sampling a new value for $\boldsymbol{\theta}_i$ according to its posterior probability given other parameters and the previous observations $D(t)$:

$$\mathbb{P}_i(\boldsymbol{\theta}_i|\boldsymbol{\theta}_{-i}, \boldsymbol{\kappa}, D(t)) \propto \prod_{\ell=1}^{L} \boldsymbol{\theta}_i^{S_{i,\ell}(t)} (1 - \boldsymbol{\theta}_i \boldsymbol{\kappa}_\ell)^{F_{i,\ell}(t)}, \tag{3}$$

where $\boldsymbol{\theta}_{-i}$ denotes the components of $\boldsymbol{\theta}$ except for the i-th one. This transition consists in two steps:

1. *draw a candidate* value $\tilde{\boldsymbol{\theta}}$ after a *proposal* probability distribution $q\left(\tilde{\boldsymbol{\theta}} \mid \boldsymbol{\theta}_i, \boldsymbol{\theta}_{-i}, \boldsymbol{\kappa}, D(t)\right)$ discussed later on;
2. *accept* that candidate or keep the previous sample:

$$\boldsymbol{\theta}_i \leftarrow \begin{cases} \tilde{\boldsymbol{\theta}}, & \text{w. prob. } \min\left(1, \frac{\mathbb{P}_i(\tilde{\boldsymbol{\theta}}|\boldsymbol{\theta}_{-i}, \boldsymbol{\kappa}, D(t))}{\mathbb{P}_i(\boldsymbol{\theta}_i|\boldsymbol{\theta}_{-i}, \boldsymbol{\kappa}, D(t))} \frac{q(\boldsymbol{\theta}_i|\tilde{\boldsymbol{\theta}}, \boldsymbol{\theta}_{-i}, \boldsymbol{\kappa}, D(t))}{q(\tilde{\boldsymbol{\theta}}|\boldsymbol{\theta}_i, \boldsymbol{\theta}_{-i}, \boldsymbol{\kappa}, D(t))}\right). \\ \boldsymbol{\theta}_{i-1}, & \text{otherwise} \end{cases}$$

Algorithm 2. Metropolis-Hastings applied to the distribution of Equation (2)

Require: $D(t)$: previous recommendations and rewards
Require: $\sigma = c/\sqrt{t}$: Gaussian random-walk steps width
Require: m: number of iterations
 1: draw $(\boldsymbol{\theta}, \boldsymbol{\kappa})$ after uniform distribution
 2: $\boldsymbol{\kappa}_1 \leftarrow 1$
 3: **for** $s = 1, \ldots, m$ **do**
 4:     **for** $i = 1, \ldots, N$ **do**
 5:         **repeat**
 6:             draw $\tilde{\boldsymbol{\theta}} \sim \mathcal{N}(\boldsymbol{\theta}_i, \sigma)$
 7:         **until** $0 \leqslant \tilde{\boldsymbol{\theta}} \leqslant 1$
 8:         **with prob.** $\min\left(1, \dfrac{\mathbb{P}_i(\tilde{\boldsymbol{\theta}}|\boldsymbol{\theta}_{-i}, \boldsymbol{\kappa}, D(t))}{\mathbb{P}_i(\boldsymbol{\theta}_i|\boldsymbol{\theta}_{-i}, \boldsymbol{\kappa}, D(t))} \dfrac{\Delta\Phi_\sigma(\boldsymbol{\theta}_i)}{\Delta\Phi_\sigma(\tilde{\boldsymbol{\theta}})}\right)$
 9:             $\boldsymbol{\theta}_i \leftarrow \tilde{\boldsymbol{\theta}}$
10:     **end for**
11:     **for** $\ell = 2, \ldots, L$ **do**
12:         **repeat**
13:             draw $\tilde{\boldsymbol{\kappa}} \sim \mathcal{N}(\boldsymbol{\kappa}_\ell, \sigma)$
14:         **until** $0 \leqslant \tilde{\boldsymbol{\kappa}} \leqslant 1$
15:         **with prob.** $\min\left(1, \dfrac{\mathbb{P}_\ell(\tilde{\boldsymbol{\kappa}}|\boldsymbol{\theta}, \boldsymbol{\kappa}_{-\ell}, D(t))}{\mathbb{P}_\ell(\boldsymbol{\kappa}_\ell|\boldsymbol{\theta}, \boldsymbol{\kappa}_{-\ell}, D(t))} \dfrac{\Delta\Phi_\sigma(\boldsymbol{\kappa}_\ell)}{\Delta\Phi_\sigma(\tilde{\boldsymbol{\kappa}})}\right)$
16:             $\boldsymbol{\kappa}_\ell \leftarrow \tilde{\boldsymbol{\kappa}}$
17:     **end for**
18: **end for**
19: **return** $(\boldsymbol{\theta}, \boldsymbol{\kappa})$

This acceptance step yields two behaviours:

- $\dfrac{\mathbb{P}_i(\tilde{\boldsymbol{\theta}}|\boldsymbol{\theta}_{-i}, \boldsymbol{\kappa}, D(t))}{\mathbb{P}_i(\boldsymbol{\theta}_i|\boldsymbol{\theta}_{-i}, \boldsymbol{\kappa}, D(t))}$ measures how likely the candidate value is compared to the previous one, w.r.t. the posterior distribution,

- $\dfrac{q(\boldsymbol{\theta}_i|\tilde{\boldsymbol{\theta}}, \boldsymbol{\theta}_{-i}, \boldsymbol{\kappa}, D(t))}{q(\tilde{\boldsymbol{\theta}}|\boldsymbol{\theta}_i, \boldsymbol{\theta}_{-i}, \boldsymbol{\kappa}, D(t))}$ downgrades candidates easily reached by the proposal q.

Algorithm 2 uses a truncated Gaussian random-walk proposal for the parameter $\boldsymbol{\theta}_i$, with a Gaussian step of *standard deviation* σ (see Lines 5–7). Note that due to the truncation, the probability to get the proposal $\tilde{\boldsymbol{\theta}}$ starting from $\boldsymbol{\theta}_i$ is $q\left(\tilde{\boldsymbol{\theta}} \mid \boldsymbol{\theta}_i, \boldsymbol{\theta}_{-i}, \boldsymbol{\kappa}, D(t)\right) = \phi(\tilde{\boldsymbol{\theta}} \mid \boldsymbol{\theta}_i, \sigma)/\Delta\Phi_\sigma(\boldsymbol{\theta}_i)$, where $\phi(\cdot \mid \boldsymbol{\theta}_i, \sigma)$ is the probability associated to the Gaussian distribution with mean $\boldsymbol{\theta}_i$ and standard deviation σ, $\Phi(\cdot \mid \boldsymbol{\theta}_i, \sigma)$ is its cumulative distribution function, and $\Delta\Phi_\sigma(\boldsymbol{\theta}_i) = \Phi(1 \mid \boldsymbol{\theta}_i, \sigma) - \Phi(0 \mid \boldsymbol{\theta}_i, \sigma)$. The probability to get the proposal $\boldsymbol{\theta}_i$ starting from $\tilde{\boldsymbol{\theta}}$ is similar, which reduces the ratio of proposal probabilities at Line 8 to

$$\frac{q\left(\boldsymbol{\theta}_i \mid \tilde{\boldsymbol{\theta}}, \boldsymbol{\theta}_{-i}, \boldsymbol{\kappa}, D(t)\right)}{q\left(\tilde{\boldsymbol{\theta}} \mid \boldsymbol{\theta}_i, \boldsymbol{\theta}_{-i}, \boldsymbol{\kappa}, D(t)\right)} = \frac{\Delta\Phi_\sigma(\boldsymbol{\theta}_i)}{\Delta\Phi_\sigma(\tilde{\boldsymbol{\theta}})}.$$

The transition regarding parameter κ_ℓ involves the same framework: the proposal is a truncated Gaussian random-walk step and aims at the probability

$$\mathbb{P}_\ell\left(\kappa_\ell|\boldsymbol{\theta},\kappa_{-\ell},D(t)\right) \propto \prod_{i=1}^{N} \kappa_\ell^{S_{i,\ell}(t)}\left(1-\theta_i\kappa_\ell\right)^{F_{i,\ell}(t)}. \tag{4}$$

4.2 Overall Complexity

The computational complexity of Algorithm 1 is driven by the number of random-walk steps done per recommendation: $m(N+L-1)$, which is controlled by the parameter m. This parameter corresponds to the burning period: the number of iterations required by the Metropolis-Hastings algorithm to draw a point $(\boldsymbol{\theta}^{(m)},\kappa^{(m)})$ almost independent from the initial one. While the requirement for a burning period may refrain us from using a Metropolis-Hasting algorithm in such recommendation setting, we demonstrate in the following experiments that the required value for m remains reasonable. We drastically reduce m by starting the Metropolis-Hasting call from the point used to recommend at previous time-stamp. This corresponds to replacing Line 1 in Algorithm 2 by:

1: $(\boldsymbol{\theta},\kappa) \leftarrow (\tilde{\boldsymbol{\theta}},\tilde{\kappa})$ used for the previous recommendation .

5 Experiments

In this section we demonstrate the benefit of the proposed approach both on two artificial and two real-life datasets. Note that whatever real-life data we are using, we can only use them to compute the parameters $\boldsymbol{\theta}$ and κ and simulate at each time-stamp a "real" user feedback (i.e. clicks) by applying PBM with these parameters. This is what is usually done in the literature since the recommendations done by a bandit are very unlikely to match the recommendations logged in the ground truth data and without a good matching, it would be impossible to compute a relevant reward for each interaction. Code and data for replicating our experiments are available at https://github.com/gaudel/ranking_bandits.

5.1 Datasets

In the experiments, the online recommender systems are required to deliver T consecutive recommendations, their feedbacks being drawn from a PBM distribution. We consider two settings denoted *purely simulated* and *behavioral* in the remaining. With the *purely simulated* setting, we choose the value of the parameters $(\boldsymbol{\theta},\kappa)$ to highlight the stability of the proposed approach even for extreme settings. Namely, we consider $N = 10$ items, $L = 5$ positions, and $\kappa = [1, 0.75, 0.6, 0.3, 0.1]$. The range of values for $\boldsymbol{\theta}$ is either close to zero ($\boldsymbol{\theta}^- = [10^{-3}, 5.10^{-4}, 10^{-4}, 5.10^{-5}, 10^{-5}, 10^{-6}, \ldots, 10^{-6}]$) or close to one ($\boldsymbol{\theta}^+ = [0.99, 0.95, 0.9, 0.85, 0.8, 0.75, \ldots, 0.75]$).

With the *behavioral* setting, the values for $\boldsymbol{\kappa}$ and $\boldsymbol{\theta}$ are obtained from true users behavior as in [14,17]. Two behavioral datasets are considered and presented hereafter. The first one is *KDD Cup 2012 track 2* dataset, which consists of session logs of *soso.com*, a Tencent's search engine. It tracks clicks and displays of advertisements on a search engine result web-page, w.r.t. the user query. For each query, 3 positions are available for a various number of ads to display.

To follow previous works, instead of looking for the probability to be clicked per display, we target the probability to be clicked per session. This amounts to discarding the information *Impression*. We also filter the logs to restrict the analysis to (query, ad) couples with enough information: for each query, ads are excluded if they were displayed less than 1,000 times at any of the 3 possible positions. Then, we filter queries that have less than 5 ads satisfying the previous condition. We end up with 8 queries and from 5 to 11 ads per query. Finally, for each query q, the parameters $(\boldsymbol{\theta}^{[q]}, \boldsymbol{\kappa}^{[q]})$ are set from the *Singular Value Decomposition* (SVD) of the matrix $\boldsymbol{M}^{[q]} \in \mathbb{R}^{N \times L}$ which contains the probability to be clicked for each item in each position. By denoting $\zeta^{[q]}$, the greatest singular value of $\boldsymbol{M}^{[q]}$, and $\boldsymbol{u}^{[q]}$ (respectively $\boldsymbol{v}^{[q]}$) the left (resp. right) singular vector associated to $\zeta^{[q]}$, we set $\boldsymbol{\theta}^{[q]} \stackrel{def}{=} \boldsymbol{v}_1^{[q]} \zeta^{[q]} \boldsymbol{u}^{[q]}$ and $\boldsymbol{\kappa}^{[q]} \stackrel{def}{=} \boldsymbol{v}^{[q]}/\boldsymbol{v}_1^{[q]}$, such that $\boldsymbol{\kappa}_1^{[q]} = 1$, and $\boldsymbol{\theta}^{[q]T} \boldsymbol{\kappa}^{[q]} = \zeta \boldsymbol{u}^{[q]T} \boldsymbol{v}^{[q]}$. This leads to $\boldsymbol{\theta}_i$ values ranging from 0.004 to 0.149, depending on the query.

The second behavioral dataset is Yandex[4]. As in [18], we select the 10 most frequent queries, and for each query the ORS displays 5 items peeked among the 10 most attractive ones. As for KDD dataset, the parameters $(\boldsymbol{\theta}^{[q]}, \boldsymbol{\kappa}^{[q]})$ are set from an SVD. This leads to $\boldsymbol{\theta}_i$ values ranging from 0.070 to 0.936, depending on the query.

5.2   Competitors

We compare the performance of PB-MHB with the performance of PMED [14], TopRank [18], and the standard baseline ε_n-greedy [3].

PMED is designed to match a lower-bound on the expected regret of any reasonable algorithm under the PBM assumption. Let us recall that it assumes $\boldsymbol{\kappa}_\ell$ values to be decreasing, which means the ORS knows in advance which is the most observed position, which is the second most observed position, and so on. PB-MHB does not require this ordering, it learns it from interactions with users. PMED uniform-exploration parameter α is fixed to 1. Due to its very high time complexity, experiments with PMED are stopped after 5 h for each dataset (which corresponds to about 10^5 recommendations).

TopRank handles a wider range of click models than PB-MHB, but it also assumes the knowledge of the order on positions. TopRank hyper-parameter δ is set to $1/T$ as recommended by Theorem 1 in [18].

Finally, we compare PB-MHB to ϵ_n-Greedy. At each time-stamp t, an estimation $(\hat{\boldsymbol{\theta}}, \hat{\boldsymbol{\kappa}})$ of parameters $(\boldsymbol{\theta}, \boldsymbol{\kappa})$ is obtained applying SVD to the collected data.

---

[4] Yandex personalized web search challenge, 2013. https://www.kaggle.com/c/yandex-personalized-web-search-challenge.

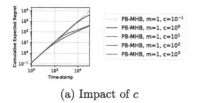   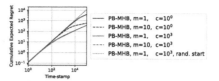

(a) Impact of c (b) Impact of m and random start

Fig. 1. Cumulative regret w.r.t. time-stamp on Yandex data. Impact of the width $c/\sqrt{t}$ of Gaussian random-walk steps (left). Impact of the use of the parameters from the previous time-stamp to warm-up the Metropolis-Hasting algorithm and of the number m of Metropolis-Hastings iterations per recommendation (right). The shaded area depicts the standard error of our regret estimates. (Color figure online)

Let us denote $\hat{i}(t)$ the recommendation with the highest expected reward given the inferred values $(\hat{\theta}, \hat{\kappa})$. A greedy algorithm would recommend $\hat{i}(t)$. Since this algorithm never explores, it may end-up recommending a sub-optimal affectation. ϵ_n-Greedy counters this by randomly replacing each item of the recommendation with probability $\varepsilon(t) = c/t$, where c is a hyper-parameter to be tuned. In the following, we plot the results obtained with the best possible value for c, while trying c in $\{10^0, 10^1, \ldots, 10^6\}$. Note that the best value for c varies a lot from a dataset to another.

In the experiments presented hereafter the requirements of each algorithm are enforced. Namely, κ_ℓ values are decreasing when running experiments with PMED and TopRank.

5.3   Results

We compare the previously presented algorithms on the basis of the *cumulative regret* (see Eq. (1)), which is the sum, over T consecutive recommendations, of the difference between the expected reward of the best possible answer and of the answer of a given recommender system. The regret will be plotted with respect to T on a log-scale basis. The best algorithm is the one with the lowest regret. The regret plots are bounded by the regret of the oracle (0) and the regret of a recommender system choosing the items uniformly at random. We average the results of each algorithm over 20 independent sequences of recommendations per query.

PB-MHB Hyper-parameters. PB-MHB behavior is affected by two hyper-parameters: the width $c/\sqrt{t}$ of the Gaussian random-walk steps, and the number m of Metropolis-Hastings iterations per recommendation. Overall, when Metropolis-Hastings runs start from the couple $(\tilde{\theta}, \tilde{\kappa})$ from the previous time-stamp, we show in Fig. 1a that PB-MHB exhibits the smallest regret on Yandex as soon as $c > 1000$ and $m = 1$. Note that $m = 1$ is also the setting which minimizes the computation time of PB-MHB. These hyper-parameter choices also hold for the 3 other datasets (not shown here for lack of space).

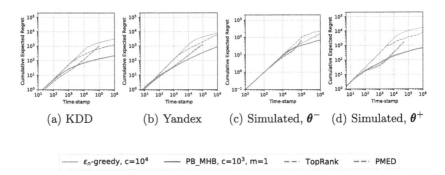

(a) KDD   (b) Yandex   (c) Simulated, $\boldsymbol{\theta}^-$ (d) Simulated, $\boldsymbol{\theta}^+$

——— ε_n-greedy, c=10^4 ——— PB_MHB, c=10^3, m=1   — — · TopRank   — — · PMED

Fig. 2. Cumulative regret w.r.t. time-stamp on five different settings for all competitors. The plotted curves correspond to the average over 20 independent sequences of recommendations per query (in total: 20 sequences for simulated data, 160 sequences for KDD and 200 sequences for Yandex). The shaded area depicts the standard error of our regret estimates. For ε_n-Greedy, c is set to 10^4 for KDD and Yandex settings, to 10^5 when $\boldsymbol{\theta}$ is close to 0, and to 10^3 when $\boldsymbol{\theta}$ is close to 1. (Color figure online)

We now discuss the impact of choosing other hyper-parameter values on Yandex data. The regret is the smallest as soon as c is large enough ($c \geq 100$). In Fig. 1b, we illustrate the impact of m. It yields a high regret only when c and m are both too small (full blue curve): when the random-walk steps are too small the Metropolis-Hasting algorithm requires more iterations to get uncorrelated samples $(\tilde{\boldsymbol{\theta}}, \tilde{\boldsymbol{\kappa}})$. For reasonable values of c, m has no impact on the regret. Figure 1b also shows the impact of keeping the parameters from the previous time-stamp compared to a purely random start. Starting from a new randomly drawn set of parameters would require more than $m = 10$ iterations to obtain the same result, meaning a computation budget more than 10 times higher. This behavior is explained by the gap between the uniform law (which is used to draw the starting set of parameters) and the targeted law (*a posteriori* law of these parameters) which concentrates around its MAP. Even worse, this gap increases while getting more and more data since the *a posteriori* law concentrates with the increase of data. As a consequence, the required value for m increases along time when applying a standard Metropolis-Hasting initialisation, which explains why the dotted red line diverges from the solid one around time-stamp 30.

Comparison with Competitors. Figure 2 compares the regret obtained by PB-MHB and its competitors on datasets with various click and observation probabilities. Up to time-stamp 10^4, PMED and PB-MHB exhibit the smallest regret on all settings. Thereafter, PMED is by far the algorithm with the smallest regret. Regarding computation time, apart from PMED all the algorithms require less than 20 ms per recommendation which remains affordable: ε_n-Greedy is the fastest with less than 0.5 ms per recommendation[5]; then TopRank and PB-MHB require 10 to 40 times more computation time than ϵ_n-Greedy; finally, PMED requires more than 150 ms per recommendation which makes it impractical regardless of its low regret.

6 Conclusion

We have introduced a new bandit-based algorithm, PB-MHB, for online recommender systems in the PBM which uses a Thompson sampling framework to learn the κ and θ parameters of this model instead of assuming them given. Experiments on simulated and real datasets show that our method (i) suffers a smaller regret than its competitors having access to the same information, and (ii) suffers a similar regret as its competitors using more prior information.

These results are still empirical but we plan to formally prove them in future work. Indeed, [21] upper-bounded the regret of a Thompson Sampling bandit algorithm, while using Langevin Monte-Carlo to sample posterior values of parameters. That could be a good starting point for theoretically studying the convergence of PB-MHB. We also would like to improve our algorithm by further working on the proposal law to draw candidates for the sampling part. The proposal is currently a truncated random walk. By managing it differently (with a logit transformation for instance) we could improve both the time and precision performance. On the other hand, with a better understanding of the evolution of the target distribution, we could also improve the sampling part. Moreover, we would like to apply PB-MHB to environments where κ is evolving with time (with new marketing trends) and where our learning setting could develop its full potential.

References

1. Agrawal, S., Goyal, N.: Thompson sampling for contextual bandits with linear payoffs. In: Proceedings of the 30th International Conference on Machine Learning, ICML 2013 (2013)
2. Agrawal, S., Goyal, N.: Near-optimal regret bounds for Thompson sampling. J. ACM **64**(5), 30:1–30:24 (2017)
3. Auer, P., Cesa-Bianchi, N., Fischer, P.: Finite-time analysis of the multiarmed bandit problem. Mach. Learn. **47**(2), 235–256 (2002)
4. Chapelle, O., Li, L.: An empirical evaluation of Thompson sampling. In: Advances in Neural Information Processing Systems 24, NIPS 2011 (2011)
5. Chen, W., Wang, Y., Yuan, Y.: Combinatorial multi-armed bandit: general framework and applications. In: Proceedings of the 30th International Conference on Machine Learning, ICML 2013 (2013)

---

[5] Computation time for a sequence of 10^7 recommendations vs. the first query of Yandex data, on an Intel Xeon E5640 CPU 2.67 GHz with 50 GB RAM. The algorithms are implemented in Python.

6. Cheung, W.C., Tan, V., Zhong, Z.: A Thompson sampling algorithm for cascading bandits. In: Proceedings of the 22nd International Conference on Artificial Intelligence and Statistics, AISTATS 2019 (2019)
7. Chuklin, A., Markov, I., de Rijke, M.: Click Models for Web Search. Morgan & Claypool Publishers, San Rafael (2015)
8. Combes, R., Magureanu, S., Proutière, A., Laroche, C.: Learning to rank: regret lower bounds and efficient algorithms. In: Proceedings of the 2015 ACM SIG-METRICS International Conference on Measurement and Modeling of Computer Systems (2015)
9. Craswell, N., Zoeter, O., Taylor, M., Ramsey, B.: An experimental comparison of click position-bias models. In: Proceedings of the 2008 International Conference on Web Search and Data Mining, WSDM 2008 (2008)
10. Dumitrascu, B., Feng, K., Engelhardt, B.: PG-TS: improved Thompson sampling for logistic contextual bandits. In: Advances in Neural Information Processing Systems 31, NIPS 2018 (2018)
11. Katariya, S., Kveton, B., Szepesvári, C., Wen, Z.: DCM bandits: learning to rank with multiple clicks. In: Proceedings of the International Conference on Machine Learning, ICML (2016)
12. Kawale, J., Bui, H.H., Kveton, B., Tran-Thanh, L., Chawla, S.: Efficient Thompson sampling for online matrix factorization recommendation. In: Advances in Neural Information Processing Systems 28, NIPS 2015 (2015)
13. Komiyama, J., Honda, J., Nakagawa, H.: Optimal regret analysis of Thompson sampling in stochastic multi-armed bandit problem with multiple plays. In: Proceedings of the 32nd International Conference on Machine Learning, ICML 2015 (2015)
14. Komiyama, J., Honda, J., Takeda, A.: Position-based multiple-play bandit problem with unknown position bias. In: Advances in Neural Information Processing Systems 30, NIPS 2017 (2017)
15. Kveton, B., Szepesvári, C., Wen, Z., Ashkan, A.: Cascading bandits: learning to rank in the cascade model. In: Proceedings of the 32nd International Conference on Machine Learning, ICML 2015 (2015)
16. Kveton, B., Wen, Z., Ashkan, A., Szepesvári, C.: Combinatorial cascading bandits. In: Advances in Neural Information Processing Systems 28, NIPS 2015 (2015)
17. Lagrée, P., Vernade, C., Cappé, O.: Multiple-play bandits in the position-based model. In: Advances in Neural Information Processing Systems 30, NIPS 2016 (2016)
18. Lattimore, T., Kveton, B., Li, S., Szepesvari, C.: TopRank: a practical algorithm for online stochastic ranking. In: Advances in Neural Information Processing Systems 31, NIPS 2018 (2018)
19. Li, C., Kveton, B., Lattimore, T., Markov, I., de Rijke, M., Szepesvári, C., Zoghi, M.: BubbleRank: safe online learning to re-rank via implicit click feedback. In: Proceedings of the 35th Uncertainty in Artificial Intelligence Conference, UAI 2019 (2019)
20. Li, S., Wang, B., Zhang, S., Chen, W.: Contextual combinatorial cascading bandits. In: Proceedings of the 33rd International Conference on Machine Learning, ICML 2016 (2016)
21. Mazumdar, E., Pacchiano, A., Ma, Y., Bartlett, P.L., Jordan, M.I.: On Thompson sampling with Langevin algorithms. In: Proceedings of the 37th International Conference on Machine Learning, ICML 2020 (2020)
22. Neal, R.M.: Probabilistic inference using Markov chain Monte Carlo methods. Technical report, University of Zurich, Department of Informatics, September 1993

23. Richardson, M., Dominowska, E., Ragno, R.: Predicting clicks: estimating the click-through rate for new ads. In: Proceedings of the 16th International World Wide Web Conference, WWW 2007 (2007)
24. Riquelme, C., Tucker, G., Snoek, J.: Deep Bayesian bandits showdown: an empirical comparison of Bayesian deep networks for Thompson sampling. In: Proceedings of the International Conference on Learning Representations, ICLR 2018 (2018)
25. Thompson, W.R.: On the likelihood that one unknown probability exceeds another in view of the evidence of two samples. Biometrika **25**(3/4), 285–294 (1933)
26. Zoghi, M., Tunys, T., Ghavamzadeh, M., Kveton, B., Szepesvari, C., Wen, Z.: Online learning to rank in stochastic click models. In: Proceedings of the 34th International Conference on Machine Learning, ICML 2017 (2017)
27. Zong, S., Ni, H., Sung, K., Ke, N.R., Wen, Z., Kveton, B.: Cascading bandits for large-scale recommendation problems. In: Proceedings of the 32nd Conference on Uncertainty in Artificial Intelligence, UAI 2016 (2016)

Performance Prediction for Hardware-Software Configurations: A Case Study for Video Games

Sven Peeters[1], Vitalik Melnikov[1], and Eyke Hüllermeier[2]([⊠])

[1] Department of Computer Science, Paderborn University, Paderborn, Germany
{speeters,melnikov}@mail.uni-paderborn.de
[2] Institute of Informatics, LMU Munich, Munich, Germany
eyke@ifi.lmu.de

Abstract. Performance prediction for hardware-software configurations is a relevant and practically important problem. With an increasing availability of data in the form of performance measurements, this problem becomes amenable to machine learning, i.e., the data-driven construction of predictive models. In this paper, we propose a learning method that is specifically tailored to the task of performance prediction and takes two important characteristics of this problem into account: (i) prior knowledge in the form of monotonicity constraints, suggesting that certain properties of hard- or software can influence performance only positively or negatively, and (ii) strong differences in the precision and reliability of performance measurements available as training data. We evaluate our method on a real-world dataset from the domain of performance prediction in video games, which we specifically collected for this purpose.

Keywords: Performance prediction · Imprecise data · Monotonicity

1 Introduction

Innovations in the field of hardware architecture and systems design lead to a growing number of hardware components like central processing units (CPU) or graphical processing units (GPU). For example, Intel alone released 29 different consumer desktop CPUs in the year 2019[1].

The amount of newly published software also grows rapidly. Statistics of the digital distribution service Steam indicate that 9050 new video games were published on Steam[2] in 2018. Many of them require powerful hardware in order to guarantee the fulfillment of major non-functional software properties. One example for such a non-functional software property in video games is the achieved

---

[1] https://ark.intel.com.
[2] https://store.steampowered.com.

Supported by the German Research Foundation (DFG) through CRC 901.

P. H. Abreu et al. (Eds.): IDA 2021, LNCS 12695, pp. 222–234, 2021.
https://doi.org/10.1007/978-3-030-74251-5_18

frames per second (FPS), which has to exceed some threshold to make a video game enjoyable for a user.

A common practical problem is to find a suitable hardware configuration that allows for running a certain software in a proper way. However, corresponding recommendations are not always easy to make, even by specialists, due to the complex interrelationships between hard- and software components. An interesting question, therefore, is whether this problem could perhaps be supported by machine learning methods. This idea is especially motivated by the fact that many companies and user communities have build up a huge amount of benchmark data for different hardware configurations. In addition, there are many data collections that relate hardware configurations to non-functional software properties, such as maximum or average achieved FPS[3] in video games.

In this paper, we tackle the problem of predicting non-functional properties of software from a machine learning perspective, and propose a learning method specifically tailored to that purpose. More specifically, our approach puts special emphasis on the following properties, which are typical for problems of this kind:

- Monotonicity: Non-functional properties are often monotone with respect to some features of hardware or software. For example, a higher display resolution lowers the achieved FPS, since more pixels have to be processed for every displayed frame. Analogously, using a game configuration that increases the graphics quality also lowers the achieved FPS. Besides such monotonic relationships, there are many other features that may influence a non-functional property, albeit the effect is unknown or can at best be assumed. A learning model that only imposes soft constrains or penalties on non-monotonic behavior, instead of hard monotonicity constrains, would be beneficial in this domain.

- Imprecision: Compared with benchmark data provided by companies, data collections relating hardware configurations to non-functional software properties have a different level of precision. In particular, user-generated data is often imprecise due to mistakes in the measurement protocol. However, if a measurement was taken improperly, for instance if the CPU was not cooled efficiently or the computational load on CPU was increased by another applications, the same hardware-software configuration would be reported with different FPS values. It is therefore important to have a model which can benefit from learning on such imprecise observations. An additional contribution of this paper is a novel dataset from the domain of video games which contains such imprecise observations. We believe, that this dataset can be used for evaluating a wide range of performance prediction models.

The paper is structured as follows. In the next section, we state the learning problem in a more formal way. To tackle this problem, we then introduce a novel learning model based on the principles of generalized loss minimization and monotonicity approximation in Sect. 3. In Sect. 4, we empirically investigate the performance of that model on a real-world dataset from the domain of video

---

[3] https://www.userbenchmark.com.

games. Section 5 contains a brief overview of a related work focused on the prediction of non-functional software properties. Finally, Sect. 6 summarizes the paper and suggests some directions for future research.

2   Learning Problem

We essentially proceed from the standard setting of supervised learning, where instances are feature vectors $\mathbf{x} = (x_1, \ldots, x_m) \in \mathcal{X} = \mathcal{X}_1 \times \ldots \times \mathcal{X}_m$, i.e., an instance is characterized by some value $x_i \in \mathcal{X}_i$ for each feature X_i. The only property specific to our application is the fact that two types of features can be distinguished, those describing characteristics of a hardware, and those representing properties of the software. Correspondingly, $\mathcal{X} = \mathcal{X}_H \times \mathcal{X}_S$ is a compound instance space defined by two subspaces $\mathcal{X}_H$ and $\mathcal{X}_S$, and a software $\mathbf{x}_S \in \mathcal{X}_S$ executed on a hardware $\mathbf{x}_H \in \mathcal{X}_H$ is described by a tuple $(\mathbf{x}_H, \mathbf{x}_S) \in \mathcal{X}_H \times \mathcal{X}_S = \mathcal{X} = \mathcal{X}_1 \times \ldots \times \mathcal{X}_m$. An instance of that kind is associated with a non-functional software property of interest (such as an FPS measurement), playing the role of the target variable Y. We assume this variable to be real-valued, taking values in $\mathcal{Y} \subseteq \mathbb{R}$.

We are interested in modeling the dependency between features and target variable. To this end, let $\mathcal{H} = \{h \mid h : \mathcal{X} \to \mathcal{Y}\}$ be an underlying hypothesis space, i.e., a set of predictive models the learner can choose from. This choice is guided by the principle of risk minimization, i.e., the learner seeks to find

$$h^* \in \underset{h \in \mathcal{H}}{\operatorname{argmin}} \int_{(\mathbf{x},y) \in \mathcal{X} \times \mathcal{Y}} \mathcal{L}(h(\mathbf{x}), y) \, d\,\mathbb{P}(\mathbf{x}, y), \tag{1}$$

where $\mathcal{L} : \mathcal{Y} \times \mathcal{Y} \to \mathbb{R}$ is a point-wise loss function and $\mathbb{P}$ an unknown joint probability distribution $\mathbb{P}(\mathbf{x}, y) = \mathbb{P}(\mathbf{x})\mathbb{P}(y \mid \mathbf{x})$ on $\mathcal{X} \times \mathcal{Y}$ characterizing the data-generating process. In the next section, we propose an algorithm for tackling this learning problem. Before doing so, we discuss two properties that are specific for our learning task.

Monotonicity. One property our learning algorithm is supposed to obey is monotonicity: We assume that the target property is monotone, not necessarily in all but at least in some of the features X_i. To specify what we mean by this, recall that we assume a stochastic dependency of the target variable on the features $\mathbf{x} \in \mathcal{X}$, i.e., the property can be seen as a random variable Y with conditional distribution $\mathbb{P}(Y \mid \mathbf{x})$.

Let $y^*(\mathbf{x}) = \mathbb{E}(Y \mid \mathbf{x})$ denote the conditional expectation of the target given features $\mathbf{x}$. We call the target monotone increasing in the ith feature if the following holds: $y^*(\mathbf{x}) \leq y^*(\mathbf{x}')$ for all $\mathbf{x} = (x_1, \ldots, x_{i-1}, x_i, x_{i+1}, \ldots, x_m)$ and $\mathbf{x} = (x_1, \ldots, x_{i-1}, x_i', x_{i+1}, \ldots, x_m)$ such that $x_i \leq x_i'$. The case of a monotone decreasing dependency is defined analogously.

Imprecise Training Data. A second property of the learning task concerns the data available for training. In the standard setting of supervised learning, training data is of the form $(\mathbf{x}, y) \in \mathcal{X} \times \mathcal{Y}$, where y is a precise albeit noisy measurement of the target variable. Here, we instead assume that the target is only observed imprecisely. More specifically, given an instance $\mathbf{x} \in \mathcal{X}$, we assume observations to be characterized by subsets $Y \subseteq \mathcal{Y}$, i.e., training data is of the form $\mathcal{D}_{\mathrm{train}} = \{(\mathbf{x}_n, Y_n)\}_{n=1}^{N}$. Concretely, the subsets Y will take the form of intervals $[y^l, y^u]$ in our application (cf. Sect. 3.1). Such intervals are not observed directly, i.e., they are not produced as an outcome of an automatic measurement process. Instead, they should be considered as the result of a *modeling process* aimed at finding a "consensus" among a set of precise though partly contradicting or incoherent observations.

To be more specific, suppose that, for a given instance $\mathbf{x}$ (in our case a hardware/software configuration), not only a single value is observed for the target, but a complete set of values $y^{(1)}, \ldots, y^{(k)}$ (for example, FPS measurements by different users). The corresponding data could be used for learning in different ways. Perhaps most obviously, all combinations $(\mathbf{x}, y^{(1)}), \ldots, (\mathbf{x}, y^{(k)})$ could be added to the training data, resulting in a standard data set amenable to standard learning algorithms. This, however, would lead to an implicit weighting of the instance $\mathbf{x}$, which is not necessarily desirable. Alternatively, the observed values could be replaced by the mean $\bar{y} = (y^{(1)} + \ldots + y^{(k)})/k$ as a consensus, giving rise to a single training example $(\mathbf{x}, \bar{y})$. Additionally, the standard deviation of the observations might be used for weighting the example, suggesting the application of methods such as heteroscedastic regression.

Approaches of that kind are clearly reasonable, provided certain statistical assumptions on the measurements $y^{(1)}, \ldots, y^{(k)}$ are fulfilled. For example, one may assume that all observations $y^{(i)}$ are noisy copies of the target $y^*(\mathbf{x})$, independent of each other and following the same distribution for the noise. Under these conditions, statistics like the mean and standard deviation are meaningful quantities. In our application, however, the validity of such assumptions is highly doubtful, and the measurements can neither be assumed to be independent nor identically distributed. Therefore, instead of pre-determining the mean $\bar{y}$ as a unique "consensus measurement", we merely summarize the data into a range $[y^l, y^u]$ of plausible candidates for such a consensus. Candidate sets of that kind are then given as input to the learning algorithm, hoping the learner itself will be able to figure out the most plausible among the candidates. Broadly speaking, we prefer feeding the learner with weaker but more reliable information of the kind "the actual measurement for $\mathbf{x}$ should be somewhere between y^l and y^u", instead of providing more precise but potentially misleading guidance in the form of a single measurement. As will be discussed in the next section, a class of methods suitable for learning from weak supervision of that kind has recently been proposed under the name *superset learning* [11].

3 Learning Model

In this section, we propose a learning model suitable for tackling both challenges outlined in the previous section, essentially by minimizing a customized loss function. The approach described below is general and independent of a concrete model class and learning algorithm. In our case study in Sect. 4, we will instantiate the approach by learning with deep feedforward neural networks.

3.1 Learning from Imprecise Observations

To address the problem of learning from imprecise observations, we adopt the approach of generalized loss minimization, which was originally proposed as a method for superset learning in [12]. The so-called *optimistic superset loss* (OSL) is a generalization of the original loss $\mathcal{L}$ in (1) defined as follows:

$$\mathcal{L}^\star(\hat{y}, Y) = \inf_{y \in Y} \mathcal{L}(\hat{y}, y) \tag{2}$$

As can be seen, by looking for the candidate $y \in Y$ that is most favorable for the (precise) prediction $\hat{y}$ in terms of the original loss, the generalized loss compares $\hat{y}$ with the set-valued target in an "optimistic" way. More recently, the same generalization has been proposed in [3], where it is called *infimum loss*.

Learning can now be accomplished by minimizing the generalized loss, in the simplest case by following the principle of empirical risk minimization:

$$h^* \in \underset{h \in \mathcal{H}}{\operatorname{argmin}} \frac{1}{N} \sum_{i=1}^{N} \mathcal{L}^\star(h(\mathbf{x}_i), Y_n)$$

This way of learning from imprecise data is essentially motivated by the idea of data disambiguation, i.e., of figuring out the true observations y_n among the candidates suggested by the set-valued observations Y_n. This idea is explained in more detail in [12] and corroborated theoretically in [3].

In the case of a continuous, real-valued target variable, a set-valued observation Y may comprise an infinite number of candidate values. Likewise, to compute the generalized loss (2), an infimum must be found over a potentially infinite range. A practicable solution, both for the representation of training data and the computation of (generalized) losses, can be obtained by restricting sets to *intervals* $Y = [y^l, y^u]$. In this case, making the plausible assumption that the original loss $\mathcal{L}(\cdot, y)$ is monotone decreasing on $(-\infty, y)$, vanishing for $\hat{y} = y$, and monotone increasing on (y, ∞), the infimum in (2) is either 0 (namely if $y^l \le \hat{y} \le y^u$, or attained at the boundary points y^l or y^u. For example, for the L_1-loss, one easily verifies that

$$\mathcal{L}^\star_{\text{abs}}(\hat{y}, [y^l, y^u]) = \begin{cases} y^l - \hat{y} & \text{if } \hat{y} < y^l \\ 0 & \text{if } y^l \le \hat{y} \le y^u \\ \hat{y} - y^u & \text{if } \hat{y} > y^u \end{cases} \tag{3}$$

Note that, quite interestingly, this loss essentially corresponds to the ϵ-insensitive loss in support vector regression [17]. More specifically, the ϵ-insensitive loss is recovered by taking $y = (y^l + y^u)/2$ and $\epsilon = (y^u - y^l)/2$ in (3). However, as an important difference to standard support vector regression, also note that the margin ϵ is not constant but varies across observations. Roughly speaking, for the special case of the L_1-loss, superset learning reduces to a heteroscedastic version of standard support vector regression.

3.2 Enforcing Monotonicity Using a Penalty Term

Gupta et al. [9] propose an approach to incorporate partial and total monotone increasing relationships into a gradient descent-based training process. The approach penalizes non-monotonic behavior for features in which the target variable is assumed to be monotone increasing. The authors introduce a term called *point-wise loss* (PWL) as a new objective to be optimized. Let $\mathcal{F}$ denote the set of such features. For the set of (precise) observations $\mathcal{D} \subset \mathbb{R}^m \times \mathbb{R}$, the PWL extends the risk functional as follows:

$$\underbrace{\frac{1}{|\mathcal{D}|} \sum_{(\mathbf{x},y)\in\mathcal{D}} \mathcal{L}(h(\mathbf{x}),y)}_{\text{risk functional}} + \underbrace{\sum_{(\mathbf{x},y)\in\mathcal{D}} \max(0, -\nabla \cdot_{\mathcal{F}} h(\mathbf{x}))}_{\text{non-monotonic penalty term}},$$

where $\nabla \cdot_{\mathcal{F}} h(\mathbf{x})$ denotes the divergence of $h(\mathbf{x})$ restricted to the set of monotone increasing features $\mathcal{F}$. For an input vector $\mathbf{x} = (x_1, \cdots, x_m)^T$, the latter is defined as follows:

$$\nabla \cdot_{\mathcal{F}} h(\mathbf{x}) = \sum_{i \in \mathcal{F}} \frac{\partial h(\mathbf{x})}{\partial x_i}$$

Note that the computation of PWL only requires the input vectors $\mathbf{x}$ in order to estimate the gradient values, and therefore can also be applied to imprecise observations.

3.3 Combined Loss

The two concepts introduced above can now be combined into a single model. For an imprecise dataset $\mathcal{D} = \{(\mathbf{x}_n, Y_n)\}_{n=1}^N$ and a generalized loss function $\mathcal{L}^\star$, we can easily combine both risk functionals as follows:

$$\underbrace{\frac{1}{N} \sum_{(\mathbf{x},Y)\in\mathcal{D}} \mathcal{L}^\star(h(\mathbf{x}),Y)}_{\text{generalized loss}} + \alpha \underbrace{\sum_{(\mathbf{x},Y)\in\mathcal{D}} \max(0, -\nabla \cdot_{\mathcal{F}} h(\mathbf{x}))}_{\text{non-monotonic penalty term}}.$$

The hyper-parameter α weights the importance of the monotonic behavior of the model.

4   Case Study: Predicting FPS in Video Games

We empirically evaluate our method on a real-world dataset from the domain of performance prediction in video games.

4.1 Dataset

The considered dataset relates the non-functional software property of achieved FPS in video games to hardware, i.e., computer system configurations. It was created by combining FPS measurements from the two websites *userbenchmark.com* and *fpsbenchmark.com*. The former publishes user-generated measurements for a diverse range of hardware, while the latter offers reliable assumingly expert-generated measurements only for recent hardware.

Each measurement consists of a description of a hardware, a video game, and the measured FPS value. The hardware is characterized by technical specifications of the built-in CPU and GPU. For instance, such specifications include the clock frequency of both components. The game is characterized by the name, the screen resolution, and the graphics quality setting. The dataset contains multiple measurements with different outcomes for the same hardware and game. The whole dataset including a detailed description of the features can be downloaded from the database OpenML[4]. We assume FPS to be monotone in 8 features provided in Fig. 3.

We have created two different scenarios from the whole dataset to imitate two real-world situations. In the first scenario, only user-generated (i.e., imprecise) measurements are used for learning. The training set therefore consists of the measurements from *userbenchmark.com*. Expert data from *fpsbenchmark.com* is used as the test set. The second scenario simulates a situation, in which both precise and imprecise data, i.e., user- and expert-generated measurements, are combined. The training set consists of the measurements from u*serbenchmark.com* and half of the measurements from *fpsbenchmark.com*. The remaining measurements from *fpsbenchmark.com* are used as the test set. Due to the lack of computational resources, training and test sets were reduced to 7,500 instances each in both scenarios. Multiple FPS measurements for the same pair of a hardware and a game count as one instance.

4.2 Modeling Imprecise Observations

Recall our discussion about the modeling of imprecise data in Sect. 2. Moreover, recall that, for an instance $\mathbf{x}$, measurements typically come in the form of a multiset $M = \{y^{(1)}, \ldots, y^{(k)}\}$. Here, we construct intervals $Y = [y^l, y^u]$ as follows: We first reduce the set M to a set $M' \subseteq M$ by removing outliers, using a well-known outlier detection technique based on a *modified Z-score* [13]. Then the interval is determined by letting $[y^l, y^u] = [\min M', \max M']$.

4.3 Experimental Design

We evaluate the concepts from Sect. 3 independently and in a combination. In a baseline model, MEANDFN, multiset instances are transformed to precise ones by applying the arithmetic mean. Afterwards a conventional DFN is trained.

---

[4] https://www.openml.org/d/42737.

The model INTDFN utilizes only the principle of generalized loss minimization. MONOINTDFN combines the principle of generalized loss minimization with the approach to enforce monotonicity relationships. MONOMEANDFN combines the baseline model and the approach to enforce monotonicity relationships. All models are implemented in Python 3.8 using TensorFlow 2.2[5]. The source code containing the models and the evaluation scheme is available at GitHub[6].

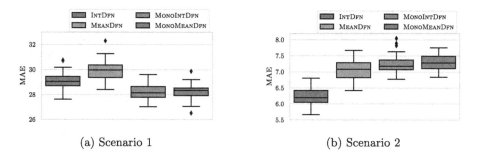

(a) Scenario 1   (b) Scenario 2

Fig. 1. Mean average error (MAE) of the models.

In both scenarios, the test set is predetermined. On every training set D_{train}, we apply a 5-fold CV scheme. A model is trained on four differently composed folds of D_{train} and the remaining fold is used for early stopping with threshold 50 of the training procedure. All models are trained using the Adam optimizer [14]. The batch size is set to 64 and the maximum training epochs to 10,000 for each model. For the sake of interpretation[7], we use the absolute (L_1) loss and its generalized counterpart (3). To guarantee a fair comparison of the models, we optimize hyper-parameters using Bayesian optimization [6] on the complete training set. The DFN architecture of each model is optimized within the following ranges: the number of hidden layers 2 to 4, the number of neurons in the first hidden layer 10 to 350, the number of neurons in the other hidden layers 5 to 200, and the dropout ratio 0.0 to 0.5. Additionally, for MONOMEANDFN and MONOINTDFN, the penalty weight α was chosen from 0.0 to 100. For MEANDFN and INTDFN 500, and for MONOMEANDFN and MONOINTDFN 625 optimization iterations were executed.

In addition to the mean absolute loss (MAE), the monotonicity behavior of each model is assessed by the monotonicity metric M_k [9]. For the kth feature, the metric M_k is an empirical measure on D_{train} that indicates to which degree the monotonicity relationship of the kth feature and the target variable is fulfilled for the instances from D_{train}. The value of M_k ranges between 0 and 1, with a value of 0 indicating that the monotonicity relationship is fulfilled for no instance, and a value of 1 indicating that it is fulfilled for every instance in D_{train}.

---

[5] https://www.tensorflow.org/.

[6] https://github.com/svpeeters/performance_prediction.

[7] Prediction errors are measured in the same unit as the target variable, namely FPS.

The 5-fold CV scheme is repeated 10 times by reshuffling D_{train} randomly. To minimize initiation influence on all of the total 50 data splits we randomly initiate every model four times and take average error values. Based on these values, we analyze the statistical significance of the results for the MAE by first performing a Friedman test [8] and afterwards a post-hoc Nemenyi test [15]. Both tests have a significance level of $p = 0.05$.

4.4   Results

In the first scenario, each model achieves on average an MAE between 28 and 30 FPS. The MAE values for each model are presented in the form of boxplots in Fig. 1(a). With a mean of approximately 28.1, MONOINTDFN achieves the lowest MAE. The monotonic models MONOMEANDFN and MONOINTDFN perform statistically significantly better than their non-monotonic counterpart INTDFN and MEANDFN, respectively. The combined model also MONOINTDFN statistically significantly outperforms the baseline MEANDFN. The average model ranks as well as the critical distance are presented in Fig. 2(a). The results show that the generalized loss principle leads to a significantly better performance in this scenario.

(a) Scenario 1   (b) Scenario 2

Fig. 2. Average ranks of the models and the critical distance (CD).

In the second scenario, including expert data into D_{train}, strongly improves the MAE of all models. All models achieve an average MAE between 6.1 and 7.3 as shown in Fig. 1(b). For this scenario, INTDFN performs statistically significantly better than the baseline MEANDFN and the two monotone models MONOMEANDFN and MONOINTDFN. In contrast to the first scenario, the two monotone models perform worse than their non-monotone counterparts. However, they do not perform significantly worse than the baseline MEANDFN. One can speculate that including the precise expert data in D_{train} limits model flexibility, and therefore makes a falsely assumed monotonicity to an obstacle while training. This hypothesis is partially supported by the analysis of the averaged monotonicity metric M_k in Fig. 3. As can be seen, the monotone models generally have higher M_k values compared to their non-monotonic counterpart. For the second scenario, we observe that the model monotonicity in features like *CPU Frequency* and *GPU Bandwidth* is much lower than in the first scenario, indicating that the assumed monotonicity does probably not hold in the combined dataset.

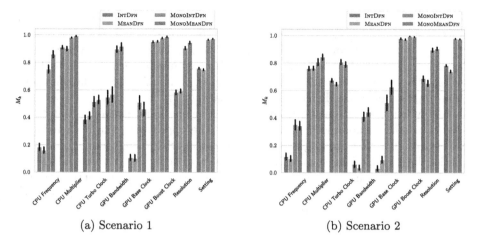

(a) Scenario 1   (b) Scenario 2

Fig. 3. Monotonicity metric for the features from $\mathcal{F}$.

5 Related Work

The predictive analysis of non-functional properties is typically limited to a certain hardware or software. The induced model can therefore only predict properties for the predetermined set of configurations. For instance, Sharkarwi et al. [19] present an approach for a particular predefined software. Based on executions of the SPEC CPU 2006 benchmark suite[8] they characterize computational and memory critical properties of the software to induce a predictive model. Wang et al. [23] present a predictive model which utilizes the CPU features, e.g., cache size, core count and core frequency, in order to predict SPEC CPU 2006 and Geekbench 3[9] benchmark scores and workload performance for different CPU models and workloads. In [22] Thereska et al. propose a general framework for performance prediction. The framework includes many non-functional software properties like response time or start-up time of the application. The framework in addition captures the relationship between different hardware system configurations and non-functional software properties. However, due to the used models only predictions for already known computer systems and applications are possible. Arndt et al. [1] propose a model in which hardware and software are undetermined. They predict the parallel execution time of applications on a target system using distance metrics on the software scalability characteristics. Likewise all target hardware have to be profiled using a proposed set of benchmarks.

To cope with uncertain data complete frameworks, like *weakly supervised learning* [25], have been proposed. In this framework three types of weak supervision are considered: (i) a subset of the training instances is labeled, (ii) the

---

[8] https://www.spec.org/cpu2006/.
[9] https://www.geekbench.com/geekbench3/.

labels of the training instances are coarse, and (iii) the training instances are not ground truth, i.e. falsely labeled observations are expected. For each of the three types different solution strategies can be applied: for (i) active learning [18] and semi-supervised learning [26], for (ii) multi-instance learning [5] and for (iii) solution strategies that incorporate label noise in the case of classification [7] or approaches to handle crowd-sourced data [2].

Lately, much effort has been invested to develop neural networks that obey total or partial monotonicity constraints [4]. The approaches can be divided in two groups. The first group guarantees compliance with the given monotonicity relationships by altering the architecture of neural networks. The second group only penalizes non-monotonic behavior during the training of the neural network and therefore does not guarantee compliance. Examples of the first group are the approach proposed by You et al. in [24] (deep lattice networks) and the approach proposed by Sill in [20] (min-max architecture). An example of the second group is proposed by Sill and Abu-Mostafa in [21] or by Gupta et al. in [9]. Both approaches seek to penalize the non-monotonic behavior of the model during the learning process.

6   Conclusion

We proposed a new approach to performance prediction for hardware-software configurations, which extends deep feedforward networks based on two recent methodological advances in machine learning, one from the field of weakly supervised learning (generalized loss minimization for superset learning) and another one from learning monotone models (penalty-based monotonicity approximation). In an empirical study on performance prediction in video games, our approach significantly outperforms a state-of-the-art baseline. The real-world dataset was specifically collected for this purpose, and might also be interesting for evaluating other types of performance prediction models.

There are several directions for future work. Perhaps most obviously, it would be interesting to try our approach for other performance metrics and other types of non-functional software properties. Besides, there is also potential for further methodological improvement. For example, putting more emphasis on the "dyadic" nature of instances (consisting of a hardware and a software component), one may think of leveraging methods specialized on dyadic prediction [16]. Another idea is to tackle the problem as a ranking instead of a regression problem, which is meaningful if predictions are only used to compare configurations with each other [10]. Last but not least, the aspect of explainability might be of interest: In addition to making a performance prediction, the learner should be able to provide an explanation of that prediction, for example by quantifying the importance of features or highlighting components that appear to be critical.

References

1. Arndt, O., Lüders, M., Blume, H.: Statistical performance prediction for multicore applications based on scalability characteristics. In: ASAP 2019 (2019)
2. Brabham, D.C.: Crowdsourcing as a model for problem solving: an introduction and cases. Convergence **14**, 75–90 (2008)
3. Cabannes, V., Rudi, A., Bach, F.: Structured prediction with partial labelling through the infimum loss. In: ICML (2020)
4. Cano, J., Gutiérrez, P., Krawczyk, B., Wozniak, M., García, S.: Monotonic classification: an overview on algorithms, performance measures and data sets. Neurocomputing **341**, 168–182 (2019)
5. Foulds, J., Frank, E.: A review of multi-instance learning assumptions. In: The Knowledge Engineering Review (2010)
6. Frazier, P.I.: A tutorial on Bayesian optimization. CoRR (2018)
7. Frenay, B., Verleysen, M.: Classification in the presence of label noise: a survey. IEEE Trans. Neural Netw. Learn. Syst. **25**, 845–869 (2014)
8. Friedman, M.: The use of ranks to avoid the assumption of normality implicit in the analysis of variance. J. Am. Stat. Assoc. **32**, 675–701 (1937)
9. Gupta, A., Shukla, N., Marla, L., Kolbeinsson, A., Yellepeddi, K.: How to incorporate monotonicity in deep networks while preserving flexibility? CoRR (2019)
10. Hanselle, J., Tornede, A., Wever, M., Hüllermeier, E.: Hybrid ranking and regression for algorithm selection. In: Schmid, U., Klügl, F., Wolter, D. (eds.) KI 2020. LNCS (LNAI), vol. 12325, pp. 59–72. Springer, Cham (2020). https://doi.org/10.1007/978-3-030-58285-2_5
11. Hüllermeier, E., Cheng, W.: Superset learning based on generalized loss minimization. In: ECML/PKDD 2015 (2015)
12. Hüllermeier, E.: Learning from imprecise and fuzzy observations: Data disambiguation through generalized loss minimization. Int. J. Appr. Reason. **55**, 1519–1534 (2014)
13. Iglewicz, B., Hoaglin, D.: How to Detect and Handle Outliers. ASQC Basic References in Quality Control. ASQC Quality Press, Milwaukee (1993)
14. Kingma, D.P., Ba, J.: Adam: a method for stochastic optimization. In: 3rd International Conference on Learning Representations (2015)
15. Nemenyi, P.: Distribution-free multiple comparisons. In: Biometrics (1962)
16. Schäfer, D., Hüllermeier, E.: Dyad ranking using Plackett-Luce models based on joint feature representations. Mach. Learn. **107**, 903–941 (2018)
17. Schölkopf, B., Smola, A.: Learning with kernels: support vector machines, regularization, optimization, and beyond. MIT Press, Cambridge (2001)
18. Settles, B.: Active learning literature survey. Technical report (2009)
19. Sharkawi, S., et al.: Performance projection of HPC applications using spec CFP 2006 benchmarks. In: 2009 IEEE International Symposium on Parallel Distributed Processing (2009)
20. Sill, J.: Monotonic networks. In: NIPS 10 (1997)
21. Sill, J., Abu-Mostafa, Y.S.: Monotonicity hints. In: NIPS 9 (1996)
22. Thereska, E., Doebel, B., Zheng, A.X., Nobel, P.: Practical performance models for complex, popular applications. SIGMETRICS Perform. Eval. Rev. **38**, 1–12 (2010)
23. Wang, Y., Lee, V., Wei, G.Y., Brooks, D.: Predicting new workload or CPU performance by analyzing public datasets. ACM Trans. Archit. Code Optim. **15**, 1–21 (2019)

24. You, S., Ding, D., Canini, K., Pfeifer, J., Gupta, M.: Deep lattice networks and partial monotonic functions. In: NIPS 30 (2017)
25. Zhou, Z.H.: A brief introduction to weakly supervised learning. Natl. Sci. Rev. **5**, 44–53 (2017)
26. Zhu, X., Goldberg, A.B.: Introduction to semi-supervised learning. Synth. Lect. Artif. Intell. Mach. Learn. **3**, 1–130 (2009)

AVATAR—Automated Feature Wrangling for Machine Learning

Gust Verbruggen[1,2](✉) , Elia Van Wolputte[1,2] , Sebastijan Dumančić[1,2] ,
and Luc De Raedt[1,2]

[1] Department of Computer Science, KU Leuven, Leuven, Belgium
[2] Leuven.AI—KU Leuven Institute for AI, Leuven, Belgium
{gust.verbruggen,eliavan.wolputte,
sebastijan.dumancic,lucde.raedt}@kuleuven.be

Abstract. A large part of the time invested in data science is spent on manual preparation of data. Transforming wrongly formatted columns into useful features takes up a significant part of this time. We present the AVATAR algorithm for automatically learning programs that perform this type of *feature wrangling*. Instead of relying on users to guide the wrangling process, AVATAR directly uses the predictive performance of machine learning models to measure its progress during wrangling. We use datasets from Kaggle to show that AVATAR improves raw data for prediction, and square it off against human data scientists.

Keywords: Data wrangling · Program synthesis · Machine learning

1 Introduction

Data scientists spend a lot of time simply preparing data for analysis. Even before exploratory analysis, data cleaning and feature engineering, an additional step of *data wrangling* is often required. This step consists of taking raw data and *wrangling* it into a format that can be used for data science tasks, such as visualisation and prediction. Data wrangling is typically carried out by writing a program that transforms part of the data into the desired format. Writing these programs is very time consuming to data scientists—according to popular statistic, up to 80% of the time in the whole data science pipeline is invested in wrangling [2], which explains the interest in automated data wrangling [5,10].

The existing work on automated data wrangling, however, assumes that a user knows which format the data should take and can provide input. This input can take many forms. Early methods interactively propose transformations based on data that the user selects and require the wrangling algorithm to learn how to extract the selection [7,14]. Other methods allow the user to give an example of what the output should look like in order to learn a program that correctly produces this output [3,5]. This is clearly a strong assumption: the big lesson of feature engineering is that users rarely know which features, and in which form, are useful for the target task.

© Springer Nature Switzerland AG 2021
P. H. Abreu et al. (Eds.): IDA 2021, LNCS 12695, pp. 235–247, 2021.
https://doi.org/10.1007/978-3-030-74251-5_19

Taking inspiration from both feature engineering and data wrangling, we introduce the problem of *feature wrangling*, which is concerned with wrangling at the feature level. More specifically, we automatically search for transformations that wrangle individual columns into features of high quality to be used in predictive models. For example, a date formatted as "01/01/2001" would be split in its constituent day, month and year parts and these should be marked as ordinal (day and month) or numerical (year) features. As the resulting features are to be used in supervised machine learning, the quality of the generated features can be assessed using the predictive performance of the resulting model. A major benefit of our approach is that it eliminates the need for user interaction.

Motivational Example. Consider the excerpt of basketball data in Fig. 1a. Regardless of the task, we can see that it is not very suited for further analysis. The **height** feature is not numerical and **position** is ambiguous—is "G-F" a position on its own or is this player comfortable in multiple positions?

Suppose a fourth column **salary** exists that we want to predict. We can then try different possibilities of representations for **position** and **height** and use their performance in predicting **salary** to choose the most appropriate one. For example, **position** can be one-hot encoded or split on "-" and then encoded with a dummy variable for every symbol.

Whereas previous approaches would require the user to provide an example of the desired feature, AVATAR generates and tries different alternatives to see which ones yield the best performance. In this example, it will also discover that splitting **height** by a "-" yields new columns that, after being made numerical in a second iteration, are good features. The full wrangling program and its result are respectively shown in Figs. 1b and 1c.

name	position	height
Kuzma	F	6-9
Wagner	C	6-11
Ingram	G-F	5-11

(a) Initial dataset D

```
splitDummies(position, "-")
split(height, "-")
makeNumeric(s_1)
makeNumeric(s_2)
drop(position)
drop(height)
```

(b) Wrangling program

name	s_3	s_4	s_5	s_1	s_2
Kuzma	1	0	0	6.0	9.0
Wagner	0	1	0	6.0	11.0
Ingram	1	0	1	5.0	11.0

(c) Wrangled dataset D'

Fig. 1. Example of data wrangling for machine learning.

Contributions. In this paper, we make the following contributions.

- We introduce the problem of automated feature wrangling, which is concerned with wrangling at the individual feature level and uses the performance of the predictive models to evaluate alternative feature sets.
- We implement this idea in a prototype feature wrangling tool called AVATAR— the Automated VAlue Transformator And extractoR. Given only a dataset and a prediction task, it returns a new dataset with wranlged features that are more suitable for the given task.
- We evaluate AVATAR on real datasets from the Kaggle[1] data science platform.

---

[1] www.kaggle.com.

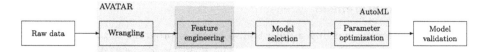

Fig. 2. Overview of the data science pipeline.

2   Related Work

Feature engineering aims to improve the performance of predictive models by transforming and combining existing features into new features that are easier for the model to use. Being a laborious process, automating it is an active area of research [8,9]. The goal of feature wrangling is to use wrangling transformations in order to extract new features from previously unusable columns. Feature wrangling therefore lies at the intersection of data wrangling and feature engineering.

AutoML is concerned with automating the data science pipeline as a whole. The general structure of such a pipeline is shown in Fig. 2. These systems start either from the feature engineering or model selection steps and build a data science pipeline with the goal of optimising performance on a prediction task. Some examples of methods are TPOT [13], auto-sklearn [4] and OBOE [18]. Automated feature wrangling can be viewed as extending these approaches to include wrangling transformations in the feature engineering process.

Two types of wrangling approaches aim to prepare data for the data science pipeline. The first is concerned with extracting and restructuring data, as lots of information is still stuck in inconvenient formats such as spreadsheets, XML or json. Selecting a few examples of desired rows allows methods like FlashExtract [10] to learn a program that extracts all similar rows. Auto-Suggest recommends data preparation steps, such as pivot and join, for raw tables [17]. Foofah [6] and AutoPandas [1] learn full transformation programs if an output example can be given. A second type of wrangling is concerned with transforming and normalizing individual columns based on examples provided by a user [3,5]. Approaches in both types of wrangling assume that a user knows how to represent their data and provide a shortcut to obtain this representation. AVATAR, on the other hand, automatically determines a suitable representation at the feature level.

3   Data Wrangling for Machine Learning

Data wrangling in general is concerned with preparing raw data for data science. In this paper, we focus on the specific task of transforming wrongly formatted columns into usable features by automatically constructing a transformation program—similar to how a human data scientist would perform the same task. We formally describe this problem and present a simple language capable of performing common data wrangling tasks in the following two sections.

3.1   Problem Statement

We are interested in learning a data transformation program $P : \mathcal{X} \to \mathcal{X}'$ that transforms a dataset D with instances of the form $(\mathbf{x}, y) \in (\mathcal{X}, \mathcal{Y})$ into a new dataset D'. The goal is to obtain a dataset D' with a better feature representation than the original dataset D to perform a given machine learning task. In this paper, we consider the task of supervised learning. The dataset D is used to learn a model $m : \mathcal{X} \to \mathcal{Y}$ that predicts the value of y given its features $\mathbf{x}$. This model m is learned using a learner $\mathcal{F}$ on the dataset D, written as $m = \mathcal{F}(D)$.

Assessing whether a dataset D' contains better features than D is possible in the existence of a scoring function $s : (\mathcal{F}, D) \to \mathbb{R}$ that estimates the performance of a model $\mathcal{F}(D)$. The score of a model trained on a dataset then serves as a proxy to evaluate the quality of the features of this dataset—better features will result in better predictions. We assume the learner and scoring function to be given, for example, a decision tree classifier and predictive accuracy.

The problem of feature wrangling for machine learning is then as follows. **Given** a dataset D and a transformation language $\mathcal{L}$, **find** a program $P^* = \arg\max_{P \in \mathcal{L}} s(\mathcal{F}, P(D))$ that transforms D into a dataset $D^* = P^*(D)$ on which an optimal model $\mathcal{F}(D^*)$ can be learned.

It is intractable to find the optimal program, however, as an infinite number of programs can be generated. Any program P such that $s(\mathcal{F}, P(D)) > s(\mathcal{F}, D)$ is an improvement over using the raw data.

3.2   A Language for Feature Wrangling

Let us write $D = [X_1, \dots, X_m]$ when referring to columns of data. Let $t(X, \mathbf{a})$ be a transformation that takes a column X and (optional) arguments $\mathbf{a}$, and returns a new matrix of columns $\mathbf{X}$. A transformation with fixed arguments is called a *wrangling transformation* and written as $t(\mathbf{a})$. This wrangling transformation is *valid* for X if $t(X, \mathbf{a}) \neq X$.

Example 1. The $\mathsf{split}(X, d)$ transformation takes a column X and a delimiter d. It returns a set of columns obtained by splitting each row of X at every occurrence of d. An example of a wrangling transformation is $\mathsf{split}(\text{"-"})$. It is valid for the **height** and **position** columns in Fig. 1a, but not for the **name** column.

A wrangling program is simply a sequence of wrangling transformations. Data scientists typically build such programs by iteratively picking a transformation t and arguments $\mathbf{a}$ for a target column X_i such that $t(X_i, \mathbf{a})$ yields new columns. Each of these new columns is given a unique identifier and added to the data.

Example 2. An example of a dataset, wrangling program and its result is shown in Fig. 1a. Table 1 shows an overview of transformations currently supported by AVATAR.

Table 1. Overview of transformations supported by AVATAR and their generators. The implicit column parameter is not mentioned. Argument d is a string, p is a regular expression and L is a list of strings.

Transformation	Description	Generator
makeNumerical	Make column numerical	true if X_i contains a number
oneHot	One hot encode	true if X_i contains limited number of unique values
NaN	Encode value as hidden missing value	Values in X_i that match a predefined set of patterns, such as "?" and "111"
split(d)	Split on delimiter	Strings consisting of subsequent, non-alphanumeric characters found in X_i
splitDummies(d)	Split on delimiter and dummy encode the resulting categorical features	Same as split
extractNumber(p)	Extract numbers that follow a regular expression pattern	Extract numbers from X_i and generate regexes from them by mapping digits to \d. Additionally, generate patterns where consecutive \d are mapped to \d+
extractWord(L)	Extract a specific word from L in each row	Greedily look for combinations of words such that each row contains exactly one of these words
wordToNumber	Convert written numbers to numerical	true if at least one written number is found

3.3 Generating Arguments

To compose valid wrangling programs, we need to tractably identify the possible arguments of transformation functions. We do so by following a generator-based approach [1]. For each transformation t, we define a generator $\mathcal{G}_t(X)$ that takes a column X as input and yields arguments **a** such that $t(\mathbf{a})$ is a valid wrangling transformation for X. In other words, the arguments of wrangling transformations are generated from data and are not predefined by a user. Generators in AVATAR are only allowed to yield a finite number of arguments.

Example 3. The generator for split yields strings of consecutive, non-alphanumeric characters from rows in the input column, one at a time. Given either position or height columns from Fig. 1a, only a single argument is generated: "-".

Generators for all transformations that AVATAR supports are described in Table 1. A generator for a transformation without additional arguments returns true if the function can be applied to X.

4   Machine Learning for Feature Wrangling

At the core of AVATAR is the use of machine learning models for evaluating progress during wrangling. As opposed to looking for a single transformation at a time, multiple transformations are considered in parallel to allow feature interactions to be considered when evaluating progress. In order to do so, AVATAR explores the space of wrangling programs by exploiting the fact that, starting from a dataset, the order in which transformations are applied to this dataset does not matter. At each iteration, a large wrangling program is generated, which is then pruned by subsequent steps. A high level overview of AVATAR is shown in Fig. 3 and the following sections describe each of these steps in detail.

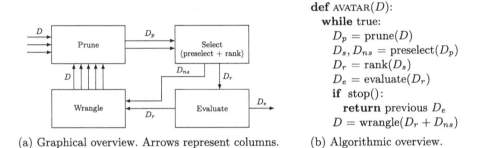

(a) Graphical overview. Arrows represent columns.

```
def AVATAR(D):
    while true:
        D_p = prune(D)
        D_s, D_ns = preselect(D_p)
        D_r = rank(D_s)
        D_e = evaluate(D_r)
        if stop():
            return previous D_e
        D = wrangle(D_r + D_ns)
```

(b) Algorithmic overview.

Fig. 3. The AVATAR algorithm.

4.1   Prune

Pruning aims to remove columns that are not and will never become useful features. This step allows the generators for transformations to be significantly less complex, as different edge cases don't have to be explicitly considered. The following columns are removed from the dataset.

1. Columns that are constant.
2. Columns in which more than p_{nan} percent of values is missing.
3. Columns that are more than p_{id} percent identical to another column.

4.2   Select

From all remaining columns, the selection step aims to find promising features—those that have at least some predictive power. Selection happens in two steps: preselection and feature ranking. This ranking of features is then used in the next step to evaluate the fitness of the current dataset.

Preselection. This step heuristically excludes the following bad columns.

1. Categorical columns that contain more than p_u percent unique values.
2. Categorical columns X_j for which there exists a column X_i with $i < j$ such that a bijective mapping exists between these columns for at least p_{bi} of rows.

Preselection serves to reduce the effort required by the feature ranking step that follows. As opposed to the pruning step, columns excluded by preselection are not removed from the dataset; instead, they remain available to subsequent wrangling steps, as they may still become useful features after more transformations.

Feature Ranking. The aim of this step is to quickly rank columns by potential relevance. To do so, AVATAR uses a wrapper approach—learning shallow models on subsets of features and aggregating the feature importances extracted from these models. In every iteration, n rows are randomly sampled from a random subset of columns. On this subset of data, we perform k-fold cross-validation with a shallow learner $\mathcal{F}_r$. In each of the folds, feature importances are estimated from these learned models, averaged for each column and weighted by the cross-validation performance. Final importances for each column are obtained by averaging the weighted importances over multiple iterations.

To estimate model performance, we use accuracy in case of classification and $\max(0, R^2)$ in case of regression. Feature importances within each model are estimated using SHAP values [11,12]. They are a practical implementation of the game-theoretic concept of Shapley values, which quantify an individual player's contribution towards the final outcome in a cooperative game [15]. Each feature takes the role of a player and a prediction is considered the outcome of a game.

4.3 Evaluate

Given the ranking of features, AVATAR now heuristically evaluates its progress on the current dataset. It looks for a k such that the top-k ranked features result in the best performance. Performance for a set of features is evaluated using cross validation on all rows of the dataset using a learner $\mathcal{F}_e$. Accuracy is used for classification and RMSE for regression.

If performance decreases with respect to previous iteration, AVATAR terminates and returns the set of features that achieved the highest performance. A user can easily request more features from AVATAR, which are returned in order of their rank. The wrangling program is also generated from these selected features by adding drop transformations for columns that are generated but not selected, as was shown in Fig. 1b.

4.4 Wrangle

In this step, AVATAR generates new candidate features by transforming the columns of the current dataset. We exhaust the generators for all transformations on all columns that were not wrangled before and apply the transformations to obtain new columns. These new columns are appended to the current dataset, ensuring that more complex features—obtained by applying more transformations—are pruned over simpler ones.

5   Evaluation

We perform experiments to answer the following questions.

Q1 Is AVATAR able to find new and useful features?
Q2 How does AVATAR compare to human wranglers?

Data. We use datasets from Kaggle, a popular data science platform. Kaggle allows users to publish datasets and provides *public notebooks* which contain snippets of code executing the data science steps. We search for datasets that (1) contain scraped data, (2) have a single file, and (3) a clear prediction target. We focus on evaluating AVATAR's ability to wrangle interesting features and, therefore, only use the datasets that have at least one column that requires wrangling. An overview of datasets is shown in Table 2a.

Table 2. Data used for evaluating AVATAR.

(a) Classification (C) and regression (R) datasets.

Dataset	Type	Columns Total	Text	Rows
Android	R	10	8	984
Car features	R	17	8	11914
Car price	R	27	10	205
Food choices	R	61	13	121
GSM	R	40	39	8628
House	R	82	43	1460
Melbourne housing	R	22	8	13580
NBA	C	21	7	128069
NBA2K	R	15	11	429
Pet	C	11	4	18834
Shelter animals	C	10	10	26729
Titanic	C	12	5	891
iPhone 11	R	7	3	247

(b) Notebooks compared with AVATAR.

Dataset	Lines of code	# features Human	AVATAR
iPhone 11	28	6	7
NBA	34	10	9
Pet	44	66	10
Car features	42	3	26
Food choices	57	133	17
GSM	277	14	42

Models and Metrics. As we are interested in AVATAR's ability to wrangle new features, not in obtaining the best possible performance on a dataset, our primary concern when choosing the model for estimating feature importance is its speed (as we need to train it frequently) and ability to identify useful features. We assume that even low-capacity models are capable of identifying useful features, though their estimate might be less robust compared to complex models. For this reason, we focus on decision trees and limit their depth to 4 when evaluating feature importance and to 12 when training the final model. We report the relative performance over the absolute performance.

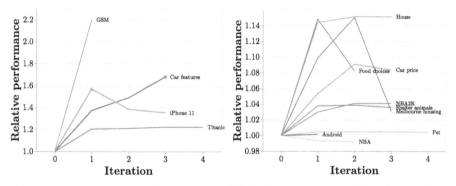

(a) Performance gain of 20% or more.   (b) Performance gain of less than 20% or
performance loss.

Fig. 4. Relative performance of AVATAR after iterations of wrangling new features when compared to the original dataset (iteration 0). Feature importances for marked data points are shown in Fig. 5a.

Experimental Setup. Experiments were performed on a laptop with a prototype implemented in Python. Code, data and results are available on GitHub.[2] We ran AVATAR for four iterations, with 1600 iterations of feature selection on samples of 1000 rows. In some datasets with many columns containing long strings, the number of columns can quickly explode after a few iterations. If the pruning step took longer than two hours, AVATAR was stopped early.

5.1   Wrangling New Features

Evaluating the quality of features is impossible to do directly; instead, we evaluate their quality implicitly through the performance of a model trained on the features. More precisely, we compare performance of the model training the raw data versus the model trained on data wrangled by AVATAR. The relative performance after each iteration is shown in Fig. 4. Note that AVATAR starts with pruning and selection, and the baseline result at iteration 0 is thus also obtained after greedily selecting features for the best performance without wrangling.

The results show that AVATAR consistently improves predictive performance by wrangling new features. A single exception is the NBA dataset, where wrangled features are not relevant to the target. This is reinforced in the next experiment, where AVATAR performs on par with human wranglers. We observe a general trend where performance drops after multiple wrangling iterations. The reason for that is the noise in feature importance estimation: our estimate becomes less robust with the increase of the number of features because AVATAR repeatedly uses uniformly sampled subsets of features to estimate their importance. With the increase in the number of features, there is a higher chance of a spurious interaction between the features. This negatively impacts the performance

---

[2] https://github.com/pidgeyusedgust/avatar-ida21.

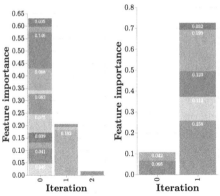

(a) Feature importances after wrangling for the Melbourne housing (left) and iPhone 11 datasets (right). Each colored segment is one feature.

(b) Original columns from (top) iPhone 11 and (bottom) Melbourne housing datasets.

Fig. 5. A closer look at selected features for two datasets.

of the final model due to overfitting. AVATAR then terminates and returns the ranked features from the previous iteration.

As a small case study, we take a closer look at the best performing features for the Melbourne housing and iPhone 11 datasets in Fig. 5a. One column from their original datasets is shown in Fig. 5b. For the Melbourne housing dataset, the dummy encoded feature for "Southern" after splitting **Regionname** on "" is found to be the most relevant one. The selected feature in the second iteration first splits this column by "-" and then extracts the word "Metropolitan", "South" or "Victoria". This results in "South-Eastern Metropolitan" and "Southern Metropolitan" being projected to the same "South" feature, which a human might not think of. On the iPhone 11 dataset, many features are extracted from the **Description**. Very relevant is the full model name "iPhone 11 256GB" as obtained by splitting on "-". Human data scientists might expect that this feature requires to be split up further. It is, however, an ordinal feature on its own and provides a strong signal.

5.2   Comparison with Humans

In the second experiment, we compare the performance of a predictive model on a dataset wrangled by (1) human experts on Kaggle and (2) by AVATAR. We obtain expert-wrangled datasets from the corresponding notebooks on Kaggle. As we are interested in the ability to wrangle features, any feature engineering steps are removed from the notebooks, but any feature selection is left untouched. A list of notebooks and number of lines of wrangling code is given in Table 2b. We compare the relative performance of the same model trained on features wrangled by humans versus features wrangled by AVATAR and show them in Fig. 6.

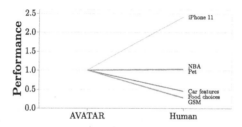

Fig. 6. Comparing the relative performance of human wranglers to AVATAR. Downward slopes indicates that AVATAR is better, which happens for half of the datasets. For the NBA and Pet dataset, the previous experiment has already shown that little additional information is present in wrangled features.

The results show that AVATAR performs similarly or better than human data wranglers. The only exception is the iPhone 11 dataset. AVATAR still identifies interesting features, but the main reason for bad performance are noisy examples—iPhone 11 covers instead of phones—which negatively impacts the performance of AVATAR. For the NBA and Pet datasets, human performance is marginally better. Wrangled features are not representative of the target, which further explains their small performance differences in Fig. 4b. On datasets where AVATAR greatly improves with respect to the baseline, it also beats human wrangling.

6   Conclusion and Future Work

In order to cope with data scientists spending valuable time on this tedious process, we present the AVATAR algorithm for automatically wrangling features from raw columns. We show that AVATAR is able to wrangle features that improve predictive performance when compared to the original dataset. On datasets that require heavy wrangling, it even outperforms some human wranglers.

Future Work. Two immediate pointers for extensions are expanding AVATAR to the multi-relational setting, allowing different tables to be joined, and exploring the unsupervised case, for example, by using multi-directional ensembles of decision trees [16]. Unsupervised data wrangling would allow AVATAR to aid exploratory data analysis, another significant time sink for data scientists. Quickly selecting relevant features from high-dimensional data with high multicollinearity plays an important role in AVATAR. Our repository contains the intermediate, wrangled datasets to encourage further research on this topic. The main technical limitation for AVATAR is that the search space quickly explodes when many columns with long, textual values are present. Being more strict on the generators and pruning rules can trade off speed for expressive power.

Acknowledgements. This work has received funding from the European Research Council (ERC) under the European Union's Horizon 2020 research and innovation programme (grant agreement No [694980] SYNTH: Synthesising Inductive Data Models).

This research received funding from the Flemish Government (AI Research Program). Sebastijan Dumancic is funded by the Research Foundation-Flanders (FWO).

References

1. Bavishi, R., Lemieux, C., Fox, R., Sen, K., Stoica, I.: Autopandas: neural-backed generators for program synthesis. In: Proceedings of the ACM on Programming Languages 3(OOPSLA), pp. 1–27 (2019)
2. Dasu, T., Johnson, T.: Exploratory Data Mining and Data Cleaning, vol. 479. Wiley, New York (2003)
3. Drosos, I., Barik, T., Guo, P.J., DeLine, R., Gulwani, S.: Wrex: a unified programming-by-example interaction for synthesizing readable code for data scientists. In: Proceedings of the 2020 CHI Conference on Human Factors in Computing Systems, pp. 1–12 (2020)
4. Feurer, M., Klein, A., Eggensperger, K., Springenberg, J.T., Blum, M., Hutter, F.: Auto-sklearn: efficient and robust automated machine learning. In: Hutter, F., Kotthoff, L., Vanschoren, J. (eds.) Automated Machine Learning. TSSCML, pp. 113–134. Springer, Cham (2019). https://doi.org/10.1007/978-3-030-05318-5_6
5. He, Y., Chu, X., Ganjam, K., Zheng, Y., Narasayya, V., Chaudhuri, S.: Transform-data-by-example (TDE) an extensible search engine for data transformations. Proc. VLDB Endow. 11(10), 1165–1177 (2018)
6. Jin, Z., Anderson, M.R., Cafarella, M., Jagadish, H.: Foofah: transforming data by example. In: Proceedings of the 2017 ACM International Conference on Management of Data, pp. 683–698 (2017)
7. Kandel, S., Paepcke, A., Hellerstein, J., Heer, J.: Wrangler: interactive visual specification of data transformation scripts. In: Proceedings of the SIGCHI Conference on Human Factors in Computing Systems, pp. 3363–3372 (2011)
8. Kanter, J.M., Veeramachaneni, K.: Deep feature synthesis: towards automating data science endeavors. In: 2015 IEEE International Conference on Data Science and Advanced Analytics (DSAA), pp. 1–10. IEEE (2015)
9. Kaul, A., Maheshwary, S., Pudi, V.: Autolearn–automated feature generation and selection. In: 2017 IEEE International Conference on Data Mining (ICDM), pp. 217–226. IEEE (2017)
10. Le, V., Gulwani, S.: Flashextract: a framework for data extraction by examples. In: Proceedings of the 35th ACM SIGPLAN Conference on Programming Language Design and Implementation, pp. 542–553 (2014)
11. Lundberg, S.M., et al.: From local explanations to global understanding with explainable AI for trees. Nat. Mach. Intell. 2(1), 2522–5839 (2020)
12. Lundberg, S.M., Lee, S.I.: A unified approach to interpreting model predictions. In: Advances in Neural Information Processing Systems, pp. 4765–4774 (2017)
13. Olson, R.S., Moore, J.H.: TPOt: a tree-based pipeline optimization tool for automating machine learning. In: Workshop on Automatic Machine Learning, pp. 66–74. PMLR (2016)
14. Raman, V., Hellerstein, J.M.: Potter's wheel: an interactive data cleaning system. VLDB 1, 381–390 (2001)
15. Shapley, L.S.: A value for n-person games. Contrib. Theor. Games 2(28), 307–317 (1953)

16. Van Wolputte, E., Korneva, E., Blockeel, H.: Mercs: multi-directional ensembles of regression and classification trees. In: Proceedings of the Thirty-Second AAAI Conference on Artificial Intelligence, pp. 4276–4283. AAAI Publications, New Orleans, Louisiana, USA (2018)
17. Yan, C., He, Y.: Auto-suggest: learning-to-recommend data preparation steps using data science notebooks. In: Proceedings of the 2020 ACM SIGMOD International Conference on Management of Data, pp. 1539–1554 (2020)
18. Yang, C., Akimoto, Y., Kim, D.W., Udell, M.: Oboe: collaborative filtering for autoML model selection. In: Proceedings of the 25th ACM SIGKDD International Conference on Knowledge Discovery & Data Mining, pp. 1173–1183 (2019)

Modeling Language and Graphs

Semantically Enriching Embeddings of Highly Inflectable Verbs for Improving Intent Detection in a Romanian Home Assistant Scenario

Andrei-Cristian Rad[✉], Ioan-Horia-Mihai Muntean, Anda-Diana Stoica, Camelia Lemnaru, Rodica Potolea, and Mihaela Dînșoreanu

Computer Science Department, Technical University of Cluj -Napoca, Cluj-Napoca, Romania

Abstract. Word embeddings are known to encapsulate semantic similarity and have become the preferred representation solution for NLP models. However, they fail to identify the type of semantic relationship, which – in some applications – might be crucial. This paper adapts an existing solution for enhancing word embedding representations such as to better separate between synonyms and antonyms in an intent detection task applied to a Romanian home assistant scenario. Accounting for the morphological richness of the Romanian language, our method proposes an additional augmentation step, in order to generate conjugated pairs of antonym and synonym verbs. The generated pairs are run through the counterfitting step (inspired from literature), for which we propose a justified improvement for one of the hyperparameters. The evaluations performed on the home assistant scenario have shown that the pre-processing step has an essential role in reducing opposing intent errors in the classification model (by almost two thirds).

Keywords: Intent detection · Slot labeling · Word embeddings · Semantic lexicons · RASA NLU · Antonyms · Synonyms · Romanian home assistant

1 Introduction

Natural Language Understanding (NLU) systems can be found in many domain-specific applications nowadays, such as Google Assistant, Microsoft Cortana, or Apple's Siri, which can handle a variety of requests, ranging from calendar management to query answering (if interfaced with a search engine). Another application of NLU systems are conversational bots such as Pepper, Sophia or Erica, which are equipped with the ability to chat with humans. These systems require more breadth and depth of understanding, as they aim to mimic the language understanding level of humans and they are not necessarily tied to a specific domain. Last but not least, NLU systems can be deployed in the context of smart home assistants. Used together with smart IoT devices such as smart

P. H. Abreu et al. (Eds.): IDA 2021, LNCS 12695, pp. 251–262, 2021.
https://doi.org/10.1007/978-3-030-74251-5_20

lights or thermostats, home assistants are able to automate an entire home, thus increasing efficiency, convenience, and security. All the above mentioned examples have become proficient in specific use-cases for the English and Chinese languages, but there have been significantly fewer to no attempts of such applications for less spread languages, such as Romanian.

In [1], a home assistant scenario for the Romanian language was proposed and implemented. Corresponding datasets were generated and labeled, in order to train machine learning models for intent detection and slot filling. These datasets included several data and language-specific complexities expected to occur in such a scenario. The end goal was to develop an efficient solution for intent detection and slot filling for the Romanian language. After the most prominent existing solutions for intent detection and slot filling were evaluated on the dataset, the aim diverged towards exploring additional complexities [2] and improving the performance by addressing common causes of errors.

In this paper, we analyze the most common class of errors, represented by the frequent confusion between opposing intents, and propose, implement and evaluate an adapted solution, based on the method described in [3]. The solution involves applying a pre-processing step at word representation level, aimed towards better distinguishing between synonym and antonym verbs, as they appear to be driving the prediction towards one of the opposing intent classes or the other. Both the original and enhanced word embeddings were run through the same intent detection and slot labeling pipeline and the results are analyzed.

The results of the experiments indicate a significant decrease in the number of errors caused by the misclassification of opposing intents when using the enhanced embeddings. Moreover, other frequent misclassifications that did not involve opposing intents were also corrected, as a side effect of the enhanced word embeddings. As expected, the slot filling results are not affected by the addition of the pre-processing step.

2   Related Work

Due to the recent surge in conversational AI systems, we can find a relatively rich body of work on NLU tasks, resulting in both theoretical approaches and standalone tools. The goal of our current research was not to develop a novel intent detection and slot filling approach, but to improve the quality of this step, given a set of previously discovered shortcomings, in a Romanian home assistant scenario. To that end, we employed an existing solution for the learning tasks (classification – for intent detection and sequence tagging – for slot filling). For evaluation, the methodology is the same as described in [1] and [2], as RASA NLU [4] was used. More information regarding the datasets used in the experiments can be found in Sect. 3.

Static word embedding representations from the Word2Vec family (CBoW [5], SkipGram [5,6], FastText [7,8]) are generated according to the assumption that words which are semantically related tend to be distributionally related also, without making any distinction between the type of semantic relation. Relatedness is normally measured with the vector cosine similarity. Consequently, the cosine distance between the embeddings of both synonym and antonym pairs is close to 0, which makes the opposing relation between them indistinguishable.

Solutions which classify synonyms and antonyms, such as [9] and [10], are not suitable as a pre-processing step for the intent detection task, since the goal here is to make the distinction between them directly in the word embeddings.

A method for in-place modification of word embeddings is proposed in [3]. Using a thesaurus of known synonym and antonym pairs, the model uses gradient descent to minimize the distance between synonyms and maximize the distance between antonyms, while keeping the vector space representation as close to the original as possible. The benefit of intent classification provided by the modified embeddings was proved in [11], where the authors used the in-place modification method on the GloVe [12] embeddings, for the English language.

A more recent strategy [13] takes the counter-fitting procedure further, by considering the relations between synonym/antonym pairs and other vectors as well, and updating not only the synonym/antonym word pairs, but also – potentially – the word vectors in the neighborhood of the pairs. L_2 regularization is also used in [13], to prevent the changes injected by the linguistic constraints from cancelling the rich semantic content in the initial (distributional) vector space, as long as that content does not contradict the linguistic constraints.

In the counter-fitting approach from [3], only the base form of the verbs is extracted from the lexicon, therefore only the vectors corresponding to those forms are updated. This approach works somewhat consistently on morphologically poor languages, such as English, where verbs have at most five different forms. For the Romanian home assistant scenario, the base form only accounts for roughly 20% of the total number of verbs in the dataset. Therefore, taking into account the morphological richness of the Romanian language, we propose a customized solution for altering the word representations of synonyms and antonyms, starting from the counter-fitting procedure proposed in [3].

3   Home Assistant Scenario and Challenges

Language resources for the Romanian language are far scarcer than for English. For the concrete home assistant scenario, no standard intent detection dataset existed prior to the one introduced in [1]. To the best of our knowledge, no alternative dataset has been proposed since. The dataset and the code corresponding to the implementation of the methods presented in this paper can be found on the project's GitHub page[1].

In [1], various language challenges were explored, and models were trained under each of the constraints listed below. Each language challenge maps to a learning complexity, which inevitably impacts the model's performance. These challenges are mapped to *scenarios*, each scenario adding a new complexity on top of the previous one. Different datasets were generated for each scenario, using Chatito,[2] thus learning models were trained and evaluated on each scenario separately.

---

[1] https://github.com/eaaskt/nlu/tree/master/rad-antonyms.
[2] https://rodrigopivi.github.io/Chatito/ - Generate datasets for NLU models using a simple DSL.

- Scenario 0 - **No added complexity**. Both the train and the test data are drawn from the same distribution. This is the *best-case scenario*.
- Scenario 1 - **Different formulations**. The train and the test data are drawn from different distributions. Test data contains utterances having different structure, or which employ synonyms for the predicate verbs.
- Scenario 2 - **Missing and differing slots**. The slots in the test data are either different from the train distribution, or are completely missing.
- Scenario 3 - **Class imbalance**. To illustrate class imbalance, three sub-scenarios were proposed. Each sub-scenario has reduced number of training examples from one of the intent super-classes.

A complete quantitative and qualitative analysis can be found in [1]. In this paper we address the most important limitation identified in [1]: distinguishing between opposing intents. This confusion appeared in all the models trained in [1]. Moreover, as presented in [2], the addition of Romanian diacritics has increased the frequency of this confusion, increasing the need for a solution to address this issue.

From a structural and morphological point of view, the only significant difference between sentences belonging to opposing intent classes is the predicate verb. Consider, for example, the sentences in Table 1. The prediction confidence of the last sentence is close for both the L_HI and the L_LO classes. What gives an edge to the latter is that the verb contained in the sentence is more similar to the verb in the second sentence (see Table 2). This is because embeddings do not explicitly indicate the nature of the semantic relationship between the verbs. This example reflects the phenomenon that happens during the learning procedure, predicting the class of the last sentence corresponding to the inference stage.

Table 1. Different formulation for opposing intents

Sentence	Intent
Salut, **creşte** lumina cu un nivel în pivniţă Hello, **increase** the light with one level in the basement	L_HI
Salut, **scade** lumina cu un nivel în pivniţă Hello, **decrease** the light with one level in the basement	L_LO
Salut, **îmbunătăţeşte** lumina cu un nivel în pivniţă Hello, **improve** the light with one level in the basement	?

4 Proposed Solution

We propose an extension to the solution presented in [3], to address the additional constraints induced by morphologically rich languages, for the home assistant scenario. Figure 1 presents an overview of the processing modules employed

Table 2. Cosine distance of opposing verbs

Verb 1	Verb 2	Cosine sim (Diacritics)	Cosine sim (No Diacritics)	Pair relation
creşte (increase)	scade (decrease)	0.3238	0.4108	Antonyms
creşte (increase)	îmbunătăţeşte (increase)	0.4631	0.5401	Synonyms
scade (decrease)	îmbunătăţeşte (increase)	0.5453	0.5638	Antonyms

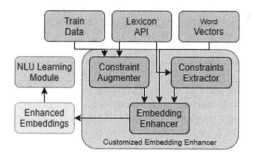

Fig. 1. Employed processing pipeline. The solution presented in this paper is composed by the modules in orange (Color figure online)

in the evaluation part, including the modules implementing the proposed pre-processing steps: constraints generation, constraints augmentation and embedding enhancement.

The first step only requires synonym and antonym pairs to be extracted from a lexicon. RoWordNet [14] provides a simple lexicon API for the Romanian language, but as expected, only the base form of the verbs are extracted.

The constraints augmentation step generates pairs of synonyms and antonyms from the verbal times and moods in the train data. All the verbs in the train data are extracted, and using MlConjug[3], the lemmas and verbal times are separated. After the separation, the synonyms and antonyms pairs of each extracted lemma are retrieved from the lexicon.

Following, for all synonym and antonym pairs retrieved, both words are conjugated sequentially to all the extracted verbal times. The conjugated pairs are added to the final synonym and antonym pair lists. The proposed algorithm is described by the pseudocode in Algorithm 1.

Alternatively, all the pairs could be conjugated at all the existing verbal times, but that would drastically increase the total number of pairs by a factor of around 50, making it infeasible, considering the available resources. The embedding enhancement procedure follows the one described in [3], however the vector space preservation step was discarded, as its time complexity is quadratic with respect to the vocabulary size. Therefore, the loss function is the following:

---

[3] https://pypi.org/project/mlconjug/ - A Python library to conjugate verbs using Machine Learning techniques.

$$J(V, V') = k_1 \sum_{(u,w) \in ant} max(0, \delta - CosineDist(V'_u, V'_w))$$
$$+ k_2 \sum_{(u,w) \in syn} max(0, CosineDist(V'_u, V'_w) - \gamma) \tag{1}$$

Where δ describes the ideal antonym distance, γ describes the ideal synonym distance, and k1, respectively k2 represent weighting coefficients.

An improvement that has had a significant impact on the results was stretching the distance between vectors corresponding to antonyms towards anti-parallelism,

---

Algorithm 1. Linguistic Constraints Augmenter

Result: Conjugated pairs of verbs, according to times and verbs extracted.

Initialize *verbal_times, lemmas* with empty_set

Initialize *conjugated_synonyms, conjugated_antonyms* with empty_set

for *sentence in train_sentences* **do**

  for *verb in sentence* **do**

    lemma ← lemmatize(verb)

    Add *lemma* to *lemmas*

    for *time in language_verbal_times* **do**

      if *conjugate(lemma, time) = verb* **then**

        | Insert *time* in *verbal_times*

      end

    end

  end

end

for *lemma in lemmas* **do**

  lemma_syn ← extract_lexicon_synonym_pairs(lemma)

  for *synonym_pair in lemma_syn* **do**

    for *time in verbal_times* **do**

      conjugated_first ← conjugate(synonym_pair[0], time)

      conjugated_second ← conjugate(synonym_pair[1], time)

      Insert *tuple(conjugated_first, conjugated_second)* in

        conjugated_synonyms

    end

  end

  lemma_ant ← extract_lexicon_antonym_pairs(lemma)

  for *antonym_pair in lemma_ant* **do**

    for *time in verbal_times* **do**

      conjugated_first ← conjugate(antonym_pair[0], time)

      conjugated_second ← conjugate(antonym_pair[1], time)

      Insert *tuple(conjugated_first, conjugated_second)* in

        conjugated_antonyms

    end

  end

end

return conjugated_antonyms, conjugated_synonyms

---

instead of orthogonality, as initially proposed in [3]. This implies setting the δ hyperparameter to 2, instead of 1.

As opposed to [3], the vector space preservation step was skipped. If we compare their experiment to ours, a few conclusions can be drawn: the vocabulary they used was of smaller size (under 100K words), but the number of synonym and antonym pairs extracted was much larger (more than 100K). For their experiment, it makes sense to try to preserve the vector space, as most of the words are impacted by this procedure. The justification for skipping the VSP step in our case is two-fold. First, the complexity of extracting these pairs is at worst $O(n^2)$ with respect to the vocabulary size, and it is very challenging to scale it with a vocabulary of millions of words (as was used in our case). Moreover, we modify a much smaller percent of the total vocabulary, and the vector space itself does not shift that much.

Figure 2 provides a visualization of the proposed word embedding enhancement solution. In reality, these word embeddings used are 300-dimensional, but for visualization purposes, we can use 2-dimensional vectors, the similarity principle being the same. The words "creşte" and "îmbunătăţeşte", corresponding to the red and blue arrows are synonyms, and the word "scade", corresponding to the green arrow, is their antonym.

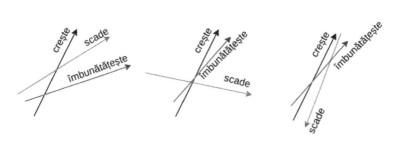

(a) Original Embeddings   (b) Solution presented in [3]   (c) Adapted solution (ours)

Fig. 2. Word embeddings visualization for different approaches. (Color figure online)

5   Empirical Evaluations

5.1   Experimental Setup

As stated previously, *RASA NLU's* intent classification and slot labeling modules were chosen for evaluation. Both the data and the pipelines were identical in all the experiments, the only difference being in the word embeddings. Using RASA NLU, a different language model was generated for each set of embeddings, using the underlying SpaCy[4] library. Henceforth, the following four embedding sets were defined and used:

---

[4] https://spacy.io - Industrial-Strength Natural Language Processing.

- **FT** (FastText): FastText[8] embeddings for the Romanian language.
- **CF** (Counterfit): FastText embeddings, enhanced as described in [3].
- **TS** (Three-step): FastText embeddings, enhanced with the three-step procedure described in Sect. 4, with $\delta = 1$.
- **TSM** (Three-step, maximum distance): Same as **TS**, but with $\delta = 2$.

For the evaluation metric, the F1-score was chosen for both the intent classification and the slot labeling tasks. The evaluation was done using a 5-fold cross-validation loop.

5.2 Results and Discussions

Quantitative Analysis. In this sub-section, the impact of the enhanced embeddings is presented in order to emphasise how each additional step increases the performance of the model (Tables 3 and 4). An increase in performance for the intent detection task can be seen between every two consecutive embedding sets, throughout all the scenarios, with one exception in scenario 3.1. The reported F1 scores have had an increase ranging from 0.01 to 0.12 from one set of embeddings to another, with the highest overall improvement of 0.2277 in scenario 3.1.

Comparing the total number of misclassified opposing intents between the **FT** and the **TSM** embeddings, it can be seen that almost two thirds of the initial errors were fixed. The number of errors decreases between every two consecutive embedding types in most cases. Looking at both the intent F1-score and the number of opposing intent confusions, we can observe that each of the additional steps taken has had a positive impact on the performance of the system. Visually, this can be confirmed by inspecting the confusion matrices in appendix A, as the values on the main diagonal, corresponding to the correct prediction, are increasingly larger with each embedding set.

The F1-score of slot filling did not change with the enhancement of the embeddings, as opposing intents share the same slots, and the representations of those words are not modified by the proposed procedure.

Table 3. Intent detection results for the proposed embedding types.

Scenario	0	1	2	3.1	3.2	3.3
Intent F1 - FT	0.9862	0.5112	0.4201	0.3176	0.3582	0.2905
Intent F1 - CF	0.9964	0.5897	0.4895	0.3525	0.4725	0.3455
Intent F1 - TS	0.998	0.6562	0.5666	0.3424	0.5129	0.3653
Intent F1 - TSM	**0.9988**	**0.7081**	**0.6773**	**0.4663**	**0.5859**	**0.4116**

Qualitative Analysis. We have also analyzed the confidence of the intent predictions for the opposing intent misclassifications. The three following confidence groups are defined:

Table 4. Absolute number of errors caused by opposing intent confusion for the previously described pipelines.

Scenario	0	1	2	3.1	3.2	3.3	Total
Number of Opposing Intent Confusions - FT	2	67	98	70	66	80	383
Number of Opposing Intent Confusions - CF	1	70	85	59	61	55	331
Number of Opposing Intent Confusions - TS	**0**	45	44	42	37	31	199
Number of Opposing Intent Confusions - TSM	1	**41**	**28**	**17**	**24**	**24**	**135**

1. Low: The intent is predicted with confidence less than 0.3.
2. Medium: The intent is predicted with a confidence between 0.3 and 0.7.
3. High: The intent is predicted with a confidence greater than 0.7.

For the misclassifications that involved base forms of the verbs, the **CF** embeddings solved most of the misclassifications in the low confidence group, while significantly reducing the prediction confidence of most predictions in the medium and high confidence groups, as expected. For misclassifications that involved other forms of the verbs, the **TS** and **TSM** embeddings had the same effect, of solving most of the misclassifications in the low confidence groups, while decreasing the confidence for the other two groups. For certain sentences belonging to the high confidence group, the confidence has decreased with each additional step of the embedding enhancement procedure.

Regardless of the scenario and the embedding type, sentences that contained phrasal verbs did not change in confidence of the prediction. As phrasal verbs are made of more words that do not get modified during the procedure, the confidence and the prediction are not impacted. This shows the first limitation of our approach, the ability to update the representation of phrasal verbs.

Sentences containing specific verbs – "a reduce" (to reduce) and "a porni" (to start) – were not corrected by either embedding set. This was most likely caused by the lexicon not providing any semantic relationships between these and any other verbs in the training set. This shows the second limitation of our approach, the dependency on the lexicon, and the inability to capture all the semantic relationships one could think of.

These conclusions are reflected in the confidence histograms in appendix A. When using the **TSM** embedding set, there are fewer wrong predictions with high confidence – corresponding to the red bars on the right – (which most likely belong to the two limitations described above), than when using the **FT** embedding set.

In terms of computational complexity, significant differences exist between the **CF** pipeline and the **TS/TSM** pipelines. The complexity of the **CF** approach is determined solely by the number of pairs, p, and the number of epochs, e, considering the pairs are already extracted and accessed by simply loading them, thus being $O(p * e)$. The complexity of the other two pipelines is increased by the pair conjugation step described in Algorithm 1, resulting in $O(ts * vb * ti + l * (es + s + ea + a) * ti)$. We argue that the number of verbs per sentence, **vb**, the number of verbal times, **ti**, the number of antonyms and synonyms of a word, **s** and **a**, as well as the per-word extraction steps, **es** and **ea**, respectively, are constant. The time complexity can be reduced to $O(ts+l)$, where **ts** is the number of train samples, **l** is the number of lemmas, and **es/ea** represent the complexity of the extraction step. Therefore, the **TS/TSM** pipelines have a complexity of $O(p * e + ts + l)$.

Compared to the original counterfitting approach which includes the VSP step, and has a worst case complexity of $O(n^2)$, n being the size of the vocabulary, our approach is linear with respect to the size of train data and the number of verb lemmas extracted. The main disadvantage is that our approach needs to be re-run with every different set of training data.

6   Conclusions, Limitations, and Further Work

In this paper, we adapt an existing solution for enriching word embedding representations used as features for intent detection and slot filling in a Romanian home assistant scenario. The solution aims to enrich the semantic information captured by the embeddings, by implicitly distinguishing between the synonymy and the antonymy relationship. Moreover, we argue that antonyms should be represented by vectors having the same direction but reverse orientations, as opposed to being orthogonal, assumption which is empirically evaluated. Experiments have revealed an increased F1-score (by up to 0.2277) and a reduced number of opposing intent confusions (by almost two thirds).

The major drawback of the proposed approach is that is tailored to a domain-specific problem, which only uses a small part of the language's vocabulary. In this case, as it is unlikely to extend the system so that it supports a much larger number of intents, going towards a domain over-fitting of certain words is justified. This approach could, in theory, work for any language, provided we have the lexicon, the conjugation rules, and a trained lemmatizer.

A direction for further investigations would be applying approaches similar to this on phrasal verbs. Such constructions do not change their representation with these kind of approaches, and rightfully so, as the words that compose them are not part of the antonym/synonym pairs.

Acknowledgment. The work presented in this paper was supported by grant no. 72PCCDI/01.03.2018, *ROBIN - Robots and Society: Cognitive Systems for Personal Robots and Autonomous Vehicles.*

Appendix A   Confusion matrices and histograms

The evolution of the confusion matrices (for evaluation Scenario 1) display the reduction in number of errors, as there are more elements on the main diagonal. The evolution of the confidence histograms (for evaluation Scenario 2) depict less wrong predictions with high and low confidences – most low margin misclassifications were solved, and confidence for those with high confidence was mostly reduced.

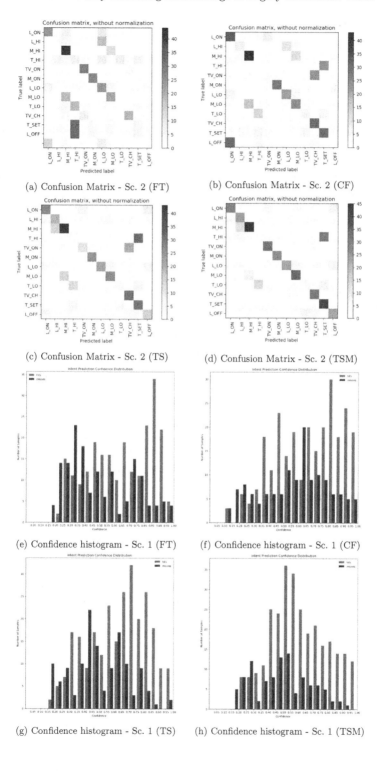

(a) Confusion Matrix - Sc. 2 (FT)   (b) Confusion Matrix - Sc. 2 (CF)

(c) Confusion Matrix - Sc. 2 (TS)   (d) Confusion Matrix - Sc. 2 (TSM)

(e) Confidence histogram - Sc. 1 (FT)   (f) Confidence histogram - Sc. 1 (CF)

(g) Confidence histogram - Sc. 1 (TS)   (h) Confidence histogram - Sc. 1 (TSM)

References

1. Stoica, A., Kadar, T., Lemnaru, C., Potolea, R., Dînşoreanu, M.: The impact of data challenges on intent detection and slot filling for the home assistant scenario. In: IEEE 15th International Conference on Intelligent Computer Communication and Processing (ICCP), pp. 41–47. IEEE (2019)
2. Stoica, A.D., et al.: The impact of Romanian diacritics on intent detection and slot filling. In: IEEE International Conference on Automation, Quality and Testing, Robotics (AQTR), pp. 1–6 (2020)
3. Mrkšić, N., et al.: Counter-fitting word vectors to linguistic constraints. In: Proceedings of the 2016 Conference of the North American Chapter of the Association for Computational Linguistics: Human Language Technologies (2016)
4. Bocklisch, T., Faulkner, J., Pawlowski, N., Nichol, A.: Rasa: open source language understanding and dialogue management. arXiv preprint arXiv:1712.05181 (2017)
5. Mikolov, T., Chen, K., Corrado, G., Dean, J.: Efficient estimation of word representations in vector space. arXiv preprint arXiv:1301.3781 (2013)
6. Mikolov, T., Sutskever, I., Chen, K., Corrado, G., Dean, J.: Distributed representations of words and phrases and their compositionality. In: Advances in Neural Information Processing Systems, p. 26 (2013)
7. Joulin, A., Grave, E., Bojanowski, P., Mikolov, T.: Bag of tricks for efficient text classification. arXiv preprint arXiv:1607.01759 (2016)
8. Joulin, A., Grave, E., Bojanowski, P., Douze, M., Jégou, H., Mikolov, T.: Fasttext.zip: compressing text classification models. arXiv preprint arXiv:1612.03651 (2016)
9. Ali, M.A., Sun, Y., Zhou, X., Wang, W. and Zhao, X.: Antonym-synonym classification based on new sub-space embeddings. arXiv preprint arXiv:1612.03651 (2019)
10. Nguyen, K.A., Walde, S.S.I., Vu, N.T.: Distinguishing antonyms and synonyms in a pattern-based neural network. In: Proceedings of the 15th Conference of the European Chapter of the Association for Computational Linguistics: Volume 1, Long Papers (2017)
11. Kim, J., Tur, G., Celikyilmaz, A., Cao, B., Wang, Y.: Intent detection using semantically enriched word embeddings. In: IEEE Spoken Language Technology Workshop (SLT) **2016**, pp. 414–419 (2016)
12. Pennington, J., Socher, R., Manning, C.D.: Glove: global vectors for word representation. In: EMNLP, pp. 1532–1543 (2014)
13. Mrkšić, N., et al.: Semantic specialization of distributional word vector spaces using monolingual and cross-lingual constraints. Trans. Assoc. Comput. Linguis. **5**, 309–324 (2017). https://www.aclweb.org/anthology/Q17-1022
14. Dumitrescu, S.D., Avram, A.M., Morogan, L., Toma, S.A.: Rowordnet-a python api for the romanian wordnet. In: Proceedings of the 10th International Conference on Electronics, Computers and Artificial Intelligence (ECAI), pp. 1–6. IEEE (2018)

BoneBert: A BERT-based Automated Information Extraction System of Radiology Reports for Bone Fracture Detection and Diagnosis

Zhihao Dai[1] , Zhong Li[2], and Lianghao Han[3(✉)]

[1] Department of Computer Science, University of Warwick, Coventry CV4 7AL, UK
zhihao.dai@warwick.ac.uk
[2] InterSystem, Eton SL4 6BB, UK
[3] Department of Computer Science, Brunel University, Uxbridge UB8 3PH, UK
lianghao.han@brunel.ac.uk

Abstract. Radiologists make the diagnoses of bone fractures through examining X-ray radiographs and document them in radiology reports. Applying information extraction techniques on such radiology reports to retrieve the information of bone fracture diagnosis could yield a source of structured data for medical cohort studies, image labelling and decision support concerning bone fractures. In this study, we proposed an information extraction system of Bone X-ray radiology reports to retrieve the details of bone fracture detection and diagnosis, based on a bio-medically pre-trained Bidirectional Encoder Representations from Transformers (BERT) natural language processing (NLP) model by Google. The model, named as BoneBert, was first trained on annotations automatically generated by a handcrafted rule-based labelling system using a dataset of 6,048 X-ray radiology reports and then fine-tuned on a small set of 4,890 expert annotations. Thus, the model was trained in a "semi-supervised" fashion. We evaluated the performance of the proposed model and compared it with the conventional rule-based labelling system on two typical tasks: Assertion Classification (AC) for bone fracture status detection (positive, negative or uncertainty) and Named Entity Recognition (NER) related to the fracture type, the bone type and location of a fracture occurs. BoneBert outperformed the rule-based system in both tasks, showing great potential for automated information extraction of the detection and diagnosis of bone fracture from radiology reports, such as, the clinical status, type and location of bone fracture, and more related observations.

Keywords: Electronic medical records · Machine learning · Natural language processing · Semisupervised learning

© Springer Nature Switzerland AG 2021
P. H. Abreu et al. (Eds.): IDA 2021, LNCS 12695, pp. 263–274, 2021.
https://doi.org/10.1007/978-3-030-74251-5_21

1   Introduction

Radiology reports in the form of Electronic Health Report (EHR) can be a rich source of data for medical cohort studies, image labelling, and decision support after information extraction techniques are applied for automatic annotation and labeling. Despite abundant researches in recent years, existing information extraction systems of radiology reports are developed for either general [2,19] or Chest X-ray radiology reports [1,5,9,10,12–14,20]. Although some of these system can capture the presence or absence of bone fracture, they either do not extract other significant observations [8,25], such as the uncertainty, type and location of bone fracture, or rely on regular expressions [22–24], which hamper their performance.

In this study, we have developed a BERT-based information extraction system to retrieve the details related to the detection and diagnosis of bone fracture from bone X-ray radiology reports. It is informed by a large-scale biomedical corpus and syntactic structures of sentences. More specifically, we implement the automated information extraction on the clinical status, type and location of bone fracture. The aim of this study is to convert the information for each fracture recorded from the free-text format into a structured one, such as the following template used by radiologists in the UK:

There is (not/possibly) [STATUS] a [TYPE] fracture of the
[LOCATION-BONE-PART] part of the [LOCATION-BONE] bone.

The proposed system employed a BERT-based model which was pre-trained on the PubMed abstracts and MIMIC-III. It was first trained with the annotations automatically generated by a conventional handcrafted rule-based labelling system from a dataset of radiology reports, and then fine-tuned with a small set of expert annotations. The conventional rule-based labelling system was developed to alleviate the burden of manual labelling for generating training datasets. Therefore the proposed system adopted a semi-supervised training approach. The whole dataset comprised of 13,712 Bone X-ray radiology reports in which 4,530 sentences and 4,890 mentions of "fracture" were annotated by clinical experts.

We evaluated the performance of the proposed approach and compared it with the conventional rule-based labelling system on two typical tasks: Assertion Classification (AC) for bone fracture status detection (positive, negative and uncertainty) and Named Entity Recognition (NER) related to the type and location of bone fracture.

2   Related Works

2.1   Rule-Based Approaches

NegBio [14] made uncertainty cases explicit and applied two sets of rules, one for negation and the other for uncertainty, on Universal Dependencies (UD) [6] trees of sentences. CheXpert-labeller [10] used a set of rules to automatically detect the presence of 14 common observations in Chest X-ray radiology reports, and addressed the problem of misclassification of double negation in NegBio by splitting uncertainty detection into pre-negation and post-negation stages.

2.2   Machine Learning Approaches

Earlier machine learning systems employed tradition methods such as Logistic Regression [1,8], Decision Trees [25], Support Vector Machine (SVM) [8], Random Forests [8], Conditional Markov Model (CMM) as well as Conditional Random Field (CRF) [9]. Recent advancements in Deep Neural Networks (DNNs) lead to the exploration of Recurrent Neural Network (RNN) [5,21], Convolutional Neural Network (CNN) [17], as well as Transformers [5] such as BERT [7] and XLNet [26] for information extraction.

2.3   Hybrid Approaches

Training machine learning models on labels automatically generated by rule-based systems, to which some works refer as "weak supervision," reduces the annotation costs and alleviates the burden of manual annotation. CheXbert [20] and Transfer [12], coupling supervised learning to weakly supervised learning, was a pre-trained BERT/LSTM network fine-tuned successively on labels generated by CheXpert labeller/NegBio and manually produced ground-truths.

3   Methodology

3.1   Dataset

Our dataset was a privately-owned collection of 9,435 radiology studies and 13,712 reports in the UK. All the reports have been anonymised. The dataset also contained a total of 4,890 manual annotations performed by two clinical experts. For each report used for manual annotation, the sentences, where mentions of "fracture" exist, were annotated with four categories of information per mention, and they were **assertion**, **type**, **bone** and **bone part**. Assertion was either **positive (P)**, **negative (N)**, **uncertain (U)** or **ignored (I)**. When there were two mentions and both referred to the same fracture in a sentence, the latter was assigned with an "ignored" label. Also, in the same sentence, words other than the keyword itself and describing type, bone and bone part of the fracture were paired with the mention and assigned to the corresponding categories. Each word was only paired with one mention at most.

Our task is, in effect, a combination of two subtasks, AC for the mention and NER for each of other words. Figure 1 presents an example of manual annotations for a sample report in our dataset.

We split the dataset into the training, validation and test sets consecutively, as shown in Table 1. We ensured that there was no overlap of studies across different sets.

ID: 4e402a05-4cfe-43b4-8e88-e1b7752c3a31
CLINICAL INFORMATION: Fracture review
ORDER ITEM: XLOLR, XR Tibia and fibula Rt
REPORT:

1. There is a healing **fracture** at the neck of the right fibula.
2. Position as shown.

- **ASSERTION:** positive **TYPE:** healing
- **BONE:** right, fibula **BONE PART:** neck

Fig. 1. A sample report from the annotated dataset. The annotation is in color green. (Color figure online)

Table 1. Distributions of Reports, Sentences and Mentions (Either Positive (P), Negative (N), Uncertain (U) or Ignored (I)) in Datasets

Set	Reports	Sentences	Mentions				
			Positive	Negative	Uncertain	Ignored	Sum
Training	9,389	28,000	1,155	1,888	262	27	3,332
Validation	1,903	4,000	203	501	36	4	744
Test	2,420	8,509	270	498	43	3	814
Total	13,712	40,509	1,630	2,896	341	32	4,890
Extra	6,048	51,460	4,733	5,192	365	0	10,290

Additionally, we retrieved 6,048 reports related to bone fracture. The extra set contains 10,290 mentions and is annotated by our rule-based model. Notice that the model does not assign the "ignored" assertion label.

3.2 Information Extraction

Figure 2 presents the BERT-based information extraction pipeline proposed in this study. It consists of a pre-trained BERT model as its core component and a conventional rule-based labeller for automatic annotation. The rule-based labeller applies handcrafted rules on syntactic structures of sentences and words matching to generate "weak labels" or so-called "imperfect labels" for the large extra set. As shown in Fig. 2, the proposed BERT-based model is trained in a so-called "semi-supervised" fashion, that is, first on the aforementioned weak labels and later on a small set of ground-truths annotated by clinical experts for fine-tuning. We named our BERT-based system as BoneBert.

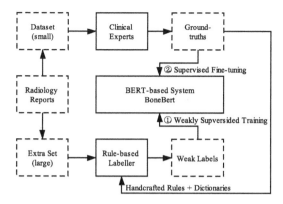

Fig. 2. BERT-based information extraction pipeline.

BERT-based Model. BoneBert was built upon the language model BlueBERT [15], a BERT model pre-trained on the PubMed abstract database and clinical notes MIMIC-III [11] and developed for clinical NLP tasks. We further trained BlueBERT on our dataset of clinical reports, in order to learn Bone X-ray radiology reports containing the information of fracture detection and diagnosis. In this BERT-based model, we converted each mention along with its context into a input-output sequence pair. In the input sequence, the keyword (e.g. fracture) was masked. In the output sequence, we assigned either "POSITIVE", "NEGA-TIVE", "UNCERTAIN", or "IGNORED" label to the masked token depending on its assertion. For the rest of tokens, we assigned labels in the "type", "bone", and "bone part" categories accordingly and empty "O" labels to others.

Rule-Based Labeller. The rule-based labeller was developed to alleviate the burden of large scale manual labelling. The proposed rule-based labeller was based on CheXpert-labeller [10], a rule-based labeller of Chest X-ray radiology reports, and simple words matching for NER.

Figure 3 illustrates the flowchart of the rule-based labeller on bone fracture labelling with a sample sentence extracted from a bone X-ray radiology report. Given a sentence in a report, we first tokenized and extracted mentions of inter-est. In this study, we looked for any token in the form of "fracture" or "frac-tures." We then parsed the sentence to produce a Universal Dependencies (UD) Tree. The tree described the syntactic relations among tokens in the sentence, whereas each arc represented a relation. The head pointed to the dependent of the relation, and the tail the governor.

For the AC task, to detect the presence of bone fracture, we fed the UD Tree into the labeller. Like the CheXpert-labeller, the proposed labeller deployed three sets of rules defined in Semgrex [3], a language for searching dependency relations, of pre-negation, negation, and post-negation consecutively on mentions in the UD Tree to determine the assertion. Mentions matching the pre-negation or post-negation rules were assigned with "uncertain" label, and those matching

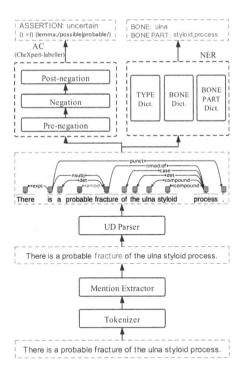

Fig. 3. Rule-based labeller.

the negation rules were assigned with "negative." Mentions that did not match any rule are considered "positive."

For the NER task, in order to label fracture type, bone type and bone part where a fracture occurs by the rule-based labeller, we first learned three dictionaries, corresponding respectively to "fracture type," "bone type," and "bone part" from the ground-truth labels of the training set. During the training stage, each token with a single NER label was assigned to the dictionary of its corresponding category. Tokens with more than one label were assigned to the dictionary of the most frequent ones only. In addition, we extracted phrases whose roots are "fracture" (type), "bone organ" (bone), and "zone of bone organ" (bone part) from RadLex[1], split them into words, and assigned each word to its corresponding category. During the prediction stage, the system, by default, looks for matches in the sentence where a mention exists. For sentences that have two or more mentions, however, the system limits the matching scope to their respective dependents.

---

[1] http://radlex.org.

3.3 Training and Evaluation

For the rule-based model, we used the "GUM" model[2] of the Stanford's Stanza toolkit [16] for tokenisation and the "GENIA+PubMed" model[3] of the BLLIP parser [4] for parsing. We converted the resulting trees into Universal Dependencies using the Stanford Dependencies Converter [18].

For the proposed model, BoneBert, we used the base version of BlueBERT as a starting point, which had 12 layers, 12 heads, and 110 million parameters in total. We adapted the original NER code in BlueBERT [4] for training. Hyperparameters are tuned on the validation set.

4 Experiments

4.1 Assertion Classification

Extra New Rules for Bone X-Ray Radiology Reports. The CheXpert-labeller came with 153 assertion rules across three stages. In our labeller, we expanded the rules bases through manually designing rules for any incorrect prediction by the labeller to account for the style and syntactic differences between our dataset and Chest X-ray reports used for developing the CheXpert-labeller. In the end, the process yielded 19 new rules, of which four were negation, 15 post-negation and no pre-negation. We found that none of the new rules resulted in an incorrect prediction on the validation set.

Table 2. Assertion classification results of the rule-based labellers and the BERT-based systems on the test set. Precision, recall, and F1 score per class as well as overall weighted F1 score are reported in percentile.

Model	Positive			Negative			Uncertain			Overall
	P	R	F1	P	R	F1	P	R	F1	F1
BonePert	80.12	**100**	88.96	99.58	94.58	97.01	0	0	0	89.19
BonePert+	97.12	**100**	98.54	99.60	**99.80**	99.70	**100**	86.05	92.50	98.93
BlueBERT	**99.63**	99.26	99.44	**100**	**99.80**	**99.90**	95.56	**100**	97.73	99.63
BoneBert	**99.63**	**100**	**99.82**	**100**	**99.80**	**99.90**	**100**	**100**	**100**	**99.88**

Table 2 compares the performance on the test set between the rule-based labeller with the CheXpert's rule base (we name it **BonePert**) and our expanded rule base (**BonePert+**). Overall, BonePert+ has a weighted average F1 score of 98.93%, a considerable leap from 89.19% by BonePert.

---

[2] https://stanfordnlp.github.io/stanza/available_models.html.
[3] https://github.com/BLLIP/bllip-parser/blob/master/MODELS.rst.
[4] https://github.com/ncbi-nlp/bluebert.

Weak Supervision for BERT. To investigate the effects of weak supervision on BERT's performance, we fine-tuned a BlueBERT model directly on the training set. We compared it against our BERT-based system (**BoneBert**) trained in the semi-supervised fashion.

Table 2 shows that BlueBERT achieves near-perfect performance on both the "positive" and "negative" classes, with 99.44% and 99.90% F1 scores respectively. The system, however, has a slightly lower F1 score of 97.73% on the "uncertain" class due to the presence of false positives. BoneBert, benefiting from weak supervision by BonePert+, improves its recall in the "positive" class and precision in the "uncertain." In comparison to BonePert+, BoneBert purges six misclassifications, all of which are uncertain, while making no new ones. Here, we provide an example of an error made by BonePert+ and later corrected by BoneBert.

A repeat lateral projection is advised to confirm or exclude **fracture**.

The "fracture" in the sentence is incorrectly matched to a negation rule and thus classified as "negative" by BonePert+. Both BlueBERT and BoneBert correctly produce an "uncertain" label. As a result, BoneBert has the highest weighted average F1 score of 99.88% thus far.

4.2   Named Entity Recognition

Dictionary Compilation. In the NER subtask, BonePert(+) learned 128 words for "type," 201 for "bone," 335 for "bone part" from the training set and RadLex.

Table 3. Named Entity Recognition Results of the rule-based labeller and the BERT-based Systems on the Test Set. Precision, Recall, and F1 score per category as well as average F1 score are reported in percentile.

Model	TYPE			BONE			BONE PART			Average
	P	R	F1	P	R	F1	P	R	F1	F1
BonePert(+)	88.44	**95.65**	91.91	79.26	91.36	84.88	69.98	**97.61**	81.52	86.10
BlueBERT	98.29	93.75	95.97	86.44	91.86	89.07	85.56	92.10	88.71	91.24
BoneBert	**98.57**	93.75	**96.10**	**89.18**	**92.20**	**90.67**	**89.70**	93.78	**91.70**	**92.82**

Table 3 presents the performance of the BonePert(+) model per category on average. Overall, the model has an average F1 score of 86.10%.

On the test set, 19.71% predicted as "bone" and 25.09% "bone part" in fact do not belong to any category, compared to 11.56% for "type." Further analysis reveals that most such errors arise from spatial information linked to observations other than bone fractures being constantly mislabelled as "bone" or "bone part" for bone fractures, which explains the relatively lower precision scores in the former two categories.

Weak Supervision for BERT. BlueBERT, informed by large-scale biomedical knowledge, produces 95.97% F1 score for "type", 89.07% for "bone" and 88.71% for the "bone part." In contrast, BoneBert, with additional weak supervision from BonePert+, has higher F1 scores of 96.10% for "type", 91.06% for "bone" and 92.08% for "bone part." Overall, BlueBERT has an average F1 score of 91.24%, whereas BoneBert has a higher score of 92.95%.

Weak supervision enables BoneBert to capture concepts present in BonePert(+)'s dictionary with greater confidence. Here, we present an example where BlueBERT misses "base" and "fifth" in "base of the fifth metatarsal."

Left foot- there is a **fracture** through the base of the fifth metatarsal.

Both BonePert(+) and BoneBert correctly identify the words as "bone part" and "bone" respectively since they are included in the corresponding dictionaries.

Since BoneBert is better in separating relevant information from information tied to other observations than BonePert(+), it achieves higher precision scores across all categories. Let's look at the following sentence in a radiology report as an example,

Left total knee replacement in situ, no **fracture**, dislocation, periprosthetic fracture or evidence of loosening identified.

BonePert(+) mistakes "Left", "knee," and "replacement" for the observation of "Left total knee replacement in situ" as the "bone" and "bone part" related to the "fracture," whereas BoneBert ignores the irrelevant spatial concepts.

The improvements in precision, in comparison to losses in recall, is so significant that the unweighted average F1 score of BoneBert is +6.72% higher than BonePert(+)'s.

5   Discussion

Admittedly, several limitations have arisen in this research. First, our information model covered only the assertion, type and location of bone fractures whereas more information, such as plurality, measurements, and imaging characteristics, could be considered. Second, we developed the expanded rule base for BonePert+ manually. The process was inefficient and hard to scale up if the training set was large. There was no guarantee that the new rules were general enough. Algorithms for learning rules from the training set remains an open task. Last, we considered "fracture" to be the only keyword since it was the most significant indicator of itself. In some rare cases, other words or phrases, say, "bone injury," might be used to indicate a bone fracture.

6 Conclusion

In this study, we have designed and implemented a BERT-based automatic information extraction system on bone fracture detection and diagnosis from radiology reports, BoneBert. We have also proposed a rule-based labeller for automated annotation to be used for training the proposed model in a weakly supervised fashion.

We evaluated the performance of the model (BoneBert) against the rule-based approach with and without rules specific for fracture diagnosis (named as BonePert+ and BonePert, respectively) on two tasks, namely, AC for detecting the presence of bone fracture and NER for extracting the information about the fracture type, bone type and bone part that a fracture occurs. For the AC task, BoneBert achieved a weighted average F1 score of 99.88%. For the NER task, BoneBert had a higher average F1 score of 92.82%. The proposed approach has shown great potential for automated information extraction on bone fracture detection and diagnosis from bone X-ray radiology reports.

Acknowledgements. This work was supported in part by the SBRI competition: AI supporting early detection and diagnosis in heart failure management.

References

1. Banerjee, I., Chen, M.C., Lungren, M.P., Rubin, D.L.: Radiology report annotation using intelligent word embeddings: applied to multi-institutional chest CT cohort. J. Biomed. Inform. **77**, 11–20 (2018). https://doi.org/10.1016/j.jbi.2017.11.012, https://linkinghub.elsevier.com/retrieve/pii/S1532046417302575
2. Bozkurt, S., Alkim, E., Banerjee, I., Rubin, D.L.: Automated detection of measurements and their descriptors in radiology reports using a hybrid natural language processing algorithm. Journal of Digital Imaging **32**(4), 544–553 (2019). https://doi.org/10.1007/s10278-019-00237-9
3. Chambers, N., et al.: Learning alignments and leveraging natural logic. In: Proceedings of the ACL-PASCAL Workshop on Textual Entailment and Paraphrasing - RTE 2007. Association for Computational Linguistics, Morristown, NJ, USA, pp. 165–170 (2007). https://doi.org/10.3115/1654536.1654570
4. Charniak, E., Johnson, M.: Coarse-to-fine n-best parsing and MaxEnt discriminative reranking. In: Proceedings of the 43rd Annual Meeting on Association for Computational Linguistics - ACL 2005. Association for Computational Linguistics, Morristown, NJ, USA, vol. 1, pp. 173–180 (2005). https://doi.org/10.3115/1219840.1219862
5. Datta, S., Si, Y., Rodriguez, L., Shooshan, S.E., Demner-Fushman, D., Roberts, K.: Understanding spatial language in radiology: representation framework, annotation, and spatial relation extraction from chest X-ray reports using deep learning. J. Biomed. Inform. **108**, 103473 (2019). https://doi.org/10.1016/j.jbi.2020.103473, http://arxiv.org/abs/1908.04485
6. De Marneffe, M.C., et al.: Universal stanford dependencies: a cross-linguistic typology. In: Proceedings of the 9th International Conference on Language Resources and Evaluation, LREC 2014, pp. 4585–4592 (2014)

7. Devlin, J., Chang, M.W., Lee, K., Toutanova, K.: BERT: pre-training of deep bidirectional transformers for language understanding. arXiv preprint arXiv:1810.04805 (2018)

8. Grundmeier, R., et al.: Identification of long bone fractures in radiology reports using natural language processing to support healthcare quality improvement. Appl. Clin. Inform. **7**(4), 1051–1068 (2016). https://doi.org/10.4338/ACI-2016-08-RA-0129

9. Hassanpour, S., Langlotz, C.P.: Information extraction from multi-institutional radiology reports. Artif. Intell. Med. **66**, 29–39 (2016). https://doi.org/10.1016/j.artmed.2015.09.007, https://linkinghub.elsevier.com/retrieve/pii/S0933365715001244

10. Irvin, J., et al.: CheXpert: A large chest radiograph dataset with uncertainty labels and expert comparison. In: Proceedings of the AAAI Conference on Artificial Intelligence, Vol. 33, pp. 590–597 (2019). https://doi.org/10.1609/aaai.v33i01.3301590, https://aaai.org/ojs/index.php/AAAI/article/view/3834

11. Johnson, A.E., et al.: MIMIC-III, a freely accessible critical care database. Sci. Data **3**(1), 160035 (2016). https://doi.org/10.1038/sdata.2016.35

12. Liventsev, V., Fedulova, I., Dylov, D.: Deep text prior: weakly supervised learning for assertion classification. In: Tetko, I.V., Kůrková, V., Karpov, P., Theis, F. (eds.) ICANN 2019. LNCS, vol. 11731, pp. 243–257. Springer, Cham (2019). https://doi.org/10.1007/978-3-030-30493-5_26

13. McDermott, M.B.A., Hsu, T.M.H., Weng, W.H., Ghassemi, M., Szolovits, P.: CheXpert++: approximating the cheXpert labeler for speed, differentiability, and probabilistic output. arXiv preprint arXiv:2006.15229 (2020)

14. Peng, Y., Wang, X., Lu, L., Bagheri, M., Summers, R., Lu, Z.: NegBio: a high-performance tool for negation and uncertainty detection in radiology reports. AMIA Joint Summits Trans. Sci. Proc. **2017**, 188–196 (2018). http://www.ncbi.nlm.nih.gov/pubmed/29888070

15. Peng, Y., Yan, S., Lu, Z.: Transfer learning in biomedical natural language processing: an evaluation of BERT and ELMo on ten benchmarking datasets. In: Proceedings of the 18th BioNLP Workshop and Shared Task. Association for Computational Linguistics, Stroudsburg, PA, USA, pp. 58–65 (2019). https://doi.org/10.18653/v1/W19-5006

16. Qi, P., Zhang, Y., Zhang, Y., Bolton, J., Manning, C.D.: Stanza: a Python natural language processing toolkit for many human languages. arXiv preprint arXiv:2003.07082 (2020)

17. Santus, E., et al.: Do neural information extraction algorithms generalize across institutions? JCO Clin. Cancer Inform. **3**, 1–8 (2019). https://doi.org/10.1200/CCI.18.00160

18. Schuster, S., Manning, C.D.: Enhanced English universal dependencies: an improved representation for natural language understanding tasks. In: Proceedings of the 10th International Conference on Language Resources and Evaluation, LREC 2016, pp. 2371–2378 (2016)

19. Sevenster, M., Buurman, J., Liu, P., Peters, J., Chang, P.: Natural language processing techniques for extracting and categorizing finding measurements in narrative radiology reports. Appl. Clin. Inform. **6**(3), 600–610 (2015). https://doi.org/10.4338/ACI-2014-11-RA-0110

20. Smit, A., Jain, S., Rajpurkar, P., Pareek, A., Ng, A.Y., Lungren, M.P.: CheXbert: combining automatic labelers and expert annotations for accurate radiology report labeling using BERT. arXiv preprint arXiv:2004.09167 (2020)

21. Steinkamp, J.M., Chambers, C., Lalevic, D., Zafar, H.M., Cook, T.S.: Toward complete structured information extraction from radiology reports using machine learning. J. Digit. Imaging **32**(4), 554–564 (2019). https://doi.org/10.1007/s10278-019-00234-y

22. Tibbo, M.E., et al.: Use of natural language processing tools to identify and classify periprosthetic femur fractures. J. Arthroplasty **34**(10), 2216–2219 (2019). https://doi.org/10.1016/j.arth.2019.07.025, https://linkinghub.elsevier.com/retrieve/pii/S0883540319307090

23. Wang, Y., Mehrabi, S., Sohn, S., Atkinson, E.J., Amin, S., Liu, H.: Natural language processing of radiology reports for identification of skeletal site-specific fractures. BMC Med. Inform. Decis. Making **19**(S3), 73 (2019). https://doi.org/10.1186/s12911-019-0780-5

24. Wang, Y., et al.: A clinical text classification paradigm using weak supervision and deep representation. BMC Med. Inform. Decis. Making **19**(1), 1 (2019). https://doi.org/10.1186/s12911-018-0723-6

25. Yadav, K., Sarioglu, E., Smith, M., Choi, H.A.: Automated outcome classification of emergency department computed tomography imaging reports. Acad. Emerg. Med. **20**(8), 848–854 (2013). https://doi.org/10.1111/acem.12174

26. Yang, Z., Dai, Z., Yang, Y., Carbonell, J., Salakhutdinov, R., Le, Q.V.: XLNet: Generalized autoregressive pretraining for language understanding. arXiv preprint arXiv:1906.08237 pp. 1–11 (2019)

Linking the Dynamics of User Stance to the Structure of Online Discussions

Christine Largeron[1], Andrei Mardale[1], and Marian-Andrei Rizoiu[2(✉)] (iD)

[1] Univ Lyon, UJM -Saint -Etienne, CNRS, OGS, Saint-Etienne, France
`Christine.Largeron@univ-st-etienne.fr`
[2] Data Science Institute, University of Technology Sydney, Sydney, Australia
`Marian-Andrei.Rizoiu@uts.edu.au`

Abstract. This paper studies the dynamics of opinion formation and polarization in social media. We investigate whether users' stance concerning contentious subjects is influenced by the online discussions they are exposed to and interactions with users supporting different stances. We set up a series of predictive exercises based on machine learning models. Users are described using several posting activities features capturing their overall activity levels, posting success, the reactions their posts attract from users of different stances, and the types of discussions in which they engage. Given the user description at present, the purpose is to predict their stance in the future. Using a dataset of Brexit discussions on the Reddit platform, we show that the activity features regularly outperform the textual baseline, confirming the link between exposure to discussion and opinion. We find that the most informative features relate to the stance composition of the discussion in which users prefer to engage.

Keywords: Online polarization dynamics · Online controversy · Social network analysis · Graph mining · Information diffusion

1 Introduction

In the twenty-first century, offline events are increasingly shaped by the discussions occurring on online social media. The outcome of significant events—such as the presidential elections in the United States of America [19,20,28] or the decision of the United Kingdom to leave the European Union [18]—were influenced by the opinions that voters formed using a wide array of online sources, including on social media.

Contentious subjects usually lead to heated arguments on social media, which in turn polarize public opinion. The prevailing theory is that online polarization emerges due to filter bubbles, which only expose users to peers with the same views [3]. This led to a body of work that believes that online polarization can be addressed by exposing users to contrary news and views [13,16,22]. However, participatory studies concluded that exposure to opposing views on social media could increase polarization [2,21]. There is still an open gap concerning opinion formation on social media.

© Springer Nature Switzerland AG 2021
P. H. Abreu et al. (Eds.): IDA 2021, LNCS 12695, pp. 275–286, 2021.
https://doi.org/10.1007/978-3-030-74251-5_22

This work addresses two specific open questions concerning the dynamics of polarized opinion formation in the context of Reddit discussions around Brexit. The first open question deals with how users form polarized opinions. Some works claim that social media increases polarization [8, 23], while other studies find that the usage of social media reduces polarization [4]. Furthermore, participatory and measurement studies [9] challenge this idea altogether, indicating that information savvy people leverage diverse sources of information and escape the filter bubble. The question is **are the stances of users concerning contentious subjects influenced by the discussions they are exposed to?** The second open question focuses on the dynamics of polarization. Previous work concentrates mainly on detecting and forecasting opinion polarization based on content diffusion in online social networks [11, 27]; little work concentrates on detecting polarization dynamics. **Can we predict the future stance of users based on their present activity? and what are the factors that influence the changes of stances?**

We answer the questions mentioned above on a longitudinal dataset containing discussions around Brexit on Reddit, spanning from November 2015 until April 2019. Our work assumes two factors that determine users' stance towards contentious subjects. First, user stance has inertia, i.e., the stance at a given time is dependent on their past stance. Second, user stance depends on the stance of other users with whom the said user interacts. Consequently, the interactions with users of known stances indicate the future user stance, even without observing the textual content of these interactions.

We first divide the dataset time extent into fourteen time-periods, based on the notable events in the real-life Brexit timeline, such as the referendum, the triggering of Article 50, or the EU rejecting the UK's white paper. We investigate whether users' stance concerning contentious subjects is influenced by the online discussions they are exposed to and interactions with users supporting different stances. As there are no annotations available, we transfer a textual classifier trained on Twitter data to classify user stances in Reddit. Next, we answer the first open question by building three feature sets to describe user activity during each period. The purpose of these features is to capture a user's interaction with the other users of known stance in the community. The constructed features include overall activity levels, posting success, the reactions their posts attract from users of different stances, and the types of discussions in which users engage. We answer the second open question by setting up a series of predictive exercises that forecast the user stance in the next period based on the user description in the current period. We show that the activity features regularly outperform the textual baseline, indicating that user opinions are influenced by the discussions they are exposed to. We find that the discussion's stance composition that users prefer to engage in is the most informative feature. Notably, the content posted by a user during a time period appears to be less informative about the next period's user stance.

The main contributions of this work are as follows:

- We propose three feature sets predictive of the user stance that leverage solely the structure of the discussion (i.e., not the textual content emitted by the user).
- We show that all three feature sets are more predictive of the future stance than a textual baseline trained on the content emitted in the present.
- We provide predictive evidence that user polarization dynamics are linked to the stance composition of the discussions that the users are exposed to.

2   Related Work

We structure the discussion of the related works into two categories: detecting and alleviating polarization, and opinion and polarization dynamics.

Detecting and Alleviating Online Polarization. Previous work concentrates on detecting and reducing online polarization. Detection methods usually start from the social graph of the users. If the graph is presented as a signed network—i.e., the nodes are users, and the edges between users of the same polarity have a positive sign, while the edges across two polarities have a negative sign—community detection uncovers polarized communities [5]. The idea is to search for two communities (subsets of the network vertices) where within communities there are mostly positive edges while across communities there are mostly negative edges. When the sign of edges is not available, Garimella et al. [13] propose to use the diffusion cascades that occur on top of the social graph to detect the communities of users that participate together in the same cascades. Finally, they create a controversy score for discussion topics based on how polarized apart the communities are. In this work, we use a supervised approach to detect user polarization based on their emitted text: we use a textual classifier trained on annotated Twitter data to label the stance of Reddit users.

When it comes to reducing online polarization, it is generally assumed that exposing users to opposite views reduces their polarization [15,22]. Garimella et al. [12] devised tools and algorithms to bridge the polarized echo chambers and reduce controversy. They represent online discussions on controversial issues with an endorsement graph, and they cast the problem as an edge-recommendation problem on this graph. Graells-Garrido et al. [16] study how to take advantage of partial homophily to suggest agreeable content to users authored by people with opposite views on sensitive issues, while Musco et al. [25] search for the structure of a social network that minimizes disagreement and controversy simultaneously. However, empirical studies appear to contradict the fundamental thesis that users exposed to contrary views temper their polarization. Bail et al. [2] performed a participatory study on Twitter users, where they paid users to follow bots emitting tweets of the opposing opinion. They found that most users reinforced their previously held opinions and that exposure to opposing views on social media can increase political polarization.

Opinion and Polarization Dynamics. The prior work most relevant to this paper concerns the political polarization around Brexit and the study of polarization dynamics. Grčar et al. [17] studied the relation between the Twitter mood and the referendum outcome and who were the most influential Twitter users in the Pro- and Against- Brexit camps. They constructed a stance classification model, and they predicted the stance of about one million UK-based Twitter users. They found that the top pro-Brexit communities are considerably more polarized than the contra-Brexit camp. Amador Diaz Lopez et al. [1] collected 23 million Tweets related to the EU referendum in the UK to predict the Brexit vote. They used user-generated hashtags to build training sets related to the Leave/Remain campaign, and they trained an SVM to classify tweets. The above work uses textual content to decide the stance of a user. In contrast, our work leverages the structure of the discussion in which users engage without observing the textual content. In our experiments in Sect. 5 we show that our methods consistently outperform content-based methods.

When modeling the dynamics of opinion polarization, Das et al. [7] start from the conformity theory – i.e., a user will adopt the majority of their neighbors' opinion – and propose a biased voter model. They show preliminary theoretical and simulation results on the convergence and structure of opinions in the entire network. On the empirical side, longitudinal study of controversy on Twitter [14] did not find long-term trends. However, they find that for particular subjects, polarization increased. By comparison, our work deals with the short-term polarization dynamics: we are interested in how users update their polarity concerning controversial topics based on their exposure to the content of different polarities.

3   The Dynamics of User Stance and Dataset

This section introduces our hypotheses around the dynamics of user stances, the structure of online discussions (on Reddit), and the dataset that we collected for the Brexit case study.

User Stance Dynamics. When faced with contentious subjects, users usually have opinions—dubbed here as *stances*; in the case of our study (i.e., Brexit) we define the following set of stances: **A**gainst-Brexit, **P**ro-Brexit, or **N**eutral. Our work's central hypothesis is that users can update their stance as time passes by (for example, from Neutral to pro- or against- Brexit). Furthermore, we hypothesize that the change occurs partly due to the discussions the users are exposed to at present. We posit that stance changes occur on a much longer time scale than that of diffusions and threads. Without loss of generality, we assume that the time extent $\mathcal{O}$ of our dataset is divided into periods (or time frames) during which each user's stance is constant. The time periods are defined by a set of cutoff times $o_j \in \mathcal{O}$ such that $[o_j, o_{j+1}]$ defines an interval t. We denote the stance of a user u in a given time interval t as $c_t(u) \in \{A, P, N\}$. When passing from one period to the next, the users update their stance or maintain the stance from the previous period – in other words, the user u updates their stance from $c_t(u)$ to $c_{t+1}(u)$.

Structure of Discussion on Online Social Media. Online social networks can be viewed as meeting places where users have online discussions, submit content and articles in the form of text, link or media. In these meeting places, users interact with their peers, form and update opinions and stances towards topics. For example, on Reddit, users can start threads similar to forum environments or post comments on existing threads. Consequently, the discussions present themselves as hierarchies of posts in a tree-like structure. Figure 1a shows an example of a real Reddit discussion, containing an initial post (n_0) and five comments (n_1 to n_5). For instance, comment n_3 is a reply to comment n_1. The resulted tree structure is shown in Fig. 1b, and leveraged in Sect. 4 to construct the non-textual features describing the activity of users. In the rest of this paper, we denote a tree of posts as *a thread*, which is started by *a post* – also known as *submission* in Reddit terminology, the root of the tree. We denote all the other nodes as *comments* – chronologically subsequent messages posted as replies to a post or other comments in the same thread.

We collectively denote posts and comments as *entries*. An entry is a triplet $s_j = (u_j, pc_j, d_j)$, where u_j denotes the user name, pc_j the published content, and d_j is the

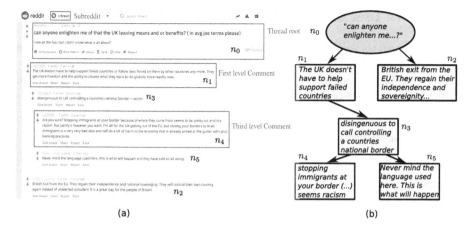

Fig. 1. (a) Elements of the Reddit platform. Structure of a discussion thread, with multi-level comments, inside a subreddit. (b) Logical structure used for analyzing the data.

time stamp of the entry s_j. We further define a *diffusion* δ_i as a temporally ordered sequence of entries, starting with a post, ending with a leaf comment and containing all comments on the path connecting the post and the leaf comment. Formally, it is defined as $\delta_i = \{s_j = (u_j, pc_j, d_j) | j = 1, 2, ..\}$. Visibly, there are as many diffusions in a thread as there are leaf nodes. For example, in Fig. 1b there are three diffusions: $\{n_0, n_1, n_3, n_4\}$, $\{n_0, n_1, n_3, n_5\}$ and $\{n_0, n_2\}$. Finally, a thread is a set of diffusions $S = \{\delta_i | i = 1, .., N\}$.

Dataset: Brexit Discussions on Reddit. We collected the Reddit dataset used in our case study using the Pushshift API [26]. It contains 229,619 entries (21,725 posts and 207,894 comments) posted between November 2015 and April 2019 on the *brexit* subreddit (https://www.reddit.com/r/brexit/). Each entry has the following variables: entry id, text, timestamp, author, parent id (useful for building the tree structure as shown in Fig. 1a), Reddit score, and the number of comments for the entry. A total of 14,362 unique authors participated in these discussions. We have divided the dataset's time extent into 15 intervals based on the occurrence date of real events, such as the UK referendum of 23 June 2016, the nomination of M. Barnier as Chief Negotiator, beginning of the Brexit negotiations, rejection of the UK white paper by EU, the publication of the Brexit withdrawal agreement, first and second meaningful votes, etc. We split the entries into 15 subsets according to the time interval in which they were posted. Due to space constraints, we further profile the dataset and the 15 intervals in the online supplement[1]. Also note that the constructed dataset, together with the code to build the feature sets detailed in Sect. 4.2 are publicly available[2].

---

[1] Supplementary Information available online: https://arxiv.org/pdf/2101.09852.pdf#page=13.
[2] Code and data publicly available: https://github.com/behavioral-ds/online-opinion-dynamics.

4 Forecast User Stance Dynamics

This section tackles the two research questions by posing them as supervised machine learning problems. We first describe the learning problem (Sect. 4.1); next, we build predictive features that embed user interactions with users of different stances (Sect. 4.2); finally, we describe the predictive setup (Sect. 4.4).

Table 1. Constructed feature sets describing user interactions with information diffusions.

Feature set	Features
FS1 (User activity)	– number of initiated diffusions $ID_t(u)$
	– number of submitted comments $CS_t(u)$
	– quantiles of the number of received comments per entry $R_t^1(u), ..., R_t^5(u)$
	– stance at current time-frame $c_t(u)$
FS2 (User activity per stance)	– number of comments submitted to entries from each stance $CS_t^A(u), CS_t^P(u), CS_t^N(u)$
	– quantiles of the number of received comments per entry, tallied by commentator stance $R_t^{x1}(u), ..., R_t^{x5}(u)$, $x \in \{A, P, N\}$
	– stance at current time-frame $c_t(u)$
FS3 (Structure of diffusion)	– quantiles of the number of submitted comments in diffusions per stance $UP_t^{x1}(u), ..., UP_t^{x5}(u)$, $x \in \{A, P, N\}$
	– stance at current time-frame $c_t(u)$
FS4 (Relational features)	FS1 + FS2 + FS3
FS0 (Textual features)	100 top words + $c_t(u)$
FS5 (All features)	FS0 + FS4

4.1 A Supervised Machine Learning Problem

We cast the problem of forecasting the future stance of users as a supervised machine learning problem. Each user u is represented by a set of features $FS_t(u)$ describing her Reddit activity during the time interval t. The feature set also includes the user stance at the current time t, i.e., $c_t(u)$. The task consists in forecasting the user stance at the next time interval $t + 1$, i.e., $c_{t+1}(u)$, using the features at time t, i.e., $FS_t(u)$. Off-the-shelf classifiers are used to learn a model from $FS_t(u)$ to $c_{t+1}(u)$. The difficulty lies in defining the features that describe the user's activity during a period and obtaining the ground truth labels to build the training set and the test set. To determine user stances, we use a textual classifier trained on Twitter data (further detailed in Sect. 4.3). In the next section, we design several feature sets that capture users' activity and their interactions with other users of different stances.

4.2 Predictive Features

We introduce three sets of features (denoted as **FS1**, .., **FS4**, shown in Table 1) aimed at capturing increasingly complex information concerning user activity. **FS1** serves as an activity baseline, tallying user posting activity and the comments they receive. **FS2** aims to capture how the user interacts with users of different stances (e.g. do they prefer to comment on entries with similar stances to their own? to the opposite stance?), and whether they elicit more comments from users with the same polarity or the opposite. **FS3** aims to capture the type of threads in which the user engages (e.g., do they like to engage in discussion with a single stance or deliberative threads?). We detail each set.

FS1 focuses on the activity of the user at the global level. For a given user u and a time interval t, we count $ID_t(u)$, the number of diffusions initiated by u during the interval t (*i.e.*, the number of posts sent by u) and $CS_t(u)$, the number of comments submitted by u during the interval t by excluding auto-comments. Thus, the number of entries submitted by u during the period is denoted $N_t(u)$ with $N_t(u) = ID_t(u) + CS_t(u)$. We also consider the user's success defined as the number of replies generated by his activity and quantified by the direct or indirect comments received by each entry (post or comment) submitted by u during the period. Formally, if r_i denotes the number of replies following the entry m_i submitted by u during the period t, we obtain the set $\{r_i | i = 1, .., N_t\}$ and we compute the quantiles $R_t^1(u), ..., R_t^5(u)$ corresponding respectively to 0%, 25%, 50%, 75% and 100% of its distribution. Thus, **FS1** contains 8 features including $c_t(u)$ (the user stance at the current time).

FS2 aims to capture how the user interacts with users of different stances: **A**gainst, **P**ro or **N**eutral in our case study. First, we measure how the user engages with content from other users by counting the comments sent by user u during the period t in response to entries posted by each group denoted respectively $CS_t^A(u), CS_t^P(u)$ and $CS_t^N(u)$. Thus, $CS_t(u) = CS_t^A(u) + CS_t^P(u) + CS_t^N(u)$, where $CS_t(u)$ has been defined in **FS1**. The underlying idea is to capture whether u exchanges more with users having the same stance as him or with users having a different stance. Second, we measure how the users of the different stances engage with u by counting the number of comments received from each group in response to entries sent by u during the period t. Thus, if r_i^x denotes the number of replies from group $x \in \{A, P, N\}$ following the entry m_i submitted by u during the period t, we obtain the distribution $\{r_i^x, i = 1, .., N_t\}$ and we compute the quantiles $R_t^{x1}(u), ..., R_t^{x5}(u)$ corresponding respectively to 0%, 25%, 50%, 75% and 100% of this distribution. With this second set composed of 19 features, the objective is to capture whether content emitted by u attracts comments from the group of users of similar stance or from the other stances.

FS3 aims to capture the type of threads in which the user u engages. For each threads in which u posted an entry (post or comment) during the period, we compute the number of entries per group. More precisely, if NS denotes the number of threads in which u sent at least one entry during the period and S_i is one of these threads, we compute the number of entries A_i, P_i, N_i respectively emitted by each group in S_i. By this way, we obtain three sets $\{A_i | i = 1, .., NS\}, \{P_i | i = 1, .., NS\}, \{N_i | i = 1, .., NS\}$ that we can summarized by their respective quantiles $UP_t^{x1}(u), ..., UP_t^{x5}(u)$, $x \in \{A, P, N\}$. Thus, if a user with a given stance, for example **A**nti-Brexit, prefers to exchange with the other anti-brexit users, the features $UP_t^{A1}(u), ..., UP_t^{A5}(u)$ will

Table 2. Hashtags used by Amador Diaz Lopez et al. [1] for splitting Twitter users in two categories, to train the Naive Bayes Classifier.

Stance	Hashtags
Pro Brexit	#voteleave #inorout #voteout #takecontrol #borisjohnson #lexit #independenceday #ivotedleave #projectfear #britain #boris #go #projecthope #takebackcontrol #labourleave #no2eu #betteroffout #june23 #democracy
Against Brexit	#strongerin #intogether #infor #votein #libdems #voting #incrowd #bremain #greenerin

have higher values than $UP_t^{P1}(u)$, ..., $UP_t^{P5}(u)$, $UP_t^{N1}(u)$, ..., $UP_t^{N5}(u)$. So, **FS3** contains 16 features, including $c_t(u)$. We also build **FS4**, the union of the above mentioned feature sets: **FS4 = FS1 ∪ FS2 ∪ FS3**.

We also build a textual baseline based on the user's content in the current period. We first extract the top 100 most frequent words (stop words removed) from all the Reddit dataset entries over all the time intervals. Next, we aggregate the text of all the entries of each user into a single document, and we compute the TF-IDF scores for the selected top 100 most frequent words. Consequently, **FS0** contains 101 features, including the user stance at the current time-frame $c_t(u)$. Finally, we also consider **FS5** composed of all the textual and relational features: **FS5 = FS4 ∪ FS0**.

4.3   Learning Stance in Twitter

One of the main challenges of this work is the lack of ground truth, *i.e.*, the stance for Reddit users at each time interval. We transfer to our Reddit dataset a model trained on Twitter and initially introduced by Amador Diaz Lopez et al. [1].

The Twitter Dataset. Amador Diaz Lopez et al. [1] collected the Twitter dataset from 6 January 2016 to July 2016 using the Twitter Firehose API. They crawled all the tweets using three search criteria related to Brexit: the general search term *Brexit*, hashtags such as *#leaveeu* or *#yes2eu* and Twitter usernames of groups and users set up to communicate about Brexit (e.g., *@voteleave* or *@yesforeurope*. The resulted dataset contains 26.5 million tweets emitted by 1.5 million users.

Build a Stance Predictor in Twitter. We build a Twitter stance predictor following the methodology proposed by Amador Diaz Lopez et al. [1], which we briefly summarize below. Amador Diaz Lopez et al. [1] curated two sets of hashtags, shown in Table 2, which indicate the user stance and utilized in 136 thousand tweets. We filter out occasional users – who emit less than 50 tweets – and users who do not employ any of the hashtags. For each of the remaining 11,277 users, we compute a 'leave' score equal to the difference between the number of used Pro-Brexit hashtags and Against-Brexit hashtags. We rank the users based on the score, and we select the 10% users with the lowest (negative) score as Against-Brexit users and the 10% of users with the highest (positive) score as Pro-Brexit users. The resulting set contains the aggregated tweets (one document per user) for 2,257 users. We first perform the usual text preprocessing: we remove stopwords, punctuation signs, hashtags, mentions, and other diacritics; we convert all letters to lower case, remove rare words, and perform stemming. Next, we train a Naive Bayes classifier using 80% of the data, and we evaluate using the remaining 20% of the data. The model outputs the probability for a document (*i.e.*, a user) to belong to one of the classes (Against-Brexit or Pro-Brexit). Following the methodology proposed by Amador Diaz Lopez et al. [1], we convert this output probability into a discrete label: if the *leave* probability is below 0.25, we label the user as Against-Brexit; if it is greater than 0.75, we label the users as Pro-Brexit. Otherwise, the label is Neutral. On the test set, the trained model obtains a prediction macro-accuracy of 89.36% and a macro-F1-score of 88.68%. As shown in the next section, we transfer the trained model to compute $c_t(u)$, the users' stance in each period in the Reddit dataset. We use a Naive Bayes classifier because it is somewhat robust to concept drift and noisy features [29] – here, vocabulary change between Twitter and Reddit. The robustness is because rank scores are typically correct even if the conditional independence assumption is violated. We use cut-offs on the Naive Bayes score rather than interpreting the score as a probability in absolute terms.

4.4   Predictive Setup

Building Reddit Learning and Testing Sets. For each timeframe, we first aggregate all the Reddit messages of each user into a single document. Next, we assign them a Brexit stance using the Naive Bayes classifier trained on the Twitter dataset (detailed in Sect. 4.3). As we perform this procedure for each interval, we obtain not only the present stance of the user $c_t(u)$ but also the stance at the next timeframe $c_{t+1}(u)$. Finally, we compute the predictive feature sets **FS1**, ...**FS5** for each user and each period from the Reddit dataset.

Models and Evaluation. We predict users' stance in the next timeframe using each feature set computed on the current timeframe. We train and test five different algorithms – Logistic Regression, KNN, Random Forest, Gradient Boosting [10], XGBoost [6]. We evaluate using a double Cross-Validation. First, we use a 10-fold outer Cross-Validation to split the data into training and testing sets. At each fold, we tune hyper-parameters using an inner 5-fold Cross-Validation together with Random Search with 500 iterations. We measure performance using standard evaluation metrics and their standard deviation: macro-F1, macro-Accuracy, macro-Precision, and macro-Recall.

5   Results

This section presents the obtained performances for predicting the future stance of users. The Reddit dataset is imbalanced, with most of the user having a Neutral stance. Therefore, Fig. 2 plots the macro versions of accuracy and F1 score (macro-precision and macro-recall are shown in the Supplementary Information[1]). Note that we use the macro version of the metrics, which gives equal representation to minority classes and alleviate the class imbalance in our dataset. Note that for a three-class classification problem (here Against, Neutral, Brexit), an unweighted, random classifier is expected to obtain an F1 score and accuracy score of 33%.

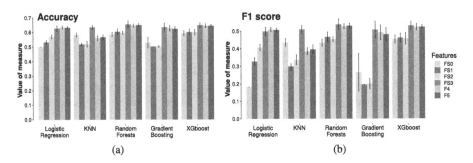

Fig. 2. Evaluation metrics for the developed models: accuracy (**a**) and F1-Score (**b**).

Table 3. F1 score of predicting next stance, tabulated per current stance.

Stance at t	Stance at t+1		
	Against	Neutral	Brexit
Against	0.68	0.34	0.35
Neutral	0.51	0.62	0.45
Brexit	0.44	0.34	0.59

Analysis of the Relational Features. Figure 2 shows that the best classifier reaches 53.9% F1 score, which is double the random score. As the data is imbalanced, the accuracy is higher at 65%. For most classifiers, the performance improves from FS1 to **FS3**, with **FS3** providing the best performance for all methods, except KNN. This indicates that the stance composition of the threads that the user prefers to engage in best indicates her future stance. The best performing classifiers are Random Forest and XGBoost. Interestingly, the combination of all activity features (denoted as **FS4**) does not further improve results.

Relational and Textual Features. Figure 2 shows that relational features (**FS1** to **FS4**) have higher predictive power than textual features (FS0), for the best performing method (Random Forest and XGBoost). While the conclusions are more nuanced for the other classifiers, **FS3** outperforms FS0 for all classifiers and all metrics. This result suggests that the type of discussions users engage in indicates their future stance more than the content they emit at present. Moreover, we observe that using textual together with relational features (**FS5**) does not improve results significantly as the performances of **FS5** are equal to **FS3**.

Analysis per Stance. We analyze in more detail the performances of the best performing classifier (XGBoost) on the best features set (**FS3**). We compute the prediction performances for each combination of present and future stance – i.e., the nine combination $\{(c_t(u), c_{t+1}(u))|c_t(u), c_{t+1}(u) \in \{A, B, N\}\}$. The values are reported in Table 3. We see that the classifier performs well for the users who maintain their opinion between two subsequent timeframes (shown by the main diagonal of Table 3). Noteworthy, it also performs well for the transitions from Neutral to Pro- or Against-Brexit, with F1 scores equal to 0.51 and 0.45, respectively. The result implies that we can predict the future stance of the currently undecided participants in online debates. The implications are significant, as most democratic processes tend to be decided by swaying undecided voters.

6   Conclusion

In this paper, we analyzed information diffusion in social media platforms, and we studied whether the stances of users are influenced by the discussions to which they are exposed. To capture the dynamics of the opinions of online communities, we chose the Reddit platform and Brexit as a case study due to its polarity. To better understand why users change their stance, we predict the future user stance using supervised machine learning algorithms. We construct three feature sets that capture different aspects of the user activity in the diffusion process. Our experiments showed that the best-performing feature set accounts for the stance composition of the threads in which a user chooses to engage. Notably, our activity feature sets outperform a textual baseline that encodes the content that the user emits.

One difficulty we met is the lack of ground truth, i.e., the stance for Reddit users at each time interval. To obtain the ground truth, we transferred a model trained on a Twitter dataset. However, the underlying distribution of language and structure of the two platforms differ. The transfer labeling risks introducing inaccuracies, and the performances would probably be better if the Reddit users' correct labels were available. This is a perspective of this work.

Acknowledgement. This work was partially supported by IDEXLYON ACADEMICS Project ANR-16-IDEX-0005 of the French National Research Agency, Facebook Research under the Content Policy Research Initiative grants, and the Defence Science and Technology Group of the Australian Department of Defence. We thank Keneth Benoit, who generously shared the Twitter dataset of Brexit discussions [1].

References

1. Amador Diaz Lopez, J.C., Collignon-Delmar, S., Benoit, K., Matsuo, A.: Predicting the Brexit vote by tracking and classifying public opinion using Twitter data. Stat. Polit. Policy **8**(1), 85–104 (2017). ISSN 2194–6299
2. Bail, C.A., et al.: Exposure to opposing views on social media can increase political polarization. PNAS **115**(37), 9216–9221 (2018)
3. Banisch, S., Olbrich, E.: Opinion polarization by learning from social feedback. J. Math. Sociol. **43**(2), 76–103 (2019). ISSN 0022–250X
4. Barberá, P.: How social media reduces mass political polarization. Evidence from Germany, Spain, and the US. Midwest Pol. Sci. Assoc. p. 44 (2014)
5. Bonchi, F., Gionis, A., Ordozgoiti, B., Galimberti, E., Ruffo, G.: Discovering polarized communities in signed networks. In: CIKM, pp. 961–970 (2019)
6. Chen, T., Guestrin, C.: Xgboost: a scalable tree boosting system. In: KDD, pp. 785–794. ACM (2016)
7. Das, A., Gollapudi, S., Munagala, K.: Modeling opinion dynamics in social networks. In: WSDM, pp. 403–412 (2014)

8. De-Wit, L., Brick, C., Van Der Linden, S.: Are social media driving political polarization? Battles (2019)
9. Dubois, E., Blank, G.: The echo chamber is overstated: the moderating effect of political interest and diverse media. Inf. Comm. Soc. **21**(5), 729–745 (2018)
10. Friedman, J.H.: Greedy function approximation: a gradient boosting machine. Ann. Stat. 1189–1232 (2001)
11. Garimella, K., De Francisci Morales, G., Gionis, A., Mathioudakis, M.: Quantifying controversy in social media. In: WSDM, vol. 1, pp. 33–42 (2016)
12. Garimella, K., De Francisci Morales, G., Gionis, A., Mathioudakis, M.: Reducing controversy by connecting opposing views. In: WSDM, pp. 81–90 (2017)
13. Garimella, K., Morales, G.D.F., Gionis, A., Mathioudakis, M.: Exposing twitter users to contrarian news (2017)
14. Garimella, K., Morales, G.D.F., Gionis, A., Mathioudakis, M.: The EBB and flow of controversial debates on social media. In: ICWSM, pp. 524–527 (2017)
15. Gillani, N., Yuan, A., Saveski, M., Vosoughi, S., Roy, D.: Me, my echo chamber, and I. In: WWW, pp. 823–831. ACM (2018)
16. Graells-Garrido, E., Lalmas, M., Quercia, D.: Data portraits: connecting people of opposing views. In: International Conference on Intelligent User Interfaces (2016)
17. Grčar, M., Cherepnalkoski, D., Mozetič, I., Kralj Novak, P.: Stance and influence of twitter users regarding the Brexit referendum. Comp. Soc. Net. **4**(1), 1–25 (2017)
18. Howard, P.N., Kollanyi, B.: Bots, #StrongerIn, and #Brexit: computationalpropaganda during the UK-EU referendum. Available at SSRN 2798311 (2016)
19. Hughes, A.L., Palen, L.: Twitter adoption and use in mass convergence and emergency events. Int. J. Emerg. Manage. **6**(3–4), 248–260 (2009)
20. Kim, D., Graham, T., Wan, Z., Rizoiu, M.A.: Analysing user identity via time-sensitive semantic edit distance (t-SED): a case study of Russian trolls on Twitter. J. Comput. Soc. Sci. **2**(2), 331–351 (2019)
21. Liao, Q.V., Fu, W.T.: Beyond the filter bubble: interactive effects of perceived threat and topic involvement on selective exposure to information. In: Human Factors in Computing Systems, pp. 2359–2368 (2013)
22. Matakos, A., Terzi, E., Tsaparas, P.: Measuring and moderating opinion polarization in social networks. Data Min. Knowl. Disc. **31**(5), 1480–1505 (2017). https://doi.org/10.1007/s10618-017-0527-9
23. Messing, S., Westwood, S.J.: Selective exposure in the age of social media. Commun. Res. **41**(8), 1042–1063 (2014). ISSN 0093–6502
24. Mishra, S., Rizoiu, M.A., Xie, L.: Modeling popularity in asynchronous social media streams with recurrent neural networks. In: ICWSM, pp. 1–10 (2018)
25. Musco, C., Musco, C., Tsourakakis, C.E.: Minimizing polarization and disagreement in social networks. In: WWW, pp. 369–378 (2018)
26. Pushshift: Pushshift. https://pushshift.io/ (2019)
27. Rama, V., Garimella, K., Weber, I.: A long-term analysis of polarization on Twitter. In: ICWSM, pp. 528–531 (2017)
28. Rizoiu, M.A., Graham, T., Zhang, R., Zhang, Y., Ackland, R., Xie, L.: #DebateNight: The role and influence of socialbots on twitter during the 1st 2016 us presidential debate. In: ICWSM, pp. 1–10 (2018)
29. Schütze, H., Manning, C.D., Raghavan, P.: Introduction to Information Retrieval. Vol. 39. Cambridge University Press Cambridge (2008)

Unsupervised Methods for the Study of Transformer Embeddings

Mira Ait Saada[1,2]([✉]), François Role[1], and Mohamed Nadif[1]

[1] Université de Paris, CNRS, Centre Borelli, 75006 Paris, France
{mira.ait-saada,francois.role,mohamed.nadif}@u-paris.fr
[2] Groupe Caisse des Dépôts, Paris, France

Abstract. Over the last decade neural word embeddings have become a cornerstone of many important text mining applications such as text classification, sentiment analysis, named entity recognition, question answering systems, etc. Particularly, Transformer-based contextual word embeddings have gained much attention with several works trying to understanding how such models work, through the use of supervised probing tasks, and usually emphasizing on BERT. In this paper, we propose a fully unsupervised manner to analyze Transformer-based embedding models in their bare state with no fine-tuning. We more precisely focus on characterizing and identifying groups of Transformer layers across 6 different Transformer models.

Keywords: Transformer-based language models · Unsupervised learning · Word embeddings

1 Introduction

Transformer-based word embeddings provided by neural language models are today increasingly used as the initial input to many text mining applications where they greatly contribute to achieve impressing performance levels. This has motivated a growing number of researchers to investigate the reasons behind this effectiveness as part of the general effort to unlock the black box of AI models. Since a Transformer model produces several embeddings for each word (one for each layer of its deep architecture), it is natural to study the nature of the embeddings learned at the different layers of the model. So far, the common way of doing this is to feed them as input to some supervised probing tasks (text classification, question answering, etc.) and then measure how well they perform on these tasks. From the observed performance, and depending on the probing task used, one may deduce, for example, that a given set of layers seems to be good at capturing some features of language while another set seems to encode another kind of information. While these experiments have allowed to draw some conclusions, the observed results depend both on the tasks and the train and test datasets, and so are not always generalizable. This observation prompted us to explore if it could be possible to gain additional insight into the behavior of the

© Springer Nature Switzerland AG 2021
P. H. Abreu et al. (Eds.): IDA 2021, LNCS 12695, pp. 287–300, 2021.
https://doi.org/10.1007/978-3-030-74251-5_23

layers without having to rely on supervised probing tasks and external datasets. In this paper, we propose unsupervised techniques that completely dispense of probing tasks, and demonstrate their interest by applying them to real datasets and several widely used Transformer models. The contributions of the paper are as follows:

1. We propose a set of unsupervised methods that allow to gain insights into the nature of the embeddings available at the different layers of a Transformer model, and how these embedding layers relate to each other. This approach, which directly leverages the intrinsic features of the layers, is in contrast to other studies that rely on probing tasks.
2. The experimental section shows that applying these methods on real datasets allows to acquire new knowledge about the layers of several Transformer models that seem to best perform on the important word clustering task.
3. Also, while most layer interpretation studies have so far focused mainly on BERT we provide a performance comparison for 3 different models namely BERT, RoBERTa and ALBERT, in both their base and large flavors.

2   Related Work

In the supervised learning realm, a growing body of research has been devoted to investigating the linguistic features learned by contextual word embedding models including LSTM-based models as in [9] and Transformer-based models like BERT as in [12]. Both authors agree to say that early layers encode most local syntactic phenomena while more complex semantics appear at the higher layers. In [8], the authors evaluate the performance of contextualized word representations on several supervised tasks and compare layers with each other, including ELMo, BERT (base and large) and OpenAI Transformer models. They especially observe that Transformers' middle layers allow for a better transferability. On the other hand, the authors in [5] observe that the early layers of BERT are more invariant across tasks and hence more transferable. It has also been shown in [1] that, after fine tuning BERT on Question Answering, the model acts in different phases starting from capturing the semantic meaning of tokens in the first layers to separating the answer token from the others in the last layers. It has been concluded that the closer we get to the last layer, the more task specific the representations are. This explains the results obtained in [7] which studies the changes between pre-trained and fine-tuned BERT-base model in terms of attention weights. A significant change in the two last layers in terms of cosine similarity between original and fine-tuned attention weights has been observed on 6 GLUE tasks. The authors deduced that the BERT-base's two last layers learn more task specific features. Several papers focus on identifying the linguistic structure implicitly learned by the models [2,6]. For example, Goldberg [4] evaluates how well BERT captures syntactic information for subject-verb agreement. Ethayarajh et al. [3] try to assess how context-specific are the representations at the different layers of ELMo, BERT and GPT-2.

In contrast to the above studies we propose to identify coherent groupings of layers, based on the intrinsic characteristics of the layers and not by resorting to external probing tasks.

3 Unsupervised Methods for Layer Analysis

Deep Transformer models may have dozens of layers (see Table 3). In order to better understand their behavior we argue that it is useful to compare them, and try to identify groups with similar characteristics.

3.1 Matrix and Vector Representation of Layers

In this section, we propose several alternative (matrix- and vector-based) representations for a Transformer layer, thus allowing to study their correlations from multiple points of view. Given a dataset of n words, and a Transformer model with b layers and embedding dimension d, the dataset can be represented by b different matrices $\mathbf{X}_1, \ldots, \mathbf{X}_b$ of size $n \times d$, where each matrix $\mathbf{X}_\ell$ corresponds to the dataset at the ℓ-th layer. An alternative way of representing a layer ℓ is by averaging the rows of its $\mathbf{X}_\ell$ matrix, leading to a vector representation $\mathbf{v}_\ell$ of the layer. Additional intermediate data structures are then computed from these initial representations (Table 1). The pseudo-code in Algorithm 1 describes in detail how these data structures are created and used during the analysis process.

Table 1. Definitions and notations

Symbol	Description
n	Number of words of the dataset
d	Number of dimensions: 768 for base models and 1024 for large ones
b	Number of layers: 12 for base models and 24 for large ones
$\mathbf{X}_\ell$	Matrix of size $(n \times d)$: data matrix of layer ℓ (cf. Fig. 1)
$\mathbf{x}_{\ell i}$	The ith row of $\mathbf{X}_\ell$
$\mathbf{S}_\ell$	Matrix of size $(n \times n)$: corresponds to the square matrix of $\mathbf{X}_\ell$
$\mathbf{v}_\ell$	Vector of size d: computed for a layer ℓ as the average of rows of $\mathbf{X}_\ell$
$\mathbf{r}_\ell$	Vector of size n: similarity ranks of words regarding $\mathbf{v}_\ell$

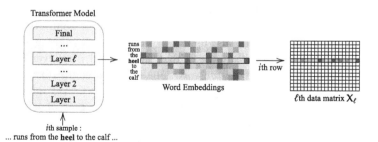

Fig. 1. Construction of the data matrices from contextual word embeddings

---

Algorithm 1: Unsupervised Process of Layers' Analysis

Input: a dataset D of n words; a Transformer model M with b layers and embedding dimension d; a clustering algorithm $\mathcal{C}$; a ranking function $rank$.

Step 1. Build matrix and vector representations of layers, for each $\ell = 1 \ldots b$:

$\mathbf{X}_\ell \leftarrow$ vertical stacking of the n word embeddings provided by the ℓth layer

$\mathbf{S}_\ell \leftarrow \mathbf{X}_\ell \mathbf{X}_\ell^T$

$\mathbf{v}_\ell \leftarrow \sum_i \mathbf{x}_{\ell i}$, where $\mathbf{x}_{\ell i}$ is the ith row of $\mathbf{X}_\ell$

$\mathbf{e}_{\ell i} \leftarrow$ cosine similarity between the word vectors $\mathbf{x}_{\ell i}$ and $\mathbf{v}_\ell$, $i = 1 \ldots, n$

$\mathbf{r}_{\ell i} \leftarrow rank(\mathbf{e}_{\ell i})$, $i = 1 \ldots, n$

$R_v(\mathbf{X}_\ell, \mathbf{X}_{\ell'}) = \dfrac{trace(\mathbf{S}_\ell \times \mathbf{S}_{\ell'})}{\sqrt{trace(\mathbf{S}_\ell^2) \times trace(\mathbf{S}_{\ell'}^2)}}$, $\ell, \ell' = 1, \ldots, b$

$\rho(\mathbf{r}_\ell, \mathbf{r}_{\ell'}) = \dfrac{6 \sum_{i=1}^n (\mathbf{r}_{\ell i} - \mathbf{r}_{\ell' i})^2}{n(n^2 - 1)}$, $\ell, \ell' = 1, \ldots, b$ where ρ is the Spearman coefficient

Step 2. Identify groups of layers

Visualize the R_v and Spearman coefficients as heatmap matrices.

$\mathbf{V} \leftarrow$ vertical stacking of the b vectors $\mathbf{v}_\ell$, $\ell = 1 \ldots b$

$clusters \leftarrow \mathcal{C}(\mathbf{V})$

Visualise $clusters$

Step 3. Interpret the groups identified in step 2.

3.2 Measuring the Correlations Between Layers

In this section and the following one, we propose unsupervised methods for comparing the layers against each other the goal being to exhibit layers that share some characteristics.

When using a matrix representation for the layers (the $\mathbf{X}_\ell$ matrices of Table 1), an appropriate correlation measure is the R_v coefficient [10] which can be used in order to visualize the layers' similarities and distinguish any possible bloc structures. The R_v coefficient can be interpreted as a non centered squared coefficient of correlation between two given data matrices $\mathbf{X}_\ell$ and $\mathbf{X}_{\ell'}$ (cf. Algorithm 1). This proportion varies between 0 and 1 and the closer to 1 it is, the better is $\mathbf{X}_{\ell'}$ as a substitute for $\mathbf{X}_\ell$ (and *vice-versa*) to characterize the n samples of the dataset. In order to draw a similarity tendency across layers, we compute for each layer ℓ an *Average-R_v* which corresponds to the mean of R_v values between the layer ℓ and the rest of the layers. The heatmap representation of these values allows to spot groupings of layers.

The vector representation of the layers (the $\mathbf{v}_\ell$ vectors) allow for other possibilities. They can be used as input to a clustering algorithm (this will be described in Sects. 3.3 and 4.3). But they can also serve as a basis for measuring the correlations between layers. For each layer ℓ, we first compute the cosine similarity of its vector $\mathbf{v}_\ell$ with all the word vector $\mathbf{x}_{\ell i}$. A ranking vector $\mathbf{r}_\ell$ is then computed where $\mathbf{r}_{\ell i}$ is the ranking assigned to word i by layer ℓ. Since for two layers ℓ and ℓ' $\mathbf{r}_\ell$ and $\mathbf{r}_{\ell'}$ contain word ranks, a suitable measure of comparison is the Spearman correlation coefficient ρ that measures the rank correlation between two variables. From the ρ values between each pair of layers we can construct a heatmap matrix of size $b \times b$ which, as with the matrix of R_v values, also allows to identify groupings of layers (cf. Algorithm 1).

3.3 Clustering Layers

The next step of the study is to perform a cluster analysis to confirm the potential groups using the techniques described in the previous section. The data samples are the b layers of a given model where each layer ℓ is represented by its corresponding average vector $\mathbf{v}_\ell$. In theory, any kind of clustering algorithm could be used at this stage. In practice, since the number of layers is relatively low and the number of cluster is unknown (although the techniques of the previous section can give an estimate of it), we often used Agglomerative Hierarchical Clustering (AHC) methods in our experiments. The hierarchical arrangement of the samples provided by the dendrograms indeed allows for a better interpretation of the clustering results as will be shown in the experiments section.

3.4 Interpreting Layers

In order to provide a more qualitative analysis of layers' behavior, we use the vector representation $\mathbf{r}_\ell$ and visualize the ranking of the first m words regarding their similarity to $\mathbf{v}_\ell$. We can also deepen our analysis of layers by using the interpretation abilities offered by dimension reduction techniques such as the Principal Component Analysis (PCA). When applying PCA on the $\mathbf{X}_\ell$ matrices, the samples are the word representations and the features represent the dimensions of the embeddings. The cos^2 measure denotes the correlation between a principal component and a given dimension (feature). It also measures the quality of representation of the feature, which allows us to select only the features that are more influential for interpretation.

4 Experiments

In this section, we first apply the process described in Algorithm 1 to several word datasets, in a step by step manner. Then, in order to validate the above methods and better understand the results they provide, we cluster our word datasets and evaluate each layer in terms of clustering performance. To achieve that, we perform word clustering experiments on the $\mathbf{X}_\ell$ matrices. Each clustering run provides a partition containing the cluster label of each word. To evaluate the partition obtained with each layer, we rely on a standard external measure for assessing clustering quality, namely Normalized Mutual Information (NMI) measure [11].

4.1 Datasets and Models Used

The datasets of size n used in the experiments are described in Table 2. The first dataset, referred to as UFSAC3, is extracted from the UFSAC dataset [13] which consolidates multiple popular datasets annotated with WordNet (such as SemEval and SensEval) into a uniform format. The examples are manually divided into three topics: Body, Botany and Geography. The second dataset,

UFSAC4, is a slightly more difficult dataset since it includes a fourth class (words related to Information Technology) and is augmented with some polysemous examples (such as "lobes" which appears in Body and Botany with different contexts). The third dataset yahoo4, is extracted from the Yahoo! Answers dataset [14] by manually selecting sets of words for each category and some corresponding contexts.

Table 3 describes the 6 pre-trained Transformer-based embedding models used for the experiments, without any fine-tuning.

Table 2. Datasets description: k denotes the number of clusters.

Datasets	n	k	Clusters' sizes
UFSAC3	583	3	Body: 266, geo: 227, Botany: 90
UFSAC4	691	4	Body: 275, geo: 227, Botany: 99, IT:90
yahoo4	528	4	Finance: 150 Science-maths.: 152 Computers-internet: 144 Music: 82

Table 3. Transformer models' description.

	b	d	vocab size
BERT-base-cased	12	768	28,996
RoBERTa-base			50,265
ALBERT-base-v2			30,000
BERT-large-cased	24	1024	28,996
RoBERTa-large			50,265
ALBERT-large-v2			30,000

4.2 Investigating the Correlations Between Layers

For comparing the layers with each other, we experimented with the R_v coefficient and the Spearman's rank correlation coefficient (cf. Sect. 3.2). Figure 2 shows the similarities computed between the layers of each model in terms of the R_v coefficient which uses the matrix-based representations of the layers.

As a result of the way in which Transformer models operate, one would expect that a layer is similar to the one following it. This is indeed what is observed globally in Fig. 2. However, when taking a closer look, some interesting remarks can be made:

- Several rectangular blocks can be spotted. This is confirmed by the curve of the average R_v value which is drawn on top of the heatmaps. Clearly there are breakpoints separating groups of layers that share common characteristics in terms of affinities with other layers.
- One can observe a significant decrease of average similarity on the three last layers with the last layer sometimes having a distinctive behavior.
- ALBERT models and especially ALBERT-large are very different from the other models in terms of layer-wise similarity[1].

Additional insights can be gained from the Spearman correlation coefficients computed on pairs of layers using their ranking vectors r_ℓ (Fig. 3).

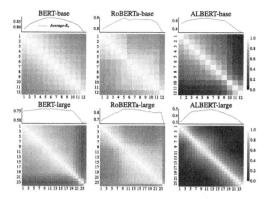

Fig. 2. R_v-coefficient based layer-wise similarity computed between UFSAC4's data matrices $\mathbf{X}_\ell$.

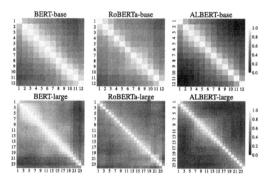

Fig. 3. Layer-wise agreements using Spearman correlation coefficient: the agreement coefficient between two layers ℓ and ℓ' is the Spearman correlation coefficients ρ calculated between $\mathbf{r}_\ell$ and $\mathbf{r}_{\ell'}$.

These coefficients allow to refine the observations made on Fig. 2, we can notice an even bigger difference between the 1st layer and the rest of the network in terms of correlation for BERT-base, moving from $\rho = 0.82$ between layers 1 and 2 to $\rho = 0.95$ between 2 and 3. Overall, Fig. 3 reveals a certain block structure with groups $\{1\}$, $\{2, 3, 4\}$ and $\{5, 6, 7, 8\}$. Finally, another break can be observed between layers 11 and 12 where $\rho = 0.88$ while it was $\rho = 0.94$ between layers 10 and 11 leading to two new groups $\{9, 10, 11\}$ and $\{12\}$. The same kind of block structure can also be observed when looking at the other models.

4.3 Identifying Clusters of Layers

In order to have another look at the possible groupings of layers, we perform an AHC and draw the associated dendrograms (cf. Sect. 3.3). Figure 4 shows the

---

[1] This could be explained by the parameter sharing technique used to train the ALBERT model, which consists of duplicating the same parameters for all layers [5].

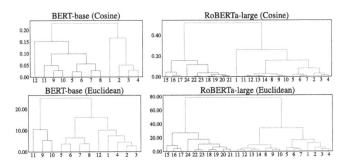

Fig. 4. Dendrograms obtained with AHC from the set of layers where each layer is represented by $\mathbf{v}_\ell$ a $d-$dimensional vector computed on UFSAC4.

results obtained using the Ward and Average linkage criteria, used respectively with the euclidean and cosine distances. If we look at the results for BERT-base that are obtained using the Euclidean distance, we can see that the clusters are close to the groupings suggested by the methods of Sect. 4.2 (compare with the top-left heatmap in Fig. 3), with the exception of layer 12 which strangely seems to be close to layer 1. This can be explained by the fact that we use the euclidean distance, which tends to be sensitive to the amplitude of data. If we look at BERT-base's box plots in Fig. 5, it can be seen that the variance of the last layer is very close to that of the 1st layer. To confirm that this wrong assignment was due to an amplitude issue, we experimented with the same AHC algorithm using a cosine distance (known to be insensitive to vector magnitude) with the "average" linkage strategy. With this configuration, the 1st layer is even more separated from the following ones and as expected, the last layer is much less close to the 1st and is assigned to a separate cluster, which is coherent with the previous observations (Sect. 4.2). This intuition is confirmed when looking at RoBERTa-large, for which we don't have the problem of differing variances across layers (Fig. 5) and hence presenting almost the same groupings using the two distances. Overall, clustering the layers leads to the following observations:

- As shown in Fig. 4 for BERT-base, the 4th layer is merged with the $\{2,3\}$ cluster before the 1st layer, which confirms the break between the first layer and the following ones. In fact, the first layer is, for most models, isolated in its own cluster. This behavior is visible in Fig. 2 and even more in Fig. 3 where the 1st layer (1st row) has darker colors than its following neighbors, which indicates lower correlation values compared to the other layers.
- For RoBERTa-large we can also see that the 1st layer joins the 2nd only after layers 3 and 4 (especially in the Cosine version). The last layer is also isolated, joining a cluster only at the 3rd merge of the AHC. The rest of the clusters generally contain successive layers (like $\{5,6,7\}$). When cutting at the second merge level we end up with the following partition $\{1\}$, $\{2,3,4\}$, $\{5,6,7\}$, $\{8,9,10\}$, $\{11,12,13,14\}$, $\{15,16,17\}$, $\{18,19,20,21\}$, $\{22,23\}$, $\{24\}$.

In Fig. 5, we use the vector representation $\mathbf{v}_\ell$ to draw box plots to analyze the distribution's evolution of layers over the network. We first observe that the three models present different behaviors in terms of variance with from the smallest to the largest: RoBERTa, BERT and ALBERT. Despite that, all distributions are centered around zero with the lower and upper boundaries being quite symmetric. Besides, for BERT (base and large), we can observe a certain break at the last layers (progressive increase followed by a sudden drop) corresponding to the breaks of similarity observed in Figs. 2 and 3.

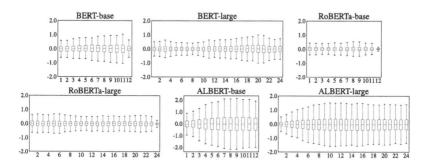

Fig. 5. Evolution of box plots (without outliers) over layers: each layer is represented by its average vector $\mathbf{v}_\ell$ of the UFSAC4 dataset.

4.4   Qualitative Interpretation

Table 4 shows the first $m = 30$ words that are the closest to the $\mathbf{v}_\ell$ representations of a selection of layers (due to space limitations) of BERT-base for the UFSAC4 dataset. Confirming the insights provided by the previous rank-based comparisons between layers as well as the clustering experiments, one can note a significant break between layer 1 and its immediate neighbors. Layers 2, 3 and 4 resemble each other more than they resemble layer 1, and share more words such as axons, sclera and scrotum. The correlation scores displayed on top of each pair of layers in Table 4 confirm this visual inspection. Between layers 5 and 8 (not shown here), we observed a continuous shift of words in the sense that a limited number of words appeared and disappeared from a layer to another, with the vanishing of Botany words from the 5th layer.

More new words start to appear on the 9th layer like Bermuda, sinus and hepatic with an increasing number of Geography words, until layer 11 inclusive. Layer 12 includes new words that do not appear before like ribs, Carpal and gallbladder and fewer number of Geography words. Overall, the qualitative analysis seems to be in good agreement with what was observed with the previous methods. For example, it seems to attest to the existence of five groups of layers in the standard BERT-base model, namely $\{1\}$, $\{2, 3, 4\}$, $\{5, 6, 7, 8\}$, $\{9, 10, 11\}$ and $\{12\}$.

Table 4. Ranking of the words (colored according to their topic) that are closest to $\mathbf{v}_\ell$ representations the BERT-base layers for the UFSAC4 dataset. The first row contains the pairwise Spearman correlation coefficient.

$\rho = 0.82$		$\rho = 0.95$		$\rho = 0.94$		$\rho = 0.93$		$\rho = 0.94$		$\rho = 0.88$
1	2	3	4	9	10	11	12
cerebellar	cerebellar	cerebellar	bronchial	adenoids	adenoids	anus	penis
bulbs	kernels	bronchial	cerebellar	atrium	cerebellum	eardrum	eardrum
perennials	maxillae	sclera	molars	hipbones	anus	penis	anus
orchids	bronchial	bronchioles	cranial	anus	Bermuda	armpit	ribs
bronchioles	sclera	clavicles	axons	cerebellum	atrium	cortical	cortical
lymphocyte	cerebellum	cerebellum	arterioles	armpit	eardrum	Bermuda	sphincter
mosses	deserts	cranial	sclera	gyral	armpit	cerebellum	clitoris
rootstocks	clavicles	molars	bronchioles	Bermuda	penis	atrium	pelvic
bronchial	axons	axons	clavicles	sinus	gyral	skull	bulbar
clavicle	bronchioles	arterioles	cerebellum	sphincter	sphincter	Egyptian	calf
leaflets	arterioles	brachial	follicle	leg	Armenia	breastbone	skull
follicle	molars	maxillae	epidermis	clitoris	clitoris	adenoids	armpit
arteriovenous	hindbrain	axon	axon	brachial	pelvic	pelvic	peritoneum
occipital	interface	cervical	brachial	breastbone	hipbones	clitoris	palmar
maxillae	bulbs	rootstocks	scrotum	incisors	breastbone	Armenia	cerebellum
cheekbone	scrotum	kernels	cervical	skull	calf	gyral	Carpal
cerebellum	cranial	scrotum	cheekbone	eardrum	skull	sphincter	gallbladder
cranial	pods	interface	hindbrain	hepatic	sinus	liver	distal
epidermis	sphincter	cerebrum	maxillae	brain	arteriovenous	calf	leg
mucosa	pylorus	deserts	peritoneum	arcuate	Egyptian	peritoneum	wrist
clavicles	rootstocks	epidermis	saliva	cheekbone	leg	sinus	hips
pods	epidermis	follicle	incisors	eye	Bavaria	membrane	gut
herbaceous	areolae	sphincter	triceps	muscles	cortical	Syria	bronchial
brachial	follicle	peritoneum	aorta	bones	arcuate	bulbar	anal
metatarsal	axon	hindbrain	rootstocks	rump	body	arcuate	scrotum
kernels	glomeruli	saliva	atrium	liver	liver	leg	brachial
arterioles	peritoneum	cheekbone	lumbar	cilia	CNS	hipbones	fibula
pylorus	lymphocyte	triceps	cerebrovascular	Armenia	hepatic	palmar	Bermuda
metatarsus	arteriovenous	cerebrovascular	gyral	ribs	rump	hips	liver
molars	occipital	arteriovenous	kernels	dental	cardiovascular	hips	basal

4.5   Quantitative Interpretation Using Dimension Reduction

In this section, relying on PCA, the objective is to go further in the unsupervised analysis of embeddings at different layers. Figure 6 presents visual representations provided by PCA applied to the $\mathbf{X}_\ell$ matrices of each layer. First, on the projections of samples, one can observe a significant enhancement of the separability of samples between the layers 1 and 2 whereas it is almost the same between 2 and 3. We noticed another difference between layers 4 and 5 with a sort of rotation of samples along with a higher increase of variance explained by the two first components. The separability remains more or less stable until layer 11 inclusive and deteriorates in the 12th layer, which also knows a significant increase of explained variance. These differences in separability indicate that the extremities of the network are not only different, but may be much less efficient. Concerning the correlation circles, we notice more differences between layers 1 and 2 than between 2 and 3, this confirms that the 1st layer constitutes a singleton. We also observe a shift across layers with many dimensions that appear in few consecutive layers and then disappear (like 643 appearing in the 2nd layer and disappearing in the 5th layer). Another significant break is observed at the last layer, where dimensions like 223 and 636 disappear while being important for layers 9, 10 and 11. These observations reinforce our previous groupings for BERT-base.

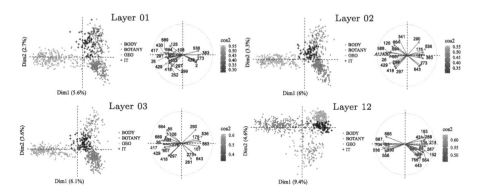

Fig. 6. PCA on BERT-base's data matrices $\mathbf{X}_\ell$, $\ell = 1, \ldots, b$ - Projections (left): coordinates of words on the two first principal components colored w.r.t. their topic. - Correlation circle (right): only the 20 dimensions that are most correlated with the two first components are displayed.

4.6 Results Validation Using a Clustering Performance Metric

In this section, we provide numerical results assessing the layer-wise performance on word clustering using NMI scores (Fig. 7) on clustering partitions obtained with K-means applied to $\mathbf{X}_\ell$ matrices. In doing so, we aim to validate the layer groups that have been identified in the previous sections. The main question we try to answer is: Do the previously identified groups share characteristics in terms of clustering performance? This study also gives us an idea of the transferability of each layer and each model for the unsupervised task of word clustering. By separating layers into groups based on the NMI scores they achieve, one can find clusters of layers that quite resemble the breakdown suggested by the dendograms in Sect. 4.3 (compare the values in Table 5 with the corresponding dendograms depicted in Fig. 4). For BERT-base, in the same way as layer 1 is isolated in its own singleton cluster, its NMI score is also the worst. The group formed by 1, 2 and 3 achieves values between 0.78 and 0.88, while the best performers are the layers from 5 to 8. Performance then decreases, with a marked drop at the last layer, again in agreement with the grouping patterns observed in Figs. 3 and 4. The same observations extend to RoBERTa-large where the cluster {5, 6, 7} contains the best performing layers. We also clearly see a breaking point of performance between the 1st layer and the following, and another one (more acute) at the last layer. These breaking points are visible in Figs. 2 and 3.

Table 5. NMI scores on blocks of layers with UFSAC4 - The first table corresponds to BERT-base and the second to RoBERTa-large. The groups obtained based on word clustering performance fairly closely correspond to the groups that had been spotted using correlation and cluster analyses.

ℓ	01	02	03	04	05	06	07	08	09	10	11	12
NMI	0.64	0.78	0.81	0.88	0.9	0.94	0.9	0.92	0.91	0.91	0.88	0.83

ℓ	01	02	03	04	05	06	07	08	09	10	11	12	13	14	15	16	17	18	19	20	21	22	23	24
NMI	0.51	0.57	0.55	0.61	0.81	0.87	0.9	0.7	0.64	0.62	0.63	0.62	0.61	0.62	0.61	0.55	0.53	0.51	0.48	0.41	0.41	0.58	0.57	0.38

In addition, these observations allow us to confirm some findings presented in the supervised study [8] showing that BERT models achieve their best performance on the intermediate layers. We also extend this observation to RoBERTa with fewer well performing layers, situated more earlier in the network.

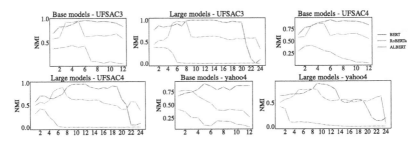

Fig. 7. NMI scores obtained by the word clustering on the $\mathbf{X}_\ell$ data matrices for each layer ℓ.

More generally, on both base and large versions, BERT outperforms the three other models, followed by RoBERTa and far away by ALBERT. This is surprising considering that ALBERT is supposed to outperform BERT and RoBERTa when fine-tuned on supervised tasks. We then show that in a no fine-tuning configuration, BERT word embeddings are of higher quality (BERT-large is the only model to achieved the perfect score on UFSAC3). Finally, ALBERT is the only model for which the base version is better than the large one. Moreover, both versions present very poor results on word clustering (especially the large version) and we can notice a better (but still poor) performance with the first layers. One possible explanation is that ALBERT's layers start to be task specific from the beginning of the network, particularly in view of the architecture of ALBERT where all parameters (including attention parameters) are shared across layers.

5   Conclusion

Knowing more about contextualized word embeddings and what can really be expected from them is an important topic. This paper provides a novel way of analysing Transformer embeddings, based on unsupervised methods, more specifically a correlation and cluster analysis of the layers. Applying these methods to real datasets made it possible to spot precise groups of layers (e.g. 5 groups of layers in BERT-base and 9 in RoBERTa-large) which subsequently proved to fairly closely match the groups obtained when grouping layers based on their clustering performance. This suggests that the proposed method, when applied to a dataset is capable of identifying in advance groups of layers that are likely to best or worst perform on the clustering task. This study also allowed to bring out major differences between Transformer models on the important text clustering task, for example the specificity of ALBERT, which is most likely due to its different network architecture, or the fact that BERT seems to outperform RoBERTa on the clustering task. Future path for research is to further investigate these differences as well as the potential of dimension reduction techniques on contextual word embeddings, an issue that deserves to be the subject of further study, allowing in particular to highlight the potential redundancies present in the Transformer networks.

References

1. van Aken, B., Winter, B., Löser, A., Gers, F.A.: How does BERT answer questions? A layer-wise analysis of transformer representations. In: CIKM, pp. 1823–1832 (2019)
2. Clark, K., Khandelwal, U., Levy, O., Manning, C.D.: What does BERT look at? An analysis of Bert's attention. arXiv preprint arXiv:1906.04341 (2019)
3. Ethayarajh, K., Duvenaud, D., Hirst, G.: Understanding undesirable word embedding associations. arXiv preprint arXiv:1908.06361 (2019)
4. Goldberg, Y.: Assessing BERT's syntactic abilities. arXiv preprint arXiv:1901.05287 (2019)
5. Hao, Y., Dong, L., Wei, F., Xu, K.: Visualizing and understanding the effectiveness of BERT. arXiv preprint arXiv:1908.05620 (2019)
6. Jawahar, G., Sagot, B., Seddah, D.: What does bert learn about the structure of language? In: ACL 2019-57th Annual Meeting of the Association for Computational Linguistics (2019)
7. Kovaleva, O., Romanov, A., Rogers, A., Rumshisky, A.: Revealing the dark secrets of BERT. arXiv preprint arXiv:1908.08593 (2019)
8. Liu, N.F., Gardner, M., Belinkov, Y., Peters, M.E., Smith, N.A.: Linguistic knowledge and transferability of contextual representations. arXiv preprint arXiv:1903.08855 (2019)
9. Peters, M.E., Neumann, M., Zettlemoyer, L., Yih, W.T.: Dissecting contextual word embeddings: architecture and representation. arXiv preprint arXiv:1808.08949 (2018)
10. Robert, P., Escoufier, Y.: A unifying tool for linear multivariate statistical methods: the RV-coefficient. J. R. Stat. Soc. **25**(3), 257–265 (1976)

11. Strehl, A., Ghosh, J.: Cluster ensembles–a knowledge reuse framework for combining multiple partitions. J. Mach. Learn. Res. **3**, 583–617 (2002)
12. Tenney, I., Das, D., Pavlick, E.: BERT rediscovers the classical NLP pipeline. arXiv preprint arXiv:1905.05950 (2019)
13. Vial, L., Lecouteux, B., Schwab, D.: UFSAC: unification of sense annotated corpora and tools. In: Language Resources and Evaluation Conference (LREC) (2018)
14. Zhang, X., Zhao, J., LeCun, Y.: Character-level convolutional networks for text classification. In: Advances in Neural Information Processing Systems (2015)

A Framework for Authorial Clustering of Shorter Texts in Latent Semantic Spaces

Rafi Trad[(✉)] [iD] and Myra Spiliopoulou[(✉)] [iD]

Otto von Guericke University Magdeburg, Magdeburg, Germany
`rafi.trad@ovgu.de`

Abstract. Authorial clustering involves the grouping of documents written by the same author or team of authors without any prior positive examples of an author's writing style or thematic preferences. For authorial clustering on shorter texts (paragraph-length texts that are typically shorter than conventional documents), the document representation is particularly important. We propose a high-level framework which utilizes a compact data representation in a latent feature space derived with non-parametric topic modeling. Authorial clusters are identified thereafter in two scenarios: (a) fully unsupervised and (b) semi-supervised where a small number of shorter texts are known to belong to the same author (must-link constraints) or not (cannot-link constraints).

We report on experiments with 120 collections in three languages and two genres and show that the topic-based latent feature space provides a promising level of performance while reducing the dimensionality by a factor of 1500 compared to state-of-the-art. We also demonstrate that little knowledge on constraints in authorial clusters memberships leads to auspicious improvements in front of this difficult task.

Keywords: Authorial clustering · Document clustering · Authorship analysis

1 Introduction

As users contribute news, opinions and arguments online, it is important to ascribe each text to its author towards protecting an author's statements from misuse by others and towards guarding the online community by advancing digital forensics. It is reasonable to assume that authors demonstrate distinct writing styles, which can be used for automated authorship analysis [21].

Authorial clustering assumes that information on authors of documents is unavailable or unreliable, and seeks to partition the set of documents into clusters such that each cluster corresponds to one author [22]. Stamatatos et al. term the process of discerning the number of authors/clusters and then assigning the documents to clusters as "complete authorial clustering" [22]. Our approach is a complete authorial clustering approach, since we also derive the number

© Springer Nature Switzerland AG 2021
P. H. Abreu et al. (Eds.): IDA 2021, LNCS 12695, pp. 301–312, 2021.
https://doi.org/10.1007/978-3-030-74251-5_24

of clusters. We use the terms "complete authorial clustering" and "authorial clustering" interchangeably and prefer the latter for brevity.

Many authorial clustering approaches invest on advanced machine learning methods, like recurrent neural networks [4], word embedding [1] and sophisticated document representations [4,10,20] with thousands of dimensions. High-dimensional feature spaces, however, tend to get sparser as the texts get shorter and suffer from consequences like the curse of dimensionality. In this work, we propose a new high-level framework for authorial clustering. We represent texts in a dense feature space derived with non-parametric topic modeling which automatically infer the number of topics spoken about, and cluster them by authorship with known unsupervised and a semi-supervised algorithms.

We use the term "shorter texts" to indicate the kind of texts we may read in micro-blogs, online reviews and social media which are around one paragraph in length. These texts are *shorter* than ordinary texts but are still long enough to be useful for authorship analyses that are difficult even for humans [18]. Through non-parametric topic modeling we thus represent texts as denser vectors in a low-dimensional feature space, the size of which is also automatically induced.

Our contributions are as follows: (i) proposing a simple high-level pipeline for authorial clustering in latent feature spaces whose size (i.e. number of latent factors) is automatically inferred from the data; (ii) measuring the benefit of annotating a small portion of the data via semi-supervision, which capitalizes on minimal expert knowledge in the form of constraints and (iii) thorough evaluation of the framework against naive and state-of-the-art (SOTA) baselines for text collections in different languages and genres.

The remainder of the paper is organized as follows: Sect. 2 describes advances of authorial clustering and other relevant works. Our approach is presented in Sect. 3, followed by experimental design and evaluation in Sect. 4. We close with a discussion and suggested improvements in Sect. 5.

2   Related Work

Authorial clustering was one of the 2016 and 2017 tasks of the PAN competition[1]. For this competition task, Bagnall et al. proposed a character-level multi-headed recurrent neural network (RNN) as a language model and showed that this approach recognized authorship idiosyncrasies even with short texts discussing different topics [4]. Sari and Stevenson used k-means for authorial clustering, and investigated the potential of word embedding in comparison to a tf-idf n-gram language model (at character level) [20]. They showed that the former was beneficial for multi-topic texts but it was also more computationally demanding without achieving substantially better performance [20]. Agarwal et al. utilized word embedding with tf-idf weights and employed hierarchical clustering algorithms to perform authorship clustering [1]. Kocher and Savoy adopted a simple set of features of the most frequent terms (words and punctuation) to represent the authorship and writing styles [14].

---

[1] https://pan.webis.de.

García-Mondeja et al. used a Bag-of-Words language model with binary features, because the documents were too short to use frequencies, and then applied a β-compact algorithm that placed documents in the same cluster if they were maximally similar and more proximal than the threshold β [9]. Aldebei et al. proposed a two-level HMM to model relations of sequential sentences in order to cluster single-author documents by authorship [2]. While the approach was for long documents, they also tested it on smaller segments of texts as well [2]. Gómez-Adorno et al. used a hierarchical agglomerative clustering algorithm with average linkage and cosine similarity, and with the Calinski-Harabasz optimization criterion to determine the cut-off layer of the dendrogram [10]. They considered two language models at term level, tf-idf and log entropy, and showed that the latter had best performance when used with the most frequent 20,000 terms in the vocabulary [10]. The aforementioned algorithms build clusters from vectors drawn on elaborately crafted language models.

To the best of our knowledge, topic modeling has not been used for authorial clustering thus far, but it has been applied successfully for authorship verification [15–17]. Potha and Stamatatos pointed out that the topic space to which they reduced the original high dimensional space was less sparse, less noisy and appropriate for language-independent learning [15]. In their follow-up work [17], they showed that topic modeling lifted up the performance [17]. Hence, the potential of low-dimensional document representation in the topic space [15,17] makes topic modeling worthy of investigation for authorial clustering as well. In addition, and similarly to authorial clustering, recent solutions to authorship verification invest on sophisticated text representations, as proposed by Ding et al. [8], and on combinations of text representation and complex (dis)similarity functions, as proposed e.g. by Halvani et al. in [11].

On the front of topic modeling, LDA, a mainstay therein, was introduced by Blei et al. as a 3-level hierarchical parametric Bayesian model for collections of discrete data, which models the generative probabilistic process that is believed to generate the data items, or documents [7]. HDP (Hierarchical Dirichlet Processes) was introduced by Teh et al. to extend the well-known Latent Dirichlet Allocation (LDA) and capture the uncertainty pertaining to the number of topics via an additional Dirichlet process [28].

Conventional topic modeling, let it be parametric (e.g. LDA) or nonparametric (e.g. HDP), is generally used with long typical texts. Furthermore, Hong and Davison showed that LDA-based parametric topic models perform poorly on micro-blog texts [13]. LDA was extended by Rosen-Zvi et al. in their Author-Topic Model (AT), which inferred topics and authors from large corpora simultaneously [19]; however, it was shown that the potential of AT didn't exceed that of standard LDA with short texts when LDA was trained on aggregated short texts [13]. An improvement in terms of the coherence and interpretability of inferred topics from very short texts, e.g. document titles, was achieved with the biterm topic model (BTM) by Yan et al. [29] relying on co-occurrences of terms at corpus level rather than document level.

3   Our Approach

Our approach encompasses the following components: (1) A method of latent semantic representation (LSSR) of texts in a low-dimensional, dense feature space after vectorizing with word unigrams. The number of latent topic-based dimensions is inferred via a non-parametric topic model. (2) A method for deriving authorial clusters in this feature space in two variants with respect to the learning model: fully unsupervised or semi-unsupervised with a restricted amount of background knowledge.

To test how good we can select the number of authors k in the corpus[2], we also supply the true k to each variant to test the differences in performance. Doing so isolates the effects of any suboptimal k estimations, and thus monitors the severity of any consequent losses in performance. While LSSR is the only input to the unsupervised variant, the semi-supervised clustering variant takes advantage of a *small* number of must-link and cannot-link (ML/CL) constraints to form the authorial clusters. We describe our approach in detail hereafter.

3.1   Building a Dense Feature Space with Non-parametric Topic Modeling

The first step is to vectorize the documents. We use word unigrams because they perform well in authorship verification settings [15], weighted by term frequencies. Furthermore, no punctuation is removed as it can contribute to the writing style of authors. On the other hand, too infrequent words which occur only once in a corpus are removed as they are most likely specific keywords that do not relate to the style of writing. Empirically we found this profitable while developing the approach with the dataset at hand.

Topic modeling is exploited afterwards as a dimensionality reduction technique to produce LSSR, the low-dimensional representation of texts with latent topics, which is also language-independent and less noisy. To this end, we use a non-parametric Bayesian topic model, namely Hierarchical Dirichlet Processes (HDP), implementing Gibbs sampling and inferring the number of topics t automatically [23]. After this stage, each document d is represented as $\vec{d_t}$ in terms of its weighted latent topics instead of observed words, and the weight of a topic in $\vec{d_t}$ is the count of that topic's words in d (see Table 1). $\vec{d_t}$ characterizes d in the low-dimensional latent semantic space which is manifested by the word-topic and document-topic matrices calculated by HDP.

3.2   Unsupervised Authorial Clustering Variant

Determining the number of authors k, i.e. authorial clusters, that governs a group of data points is a challenging task. We use two methods to select k: the G-means algorithm [12] and the Gap statistic [24]. In addition, we couple k selection with *Spherical K-Means* algorithm (SPKMeans), which can be

---

[2] Please note that k is different from number of topics t.

Table 1. An example LSSR of a corpus embracing four documents, each of which contains #w terms. LSSR is comprised of five dimensions in this example as per the number of inferred ulterior topics.

doc	#w	t1	t2	t3	t4	t5
d1	74	7	14	19	11	23
d2	50	8	11	9	12	10
d3	44	4	6	7	1	26
d4	60	11	15	7	15	12

regarded as K-Means but with cosine similarity [5], to complete our workflow for unsupervised authorial clustering. SPKMeans better suits the clustering of intrinsically directional data, like document vectors, and we found it superior to other clustering algorithms in preliminary experiments.

3.3 Semi-supervised Authorial Clustering Variant

The main difference between the semi-supervised variant and the unsupervised variant is that we assume access to little expert knowledge as constraints in the former. We select the best k in a constraint-compliant manner by *optimization of an intrinsic clustering evaluation method*, and thus add a preparatory step to derive instance-level must-link and cannot-link (ML/CL) constraints. A ML constraint indicates that a pair of documents must belong to the same cluster, while a CL one states that a pair of documents cannot be related [26]. We did a small manual experiment and found CL constraints easier to construct.

A ground truth must be used to derive ML/CL constraints from. The number of constraints should be "small" enough to be practical, because in reality experts would need to annotate these texts. The details whereby we elicit these constraints are described in Sect. 4.2. We thereupon employ Constrained K-means (COP K-Means) [26] which enhances K-Means by ML/CL.

4   Experimental Design

In our experiments, we quantified the performance of the various configurations within the approach, and compared them to naive and state-of-the-art baselines. Comparisons were made in terms of the quality of their clusterings against the true clusterings, so we utilized extrinsic evaluation metrics.

4.1   The Dataset

We used PAN17-Clustering dataset [25] as it was the only suitable and publicly available[3] dataset with an appropriate ground truth for the experiments. It comprises a number of clustering problems –sets of texts– spanning three languages

---

[3] https://pan.webis.de/data.html.

(English, Dutch and Greek) and two genres ("articles" and "reviews"). There are 60 problems reserved for development and tuning purposes and 120 for the final evaluation, allocated equally to the six language-genre combinations. This means there are 10 problems for each language-genre in the train segment and 20 in the test segment. Each problem consists mostly of 20 single-authored texts in a specific language and genre, written by six authors on average [25]. We referred only to the training dataset to tune the proposed approach.

Document lengths fall between 100 and 500 characters. On average, English and Dutch "articles" exhibit shorter texts than "reviews" whilst the contrary holds for Greek "articles" [25]. Most of the ground truth authorial clusters contain between 1 and 4 documents, with singleton clusters (where an author writes only one document) making up more than 25% of the 1075 clusters in the dataset.

As PAN17-Clustering is commonly used for authorship clustering, we want to re-state that English and Greek corpora were built by segmenting longer texts into paragraphs. For this reason, it is considerably easier to reassemble such texts following some thematic hints and unique keywords/phrases found in the original documents. Tschuggnal et al. acknowledge this fact [25] and we have observed this first-hand when attempting the task manually.

Table 2. Overview of the compared methods. "BL" stands for "baseline".

Method's acronym	Learning model	Description of the method	Selection method of k
BL_r	–	Naive BaseLine from [22, 25]: it chooses a random number as k and builds k clusters randomly	Random choice
BL_s	–	Naive BaseLine from [22, 25]: each document is a singleton cluster	$k = |Corpus|$
BL_SOTA	Unsupervised	State-Of-The-Art as BaseLine: the winner of the PAN-2017 competition [10, 25]	Optimal k was chosen by the baseline itself through optimizing the Calinski-Harabasz (CH) index
SPKMeans	Unsupervised	SPherical KMeans clustering	Averaging out the estimations of G-Means and Gap
COP-KMeans	Semi-supervised	Constrained COP-KMEANS with 12% of pairwise document links revealed as ML/CL constraints	Minimizing Davies–Bouldin index (DBI) penalized by k (i.e. $DBI * k$)

4.2 Configurations and Baselines

We compare the approach to two baseline methods and to the winner of the PAN-2017 competition as the state-of-the-art [10, 25] (Table 2) since PAN-2018 and later iterations don't include authorial clustering as a shared task.

HDP topic model with Gibbs sampling is a cornerstone in the proposed framework and generates the main inputs to SPKMeans and COP-KMeans variants. It was shown in [28] that HDP is on a par with the best selected LDA model through a model selection mechanism, and also that non-parametric methods outperform LDA in [6]. For these reasons, we weren't encouraged to additionally implement our approach with LDA as a baseline, noting that it would need an additional model selection scheme to determine t.

We tried BTM instead of HDP in an experiment since it should produce more coherent and interpretable topics with extremely short texts according to [29]. To this end, we used PAN-17 train data and set $t = 5$, but didn't find promising improvements in the resultant authorial clusters as judged by our adopted evaluation metrics. As a possible explanation, BTM relies on corpus-level words co-occurrences rather than operating on the document level, and such co-occurrences aren't as effective as document-level ones when grouping texts by distinctive writing styles. Besides, we use topic modeling as a means for intelligent reduction and densification of the sparse high-dimensional feature space, which is orthogonal to the formation of interpretable, author-independent topics.

Implementation. We used the original implementation of Hierarchical Dirichlet Processes (HDP) with Gibbs sampling [23,27][4]. Additionally, we utilized publicly available implementations of the core algorithms: G-Means[5], Gap[6], SPKMeans[7] and COP-KMeans[8] in a novel pipeline.

For the components which utilize randomness, we fixed the random seed in HDP and COP-KMeans and averaged out 5 full runs of SPKMeans which included running Gap and G-Means to select k. Our code is written mostly in Python and is hereby made available[9].

Selecting k. Since we had two clustering variants of different natures, we opted for different methods to select the best k which led to optimal results on the training data. To determine k for SPKMeans, the estimates of G-means and Gap were averaged out and initial seeds were chosen with K-means++. For COP-KMeans, a grid search for k in the range $[2, n - 1]$, where $n = |Corpus|$, was performed to minimize the quantity $(DBI * k)$ –DBI: Davies-Bouldin index– without causing the clustering to fail. By "fail" we mean the inability to satisfy all constraints at a proposed k, and $DBI * k$ quantity was inspired by the original COP-KMeans paper [26].

Derivation of ML and CL Constraints. Let there be n documents in a corpus, then we have $l = \frac{n}{2} \times (n-1)$ pairwise links therein. We relied on these l pairwise links to form ML and CL constraints among documents while covering only a small percentage of l. We exercised no influence on how many MLs or CLs we

---

[4] https://github.com/blei-lab/hdp.
[5] https://github.com/flylo/g-means.
[6] https://github.com/milesgranger/gap_statistic.
[7] https://github.com/jasonlaska/spherecluster.
[8] https://github.com/Behrouz-Babaki/COP-Kmeans.
[9] Code of the study: https://github.com/rtrad89/authorship_clustering_code_repo.

ended up with. Choosing the percentage of l to cover has its issues because COP-KMeans cannot backtrack, and its underlying sequential decisions are order-sensitive [26] which can lead to a clustering fail.

As a result, we tried several percentages using the training data and true k values, and adopted 12% after it had demonstrated minimum fails while being practically possible to attain – say via experts annotating documents. While testing, and since k was selected dynamically, we skipped those k values which caused a fail at 12% of l. As a note, we observed that COP-KMeans clustering fail was not monotonic: 10% of l may fail but 12% can still succeed. Furthermore, the higher the percentage, the better the performance at the cost of real-world practicality.

Evaluation Criteria. When the ground truth is available, extrinsic clustering evaluation measures are the ones to use to assess the quality of clusterings. Besides, Amigo et al. identified four criteria for judging a clustering evaluation metric [3] (*cluster homogeneity, cluster completeness, rag bag* and *cluster size vs. quantity*) and found that $\boldsymbol{B^3F}$ satisfies all. Therefore, B^3F was adopted[10] in our experiments.

B^3F is formally defined as follows: let $\mathbb{D}$ be a corpus of N documents. More-over, let $C(d.)$ be the cluster to which the document $d.$ is ascribed and $A(d.)$ be the author of the document in question. Furthermore, let d_i and d_j be two document from $\mathbb{D}$, where $i \in [1, N] \wedge j \in [1, N] \wedge i \neq j$, and let C_i be the cluster of documents in $C(d_i)$, and A_i be the collection of documents written by A_i. We can now define a correctness function as in Eq. 1 and use it to define B^3F in Eq. 2 [22].

$$correct(d_i, d_j) = \begin{cases} 1 & when\ A(d_i) = A(d_j) \wedge C(d_i) = C(d_j) \\ 0 & Otherwise. \end{cases} \tag{1}$$

$$B^3F = 2 \times \frac{\frac{1}{N}\sum_{i=1}^{N}\frac{\sum_{d_j \in C_i} correct(d_i,d_j)}{|C_i|} \times \frac{1}{N}\sum_{i=1}^{N}\frac{\sum_{d_j \in C_i} correct(d_i,d_j)}{|A_i|}}{\frac{1}{N}\sum_{i=1}^{N}\frac{\sum_{d_j \in C_i} correct(d_i,d_j)}{|C_i|} + \frac{1}{N}\sum_{i=1}^{N}\frac{\sum_{d_j \in C_i} correct(d_i,d_j)}{|A_i|}} \tag{2}$$

We also incorporated the mean rank of the methods $\overline{r}^{11}$; a simple metric that averages out the six B^3F relative ranks (in the six language-genres of the test data), and it thus helps to consider the consistency of exhibited performances when comparing the methods.

4.3   Results

Table 3 encompasses the results of our experiments. The first "k acq." column tells whether the number of authors k has been dynamically selected –"Selected"

---

[10] https://github.com/hhromic/python-bcubed.
[11] We also measured the Adjusted Rand Index (ARI) but omitted it due to space limitations. It is available in our preprint on https://arxiv.org/pdf/2011.15038.pdf.

segment– or input from the ground truth –"Input" segment–. In the second column we enlist the algorithms, followed by the mean ranks in the third column and B^3F values in rightmost columns.

Table 3. The overall mean rank $\bar{r}$ (lower is better) and averaged $B^3 F$ scores (higher is better) of the different methods over the 120 test problem sets; en: English, gr: Greek, nl: Dutch; ar: Articles and re: Reviews. k acquisition (abbreviated as k acq.) is how k is provided to the methods.

k acq.	Algorithm	$\bar{r}$	B^3F						
			Overall mean	en-ar	en-re	gr-ar	gr-re	nl-ar	nl-re
Selected	BL_r	4.7	0.435	0.466	0.444	0.411	0.418	0.428	0.441
	BL_s	3.8	0.458	0.436	0.475	0.403	0.455	0.438	**0.543**
	BL_SOTA_le	2.3	0.562	0.602	0.570	0.532	0.535	**0.670**	0.461
	SPKMeans	2.8	0.542	0.556	0.552	0.569	0.514	0.553	0.507
	COP-KMeans	*1.3*	*0.626*	**0.682**	**0.635**	**0.676**	**0.590**	0.643	0.530
Input	SPKMeans	-	0.562	0.574	0.569	0.580	0.530	0.579	0.540
	COP-KMeans	-	0.649	0.700	0.654	0.709	0.603	0.642	0.585

Comparative Study of Performance Levels. "Selected" segment in Table 3 shows the average B^3F of the methods in Table 2 over the 120 test clustering problems when k is dynamically selected. The $\overline{B^3F}$ performance of BL_SOTA as reported in [25] is *0.573*, but even though we use the same data, configuration and number of dimensions (20000) as in [10] without changing any preprocessing steps, we have observed lower $\overline{B^3F}$ scores which we report here.

$\overline{B^3F}$ results indicate that our unsupervised variant is better than BL_r and BL_s, whilst the constrained-based variant COP-KMeans performs remarkably better. COP-KMeans scores the best $\overline{B^3F}$ at *0.626* and ranks first, followed in rank by BL_SOTA and closely by SPKMeans in that order.

COP-KMeans expectedly tops the scores in all sub-datasets but the Dutch documents, where it is still competitive. In addition, our variants are particularly better than state-of-the-art in Greek sub-dataset and especially "articles". Since Dutch "articles" were built without segmentation in PAN-17 (cf. Sect. 4.1), they are the closest to reality. SPKmeans is superior to SOTA in the Dutch "reviews" genre which also tends to be less structured usually, but not in Dutch "articles". It is important to remember that our pipeline works in ≤ 13 latent dimensions *compared to 20000 dimensions* in SOTA, which emphasizes how intriguing it is for the proposed methods to still be competitive to SOTA.

Finally, segment "Input" in Table 3 monitors the gain in performance should the true k is known rather than selected, representing an ideal case for our k selection component and thus isolating its adverse effects. We observe that SPKMeans and COP-KMeans could capitalize on true k values only slightly.

Statistical Significance Tests. In Fig. 1 we show the critical difference plot when applying Friedman-Nemenyi non-parametric post-hoc tests. At $\alpha_{corrected} = \frac{0.1}{2}$, our methods and SOTA demonstrate a significantly better performance than the naive baselines BL_r and BL_s. COP-KMeans is not significantly different from BL_SOTA but is significantly better than SPKMeans.

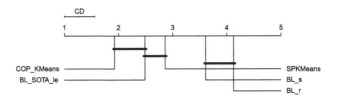

Fig. 1. The critical difference diagram of the methods on the 120 test problems ($\alpha_{corrected} = \frac{0.1}{2}$). Methods are ordered from best (leftmost) to worst (rightmost) and those that are not significantly different are connected with horizontal lines.

5   Discussion and Conclusion

This work is the first to study non-parametric topic modeling for authorial clustering of paragraph-long shorter texts. Our high-level framework highlights the potential of non-parametric topical dimensions to tackle authorial clustering with high efficiency, while grabbing the attention to how semi-supervised attempts fare.

We have used B^3F for evaluation purposes, which is a common metric in authorial clustering literature to this end. Best performance is attained by our semi-supervised COP-KMeans, and while it is indeed not directly comparable to SOTA, it is statistically significantly better than our unsupervised variant SPKMeans. *This suggests that when operating in low-dimensional topic-based vector spaces, capitalizing on little prior expert knowledge is beneficial for authorial clustering of shorter texts.*

When focusing on SPKMeans vs. BL_SOTA, it is clear that the latter reached higher $\overline{B^3F}$ but *the two are still comparable in terms of B^3F.* Please note that: (1) Both are significantly better than the naive baselines and produce comparable B^3F scores, and (2) SPKMeans with LSSR alleviates the need to engineer and tune down the dimensionality, because it operates in a dynamically-inferred lower dimensional space. The maximum number of topics whereby test documents were represented was *13* in LSSR; *1500x less than BL_SOTA's 20000.*

B^3F scores of elaborate methods do not exceed those of naive baselines (BL_r and BL_s) by much, which indicates the difficulty of authorial clustering with shorter texts, and marks the need for more substantial work. To acquire more insights on the nature of the challenges, we have asked four annotators to cluster one problem from PAN17-Clustering training data, and have found that identifying dissimilarities among texts is the best feasible strategy. As a result, we want to investigate *similarity/metric learning* in future works and craft a (dis)similarity function that ascertains how (dis)similar two texts are in stylometric terms. Once done, authorial clustering can follow using that effective and specialized function.

References

1. Agarwal, L., Thakral, K., Bhatt, G., Mittal, A.: Authorship clustering using tf-idf weighted word-embeddings. In: Proceedings of the 11th Forum for Information Retrieval Evaluation, pp. 24–29 (2019)
2. Aldebei, K., Farhood, H., Jia, W., Nanda, P., He, X.: Sequential and unsupervised document authorial clustering based on hidden Markov model. In: 2017 IEEE Trustcom/BigDataSE/ICESS, pp. 379–385. IEEE (2017)
3. Amigó, E., Gonzalo, J., Artiles, J., Verdejo, F.: A comparison of extrinsic clustering evaluation metrics based on formal constraints. Inf. Retr. **12**(4), 461–486 (2009). https://doi.org/10.1007/s10791-008-9066-8
4. Bagnall, D.: Authorship clustering using multi-headed recurrent neural networks. arXiv preprint arXiv:1608.04485 (2016)
5. Banerjee, A., Dhillon, I.S., Ghosh, J., Sra, S.: Clustering on the unit hypersphere using von Mises-fisher distributions. J. Mach. Learn. Res. **6**, 1345–1382 (2005)
6. Blei, D.M., Griffiths, T.L., Jordan, M.I., Tenenbaum, J.B.: Hierarchical topic models and the nested Chinese restaurant process. In: Advances in Neural Information Processing Systems, pp. 17–24 (2004)
7. Blei, D.M., Ng, A.Y., Jordan, M.I.: Latent Dirichlet allocation. J. Mach. Learn. Res. **3**, 993–1022 (2003)
8. Ding, S.H.H., Fung, B.C.M., Iqbal, F., Cheung, W.K.: Learning stylometric representations for authorship analysis. IEEE Trans. Cybern. **49**(1), 107–121 (2019). https://doi.org/10.1109/TCYB.2017.2766189
9. García-Mondeja, Y., Castro-Castro, D., Lavielle-Castro, V., Muñoz, R.: Discovering author groups using a β-compact graph-based clustering. In: CLEF (Working Notes), CEUR Workshop Proceedings, vol. 1866 (2017)
10. Gómez-Adorno, H., Martín-del-Campo-Rodríguez, C., Sidorov, G., Alemán, Y., Vilariño, D., Pinto, D.: Hierarchical clustering analysis: the best-performing approach at PAN 2017 author clustering task. In: Bellot, P., et al. (eds.) CLEF 2018. LNCS, vol. 11018, pp. 216–223. Springer, Cham (2018). https://doi.org/10.1007/978-3-319-98932-7_20
11. Halvani, O., Winter, C., Graner, L.: Authorship verification based on compression-models. arXiv preprint arXiv:1706.00516 (2017)
12. Hamerly, G., Elkan, C.: Learning the k in k-means. In: Advances in Neural Information Processing Systems, pp. 281–288 (2004)
13. Hong, L., Davison, B.D.: Empirical study of topic modeling in Twitter. In: Proceedings of the First Workshop on Social Media Analytics, SOMA 2010, pp. 80–88. ACM, New York (2010). https://doi.org/10.1145/1964858.1964870, http://doi.acm.org/10.1145/1964858.1964870
14. Kocher, M., Savoy, J.: Unine at clef 2016: author clustering. In: CLEF (Working Notes), pp. 895–902 (2016)
15. Potha, N., Stamatatos, E.: Intrinsic author verification using topic modeling. In: Proceedings of the 10th Hellenic Conference on Artificial Intelligence, p. 20. ACM (2018)

16. Potha, N., Stamatatos, E.: Dynamic ensemble selection for author verification.·In: Azzopardi, L., Stein, B., Fuhr, N., Mayr, P., Hauff, C., Hiemstra, D. (eds.) ECIR 2019. LNCS, vol. 11437, pp. 102–115. Springer, Cham (2019). https://doi.org/10.1007/978-3-030-15712-8_7

17. Potha, N., Stamatatos, E.: Improving author verification based on topic modeling. J. Assoc. Inf. Sci. Technol. **70**, 1074–1088 (2019)

18. Rexha, A., Kröll, M., Ziak, H., Kern, R.: Authorship identification of documents with high content similarity. Scientometrics **115**(1), 223–237 (2018)

19. Rosen-Zvi, M., Chemudugunta, C., Griffiths, T., Smyth, P., Steyvers, M.: Learning author-topic models from text corpora. ACM Trans. Inf. Syst. **28**(1), 4:1–4:38 (2010). https://doi.org/10.1145/1658377.1658381, http://doi.acm.org/10.1145/1658377.1658381

20. Sari, Y., Stevenson, M.: Exploring word embeddings and character n-grams for author clustering. In: CLEF (Working Notes), pp. 984–991 (2016)

21. Stamatatos, E.: A survey of modern authorship attribution methods. J. Am. Soc. Inf. Sci. Technol. **60**(3), 538–556 (2009). https://doi.org/10.1002/asi.21001, https://onlinelibrary.wiley.com/doi/abs/10.1002/asi.21001

22. Stamatatos, E., et al.: Clustering by authorship within and across documents. In: Working Notes Papers of the CLEF 2016 Evaluation Labs. CEUR Workshop Proceedings/Balog, Krisztian [edit.] et al., pp. 691–715 (2016)

23. Teh, Y.W., Jordan, M.I., Beal, M.J., Blei, D.M.: Hierarchical Dirichlet processes. J. Am. Stat. Assoc. **101**(476), 1566–1581 (2006). https://doi.org/10.1198/016214506000000302

24. Tibshirani, R., Walther, G., Hastie, T.: Estimating the number of clusters in a data set via the gap statistic. J. R. Stat. Soc.: Ser. B (Stat. Methodol.) **63**(2), 411–423 (2001)

25. Tschuggnall, M., et al.: Overview of the author identification task at pan-2017: style breach detection and author clustering. In: Working Notes Papers of the CLEF 2017 Evaluation Labs/Cappellato, Linda [edit.] et al., pp. 1–22 (2017)

26. Wagstaff, K., Cardie, C., Rogers, S., Schrödl, S., et al.: Constrained k-means clustering with background knowledge. In: ICML, vol. 1, pp. 577–584 (2001)

27. Wang, C., Blei, D.M.: A split-merge MCMC algorithm for the hierarchical Dirichlet process. Stat, vol. 1050, p. 8 (2012)

28. Teh, Y.W., Jordan, M.I., Beal, M.J., Blei, D.M.: Hierarchical Dirichlet processes. J. Am. Stat. Assoc. **101**, 476–1566 (2006). https://doi.org/10.1198/016214506000000302, http://amstat.tandfonline.com/action/journalInformation?journalCode=uasa20

29. Yan, X., Guo, J., Lan, Y., Cheng, X.: A biterm topic model for short texts. In: Proceedings of the 22nd International Conference on World Wide Web, WWW 2013, pp. 1445–1456. ACM, New York (2013). https://doi.org/10.1145/2488388.2488514, http://doi.acm.org/10.1145/2488388.2488514

DeepGG: A Deep Graph Generator

Julian Stier$^{(\boxtimes)}$ and Michael Granitzer

University of Passau, Innstraße 41, 94032 Passau, Germany
julian.stier@uni-passau.de

Abstract. Learning distributions of graphs can be used for automatic drug discovery, molecular design, complex network analysis, and much more. We present an improved framework for learning generative models of graphs based on the idea of deep state machines. To learn state transition decisions we use a set of graph and node embedding techniques as memory of the state machine.

Our analysis is based on learning the distribution of random graph generators for which we provide statistical tests to determine which properties can be learned and how well the original distribution of graphs is represented. We show that the design of the state machine favors specific distributions. Models of graphs of size up to 150 vertices are learned. Code and parameters are publicly available to reproduce our results.

1 Introduction

We aim to learn generative models of graphs from an empirical set for which we assume a characteristic underlying distribution. These desirable models find applications in the discovery of chemical compounds such as drugs and various other application areas for which the discovery is based on profound expert knowledge, empirical testing and complex underlying rules of how the graphs emerge.

We present a generalized generative model for graphs based on DGMG [19] trained on sets of representative graphs and evaluate it on existing probabilistic random graph generators with various graph sizes of up to several hundred vertices. For this, we represent graphs in construction sequences and discuss three variants to obtain such sequences. Construction sequences are possible representations of graphs like the commonly used adjacency matrix of a graph and explained in Sect. 3. Equivalent or similar representations are used by various auto-regressive models as mentioned in Sect. 2. Our **contributions** comprise

1. a generative model for graphs learned from graph construction sequences,
2. an introduction to and an analysis of three variants of graph construction sequences,
3. an analysis of generated graphs obtained through examples from graph distributions of the probabilistic models of Erdős-Rényi, Barabasi-Albert and Watts-Strogatz,
4. and accessible source code and reproducible evaluations[1].

---

[1] Our source code is published at https://github.com/innvariant/deepgg.

© Springer Nature Switzerland AG 2021
P. H. Abreu et al. (Eds.): IDA 2021, LNCS 12695, pp. 313–324, 2021.
https://doi.org/10.1007/978-3-030-74251-5_25

2   Related Work

For understanding our work and its embedding in its research field, we differentiate between two families of random models of graphs: imprecisely, we call them *probabilistic* models of graphs and *generative* models of graphs although usually the latter are subsets of the former and both terms refer to statistical and thus mathematical models. Here, we consider models as *probabilistic* if they consist of an algorithmic description and if their draws of random samples are based on simple distributions. Examples for probabilistic models of graphs are the Erdős-Rényi model [7] for random graphs, a special case of exponential random graph models [23], the Watts-Strogatz model for small-world networks [24], the Kleinberg model [15], the Barabasi-Albert model for scale-free networks [1] Probabilistic models of graphs provide a distribution of graphs with a usually small set of parameters controlling a core principle of the model. A major intend to study those models are statistical analyses in network science.

We consider models as *generative* models of graphs if they are intended to be able to learn characteristic distributions of graphs based on an observed set of graphs from an underlying unknown distribution of graphs. These generative models are usually of a magnitude higher in terms of their number of parameters. While Liao et al. [20] differentiate between auto-regressive and non-autoregressive models, we currently prefer to categorize generative models of graphs further into popular types of deep learning models which we identified as *Recurrent Neural Networks* (RNN), *Variational Auto-Encoder* (VAE), *Generative Adversarial Networks* (GAN), *Policy Networks* (PI) or a mixture of them. Furthermore, it is important to know of techniques such as Graph Neural Networks [10], Graph Convolution [14] and the Message Passing Framework [9], in general, as they provide embedding techniques which are now widely used among above generative models.

An early work which provides a model that "can generate graphs that obey many of the patterns found in real graphs" is based on kronecker multiplication [17] and called *KronFit*. However, the model is fitted towards a single graph with maximum likelihood. To our understanding the original intend of it was not to learn the hidden distribution of graphs but the exemplary graph itself and despite it can "sample of the real graph" by "using a smaller exponent in the Kronecker exponentiation" it can be assumed that the distribution is close to this particular single objective graph and not an underlying distribution of graphs from which the graph might have been sampled [16].

The most important work related to our model and analysis are Learning Deep Generative Models of Graphs (DGMG) [19], Graph Recurrent Neural Networks (GraphRNN) [26] and Efficient Graph Generation with Graph Recurrent Attention Networks (GRANs) [20]. DGMG is the model framework we extended, generalized and provided new experiments for and which computational issues Li et al. have again tackled with the successful GRAN in [20]. GraphRNN [26] is a highly successful auto-regressive model and was experimentally compared on three types of datasets called "grid dataset", "community dataset" and "ego dataset". The model captures a graph distribution in "an autoregressive (recurrent) manner as a sequence of additions of new nodes and edges". Liao et al. identify some major issues of GraphRNN and explain that "handling permutation invariance is vital for generative models on graphs" [20]. GRAN is a recent efficient auto-regressive model "generating large graphs of up to 5k vertices" by generating a sequence of vectors representing "one row or one block of rows" of the lower triangular matrix at a time [20].

Besides those three works, there is also structure2vec [5], Graphite [11] and GraphGAN [21] for generically learning models of graphs. There exist various generative models which are mostly tailored specifically to applications such as molecular designs. We found [4] (RNN), [12] (RNN), [13] (VAE), [3] (VAE), [25] (PI), [18] worthy to mention here.

We also want to refer to two frameworks which provide a lot of tools for differentiable computation on graph structures such as the Deep Graph Library [22], Euler [2] and StellarGraph [6].

3 Graph Construction Sequences

To learn the hidden distribution of graphs given a set of exemplary graphs we need a suitable representation from which we can learn from. Using the flattened adjacency matrix of the graph would be one approach but "suffers from serious drawbacks: it cannot naturally generalize to graphs of varying size, and requires training on all possible vertex permutations or specifying a canonical permutation" [26].

We follow a similar approach as in [26] and [19] and learn a distribution of graphs from a sequence we call *actionable construction sequence*[2]. In other contexts of network science this representation is also viewed under the perspective of graph evolution.

An action denotes a graph operation on an initially empty graph. Each operation can be parameterized by a fixed number of values in the sequence and thus has at least length one but at most a finite number of values. Each action modifies the current graph by applying the graph operation on it. Many probabilistic graph models can be represented with two graph operations: adding a node and adding an edge. Models such as the Watts-Strogatz model additionally require the operation to remove nodes. All probabilistic graph models examined in our work can be learned by those three operations of adding a node, adding an edge or removing a node. The construction sequence of a graph can be seen as the transition sequence of a (finite) state machine, but with parameterized decisions in each state – making it a state machine with memory.

To describe a graph construction sequence we label those operations **N** (add node), **E** (add edge) and **R** (remove node). Technically the labels are encoded as natural numbers in the construction sequence along with all other information which are also natural numbers. One can easily extend the model to also learn to

---

[2] Like with all representations of graphs there is no *easy* canonical representation of a graph, otherwise the graph isomorphism problem could be solved in polynomial time.

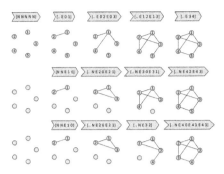

Fig. 1. Variants for obtaining construction sequences representing the same graph (under ismorphism). The first graph evolution shows the steps of an Erdős-Rényi model which at first generates five vertices and then adds edges in order of the vertex numbers with an unknown probability p. The second graph evolution shows a traversal with breadth-first-search (*bfs*) through the same graph and the third graph evolution shows a traversal with depth-first-search (*dfs*). Notice, that *dfs* comes up with a different vertex ordering than *bfs* at the end (vertices four and five are flipped).

remove edges or perform other graph operations but it has to be considered that this adds more state decisions to the model and thus more learnable parameters. While N needs no further parameters, E is followed by two parameters indicating the source and target vertex and R is followed by one parameter denoting the affected vertex which will be removed from the graph. Those three operations are sufficient for the most well-known probabilistic models of graphs such as the ones of Erdős-Rényi, Barabasi-Albert or Watts-Strogatz.

The null or empty graph is represented by the empty sequence [ ]. With the introduced labels, a graph with a single node is represented by [N] and a graph with two connected nodes with [N N E 0 1]. The representation encodes undirected graphs if not otherwise stated. For a directed graph with two edges between two nodes the sequence extends to [N N E 0 1 E 1 0].

We consider three variants through which we obtain construction sequences of graphs: firstly, through the **construction process** of the particular probabilistic model, secondly through a breadth-first-search **traversal** of any given graph, and thirdly through a depth-first-search traversal of any given graph.

Construction Process. Given a probabilistic model for graphs – such as the Erdős-Rényi model with a finite number of vertices – one can follow the algorithmic rules to build a construction sequence for each draw from the model. If the model starts with an initial number of n_{v_0} vertices the construction sequence starts with $[N] * n_{v_0}$ – which we understand as repeating the sequence of contained operations repeated n_{v_0} times. In the appendix we provide peusodcode for generating construction sequences following the rules of the probabilistic model of Barabasi-Albert.

Graph Traversal. In application cases we usually do not know the underlying process used to come up with the observed graphs. Thus, we need to transform graphs into construction sequences and we can do this by using common graph traversal algorithms. The nature of the chosen traversal algorithm has most likely a major impact on our subsequent deep graph generator model (DeepGG) as the decision functions for state transitions in DeepGG are learned based on exactly those exemplary steps.

4   Deep Graph Generator

We follow the sequential and auto-regressive generation model "Deep Generative Models of Graphs" (DGMG) of Li et al. [19] to learn decisions from construction sequences based on a representation of the current graph state. Our generative model – which we will refer to as *DeepGG* – has three major differences to DGMG: (1) we use a more relaxed notion of a finite state machine in which the model can learn to add edges from a source vertex at any step and not just at the point in which the source vertex was added to the graph, and (2) to avoid exploding losses we reduce the negative log-likelihood loss from choosing a source or target vertex in a growing graph by dividing it with the logarithmic number of vertices at that moment, and (3) we describe the possibility to add another state to also learn to remove vertices from the graph, which is a necessary step to learn probabilistic graph models such as the Watts-Strogatz model.

The essence of learning categorical decisions for the state transitions lies in the representational power of its memory. Memory refers to a set of real-valued vectors (embeddings) associated with a graph. During inference steps, a graph and associated embeddings are initialized and updated. We use the message passing framework to learn embeddings of vertices and edges to combine them to an graph embedding. This graph embedding and possibly a context embedding of a vertex are used to learn a transition function for states.

For a graph $G = (V, E)$ with vertices $v \in V$ and edges $e \in E = \{(s, t) \in V \times V \mid s$ has edge to $t\}$ we have embeddings $\boldsymbol{h}_v \in \mathbb{R}^{H_v}$ and $\boldsymbol{h}_e \in \mathbb{R}^{H_e}$ for hyperparameters $H_v, H_e \in \mathbb{N}^+$ for which we chose $H_v = H_e = 16$ in accordance with [19]. The number of vertices is given as $n_v = |V|$. The graph embedding is denoted as $\boldsymbol{h}_g \in \mathbb{R}^{H_g}$ with $H_g \in \mathbb{N}^+$ for which we chose $H_g = 2 \cdot H_v$. For an empty graph we set $\boldsymbol{h}_g = (0, \ldots, 0)$ (a zero vector). Like every construction sequence as depicted in Fig. 1 *DeepGG* starts with an empty graph and iteratively adds edges or vertices.

Initializing Vertices and Edges. Like in DGMG [19, 4.1] we use a simple differentiable model such as a Multi-Layer Perceptron (MLP) to learn one initialization function for vertices and one for edges. Each time *DeepGG* adds a vertex v_{new} or an edge e_{new} an embedding for it is initialized. While the empty graph is initialized with a zero vector, embeddings for v_{new} or e_{new} can be initialized from a learnable function based on the current memory state – the graph embedding $\boldsymbol{h}_g$. We call this initialization functions $f_{init,v}$ and $f_{init,e}$, respectively:

$$f_{init,v} : \mathbb{R}^{H_g} \rightarrow \mathbb{R}^{H_v}$$

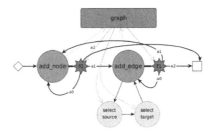

Fig. 2. *DeepGG* is a sequential generative model based on the notion of a state machine with memory. As we are generating a graph step by step, the memory in our case consists of a graph structure with node and graph embeddings on which message passing updates are performed. The figure shows two states (dark circles) *add_node* and *add_edge* with possible state transitions prefixed with "*a*" between those states. The lighter circles depict sub-states which can read from memory to derive a categorical decision and contribute loss to the overall end-to-end model. Operations (or actions) from the construction sequence control which decision a state has to take given the current memory.

In case of a MLP with non-linear activation function σ this could be a function mapping a graph representation $\boldsymbol{h}_g \in \mathbb{R}^{H_g}$ to $\sigma\left(W_{init,v} \cdot \boldsymbol{h}_g + b_{init,v}\right)$. Equivalently we define $f_{init,e} : (\mathbb{R}^{H_v}, \mathbb{R}^{H_v}) \rightarrow \mathbb{R}^{H_e}$ with $(\boldsymbol{h}_s, \boldsymbol{h}_t) \in \mathbb{R}^{H_v} \times \mathbb{R}^{H_v} \mapsto \sigma\left(W_{init,e} \cdot (\boldsymbol{h}_s \oplus \boldsymbol{h}_t) + b_{init,e}\right)$. The learnable models $f_{init,v}$ and $f_{init,e}$ are often called sub-modules. Parameters of $f_{init,v}$ and $f_{init,e}$ such as $W_{init,v}$, $b_{init,v}$, $W_{init,e}$ and $b_{init,e}$ are then learnable parameters of *DeepGG* and their dimensions can be easily inferred by definition of our parameter choices.

Deep State Decisions. We identify a state with index $\kappa \in \mathbb{N}$ as s_κ. Its transition decision function draws from a categorical distribution based on an embedding vector which is either a graph embedding $\boldsymbol{h}_g$, a composition of vertex embeddings $\boldsymbol{h}_v$ or a mixture of both. Therefore, its input dimension is denoted with H_{s_κ} and for each state it has to be described how to aggregate information from the memory to the particular input embedding from which the decision is derived. The decision function f_{s_κ} is given as

$$f_{s_\kappa} : \mathbb{R}^{H_{s_\kappa}} \rightarrow \{1, \dots, n_{s_\kappa}\}$$

in which n_{s_κ} is the number of possible categorical actions for that state. During learning, the cross-entropy loss of this state decision and the observed action from the construction sequence contributes to the overall optimization objective.

A critical part of sequential state models such as *DGMG* and *DeepGG* besides their state transition decisions are additional objectives to learn making a choice from a growing space – such as choosing a target vertex from a growing graph. While *DGMG* makes only target vertex decisions from the recently added vertex, *DeepGG* makes two decisions when adding an edge to the graph: one for a source and one for a target vertex. This makes the model more generic and facilitates to more precisely follow a possibly underlying construction rule. For example, in the Erdős-Rényi model first n_v vertices are created and then edges are "activated" based on a probability and in order of their enumeration. *DGMG* would have arguably struggles learning from construction sequences following this process but most likely could learn from this distribution of graphs when traversing them with *bfs* or *dfs*. On the other hand, more decisions with growing choices also increases the number of learnable parameters and adds an additional objective. We compensate for exploding losses which we observed in a first version of *DeepGG* by dividing the cross-entropy loss with the logarithm of possible vertex choices – which will arguably also penalize early wrong choices over wrong choices made later on a large graph. For one vertex choice $\delta \in \mathbb{N}$ as c_δ we have a categorical choice based on the current graph state given as:

$$f_{c_\delta} : \mathbb{R}^{H_{c_\delta}} \to \{1, \ldots, n_v\}$$

Note, that with a growing graph as memory during the generation process n_v grows linearly. When adding edges, we used two vertex choice functions f_{c_1} and f_{c_2} which can be seen in Fig. 2 as *select source* and *select target*. For the memory readout we chose $H_{c_\delta} = H_g + H_v + H_v$ for each vertex v under consideration and used the current graph embedding $\boldsymbol{h}_g$, the vertex embedding $\boldsymbol{h}_v$ and an additional contextual vertex v_c embedding $\boldsymbol{h}_{v_c}$.

Equivalently to the initialisation functions for vertices and edges above, we chose single-layered MLPs as differentiable and learnable functions for all f_{s_κ} and f_{c_δ}.

Memory Update. In each step of a construction sequence *DeepGG* and *DGMG* compute a graph embedding based on the current vertex embeddings in memory. While *DGMG* aggregate a graph embedding with a "gated sum $R(\boldsymbol{h}_v, G)$" *DeepGG* uses a gated vertex embedding in conjunction with a graph convolution [14] which is then reduced to its mean. For the gated vertex embedding we use a sub-module f_{reduc}:

$$f_{reduc} : \mathbb{R}^{H_v} \to \mathbb{R}^{H_r}, \boldsymbol{h}_v \mapsto \sigma\left(W_{reduc} \cdot \boldsymbol{h}_v + b_{reduc}\right)$$

for which we chose $H_r = 7$ which then specifies the feature dimensions of the subsequent graph convolution. We chose the mean instead of the sum as in *DGMG* because we observed exploding sums for resulting graph embeddings. Given the adjacency matrix $A \in \mathbb{R}^{n_v \times n_v}$ of a graph and input features of dimension $\mathbb{R}^{d_{in}}$ a graph convolution computes $f_{conv} : \mathbb{R}^{n_v \times d_{in}} \to \mathbb{R}^{n_v \times d_{out}}$.

$$f_{conv}(H^{(l)}, A) = \sigma\left(D^{-\frac{1}{2}} \hat{A} D^{-\frac{1}{2}} H^{(l)} W^{(l)}\right)$$

with $\hat{A} = A + I$ (see [14] for details). We used one single graph convolution f_{conv} with reduced vertex representations for each vertex in graph G, making up $H^{(l)}$. A is the graphs adjacency matrix.

When the current graph G (the memory) is modified, we perform an update step based on the message passing framework [9] to update vertex representations. The graph propagation (update) step in *DeepGG* is kept equivalent to *DGMG*. Two propagation rounds ν_{rounds} of gated recurrent units are used and vertex embeddings are updated as illustrated in [19, figure 2].

Training Objective. The model draws from categorical distributions to decide on state transitions or choosing vertices as source or target for an edge. We use a cross-entropy loss on f_{s_κ} and f_{c_δ} and minimize the joint negative log-likelihood with stochastic gradient descent. The learning rate is $\eta = 0.0001$, we use $\nu_{epochs} = 8$ number of epochs, $\nu_{rounds} = 2$ rounds of propagations and $\nu_{n_{v\_max}} = 150$ as a hard threshold for generating a maximum number of vertices and stopping the generative process. During generative inference a minimum value $\nu_{n_{v\_min}}$ can be specified to restrain the state machine from transitioning to a halting state before reaching a lower bound in the number of vertices.

5   Experiments

Learning distributions of graphs is not only difficult because of the complexity of the combinatorial nature of graphs but also difficult to assess properly. Notably, due to the graph isomorphism problem we possibly require a computational expensive effort to compare two sets of graphs for overlapping isomorphic graphs. Although our interest is not to obtain isomorphic graphs, we are faced with this or related complex problems when formulating a notion of equivalence classes of graphs. Because we are interested in reproducing certain properties of a hidden distribution of graphs we need to investigate on if and which of those properties can statistically significantly be reproduced.

We computed 69 total *DeepGG* instances of which 24 instances have been trained on datasets with bfs-traversal, 39 with dfs-traversal and six based on the construction process of the underlying probabilistic model. 24 instances have been computed with datasets based on the Erdős-Rényi model, 26 instances on the Barabasi-Albert model and 19 on the Watts-Strogatz model. Across all computations we used the same objective, the same learning rate, the same number of epochs and other hyperparameters as stated in Sect. 4. For each computation instance we sampled new sets of graphs of size $n_v = 50$ from the ER-model with $p = 0.2$, from the WS-model with $k = 10, p = 0.2$ and from the BA-model with $m = 3$.

We argue, that it is important to investigate on multiple levels of distributions of graph properties to constitute that a certain hidden process could be reflected. In network science, complex networks are compared based on the degree distribution, clustering coefficient [24] or on the average path length distribution (or similar aggregated statistics of the underlying properties) (Fig. 3).

Degree Distribution. The three considered probabilistic graph models have distinct degree distributions. Barabasi-Albert is known to have a scale-free degree distribution. Erdős-Rényi has a binomial distribution $p_k \sim B(n_v, ER_p)$ which in our case gives $E(p_k) = 10$. The degree distribution of Watts-Strogatz graphs are similar to random graphs in shape. For selected *DeepGG* instances we find that they are able to reproduce the degree distribution very closely. However, we

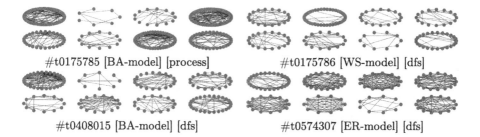

#t0175785 [BA-model] [process]   #t0175786 [WS-model] [dfs]

#t0408015 [BA-model] [dfs]   #t0574307 [ER-model] [dfs]

Fig. 3. Exemplary samples from computed *DeepGG* instances. The id is a shortened computation timestamp. Layouts are circular to provide a visual impression of the density. The original distribution is based on samples from either an Erdős-Rényi, a Watts-Strogatz or a Barabasi-Albert probabilistic model. Used traversal method are breadth-first-search (bfs), depth-first-search (dfs) or based on the process of the model as described in Sect. 3.

also encounter instances which follow a scale-free distribution when trained on ER-models. Similar to *DGMG* we find a close relationship to the degree distribution of scale-free networks but do not observe the same behaviour for WS-graphs.

Average Path Length Distribution. We observe a mean of 1.75 for the distribution of average path lengths of *DeepGG* learned on ER-graphs. This observed mean of generated graphs indeed gets close to the mean in the dataset of 1.91. According to the analytic form given by [8] it must be $l_{ER} = \frac{ln(n_v)-\gamma}{ln(p \cdot n_v)} + \frac{1}{2}$ with γ being the Euler-Mascheroni constant. We have $l_{ER} = \frac{ln(50)-\gamma}{ln(0.2 \cdot 50)} + \frac{1}{2} \approx 1.95$. For Barabasi-Albert graphs the analytical average path length is $l_{BA} = \frac{ln(n_v)-ln(m/2)-1-\gamma}{ln(ln(N))+ln(m/2)} + \frac{3}{2}$ for which we get $l_{BA} \approx 2.59$. In our dataset of BA-graphs we observe an averaged average shortest path length of 2.29 while *DeepGG* resembles 2.61, again with a high standard deviation of 1.50.

Computation Times. Overall the computation time over training datasets of 1,000 graph samples with each large construction sequences has been very high. We used GPU acceleration but did not perform batching. The average computation time was roughly 60 h with a minimum of 20 h and a maximum of 120 h. Instances trained on BA-graphs took only 40 h on average with a low standard deviation while WS-graphs took 65 h and ER-graphs over 70 h on average. We also observed significantly different distribution between computation times when using dfs- or bfs-traversal (Fig. 4).

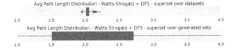

Fig. 4. For multiple instances of *DeepGG* trained on Watts-Strogatz graphs we computed the average path length of each of the 1,000 graphs used for training for both bfs- and dfs-traversal. Equivalently, we computed the average path length of each generated graph from the model (on average 171 for the BFS-instances and 170 for the DFS-instances). Seven *DeepGG* instances have been trained on bfs-traversals, twelve on dfs-traversals. Watts-Strogatz+BFS constitute a superset in which we generated 1,199 graphs, Watts-Strogatz+DFS a superset in which we computed 2,034 graphs. As to no surprise the average path length distributions for both supersets over the datasets are visually equivalent. However, we have to ascertain that the average path length distributions for generated graphs can not only be matched its dataset but also have to point out that the resulting superset distribution for different traversal choices for construction sequences differs significantly.

5.1 Findings in Our Experiments

First of all, we do find *DeepGG* instances which generate new graphs with property distributions close to the underlying probabilistic models. We even manage to generate larger graphs than reported by Li et al. of up to a few hundred vertices, although the recently published *GRAN* reportedly achieves to generate several thousand of vertices. Looking at single instances visually one could easily think that *DeepGG* (or *DGMG*) instances learn meaningful distributions of graphs. Repeated experiments and reasoning from the nature of both *DeepGG* and *DGMG*, however, leads us to the conjecture that the models are biased towards scale-free random graphs and can not repeatedly resemble the behaviour of the targeted probabilistic model – if not supervised carefully.

The choice of representation of graphs has a significant impact on learning distributions over graphs as already stated in [26] or [20]. In case of our chosen representation with construction sequences we have a huge number of possible permutations over a random ordering of vertices for a single graph. We investigated on three variants of canonical traversal methods over random orderings of vertices and observed different resulting distributions for average shortest path lengths and vertex degrees. For depth-first-search we observe a higher variance in computation times than for breadth-first-search. The difference in the mean of their computation times could be a result to the low number of overall computed instances over a rather high number of hyperparameter choices. We further observe a high computation time for ER-models over WS-models and BA-models.

Especially the message passing component to obtain vertex and graph embeddings is a computational expensive part of the model and we see possibilities for improvement there. The growing number of vertices further leads to a growing categorical choice space for f_{c_δ} which we identify as an essential step towards learning other degree distributions than the distribution of a BA-model. We see a possibility of "almost random" transitions through the state machine which might result in the generation of scale-free random networks and we will investigate further in this decision process.

6   Conclusion

We described a generative model for learning distributions of graph as a generalization of the model given in [19]. The generalization made it possible to learn distributions of graphs based on the graph construction process of the *Watts-Strogatz* model and we are confident that *DeepGG* reduced bias towards scale-free graphs. Our experiments showed, that often an underlying construction process could not be learned although single instances showed promising results – visually and based on graph property distributions. We emphasize that generative models of graphs need to be evaluated on multiple levels to reach statistical significant evidence and focussed on providing such experimental setups.

DeepGG was rendered under the perspective of a *deep state machine*, which can be seen as a state machine with learnable transitions and a memory. The decision process of such a state machine can be analysed more transparently as compared to other common end-to-end models.

We hope to contribute valuable insights for learning distributions of graphs and expect to (1) further investigate generative models of graphs and (2) apply the recently developed models in promising domains.

Acknowledgements. We thank Jörg Schlötterer for valuable discussions during the time of this research and everyone who contributed valuable feedback, including our reviewers.

References

1. Albert, R., Barabasi, A.L.: Statistical mechanics of complex networks. Rev. Mod. Phys. **74**(1), 47 (2002)
2. Alibaba: Euler: a distributed graph deep learning framework (2019). https://github.com/alibaba/euler. Accessed 12 May 2020
3. Bjerrum, E.J., Sattarov, B.: Improving chemical autoencoder latent space and molecular de novo generation diversity with heteroencoders. Biomolecules **8**(4), 131 (2018)
4. Bjerrum, E.J., Threlfall, R.: Molecular generation with recurrent neural networks (rnns). arXiv preprint arXiv:1705.04612 (2017)
5. Dai, H., Dai, B., Song, L.: Discriminative embeddings of latent variable models for structured data. In: International Conference on Machine Learning, pp. 2702–2711 (2016)
6. Data61, C.: Stellargraph machine learning library. https://github.com/stellargraph/stellargraph (2018)
7. Erdos, P.: On random graphs. Publicationes mathematicae **6**, 290–297 (1959)
8. Fronczak, A., Fronczak, P., Hołyst, J.A.: Average path length in random networks. Phys. Rev. E **70**(5), 056110 (2004)

9. Gilmer, J., Schoenholz, S.S., Riley, P.F., Vinyals, O., Dahl, G.E.: Neural message passing for quantum chemistry. In: Proceedings of the 34th International Conference on Machine Learning, vol. 70, pp. 1263–1272. JMLR. org (2017)

10. Gori, M., Monfardini, G., Scarselli, F.: A new model for learning in graph domains. In: Proceedings of 2005 IEEE International Joint Conference on Neural Networks, 2005, vol. 2, pp. 729–734. IEEE (2005)

11. Grover, A., Zweig, A., Ermon, S.: Graphite: iterative generative modeling of graphs. arXiv preprint arXiv:1803.10459 (2018)

12. Gupta, A., Müller, A.T., Huisman, B.J., Fuchs, J.A., Schneider, P., Schneider, G.: Generative recurrent networks for de novo drug design. Mol. Inform. **37**(1–2), 1700111 (2018)

13. Jin, W., Barzilay, R., Jaakkola, T.: Junction tree variational autoencoder for molecular graph generation. arXiv preprint arXiv:1802.04364 (2018)

14. Kipf, T.N., Welling, M.: Semi-supervised classification with graph convolutional networks. arXiv preprint arXiv:1609.02907 (2016)

15. Kleinberg, J.M.: Navigation in a small world. Nature **406**(6798), 845 (2000)

16. Leskovec, J., Chakrabarti, D., Kleinberg, J., Faloutsos, C., Ghahramani, Z.: Kronecker graphs: an approach to modeling networks. J. Mach. Learn. Res. **11**, 985–1042 (2010)

17. Leskovec, J., Faloutsos, C.: Scalable modeling of real graphs using kronecker multiplication. In: Proceedings of the 24th International Conference on Machine Learning, pp. 497–504 (2007)

18. Li, X., Yan, X., Gu, Q., Zhou, H., Wu, D., Xu, J.: Deepchemstable: chemical stability prediction with an attention-based graph convolution network. J. Chem. Inf. Model. **59**(3), 1044–1049 (2019)

19. Li, Y., Vinyals, O., Dyer, C., Pascanu, R., Battaglia, P.: Learning deep generative models of graphs. arXiv preprint arXiv:1803.03324 (2018)

20. Liao, R., et al.: Efficient graph generation with graph recurrent attention networks. In: Advances in Neural Information Processing Systems, pp. 4257–4267 (2019)

21. Wang, H., et al.: GraphGAN: graph representation learning with generative adversarial nets. In: Thirty-Second AAAI Conference on Artificial Intelligence (2018)

22. Wang, M., et al.: Deep graph library: towards efficient and scalable deep learning on graphs. In: ICLR Workshop on Representation Learning on Graphs and Manifolds (2019). https://arxiv.org/abs/1909.01315

23. Wasserman, S., Pattison, P.: Logit models and logistic regressions for social networks: I. An introduction to Markov graphs andp. Psychometrika **61**(3), 401–425 (1996)

24. Watts, D.J., Strogatz, S.H.: Collective dynamics of 'small-world' networks. Nature **393**(6684), 440 (1998)

25. You, J., Liu, B., Ying, Z., Pande, V., Leskovec, J.: Graph convolutional policy network for goal-directed molecular graph generation. In: Advances in Neural Information Processing Systems, pp. 6410–6421 (2018)

26. You, J., Ying, R., Ren, X., Hamilton, W.L., Leskovec, J.: GraphRNN: generating realistic graphs with deep auto-regressive models. arXiv preprint arXiv:1802.08773 (2018)

SINr: Fast Computing of Sparse Interpretable Node Representations is not a Sin!

Thibault Prouteau[1]([✉])(iD), Victor Connes[2](iD), Nicolas Dugué[1](iD),
Anthony Perez[3], Jean-Charles Lamirel[4](iD), Nathalie Camelin[1](iD),
and Sylvain Meignier[1](iD)

[1] Laboratoire d'Informatique de l'Université du Mans, LIUM, EA 4023,
Le Mans Université, Le Mans, France
thibault.prouteau@univ-lemans.fr
[2] Laboratoire des Sciences du Numérique de Nantes, Université de Nantes,
Nantes, France
victor.connes@univ-nantes.fr
[3] INSA Centre Val de Loire, LIFO EA 4022, Univ. Orléans,
45067 Orléans, France
anthony.perez@univ-orleans.fr
[4] LORIA, Equipe Synalp, Université de Strasbourg, Strasbourg, France
lamirel@loria.fr

Abstract. While graph embedding aims at learning low-dimensional representations of nodes encompassing the graph topology, word embedding focus on learning word vectors that encode semantic properties of the vocabulary. The first finds applications on tasks such as link prediction and node classification while the latter is systematically considered in natural language processing. Most of the time, graph and word embeddings are considered on their own as distinct tasks. However, word co-occurrence matrices, widely used to extract word embeddings, can be seen as graphs. Furthermore, most network embedding techniques rely either on a word embedding methodology (Word2vec) or on matrix factorization, also widely used for word embedding. These methods are usually computationally expensive, parameter dependant and the dimensions of the embedding space are not interpretable. To circumvent these issues, we introduce the Lower Dimension Bipartite Graphs Framework (LDBGF) which takes advantage of the fact that all graphs can be described as bipartite graphs, even in the case of textual data. This underlying bipartite structure may be explicit, like in coauthor networks. However, with LDBGF, we focus on uncovering *latent* bipartite structures, lying for instance in social or word co-occurrence networks, and especially such structures providing conciser and interpretable representations of the graph at hand. We further propose SINr, an efficient implementation of the LDBGF approach that extracts Sparse Interpretable Node Representations using community structure to approximate the underlying bipartite structure. In the case of graph embedding, our near-linear time method is the fastest of our benchmark, parameter-free and provides state-of-the-art results on the classical link prediction task. We also show that

P. H. Abreu et al. (Eds.): IDA 2021, LNCS 12695, pp. 325–337, 2021.
https://doi.org/10.1007/978-3-030-74251-5_26

low-dimensional vectors can be derived from `SINr` using singular value decomposition. In the case of word embedding, our approach proves to be very efficient considering the classical similarity evaluation.

1   Introduction

The aim of *graph embedding* is to learn representations of nodes encompassing the structural properties of the network. Such representations (or *embedding vectors*) can then be processed in reduced time and space and proved to be useful to deal with problems such as link prediction [14] and node classification [2].

Among the state-of-the art embedding methods, techniques adapting the `Word2vec` (for semantic representations of words) framework [15] with random walks have been extensively studied [19,20]. Matrix factorization approaches [1, 6,17] were also widely considered, some of them also inspired by the `GloVe` word embedding technique [5]. As one can see, natural language processing (NLP) literature influenced a lot the field of graph embedding, providing a solid base on which to build. Indeed, word embedding also aims to provide dense continuous representations, those being used as inputs of NLP systems for opinion mining, translation or text categorization for instance.

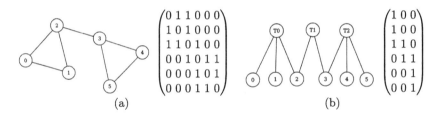

(a)   (b)

Fig. 1. Illustrating the `LDBGF`: (a) a toy graph and its adjacency matrix (b) a low-dimensional bipartite graph representation. The adjacency matrix of the $\perp$ nodes (rows) from the toy graphs are represented with their links to the $\top$ nodes (columns). The resulting adjacency matrix is smaller and is actually an interpretable embedding: dimensions represent the connectivity to $\top$ nodes which are tangible entities.

Our Approach. To the best of our knowledge, despite the connections between these tasks, graph and word embedding are usually considered as distinct tasks. In this paper, we tackle both of these tasks, considering that word co-occurrence matrices extracted from substantial text corpora can also be seen as graphs. We thus reduce the task of learning word embedding to a graph embedding problem and provide a unified approach for both tasks. Furthermore, in all aforementioned graph embedding works, authors mainly focus on getting efficient and low-dimensional dense vectors, somehow neglecting the time complexity and the interpretability of the results. Meanwhile, interpretability and green computing are major issues for the machine learning field. Taking into account these considerations, we introduce the Lower Dimension Bipartite Graphs Framework (LDBGF), a framework based on low-dimensional bipartite representations of graphs to compute sparse interpretable vectors for words and nodes.

Guillaume and Latapy [8] showed that all complex networks can be represented by a bipartite structure. Coauthoring networks are by nature represented as a bipartite graph $G = (\top, \bot, E)$ where $\top$ corresponds to the set of papers and $\bot$ to the set of authors, each author being connected to papers they co-signed. The unipartite coauthoring network can thus be retrieved by *projecting* the bipartite graph, *i.e.* by adding an edge between any two authors linked to the same paper. When considering social networks, one can reasonably assume that there is a latent bipartite structure [8]: people are connected through their school, family, firm, *etc.*. In the case of word co-occurrence networks extracted from large corpora, words are connected by syntactic rules, but also thematic or semantic fields. With LDBGF, we assume that we can uncover low-dimensional latent bipartite structures for real networks, representing them in a concise way (Fig. 1). In such a case, the graph embedding space is interpretable: nodes are represented by their connectivity to the $\top$-nodes uncovered that are tangible graph objects (Fig. 1(b)). Guillaume and Latapy [8] use cliques in the $\top$-part of the bipartite graph to encode relations between nodes. The problem considered can thus be seen as a CLIQUE COVERING problem [8]: given a network, compute a set of cliques such that each edge belongs to at least one clique (ensuring that the $\bot$-projection yields the original network). However, LDBGF enforces the number of cliques to be as small as possible in order to represent the original graph with as few $\top$-nodes as possible, and thus get a lower-dimensional embedding space. For instance, considering each edge as a clique would yield too many cliques. Thus, LDBGF is related to MINIMUM CLIQUE COVERING NUMBER, a classical NP-Hard problem [16]. Hence, one needs heuristics to obtain a satisfying covering in a reasonable time.

Our Contribution. In line with the LDBGF philosophy, we introduce the SINr[1] (SPARSE INTERPRETABLE NODE REPRESENTATIONS) method that derives sparse and interpretable word and graph embedding vectors in near-linear time, thus making a parsimonious usage of CPU resources. The main idea of SINr is to use the community structure to provide an approximate solution to the MINIMUM CLIQUE COVERING problem. Indeed, communities can be seen as clique relaxations that can be uncovered very efficiently [3], allowing SINr to run faster than the other graph embedding approaches. Basing our work on the hypothesis that nodes with similar connectivity to the communities are similar, we compute our bipartite approximation directly from community structure. This is why SINr vectors are sparse and interpretable: each dimension of the embedding vector represents the node connectivity to a community, and the number of dimensions is thus linear in the number of communities. Furthermore, if low-dimensional vectors are required, our SINr vectors can be projected in a lower-dimensional space using standard dimension reduction techniques whilst preserving their efficiency.

---

[1] https://www.github.com/anthonimes/SINr.

Outline. We first describe our SINr embedding technique (Sect. 2), and how it can be applied to deal with word and graph embeddings. We then detail the experimental setup (Sect. 3), considering graph and textual datasets, and detailing graph and word embedding approaches we compare to. We finally present the very encouraging experimental results on the classical link prediction task for graph embedding, and on the similarity task for word embedding (Sect. 4). We also demonstrate the lower computational cost of SINr when compared to the other graph embedding methods we consider.

2   SINr: Algorithmic Framework

SINr is a near-linear time implementation of LDBGF. Since communities can be seen as cliques relaxations [3], instead of relying on cliques to compute a latent bipartite structure (Fig. 2(b)), SINr relies on communities which are faster to compute. However, unlike in cliques, nodes connected to a community may not be connected to the whole community. To cope with this problem, we use a recent work by a subset of the same authors, allowing to account for the nodes connectivity to the community structure, the Node F-Measure framework [7]. The aim of our method is to produce embedding vectors where nodes with a similar behaviour towards the community structure of the network lie close in the embedding space. Thus, the approach of SINr actually consists in two steps: the first one is detecting the p communities of the network at hand (Sect. 2.1). The second, described Sect. 2.2, is computing the Node Predominance and Node Recall of each node for every community (Fig. 2(c)). This allows to obtain a $2p$ embedding vector for each node (Fig. 2(d)). This explains why SINr leads to sparse and interpretable vectors: dimensions of the embedding space are not abstract but community-related. In the remaining of this section, we describe further the two steps of SINr.

2.1   First Step: Community Detection Algorithms

We consider (un)directed and (un)weighted graphs $G = (V, E, W)$ with V the set of vertices, E the set of edges and W the weights attached to the edges. The neighbourhood of a vertex $v \in V$ is denoted by $N(v)$, and we let $d(v) = \sum_{u \in N(v)} W_{u,v}$.

The community structure of G is a *partition* $\mathcal{C} = \{C_1, \ldots, C_p\}$ of V such that each subgraph $G[C_i]$ is densely connected, while the density between C_i and C_j is low, $1 \leqslant i < j \leqslant p$. To measure the quality of such a partition, Girvan and Newman [3] introduced the modularity $Q_{\mathcal{C}}$:

$$Q_{\mathcal{C}} = \frac{1}{2m} \cdot \sum_{i,j} \left[A_{ij} - \frac{d_i \cdot d_j}{2m} \right] \cdot \delta(C_i, C_j) \tag{1}$$

where A_{ij} denotes the existence (or weight) of edge ij, and the δ-function $\delta(u, v)$ is 1 if $u = v$ and 0 otherwise. Computing a partition which maximizes modularity is NP-Hard [4] but there exist community detection algorithms which implement heuristics to maximize modularity, such as the extensively used Louvain algorithm [3].

Community structure was already successfully considered to extract graph embedding vectors: Bhowmick et al. [2] used a projection of the hierarchical community tree to obtain the network embeddings. However, our SINr approach relies directly on the community structure, defining the embedding space using the connectivity to the communities. We considered using various algorithms to detect the communities and thus ran several tests using Label Propagation [21] (LP), Infomap, and Louvain algorithms. Both LP and Louvain run fast (near-linear time), while Infomap is slower but known to perform better. Our experiments have shown that the graph embeddings extracted using Louvain with the SINr methodology perform better for link prediction while the word embeddings extracted with LP perform better on words similarity (Sect. 4).

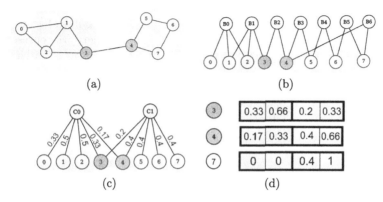

(a)   (b)

(c)   (d)

Fig. 2. SINr: (a) Toy example with oval shapes representing communities (b) Latent bipartite structure using maximum cliques (c) Approximation of such a structure using detected communities and Node predominance (d) SINr vectors with Node predominance and Node recall for both communities.

2.2 Second Step: Node Predominance and Node Recall

The Node F-measure framework introduced in [7] encompasses interesting topological properties such as centrality and community roles. It is based on **Node Predominance** (NP) and **Node Recall** (NR). Node Predominance (Eq. 2) is used to characterize the node's connectivity towards its community: the higher it is, the more a node is connected to its community. Node Recall (Eq. 3) is used to evaluate the connectivity of a node with nodes outside its community: the weaker it is, the more the node is connected to the outside. Considering $\mathcal{C} = \{C_1, \ldots, C_p\}$, and $1 \leqslant i \leqslant p$, we define NP and NR for each node u as:

$$\text{NP}_i(u) = \frac{d_{C_i}(u)}{d_{C_i}} \qquad (2) \qquad \qquad \text{NR}_i(u) = \frac{d_{C_i}(u)}{d(u)} \qquad (3)$$

where $d_{C_i}(u)$ is the degree of node u in C_i, $i.e.$ $d_{C_i}(u) = |\{uv \in E \mid v \in C_i\}|$, and d_{C_i} is the number of edges incident to vertices in community C_i.

In this work, we consider NP and NR for a given node to any community of a partition. We thus compute $2p$-dimensional embeddings (Fig. 2(d)) that encompass connectivity of the nodes towards the network's communities.

3   Experimental Setup

3.1   Datasets

Networks Considered for Graph Embedding. To conduct our experiments we use several well-known datasets from different fields described by their size ($n = |V|$ and $m = |E|$). For the sake of our experiments, we extract the largest connected component of each graph and consider them undirected.

(a) Citeseer [13] (Cts, $n = 3,312$ and $m = 4,660$) and Cora [13] ($n = 2,708$ and $m = 5,278$) are networks of citations of scientific publications.
(b) Email-eu [11] (Eu, $n = 1,005$ and $m = 16,706$) is a network representing a sender-receiver relationship w.r.t. e-mails within European research institution.
(c) arXiv [9] ($n = 18,771$ and $m = 198,050$) covers scientific collaborations between authors of papers submitted in the Astrophysics category.
(d) Facebook (Fb, $n = 63,731$ and $m = 817,035$) represents friendship data of Facebook users.

Corpora Considered for Word Embedding. Our experiments on word embedding span two corpora. For each corpus[2], words with fewer than four occurrences and stop words (words without semantic interest, $e.g.$ the, at, which) are removed. Furthermore, both corpora are lemmatized using SpaCy.

(a) text8 is made of the first 100MB of Wikipedia's March 2006 dump. After preprocessing, the corpus contains $6,039,538$ tokens for a vocabulary of $73,860$ words.
(b) OANC, the *Open American National Corpus* is a 15-million-word corpus of written and spoken American English. After preprocessing, the number of tokens of this corpus is $6,016,207$ for a vocabulary of $53,282$ words.

3.2   Extracting Word Co-occurrence Networks for Textual Corpora

When dealing with textual data, the first step is to extract a word co-occurrence network from the corpora at hand. To build this graph, in a similar way to other textual word embedding methods [12,18], we first compute the word co-occurrence matrix by applying a sliding context window to each sentence in the corpora. At the second step, in order to filter out the insignificant co-occurrences

---

[2] http://mattmahoney.net/dc/textdata.html and http://www.anc.org/data/oanc/.

from this matrix, we compute the *Pointwise Mutual Information* (PMI [12], Eq. 4) for each entry of the matrix, and set entries to 0 when the PMI value is negative. When PMI value is positive, the entry remains unchanged.

Let w_1, w_2 be two words, $p(w_1)$ the frequency of w_1 in the corpora and $p(w_1, w_2)$ the co-occurrence frequency of both w_1, w_2. The PMI is defined as follows:

$$\text{PMI}(w_1, w_2) = \log_2 \left(\frac{p(w_1, w_2)}{p(w_1)p(w_2)} \right) \tag{4}$$

The third step consists in building a weighted graph $G = (V, E, W)$ from the *filtered* matrix. The vertex set V represents words. The edge set E and the weights W attached to the edges represent the co-occurrences in the corpora: there is an edge between two vertices if these words co-occur significantly in the corpus, and the weight attached to the edge is the number of these co-occurrences.

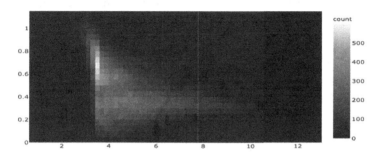

Fig. 3. Heatmap of the weighted degrees of the graph extracted on OANC after IPMI according to the weighted degrees before applying IPMI, abscissa in logarithmic scale.

The final step consists in applying a re-weighting scheme to the graph. According to our extensive experiments, such a process is necessary to extract relevant communities and thus word embeddings. We thus introduce our original IPMI (Iterative Pointwise Mutual Information) re-weighting scheme. Let E_{ord} be the edges (u, v) of E ordered from the highest to the lowest sum of its weighted degrees $d(u) + d(v)$. For each edge (u, v) ordered as in E_{ord}, we iteratively update $W_{u,v}'$ with the IPMI value:

$$\text{IPMI(u,v)} = \frac{W_{u,v}}{d(u)d(v)} \tag{5}$$

To illustrate the effect of the IPMI, we consider the graph extracted from the text8 corpus described Sect. 3. We plot the weighted degrees of the vertices of this graph after IPMI against the ones before IPMI. As one can see Fig. 3, the plot actually looks like an *inverse* function. Our experiments thus seem to show that it is important to considerably lower the weights of the hubs (nodes that are widely connected). Our hypothesis is that hubs represent very frequent words, which are more susceptible to be polysemous. It may thus be more relevant to detect communities based on more specific words by lowering the hubs influence before the community detection.

3.3 State-of-the-Art Algorithms

Graph Embedding. We use several state-of-the-art graph embedding techniques provided by the `karateclub` library [23] to compare with the results obtained by our method. We use the default implementation parameters and embedding vectors dimension number is always set to 128.

(a) `HOPE` [17] stands for *High-order proximity preserved embedding*. This approach uses generalized SVD to approximate proximity matrices such as the ones that can be obtained by using Katz or Adamic-Adar indexes. In our experiments, the proximity matrix used is the Common neighbours one.

(b) `Deepwalk` (`DW`) [19] is similar in spirit to the `Word2vec` Skip-gram approach [15]. Instead of computing Skip-gram on sentences, the authors compute it on paths given by random walks on the graph. The number of walks is fixed to 10, the walk length to 80 and the window size to 5.

(c) `Walklets` (`WL`) [20] is also based on random walks, but the authors introduce a sampling method improving the results. The parameters are the same as for `Deepwalk` except that the window size is 4.

We also ran experiments with `Diff2vec` [23], `GraRep` [6] and `Laplacian-EigenMaps` [1] but for the sake of concision, we do not report their results. Indeed, `GraRep` is similar to `Walklets` in spirit, and obtain similar results but it runs slower and requires much more memory. `LaplacianEigenmaps` and `Diff2vec` obtain poorer results than the other approaches.

Word Embedding. We compare to classical state-of-the-art methods but do not consider contextual word embeddings, since our work focuses on interpretability and parsimonious usage of computing resources. The implementations are detailed below. In all of them, the sliding context window is set to 5 words and the number of dimensions to 300.

(a) `Word2vec` (`W2V`) is one of the most popular methods to learn word embeddings [15]. We compute embeddings for each corpus using the `CBOW` architecture provided by `Gensim` [22].

(b) `GloVe` [18] stands for *Global Vectors for Word Representation* and aims at providing corpus-derived semantic models based on global word co-occurrence statistics. We use the `GloVe` implementation provided by the authors.

(c) `SVD2vec` is an implementation[3] of the approach described by Levy et al. [12] using *SVD* on a *PPMI* co-occurrence matrix to compute embeddings.

---

[3] https://git-lium.univ-lemans.fr/vpelloin/svd2vec

4 Experiments and Results

4.1 SINr is Fast: Complexity and Runtime

Given the community structure of a network, computing embeddings can be done in linear time since one only needs to parse the edges of the graphs to compute Node Predominance and Node Recall. As stated previously, we use Louvain's algorithm to compute graph embeddings, which is known to run in $O(m)$ time [2, 24]. For word embedding, we use Label propagation which is known to run in near-linear time, each propagation step running in $O(m)$ time and the algorithm converging in few steps. Altogether, the running time of our method is thus in $O(m)$. To conclude this section, we present the average time[4] (50 runs) needed to compute embeddings for SINr and graph embedding algorithms HOPE, Deepwalk and Walklets we compare to (see Sect. 3.3 for more details). As detailed Sect. 3.1, the Facebook graph contains $63,731$ vertices and $817,035$ edges. As one can see, our method is significantly faster than the other approaches.

Table 1. Average runtime in seconds (left) and CPU time taking into account parallelism (right)

	Cora	Eu	Cts	arXiv	Fb
SINr	**0.3/1.3**	**0.3/2**	**0.1/0.9**	**0.9/4**	**3/8**
HOPE	0.2/3	0.6/8	0.7/2	10/120	26/195
DW	24/36	13/18	20/30	264/378	336/422
WL	26/38	12/18	24/36	261/365	475/652

4.2 Graph Embedding: Link Prediction

Problem Description. Let $G = (V, E)$ be a simple undirected network. Let U denote the universal set containing $\frac{n(n-1)}{2}$ possible pairs of V and $\overline{E} = U \backslash E$ the set of non-edges of G. We consider link prediction as a binary classification problem where we assume that there are some missing links (or links that will appear later on) and we train a classifier to detect such links with high probability.

As in [17], we randomly separate the graph into a *training set* (containing 80% edges) and a *test set* containing the remaining edges. We train the embedding vectors on the training set, and then evaluate link prediction on the test set. Training is done using Xgboost and Logistic regression and the best results are kept in each case. For the sake of comparison, we consider the node representation algorithms detailed Sect. 3.3 with Hadamard product, as well as the following set of heuristic features which is proved to be efficient on the link prediction task (see [14]): Common Neighbours, Adamic Adar, Preferential Attachment, Jaccard index, Resource Allocation Index. The vector obtained from such features is referred to as the *heuristics* vector.

---

[4] With two Intel Xeon CPU E5-2660 2.20 GHz: 16 cores, 96 Go Ram.

Evaluation. We consider two evaluation procedures. In the first one, the test set is made of the 20% of existing edges augmented with the same number of negative examples sampled from $\overline{E}$. We run each test 50 times and present the averaged accuracy. SINr achieves the highest accuracy for most of the small datasets as one can see Table 2. On sizeable graphs, results are comparable to those of the other state-of-the-art approaches. On such graphs, the communities may be harder to detect, explaining the results. Furthermore, we can observe that results are still close to the best ones, even when applying SVD on SINr in order to get 20 dimensions. Our approach can thus provide both sparse interpretable and dense low-dimensional vectors.

Table 2. Accuracy on the link prediction task. SINr-SVD is 20-*d* SINr vectors obtained using *SVD*.

	SINr	SINr-SVD	Heuristics	DW	WL	HOPE
Cora	**0.83**	**0.83**	0.76	0.73	0.82	0.75
Eu	**0.88**	**0.88**	0.87	0.81	0.87	0.87
Cts	**0.88**	0.86	0.78	0.76	0.87	0.83
arXiv	0.92	0.90	**0.97**	0.92	0.96	0.92
Fb	0.91	0.89	**0.93**	0.86	0.92	0.90

Table 3. Number of communities p, modularity Q_C, and sparsity coefficient σ of the SINr vectors.

	p	Q_C	σ
Cora	23	0.80	0.94
Eu	6	0.41	0.44
Cts	33	0.85	0.96
arXiv	28	0.62	0.87
Fb	73	0.62	0.96

In our second evaluation procedure, we consider a test set with many more negative examples. Due to the high cardinality of the set $\overline{E}$, we randomly sample about 1% of such pairs for evaluation on most graphs, except for Facebook where we sample 0.1%. We run each test 50 times and present the averaged precision@k. The latter measures the fraction of node pairs in the top-k most probable pairs (according to our classifier) corresponding to an actual edge in the network. Figure 4 presents representative results. For most datasets introduced Sect. 3.1, experiments highlight the relevance of our method that competes with the state-of-the art approaches. On Email-eu, the lower modularity of the partitions returned (Table 3) degrades the performances of our approach. Our method obtains these encouraging results being by far the fastest (Table 1).

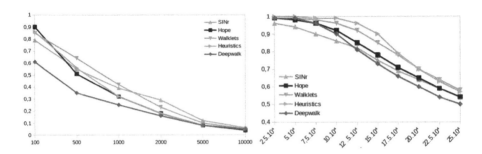

Fig. 4. precision@k, the proportion among the k most probable pairs that are edges according to the classifier trained on link prediction on Cts (at left) and Fb (at right).

4.3   Word Embedding: Similarity

To evaluate the performances of SINr word embeddings, we consider a word similarity task with datasets presented in Lastra-Diaz et al. [10]. Each dataset is composed of pairs of words associated with a similarity value assessed by humans. The evaluation consists in computing the Spearman correlation between the cosine similarity for all the pairs in the embedding space and the human value (Table 4).

Table 4. Word similarity evaluation in Spearman correlation between human judgement and cosine similarity for each model. At left, on text8 corpus, at right on OANC.

text8	W2V	GloVe	SVD2vec	SINr
MC28	0.58	0.42	0.67	**0.69**
RG65	0.52	0.48	0.57	**0.64**
MTurk771	**0.52**	0.48	0.45	0.48
WS353Rel	0.47	0.44	0.46	**0.50**
WS353Full	**0.55**	0.47	**0.55**	0.53
MEN	0.53	0.48	**0.61**	0.52

OANC	W2V	GloVe	SVD2vec	SINr
MC28	0.45	0.54	0.33	**0.62**
RG65	0.33	0.32	0.32	**0.39**
MTurk771	**0.44**	0.39	0.36	0.37
WS353Rel	0.40	0.34	**0.47**	0.41
WS353Full	0.49	0.40	**0.51**	0.44
MEN	0.44	0.46	**0.59**	0.40

The first four datasets (MC28, RG65, MTurk771and WS353Rel) are composed of pairs of names, the last two datasets (WS353Full, MEN) contain names, adjectives and verbs. On both text8 and OANC, SINr word embeddings perform best on MC28 and RG65 whose words in pairs have a similar meaning. W2V and SVD2vec achieve better results than SINr on datasets with related pairs of words (MTurk771 and WS353Rel) and datasets with names adjectives and verbs (WS353Full, MEN). Overall, the performances of SINr on this task remain encouraging and show that word embeddings extracted from co-occurrence networks can achieve good results on the similarity task.

5   Conclusion

We introduced LDBGF, a novel approach based on the underlying bipartite structure of networks to compute sparse interpretable embeddings. Moreover, we developed SINr, a near linear-time implementation of this newly introduced framework that is faster than all the other graph embedding approaches we compare to. Although embedding techniques explicitly aim to get dense low-dimensional vectors, we demonstrate that the SINr vectors achieve state-of-the-art results on classic graph and word embedding evaluation tasks whilst maintaining a sparse and interpretable representation. We also show that projecting our embedding vectors into a low-dimensional space using SVD does not significantly lower the results. These results demonstrate the relevance of the LDBGF philosophy. We thus hope for new efficient implementations of this framework. For instance, it would be interesting to extend our approach to deal with temporal networks by considering incremental clustering algorithms.

References

1. Belkin, M., Niyogi, P.: Laplacian eigenmaps and spectral techniques for embedding and clustering. In: NIPS, pp. 585–591 (2002)
2. Bhowmick, A.K., Meneni, K., Danisch, M., Guillaume, J., Mitra, B.: Louvainne: hierarchical louvain method for high quality and scalable network embedding. In: WSDM, pp. 43–51 (2020)
3. Blondel, V.D., Guillaume, J.L., Lambiotte, R., Lefebvre, E.: Fast unfolding of communities in large networks. J. Stat. Mech.: Theory Exp. **2008**, P10008 (2008)
4. Brandes, U., et al.: Maximizing modularity is hard. arXiv preprint physics/0608255 (2006)
5. Brochier, R., Guille, A., Velcin, J.: Global vectors for node representations. In: WWW, pp. 2587–2593 (2019)
6. Cao, S., Lu, W., Xu, Q.: GraRep: learning graph representations with global structural information. In: CIKM, pp. 891–900 (2015)
7. Dugué, N., Lamirel, J.-C., Perez, A.: Bringing a feature selection metric from machine learning to complex networks. In: Aiello, L.M., Cherifi, C., Cherifi, H., Lambiotte, R., Lió, P., Rocha, L.M. (eds.) Complex Networks 2018. SCI, vol. 813, pp. 107–118. Springer, Cham (2019). https://doi.org/10.1007/978-3-030-05414-4_9
8. Guillaume, J.L., Latapy, M.: Bipartite graphs as models of complex networks. Physica A **371**(2), 795–813 (2006)
9. Kunegis, J.: The Koblenz network collection. In: WWW, pp. 1343–1350 (2013)
10. Lastra-Díz, J.J., et al.: Reproducibility dataset for a large experimental survey on word embeddings and ontology-based methods for word similarity. Data Brief **26**, 104432 (2019)
11. Leskovec, J., Kleinberg, J., Faloutsos, C.: Graph evolution: densification and shrinking diameters. ACM Trans. Knowl. Discov. Data **1**(1), 2-es (2007)
12. Levy, O., Goldberg, Y., Dagan, I.: Improving distributional similarity with lessons learned from word embeddings. ACL **3**, 211–225 (2015)
13. Lu, Q., Getoor, L.: Link-based classification. In: ICML, pp. 496–503 (2003)
14. Martínez, V., Berzal, F., Talavera, J.C.C.: A survey of link prediction in complex networks. ACM Comput. Surv. **49**(4), 69:1–69:33 (2017)
15. Mikolov, T., Sutskever, I., Chen, K., Corrado, G.S., Dean, J.: Distributed representations of words and phrases and their compositionality. In: NIPS, pp. 3111–3119 (2013)
16. Monson, S.D., Pullman, N.J., Rees, R.: A survey of clique and biclique coverings and factorizations of (0, 1)-matrices. Bull. Inst. Combin. Appl. **14**, 17–86 (1995)
17. Ou, M., Cui, P., Pei, J., Zhang, Z., Zhu, W.: Asymmetric transitivity preserving graph embedding. In: SIGKDD, pp. 1105–1114 (2016)
18. Pennington, J., Socher, R., Manning, C.D.: Glove: global vectors for word representation. In: EMNLP, pp. 1532–1543 (2014)
19. Perozzi, B., Al-Rfou, R., Skiena, S.: DeepWalk: online learning of social representations. In: SIGKDD, pp. 701–710 (2014)
20. Perozzi, B., Kulkarni, V., Chen, H., Skiena, S.: Don't walk, skip! online learning of multi-scale network embeddings. In: ASONAM, pp. 258–265 (2017)
21. Raghavan, U.N., Albert, R., Kumara, S.: Near linear time algorithm to detect community structures in large-scale networks. Phys. Rev. E **76**(3), 036106 (2007)
22. Řehůřek, R., Sojka, P.: Software framework for topic modelling with large corpora. In: LREC, pp. 45–50 (2010)

23. Rozemberczki, B., Kiss, O., Sarkar, R.: An API oriented open-source python framework for unsupervised learning on graphs (2020)
24. Traag, V.A.: Faster unfolding of communities: speeding up the Louvain algorithm. Phys. Rev. E **92**(3), 032801 (2015)

Detection of Contextual Anomalies
in Attributed Graphs

Rémi Vaudaine[✉], Baptiste Jeudy, and Christine Largeron

Univ Lyon, UJM-Saint-Etienne, CNRS, Institut d Optique Graduate School
Laboratoire Hubert Curien UMR 5516, 42023 Saint-Etienne, France
{remi.vaudaine,baptiste.jeudy,christine.largeron}@univ-st-etienne.fr

Abstract. Graph anomaly detection have proved very useful in a wide range of domains. For instance, for detecting anomalous accounts (e.g. bots, terrorists, opinion spammers or social malwares) on online platforms, intrusions and failures on communication networks or suspicious and fraudulent behaviors on social networks. However, most existing methods often rely on pre-selected features built from the graph, do not necessarily use local information and do not consider context based anomalies. To overcome these limits, we present CoBaGAD, a Context-Based Graph Anomaly Detector which exploits local information to detect anomalous nodes of a graph in a semi-supervised way. We use Graph Attention Networks (GAT) with our custom attention mechanism to build local features, aggregate them and classify unlabeled nodes into normal or anomaly. Finally, we show that our algorithm is able to detect anomalies with high precision and recall and, outperforms state-of-the-art baselines.

Keywords: Graph neural network · Graph anomaly detection · Node classification

1 Introduction

Anomaly detection has been a field of intense research for the last decades, both for graph data [3] and for vector data [24]. According to these last ones, anomalies are substantial variations from the norm. In a graph, a node can be an anomaly because of its neighborhood, its attributes or a combination of both. For instance, in a graph with community structure (i.e. containing sets of highly connected nodes) an anomaly can correspond to a node which do not really belong to any community either because it is isolated or because it forms a bridge between two groups. In an attributed graph with assortativity, it can be a node whose attributes are significantly different from those of its neighbors.

Supplementary Information available online: https://github.com/vaudaine/Detection-of-contextual-anomalies-in-attributed-graphs.

P. H. Abreu et al. (Eds.): IDA 2021, LNCS 12695, pp. 338–349, 2021.
https://doi.org/10.1007/978-3-030-74251-5_27

In this paper, we introduce and study a new particular case of node anomaly: context-based anomaly. This kind of anomaly is relatively frequent in practice. For instance, in a bibliographic network where the nodes correspond to papers assigned to thematic categories and there is a link from a document node to another if the first one cites the second, a contextual anomaly can correspond to a node belonging to the category 'Fruit' (because it contains the word 'Apple') which is cited by documents belonging to the category 'computer science'. Context-based anomalies are also often associated with fraud or corruption. In those situations, experts try to use "patterns" or contexts to find these fraud or corruption cases. For instance, a company has a CEO or an accountant who has an account in a tax haven then this company is more likely to be fraudulent. To define this kind of anomaly, we consider that there exists an unknown small subgraph (a context), and a distinguished node in this subgraph, such that each time this subgraph occurs in the data, then the node corresponding to the distinguished node is an anomaly with a high probability p. In this paper, for simplicity, we consider the case $p = 1$. We call this unknown subgraph a context and the corresponding anomalies "context-based anomalies". We argue that these context-based anomalies are interesting and, as the experiments show, not always well detected by current approaches.

Their detection can be tackled in a supervised, semi-supervised or unsupervised way. The first one supposes that a training sample consisting of instances of the two classes (normal nodes and anomaly nodes) is available. In the second one, a set of unlabeled instances is also exploited during training while in the latter one, no labels are available. In this paper, we consider the semi-supervised case. More precisely, we use a transductive setting: the data consist of a single graph for which a proportion of the nodes is labeled (either "anomaly" or "normal") and other nodes have no labels. The goal is to find the labels of the unlabeled nodes. The difference with a fully supervised setting is that the learning algorithm can use the unlabeled nodes even if it has no access to their labels which is helpful since removing them would change the connectivity of the graph and thus disrupt the learning.

Generally, node anomaly detection is addressed by finding a representation of the nodes in a feature space and then identifying anomalies in this space. The features can be hand-made or automatically learned, for instance by a Graph Neural Network (GNN) which is the state of the art for node classification and more generally for solving many supervised or unsupervised problems on graphs. In this paper, we propose to use this approach to automatically and simultaneously learn a suited representation of the nodes and detect the anomalies. More precisely, we propose CoBaGAD (Context-Based Graph Anomaly Detector) a semi-supervised algorithm to detect graph anomalies. CoBaGAD is a variation of Graph Attention Networks (GAT) where the attention mechanism has been changed by a custom one allowing better feature selection.

To carry out an experimental evaluation of CoBaGAD, we need datasets. However, to our knowledge, real data for this kind of anomaly is not publicly available. Thus, we used synthetic and real graph data in which we artificially introduced context-based anomalies.

Our contributions are:

- We define a new kind of node anomaly in a graph.
- We propose a GNN architecture to detect it.
- We validate our model on several kinds of graph with different pattern anomalies and compare it with GAT, GCN, GraphSage and Node2vec + LOF.

The paper is organized as follows. First, we review related works. We define the problem in Sect. 3 and present our method to detect context-based anomaly in attributed graphs in Sect. 4. Then, we describe our evaluation protocol and the experiments carried out to evaluate the ability of our method to detect anomalies. Finally, we discuss the obtained results which are generally better than those provided by state of the art methods.

2   Related Work

We can distinguish two main fields of research in anomaly detection according to the type of data investigated. First, anomaly detection with tabular data, where the elements (or instances) are described by feature vectors and which aims at finding vectors in the space that are "far" from the others. Different criteria have been proposed to quantify the notion of "far" from the others. On the other hand, graph anomaly detection deals with relational data. While they do not use the same type of data, these fields share common ideas. In this section, we review state-of-the-art methods for both types of data and, finally, for graph mining. Both fields have variations as static and dynamic anomaly detection. Thereafter, we will focus only on static data.

2.1   Anomaly Detection with Vector Data

In the literature, a large number of methods have been proposed to solve the task of anomaly detection on vector data [17,33]. They can be classified in several families. The first family, detailed in particular in [31], uses a probability model to describe the available instances and then identifies the anomalies as elements having a low probability of occurrence according to the model generated from the data. The second approach, based on notions of distance or neighborhood detects anomalies by looking for elements that are too far from their neighbors in the representation space or whose neighborhood is not sufficiently dense [1,20,34]. Among the methods which directly exploit the neighborhood, we can mention for instance [4,20,30] and among those which estimate the density around an instance, LOF (Local Outlier Factor) [8]. We can also cite methods based on the construction of forests such as iForest [23] or iNNE [5], which consist in recursively partitioning all the instances using attributes so as to build a tree in which an instance located in a leaf far from the root is more likely to be an anomaly than a less distant instance. However, comparative studies of these methods have highlighted difficulties that can lead to a decrease in their performance, in particular the curse of dimensionality when the number of attributes is high or even the imbalance of the data.

2.2 Anomaly Detection with Graph Data

Concerning anomaly detection with graph data, the methods proposed in the literature rarely aim at finding the same type of anomalies but they can be classified into different categories depending on the kind of graph that they deal with. The first kind is plain graph which is a graph without features. Scan [39] and PAICAN [6] are graph clustering algorithms that detect anomalies as byproducts. Such anomalies are usually bridges between communities as in [37]. Structural anomalies such as anomalous edges or irregular subgraphs can be detected by Autopart [10], [27] and [12]. For its part, OddBall [2] is an approach based on power laws which detects elements of the graph whose characteristics deviate from these power laws, for instance nodes with very high degree. By this way, this method can detect near stars, near cliques, dominant edges and heavy vicinity in a weighted graph. On the other hand, some methods [26,28,29] have been proposed to deal with attributed graphs. FocusGo [29] is a method that focuses on user-specific attributes to cluster nodes that are similar. Outliers are defined as nodes which structurally belong to a cluster but deviate from its focus attributes. Recently, an extension [28] of this method has been proposed. It is able to both find communities and extract local information (find focus features). Anomalies are nodes or groups of nodes that cannot be easily summarized by a community and some focus features. GOutrank [26] and ConOut [32] are outlier ranking techniques that find subgraphs as context of nodes and subspaces of their features to focus on those that deviate from these subspaces. Thus, like in [28,29], anomalies are nodes whose features deviate a lot from those of their neighbors.

2.3 Machine Learning and Graph Mining

In recent years, machine learning has become more popular to mine graphs. In particular, the rise of Word2vec [25] to deal with textual data has also led to a renewal of graph embedding which aims to project a graph into a low-dimensional space such that each node is represented by a vector [9,13,41]. In the context of anomaly detection, any method that deals with vector data can be used afterwards. On the other hand, some embedding algorithms [18,40] have been created to both represent the nodes as vectors and find outliers. However, they are unsupervised whereas we focus on semi-supervised learning.

Today, state-of-the-art methods such as SDNE [36], GraphSAGE [15], GCN [19] or GAT [7,35] use deep learning to mine graphs and they have notably obtained very good performance on tasks such as node classification as shown in recent surveys [11,38]. But, to the best of our knowledge, these deep learning methods have not been used in anomaly detection context. Thus, in this work, we continue down this path by proposing a deep learning based method to classify nodes into two classes: anomalies and normal nodes in a semi-supervised context.

3 Problem Definition

We aim at detecting contextual anomalies which are nodes of the graph whose local context exhibits a singular arrangement.

More formally, let $G(V, E, X)$ be a graph on a set of n nodes $V = \{v_i\}$, a set of edges $E = \{e_{ij}\}$ and a feature matrix $X \in \mathbf{R}^{n \times F}$. Each row $\vec{x}_i$ in matrix X is the feature vector of node v_i. We consider that there exists an unknown small subgraph (a context), and a distinguished node in this subgraph, such that each time this subgraph occurs in the data, then the node corresponding to the distinguished node is an anomaly (we give several examples in Sect. 5.1).

We use a transductive setting: the data consists of a single graph for which a proportion of the nodes is labeled (either "anomaly" or "normal") and other nodes have no labels. The goal is to find the labels of the unlabeled nodes. However and most importantly, the conditions (i.e., the context) which make a node anomalous are not known during the training of the model.

4   Our Method: CoBaGAD

The main idea of our method is to learn simultaneously two-classes classifiers with attention mechanisms. Then, local information is aggregated to determine whether a node is normal or not. Parameters of the network are learnt with a standard classification loss in a semi-supervised fashion. For this, we propose to improve Graph Attention Networks (GAT) [35].

Global Affine Transformation: The first step is an affine transformation followed by a non linearity σ. This function σ is applied elementwise. The parameters are the matrix $W \in \mathbf{R}^{F \times F'}$ and a row vector $b \in \mathbf{R}^{1 \times F'}$. The identity matrix is denoted $\mathbb{1}$.

$$\Lambda = \sigma \left(XW + \mathbb{1}b \right) \tag{1}$$

This step transforms the features $\vec{x}_i$ independently for each node v_i. The ith row of Λ is the new representation for node v_i, and notice that since the matrix W is not necessarily square, this new representation can have more or less features than $\vec{x}_i$.

Attention Layer: It consists of k attention heads (k is an hyper-parameter). For each attention head $c \in \{0, ..., k - 1\}$, we perform a local linear transformation followed by a weighted aggregate: First, a local linear transformation $W_c \in \mathbf{R}^{F' \times F'}$ is applied on the features:

$$\Lambda_c = \Lambda W_c \tag{2}$$

Then, for each edge $(i, j) \in E$, the value $e_{i,j,c}$ is computed:

$$e_{i,j,c} = LeakyReLU \left((\vec{\lambda}_{i,c} \odot \vec{\lambda}_{j,c}).\vec{u}_c \right) \tag{3}$$

where $\odot$ is the Hadamard product, $\vec{\lambda}_{i,c}$ and $\vec{\lambda}_{j,c}$ are resp. the ith and jth rows of Λ_c, and $\vec{u}_c \in \mathbf{R}^{F'}$ is a parameter column vector. The Hadamard product multiplied by $\vec{u}_c$ corresponds to a weighted dot-product similarity.

The attention weights $\alpha_{i,j,c}$ are defined as a normalized version of $e_{i,j,c}$ such that for each node v_i and each head c, they are positive and sum to 1:

$$\alpha_{i,j,c} = \frac{\exp(e_{i,j,c})}{\sum_{k \in N(i)} \exp(e_{i,k,c})} \tag{4}$$

where $N(i)$ is the set of the neighbors of node v_i.

The next step is to compute for each node v_i, a convex combination of the $\vec{\lambda}_{j,c}$ for all neighbors v_j of v_i using the attention weights. These weights can be seen as the amount of information that flows between nodes. Finally, the new representation $\vec{h_i}$ of the node v_i is given by the concatenation of all the representations given by the k attention heads. i.e., each node v_i is represented by a row vector of $F'k$ features.

$$\vec{h_{i,c}} = \sum_{j \in N(i)} \alpha_{i,j,c} \vec{\lambda}_{j,c} \text{ and } \vec{h_i} = \sigma' \left(\|_{c=0}^{k-1} \vec{h_{i,c}} \right) \tag{5}$$

where σ' is an activation function and $\|$ is vector concatenation.

The network can be a stack of several such attention layers, the output of each layer being the input of the next layer.

Classification: To detect anomalies, we consider that each of the head in the last layer is a 2-classes classifier (thus each $\vec{h_{i,c}} \in \mathbf{R}^2$) and we combine these classifiers by taking the argmax. i.e., if the maximum component in vector $\vec{h_i}$ is in an odd index, v_i is classified as an anomaly. If the maximum is in an even index, then it is a normal node.

The parameters that must be learnt are: W, b, and for each of the k attention heads in each attention layer: the matrix W_c and the vector $\vec{u_c}$. The hyperparameters are F', the number of attention layers, and the number k of heads in each attention layer. The activation functions σ and σ' can also be chosen by the user.

CoBaGAD differs from GAT by two major points. First, we added a global affine transformation (Eq. 1) to embed the original features in a new space. This operation improves the ability to detect anomalies and allows to reduce the dimension of the problem. Then, we use a custom attention mechanism in Eq. 3. Rather than concatenating the new representations of a pair of nodes, we compute a similarity between them with the Hadamard product. The attribute weight vector $\vec{u_c}$ focuses on most important part of this product for classification.

5   Experiments

5.1   Dataset Generation and Description

As benchmarks corresponding to the kind of anomaly considered in this paper are not publicly available, to experimentally evaluate our model and compare it with the state of the art, we have artificially introduced context-based anomalies in many different graphs, real or synthetic. Table 1 gives the name, the number of nodes and the number of edges of these graphs. G_0 is a random Erods-Renyi graph. G_1 and G_4 are also generated, respectively with Dancer [22] and LFR [21], which mimic real-world graph's behaviour. Moreover, we chose real world graphs that are common in the literature: Polblogs[1], Cora[2] and Facebook[3].

The following process has been applied to transform each of these graphs $G(V, E)$ into an attributed graph $G(V, E, X)$. The feature vector $\vec{x}_i$ of node v_i is defined as a one-hot vector of dimension 5. In our illustrative example related to fraud detection, such features can be interpreted as the role in a company (e.g. $[0, 0, 1, 0, 0]$ represents the CEO and $[0, 1, 0, 0, 0]$ represents an employee). In the following, these one-hot vectors are flagged as colors: blue (B), green (G), red (R), yellow (Y) and purple (P).

Among the nodes of the graph, a few percent (between 4% and 6%) are flagged as anomalies if they follow a simple rule described by a context. These rules are presented in Table 2. In this table, $\bar{Y}$ means that anomalies are nodes that have colour $Yellow$ whereas B means that anomalies have at least one

Table 1. Datasets characteristics: name of the graphs, number of nodes and edges.

Graph	Name	Nodes	Edges
G_0	Erdos-Renyi	10000	24907
G_1	Dancer	10000	189886
G_2	Facebook	4039	88234
G_3	Polblogs	1224	16715
G_4	LFR	1000	5622
G_5	Cora	1433	5429

Table 2. Anomalies characteristics. B = blue, G = green, R = red, Y = yellow, P = purple. $\bar{Y}$ means that anomalies are nodes that have colour Y. B means that anomalies have at least one neighbor whose colour is B.

Anomalies	Definition
A_0	$B \wedge G$
A_1	$(B \wedge G) \vee (B \wedge R)$
A_2	$(B \wedge G) \vee (R \wedge Y)$
A_3	$\bar{Y}$
A_4	$\bar{Y} \wedge B$
A_5	$\bar{Y} \wedge B \wedge Y$
A_6	$\bar{Y} \vee (B \wedge Y)$

---

[1] http://konect.cc/networks/dimacs10-polblogs/.
[2] https://relational.fit.cvut.cz/dataset/CORA.
[3] https://snap.stanford.edu/data/egonets-Facebook.html.

neighbor whose colour is *Blue*. For example, A_6 represent nodes that have the colour yellow (Y) or have at least one neighbor with colour blue (B) and at least one neighbor with colour yellow (Y).

Note that our algorithm CoBaGAD does not know how the anomalies have been created. Indeed, in a real-world case, the expert would flag some nodes as anomalies but he does not necessary know the conditions which make a node anomalous. Thus the goal of our algorithm is to recognize these anomalies without this contextual knowledge.

5.2 Experimental Setup

All nodes of the graphs belong to either the set of anomalies or the set of normal nodes. In a transductive setup, nodes are split into train, validation and test sets. The train set is made of 50% of the total anomalies. Then, we add as many normal nodes as there are anomalies. The same applies for validation set with 25% of anomalies. The test set is composed of the remaining 25% of anomalies and 25% of normal nodes of the graph. Balancing train and validation sets in order to have as many normal nodes as anomalies improved a lot the results. Thus a part of negative examples (normal nodes) is ignored during training. Due to space limitations, we only show the results using this sampling strategy. To ensure the reproducibility of our results, code and datasets are available in our GitHub[4]. We compare our algorithm, CoBaGAD, with state-of-the-art methods in node classification: Graph Convolution Networks [19] (GCN), Graph Attention Networks [35] (GAT), GraphSAGE [15] with mean aggregator and an unsupervised anomaly detection approach based on Node2vec [14] and LOF [8]. For every deep learning method, we learn a single layer. Given the kind of studied pattern, add more layers seems not relevant. For CoBaGAD, we use GELU [16] as activation function σ and softmax as activation function σ', $F' = 2$, $k = 2$ as we learn two 2-classes classifiers for both anomalies and normal nodes. For GAT and GraphSAGE, we use the same parameters. For GCN, we use *localpool* filter, softmax as activation function and output of dimension 2. For every algorithm, we tried two versions: without self-loop and with self-loops by adding the identity matrix to the adjacency matrix and we present the best results. We train for 1000 epochs with Adam optimizer and a learning rate of $5e{-}3$ on the train set and validate it at each step. The weights of the networks are kept when the accuracy on the validation set is the highest. We use the standard categorical cross-entropy loss: $L(Y^{true}, Y^{pred}) = - \sum_{j=1}^{k} \sum_{i}^{N} (y_{ij}^{true} \times log(y_{ij}^{pred}))$. Concerning the unsupervised approach, it is an association of Node2vec embedding and LOF anomaly detection. First, we compute an embedding of the graph using Node2vec with $p = 1, q = 1$ and dimension 128. It outputs a new representation for every node v_i. This representation is concatenated with its feature vector $\tilde{x}_i$. Finally, these vectors are fed to a LOF classifier in order to detect anomalies.

---

[4] https://github.com/vaudaine/Detection-of-contextual-anomalies-in-attributed-graphs.

6   Results

For each model, each dataset and each type of anomaly, experiments are conducted 12 times by changing the train/validation/test split. We choose the 3 best results on the validation and report the mean and standard deviation of precision obtained on the test set. These results can be found in Table 3. Due to space constraints, we did not report results for the unsupervised approach combining Node2vec and LOF since the precision was very low as expected (between

Table 3. Precision of the detection of anomalies A_0–A_6 on several graphs (G_0–G_5) in the testing set. **Bold**: best in column.

A_0	G_0	G_1	G_2	G_3	G_4	G_5
CoBaGAD	$\mathbf{0.98 \pm 0.03}$	$\mathbf{0.96 \pm 0.03}$	$\mathbf{0.95 \pm 0.03}$	$\mathbf{0.87 \pm 0.09}$	$\mathbf{0.85 \pm 0.13}$	0.92 ± 0.12
GAT	0.96 ± 0.04	0.83 ± 0.02	0.33 ± 0.08	0.55 ± 0.08	0.59 ± 0.13	$\mathbf{0.93 \pm 0.1}$
GCN	0.34 ± 0.02	0.12 ± 0.01	0.11 ± 0.0	0.18 ± 0.02	0.31 ± 0.03	0.26 ± 0.02
GraphSage	0.53 ± 0.01	0.56 ± 0.03	0.63 ± 0.05	0.44 ± 0.08	0.36 ± 0.08	0.52 ± 0.03
A_1	G_0	G_1	G_2	G_3	G_4	G_5
CoBaGAD	$\mathbf{0.96 \pm 0.03}$	$\mathbf{0.98 \pm 0.02}$	$\mathbf{0.78 \pm 0.1}$	$\mathbf{0.73 \pm 0.05}$	$\mathbf{0.72 \pm 0.15}$	$\mathbf{0.85 \pm 0.12}$
GAT	0.74 ± 0.3	0.55 ± 0.21	0.51 ± 0.14	0.63 ± 0.07	0.46 ± 0.19	0.8 ± 0.18
GCN	0.34 ± 0.02	0.19 ± 0.03	0.13 ± 0.02	0.19 ± 0.03	0.34 ± 0.04	0.26 ± 0.01
GraphSage	0.46 ± 0.04	0.5 ± 0.02	0.51 ± 0.06	0.39 ± 0.06	0.38 ± 0.07	0.47 ± 0.03
A_2	G_0	G_1	G_2	G_3	G_4	G_5
CoBaGAD	$\mathbf{0.61 \pm 0.04}$	$\mathbf{0.62 \pm 0.06}$	$\mathbf{0.58 \pm 0.2}$	$\mathbf{0.47 \pm 0.14}$	$\mathbf{0.64 \pm 0.15}$	$\mathbf{0.72 \pm 0.06}$
GAT	0.52 ± 0.02	0.42 ± 0.1	0.29 ± 0.03	0.35 ± 0.06	0.3 ± 0.03	0.51 ± 0.11
GCN	0.27 ± 0.02	0.12 ± 0.0	0.14 ± 0.01	0.2 ± 0.04	0.25 ± 0.02	0.23 ± 0.03
GraphSage	0.33 ± 0.01	0.38 ± 0.02	0.44 ± 0.03	0.44 ± 0.05	0.33 ± 0.03	0.38 ± 0.01
A_3	G_0	G_1	G_2	G_3	G_4	G_5
CoBaGAD	0.99 ± 0.01	$\mathbf{0.99 \pm 0.01}$	0.95 ± 0.05	$\mathbf{0.91 \pm 0.13}$	0.89 ± 0.15	0.93 ± 0.02
GAT	0.82 ± 0.07	0.79 ± 0.03	0.78 ± 0.07	0.55 ± 0.03	0.43 ± 0.01	0.61 ± 0.09
GCN	0.95 ± 0.02	0.97 ± 0.02	0.91 ± 0.07	0.8 ± 0.21	$\mathbf{0.94 \pm 0.08}$	0.78 ± 0.04
GraphSage	$\mathbf{1.0 \pm 0.0}$	$\mathbf{0.99 \pm 0.01}$	$\mathbf{0.97 \pm 0.04}$	0.71 ± 0.1	0.68 ± 0.24	$\mathbf{0.97 \pm 0.03}$
A_4	G_0	G_1	G_2	G_3	G_4	G_5
CoBaGAD	$\mathbf{0.9 \pm 0.1}$	$\mathbf{0.95 \pm 0.04}$	$\mathbf{0.97 \pm 0.04}$	$\mathbf{0.8 \pm 0.07}$	0.62 ± 0.1	$\mathbf{0.89 \pm 0.09}$
GAT	0.5 ± 0.07	0.77 ± 0.15	0.77 ± 0.03	0.67 ± 0.23	0.51 ± 0.1	0.43 ± 0.05
GCN	0.44 ± 0.01	0.7 ± 0.03	0.71 ± 0.12	0.6 ± 0.12	$\mathbf{0.65 \pm 0.07}$	0.35 ± 0.02
GraphSage	0.46 ± 0.03	0.73 ± 0.02	0.72 ± 0.02	0.58 ± 0.11	0.61 ± 0.04	0.41 ± 0.03
A_5	G_0	G_1	G_2	G_3	G_4	G_5
CoBaGAD	$\mathbf{0.84 \pm 0.02}$	$\mathbf{0.9 \pm 0.03}$	$\mathbf{0.82 \pm 0.07}$	$\mathbf{0.61 \pm 0.03}$	0.51 ± 0.23	$\mathbf{0.84 \pm 0.22}$
GAT	0.69 ± 0.11	0.74 ± 0.07	0.71 ± 0.09	0.57 ± 0.07	0.52 ± 0.09	0.46 ± 0.1
GCN	0.35 ± 0.01	0.67 ± 0.04	0.62 ± 0.07	0.6 ± 0.04	0.46 ± 0.13	0.23 ± 0.02
GraphSage	0.34 ± 0.01	0.68 ± 0.0	0.68 ± 0.06	0.51 ± 0.04	$\mathbf{0.56 \pm 0.06}$	0.3 ± 0.04
A_6	G_0	G_1	G_2	G_3	G_4	G_5
CoBaGAD	$\mathbf{0.9 \pm 0.01}$	$\mathbf{0.89 \pm 0.05}$	$\mathbf{0.54 \pm 0.27}$	$\mathbf{0.62 \pm 0.2}$	0.26 ± 0.09	0.4 ± 0.04
GAT	0.55 ± 0.12	0.59 ± 0.12	0.39 ± 0.05	0.48 ± 0.1	0.27 ± 0.03	0.39 ± 0.03
GCN	0.38 ± 0.05	0.26 ± 0.09	0.2 ± 0.07	0.21 ± 0.01	0.32 ± 0.13	0.46 ± 0.11
GraphSage	0.67 ± 0.04	0.58 ± 0.05	0.48 ± 0.06	0.49 ± 0.16	$\mathbf{0.48 \pm 0.06}$	$\mathbf{0.65 \pm 0.14}$

0% and 20%). Also, the recall on anomalies, and the recall and precision on normal nodes are not reported. They are indeed very high for all graphs and type of anomaly (most of the time above 98%) and no significant differences can be observed between the different models. These results are however available in additional materials[5].

The results show that our algorithm achieves state-of-the-art performance across all datasets and anomalies. More specifically, for A_0, A_1 and A_2 which all are anomalies based on the pattern $B \wedge G$, our method always outperforms the other competitors (except for A_0, G_5 where it is still very relevant). We are able to improve upon GAT, our principal contendor, by at least 2% on A_0, G_0 up to 62% on A_0, G_2. Attention based methods are better than the others (GCN, GraphSage, Node2vec + LOF) when dealing with these types of anomaly.

Anomalies A_3 to A_6 rely on the pattern $\bar{Y}$ which means that the considered nodes are yellow. This means that the information about the node itself is required. A_3 is a very simple pattern where anomalies are defined by the simplest pattern: nodes are just yellow. In that case, we can suppose that it is easy for many algorithms to perform well on detecting those nodes. In fact, GraphSAGE shows good performance for most of the graphs but lack a bit of consistency. GCN is more consistent but results are worse than those provided by GraphSAGE. While GAT fails to show good performance, our method is the most consistent and show very good results in general. Then, for A_4 to A_6, as the pattern becomes more complex, CoBaGAD remains the only method that, except a few cases, correctly detects the anomalies.

7   Conclusion

We have defined a new kind of anomaly based on a context. Such anomalies follow a simple pattern. Then, we have presented Context Based Graph Anomaly Detector, CoBaGAD, an extension of the Graph Attention Networks that focuses on detecting those anomalies. Through intensive transductive experiments, we demonstrate the ability of our method to identify such pattern anomalies and to outperform state-of-the-art algorithms.

Different improvements can be addressed as future work such as scoring anomalies instead of binary classifying. Another particularly interesting field of research in the domain of anomaly detection is the interpretability of the detected anomalies. The objective would be to be able to recover the context that defines anomalies. Then, we will also study anomaly defined by contexts of larger diameter. This will involve using networks with more layers to increase the "field of view".

Acknowledgement. This work has been supported by IDEXLYON ACADEMICS Project ANR-16-IDEX-0005 of the French National Research Agency.

---

[5] https://github.com/vaudaine/Detection-of-contextual-anomalies-in-attributed-graphs.

References

1. Aggarwal, C.C.: Time Series and Multidimensional Streaming Outlier Detection. Outlier Analysis, pp. 273–310. Springer, Cham (2017). https://doi.org/10.1007/978-3-319-47578-3_9

2. Akoglu, L., McGlohon, M., Faloutsos, C.: oddball: spotting anomalies in weighted graphs. In: Zaki, M.J., Yu, J.X., Ravindran, B., Pudi, V. (eds.) PAKDD 2010. LNCS (LNAI), vol. 6119, pp. 410–421. Springer, Heidelberg (2010). https://doi.org/10.1007/978-3-642-13672-6_40

3. Akoglu, L., Tong, H., Koutra, D.: Graph based anomaly detection and description: a survey. Data Min. Knowl. Disc. **29**(3), 626–688 (2014). https://doi.org/10.1007/s10618-014-0365-y

4. Angiulli, F., Pizzuti, C.: Fast outlier detection in high dimensional spaces. In: PKDD, pp. 15–26 (2002)

5. Bandaragoda, T.R., Ting, K.M., Albrecht, D., Liu, F.T., Zhu, Y., Wells, J.R.: Isolation-based anomaly detection using nearest-neighbor ensembles. Comput. Intell. **34**(4), 968–998 (2018)

6. Bojchevski, A., Günnemann, S.: Bayesian robust attributed graph clustering: joint learning of partial anomalies and group structure. In: AAAI Conference on Artificial Intelligence, pp. 2738–2745 (2018)

7. Bresson, X., Laurent, T.: Residual gated graph convnets. In: ICLR (2018)

8. Breunig, M., Kriegel, H.P., Ng, R.T., Sander, J.: LOF: identifying density-based local outliers. In: ICMD, pp. 93–104 (2000)

9. Cai, H., Zheng, V., Chen-Chuan Chang, K.: A comprehensive survey of graph embedding: problems, techniques, and applications. TKDE **30**(9), 1616–1637 (2018)

10. Chakrabarti, D.: AutoPart: parameter-free graph partitioning and outlier detection. In: PKDD, pp. 112–124 (2004)

11. Dwivedi, V.P., Joshi, C.K., Laurent, T., Bengio, Y., Bresson, X.: Benchmarking graph neural networks (2020). https://arxiv.org/abs/2003.00982

12. Eberle, W., Holder, L.: Discovering structural anomalies in graph-based data. In: ICDMW 2007. IEEE (2007)

13. Goyal, P., Ferrara, E.: Graph embedding techniques, applications, and performance: a survey. Knowl.-Based Syst. **151**, 78–94 (2018)

14. Grover, A., Leskovec, J.: Node2vec: scalable feature learning for networks. In: SIGKDD, pp. 855–864. ACM (2016)

15. Hamilton, W.L., Ying, R., Leskovec, J.: Inductive representation learning on large graphs. NeurIPS **30**, 1024–1034 (2017)

16. Hendrycks, D., Gimpel, K.: Gaussian error linear units (GELUs) (2020). https://arxiv.org/abs/1606.08415v3

17. Hodge, V., Austin, J.: A survey of outlier detection methodologies. Artifi. Intell. Rev. **22**, 85–126 (2004)

18. Hu, R., Aggarwal, C.C., Ma, S., Huai, J.: An embedding approach to anomaly detection. In: ICDE, pp. 385–396 (2016)

19. Kipf, T., Welling, M.: Semi-supervised classification with graph convolutional networks. In: ICLR (2017)

20. Knorr, E.M., Ng, R.T., Tucakov, V.: Distance-based outliers: algorithms and applications. VLDB J. **8**, 237–253 (2000)

21. Lancichinetti, A., Fortunato, S., Radicchi, F.: Benchmark graphs for testing community detection algorithms. Phys. Rev. E **78**, 046110 (2008)

22. Largeron, M.: Dancer: dynamic attributed networks with community structure generation. Knowl. Inf. Syst. **53**, 109–151 (2017)
23. Liu, F., Ting, K., Zhou, Z.: Isolation Forest. In: ICDM, pp. 413–422 (2008)
24. Mehrotra, K.G., Mohan, C.K., Huang, H.M.: Algorithms for time series data. Anomaly Detection Principles and Algorithms. TSC, pp. 153–189. Springer, Cham (2017). https://doi.org/10.1007/978-3-319-67526-8_9
25. Mikolov, T., Sutskever, I., Chen, K., Corrado, G., Dean, J.: Distributed representations of words and phrases and their compositionality. In: NeurIPS, pp. 3111–3119 (2013)
26. Müller, E., Sánchez, P., Mülle, Y., Böhm, K.: Ranking outlier nodes in subspaces of attributed graphs. In: ICDEW, pp. 216–222 (2013)
27. Noble, C.C., Cook, D.J.: Graph-based anomaly detection. In: SIGKDD, pp. 631–636. Association for Computing Machinery (2003)
28. Perozzi, B., Akoglu, L.: Discovering communities and anomalies in attributed graphs: interactive visual exploration and summarization. ACM TKDD **12**(2), 1–40 (2018)
29. Perozzi, B., Akoglu, L., Iglesias Sánchez, P., Müller, E.: Focused clustering and outlier detection in large attributed graphs. In: SIGKDD, pp. 1346–1355 (2014)
30. Ramaswamy, S., Rastogi, R., Shim, K.: Efficient algorithms for mining outliers from large data sets. SIGMOD Rec. **29**(2), 427–438 (2000)
31. Rousseeuw, P., Hubert, M.: Robust statistics for outlier detection. Wiley Interdisc. Rev. Data Mining Knowl. Disc. **1**(1), 73–79 (2011)
32. Sánchez, P.I., Müller, E., Irmler, O., Böhm, K.: Local context selection for outlier ranking in graphs with multiple numeric node attributes. In: SSDM (2014)
33. Su, X., Tsai, C.: Outlier detection. Wiley Interdisc. Rev. Data Min. Knowl. Disc. **1**(3), 264–268 (2011)
34. Ting, K., Aryal, S., Washio, T.: Which outlier detector should i use? In: ICDM, p. 8 (2018)
35. Veličković, P., Cucurull, G., Casanova, A., Romero, A., Liò, P., Bengio, Y.: Graph attention networks. In: International Conference on Learning Representations (2018)
36. Wang, D., Cui, P., Zhu, W.: Structural deep network embedding. In: SIGKDD, pp. 1225–1234 (2016)
37. Wang, X., Davidson, I.: Discovering contexts and contextual outliers using random walks in graphs. In: ICDM, pp. 1034–1039 (2009)
38. Wu, Z., Pan, S., Chen, F., Long, G., Zhang, C., Yu, P.S.: A comprehensive survey on graph neural networks. IEEE Trans. Neural Netw. Learn. Syst. 1–21 (2020)
39. Xu, X., Yuruk, N., Feng, Z., Schweiger, T.A.J.: Scan: a structural clustering algorithm for networks. In: SIGKDD, pp. 824–833 (2007)
40. Yu, W., Cheng, W., Aggarwal, C.C., Zhang, K., Chen, H., Wang, W.: NetWalk: a flexible deep embedding approach for anomaly detection in dynamic networks. In: SIGKDD, pp. 2672–2681 (2018)
41. Zhang, D., Yin, J., Zhu, X., Zhang, C.: Network representation learning: a survey. IEEE Trans. Big Data **6**(1), 3–28 (2020)

Ising-Based Louvain Method: Clustering Large Graphs with Specialized Hardware

Pouya Rezazadeh Kalehbasti[1]([⊠]) [ID], Hayato Ushijima-Mwesigwa[2] [ID],
Avradip Mandal[2], and Indradeep Ghosh[2] [ID]

[1] School of Engineering, Stanford University, Stanford, CA 94305, USA
pouyar@stanford.edu
[2] Fujitsu Laboratories of America, Inc., Sunnyvale, CA 94085, USA
{hayato,amandal,ighosh}@fujitsu.com

Abstract. Recent advances in specialized hardware for solving optimization problems such quantum computers, quantum annealers, and CMOS annealers give rise to new ways for solving real-word complex problems. However, given current and near-term hardware limitations, the number of variables required to express a large real-world problem easily exceeds the hardware capabilities, thus hybrid methods are usually developed in order to utilize the hardware. In this work, we advocate for the development of hybrid methods that are built on top of the frameworks of existing state-of-art heuristics, thereby improving these methods. We demonstrate this by building on the so called Louvain method, which is one of the most popular algorithms for the Community detection problem and develop and Ising-based Louvain method. The proposed method outperforms two state-of-the-art community detection algorithms in clustering several small to large-scale graphs. The results show promise in adapting the same optimization approach to other unsupervised learning heuristics to improve their performance.

Keywords: Graphs · Community detection · Clustering · Ising model

1 Introduction

Graphs are powerful tools for modeling and analyzing complex systems from social networks to biological structures. In graphs, some groups of nodes can show modular behavior [16] in that nodes in these groups are highly interrelated and show similar traits and strong connections [6]. Communities or clusters are a form of these modules in graphs which are identified as clusters of nodes with a higher density of internal edges compared to external edges [8,24]. These highly inter-connected nodes reveal underlying structures within a network ranging from friend groups in social networks [22], similar proteins in biochemical structures [14], and papers of similar categories in citation graphs [30]. *Community Detection* (CD) is an unsupervised learning method which aims to identify these interwoven structures (communities, aka clusters) in graphs. CD is an NP-Hard combinatorial optimization problem.

P. R. Kalehbasti—Work done while at Fujitsu Laboratories of America, Inc.

P. H. Abreu et al. (Eds.): IDA 2021, LNCS 12695, pp. 350–361, 2021.
https://doi.org/10.1007/978-3-030-74251-5_28

In recent years, we have seen the emergence of specialized hardware designed for solving combinatorial optimization problem. Examples of these novel computing hardware include, adiabatic quantum computers, CMOS annealers, memristive circuits, and optical parametric oscillators, that are designed to solve optimization problems formulated as an Ising or QUBO mathematical model. Given that many well-known problems in graphs can easily be modeled in this form, there has been a growing interest in formulating and evaluating these problem and their subsequent QUBO models on the different specialized hardware platforms [4,15,21,32,34]. However, many real-world problems require significantly more variables than these devices can handle, thus hybrid methods are usually used.

Our Contribution: This paper introduces a hybrid method, inspired by the Louvain algorithm, for solving the community detection problem on specialized hardware. Following the work on leveraging specialized hardware for local search [18], the proposed method is expected to produce more optimal clusterings (*i.e.* communities) compared to the original algorithm. This improvement is expected since instead of using a greedy approach for assigning nodes to communities iteratively, this method creates local optimization problems for a set of multiple nodes and multiple candidate clusters concurrently. The method is used to cluster several benchmark graphs where the results will show improved modularity scores compared to Louvain algorithm across several runs.

1.1 Related Work

Researchers have developed several methods for finding high-quality communities that can reveal the interworking and internal structures of complex networks. Increasing availability of large-scale graphs, like the World Wide Web, or social networks of Twitter, Facebook, and Instagram with millions or billions of nodes and edges, have made traditional approaches for community detection unwieldy in terms of computational and spatial complexity [3]. Consequently, researchers have devised efficient algorithms, *e.g.* Girvan-Newman [8], Louvain [3], and Leiden [33] algorithms, for effectively detecting communities within large graphs. Some of the other well-known CD algorithms listed by Javed et al. [11] include Hierarchical Clustering [12], Graph Partitioning [23], Spectral Optimization [26], Simulated Annealing [9], Clique Percolation Method (CPM) [27], and Fuzzy Detection [29]. Many of these algorithm use *modularity* as a metric for solving the optimization problem of CD: such algorithms try to assign nodes to clusters which can maximize the modularity of the entire graph [23,26].

2 Methods

2.1 Modularity Maximization

The objective function selected here for clustering is Modularity which was introduced by Newman [26]. This metric favors highly interconnected nodes to be clustered together. For a graph, $G = (V, E)$, with $|V|$ the set of nodes and edge-set E, the Modularity Maximization problem maximizes the following objective function:

$$Q = \frac{1}{2m} \sum_{i,j} (A_{i,j} - \frac{k_i k_j}{2m}) \delta(c_i, c_j) \tag{1}$$

here, $A_{i,j}$ is the (i, j) element in the adjacency matrix of G, k_i is the weighted degree of node $i \in V$, and $m = |E|$. In addition, c_i is the community node i belongs to, and $\delta(c_i, c_j)$ equals 1 if $c_i = c_j$, and equals 0 otherwise.

2.2   QUBO Models

Quadratic Unconstrained Binary Optimization (QUBO) models include 0/1 binary variables q_i, biases c_i, and couplers $c_{i,j}$. The objective is to minimize the following:

$$E(q_1, \dots, q_n) = \sum_{i=1}^{n} c_i q_i + \sum_{i<j} c_{i,j} q_i q_j \tag{2}$$

QUBO models can be converted to Ising models (variables are ± 1) and vice versa [2]. The objective function of the Modularity Maximization for at most 2-clusters is naturally defined in the Ising Model [21]. In addition, the problem of at most k clusters forms a quadratic function, thus leads to a natural formulation as a QUBO. Subsequently, there has been a large body of research utilizing specialized hardware for tackling this problem ranging from both small to large scale graphs [21,31,32,34,35].

2.3   Solving Community Detection on the Fujitsu Digital Annealer

The Fujitsu Digital Annealer (DA) is a specialized architecture for combinatorial optimization problems formulated as QUBO [1,7]. We use the second generation of the DA that is capable of solving problems with up to 8192 variables and up to 64 bits of precision. The DA has previously been used in different areas such as communication [20], signal processing [28], and data mining [4,5].

2.4   Baseline Method: Louvain Algorithm

Louvain Algorithm (aka Louvain) is a hierarchical clustering method that uses, mainly, modularity for clustering large graphs [3,25]. Louvain identifies the optimal clusters for nodes in an agglomerative hierarchical approach: it first assigns each node to an individual cluster, then identifies the optimal cluster for each node in its immediate neighboring clusters, and after several passes over the graph, it aggregates the nodes belonging to each cluster into super-nodes [3]. The same process is applied to these super-nodes until all clusters become singletons and no nodes can be assigned to clusters other than their own. The resulting super-nodes are the ultimate clusters for their associated sub-nodes. Blondel et al. [3] and Traag et al. [33] provide detailed illustrations of the Louvain algorithm. Next section introduces the Ising-Louvain where an optimization-based approach replaces the greedy approach in the original Louvain.

2.5   Ising-Louvain Method

The proposed method in this paper, Ising-Louvain, is an agglomerative hierarchical clustering method. This method can be summarized in the following steps

1. Initially, each node is assigned to a separate cluster
2. A breadth first Search is performed for each node to find its neighboring nodes, and selects a set of candidate clusters for each of these selected nodes
3. These candidate clusters get assigned to the selected nodes in a way that the new assignments maximize the modularity of the entire graph
4. Steps 2 and 3 are repeated until no more improvement in the modularity of the graph is possible
5. Afterwards, the nodes belonging to the same cluster get aggregated into super-nodes, and steps 2–4 are applied to these super-nodes
6. Steps 2–5 get repeated until all clusters become singletons.

In the steps above, Step 3 is where the QUBOs are formed and solved. Specialized hardware, *e.g.* Fujitsu's Digital Annealer, can effectively solve such optimization problems and yield high-quality solutions.

Figure 1 shows a case where Louvain cannot improve the clustering of a graph in its current situation, while Ising-Louvain can. Here, Ising-Louvain can find a more optimal clustering by considering two nodes [or more than one node in general] at a time and changing the clusters of both nodes from red to blue. However, Louvain only considers a single node at each step and finds no gain in modularity in assigning a new cluster to that single node, and hence can never achieve the more optimal clustering that Ising-Louvain can obtain.

(a) Louvain cannot improve modularity   (b) Improved modularity by Ising-Louvain

Fig. 1. Sample case where only Ising-Louvain can improve the graph while Louvain stalls. Ising-Louvain is able to improve the modularity in (a) from 0.163 to 0.219 in (b), whereas this scenario would be a local optima for the standard Louvain.

2.6   Formulating Ising-Louvain

Deriving the Objective Function. What follows formulates the modularity as the optimization objective for the QUBO used in Ising-Louvain algorithm. Assume we have a graph with n nodes and an edge set E. We start by selecting a set S of nodes as our 'free nodes' and by checking if they should belong to a specific community C or not. The community-membership of the rest of the nodes are assumed to be constant. Let $x \in \{0, 1\}$ be a vector of n binary variables indicating whether or not each node in the graph belongs to community C, such that $x_i = 1$ if $i \in C$ and $x_i = 0$ otherwise. Following a similar derivation as Negre et al. [21], the objective function defined in Eq. 1 can be written as follows:

$$\max(Q) \equiv \min_{x} \left(\sum_{i \in S} \sum_{j \in S} x_i (\frac{k_i k_j}{2m} - A_{i,j}) x_j + \sum_{i \in S} x_i \left(2 \sum_{j \in C} (\frac{k_i k_j}{2m} - A_{i,j}) \right) \right) \quad (3)$$

We can apply the same process to nodes in set S_l and any other cluster C_l and obtain similar phrases to Eq. 3. When considering more than one cluster in our optimization problem, we should consider the constraint that each node in S (defined as $\bigcup_l S_l$) should belong to one and only one cluster at each instant. Eq. 4 shows the objective function resulting from superposing the objective functions for a set of candidate clusters, called set L, with a penalty term imposing the mentioned constraint:

$$\min_{x} \left(\sum_{l \in L} \left(\sum_{i \in S_l} \sum_{j \in S_l} x_{i,l} (\frac{k_i k_j}{2m} - A_{i,j}) x_{j,l} + \sum_{i \in S_l} x_{i,l} \left(2 \sum_{j \in C_l} (\frac{k_i k_j}{2m} - A_{i,j}) \right) \right) \right.$$
$$\left. + \gamma \sum_{i \in S_l} (\sum_{l \in L} x_{i,l} - 1)^2 \right) \quad (4)$$

where l indicates the cluster number, S_l indicates the nodes for which cluster C_l is a candidate, $x_{i,l}$ is the i'th element of vector x_l which contains the binary variables indicating the membership of all nodes to cluster C_l. The last term in this equation imposes the constraint mentioned above with γ being the penalty coefficient.

Equation 4 has a space complexity of $O\left(\max \{|S|^2, \mathscr{L}\} \right)$ where $\mathscr{L} = \sum_l |S_l|$. The optimization objective has $\mathscr{L}$ variables, so the QUBO is of size $\mathscr{L} \times \mathscr{L}$.

Pseudocode Algorithm 1 shows the pseudocode of the proposed method [partially following the pseudocodes of Blondel et al. [3] and Traag et al. [33]]. Table 1 describes functions and auxiliary variables used in Algorithm 1, and Table 2 describes the hyperparameters defined to fine-tune the behavior of the algorithm.

Table 1. Definition of functions and auxilliary variables used in Algorithm 1

Function/Variable name	Definition
Singleton(G)	Create singleton clusters for graph G
Aggregate(G, P)	Aggregate nodes in the same clusters (based on partitioning P) in graph G into supernodes
Modularity(G, P)	Modularity of graph G with partitioning P
ModGain(P, X)	Modularity gain if partition P is updated with assignments X
Modified	Flag indicating if graph is modified throughout the inner loop
Done	Flag indicating that graph can't be improved anymore, *i.e.* all clusters have stayed as singletons after running the inner while-loop
nodes	List of nodes in graph G

Function IsingLouvain (*Graph G*):
  | P = Singleton(G);
  | P = RefineAndCoarsen(G, P);
  | **return** P

Function RefineAndCoarsen (*Graph G, Partition P*):
  | $counter_{out} = 0$;
  | $\Delta Q_{out} = \theta$;
  | $done = False$;
  | /* Outer While Loop   */
  | **while** $\big((done == False)\ \&\ (counter_{out} \leq counter\_max_{out})\ \&\ (\Delta Q_{out} \geq \theta)\big)$
  | **do**
    | $counter_{out} += 1$;
    | $counter_{in} = 0$;
    | $Q_{old,out} = modularity(G, P)$;
    | $\Delta Q_{in} = \theta$;
    | $modified = True$;
    | /* Inner While Loop   */
    | **while** $\big((modified == True)\ \&\ (counter \leq counter\_max)\ \&\ (\Delta Q_{in} \geq \theta)\big)$
    | **do**
      | $counter_{in} += 1$;
      | $modified = False$;
      | $Q_{old,in} = modularity(G, P)$;
      | /* Doing a Single Pass   */
      | P, modified = RunOnePass(G, P, modified);
      | $Q_{new,in} = modularity(G, P)$;
      | $\Delta Q_{in} = Q_{new,in} - Q_{old,in}$;
      | $Q_{old,in} = Q_{new,in}$;
    | **end**
    | $Q_{new,out} = modularity(G, P)$;
    | $\Delta Q_{out} = Q_{new,out} - Q_{old,out}$;
    | $Q_{old,out} = Q_{new,out}$;
    | **if** $|P| == n$ **then**
    | | $done \leftarrow True$;
    | **else**
    | | G = Aggregate(G, P);
    | | P = Singleton(G);
    | **end**
  | **end**
  | **return** G, P

Function RunOnePass (*Graph G, Partition P, Bool mod*):
  | **for** $i \in nodes$ **do**
    | Select S and L;
    | Calculate $\mathscr{B}_{\mathscr{L} \times \mathscr{L}}, \mathscr{B}_{\mathscr{C} \times \mathscr{L}}, \mathscr{Z}, \zeta^T$;
    | $\boldsymbol{X} = [\boldsymbol{x}_{l,S_l}]_{\mathscr{L} \times 1}$ (*i.e.* solution to Equation 4);
    | **if** $ModGain(P, X) > 0$ **then**
    | | Update P with X;
    | | $mod \leftarrow True$;
    | **end**
  | **end**
  | **return** P, mod

Algorithm 1: Ising-Louvain

Table 2. Definition of hyper-parameters used in Algorithm 1

Hyperparameter name	Definition
Max_Nodes	Maximum number of nodes that the algorithm selects as set S
Max_Clusters	Maximum number of candidate clusters that the algorithm considers for each node in set S
Max_Node_Visits	Maximum number of times the algorithm includes each node of the graph in set S over a single pass of the graph during the inner while-loop
Random_seed	Seed number used to initialize the random generator in Numpy
Solver_timeout	Timeout limit for each call to the solver
BFS_Depth	Depth of the BFS run by the algorithm (explained more in Sect. 2.7)
Gamma	The penalty coefficient in QUBO
$counter\_max_{out}$	Maximum allowed number of iterations for the outer while-loop
$counter\_max_{in}$	Maximum allowed number of iterations for the inner while-loop
θ	Minimum acceptable modularity gain over an inner or outer while-loop

2.7   Implementation Details of Ising-Louvain

This section studies the strategies tried for selecting candidate nodes and clusters, tuning the γ hyperparameter, and reducing the time complexity of the proposed method.

Node and Cluster Selection Strategies. The authors noticed that the strategy for selecting nodes and candidate clusters has a sizable impact on the run-time and performance (measured by the obtained optimal modularity value) of the devised clustering algorithm. The explored node-selection-strategies for forming set S were as follows:

1. Random strategy: selecting set S at random from the graph
2. Sliding-window strategy: selecting set S from consecutive nodes in the sorted list of nodes, and shifting the list by a random number after each pass over the entire graph [shifting would result in (probably) different selections during each pass]
3. BFS strategy: selecting set S based on a breadth-first-search (BFS), of specified depth, originating from each node selected sequentially from the shuffled list of nodes

Experiments showed that the third strategy yielded consistently better results across different graphs and across different runs on the same graphs. The experiments reported later on are conducted with this approach for node selection.

The following strategies, for selecting the cluster-set L, were considered in this work.

1. BFS strategy: selecting set L at random from clusters resulting from a BFS [of specified depth] originating in each node, while assuring the current clusters for nodes in set S are included in the candidate clusters for each node [this extra step enabled obtaining a trivial solution to the QUBO with all nodes kept in their current clusters]
2. Semi-greedy strategy: composing set L from the top k clusters for each node in set S based on a greedy search for that node [the greedy search would inspect all

neighboring clusters as well as the original cluster for the node, and would select the top k clusters which resulted in the highest gains in modularity if the node was to be moved to those clusters]

The second strategy resulted in consistently better results across different graphs and across different runs on the same graphs, so this strategy was used to conduct the experiments reported later in the paper.

Strategy for Tuning γ. Based on experiments on the graphs used in this paper, the authors devised the following rule-of-thumb for setting the initial value of γ in Eq. 4:

$$\gamma = max(k_i) \text{ for } i \in G$$

This initial value of γ resulted in consistent satisfaction of the constraint imposed on the QUBO in Eq. 4. Also, after aggregating the graph at the end of each inner while-loop (Algorithm 1), γ is updated to account for the increasing degrees of nodes:

$$\gamma_{new} = max(k_i) \text{ for } i \in G_{aggregated} \tag{5}$$

Strategies for Reducing Runtime. The majority of the different types of specialized hardware are mainly accessible via the cloud, commonly provided by some WebAPI access to the hardware. In order to make the proposed approach applicable to a variety of specialized-hardware platforms, we take this into account and outline strategies that minimize the number of calls to the hardware, and if possible, minimize the size of the QUBO per iteration.

1. When set S had only a single node, a greedy search replaced the call to the solver, and the node was assigned to the top choice determined by the greedy search. This strategies is especially helpful in reducing the number of calls to the solver when many nodes in the graph have been visited enough number of times by the algorithm, and hence the algorithm frequently selects single-member S sets.
2. When creating the candidate clusters set (L), nodes with only a single candidate cluster were excluded from set S, and instead were assigned to their single candidate clusters and were treated as normal nodes with determined clusters. After solving the QUBO for the reduced set S, the assignments for the single-candidate nodes were added back to the assignments determined by the solver. This strategy led to up to 50–60% reductions in the size of the QUBOs sent to the solver for large QUBOs, and up to 30–40% reduction in the number of calls made to the solver. This strategy yields more highlighted results after the first few passes over the graph in the inner while-loop (see Algorithm 1), when the number of clusters in the graph shrinks significantly, and consequently the algorithm identifies many single-candidate nodes.

3 Results and Discussion

3.1 Experiments

Table 3 lists the 12 benchmark graphs that are used in this paper: [Zachary's] Karate Club [36], Meredith [19], Les Miserables [13], and the rest of the graphs were selected

Table 3. Benchmark instances

Graph Name	KarateClub	Meredith	LesMiserables	Facebook	Autonomous	LastFM
$|V|$	34	70	77	4,039	6,474	7,624
$|E|$	78	140	254	88,234	13,895	27,806
Graph Name	ArXiv	ArXiv2	AstroPh	Enron	DBLP	Amazon
$|V|$	9,877	12,008	18,772	36,692	317,080	334,863
$|E|$	25,998	118,521	198,110	183,831	1,049,866	925,872

from SNAP library [17]. The original Louvain algorithm was used to produce the baseline results of clustering, and Leiden algorithm [33] (an updated version of Louvain) was used to produce rivaling results to compare the performance of the Ising-Louvain method against. To obtain the Louvain and Leiden results, each were run 20–30 times and the best results were selected. To obtain the Ising-Louvain results, several experiments were conducted to find the best combination of hyperparameters, and the results of the best experiments were reported. The Ising-Louvain algorithm was developed in Python 3.7 using NetworkX v2.4 [10] as the main library for handling the graphs, and the QUBOs were solved using Fujitsu's Digital Annealer.

3.2   Results

Table 4 shows the results of clustering the 12 benchmark graphs using Leiden, Louvain, and Ising-Louvain methods. In this table, "Optimal Modularity Results" columns show the optimal modularity obtained using the three clustering methods, "Avg QUBO Size" shows the average number of variables in QUBOs sent to the solver, and "#Solver-Calls" shows the number of calls to the solver.

Table 4 shows that in all cases, Ising-Louvain has been able to obtain a more optimal clustering than that obtained by Louvain. The only exceptions are the three smallest graphs (Karate Club, Meredith, and Les Miserables) on which both Louvain and Ising-Louvain have obtained the globally optimal clustering; thus, the final modularities obtained by both methods are equal. This is largely because Ising-Louvain, using local optimization, can consider and evaluate orders of magnitude more possible assignments of clusters to nodes than Louvain is able to consider with a greedy approach. This way, Ising-Louvain can find more optimal clusterings than the original Louvain.

Table 4 also shows that Ising-Louvain has found better results than the Leiden algorithm in 7 out of the 12 benchmark graphs. The authors hypothesize that with further hyperparameter-tuning, Ising-Louvain can surpass the Leiden algorithm in the remaining 5 cases as well, since the local optimization in Ising-Louvain can inherently outperform the greedy approach of Leiden in finding more optimal clusterings.

For a more detailed analysis of QUBO sizes, Fig. ffig:3 shows the box-plot of the sizes of all QUBOs solved when clustering the Facebook graph (*c.f.* Experiment 4 in Table 4): the box starts from the first quantile (Q1 = 4) and continues until the third quantile (Q3 = 14) of the sizes with a blue line indicating the median value (Q2 = 6). The lower and upper whiskers correspond to, respectively, $Q1 - 1.5 * (Q3 - Q1)$ and

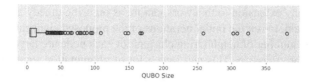

Fig. 2. Boxplot of sizes of QUBOs solved for clustering the Facebook graph

Table 4. Summary of the results of running Louvain, Leiden, and Ising-Louvain on the benchmark graphs, along with statistics of the solver

Graph	Optimal moularity results			Ising-Louvain solver Stats	
	Leiden	Louvain	Ising-Louvain	Avg QUBO size	#Solver-calls
KarateClub	0.4198	**0.4198**	**0.4198**	75	4
Meredith	0.7457	**0.7571**	**0.7571**	164	4
LesMiserables	0.5600	**0.5667**	**0.5667**	85	14
Facebook	0.8356	0.8350	**0.8358**	19	584
Autonomous	**0.6662**	0.6553	0.6572	7	1626
LastFM	**0.8170**	0.8155	0.8168	16	19036
arXiv	**0.7759**	0.7699	0.7756	11	36373
arXiv2	0.6649	0.6622	**0.6650**	32	115898
AstroPh	0.6367	0.6309	**0.6378**	44	351410
Enron	0.6265	0.6204	**0.6285**	23	146451
DBLP	**0.8301**	0.8220	0.8243	13	8369823
Amazon	**0.9309**	0.9263	0.9277	14	7812919

$Q3 + 1.5 * (Q3 - Q1)$, and the circles show the data lying outside the boundary of the whiskers. Figure 2 shows that 75% of the QUBOs sent to the solver had less than 14 variables, and most of the QUBOs had less than 50 variables.

4   Conclusion

This paper introduces a new clustering algorithm based on the popular Louvain clustering algorithm for large-scale graphs using quadratic unconstrained binary optimization (QUBO). This method, called Ising-Louvain, is particularly fit for being used with specialized hardware, including Digital Annealers, which are capable of solving combinatorial optimization problems. The method builds around replacing with local optimization a greedy approach taken by most state-of-the-art clustering algorithms. The method proves effective in obtaining improved results (as measured by modularity metric) compared to Louvain and Leiden methods—the state-of-the-art in large-scale graph clustering—when tested on 12 graphs with sizes ranging from 34 to 335k nodes. The improvement is attributed to the ability of the proposed method in evaluating orders-of-magnitude more possibilities of assigning clusters to individual nodes, and hence being able to find more optimal clusterings than the greedy method can find.

One noteworthy extension to this work can focus on using greedy approaches, like Leiden and Louvain, to run the initial iterations of the proposed algorithm on very large graphs, when the number of neighboring clusters for each node are large and hence the created QUBOs are massive. This can save a lot of computation time and can allow more experiments to be run on these graphs for obtaining more optimal solutions.

Future work can also try fitting the proposed algorithm with optimization objectives other than modularity, such as betweenness, to see the behavior of the algorithm with those objective functions. Further, the distance metric used in this paper was the adjacency matrix. Future research can try focusing on graphs in which other measures of distance between nodes, such as Euclidean distance, can be applied for selecting candidate nodes and clusters and forming the QUBOs. This can extend the application of Ising-Louvain to, especially, Geospatial Clustering.

Finally, the success of this paper in revising and improving Louvain algorithm shows promise for applying the same local-optimization-oriented approach to other unsupervised learning algorithms which depend on local search heuristics.

References

1. Aramon, M., Rosenberg, G., Valiante, E., Miyazawa, T., Tamura, H., Katzgraber, H.G.: Physics-inspired optimization for quadratic unconstrained problems using a digital annealer. Front. Phys. **7**, 48 (2019)
2. Bian, Z., Chudak, F., Macready, W.G., Rose, G.: The Ising model: teaching an old problem new tricks. D-wave Syst. **2** (2010)
3. Blondel, V.D., Guillaume, J.L., Lambiotte, R., Lefebvre, E.: Fast unfolding of communities in large networks. J. Stat. Mech: Theory Exp. **2008**(10), P10008 (2008)
4. Cohen, E., Mandal, A., Ushijima-Mwesigwa, H., Roy, A.: Ising-based consensus clustering on specialized hardware. In: Berthold, M.R., Feelders, A., Krempl, G. (eds.) IDA 2020. LNCS, vol. 12080, pp. 106–118. Springer, Cham (2020). https://doi.org/10.1007/978-3-030-44584-3_9
5. Cohen, E., Senderovich, A., Beck, J.C.: An Ising framework for constrained clustering on special purpose hardware. In: Hebrard, E., Musliu, N. (eds.) CPAIOR 2020. LNCS, vol. 12296, pp. 130–147. Springer, Cham (2020). https://doi.org/10.1007/978-3-030-58942-4_9
6. Fortunato, S.: Community detection in graphs. Phys. Rep. **486**(3–5), 75–174 (2010)
7. Fujitsu: Digital annealer. https://www.fujitsu.com/global/services/business-services/digital-annealer/
8. Girvan, M., Newman, M.E.: Community structure in social and biological networks. Proc. Natl. Acad. Sci. **99**(12), 7821–7826 (2002)
9. Guimera, R., Amaral, L.A.N.: Functional cartography of complex metabolic networks. Nature **433**(7028), 895–900 (2005)
10. Hagberg, A., Swart, P., S Chult, D.: Exploring network structure, dynamics, and function using network. Technical report, Los Alamos National Lab. (LANL), Los Alamos, NM (United States) (2008)
11. Javed, M.A., Younis, M.S., Latif, S., Qadir, J., Baig, A.: Community detection in networks: a multidisciplinary review. J. Netw. Comput. Appl. **108**, 87–111 (2018)
12. Johnson, S.C.: Hierarchical clustering schemes. Psychometrika **32**(3), 241–254 (1967)
13. Knuth, D.E.: The Stanford GraphBase: a platform for combinatorial computing. ACM Press, New York (1993)

14. Krogan, N.J., et al.: Global landscape of protein complexes in the yeast saccharomyces cerevisiae. Nature **440**(7084), 637–643 (2006)
15. Kumar, V., Bass, G., Tomlin, C., Dulny, J.: Quantum annealing for combinatorial clustering. Quantum Inf. Process. **17**(2), 1–14 (2018). https://doi.org/10.1007/s11128-017-1809-2
16. Lancichinetti, A., Fortunato, S., Radicchi, F.: Benchmark graphs for testing community detection algorithms. Phys. Rev. E **78**(4), 046110 (2008)
17. Leskovec, J., Krevl, A.: SNAP Datasets: Stanford large network dataset collection (2014). http://snap.stanford.edu/data
18. Liu, X., Ushijima-Mwesigwa, H., Mandal, A., Upadhyay, S., Safro, I., Roy, A.: On modeling local search with special-purpose combinatorial optimization hardware. arXiv preprint arXiv:1911.09810 (2019)
19. Meredith, G.H.: Regular n-valent n-connected non Hamiltonian non-n-edge-colorable graphs. J. Comb. Theory Ser. B **14**(1), 55–60 (1973)
20. Naghsh, Z., Javad-Kalbasi, M., Valaee, S.: Digitally annealed solution for the maximum clique problem with critical application in cellular v2x. In: ICC, pp. 1–7. IEEE (2019)
21. Negre, C.F., Ushijima-Mwesigwa, H., Mniszewski, S.M.: Detecting multiple communities using quantum annealing on the d-wave system. Plos one **15**(2), e0227538 (2020)
22. Newman, M.E.J.: Detecting community structure in networks. Eur. Phys. J. B **38**(2), 321–330 (2004). https://doi.org/10.1140/epjb/e2004-00124-y
23. Newman, M.E.: Spectral methods for community detection and graph partitioning. Phys. Rev. E **88**(4), 042822 (2013)
24. Newman, M.E.: Community detection in networks: modularity optimization and maximum likelihood are equivalent. arXiv preprint arXiv:1606.02319 (2016)
25. Newman, M.E.: Equivalence between modularity optimization and maximum likelihood methods for community detection. Phys. Rev. E **94**(5), 052315 (2016)
26. Newman, M.E., Girvan, M.: Finding and evaluating community structure in networks. Phys. Rev. E **69**(2), 026113 (2004)
27. Palla, G., Derényi, I., Farkas, I., Vicsek, T.: Uncovering the overlapping community structure of complex networks in nature and society. Nature **435**(7043), 814–818 (2005)
28. Rahman, M.T., Han, S., Tadayon, N., Valaee, S.: Ising model formulation of outlier rejection, with application in Wifi based positioning. In: ICASSP, pp. 4405–4409. IEEE (2019)
29. Reichardt, J., Bornholdt, S.: Detecting fuzzy community structures in complex networks with a Potts model. Phys. Rev. Lett. **93**(21), 218701 (2004)
30. Ruan, Y., Fuhry, D., Parthasarathy, S.: Efficient community detection in large networks using content and links. In: Proceedings of the 22nd International Conference on World Wide Web, pp. 1089–1098 (2013)
31. Shaydulin, R., Ushijima-Mwesigwa, H., Safro, I., Mniszewski, S., Alexeev, Y.: Community detection across emerging quantum architectures. arXiv preprint arXiv:1810.07765 (2018)
32. Shaydulin, R., Ushijima-Mwesigwa, H., Safro, I., Mniszewski, S., Alexeev, Y.: Network community detection on small quantum computers. Adv. Quantum Technol. **2**(9), 1900029 (2019)
33. Traag, V.A., Waltman, L., van Eck, N.J.: From Louvain to Leiden: guaranteeing well-connected communities. Sci. Rep. **9**(1), 1–12 (2019)
34. Ushijima-Mwesigwa, H., Negre, C.F., Mniszewski, S.M.: Graph partitioning using quantum annealing on the d-wave system. In: Proceedings of the Second International Workshop on Post Moores Era Supercomputing, pp. 22–29 (2017)
35. Ushijima-Mwesigwa, H., Shaydulin, R., Negre, C.F., Mniszewski, S.M., Alexeev, Y., Safro, I.: Multilevel combinatorial optimization across quantum architectures. arXiv preprint arXiv:1910.09985 (2019)
36. Zachary, W.W.: An information flow model for conflict and fission in small groups. J. Anthropol. Res. **33**(4), 452–473 (1977)

Modeling Special Data Formats

Reducing Negative Impact of Noise in Boolean Matrix Factorization with Association Rules

Petr Krajča[✉][ID] and Martin Trnecka[ID]

Department of Computer Science, Palacky University Olomouc,
Olomouc, Czech Republic
petr.krajca@upol.cz

Abstract. Boolean matrix factorization (BMF) is a well-established data analytical method whose goal is to decompose a single large matrix into two, preferably smaller, matrices, carrying the same or similar information as the original matrix. In essence, it can be used to reduce data dimensionality and to provide fundamental insight into data. Existing algorithms are often negatively affected by the presence of noise in the data, which is a common case for real-world datasets. We present an initial study on an algorithm for approximate BMF that uses association rules in a novel way to identify possible noise. This allows us to suppress the impact of noise and improve the quality of results. Moreover, we show that association rules provide a suitable framework allowing the handling of noise in BMF in a justified way.

Keywords: Boolean matrix factorization · Formal concept analysis · Association rules · Noise reduction

1 Introduction

The input for Boolean matrix factorization (BMF) is a Boolean matrix I of size $m \times n$ describing objects and their attributes; for instance, patients and their symptoms (see Fig. 1 for an example). The goal of BMF is to decompose I into two submatrices, A and B (of sizes $m \times k$, $k \times n$, respectively), such that composition $A \circ B$ is (approximately) equal to I. This decomposition may be interpreted as a discovery of k factors that exactly (or approximately) describe the data. The factors can be seen as rectangular areas in the data that capture non-trivial (usually hidden) dependencies. Matrices I, A, and B are interpreted as the object-attribute, object-factor, and factor-attribute matrices, respectively. Columns and rows of the last two mentioned matrices describe the factors, namely objects and

P. Krajča—was supported by the grant JG 2019 of Palacký University Olomouc, No. JG_2019_008. Martin Trnecka was supported by the grant JG 2020 of Palacký University Olomouc, No. JG_2020_003. Support by Grant No. IGA_PrF_2020_019 of IGA of Palacký University is also acknowledged.

P. H. Abreu et al. (Eds.): IDA 2021, LNCS 12695, pp. 365–375, 2021.
https://doi.org/10.1007/978-3-030-74251-5_29

attributes involved in each factor. For the patient-symptom example, each factor corresponds to a single disease; this means, object-factor matrix **A** describes patients and their diseases, factor-attribute matrix **B** describes diseases and their symptoms. In other words, diseases (factors) are described by (i) patients (objects) having the given disease and (ii) symptoms (attributes) common to patients with a given disease. Basically, BMF allows us to discover new fundamental variables (factors) describing the data in a concise and more comprehensible form.

Particular issues arise if the data contains noise (in Boolean data, it may be interpreted rather as errors [5]), as typically happens with real-world data, especially if a human factor is involved. For various reasons, input data may contain excessive 1s, or some 1s may be missing. In our example, particular symptoms may be not related to a given disease (excessive 1), or a symptom may be negligible and thus the patient does not mention it (missing 1). Closer examination of the data from Fig. 1 reveals that patients have approximately two diseases that can be identified as (i) *influenza* and (ii) a *common cold*. These are manifested by attributes (i) *rapid onset*, *fever*, and *weakness*; (ii) *sneezing* and *sore throat*. Apparently, patients #1 and #4 are suffering from influenza while patients #2 and #3 have a common cold. Patients #3 and #5 can be seen as anomalous. Patient #3 has symptoms of the common cold and reports also weakness which is not typically related to this disease. From the data we have, we are not able to decide what is the true cause of the weakness of the patient #3. On the other hand, patient #5 is very likely to suffer from influenza (due to his/her symptoms) but does not report weakness. Presence of such cases may lead to poor results of BMF, because algorithms tend to discover factors of a low importance, for example, *a common cold with weakness* or *influenza without weakness*.

patient	rapid onset	fever	weakness	sneezing	sore throat
#1	1	1	1	0	0
#2	0	0	0	1	1
#3	0	0	1	1	1
#4	1	1	1	0	0
#5	1	1	0	0	0

Fig. 1. Example of input data for BMF

Existing BMF algorithms, e.g. Asso [11], PaNDa+ [9] or Hyper+ [16], handle the aforementioned issue in various, usually ad-hoc, ways (see an overview in [4]). This means that they primarily focus on approximation of 1s and dealing with noise is only collateral. The most conservative are so-called from-below BMF algorithms [4,6]. These can gracefully handle excessive 1s, however, produce suboptimal results if there are missing 1s. This behavior of BMF algorithms can be seen as natural. Indeed, they work with available information (1s) and ignore unavailable information (0s).

The main contribution of the paper is a novel BMF algorithm using association rules to identify potentially missing 1s (noise) and utilizing this information to find better factors. Our approach allows us to conservatively, and in a user-friendly manner, describe what is acceptable noise and obtain an appropriate approximation of the input, taking potentially missing 1s into account. Note that association rules are used also in Asso, however, in a completely different way. In Asso association rules are used to describe correlations between pairs of attributes, for more details see [11].

The paper is organized as follows. First, we provide an introduction to formal concept analysis which the algorithm is built on, association rules, and BMF (Sect. 2). Then, the novel BMF algorithm is presented (Sect. 3). The paper concludes with a preliminary evaluation (Sect. 4) and discussion on results and future research (Sect. 5).

2 Preliminaries and Notation

We shall provide a necessary introduction to FCA, BMF, and the notation we use. Throughout the paper, bold capital letters $(\mathbf{I})$ denote Boolean (binary) matrices and their subscript denotes entries, i.e. $\mathbf{I}_{ij}$ denotes the entry corresponding to the row i and the column j of $\mathbf{I}$. The set of all $m \times n$ Boolean matrices is denoted by $\{0,1\}^{m \times n}$. The number of 1s in a Boolean matrix $\mathbf{I}$ is denoted by $\|\mathbf{I}\|$, i.e. $\|\mathbf{I}\| = \sum_{i,j} \mathbf{I}_{ij}$.

2.1 Formal Concept Analysis

The input of formal concept analysis (FCA) [7] is a *formal context*, a triplet $\langle X, Y, I \rangle$ where X and Y are finite non-empty sets of objects and attributes respectively, I is a relation $I \subseteq X \times Y$ such that $\langle x, y \rangle \in I$ if an object x has an attribute y. A particularly interesting output of FCA is a set of all *formal concepts*. A formal concept is a pair $\langle A, B \rangle$ where $A \subseteq X$, $B \subseteq Y$, and every object in A has all attributes from B, and all objects having all attributes from B are in A.

The formal context can be seen as a Boolean matrix where rows correspond to objects, columns to attributes, and zeros and ones indicate if an object has a given attribute. From this matrix viewpoint, formal concepts correspond to maximal sub-matrices full of ones.

Formally, let $\mathbf{I} \in \{0,1\}^{m \times n}$ be a Boolean matrix corresponding to a formal context $\langle X, Y, I \rangle$ where $X = \{1, \ldots, m\}, Y = \{1, \ldots, n\}$. Then, there exists a pair of operators $^{\uparrow} : 2^X \rightarrow 2^Y$ and $^{\downarrow} : 2^Y \rightarrow 2^X$ such that for each set $C \subseteq X$ and $D \subseteq Y$ holds:

$$C^{\uparrow} = \{j \in Y \mid \forall i \in C : \mathbf{I}_{ij} = 1\},$$
$$D^{\downarrow} = \{i \in X \mid \forall j \in D : \mathbf{I}_{ij} = 1\}.$$

In words, $C^{\uparrow}$ is the set of all attributes (columns) common to all objects (rows) in C and $D^{\downarrow}$ is the set of all objects having all the attributes from D, respectively. A formal concept is any pair $\langle A, B \rangle$, $A \subseteq X$, $B \subseteq Y$ such that $A^\uparrow = B$ and $B^\downarrow = A$.

2.2   Association Rules

Association rules [2] are typically used to process transactional databases. However, it can be easily reformulated to the terminology of FCA. Let $\mathbf{I} \in \{0,1\}^{m \times n}$ be a Boolean matrix. Then, the association rule in $\mathbf{I}$ is a rule $U \Rightarrow V$ where $U, V \subseteq Y$ has the meaning: *if an object has all attributes from U, then it is likely to have attributes from V.* To express the significance and relevance of association rules, two measures are typically used—support and confidence—given as

$$\text{supp}(U \Rightarrow V) = \frac{|(U \cup V)^\downarrow|}{|X|}, \quad \text{conf}(U \Rightarrow V) = \frac{|(U \cup V)^\downarrow|}{|U^\downarrow|}.$$

2.3   Boolean Matrix Factorization

The main objective of BMF is for a given Boolean matrix $\mathbf{I} \in \{0,1\}^{m \times n}$ to find matrices $\mathbf{A} \in \{0,1\}^{m \times k}$ and $\mathbf{B} \in \{0,1\}^{k \times n}$ for which $\mathbf{I} \approx \mathbf{A} \circ \mathbf{B}$, where $\approx$ represents approximate equality and $\circ$ is *Boolean matrix product* given as

$$(\mathbf{A} \circ \mathbf{B})_{ij} = \max_{l=1}^{k}(\min(\mathbf{A}_{il}, \mathbf{B}_{lj})).$$

The quality of approximation is typically expressed with *an approximation error*, which is a number of values that are different in $\mathbf{I}$ and $\mathbf{A} \circ \mathbf{B}$, i.e.

$$E(\mathbf{I}, \mathbf{A} \circ \mathbf{B}) = \sum_{i=1}^{m} \sum_{j=1}^{n} |\mathbf{I}_{ij} - (\mathbf{A} \circ \mathbf{B})_{ij}|.$$

We talk about *exact decomposition* if $\mathbf{I} = \mathbf{A} \circ \mathbf{B}$; that is, if and only if $E(\mathbf{I}, \mathbf{A} \circ \mathbf{B}) = 0$.

FCA gives us important insight on how to decompose Boolean matrices. It has been shown that the optimal decomposition is given as a subset of all formal concepts [6]. In essence, every Boolean matrix can be seen as a *Boolean sum* (a usual element-wise matrix sum for which $1 + 1 = 1$; denoted with $\oplus$) of matrices consisting of rectangular areas full of 1s that correspond to formal concepts. Each such area shall be called *a factor concept*, or simply, *factor*.

A set of factor concepts $\mathcal{F} = \{\langle C_1, D_1 \rangle, \ldots, \langle C_k, D_k \rangle\}$ (with a fixed indexing of the formal concepts $\langle C_l, D_l \rangle$) induces the $m \times k$ and $k \times n$ Boolean matrices $\mathbf{A}_\mathcal{F}$ and $\mathbf{B}_\mathcal{F}$, such that

$$(\mathbf{A}_\mathcal{F})_{il} = \begin{cases} 1, \text{if } i \in C_l, \\ 0, \text{if } i \notin C_l, \end{cases} \text{ and } (\mathbf{B}_\mathcal{F})_{lj} = \begin{cases} 1, \text{if } j \in D_l, \\ 0, \text{if } j \notin D_l, \end{cases}$$

for $l = 1, \ldots, k$. That is, the lth column of $\mathbf{A}_\mathcal{F}$ and lth row $\mathbf{B}_\mathcal{F}$ are the characteristic vectors of C_l and D_l, respectively. The following equation illustrates the idea of decomposition based on factor concepts of the data in Fig. 1.

$$\begin{pmatrix} 11100 \\ 00011 \\ 00111 \\ 11100 \\ 11000 \end{pmatrix} = \begin{pmatrix} 11100 \\ 00000 \\ 00000 \\ 11100 \\ 00000 \end{pmatrix} \oplus \begin{pmatrix} 00000 \\ 00011 \\ 00011 \\ 00000 \\ 00000 \end{pmatrix} \oplus \begin{pmatrix} 11000 \\ 00000 \\ 00000 \\ 11000 \\ 11000 \end{pmatrix} \oplus \begin{pmatrix} 00100 \\ 00000 \\ 00100 \\ 00100 \\ 00000 \end{pmatrix} = \begin{pmatrix} 1011 \\ 0100 \\ 0101 \\ 1011 \\ 0010 \end{pmatrix} \circ \begin{pmatrix} 11100 \\ 00011 \\ 11000 \\ 00100 \end{pmatrix}.$$

The original data (the matrix on the left side) is expressed as the element-wise matrix sum of four factor concepts (matrices with highlighted rectangular areas of 1s). These factor concepts give us information on how to construct $\mathbf{A}_\mathcal{F}$ and $\mathbf{B}_\mathcal{F}$ (matrices on the right side), i.e. each column of $\mathbf{A}_\mathcal{F}$ and corresponding row of $\mathbf{B}_\mathcal{F}$ describe one factor concept. The first column of $\mathbf{A}_\mathcal{F}$ has 1s exactly in the same rows as the first factor concept and the first row of $\mathbf{B}_\mathcal{F}$ has 1s exactly in the same columns as the first factor concept. The rest of $\mathbf{A}_\mathcal{F}$ and $\mathbf{B}_\mathcal{F}$ is obtained in the same vein.

3   Algorithm

The problem of finding optimal decomposition (with the least possible dimension k) is NP-hard [6], since it can be reduced to a set cover problem. Thus, several heuristic algorithms were proposed. One of them is GreCon (see [6], Algorithm 1), which enumerates all formal concepts first. Then, uses a greedy strategy to find factor concepts. The only criterion used to select a concept is a number of 1s that are covered by the given concept and that are not yet covered by previously discovered factors. A similar idea appears in other algorithms, e.g. GreConD [6], GreEss [4] or MDLGreConD [10], which are using different strategies for enumerating formal concepts and selecting factor concepts.

The GreCon (and similar algorithms) is able to gracefully handle additive noise. It is sufficient to stop the algorithm whenever a particular amount (e.g. 90%) of 1s is covered. In such cases, discovered factors represent an approximate matrix decomposition and uncovered ones represent noise in the data. This type of approximate decomposition covers only non-zero elements, i.e. for every element holds $(\mathbf{A} \circ \mathbf{B})_{ij} \leq \mathbf{I}_{ij}$, thus, it is called *from-below approximation*.

$$\begin{pmatrix} 1110 \\ 1111 \\ 1101 \\ 0011 \\ 0011 \end{pmatrix} = \begin{pmatrix} 1001 \\ 1111 \\ 1010 \\ 0111 \\ 0111 \end{pmatrix} \circ \begin{pmatrix} 1100 \\ 0011 \\ 0001 \\ 0010 \end{pmatrix} \approx \begin{pmatrix} 10 \\ 11 \\ 11 \\ 01 \\ 01 \end{pmatrix} \circ \begin{pmatrix} 1110 \\ 0011 \end{pmatrix}$$

Fig. 2. An example of exact decomposition of a matrix (left) and approximate decomposition of the matrix where $\mathbf{I}_{33} = 0$ and $(\mathbf{A} \circ \mathbf{B})_{33} = 1$ (right)

The search space of these algorithms is merely determined by the 1s in the input matrix. This may be a particular issue in the presence of the subtractive noise, as illustrated in Fig. 2 (left). For the given input matrix, GreCon identifies four factors $\langle\{1,2,3\},\{1,2\}\rangle$, $\langle\{2,4,5\},\{3,4\}\rangle$, $\langle\{2,3,4,5\},\{4\}\rangle$, and $\langle\{1,2,4,5\},\{3\}\rangle$. The first two factors cover 12 (of 14) ones and provide interpretation for the major part of the input. In fact, the only purpose of the remaining two factors is to deal with the last two uncovered 1s. Further, their contribution to the interpretation of the input is questionable since both are trivial, i.e. each cover only a single attribute.

3.1   New Algorithm: Grass

The matrix from Fig. 2 illustrates not only a situation where GreCon's results can be seen as unsatisfactory, but also a motivation for the new algorithm we propose. Notice that if the value $\mathbf{I}_{33}$ is set to 1, then it can be expressed as a composition of two factors, $\langle\{1,2,3\},\{1,2,3\}\rangle$ and $\langle\{2,3,4,5\},\{3,4\}\rangle$, covering all 1s. This means, these two factors explain the entire input at a cost of an approximation error equal to 1. Moreover, setting $\mathbf{I}_{33} = 1$ has merit in this context. In three of four cases, if an object has attribute 4, it also has attribute 3 (analogously, in two of three cases if an object has attributes 1 and 2, it also has attribute 3). In fact, these observations can be seen as an indication that at $\mathbf{I}_{33}$ may be missing a 1.

This leads us to the idea that if the matrix contains subtractive noise, it can be identified with association rules. An association rule $U \Rightarrow V$ can be interpreted as: *if an object has all attributes from U, then it has or should have all attributes from V*. In other words, if an object has all attributes from U and lacks any attribute from V, it can be an indication of a missing value.

We have incorporated this idea into the GreCon-like algorithm called Grass. To deal with a subtractive noise, the algorithm considers not only formal concepts as possible factors, but also submatrices induced by association rules. Specifically, if a rule $U \Rightarrow V$ has sufficient support and confidence, then the submatrix $\langle U^{\downarrow}, U \cup V\rangle$ is considered as a possible factor concept. Even though this submatrix is not a formal concept per se, it can be seen as a special kind of concept that takes into account potentially missing 1s.

As a consequence, the measure used to select factors has to reflect 0s that are (incorrectly) covered by factors induced by association rules. Thus, Grass uses a number of newly covered 1s reduced by the number of newly covered 0s as a criterion for factor selection.

The Grass algorithm is outlined in Algorithm 1. First, all formal concepts are retrieved (line 1); for instance, with the FCbO algorithm [13]. Afterwards, association rules are obtained (line 2). Note that formal concepts may be used to enumerate frequent closed itemsets which can be then used to enumerate association rules—especially a reduced set of rules of a form $U^{\downarrow\uparrow} \Rightarrow (U \cup V)^{\downarrow\uparrow}$ [17]. These rules cover all potentially missing 1s (w.r.t. our assumption) and are aligned with formal concepts. The obtained association rules are used to build new possible factor concepts, which are subsequently merged with all formal concepts (lines 3

Algorithm 1: Grass algorithm

Input: Boolean matrix **I**, *support*, *confidence*
Result: set of factor concepts
1 $\mathcal{C}_f \leftarrow$ ENUMERATEFORMALCONCEPTS(**I**)
2 $\mathcal{R} \leftarrow$ ASSOCIATIONRULES(**I**, $\mathcal{C}_f$, *support*, *confidence*)
3 $\mathcal{C}_a \leftarrow \{\langle U^\downarrow, U \cup V \rangle \mid$ for each $U \Rightarrow V \in \mathcal{R}\}$
4 $\mathcal{C} \leftarrow \mathcal{C}_f \cup \mathcal{C}_a$
5 $\mathbf{I}^+ \leftarrow \mathbf{I}$
6 $\mathbf{I}^-\leftarrow$ negation of **I**
7 $\mathcal{F} \leftarrow \emptyset$
8 **while** $\|\mathbf{I}^+\| > 0$ **do**
9    $\quad\langle A, B \rangle \leftarrow$ **select** $\langle A, B \rangle$ from $\mathcal{C}$ **where** $(coverage(\mathbf{I}^+, A, B) - coverage(\mathbf{I}^-, A, B))$ **is maximal**
10    $\quad$**foreach** $i \in A; \ j \in B$ **do**
11    $\quad\quad \mathbf{I}_{ij}^+ \leftarrow 0$
12    $\quad\quad \mathbf{I}_{ij}^- \leftarrow 0$
13    $\quad \mathcal{F} \leftarrow \mathcal{F} \cup \{\langle A, B \rangle\}$
14    $\quad \mathcal{C} \leftarrow \mathcal{C} \backslash \{\langle A, B \rangle\}$

---

and 4). Then, a copy $\mathbf{I}^+$ and a negation $\mathbf{I}^-$ (i.e. a matrix where 0s are replaced with 1s and vice versa) of the input matrix **I** is created (lines 6). The purpose of the $\mathbf{I}^+$ is to hold information on covered/uncovered 1s, whilst the matrix $\mathbf{I}^-$ contains information on covered/uncovered 0s.

The main loop of the algorithm systematically looks for a factor concept (line 9) minimizing approximation error, i.e. it selects a factor concept that covers the highest number of uncovered ones reduced by the number of newly covered 0s. Note that the number of covered ones is given as

$$coverage(\mathbf{I}, A, B) = \sum_{i \in A}\sum_{j \in B} \mathbf{I}_{ij}.$$

After an appropriate concept is found, the 1s covered by this concept are removed from $\mathbf{I}^+$ (lines 10 and 11), as well as covered zeros from the matrix $\mathbf{I}^-$ (line 12). The selected concept is inserted into a set of factor concepts $\mathcal{F}$ and removed from the set $\mathcal{C}$ (lines 13 and 14). The algorithm stops if the matrix $\mathbf{I}^+$ has no 1s to cover.

The approximation error is controlled via the parameters *support* and *confidence*, prescribing what is acceptable noise. Their values depend merely on the input data. To deal with additive noise, one can stop the algorithm when a particular coverage is reached (similarly to GreCon). It is worth noting that if the set of association rules is empty, then the algorithm becomes GreCon. In other words, Grass can be seen as a generalization of GreCon. Further, the Grass algorithm can be turned into an algorithm which returns approximation from above and below. It is sufficient to change the condition controlling the loop (line 8). If a value greater than zero is used, Grass stops when some defined number of 1s is covered. In that case, uncovered 1s correspond to an additive noise and covered 0s to an subtractive noise.

The most computationally intensive task in Grass (analogously to GreCon) is the enumeration of all formal concepts. Hence, the efficiency of Grass is mainly determined by the algorithm used for this task. Currently, the fastest algorithms for enumerating formal concepts are FCbO [13], or the In-Close family of algorithms [3]. The FCbO algorithm has worst-case time complexity $O(\mathcal{B}(\mathbf{I}) \cdot n^2 \cdot m)$ where $\mathcal{B}(\mathbf{I})$ denotes the number of all formal concepts in $\mathbf{I}$. In order to reduce the number of association rules, we consider only rules in a form $U^{\downarrow\uparrow} \Rightarrow (U \cup V)^{\downarrow\uparrow}$. The number of such rules is linear in the number of formal concepts [17]. Therefore, the set of possible factor concepts is not significantly larger when compared with the original GreCon algorithm.

4   Evaluation

We have prepared two experiments evaluating the quality of results of Grass and competing algorithms. In what follows, we used—in the BMF community well-known—real-world datasets, namely DNA [12], Ecoli [1], Mushroom [1] and Zoo [1]. Their basic characteristics are depicted in Table 1.

Table 1. Datasets and their characteristics

Dataset	Rows	Columns	Density
DNA	4590	392	0.015
Ecoli	336	34	0.068
Mushroom	8124	119	0.193
Zoo	101	28	0.309

4.1   Comparison with Competitors

We use a normalized approximation error (i.e. $E(\mathbf{I}, \mathbf{A} \circ \mathbf{B})/\|\mathbf{I}\|$) as a coverage quality measure, and compare Grass with Asso [11], GreConD [6] and MDLGreConD [10] algorithms.

Note that Asso is a state-of-the-art BMF algorithm utilizing association rules. The GreConD algorithm is widely used instead of GreCon (for more details see [4, 6]). Its modification—MDLGreConD—improves the quality of factors delivered by GreConD. All of them are direct competitors of Grass. The result of the comparison is depicted in Fig. 3.

The experiment shows that Grass outperforms GreConD and MDLGreConD on the first (the most important) factors. Note that MDLGreConD stops when a newly added factor does not improve the quality of factorization, while other algorithms stop when a prescribed parameter (number of factors, coverage) is reached. Grass (significantly) outperforms Asso for higher numbers of factors. This is a sign of a smaller number of incorrectly covered zeros by Grass.

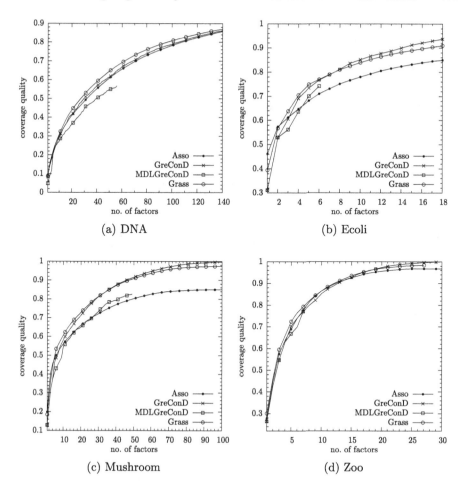

Fig. 3. Coverage quality of the first factors on real-world datasets. Larger values are better.

4.2 Ability to Handle Noise

To evaluate the ability of the algorithm to deal with noise, we reconstructed the Gupta's experiment [8]. We took three nested patterns and included noise (Fig. 4a, 4b), i.e. 5% of entries were flipped. Then, we computed factorization with each algorithm, see Figs. 4c–f for results (the parameters of Asso and Grass were selected w.r.t. input). Seemingly, GreConD is not able to discover original patterns, mainly due to subtractive noise. Better results are provided by MDLGreConD, which is unable to fully identify the middle pattern. Moreover, obtained patterns are negatively affected by noise. Asso identifies almost correctly the first and third pattern, however, the middle pattern incorrectly covers a large part of the third one. Grass identifies correctly all patterns, but one can clearly see residues of noise, however, they are not as significant as in the case of GreConD and MDLGreConD.

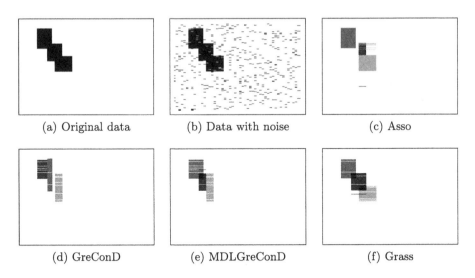

| (a) Original data | (b) Data with noise | (c) Asso |

| (d) GreConD | (e) MDLGreConD | (f) Grass |

Fig. 4. Ability of algorithms to handle noise. (a) Three nested patterns, (b) three nested patterns with added noise, (c)–(f) discovered patterns.

5   Discussion

Preliminary experiments show that the proposed algorithm in many cases outperforms state of the art algorithms. This indicates that the assumptions we have been working with are reasonable and have merits. Currently, we are just at the beginning of our research. We presented a basic algorithm that can be the subject of further study and improvements. We have identified four important areas to focus on:

(i) Despite its naïve nature, the measure used to select factors provides good results. This opens up an interesting question: whether more sophisticated measures (e.g. minimum description length [10]) can provide even better results.

(ii) Similarly, to identify missing 1s in the data, common association rules are used. However, there are other types of association rules, e.g. those described by GUHA [14]. We are going to investigate whether they may find use in Grass and improve the quality of its results.

(iii) We are to explore possible optimizations reducing memory and CPU utilization, e.g. those proposed in [15]. Besides this, we aim to develop an algorithm that does not need to compute all formal concepts or association rules in advance (like GreConD [6]).

(iv) For the preliminary evaluation, three state of the art algorithms have been chosen. Nevertheless, a thorough comparison with other BMF algorithms should be carried out.

References

1. UCI Machine Learning Repository (2020). http://archive.ics.uci.edu/ml
2. Agrawal, R., Imielinski, T., Swami, A.N.: Mining association rules between sets of items in large databases. In: Buneman, P., Jajodia, S. (eds.) Proceedings of ACM SIGMOD. ACM Press (1993)
3. Andrews, S.: A 'best-of-breed' approach for designing a fast algorithm for computing fixpoints of Galois connections. Inf. Sci. **295**, 633–649 (2015)
4. Belohlávek, R., Trnecka, M.: From-below approximations in Boolean matrix factorization: geometry and new algorithm. J. Comput. Syst. Sci. **81**(8), 1678–1697 (2015)
5. Belohlávek, R., Trnecka, M.: Handling noise in Boolean matrix factorization. Int. J. Approx. Reason. **96**, 78–94 (2018)
6. Belohlavek, R., Vychodil, V.: Discovery of optimal factors in binary data via a novel method of matrix decomposition. J. Comput. Syst. Sci. **76**(1), 3–20 (2010)
7. Ganter, B., Wille, R.: Formal Concept Analysis - Mathematical Foundations. Springer, Heidelberg (1999). https://doi.org/10.1007/978-3-642-59830-2
8. Gupta, R., Fang, G., Field, B., Steinbach, M.S., Kumar, V.: Quantitative evaluation of approximate frequent pattern mining algorithms. In: Li, Y., Liu, B., Sarawagi, S. (eds.) Proceedings of ACM SIGKDD (2008)
9. Lucchese, C., Orlando, S., Perego, R.: A unifying framework for mining approximate top-k binary patterns. IEEE Trans. Knowl. Data Eng. **26**(12), 2900–2913 (2014)
10. Makhalova, T., Trnecka, M.: From-below Boolean matrix factorization algorithm based on mdl. Adv. Data Anal. Classif. 1–20 (2020)
11. Miettinen, P., Mielikäinen, T., Gionis, A., Das, G., Mannila, H.: The discrete basis problem. IEEE Trans. Knowl. Data Eng. **20**(10), 1348–1362 (2008)
12. Myllykangas, S., Himberg, J., Böhling, T., Nagy, B., Hollmén, J., Knuutila, S.: DNA copy number amplification profiling of human neoplasms. Oncogene **25**(55), 7324–7332 (2006)
13. Outrata, J., Vychodil, V.: Fast algorithm for computing fixpoints of Galois connections induced by object-attribute relational data. Inf. Sci. **185**(1), 114–127 (2012)
14. Rauch, J.: Observational Calculi and Association Rules. Studies in Computational Intelligence, vol. 469. Springer, Heidelberg (2013). https://doi.org/10.1007/978-3-642-11737-4
15. Trnecka, M., Vyjidacek, R.: Revisiting the Grecon algorithm for Boolean matrix factorization. In: Valverde-Albacete, F.J., Trnecka, M. (eds.) Proceedings of the Fifthteenth International Conference on Concept Lattices and Their Applications, Tallinn, Estonia, June 29-July 1, 2020. CEUR Workshop Proceedings, vol. 2668, pp. 59–70. CEUR-WS.org (2020). http://ceur-ws.org/Vol-2668/paper4.pdf
16. Xiang, Y., Jin, R., Fuhry, D., Dragan, F.F.: Summarizing transactional databases with overlapped hyperrectangles. Data Min. Knowl. Discov. **23**(2), 215–251 (2011)
17. Zaki, M.J.: Mining non-redundant association rules. Data Min. Knowl. Discov. **9**(3), 223–248 (2004)

Z-Hist: A Temporal Abstraction of Multivariate Histogram Snapshots

Zed Lee[1(✉)], Nicholas Anton[2], Panagiotis Papapetrou[1], and Tony Lindgren[1]

[1] DSV, Stockholm University, Kista, Sweden
{zed.lee,panagiotis,tony}@dsv.su.se
[2] Scania CV, Turbo and Gas Exchange, Södertälje, Sweden
nicholas.anton@scania.com

Abstract. Multivariate histogram snapshots are complex data structures that frequently occur in predictive maintenance. Histogram snapshots store large amounts of data in devices with small memory capacity, though it remains a challenge to analyze them effectively. In this paper, we propose Z-Hist, a novel framework for representing and temporally abstracting histogram snapshots by converting them into a set of temporal intervals. This conversion enables the exploitation of frequent arrangement mining techniques for extracting disproportionally frequent patterns of such complex structures. Our experiments on a turbo failure dataset from a truck Original Equipment Manufacturer (OEM) demonstrate a promising use-case of Z-Hist. We also benchmark Z-Hist on six synthetic datasets for studying the relationship between distribution changes over time and disproportionality values.

Keywords: Multivariate histogram snapshots · Temporal abstraction · Disproportionality analysis

1 Introduction

Histograms are used as a means of providing compact summarizations or abstractions of complex data types [20], such as temporal data generated from sensors or multidimensional images. Their main functionality is to reduce the complexity of the original data by creating multiple bins for holding a discretized frequency representation of the original data values. In some application areas, histograms are employed together with the original data sources and function as assistive features that describe the data distribution and can lead to improvements in the target analysis tasks. Examples of such application areas include medical image analysis, i.e., MRI diagnostics [12] or tumor detection [22]. On the other hand, there are many cases where histograms are generated and stored over time without a particular analytics task in mind but rather for the purpose of data collection or monitoring; and even without the original data. Examples of such histogram data can be found in the automotive industry and are generated from, e.g., monitoring vehicle compressors [17] or sensors in heavy trucks [6]. One benefit of collecting data in the form of histograms is the ability to store larger

© Springer Nature Switzerland AG 2021
P. H. Abreu et al. (Eds.): IDA 2021, LNCS 12695, pp. 376–388, 2021.
https://doi.org/10.1007/978-3-030-74251-5_30

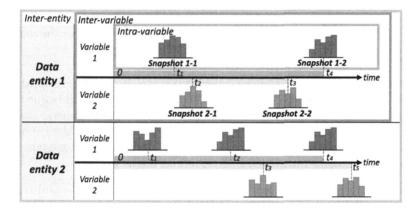

Fig. 1. An example of histogram snapshots over time comprising two data entities of two variables, with histogram snapshots generated at different time points. (Color figure online)

amounts of data in sensors and devices with small memory capacity, which is a common requirement and challenge in predictive maintenance.

Despite existing attempts at analyzing such histograms, current machine learning approaches in the automotive industry are hampered by the fact that they view them as global summaries of data variables. They hence fail to exploit the presence of multiple histograms in a single variable, each summarizing that variable over a time period. These histograms are referred to as *histogram snapshots* and can provide insights into the temporal evolution of these variables.

Example. Figure 1 depicts nine different histogram snapshots. Each data entity has the same variables as its features, and each histogram snapshot represents the summarized value of a specific feature over a time range. In Data entity 1, Snapshot 1–1 summarizes the values of Variable 1 from time point 0 to t_1. Likewise, Snapshot 1–2 summarizes the same variable from t_1 to t_4. As for Variable 2, there are two histogram snapshots (Snapshots 2–1 and 2–2) which compress the data from time point 0 to t_2, and from t_2 to t_3, respectively. The variables in Data entity 2 are summarized by five histogram snapshots in a similar manner.

Analyzing multivariate histogram snapshots can be challenging as we need to consider and exploit the temporal relations between different snapshots and across different variables. We, hence, focus on the following analysis tasks:

- **Intra-entity analysis:** This refers to explicitly extracting temporal information from each data entity so we can further compare different data entities. It consists of (1) intra-variable analysis (green box in Fig. 1), where we extract temporal trends distribution that changes over time for each variable, and (2) inter-variable analysis (orange box), where we identify varying temporal dependencies and relations among different variables over time.
- **Inter-entity analysis (yellow box):** This refers to extracting temporal information across data entities. It consists of (1) frequent arrangement min-

ing, where we extract frequently occurring temporal histogram snapshot patterns in the dataset, and (2) disproportionality analysis, where we compare the occurrences of these patterns across different groups.

Contributions. To the best of our knowledge, there is yet no principled approach for analyzing multivariate histogram snapshots. This is possibly due to the inherent complexity of the task, as we cannot directly retrofit generic machine learning methods. At the same time, current histogram analysis algorithms are not designed to capture and model temporal information across histogram snapshots in a multivariate setting. Our contributions are as follows:

- **Novelty.** We introduce Z-Hist, a novel framework for analyzing multivariate histogram snapshots by exploiting the notion of *temporal intervals* [11]. The goal is to introduce an effective way of representing and further analyzing these snapshots, using easily interpretable temporal abstraction patterns.
- **Applicability.** We further utilize disproportionality analysis in a use-case study to demonstrate the applicability of Z-Hist, on a dataset describing turbo failures in a truck Original Equipment Manufacturer (OEM). Turbo failures incur high costs to truck owners and operators due to, e.g., the need for towing to a workshop, the need for a replacement truck, or fines for late delivery. Hence, identifying trucks with a high risk of turbo failure in a timely manner could save owners and operators much money. Using our framework, the patterns we have identified can be used as early-warning indicators in a monitoring system, thus potentially avoiding undesirable turbo failures.
- **Reproducibility.** Our code is available online together with a synthetic dataset generator and six synthetic datasets [10].

Related Work. Over the past decade, histogram snapshot analysis has been performed by applying traditional machine learning algorithms, such as PCA [9], clustering based on histogram distance functions [7], and training random forests for classification [6]. However, these traditional methods do not take into account any changes in the histogram distribution over time, i.e., for each variable of each data entity, there is only one representative histogram. Moreover, histograms fall under the general class of complex data structures studied in the field of Symbolic Data Analysis (SDA) [2].

At the same time, temporal abstractions have been introduced as means to transform a time series into a set of discretized events [21], creating event sequences and event intervals. Several time series discretization techniques exist in the literature, such as Symbolic Aggregate approXimation (SAX) [23] and Symbolic Fourier Approximation (SFA) [19]. One way of exploiting the abstracted time series, or the event intervals, is by mining frequent temporal patterns, called *arrangements* [11,16], which can be further served as interpretable features for clustering or classification [3]. Arrangements have also been used in application areas such as healthcare [21] and human motion recognition [14].

Disproportionality analysis has been conducted to measure the differences in occurrences of items or patterns in one dataset from the occurrences in another dataset [15]. Disproportionality analysis has been widely used in healthcare research in various forms such as Proportional Reporting Ratio (PRR) [4], and Reporting Odds Ratio (ROR) [18]. These methods have been utilized to provide more insightful results compared to simply reporting frequencies of patterns or events in relation to electronic health record studies [8].

2   Background and Definitions

Histograms. A *histogram* $\mathcal{X}$ is a summary representation of a variable $X \in \mathbb{R}$. It is constructed by applying a function $H(X, m, \mathcal{C})$, given an integer m and a set of *coverage constraints* $\mathcal{C} = \{C_1, \ldots, C_m\}$ with $C_j = \{start_j, end_j\}$. H maps each value in $x \in X$ to m categorical bins, each containing a value count, a start and an end value, i.e., $\mathcal{X} = \{<v_1, start_1, end_1>, \ldots, <v_m, start_m, end_m>\}$. Each bin value $\mathcal{X}.v_j$ is the count of values $x \in X$ mapped to that bin if $\mathcal{X}.start_j \leq x < \mathcal{X}.end_j$. We also let $\bar{\mathcal{X}}$ denote the *normalized histogram* representation of $\mathcal{X}$, such that $\sum_{j=1}^{m} \bar{\mathcal{X}}.v_j = 1$; hence it can be regarded as a distribution.

Histogram Snapshots. *Histogram snapshots* are used as means for summarizing a variable over time by defining and employing multiple histograms instead of a single one. Let X be a temporal variable and $X[s : e]$ define a temporal slice of X containing all values between time points s and e. Assume that X is sliced into d time segments $X[s_1 : e_1], \ldots, X[s_d : e_d]$, with $s_1 = 1$ and $e_d = |X|$. For the kth time segment we can define a histogram snapshot of X as $\mathcal{S}^k = H(X[s_k : e_k], m, \mathcal{C})$ for summarizing X between time points s_k and e_k using a set of coverage points $\mathcal{C}$ and m bins.

Let $\mathcal{D} = \{X_1, \ldots, X_n\}$ define a set of n variables. For each variable $X_i \in \mathcal{D}$ we can define a set of histogram snapshots $\mathcal{S}(X_i)$. The union of these snapshots for all variables in $\mathcal{D}$, i.e., $\mathcal{S}(\mathcal{D}) = \bigcup \mathcal{S}(X_i)$ defines a *multivariate histogram snapshot* representation of $\mathcal{D}$. Multivariate histogram snapshots model three different dimensions of a dataset, i.e., the set of variables, the bins, and time, making the analysis of such data structures more complex than analyzing normal histograms, since the temporal dimension has not been handled in such contexts before. To fully exploit the nature of multivariate histogram snapshots, we introduce *temporal intervals*.

Temporal Logic. A *temporal interval* or an *event interval* $e = \{start, end, event\}$ is defined as a triplet describing the occurrence of a temporal event with a start time, an end time, and a label. In a setting where multiple variables occur concurrently and according to Allen's temporal logic [1], we can define seven types of temporal relations $R = \{$`matches`, `contains`, `follows`, `overlaps`, `meets`, `left-matches`, `right-matches`$\}$ based on their *relative* locations on the time axis. In our formulation, we only consider the temporal relations between the intervals and not their absolute positions. Depending on the task at hand, we can define other types of temporal relations or merge them accordingly.

Frequent Arrangements. An *arrangement* $A = \{A_E, A_R\}$ is a data structure composed of two elements: 1) a set of event labels A_E ordered by the start times of the corresponding temporal intervals $A_E = \{E_1, E_2, \ldots, E_n\}$, and 2) a set of temporal relations A_R, between all interval pairs in A_E, i.e., $A_R = \{r_{12}, \ldots, r_{1n}, \ldots, r_{(n-1)n}\}$. The occurrence frequency of an arrangement in a dataset $\mathcal{D}$ defines its *support*, i.e., the occurrence ratio of the arrangement over the dataset $\mathcal{D}$. Finally, an arrangement is *frequent* in $\mathcal{D}$ if its support is higher than or equal to a predefined minimum relative support threshold, *minSup*.

Disproportionality. Suppose we have two different subsets $\mathcal{D}^+, \mathcal{D}^\emptyset$ of a dataset $\mathcal{D}$. The disproportionality of an arrangement A is defined as the fraction of the support of A in $\mathcal{D}^+$ over its support in $\mathcal{D}^\emptyset$, i.e.,

$$disp(A, \mathcal{D}^+, \mathcal{D}^\emptyset) = \frac{support(A, \mathcal{D}^+)}{support(A, \mathcal{D}^\emptyset)} \tag{1}$$

Disproportionality values are used to compare relative frequencies of an arrangement in two different sets. For example, if an arrangement A occurs in $\mathcal{D}^+$ with $support(A, \mathcal{D}^+) = 0.4$ and in $\mathcal{D}^\emptyset$ with $support(A, \mathcal{D}^\emptyset) = 0.2$, the disproportionality value of this arrangement in $\mathcal{D}^+$ compared to $\mathcal{D}^\emptyset$ is $\frac{0.4}{0.2} = 2$, which means this arrangement occurs two times more in $\mathcal{D}^+$ than in $\mathcal{D}^\emptyset$.

Next, we describe how we can transform a multivariate histogram snapshot dataset into a dataset of temporal intervals.

3   The Z-Hist Framework

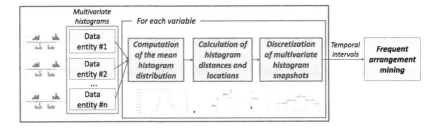

Fig. 2. Z-Hist: a three-step framework for converting multivariate histogram snapshots into sequences of temporal intervals.

We introduce Z-Hist (Fig. 2), a three-step framework for converting multivariate histogram snapshots into sequences of temporal intervals, hence exploiting the inter and intra temporal relations in the dataset. The first two steps construct the location points for histogram snapshots in each variable, while the third step converts them to temporal intervals. These steps are described next.

3.1   Step I: Computation of the Mean Histogram Distribution

To transform histogram snapshots to temporal intervals, we need to define two axes for each variable: (1) the location-axis for the histogram snapshots (y-axis) and (2) the time-axis (x-axis). Next, we compute a mean histogram distribution for each variable, the purpose of which is to give a reasonable central point c to construct the location-axis for each variable. Thus, for variable $X_i \in \mathcal{D}$ the mean is defined by using all histogram snapshots $\mathcal{S}(X_i)$ throughout the dataset. Since our histogram snapshots are not summarizing the same time range, we need to normalize each histogram snapshot to $\bar{\mathcal{S}}$ corresponding to the normalized bins of histogram snapshot $\mathcal{S}$, such that $\sum_{j=1}^{m} \bar{\mathcal{S}}(X_i)^k.v_j = 1$. We then assign a weight to each normalized histogram snapshot $\bar{\mathcal{S}}(X_i)^k$ based on its time range (s_k, e_k) to account for histograms with longer time segments. The reason for normalizing and then assigning weights is that the occurrences of histogram snapshots can be different from their time range. We eventually form a vector $\bar{c}$, which is a list of normalized weighted mean histograms for all variables. Each central point or the mean histogram distribution can be calculated as follows:

$$\bar{c}_i = \frac{\sum_{k=1}^{d_i} (e_{ik} - s_{ik}) \times \bar{\mathcal{S}}(X_i)^k}{\sum_{k=1}^{d_i} (e_{ik} - s_{ik}) \times d_i} \tag{2}$$

where d_i is the total number of histogram snapshots of variable X_i, and s_{ik} and e_{ik} are the corresponding start and end time points of the kth snapshot in X_i.

3.2   Step II: Calculation of Histogram Distances and Locations

The second step is to construct the location-axis for each variable by calculating the distance between each histogram snapshot and $\bar{c}$. This plays the same role as the y-axis of a time series, and for each variable X_i, $\bar{c}_i$ functions as the central point of each axis. For each histogram snapshot we compute the distance to $\bar{c}_i$ and regard it as its location on the y-axis. We cannot calculate the distances sequentially since snapshots may be given different locations. For example, suppose we have four snapshots of variable X_i in the following order: $\{\mathcal{S}(X_i)^{1a}, \mathcal{S}(X_i)^2, \mathcal{S}(X_i)^3, \mathcal{S}(X_i)^{1b}\}$, with two histograms having the same bin distribution $(\mathcal{S}(X_i)^{1a} = \mathcal{S}(X_i)^{1b})$. We also know that the location of $\mathcal{S}(X_i)^{1a} = \alpha$. However, when we calculate the locations sequentially, the location of $\mathcal{S}(X_i)^{1b}$ can be calculated as the sum of pairwise distances from $\mathcal{S}(X_i)^{1a}$. In this case, we cannot guarantee that the location of $\mathcal{S}(X_i)^{1b}$ will be α, since the triangular inequality dictates that the sum of distances of more than two paths reaching a point should be greater than or equal to the distance of any direct path. In other words, in our example, since $dist(\mathcal{S}(X_i)^{1a}, \mathcal{S}(X_i)^{1b}) \leq dist(\mathcal{S}(X_i)^{1a}, \mathcal{S}(X_i)^2) + dist(\mathcal{S}(X_i)^2, \mathcal{S}(X_i)^3) + dist(\mathcal{S}(X_i)^3, \mathcal{S}(X_i)^{1b})$ holds, it is unsure whether $\mathcal{S}(X_i)^{1a}$ and $\mathcal{S}(X_i)^{1b}$ always have the same location value. This problem can be solved by finding the distances of all histogram snapshots in the same variable from the same central point. Then for snapshot $\mathcal{S}(X_i)^k$, we will only get a unique location $dist(\bar{c}_i, \mathcal{S}(X_i)^k)$.

Various histogram distance functions exist, such as Chi-square, KL divergence, and Mahalanobis [5]. We use Chi-square as it makes no additional assumptions about the distance between the bins [5]. Suppose we have two histograms $\mathcal{X}_1$ and $\mathcal{X}_2$, then their Chi-square distance is computed as follows:

$$dist_{chi}(\mathcal{X}_1, \mathcal{X}_2) = \frac{1}{2} \sum_{j=1}^{m} \frac{(\mathcal{X}_1.v_j - \mathcal{X}_2.v_j)^2}{(\mathcal{X}_1.v_j + \mathcal{X}_2.v_j)} \tag{3}$$

For each histogram snapshot $S(X_i)^k$, we define a location matrix $\mathcal{L}(i, k) = sign \times dist(\bar{c}_i, S^k(X_i))$. These distances and the location matrix are used to define temporal intervals. Note that $sign$ is -1, while $mean(\bar{c}_i) > mean(S(X_i)^k)$ to represent negative distances from the central point, and 1, otherwise.

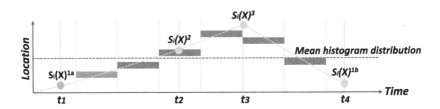

Fig. 3. The result of PAA/SAX on a histogram snapshot for one variable and one data entity. Four histograms are converted to six temporal intervals. The first interval is assigned the `low` label (yellow), while the fourth label is assigned `high` (red). (Color figure online)

3.3 Step III: Discretization of Multivariate Histogram Snapshots

So far, we have pre-processed the dataset *horizontally*, i.e., variable-wise. We will additionally pre-process it *vertically* with respect to the *data entities*. We divide the location for each data entity $\mathcal{D}_l \in \mathcal{D}$ (corresponding to dataset rows). Then for each $\mathcal{D}_l$, the locations with their time segments are converted into temporal intervals using Piecewise Aggregate Approximation (PAA) and SAX. PAA is originally used to summarize a time series of length p with the means of q consecutive, non-overlapping, equidistant segments [13]. In our case, we use PAA for each variable X_i and each data entity $\mathcal{D}_l$ to obtain fixed-length intervals before applying SAX. To calculate PAA, we must first have a continuous time series. However, we only have locations (e.g., four data points in Fig. 3) of the histogram snapshots covering a certain time range. We draw the gradual movement of these histogram locations by calculating any missing time point $\bar{t}_{ijl}$, by linearly interpolating two adjacent histogram locations as follows:

$$\bar{t}_{ijl} = (\mathcal{L}(i, k+1) - \mathcal{L}(i, k)) \times \frac{j - s_{ik}}{\frac{e_{ik} - s_{ik}}{2} + \frac{e_{i(k+1)} - s_{i(k+1)}}{2}} \tag{4}$$

where j is an absolute time point, and $(k, k + 1)$ are the consecutive indices of histogram snapshots located on either side of the jth time point. We run this approximation only when PAA needs to hit this time point to generate intervals and not for every missing time point. Since each histogram snapshot has a time range, we assume that it is located in the middle of its time range $(\frac{e_{ik} - s_{ik}}{2})$. The result of PAA is shown in Fig. 3 with six intervals.

Next, we apply SAX to all the intervals of each variable X_i. SAX maps the value of an interval (i.e., given by matrix $\mathcal{L}$) to a specific set of characters. SAX assumes that each value is sampled from a normal distribution and creates bins of a constant size on the distribution. To do this, an inverse normal transformation is applied to the position values of the intervals. An example of this transformation is depicted in Fig. 3. In this example, we divide the intervals into three parts {low, normal, high} based on their locations. The first interval is low, while the fourth one is high. Also, if two consecutive intervals are of the same SAX label, they are concatenated.

3.4 Frequent Arrangement Mining and Disproportionality Analysis

Finally, we demonstrate the applicability of Z-Hist on extracting disproportionally frequent temporal patterns from a multivariate histogram snapshot dataset. We separate the dataset into two sets, the case $\mathcal{D}^+$ and the control set $\mathcal{D}^\emptyset$. After applying Z-Hist and obtaining the interval-based representations of the original snapshots, we employ Z-Miner [11], a recently proposed algorithm for mining frequent arrangements of temporal intervals. For each frequent arrangement in $\mathcal{D}^+$ we compute its support in $\mathcal{D}^\emptyset$ and its disproportionality score (see Eq. 1). The top-k examples in $\mathcal{D}^+$ with the highest disproportionality scores are reported.

4   Experiments

Turbo Failure Dataset. We have used a real-world turbo failure dataset from a truck OEM. The 25 variables in this dataset have been selected by experts from the OEM on the basis that they could be important to the engine operation. The dataset contains almost 600,000 multivariate histogram snapshots of 33,000 trucks, with binary labels indicating whether the trucks have had a turbo failure. Among them, 30,000 (90.9%) trucks are labeled as 'normal' and 3,000 (9.1%) trucks are labeled as 'abnormal', while the class of 'abnormal' cases contains different types of failure modes of a turbo. The hypothesis is that different failure modes trigger different patterns expressed by the variables which our approach can capture. The snapshots have been produced at irregular times per vehicle without a constant cycle but on average every 100 time-units. Since the OEM has a proprietary right of the dataset, for reproducibility purposes, we provide a synthetic dataset sampled from a normal distribution with modified labels and time information that mimic the OEM dataset [10].

Our goal is to find patterns that frequently occur in the anomalous subset but rarely occur in the normal subset. To do this, we have made some adjustments to handle this dataset. First, we reduce the number of possible relations from

Table 1. The occurrences of the original seven relations and the merged relations

Relation	No. of relation	Merged relation	No. of merged relation
Matches	558, 507	**Contains**	9, 216, 580
Left-matches	1, 725, 228		
Right-matches	1, 537, 324		
Contains	5, 395, 521		
Overlaps	1, 945, 891	**Overlaps**	3, 996, 969
Meets	2, 051, 078		
Follows	16, 794, 048	**Follows**	16, 794, 048

seven to three as shown in Table 1. The reason for this is that the snapshots are generated for every 100 time-units, and it is unclear to express what happened at the same time by using seven relations, which eventually reduces the number of frequent patterns. So we have chosen three relations depending on the degree of temporal overlap between two intervals. If one interval is completely included in the other we call the relation `contains`. If only a certain period is shared we define it as `overlaps`. The `follows` relation remains the same.

Next, we have defined the parameter setup that has been used for the three steps of our framework and frequent arrangement mining. First, we have set the number of SAX labels to 3 by giving three labels: {`high`, `normal`, `low`} depending on the location of the histogram. This is the minimal setting to facilitate fast computation while still fulfilling the objective to catch abnormality. We have excluded `normal` states when we have generated arrangements for the same reason. In addition, the period of PAA has been designated as 25 time-units. For frequent arrangement mining, we have set the minimum support for the abnormal set to 30%, and a gap of 300 time-units has been accepted.

Figure 4 shows a total of 229,795 arrangements extracted from the dataset. Almost all arrangements have a disproportionality value between 0.8 and 2.1, but the black cluster on the bottom left shows 6,361 arrangements that only occur in the abnormal set.

One more interesting fact is that among 25 variables, only eight variables are found in the set of frequent arrangements as shown in Table 2. This means that we can filter out important variables that affect an actual vehicle failure through disproportionality analysis. Especially, **vehicle speed** only occurs in 1.79% of the arrangements but produces highly disproportional patterns with an average disproportionality value of 4,001. **Turbo boost pressure** shows a similar aspect with support of 1.51% and average disproportionality equal to 2,653.84. Among the variables found to be of significance, it is reassuring to find **turbo boost pressure** and **turbo speed** as they are both turbo-specific variables. The other variables may be indirectly related to the turbo operation, considering how the engine operates at different conditions. The only exception is **system voltage** which should have a negligible influence on the turbo operation.

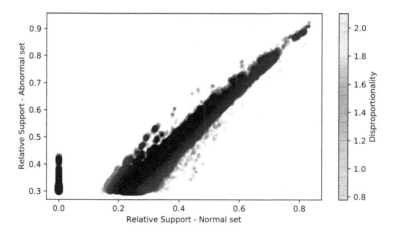

Fig. 4. A total of 229,795 arrangements with its supports in the normal set and the abnormal set of the dataset. The size of each point is proportional to the size of the arrangement, and the color of each point corresponds to a disproportionality value.

Table 2. Eight variables that appear in the experiment result with a minimum relative support of 30% for the abnormal set.

No.	Variable	Count	Support (%)	Average disprop.
1	Vehicle speed	4,110	1.79	4,001.00
2	Turbo boost pressure	3,470	1.51	2,653.84
3	Engine temperature	3,503	1.52	1,687.37
4	Turbo speed	149,091	64.88	280.22
5	Exhaust recirculation	148,424	64.59	280.11
6	Axle speed	151,731	66.03	273.12
7	System voltage	33,364	14.52	90.26
8	Ambient temperature	25,604	11.14	9.31

Next, we elaborate on the three most interesting arrangements from the top ten most disproportional ones which have occurred more than 40% in the abnormal set, together with the domain expert's opinion. The interpretation of these arrangements and other frequent arrangements can often be explained by experts as a turbo malfunction.

Figure 5a depicts the most disproportional arrangement in the experiment result. This arrangement only occurs in the abnormal set, and 43.7% of the data entities in the set have this arrangement. While **turbo boost pressure** is **high** and **contains** three different intervals that **follow** each other in turn with their **low** states. There are two **turbo speed** intervals with **low** states, which means that the **normal** and **low** states alternate as the gap between two intervals of the same label implies a **normal** state in between. To reach **high**

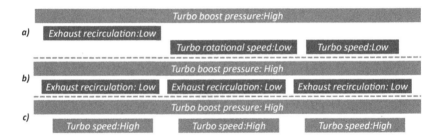

Fig. 5. Three selected arrangements from the ten most disproportional arrangements: a) the arrangement with the highest disproportionality value ($disp = 12,811$), b) an arrangement with recurring `low` exhaust recirculation under `high` turbo boost pressure ($disp = 12,811$), c) an arrangement with recurring `high` turbo speed under `high` turbo boost pressure ($disp = 12,752$).

turbo boost pressure, the turbo needs to spin at high rotational speed. The pressure build-up capability of the compressor part of the turbo is linked to the rotational speed by the governing physics. Therefore, **high turbo boost pressure** and **high turbo speed** should coincide. However, as seen, they attain values in contrary to this reasoning. Possible explanations of the arrangement could be a faulty boost pressure sensor or speed sensor. This could indicate that a faulty boost pressure or speed sensor are common failure modes pertaining to the turbo failure. However, it is unlikely that the truck is operated for a long time (considering the interval) with faulty sensors. In order to understand this specific arrangement, further studies are needed for analyzing specific trucks.

Figure 5b shows a similar pattern to Fig. 5a with one `contains` and three `follows`, but here the arrangement has three `low` **exhaust recirculation** intervals. This shows that while the high turbo boost pressure is sustained, the **exhaust recirculation** continues to move back and forth between relatively `low` and `normal` conditions. The combination of `low` **exhaust recirculation** and **high turbo boost pressure** indicates a high engine power situation. In general, this will pose additional strain on the turbo, increasing wear and reducing its life.

Figure 5c shows a slight contradiction to the arrangement we introduced first in Fig. 5a. In the first arrangement, the **turbo speed** is relatively `low`, while in this arrangement the value is constantly moving between the `high` state and the `normal` state (as they `follows` each other). It is also interesting that both conflicting patterns appear in the abnormal set with high support. Still, in this arrangement the logic of **high turbo boost pressure** and **high turbo speed** is valid. Just as in the arrangement shown in Fig. 5b, it could correspond to a high engine power and the associated increase in turbo strain and wear.

All the arrangements shown in Fig. 5 share the common state of **high turbo boost pressure** for an extensive period of time (long interval), a condition which can result in high turbo strain and therefore high wear, eventually resulting in turbo failure. Given the high values of disproportionality for the arrangements, it is reassuring to find this for the abnormal set (trucks with turbo failure).

Synthetic Datasets. To understand the phenomena in the turbo failure dataset, we have run the algorithm on six different synthetic datasets. Three datasets are for testing the movement of mean, and the other three are for the movement of standard deviation. Due to the page limit, the details of our generator and the properties of the six synthetic datasets can be found in our GitHub repository [10]. One highlight is that varying the mean of histogram snapshots does not show any meaningful differences in the mean and the variance of the disproportionality values. This suggests that the disproportionality values are robust to similar distributions, even if the central points are different. On the other hand, increasing standard deviation significantly changes the variance of disproportionality values, generating the arrangements only occurring in one set, which is what we have seen in the real-world experiment.

5 Conclusion

We proposed a novel framework for multivariate histogram snapshot datasets using temporal arrangements for the disproportionality analysis to fully exploit time information the datasets have. We showed a real world use-case using the turbo failure dataset from a truck OEM by conducting disproportionality analysis using our framework. In addition, six synthetic data were used to analyze the effect of changes in distribution on disproportionality values. Future works includes 1) more precise analysis calculating a specific time range where arrangements occur, 2) investigation on trend intervals.

References

1. Allen, J.F.: Maintaining knowledge about temporal intervals. CACM **26**(11), 832–843 (1983)
2. Billard, L., Diday, E.: Symbolic Data Analysis: Conceptual Statistics and Data Mining. Wiley, Hoboken (2007)
3. Bornemann, L., Lecerf, J., Papapetrou, P.: STIFE: a framework for feature-based classification of sequences of temporal intervals. In: Calders, T., Ceci, M., Malerba, D. (eds.) DS 2016. LNCS (LNAI), vol. 9956, pp. 85–100. Springer, Cham (2016). https://doi.org/10.1007/978-3-319-46307-0_6
4. Evans, S., Waller, P.C., Davis, S.: Use of proportional reporting ratios (PRRs) for signal generation from spontaneous adverse drug reaction reports. PDS **10**(6), 483–486 (2001)
5. Forero, M.G., Arias-Rubio, C., González, B.T.: Analytical comparison of histogram distance measures. In: Vera-Rodriguez, R., Fierrez, J., Morales, A. (eds.) CIARP 2018. LNCS, vol. 11401, pp. 81–90. Springer, Cham (2019). https://doi.org/10.1007/978-3-030-13469-3_10
6. Gurung, R.B.: Adapted random survival forest for histograms to analyze NOx sensor failure in heavy trucks. In: Nicosia, G., Pardalos, P., Umeton, R., Giuffrida, G., Sciacca, V. (eds.) LOD 2019. LNCS, vol. 11943, pp. 83–94. Springer, Cham (2019). https://doi.org/10.1007/978-3-030-37599-7_8

7. Irpino, A., Verde, R., De Carvalho, F.D.A.: Dynamic clustering of histogram data based on adaptive squared Wasserstein distances. Expert Syst. Appl. **41**(7), 3351–3366 (2014)
8. Karlsson, I., Papapetrou, P., Asker, L., Boström, H., Persson, H.E.: Mining disproportional itemsets for characterizing groups of heart failure patients from administrative health records. In: PETRA, pp. 394–398. ACM (2017)
9. Le-Rademacher, J., Billard, L.: Principal component analysis for histogram-valued data. Adv. Data Anal. Classif. **11**(2), 327–351 (2016). https://doi.org/10.1007/s11634-016-0255-9
10. Lee, Z.: Z-Hist repository (2020). https://github.com/zedshape/zhist
11. Lee, Z., Lindgren, T., Papapetrou, P.: Z-miner: an efficient method for mining frequent arrangements of event intervals. In: KDD, pp. 524–534 (2020)
12. Li, X., et al.: Meningioma grading using conventional MRI histogram analysis based on 3D tumor measurement. Eur. J. Radiol. **110**, 45–53 (2019)
13. Lin, J., Keogh, E., Wei, L., Lonardi, S.: Experiencing sax: a novel symbolic representation of time series. DMKD **15**(2), 107–144 (2007)
14. Liu, L., Wang, S., Hu, B., Qiong, Q., Wen, J., Rosenblum, D.S.: Learning structures of interval-based Bayesian networks in probabilistic generative model for human complex activity recognition. PR **81**, 545–561 (2018)
15. Montastruc, J.L., Sommet, A., Bagheri, H., Lapeyre-Mestre, M.: Benefits and strengths of the disproportionality analysis for identification of adverse drug reactions in a pharmacovigilance database. BJCP **72**(6), 905 (2011)
16. Papapetrou, P., Kollios, G., Sclaroff, S., Gunopulos, D.: Discovering frequent arrangements of temporal intervals. In: ICDM, pp. 8-pp. IEEE (2005)
17. Prytz, R., Nowaczyk, S., Rögnvaldsson, T., Byttner, S.: Predicting the need for vehicle compressor repairs using maintenance records and logged vehicle data. Eng. Appl. Artif. Intell. **41**, 139–150 (2015)
18. van Puijenbroek, E.P., Bate, A., Leufkens, H.G., Lindquist, M., Orre, R., Egberts, A.C.: A comparison of measures of disproportionality for signal detection in spontaneous reporting systems for adverse drug reactions. PDS **11**(1), 3–10 (2002)
19. Schäfer, P.: The boss is concerned with time series classification in the presence of noise. DMKD **29**(6), 1505–1530 (2015)
20. Schweizer, B.: Distributions are the numbers of the future. In: Proceedings of the Mathematics of Fuzzy Systems Meeting, pp. 137–149 (1984)
21. Sheetrit, E., Nissim, N., Klimov, D., Shahar, Y.: Temporal probabilistic profiles for sepsis prediction in the ICU. In: KDD, pp. 2961–2969 (2019)
22. Yang, L., et al.: Rectal cancer: can T2WI histogram of the primary tumor help predict the existence of lymph node metastasis? Eur. Radiol. **29**(12), 6469–6476 (2019)
23. Yu, Y., Zhu, Y., Wan, D., Liu, H., Zhao, Q.: A novel symbolic aggregate approximation for time series. In: Lee, S., Ismail, R., Choo, H. (eds.) IMCOM 2019. AISC, vol. 935, pp. 805–822. Springer, Cham (2019). https://doi.org/10.1007/978-3-030-19063-7_65

MUPPETS: Multipurpose Table Segmentation

Gust Verbruggen[1,2(✉)], Lidia Contreras-Ochando[3], Cèsar Ferri[3],
José Hernández-Orallo[3], and Luc De Raedt[1,2]

[1] Department of Computer Science, KU Leuven, Leuven, Belgium
{gust.verbruggen,luc.deraedt}@kuleuven.be
[2] Leuven.AI — KU Leuven Institute for AI, Leuven, Belgium
[3] Valencian Research Institute for Artificial Intelligence (vrAIn), Universitat
Politècnica de València, Valencia, Spain
{liconoc,cferri,jorallo}@dsic.upv.es

Abstract. We present MUPPETS, a framework for partitioning cells in a
table in segments that fulfil the same semantic role or belong to the same
semantic data type, similar to how image segmentation is used to group
pixels that represent the same semantic object in computer vision. Flexible constraints can be imposed on these segmentations for different use
cases. MUPPETS uses a hierarchical merge tree algorithm, which allows for
efficiently finding segmentations that satisfy given constraints and only
requires similarities between neighbouring cells to be computed. Three
applications are used to illustrate and evaluate MUPPETS: identifying
tables and headers, type detection and discovering semantic errors.

Keywords: Table analysis · Segmentation · Error detection · Type
detection

1 Introduction

Tables allow users to store and represent information in a general and familiar
way. Data that is often stored in tables includes measurements, data science
pipelines, logs, relational and non-relational databases. Such tables are intrinsically more complex than the grid of their values, as they may include parts that
play different roles or are associated with different domains. Unfortunately, they
rarely come with metadata describing these roles and domains.

An example of a table with cells of different roles and data types is shown
in Fig. 1. Humans easily recognise the syntactic and semantic structure in this
table, and automatically identify the coloured segments that we see on the right.
In data processing and analysis, understanding how a table is segmented in
different regions is a prerequisite for processing it. Unfortunately, this is still
mostly done manually.

The problem of segmenting a table takes inspiration from image segmentation. Images are usually composed of different objects that we would like to
delineate automatically. The goal is to assign a label to every pixel, such that

© Springer Nature Switzerland AG 2021
P. H. Abreu et al. (Eds.): IDA 2021, LNCS 12695, pp. 389–401, 2021.
https://doi.org/10.1007/978-3-030-74251-5_31

This Line is being used as a header					
ID	Date	Amount	Quantity	Status	
0042	16-Oct-17	$23.99	123	Closed	Jansen
7731	15-Jan-17	$49.99		Pending	Rho
8843	9-Mar-17	129	45		Gupta
3013	12-Feb-17		15	Pending	Harrison
4431	1-Jul-17	$99.99	1	Closed	Yang

(a) Segmentation of table in data, header and metadata.

This Line is being used as a header					
ID	Date	Amount	Quantity	Status	
0042	16-Oct-17	$23.99	123	Closed	Jansen
7731	15-Jan-17	$49.99		Pending	Rho
8843	9-Mar-17		45		Gupta
3013	12-Feb-17		15	Pending	Harrison
4431	1-Jul-17	$99.99	1	Closed	Yang

(b) Segmentation in data domains. It is easy for humans to see that the last two columns are semantically different domains.

Fig. 1. Examples of different structures of tables.

those with the same label share the same features and are different from the rest [19,22]. The imposed contiguity constraint makes image segmentation a specific kind of clustering. Additional constraints make these segments go from small *superpixels* to other more complex regions of the image. Image segmentation is a very clear and distinctive problem with many applications, such as object detection, scene understanding and compression. Table segmentation is similar to image segmentation, but instead of clustering pixels, we are clustering cells in segments that belong to the same data type or play the same semantic role.

Given that so much data is stored in tables and spreadsheets, and that image segmentation has been studied for decades, it is surprising that the problem of table segmentation has not received much attention outside of specific applications. The key contribution of this paper is that we introduce a generic, multipurpose framework for table segmentation. It can use any distance function between cells and can represent a wide range of constraints on the shape and position of segments. More specifically, we make the following contributions:

1. We introduce the problem of table segmentation subject to a set of constraints.
2. We combine a concrete class of constraints, a heuristic algorithm for finding segmentations that satisfy these constraints and a method for scoring them into a flexible framework called MUPPETS.
3. We show how table segmentation, and MUPPETS in particular, can be applied to a range of problems, such as identifying tables and headers, type detection and discovering semantic errors.

The following three sections respectively describe these contributions.

2   Table Segmentation

A table T is an $n \times m$ grid of cells. We define a *segment* $S \subseteq T$ as a set of orthogonally connected cells in this table. A segmentation $\mathbf{S}$ of T is a partitioning into mutually disjoint segments $\mathbf{S} = \{S_1, S_2, \ldots, S_k\}$ such that $\cup_i S_i = T$. This corresponds to a clustering of the cells of the table in which the elements in each cluster are orthogonally connected.

Assumptions can often be made about structural properties of tables. In spreadsheets, for example, cells of the same type are typically arranged in rectangular regions [2]. These assumptions are encoded as Boolean constraints on the segmentations.

Multiple segmentations of a table can satisfy any given constraint, but the target segmentation will have some additional, desired properties. For example, in our MUPPETS framework, we will aim for the cells within each segment to be *similar* according to some criterium. Analogous to internal evaluation methods for determining the number and quality of clusters, we thus want to assign a score to each segmentation that represents how well it exhibits these properties. The problem of table segmentation can now be defined as follows.

Given – a table

– a constraint

– a scoring function

Find a set of segmentations for the table that satisfy the constraint and that are ranked according to *score*

In the next section, we present a versatile framework for table segmentation by describing a class of constraints, a scoring function and a heuristic algorithm for finding segmentations that satisfy the constraint and have a high score.

3 The MUPPETS framework

Our MUPPETS framework consists of three key ingredients: (1) a class of supported constraints, (2) a scoring function based on the similarity between cells and (3) a heuristic search algorithm. The following sections describe these ingredients.

3.1 Constraints

A constraint C in MUPPETS consists of two parts. First, there are constraints on the possible shapes each segment in a segmentation is allowed to take. This is formalised as a Boolean function $shape(S)$ which yields true if segment S satisfies the constraint and false otherwise. All segments in the output segmentation must satisfy the constraint. The most common shape constraint is a rectangular one, which is true if the bounding box around a segment is equal to the segment itself.

Second, MUPPETS supports constraints on the spatial configuration of segments in a segmentation. This is formalised as a position constraint that must hold between pairs of segments S_i and S_j with $i \neq j$. To specify these position constraints, we resort to the well-known qualitative spatial relationships [1] that are illustrated in Fig. 2a. Each segment S_i is projected on its x- and y-coordinates, which yields two intervals on which the relations listed in Fig. 2b can be specified. In this paper, we consider first-order logic formulae over qualified variables, as shown in Example 2. This can be extended to constraints on particular segments, for example, to allow interactively specifying constraints [9].

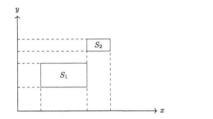

(a) Two segments and their projection.   (b) Interval algebra relations.

Fig. 2. Illustration of positional constraints using interval algebra.

Example 1. The spatial configuration of two segments S_1 and S_2 is shown in Fig. 2a. We can see that on the x axis it holds that S_1 meets S_2 and on the y axis it holds that S_1 before S_2. If no axis is specified, it should hold for both.

Example 2. We can define a *tabular* constraint by allowing only rectangular segments and prohibiting any of {overlaps, starts, finishes, during} to hold, or

$$\forall S_1, S_2 : \neg((S_1 \text{ overlaps } S_2) \vee (S_1 \text{ starts } S_2) \vee (S_1 \text{ finishes } S_2) \vee (S_1 \text{ during } S_2))$$

All segments then either align in one dimension or are completely disconnected. Similarly, a less strict *subtabular* constraint can be defined as follows.

$$\forall S_1, S_2 : \neg((S_1 \text{ starts } S_2) \vee (S_1 \text{ finishes } S_2))$$

3.2   Score

The scope of possible values in table cells is virtually endless and deciding whether two values belong to the same segment is heavily dependent on context. We therefore allow any distance function $d(c_1, c_2)$ between two cells c_1 and c_2 to be supplied as an argument. As in clustering, our goal is then to have a segmentation in which similar cells are in the same segment and vice versa. Internal cluster evaluation methods can be used to score segmentations.

Some of these distances are expensive to compute, for example, because they require search queries [6]. We present a scoring function that exploits the spatial configuration of tables and only performs $(n-1)(m-2)$ distance computations between neighbouring cells, as opposed to the $\mathcal{O}(n^2 m^2)$ computations required for popular evaluations such as the silhouette index [20].

Let $\langle c_1, c_2 \rangle$ represent the edge between two neighbouring cells c_1 and c_2. A boundary $b(S_1, \ldots, S_n)$ between segments $\{S_1, \ldots, S_n\}$ is the set of edges $\langle c_i, c_j \rangle$ such that $c_i \in S_k$, $c_j \in S_l$ and $k \neq l$. We can assign a score to a boundary b as the average distance between cells on either side of all edges that it contains

$$s(b) = \underset{\langle c_i, c_j \rangle \in b}{\text{avg}} d(c_i, c_j). \tag{1}$$

where avg denotes the mean of the values that it ranges over and avg $\varnothing = 0$.

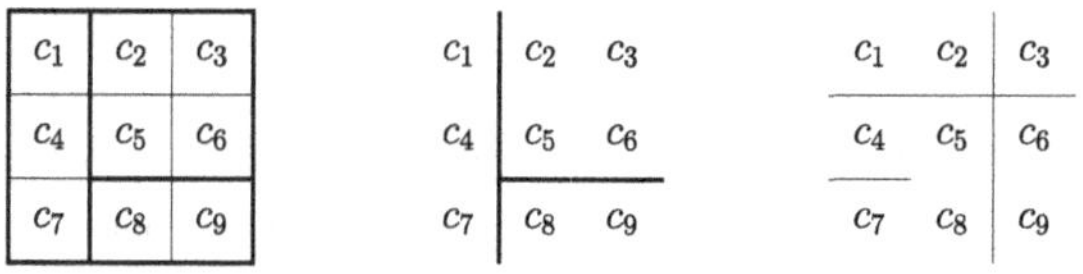

Fig. 3. (left) Table and segmentation, (middle) boundary between segments of the segmentation and (right) edges between neighbouring cells within each segment.

We compute the inter-segment score $s_e(\mathbf{S})$ of a segmentation $\mathbf{S}$ as the score of the boundary between all segments. The intra-segment score $s_a(\mathbf{S})$ is computed as the average distance of neighbouring cells within each segment. These are combined in the segmentation score

$$s(\mathbf{S}) = s_e(\mathbf{S}) - s_a(\mathbf{S}) = s(b(\mathbf{S})) - \operatorname*{avg}_{S \in \mathbf{S}} \operatorname*{avg}_{\langle c_i, c_j \rangle \in S} d(c_i, c_j) \qquad (2)$$

that we want to maximise.

Example 3. A segmentation $\mathbf{S}_e$ and its boundary are shown in Fig. 3. The inter- and intra-segment scores are computed as follows.

$$s_e(\mathbf{S}_e) = \tfrac{1}{5} \left(d(c_1, c_2) + d(c_4, c_5) + d(c_7, c_8) + d(c_5, c_8) + d(c_6, c_9) \right)$$
$$s_a(\mathbf{S}_e) = \tfrac{1}{7} \left(d(c_1, c_4) + d(c_4, c_7) + d(c_2, c_5) + d(c_3, c_6) + d(c_2, c_3) + d(c_5, c_6) + d(c_8, c_9) \right)$$

3.3   Algorithm

We combine a divisive and an agglomerative step to heuristically search for segmentations that satisfy the given constraints and have high scores. Let $\mathbf{S}_t$ be the unknown target segmentation—a segmentation that ideally maximises Eq. 2. Our algorithm consists of three main steps. First, in the divisive step, we look for a segmentation $\mathbf{S}_o$ such that (an approximation of) $\mathbf{S}_t$ can be obtained by joining as few segments of $\mathbf{S}_o$ as possible. Second, in the agglomerative step, we merge segments to search for segmentations that satisfy the given constraints. Finally, the resulting segmentations are ranked.

Divide. Inspired by *superpixels* in image segmentation, we want to find small groups of highly similar cells by iteratively splitting one segment. Let S be an $n_s \times m_s$ segment in the current segmentation $\mathbf{S}_i$. There are $(n_s - 1)(m_s - 1)$ straight boundaries that divide S in two segments. The best candidate boundary for splitting S is the one for which Eq. 1 is maximal, indicating that cells on both sides of the boundary are dissimilar. Let $\mathbf{b}(S)$ be the set of these candidate boundaries. We define the *splitting score* of a boundary $b \in \mathbf{b}(S)$ as

$$s_{split}(b) = s(b) - \operatorname*{avg}_{b' \in \mathbf{b}(S)} s(b') + \operatorname*{std}_{b' \in \mathbf{b}(S)} s(b') \qquad (3)$$

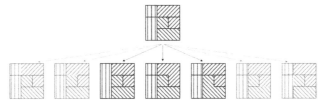

(a) Example of the divisive step. The final split and any subsequent splits will be based on a very slow splitting score.

(b) Graphical example of a single step of the merge algorithm with $w = 3$. Only candidate joins that satisfy the shape constraint are part of the merge tree. Of those, the three best candidates are added to the stack and will be expanded in the future.

Fig. 4. Graphical example of oversegmentation and merging steps using a tromino shape constraint and no position constraint.

where the boundary score $s(b)$ is adjusted for variations in the similarity between values of different types. This allows for comparing of splitting scores across different segments, as we expect the distance between cells of different types to have varying magnitudes. In other words, we look for a boundary with an unusually large boundary score *for its segment*. The divisive algorithm then works by iteratively splitting the segment with the highest scoring boundary along this boundary. It stops when the score of the chosen boundary becomes too small.

Merge. Starting from the segmentation $\mathbf{S}_o$ that was found in the previous step, we can iteratively merge segments to look for segmentations that satisfy the constraints. This corresponds to a *merge tree* as used for object segmentation in images [18]. In this tree, each node is a segmentation and its children are obtained by merging two neighbouring segments. Rather than full enumeration, we perform a heuristic beam stack search [21] with constraint checking.

Let $\mathbf{S}_i$ be the current segmentation popped from the stack. Using breadth-first search, we search the neighbourhood of every segment $S \in \mathbf{S}_i$ for the lowest number $k < k_m$ of segments that can be merged with S to create a new segment that satisfies the shape constraint, where k_m is a hyperparameter. Merging k segments at once amounts to following $k - 1$ edges in the merge tree, but the intermediate nodes are never explicitly considered. Each of these combinations of $k + 1$ candidate segments is scored using Eq. 1 and the w best ones are pushed to the stack, with w another hyperparameter. The algorithm is initialised with only $\mathbf{S}_o$ on the stack and stops when the stack is empty.

Table 1. Individual similarity functions used for training a mixed similarity.

Similarity	Description
Embedding	Cosine similarity between sum-of-word-vectors
Alignment	Global alignment similarity between strings with lowercase, uppercase and digits substituted a, A and 0, respectively
Compressed alignment	Same as alignment, but with subsequent, identical characters compressed into a single one
Prefix	Longest prefix similarity
Postfix	Longest postfix similarity
Longest common substring	Longest common substring similarity

Example 4. An example of both divide and merge of a segmentation problem is shown in Fig. 4. The shape constraint is that every segment must consist of exactly three orthogonally connected cells, there is no position constraint.

4 Evaluation

We now evaluate applicability and flexibility of MUPPETS on three use cases. In these experiments, we use the ranking of segmentations produced by MUPPETS.

4.1 Single Column Type Detection

Automatically discovering the statistical and semantic types of data in tables is a valuable tool in data preparation and information retrieval. Accordingly, methods have been presented that predict the type of a column [3,4]. These methods expect the values in a column to have the same type. If this is not the case, they will not work or perform worse.

By generating tables where data of the same type is not in one column, we show that MUPPETS is capable of detecting segments in this context. Figure 5a shows configurations of such tables. Segments of the same pattern are populated with values of a single type, randomly sampled from half of the columns used to evaluate the Sherlock [13] type detection system.

The other half of these domains was used to train a mixed syntactic and semantic distance function. For two cells c_1 and c_2, we first compute a feature vector $d(c_1, c_2)$ from k individual distance functions $\{d_1, \ldots, d_k\}$ and train a probabilistic classifier to predict whether c_1 and c_2 are taken from the same domain. Given two new values, their similarity is the probability of classifying them as being from the same domain. All considered similarity functions are shown in Table 1.

We show two results of running MUPPETS with this trained similarity measure and a tabular constraint on 60 generated problems in Fig. 5b. First, we show

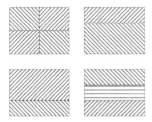   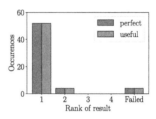

(a) Example table configurations where type detection fails without segmentation.

(b) Distribution of ranks of perfect segmentations and first segmentation in which all values of the same domain are in the same segment.

Fig. 5. Example of table configurations and results of detecting segments when generating tables from these configurations.

the rank of the perfect segmentation. Second, we also show the rank of the first segmentation in which no values of different types are in the same segment. Each segment then contains values of a single type, their types can be detected, and the segmentation is thus useful. In almost all cases, the correct segmentation is obtained as the highest ranked one. When this does not happen, we see that the similarity fails to distinguish some domains, because they contain syntactically distinct values or embeddings do not capture their semantics.

4.2   Semantic Error Detection

Error detection in spreadsheets typically happens on the basis of formulas, as these are prone to mistakes [11]. Such errors are called *spreadsheet smells* and approaches to find them often detect blocks of data that are influenced by the same formula [14]. Other errors can occur as well, however, such as copy and paste errors or artefacts of misaligned data. We call these *semantic errors*, as they require understanding of the semantics of a cell. This experiment shows how a noisy semantic similarity between words can be used by MUPPETS to detect such semantic errors in spreadsheets.

After finding a segmentation, we compute the average distance $\bar{d}(c)$ of every cell $c \in S$ to all other cells in the same segment. Additionally, we compute the average similarity $\bar{d}(S)$ between all pairs of cells in the segment. The error score of a cell $c \in S$ is then $\bar{d}(c) - \bar{d}(S)$. A high error score indicates that the cell is not like other elements in the same segment, and thus probably an error. Figures 6b and 6c show a heat map of the error scores for all cells in Fig. 6a in case of absence and presence of the segmentation as a 2×2 checkerboard.

The experiment is then performed as follows. We generate tables with errors by filling a table template with data from a pair of data domains and randomly replacing a single cell with a value from the other domain. Domain pairs are selected either two columns from the same dataset, such as movies and genres, or from the same column but with a distinct property, such as athletes from different sports. The full list of domain pairs is shown in Table 2. They were chosen to

Table 2. Domain pairs for semantic error detection.

Different columns		Different property	
Domain 1	Domain 2	Domain 1	Domain 2
Baseball players	Football players	Male gymnasts	Female gymnasts
Soccer players	Soccer clubs	American gymnasts	Russian gymnasts
Car manufacturer	Car type	Fencers	Boxers
Movie studio	Movie genre		
Pokémon name	Pokémon type		
Countries	Flavours		

Belgium	Netherlands	Vanilla	Strawberry
Spain	Poland	Pistachio	Banana
Cookie dough	Peppermint	Germany	Russia
Greece	Cherry	Austria	Spain

(a) Table following a 2 × 2 checkerboard pattern with a semantic error.

(b) no segmentation   (c) segmentation

Fig. 6. Table with a semantic error and its error scores (b) without and (a) with the segmentation using embedding similarity.

be syntactically indistinguishable. Three fairly weak semantic similarities are considered: the normalised web distance [6] using either Wikipedia or ChatNoir as search engines—that can be queried for free—and embedding similarity with spaCy [12] using the `en_core_web_lg` model.

All cells are then ranked by their error score. The distribution of ranks of the actual error for 60 iterations is shown in Fig. 7. All similarity measures are able to correctly identify close to a third of errors. We also show the lowest rank obtained for every iteration using either of the three similarities, correctly identifying 43 out of 60 errors. In cases where the actual error was not ranked first, unexpected values often confused the similarity measure. For example, in the car manufacturers and types domain, the word "pickup" yields high error scores due to its double meaning.

4.3   Table and Header Detection

A popular tool for working with tables is a Python package called **pandas**. It provides functions `read_csv` and `read_excel` for reading tables from their respective formats. Important parameters are `skiprows` that controls what part of the file to load and `header` and `index_col` for selecting the structural properties of the table. For example, the table in Fig. 1 requires `skiprows=2`, `header=0` and `index_col=0` for loading it correctly. Searching for the tags `[pandas]` and `[csv]` on StackOverflow, we found 20 questions about loading a table, where the appropriate values for these parameters was the solution.

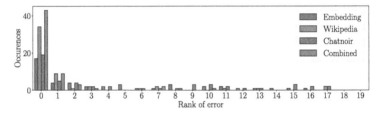

Fig. 7. Distribution of the ranks of errors when sorting by their error score.

Table 3. Parameter detection results.

Parameter	Tab	Sub	Rec	Any
skiprows	19	20	20	20
header	17	17	18	19
index_col	12	16	19	19
All	12	15	17	

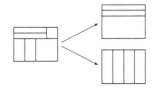

Fig. 8. Cuts based on boundaries.

We use MUPPETS to estimate the parameters for these tables as follows. First, we use the compressed alignment similarity from Table 1 and one of the tabular, subtabular or rectangular constraints to obtain the highest ranked segmentation. From this segmentation, horizontal and vertical *cuts* are made along all boundaries of segments, as visualised in Fig. 8. The **header** and **skiprows** parameters are respectively chosen to be the lowest horizontal cut and the lowest horizontal cut above which is a row that is mostly empty. On the remaining rows, **index_col** is chosen as the leftmost vertical cut such that the columns left of it are a valid index and thus contain unique rows.

For the different position constraints, Table 3 shows how often each individual parameter and all parameters together were correctly recovered, and whether it was estimated correctly using any of the constraints. Only two parameter values were never recovered. Imposing more position constraints results in coarse segmentations and information is lost. Estimating **index_col** either fails because both index and subsequent column are numerical and the distance is to small, or because the ground truth has no **index_col** and there is a vertical cut between columns of different types. Similarly, **header** either fails because data and headers are too similar or because empty cells cause superfluous segments in the data regions. In these unsuccessful cases, it is the similarity that fails to capture semantic meaning.

5   Related Work

A first line of related work is layout detection in spreadsheets, where the goal is to infer the layout of a spreadsheet and use it to extract data. Rather than distinguishing between cells, these systems take a predictive approach and try to detect their functional role—for example, whether they contain data, metadata, derived values or headers. One approach is to train a classifier using a manually curated set of syntactic and stylistic features on annotated data [16]. A more recent approach first trains context and style embeddings on unsupervised data and then uses these embeddings to make predictions with a recurrent architecture [10].

These cell roles can then be used to infer the layout using heuristics [8], graphs [15] or a genetic approach [17]. Segmentation is complementary to these approaches for detecting finer grained layouts in the *data* region, which we used to perform semantic error detection and improve semantic role detection. On a related note, the problem of detecting tables in spreadsheets [7] or CSV files [5] has recently received some attention.

Table segmentation is related to statistical and semantic type detection, where the goal is to find the data type of a set of values. Unlike our unsupervised segmentation approach, type detection generally works in a predictive setting, where the goal is to classify the statistical type of columns or to annotate them with semantic types [3,4]. As data is assumed to be grouped in sets of values that share a distinctive type, table segmentation can serve as a preprocessing step.

6   Conclusion and Future Work

We presented the flexible MUPPETS framework for the new problem of partitioning a table in segments that fulfil the same role. The framework is parametrised by a distance function between cells, which allows it to be used for different use cases. Three use cases were introduced in which MUPPETS either solves a new problem or complements existing approaches: detecting the types of cells, detecting semantic errors and easily loading tables.

Two direct pointers for future work are learning a general similarity measure between cells and learning the constraints from annotated tables. Both are aimed at making MUPPETS applicable for new use cases, such as data wrangling. Different search strategies can also be explored. For example, an evolutionary approach might be less likely to suffer from local errors that prevent the correct segmentation from being found—at the cost of performance.

Acknowledgements. This work has received funding from the European Research Council (ERC) under the European Union's Horizon 2020 research and innovation programme (grant agreement No [694980] SYNTH: Synthesising Inductive Data Models). This research received funding from the Flemish Government (AI Research Program), the EU (FEDER) and the Spanish MINECO RTI2018-094403-B-C32 and the Generalitat Valenciana PROMETEO/2019/098. LCO was also supported by the Spanish MECD grant (FPU15/03219).

References

1. Allen, J.F.: Maintaining knowledge about temporal intervals. Commun. ACM **26**(11), 832–843 (1983)

2. Barowy, D.W., Berger, E.D., Zorn, B.: ExceLint: automatically finding spreadsheet formula errors. In: Proceedings of the ACM on Programming Languages 2(OOP-SLA), pp. 148:1–148:26 (2018)

3. Ceritli, T., Williams, C.K., Geddes, J.: ptype: probabilistic type inference. Data Mining Knowl. Discov. 1–35 (2020)

4. Chen, J., Jiménez-Ruiz, E., Horrocks, I., Sutton, C.: ColNet: embedding the semantics of web tables for column type prediction. In: Proceedings of the of the 33th AAAI Conference on Artificial Intelligence (AAAI 2019) (2019)

5. Christodoulakis, C., Munson, E.B., Gabel, M., Brown, A.D., Miller, R.J.: Pytheas: pattern-based table discovery in CSV files. Proc. VLDB Endow. **13**(12), 2075–2089 (2020)

6. Cilibrasi, R.L., Vitanyi, P.M.: The google similarity distance. IEEE Trans. Knowl. Data Eng. **19**(3), 370–383 (2007)

7. Dong, H., Liu, S., Han, S., Fu, Z., Zhang, D.: Tablesense: spreadsheet table detection with convolutional neural networks. In: Proceedings of the AAAI Conference on Artificial Intelligence, vol. 33, pp. 69–76 (2019)

8. Eberius, J., Werner, C., Thiele, M., Braunschweig, K., Dannecker, L., Lehner, W.: DeExcelerator: a framework for extracting relational data from partially structured documents. In: Proceedings of the 22nd ACM International Conference on Information & Knowledge Management, pp. 2477–2480 (2013)

9. Gautrais, C., Dauxais, Y., Teso, S., Kolb, S., Verbruggen, G., De Raedt, L.: Human-machine collaboration for democratizing data science. arXiv preprint arXiv:2004.11113 (2020)

10. Gol, M.G., Pujara, J., Szekely, P.: Tabular cell classification using pre-trained cell embeddings. In: 2019 IEEE International Conference on Data Mining (ICDM), pp. 230–239. IEEE (2019)

11. Hermans, F., Pinzger, M., van Deursen, A.: Detecting code smells in spreadsheet formulas. In: 2012 28th IEEE International Conference on Software Maintenance (ICSM), pp. 409–418. IEEE (2012)

12. Honnibal, M., Montani, I.: spaCy 2: natural language understanding with Bloom embeddings, convolutional neural networks and incremental parsing (2017, to appear)

13. Hulsebos, M., et al.: Sherlock: a deep learning approach to semantic data type detection. In: Proceedings of the 25th ACM SIGKDD International Conference on Knowledge Discovery & Data Mining, pp. 1500–1508 (2019)

14. Koch, P., Hofer, B., Wotawa, F.: On the refinement of spreadsheet smells by means of structure information. J. Syst. Softw. **147**, 64–85 (2019)

15. Koci, E., Thiele, M., Lehner, W., Romero, O.: Table recognition in spreadsheets via a graph representation. In: 2018 13th IAPR International Workshop on Document Analysis Systems (DAS), pp. 139–144. IEEE (2018)

16. Koci, E., Thiele, M., Romero, O., Lehner, W.: Cell classification for layout recognition in spreadsheets. In: Fred, A., Dietz, J., Aveiro, D., Liu, K., Bernardino, J., Filipe, J. (eds.) IC3K 2016. CCIS, vol. 914, pp. 78–100. Springer, Cham (2019). https://doi.org/10.1007/978-3-319-99701-8_4

17. Koci, E., Thiele, M., Romero, O., Lehner, W.: A genetic-based search for adaptive table recognition in spreadsheets. In: 2019 International Conference on Document Analysis and Recognition (ICDAR), pp. 1274–1279. IEEE (2019)

18. Liu, T., Seyedhosseini, M., Tasdizen, T.: Image segmentation using hierarchical merge tree. IEEE Trans. Image Process. **25**(10), 4596–4607 (2016)

19. Minaee, S., Boykov, Y., Porikli, F., Plaza, A., Kehtarnavaz, N., Terzopoulos, D.: Image segmentation using deep learning: a survey. arXiv preprint arXiv:2001.05566 (2020)
20. Rousseeuw, P.J.: Silhouettes: a graphical aid to the interpretation and validation of cluster analysis. J. Comput. Appl. Math. **20**, 53–65 (1987)
21. Zhou, R., Hansen, E.A.: Beam-stack search: integrating backtracking with beam search. In: ICAPS, pp. 90–98 (2005)
22. Zhu, H., Meng, F., Cai, J., Lu, S.: Beyond pixels: a comprehensive survey from bottom-up to semantic image segmentation and cosegmentation. J. Vis. Commun. Image Represent. **34**, 12–27 (2016)

SpLyCI: Integrating Spreadsheets by Recognising and Solving Layout Constraints

Dirko Coetsee[1,2,3]($\boxtimes$) , Steve Kroon[2] , McElory Hoffmann[2,3] ,
and Luc De Raedt[1]

[1] KU Leuven, Leuven, Belgium
[2] Stellenbosch University, Stellenbosch, South Africa
[3] Praelexis, Stellenbosch, South Africa

Abstract. Valuable data are often spread out over different similar spreadsheets. Consolidating this data for further analysis can take considerable effort for a spreadsheet user without programming skills. We introduce Spreadsheet Layout Constraint Integration (SpLyCI), a system to semi-automatically merge multiple spreadsheets and lay the result out in a single output spreadsheet. SpLyCI takes advantage of the observation that spreadsheet users lay out their spreadsheets with certain implicit constraints in mind. For example, certain cells should be in the same rows or columns as other cells, or formulae should be repeated over all numbers. The system therefore identifies these implicit layout constraints, combines them, and then solves the resulting constraint satisfaction problem. The solution yields a new spreadsheet that contains the same information and the same relationships between cells as the inputs, but with formulae that are present only in some sheets extended to cover data from other sheets.

Keywords: Relational learning · Constraint learning · Spreadsheets

1 Introduction

Semi-structured data sources often contain information that would be useful if they could be converted into the right format. Spreadsheets, in particular, often have their data spread over different sheets or even files, each corresponding to a different data source or some other partitioning of the data. To work with such spreadsheets can take considerable effort, as there is not yet any tool to help consolidate data into a single sheet before further analysis can be done.

As part of a larger project to make data science more accessible to spreadsheet users [6], we aim to create a tool that can semi-automatically merge multiple spreadsheets, while handling repeated formulae correctly. A user specifies multiple input sheets and the tool (semi-)automatically transforms the input sheets into a single output sheet that non-redundantly captures the same information as the input sheets.

© Springer Nature Switzerland AG 2021
P. H. Abreu et al. (Eds.): IDA 2021, LNCS 12695, pp. 402–413, 2021.
https://doi.org/10.1007/978-3-030-74251-5_32

There are a few characteristics of spreadsheets that make them difficult to integrate: First, the same challenges that occur in relational schema matching might occur, such as changing of the schema over time or between sheets. In addition, sheets might not be in first normal form. Users might further use idiosyncratic layouts that use empty cells, text formatting, and pivoting in creative ways to represent complicated hierarchical schemas. Important information might be captured with implicit or explicit layout constraints over rows or columns. This not only includes primary-key and foreign-key constraints also present in relational databases, but also sorting on one or more row or columns, or formulae over rows or columns.

Some of these problems have been tackled in different contexts in isolation; however, as far as we know, there is as yet no end-to-end solution. This paper takes a step towards spreadsheet integration by concentrating on the last aspect—integration of spreadsheet layout constraints. To the best of our knowledge this aspect has not received any attention in the existing literature.

We propose SpLyCI—Spreadsheet Layout Constraint Integration—a framework for spreadsheet integration that is based on the view that spreadsheet integration can be represented as a constraint satisfaction problem. The layout and formula constraints in each input spreadsheet are first inferred. Next these constraints are combined, and finally the resulting constraint satisfaction problem is solved, yielding a new spreadsheet that adheres to all of the input constraints. The user is able to choose which constraints are active during the process and so can help disambiguate difficult cases or choose between contradictory constraints. We implement a prototype that is able to handle some illustrative constraints, and evaluate it on real-world data available on the web.

We contribute a description of a new task, that of interactive spreadsheet integration with formulae, a dataset and metrics to evaluate a system's performance on the task, a representation for spreadsheets based on layout constraints, and a system that uses this representation to tackle the task.

2 Problem

Figure 1 illustrates some aspects of the problem. Two spreadsheets contain similar information that the user wants to consolidate. Note the description in Cell A1 that will frustrate a naive concatenation of rows. Also note that the user would want the formulae in the first input sheet to be expanded to cover the cells introduced by the second sheet.

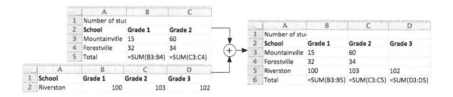

Fig. 1. Example input spreadsheets and the desired result after merging. The formulae in the first sheet have been expanded to cover new data from the second sheet.

We define *layout constraints* as the user-intended constraint on the relative row or column positions between cells. In the example in Fig. 1, the user probably intends Grade 3 to be in the same column as the number 102, because Grade 3 is (implicitly) its header. *Formulae constraints* are user-intended constraints on the extent to which the same formula is repeated in neighbouring cells, or the ranges of their arguments. For example, =SUM(.) above is repeated over all Grades, and sums over all schools for each Grade. *Match constraints* are constraints on the row or column positions between sheets. For example, the cells below Grade 1 in the first input sheet are probably intended to be in the same column as the cells below Grade 1 in the second sheet.

At a high level, the problem can now be described as follows: *Given multiple input spreadsheets, combine them so that the output satisfies the layout and formulae constraints present in each input sheet, while also satisfying match constraints between the sheets.*

3   Method

There are two main parts to our proposed technique: first the constraints present in the input sheets are recognised, and then they are combined and solved. We distinguish between two types of constraints which can be handled in two separate steps. In our system[1], formula constraints are implemented in Prolog because we represent formula generalization with logical rules which fits logic programming, and layout constraints are translated to MiniZinc[2] because the resulting constraint satisfaction problem fits the constraint programming paradigm.

We next discuss the representation and heuristics we use to solve the two subproblems in more detail. We first discuss the process for simple spreadsheets without formulae, and then show how to extend the process to handle the more interesting case where formulae are present.

Our basic notation and key concepts are defined below. Note that we will sometimes only define the columnwise concept but the corresponding rowwise concept is defined similarly.

Cuts. Each cell is indexed by a column i and row j identifier, where i or j is a unique identifier like 1, A, or A_*. Cells sharing an index represent the knowledge that the user intends those cells to be in the same column or row. To ensure that identifiers are unique across sheets, we add the sheet number as a superscript to some of the examples below, for example A^2 is a column in the second sheet.

Adjacent cells have the same column or row identifier by default, except if separated by a *cut*. A cut represents the knowledge that the cells on either side of the cut are not required to be in the same row or column of the output even if they are observed to be in the same row or column in one of the input sheets. Figure 2 shows an example of a cut.

---

[1] https://github.com/dirko/splyci.
[2] https://www.minizinc.org/.

We are unsure about what cuts the user intends without further user input. A probability distribution over cut locations could potentially be constructed, but in this paper we recognize cuts by a heuristic. We add a cut when two cells are separated by the border property and at least one empty cell. This is intended to separate independent tables embedded in a single spreadsheet.

Matches. A *match* $\mathtt{match}(i, i')$, where i and i' come from two different sheets, represent the knowledge that the user wants to align two identifiers between sheets. They can be interpreted as fields or entities that represent the same thing between sheets. A *matching algorithm* is an algorithm that takes a set of spreadsheets as input and produces a set of matches as output. The process of matching column identifiers is related to the mature fields of *schema matching* [3], and matching rows is related to *record linkage* or *entity resolution* [4], depending on the orientation of the cells in the spreadsheet.

In this paper we use a simple algorithm that matches indices when their *headers* match exactly. There is work that automatically identifies header cells in spreadsheets [7], but as a simple baseline the work in this paper takes the topmost or leftmost cells as far as necessary to produce a unique match.

Once the matching algorithm is done, for all $\mathtt{match}(i, i')$ we replace i' with i so that across all sheets we use a common set of identifiers.

Blocks. Working on the cell level is, unfortunately, slow. The number of constraints (discussion below) grows quadratically in the number of cells, which becomes impractical for large spreadsheets, even if the overall structure is simple. We therefore partition each sheet into rectangular *blocks* of cells. Each block b is associated with its position and dimensions with the $\mathtt{block}(b, i, j, w, h)$ predicate, where i is a column identifier, j a row identifier, and w and h the width and height of the block in number of cells.

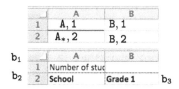

Fig. 2. An example spreadsheet (below) with a cut indicated by the red line. The column and row identifiers are shown inside each cell above. Note that $\mathtt{A}$ and $\mathtt{A}_*$ are different. Below, blue dotted lines indicate the partitions induced by the cut, namely $(1, 2)$, $(\mathtt{A}, \mathtt{B})$, and $(\mathtt{A}_*, \mathtt{B})$, and the corresponding blocks are labelled around the figure. (Color figure online)

Fig. 3. Two example sheets where row 2 (left) and row 1 (right) match, but row 3 (left) and row 2 (right) do not match. This produces a partition between the two rows, represented by the blue dotted line, as the cells on either side of these rows should be in different blocks. (Color figure online)

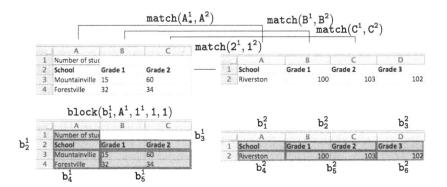

Fig. 4. Example of the proposed spreadsheet representation for two spreadsheets without formulae. The two sheets with corresponding row and column indices are given above, with the extracted blocks below. Note that the sheet is partitioned both by the cut below Cell A1 in the left sheet and the matches. Of the block facts, only the b_1^1 block is shown fully.

In general, cuts do not divide a spreadsheet into rectangular blocks, as can be seen in the example in Fig. 2. We therefore add *sheet partitions*, which we define as column or row pairs, to ensure that each spreadsheet is partitioned into blocks. The block-level representation of a spreadsheet should keep some of the properties created by cuts and matches on the cell level. For cuts, cells on either side of the cut have different indices. There should therefore be different blocks on either side of a cut. We therefore add a partition along each cut, and perpendicular to cut ends to divide the spreadsheet into four blocks, as is illustrated in Fig. 2. For matches, cells containing a matching index should be in a block that is free to align with matching cells in another block. We therefore also add partitions between indices where one of the indices match an index in another sheet but the other one does not match the adjacent index in the other sheet, as shown in Fig. 3.

Constraint Satisfaction Problem (CSP). For each input column i or row j we construct a decision variable x_i or x_j that can take values in $\{1, \ldots, m_i\}$ and $\{1, \ldots, m_j\}$ respectively, where m_i and m_j are maximum dimensions for the output spreadsheet, which we set to the sum of all block widths and heights respectively. We avoid re-using the column and row identifiers as decision variables directly and rather create new variables to make a distinction between the identifiers that are used to index cells, and variables with domains in the positive integers.

A major constraint on the values of the index variables is that the blocks should not overlap. We therefore add a disjoint_rectangles(R) constraint on the set of rectangles $R = \{(x_i, x_j, w, h) \mid \text{block}(b, i, j, w, h)\}$. Note that x_i and x_j are decision variables, but w and h are constants in terms of the CSP.

Other than this non-overlapping constraint, we add match constraints and the layout constraints present in the input spreadsheets. Our system currently recognises the following constraints, but more could be added: $\texttt{left}(i, i')$ if column i is to the left of i' in an original sheet, and $\texttt{above}(j, j')$ if row j is above j'. This defines a partial ordering of row and column identifiers.

The constraint satisfaction problem is summarised as follows:

variables	$X = \{x_i\} \cup \{x_j\}, \quad i, j$ over all input sheets,
domains	$x_i \in \{1 \ldots m_i\}, x_j \in \{1 \ldots m_j\},$
subject to	$\texttt{disjoint\_rectangles}(R),$
	$R = \{(x_i, x_j, w, h) \mid \texttt{block}(b, i, j, w, h)\}$
	$\wedge\, (\texttt{left}(j, j') \to x_j < x_{j'}) \wedge (\texttt{above}(i, i') \to x_i < x_{i'}).$

For example, the constraint satisfaction problem for Fig. 4 is

variables	$X = \{x_{A^1}, x_{A^1_*}, x_{B^1}, x_{D^2}, x_{1^1}, x_{2^1}, x_{3^1}, x_{2^2}\},$
domains	$x_i \in \{1 \ldots 15\}$ for x_i in$\{x_{A^1}, x_{A^1_*}, x_{B^1}, x_{D^2}\}$
	$x_j \in \{1 \ldots 13\}$ for x_j in$\{x_{1^1}, x_{2^1}, x_{3^1}, x_{2^2}\}$
subject to	$\texttt{disjoint\_rectangles}(R), R = \{(x_i, x_j, w, h) \mid \texttt{block}(b, i, j, w, h)\}$
	$\wedge\, x_{A^1_*} < x_{B^1} \wedge x_{1^1} < x_{2^1} \wedge x_{2^1} < x_{3^1} \wedge x_{B^1} < x_{D^2} \wedge x_{2^1} < x_{2^2}.$

Note that x_{A^2}, x_{B^2}, x_{C^2}, and x_{1^2} are not present because they were replaced by matching identifiers in the other sheet, and that x_{C^1} and x_{4^1} could be removed from the CSP as an optimisation because they occur only inside blocks.

Since the $\texttt{disjoint\_rectangles}$ constraint is usually built-in using efficient internal representations, standard constraint satisfaction solvers can be used to solve this layout problem. Our implementation is in MiniZinc.

An instantiation of the decision variables represents a possible output layout. Once we have an instantiation, the output spreadsheet is constructed by looking up the values in the original cells and copying them to the output sheet in their new position. Note that this scheme copies each cell in the original sheet to a single cell in the output sheet: it only represents a reordering of cells and cannot duplicate cells.

Formula Blocks. The scheme described above is able to represent and merge simple spreadsheets without any formulae. We now turn to the problem of representing and merging spreadsheets containing formulae.

The following steps encode formula blocks:

1. Find formula blocks. Add partitions to create blocks where all the cells have the same R1C1[3] representation. When formulae are repeated over different

---

[3] https://wiki.openoffice.org/wiki/Documentation/How_Tos/Calc:_R1C1_notation
   Absolute column or row values are replaced with values relative to the formula cell, for example "=SUM(R[-2]C[0]:R[-1]C[0])" instead of "=SUM(B3:B4)" in the B5 cell.

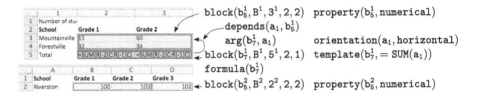

Fig. 5. Example sheets where one sheet now contains a repeated formula. The formula block is colored green and all the blocks with the `numerical` property are colored orange. Note that only one property of b_5^1 and b_5^2 is listed, as all the various properties of each of the blocks would take too much space to show here.

cells with just the row or column incrementing, the R1C1 representation will be the same for all of them.

2. Denote a block b to be a formula with the `formula`(b) predicate, and its template with `template`(b, t), where t is a string where the formula argument ranges are replaced by placeholders, so "`=SUM(R[-2]C:R[-1]C)`" becomes "$= \mathtt{SUM}(a_1)$" for example.

3. Associate the formula block b with its argument identifiers with `arg`(b, a), where a is a unique argument identifier, for example a_1.

4. Create argument blocks by adding partitions between two cells if they are arguments to two different formulae.

5. Associate the argument identifiers a with argument blocks b_a, `depends`(a, b_a).

6. Associate each argument with its orientation, `orientation`(a, r), where r is either "`vertical`" or "`horizontal`". This determines how block-level arguments map to cell-level arguments. A horizontal argument means that argument cells increment horizontally as formula cells increment horizontally. The left-most cell in the argument block is the argument to the left-most cell in the corresponding formula block, the cell to the right of that is the argument to the formula cell to the right, and so forth.

The representation is summarized in the example in Fig. 6.

Properties. Raw cells have properties like color, font, type, and other implicit properties like their semantic categories. Our main assumption when generalizing formulae is that all cells with a certain property should be the argument to a certain formula template. Block properties, denoted `property`(b, p), where b is a block and p a property, are the properties that all the cells in that block have in common. The system currently supports cell color, cell type, and properties for each column or row.

Formulae Generalisation. Now we can construct rules that generalise formulae to new data. For each formula block, we assume that if it has arguments, the height or width of its arguments determine its own height or width. At a high level, we therefore search for rules of the form,

$$\{\text{formula block facts}\} \leftarrow \{\text{argument block facts}\}. \tag{1}$$

$\text{block}(f, i, 5^1, w, 1) \leftarrow \text{block}(b, i, j, w, h), \text{property}(b, \text{numerical}), f = \text{bid}(b_7^1, i).$

$\text{arg}(f, a) \leftarrow \text{block}(b, i, j, w, h), \text{property}(b, \text{numerical}), f = \text{bid}(b_7^1, i), a = \text{aid}(a_1, i).$

$\text{depends}(a, b) \leftarrow \text{block}(b, i, j, w, h), \text{property}(b, \text{numerical}), a = \text{aid}(a_1, i).$

(a) Prolog rules that replace some of the facts in Figure 5. These rules add formula blocks in the same columns as all numerical blocks. The first line states that, if there exists a block at some location and with some width and height, and that block has the numerical property, then a block f in the same column and with the same width, but in row 5^1 should also exist, where f is an identifier that combines the original block identifier with the column it is in so that f will be unique for each block-column combination produced by the rule.

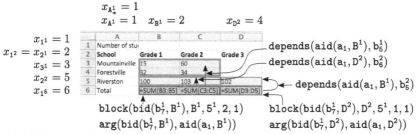

(b) The facts produced by the rules above on the two spreadsheets in Figure 5, with a solution to the accompanying CSP. Since B^2 matches B^1 and was therefore replaced by it, the rule produces a block $\text{bid}(b_7^1, B^1)$ that depends on two blocks, namely b_5^1 and b_5^2.

Fig. 6. Example of the proposed representation where one sheet contains a formula.

Since the head is a conjunction with free variables which cannot directly be implemented in Prolog, we implement these rules by splitting the conjunction into separate rules and creating compound terms *block ID* $\text{bid}(f, i)$ and *argument ID* $\text{aid}(a, i)$ to represent identifiers for the new formula blocks and arguments. f is the original formula block, i is the column of the argument, and a the original argument identifier. These terms are necessary because a rule can generate new formula blocks and their corresponding arguments, and we need a unique way to identify each block and argument. See Fig. 6a for an example of a rule that covers a single formula block and its implementation in Prolog.

Techniques from *inductive logic programming* [10] can be used to learn these rules to cover the spreadsheet formulae, but since our desired rule format is fixed we implement a custom search algorithm. The main challenge is in finding the property of the argument blocks that "explains" each formula. For a specific formula block, we first find all its argument blocks with the same width or height as itself. For each of these argument blocks, which we assume are the blocks that determine the formula's extent, we find the set of properties that uniquely identify it by taking the properties of the argument block that are not properties of any other blocks.

The facts and rules that represent each sheet are now merged by taking their union, before grounding and finding all blocks to pass to the constraint solving phase. Note that rules can depend on the result of other rules, as formulae can be arguments to other formulae.

Constraint Satisfaction Problem. With formulae, the CSP step is the same as previously, as the generalisation of formulae happens independently of the assignment of values to columns and rows. The argument templates of formulae are then filled in according to their orientations.

4   Experiments

The prototype is evaluated by comparing its output to that obtained by manually integrating multiple spreadsheets.

The Fuse corpus[4] [1] is a collection of publicly available spreadsheets scraped from the web. Since not every spreadsheet in this corpus is mergeable with every other spreadsheet (because of different domains and contents), we manually constructed a set of 15 mergeable spreadsheet pairs. We draw a random sample of spreadsheets, split suitable sheets horizontally or vertically to create two mergeable sheets, and remove formulae from the second sheet. The smallest sheet in the sample is $8 \times 17 = 136$ cells and the largest $12 \times 512 = 6144$. The experimental process is illustrated with an actual sheet from the evaluation set in Fig. 7.

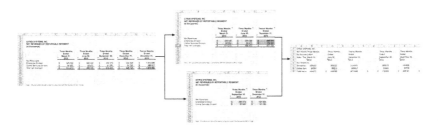

Fig. 7. The experimental process illustrated with a spreadsheet from the evaluation set. A sheet is manually split, then the two sheets are manually annotated as necessary to merge with the system.

We annotate the sheets with the necessary information if the default heuristics fail and note the number of annotations that is necessary as a measure of the manual effort that can be saved in the future with better property, cut, and constraint recognisers. Cut annotations, implemented as comments in the spreadsheet file, are added between multiple tables embedded in a single sheet, and between descriptive cells and headers. Matches are annotated by adding matching column or row identifiers as comments when the match heuristic fails,

---

[4] http://static.barik.net/fuse/.

Table 1. Result summary

	Total	Correct	Avg. %
Cuts	15	8	30%
Possible matches	3588	3498	73%
Properties	169	1	1%
Blocks correctly laid out	1155	870	90%
Sheets layout	15	7	47%
Sheets layout (ignoring order)	15	10	67%

(a) Integration results. The average column is the micro average, in other words the average percentage correct per sheet. Note that the match heuristic is much more successful than the cut or property heuristics at avoiding user input.

# annotations	# sheets
None	4
1 to 5	5
6 to 15	2
More than 15	4

(b) A frequency table of the number of annotations necessary to solve each spreadsheet pair.

while cells are colored manually when there is no other default property that uniquely covers a formula argument. We count a contiguous rectangle of cells that had to be colored as one annotation.

The results are summarised in Table 1. Over half of the sheets were solvable with 5 or fewer annotations. We distinguish between two types of correct layout results: fully correct layout and correct when ignoring the ordering of some blocks. In some cases, like in Fig. 7, the system produced a layout that had the correct meaning but not exactly the same column or row order as the original. A human would put the year-total to the right of all the months, but the system added the total in the middle. Such cases could be handled within the current framework by allowing more specific layout constraints such as that a formula is to the right, or below, its arguments.

On average, it took 22 s to process a sheet pair, with most pairs correctly merged within a few seconds, which means that a system like this has the potential to be useful in an interactive setting where it takes longer to add annotations or manually merge sheets than the system takes to compute merge proposals.

5 Related Work

Chen et al. [5] were the first to undertake automatic spreadsheet integration. They separate the problem into *extraction* and *integration* phases. They concentrate on the extraction of relational data from spreadsheets and use off-the-shelf database integration tools for the integration phase. To extract relational data from spreadsheets, they identify pivoted tabular data with machine learning techniques. They do not, however, address the integration of formulae or other constraints that we address in this work, and do not present the result as a spreadsheet again for the end-user.

Other approaches for extracting relations from spreadsheets include FLASHRELATE [2], which allows a user to visually specify transformations,

FOOFAH [8], which learns transformations by example, and the predictive program synthesis approach in [12], which searches for type-consistent relations with a zero-information-loss constraint. None of these extraction techniques take formulae into account, in contrast with our work.

Kolb et al. [9] developed a system that is able to automatically extract constraints from spreadsheets where the formula information is not present. It searches for possible constraints over blocks of cells, limiting the search space to only sub-blocks of the correct shape. Their view that spreadsheets can contain constraints inspired the current work, although we take the idea further by including layout constraints.

There is a vast literature on schema matching and mapping for relational data [3]. A recent take on the problem is in the context of data science, where Sutton et al. [11] created a tool to synthesise executable summaries of changes between tables. In contrast to our work, they do not take spreadsheet formulae into account, consider layouts other than relational data that are already in first normal form, or do the merge after calculating the changes.

6   Conclusions and Future Work

We have introduced the spreadsheet integration problem as the problem of merging multiple spreadsheets to obtain a new spreadsheet while generalising formulae so that they take data from the other sheets into account. We proposed a layout constraint representation in which merging sheets is achieved by solving the resulting constraint satisfaction problem. We present results of a system prototype that uses baseline heuristics to solve some of the sub-problems and show that it is able to correctly recover artificially split spreadsheets. We use the number of manual annotations that had to be added as a measure of user effort.

Going forward, the validation framework should be extended to include naturally occurring spreadsheet pairs, and the measure should be refined to better reflect saved user effort. We also made some strong assumptions such as identical column or row headers, and the system could be extended in a natural way allowing for soft matches between headers and determining their effects. This is a challenge that is shared with database integration.

In the future, the performance of the system can be improved by using better heuristics or machine learning approaches to lower the number of manual annotations required. The use of soft constraints can be investigated to handle duplicate or contradictory data gracefully, and under-specified constraints can be disambiguated by using a cost function to rank solutions.

Seeing spreadsheets as user-intended layout constraints opens up the possibility of investigating exactly which layout constraints are used in typical spreadsheets. So far, we have identified only simple same-column and same-row constraints together with some ordering on the columns and rows. But a more complete understanding of the constraints users typically use in spreadsheets will enable better integration of sheets and might enable other automated applications on spreadsheets.

Acknowledgements. This work was funded by the European Research Council (ERC) under the European Union's Horizon 2020 research and innovation programme (grant agreement No [694980] SYNTH: Synthesising Inductive Data Models). LDR is also funded by the Flemish Government (AI Research Program).

References

1. Barik, T., Lubick, K., Smith, J., Slankas, J., Murphy-Hill, E.: Fuse: a reproducible, extendable, internet-scale corpus of spreadsheets. In: 2015 IEEE/ACM 12th Working Conference on Mining Software Repositories, pp. 486–489 (2015)

2. Barowy, D.W., Gulwani, S., Hart, T., Zorn, B.: FlashRelate: extracting relational data from semi-structured spreadsheets using examples. SIGPLAN Not. **50**(6), 218–228 (2015)

3. Bernstein, P.A., Madhavan, J., Rahm, E.: Generic schema matching, ten years later. Proc. VLDB Endowment **4**(11), 695–701 (2011)

4. Brizan, D.G., Tansel, A.: A survey of entity resolution and record linkage methodologies. In: Communications of the International Information Management Association, vol. 6, January 2006

5. Chen, Z., Cafarella, M.: Integrating spreadsheet data via accurate and low-effort extraction. In: Proceedings of the 20th ACM SIGKDD, KDD 2014, New York, NY, USA, pp. 1126–1135, ACM (2014)

6. De Raedt, L., Blockeel, H., Kolb, S., Teso, S., Verbruggen, G.: Elements of an automatic data scientist. In: 17th International Symposium, Advances in Intelligent Data Analysis XVII (2018)

7. Doush, I.A., Pontelli, E.: Detecting and recognizing tables in spreadsheets. In: Proceedings of the 9th IAPR International Workshop on Document Analysis Systems, DAS 2010, New York, NY, USA, pp. 471–478. ACM (2010)

8. Jin, Z., Anderson, M.R., Cafarella, M., Jagadish, H.V.: Foofah: transforming data by example. In: Proceedings of the 2017 ACM SIGMOD, SIGMOD 2017, New York, NY, USA, pp. 683–698. ACM (2017)

9. Kolb, S., Paramonov, S., Guns, T., De Raedt, L.: Learning constraints in spreadsheets and tabular data. Mach. Learn. **106**(9-10), 1441–1468 (2017)

10. Muggleton, S., De Raedt, L.: Inductive logic programming: theory and methods. J. Logic Program. **19–20**, 629–679 (1994)

11. Sutton, C., Hobson, T., Geddes, J., Caruana, R.: Data diff: interpretable, executable summaries of changes in distributions for data wrangling. In: Proceedings of the 24th ACM SIGKDD, KDD 2018, New York, NY, USA, pp. 2279–2288. ACM (2018)

12. Verbruggen, G., De Raedt, L.: Towards automated relational data wrangling. In: Proceedings of AutoML@PKDD/ECML 2017, Skopje, Macedonia, September 22, 2017, pp. 12–20 (2017)

RTL: A Robust Time Series Labeling Algorithm

Frederique van Leeuwen[1,2]([✉]) [iD], Bas Bosma[3] [iD], Arjan van den Born[1,2] [iD], and Eric Postma[1,2] [iD]

[1] Jheronimus Academy of Data Science, 's-Hertogenbosch, The Netherlands
f.c.a.v.leeuwen@JADS.nl
[2] Tilburg University, Tilburg, The Netherlands
[3] VU Amsterdam, Amsterdam, The Netherlands

Abstract. Time series classification is one of the most important problems in data mining. With the growth in availability of time series data, many novel classification algorithms have been proposed. Despite the promising progress in accuracy, the performance of many algorithms still strongly depends on an initial training session containing labeled examples of all classes to be learned. In most realistic applications, however, labels are lacking or only partially available; limiting the practical applicability of time series classification algorithms with this requirement. To remedy this, we introduce the Robust Time series Labeling (RTL) algorithm and show its ability to increase labeling accuracy and robustness across a wide variety of time series datasets. Given its flexibility, the RTL algorithm can successfully be applied in many real-life situations.

Keywords: Time Series · Labeling · Classification

1   Introduction

Time Series Classification (TSC) is arguably one of the most interesting, common, and challenging problems in data mining. With the growth in availability of time series data, many novel TSC algorithms have been proposed, increasing the accuracy of classification significantly. Although this progress is promising, the performance of many algorithms still strongly depends on an initial training session containing labeled examples of all classes (or concepts) to be learned. In most real-life situations, however, this is unrealistic; severely limiting the practical applicability of these TSC algorithms.

To deal with situations without prior understanding of the concepts involved, TSC algorithms need to interactively invoke human expertise. While humans have an innate ability to extract meaningful knowledge from the shape of time series, this remains a complex problem for computers [3]. Unlike humans, TSC algorithms are not able to understand the context of the time series. However, in ever more real-life situations data is generated at such high rates that unassisted labeling by experts is no longer feasible. To be applicable in practice, TSC

© Springer Nature Switzerland AG 2021
P. H. Abreu et al. (Eds.): IDA 2021, LNCS 12695, pp. 414–425, 2021.
https://doi.org/10.1007/978-3-030-74251-5_33

algorithms thus need to support the expert in labeling efficiently and effectively. In other words, the *relative labeling effort* – which is defined as the fraction of machine- and human-based labeling relative to complete human labeling of a time series—should be minimized.

In this paper we introduce the Robust Time series Labeling (RTL) algorithm, that aims to minimize the labeling effort without affecting the overall quality of TSC tasks. The contribution of the paper is fourfold: (1) through an extensive review of an existing time series labeling algorithm we identify the key features needed to have a robust method for reducing the labeling effort while maintaining high quality labels, (2) we present the RTL algorithm that is based on these key features, (3) as part of the RTL algorithm we introduce a novel *zoom-in step* that secures the quality of the assigned labels, and (4) we show RTL's ability to increase the efficiency and robustness of the labeling procedure across a wide variety of time series datasets. RTL clears the path for TSC tasks in many application domains where large amounts of complex data are generated and need to be labeled continuously.

The outline of the remainder of the paper is as follows. In Sect. 2 we review related work. Then, in Sect. 3 we review the Like-Behaviors Labeling Routine (LBLR) introduced by Madrid et al. [9] and discuss possible improvements, which we use as starting point for the introduction of the RTL algorithm in Sect. 4. In Sects. 5 and 6 we evaluate and discuss the RTL algorithm and finally, we conclude and mention future research directions in Sect. 7.

2   Related Work

While the detection and classification of (anomalous) sub-sequences has been researched extensively (see e.g. [3]), there is almost no research dedicated to time series labeling. As far as we are aware, there are four papers on time series labeling [1,9,12,13].

Peng et al. [12] proposed the Active Learning for Time Series (ACTS) algorithm and showed that it achieved a higher classification accuracy than traditional active learning methods. Unlike our focus, theirs was on supervised active learning. Moreover, their method is built on the assumption that all classes to be learned are known before the learning procedure starts and that the time series data is perfectly arranged into segments having equal length and approximate alignment. In practice, this is seldom the case [1]. While Souza et al. [13] focus on unsupervised active learning, their experiments, like those of Peng et al. [12], were based on the perfectly segmented data from the UCR TSC Archive [2]. As stressed before, such perfectly segmented data is quite unlike the data encountered in real-life situations. In fact, segmentation is part of the challenge to find proper labels [6].

Chen et al. [1] and Madrid et al. [9] proposed the use of *motif discovery* for time series labeling. While computers are not able to understand the context of the time series, they are very proficient in motif discovery. A motif refers to pairs of sub-sequences of one or more time series that are highly similar[11] and may therefore reflect a common underlying cause. By combining the ability of algorithms to detect motifs with the ability of experts to label these motifs, the efficiency and effectiveness of labeling may increase significantly. Chen et al. [1] proposed an algorithm in which an agent examines an unbounded stream of data and occasionally asks a teacher – human or algorithm – for a label. Compared to Peng et al. [12], they do consider the case where no prior knowledge about the concepts to be learned is available. Likewise, Madrid et al. [9] proposed the LBLR algorithm to label an entire time series dataset with minimum human effort. Both algorithms, however, require the lengths of the motifs as input. Whilst the LBLR is closest to the aim of our RTL algorithm to deal with realistic unsegmented and unlabeled data, the empirical realities of different length motifs and a lack of a priori knowledge on what is to be discovered [4,5,10], suggest room for further improvement. Before introducing our RTL algorithm, we review the LBLR [9] and suggest improvements to it.

3   Requirements for a Robust Time Series Labeling Method

In this section we identify the strengths and potential shortcomings of the LBLR. To quantify the effects of these potential shortcomings, we introduce a variant called LBLR'. Subsequently, we define the two measures used for evaluating LBLR's performance. Based on the results obtained through a diverse set of experiments, we conclude with the key features needed to have a robust method for reducing labeling effort while maintaining high quality labels.

The LBLR increases the labeling efficiency of TSC by using the Matrix Profile (MP) and Minimum Description Length (MDL). The former is a method to perform motif discovery efficiently (see [14] for a detailed explanation), the latter is an information-theoretic measure to determine which motifs carry the same information content. When a set of sub-sequences is similar in terms of MDL (referred to as "semantically similar"), the whole set is assigned a single label by the user. However, during this procedure, the LBLR allows for an *extra user interaction* in which the user can add or remove sub-sequences from the elements in this set. This enables the user to remove misclassifications during the labeling procedure, which assumes that the user is able to do so. While such user-based removal could improve the quality of the assigned labels, it undeniably increases the labeling effort.

The use of motif discovery techniques helps to decrease the labeling effort. However, it also may negatively affect the quality of the labels. In the LBLR, labeled motifs are assumed to be all of a certain fixed length l. Not surprisingly, though, motifs can vary considerably in length. Assuming otherwise thus may affect the operation of LBLR during two phases: the detection of motifs and the so-called *cleanup phase*. The latter refers to the action in which all unlabeled sub-sequences of length less than l get assigned their neighboring labels automatically. Put differently, the cleanup phase labels heuristically, without any use of machine or human expertise.

To measure the effect of the extra user interaction, we compare the performance of the original LBLR with LBLR'. In the latter, all the selected motifs, misclassifications or not, receive the same label given by the user. This provides insight into the actual labeling effort of the expert. To assess how the use of fixed-length motifs affects the performance of LBLR, we vary the predefined motif lengths. To evaluate the performance of LBLR and LBLR', two measures are used: the relative labeling effort and labeling accuracy.

– **Relative Labeling Effort (RLE)** is defined as the fraction of machine- and human-based labeling to complete human labeling of a time series. Given a time series of length n and fixed motif length l, the maximum number of Labeling Rounds is defined as $LR_{max} = \frac{n}{l}$. Automatically detecting and labeling semantically similar motifs gives rise to a reduced number of labeling rounds LR. The Relative Labeling Effort is defined as $RLE = \frac{LR}{LR_{max}}$.
– **Labeling Accuracy (LA)** is defined as the percentage of correctly labeled instances and is therefore directly related to the label quality. It is important to remark that we can only determine accuracy, because we select labeled datasets for evaluation. As stated in the introduction, in most realistic applications, labels are lacking or only partially available.

In the following we will determine how fixed length motifs and the extra user interaction affect the labeling performance of LBLR. To do this, we use the following six different pre-labeled time series datasets.

1. **ACP1:** Entomology dataset. Data from an Asian Citrus Psyllid (snippet 1).
2. **ACP5:** Entomology dataset. Data from an Asian Citrus Psyllid (snippet 5).
3. **EER:** Epilepsy dataset representing distinct epilepsy episodes.
4. **ECG:** Electrocardiogram dataset. Each series traces the electrical activity recorded during one heartbeat.
5. **SLC:** Part of the StarLight Curves dataset.
6. **HCS:** A Hydraulic Control System dataset.

The datasets $ACP1$, $ACP5$, and EER have been used by Madrid et al. to evaluate their algorithm.[1] Datasets ECG and SLC are from the UCR Archive [2], and dataset HCS is a real-world industrial dataset collected by the authors.[2] These datasets were selected to cover as broad a range of characteristics as possible. Labeling each dataset with its numerical characteristics as a sequence of numbers, i.e., {number of classes, number of class transitions, length of the time series}, yields: $ACP1_{\{2,1,5203\}}$, $ACP5_{\{2,1,13126\}}$, $EER_{\{3,2,2734\}}$, $ECG_{\{2,41,9600\}}$, $SLC_{\{3,11,20480\}}$ and $HCS_{\{2,15,25000\}}$ (cf. Fig. 1). This diversity enables us to assess the performance of LBLR across different domains and situations.

Table 1 contains six sub-tables representing the performances of LBLR and LBLR' for each of the six datasets and four motif lengths. We make four observations from these results. First, rejecting the **extra user interaction**

---

[1] The datasets are downloaded from the web-page of the authors (www.cs.ucr.edu/~fmadr002/LBLR.html), where the names of some datasets differ from the original naming convention.
[2] Due to the nature of the ECG and SLC datasets, we needed to concatenate the separate sequences into a single time series.

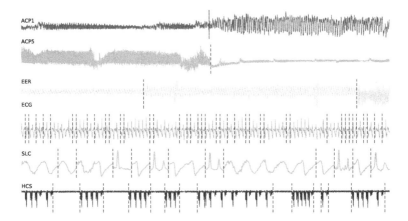

Fig. 1. The time series of the six datasets. Different time scales are depicted, due to the different time series lengths. The black vertical lines indicate the class transitions; clearly visible for the first three datasets, less so for the last three.

(LBLR vs. LBLR') results in a drop in LA that varies from zero ($APC1(l = 200)$) to huge ($EER(l = 10)$). Second, using **fixed-length motif discovery** yields a decrease in LA of LBLR for some datasets. This (negative) effect is even more substantial for the LBLR', revealing that the combined effect of abandoning both the extra user interaction and fixed-length motif discovery is large. Third, LBLR and LBLR' perform well on the datasets selected by Madrid et al., but the accuracy drops significantly on the additional datasets we tested. This drop in performance is due to the cleanup phase. As the three additional datasets include many class transitions, the chance of wrongly labeling motifs of length less than l increases. Fourth, the RLE decreases for almost all dataset-motif length combinations, and especially for LBLR'. Whilst in itself a positive effect, it only materializes in combination with a (possibly severely) reduced LA.

There are three surprising results worth mentioning. First, the LA of 34.8% for $EER(l = 20)$ and 57.4% for $HCS(l = 500)$ is lower than the *baseline accuracy*, that is obtained by assigning the majority label to the entire time series. Second, for the two pre-processed datasets, i.e. ECG and SLC, the fixed motif length ($l = 96$ and $l = 1024$, respectively) does *not* provide the best results. This even led to a substantial drop from 74.0% ($l = 100$) to 69.5% ($l = 96$) for the ECG dataset. So, even when the data is perfectly segmented and arranged into patterns of fixed length, this fixed motif length does not return the best results in terms of accuracy. Third, for $ACP1(l = 200)$ the RLE is close to 100%. This means that using the LBLR for this specific motif length is as efficient as just labeling all the sub-sequences separately.

As these results indicate, there is room for improvement with regards to: a) not being dependent on extra user interactions; and b) being able to robustly handle various situations, including varying motif lengths.

Table 1. The Labeling Accuracy LA (higher is better) and Relative Labeling Effort RLE (lower is better) per motif length l of both LBLR and LBLR'.

ACP1

l	LA LBLR	LA LBLR'	RLE LBLR	RLE LBLR'
50	99.6	90.3	34.6	28.8
100	99.5	83.9	44.2	36.5
150	98.5	77.0	75.0	54.8
200	98.9	98.9	99.9	99.9

ACP5

l	LA LBLR	LA LBLR'	RLE LBLR	RLE LBLR'
50	99.8	90.5	50.3	36.9
100	99.3	87.3	48.8	40.4
150	99.8	88.8	57.1	48.0
200	98.8	90.0	70.1	50.3

EER

l	LA LBLR	LA LBLR'	RLE LBLR	RLE LBLR'
10	99.5	34.8	19.4	1.8
20	99.6	88.2	11.7	2.2
40	99.4	72.7	21.9	8.7
50	98.1	80.7	21.9	11.0

ECG

l	LA LBLR	LA LBLR'	RLE LBLR	RLE LBLR'
50	85.9	70.0	34.4	1.6
96	85.3	69.5	25.0	3.0
100	79.6	74.0	20.8	3.1
200	74.7	69.1	20.8	6.2

SLC

l	LA LBLR	LA LBLR'	RLE LBLR	RLE LBLR'
500	79.1	75.6	34.2	7.3
1000	78.8	68.3	29.3	9.8
1024	78.9	68.4	30.0	10.0
1500	63.6	65.0	43.9	14.6

HCS

l	LA LBLR	LA LBLR'	RLE LBLR	RLE LBLR'
100	95.9	80.1	27.2	18.4
200	93.9	87.1	33.6	26.4
250	91.0	82.7	34.0	35.0
500	81.9	57.4	24.0	28.0

4 Robust Time Series Labeling

In this section we introduce a novel algorithm to efficiently and effectively label time series. It is based on a motif discovery method that groups motifs, and allows experts to label them efficiently. Motifs of variable length are considered and high labeling accuracy is maintained by the introduction of a *zooming in* function for the detected motifs.

Introducing some notation, we define a time series T as an ordered sequence of n real-valued numbers, often measured at fixed intervals. Given $T = \{t_1, \ldots, t_n\}$, we want to detect motifs of different lengths l for labeling. The steps included in the RTL algorithm are summarized in Algorithm 1.[3]

As an initial pre-processing step to raise efficiency, RTL discretizes T into a symbolic representation D (line 1). The details of this step are provided in Sect. 4.1 below. The procedure of finding motifs for labeling starts on line 2 and continues until an automatic stopping criterion is met (cf. Sect. 4.3). On line 3, variable length motifs are detected within an automatically updated range of lengths $L = \{MIN, MAX\}$ and are saved in M_L (cf. Sect. 4.1). Note that

---

[3] The code and datasets have been made publicly available at ⌂GitHub.

Algorithm 1. The RTL algorithm

Require: Time Series T
1: $D = $ SymbolicRepresentation(T)
2: **while** T has unlabeled data $\wedge \neg$ algorithm(quits) **do**
3:      $M_L = $ FindMotifs(D*, L)
4:      $M'_L = $ Zoom-in(M_L)
5:      $S = $ SelectandLabelMotif(M'_L)
6:      Update(D*)
7: **end while**
8: **return** S: Labels corresponding to T

---

only those parts of D not yet labeled are considered to be candidates for motif discovery (D*, line 6). To secure the quality of the assigned labels, the *zoom-in* step mentioned above is introduced (line 4). In fact, based on the (dis)similarity between all motifs which belong to a motif group, only the so-called *representative* motifs are selected and saved in M'_L (cf. Sect. 4.2). Within this set of motifs, the longest motif is selected to be labeled (line 5, cf. Sect. 4.3). These labels are saved in S, which includes the label (or not-yet-labeled) information per data point n of T. Unlike LBLR, no *cleanup phase* is included. All data is labeled under supervision of the user and no labels are automatically assigned. As a consequence, LBLR returns an entire labeled dataset, while RTL returns S containing not-yet-labeled data points.

In our experiments in which we evaluate RTL and LBLR (cf. Sect. 5), we use an extra step between lines 7 and 8 in Algorithm 1. This step is purely for comparison and ensures RTL, like LBLR, returns a fully labeled dataset. In the extra step all not-yet-labeled data in S is labeled automatically based on their neighbors.

4.1 Variable-Length Motifs

To transform our time series into a symbolic representation, we use SAX (Symbolic Aggregate approXimation) [8]. The SAX algorithm has two parameters: w and a, which control the number of segments (PAA-size) and alphabet-size, respectively. Based on the extensive experiments carried out in [7], we set $a = 3$ for all experiments. The best value of w depends on the data (relatively smooth and slowly changing datasets favor a small value of w). We determine the value of w as follows: all data points n of the time series are transformed into a sequence of symbols of equal length n, for which we calculate the average number of consecutive identical symbols (q). This average is rounded to the closest integer for which it holds that $n\%q = 0$. w is then set to $w = \frac{n}{q}$. This procedure ensures that the running time of creating SAX strings remains low, and complex time series showing a lower average of consecutive identical symbols, i.e. more variability, receive a larger w.

To detect variable length motifs, we split the *string* representation of T, into so-called *words* of two symbols. For example, the string *ccaaaabb* becomes *cc aa aa bb*. Subsequently, we count the number of occurrences of (successive) word(s), e.g. $\{cc:1\}, \{aa:2\}, \{ccaa:1\}, \{aaaabb:1\}$ and so on.[4] In this way, any word that occurs more than once in the string is considered to be a motif. While short words are likely to occur frequently in the string, they may be less representative of the underlying shape of the time series than longer motifs. Therefore, we start by labeling the longer – more unique – motifs and only subsequently label shorter motifs. To achieve this, we introduce $L = \{MIN, MAX\}$, with MIN being the minimum considered motif length and MAX the maximum per labeling round. Every labeling round the procedure starts with searching the longest word that appears twice (set the length of this word to MAX) and keeps searching until a word of smaller length appearing more than twice is found (set this value to MIN). In this way, a set of motifs M_L with different lengths is created in which longer motifs are prioritized over shorter ones.

4.2 Representative Motifs

Although the use of (symbolic) motif discovery techniques helps to increase the efficiency of the labeling procedure, important details within the motifs may be overlooked. More specifically, the selected motifs (Algorithm 1, line 3) may reveal significant variance when we consider more details by means of the *zoom-in* step (line 4). The zoom-in step is needed as grouped motifs may be very similar when compared to the rest of the time series, but may differ a lot when compared directly to each other. Hence, to safeguard the labeling accuracy, we need a method which is able to perceive detailed differences within the motif groups so that potential missclasifications can be removed. To achieve this, all motifs within the motif group are discretized into a small SAX string (e.g. $w = 3$: *bbb*). If these newly created strings are all the same, these so called *representative* motifs are considered to be candidates for labeling.

4.3 Motif Selection and Stopping Criteria

Every iteration round, a set M'_L of representative motifs is created (Algorithm 1, line 4). From this set, the motif group which includes most data points (motif frequency × motif length) is chosen to be labeled (line 5). This motif group is considered to be the *optimal* motif in terms of efficient labeling, as it contributes most to the goal of minimizing the labeling effort. After the motif is labeled by the human annotator, the initial discretized time series is updated (D*), so that in the next round the labeled data is not considered for labeling anymore. This procedure repeats until no more *representative* motifs can be found.

5   Results

We compare the RTL algorithm to the adjusted LBLR' algorithm, as they are both independent of (unquantifiable) extra user interactions. In this way, the

---

[4] We use the commonly used text analytics method *CountVectorizer* for this, but other methods may also work. CountVectorizer requires input words of at least size two.

actual LA and *RLE* of using motif discovery for efficient time series labeling is unveiled. We compare the performances of the RTL algorithm and LBLR' by plotting the *LA* against percentage labeled (Fig. 2) and listing the *RLE* per dataset (Table 2). In order to simplify the comparison and to unveil the robustness of the algorithms, we report the best and worst *LA* results obtained with the augmented LBLR' in Table 1.

Figure 2 shows the results for all datasets (Sect. 3) and can be interpreted as follows. The dots, interconnected by the lines, represent the percentage labeled (*x*-axis) and *LA* (*y*-axis) for each labeling round. The procedure starts in the upper left corner with 100% *LA*, i.e. correctly labeled data, and each following dot represents the *LA* of the (already) labeled part. The printed percentages at the end of the orange and red each curves express the *LA* of LBLR' after the labeling procedure was terminated. For RTL, the values at the end of the solid line represent the *LA* after the algorithm is terminated and thus before all left-overs are labeled automatically based on their neighboring behaviors (represented by dotted lines). As a reminder, automatic labeling is not part of the RTL algorithm and is only done so that RTL can be more easily compared to LBLR'.

The challenge in achieving a minimum *RLE* with a maximum *LA*, lies in managing their trade-off. In Fig. 2, we can see that RTL (blue line) outperforms LBLR' (orange and red lines) with respect to the *LA* on all datasets, except *SLC*. In some cases (*ACP5* and *ECG*) the improvement is substantial, in others it is relatively small (*ACP1*). However, the performance of LBLR' depends strongly on the chosen fixed motif length – as is evident from the considerable gaps between the orange and red curves – and is therefore not as robust as RTL. So, concerning *LA*, RTL is recommended over LBLR'.

Compared to LBLR', the *RLE* (Table 2) for RTL is significantly lower on datasets *ACP1* and *ACP5*.[5] This observation, together with a higher *LA*, implies that on similar datasets RTL outperforms LBLR'. For the other datasets, RTL requires a higher *RLE*, which generally leads to a higher *LA*. Since the *RLE* is still not excessive, ranging from 8.0% to 29.6%, the higher *LA* may be worth the extra effort.

Table 2. Relative labeling effort %

	ACP1	ACP5	EER	ECG	SLC	HCS
RTL	20.2	8.0	13.9	25.0	9.8	29.6
LBLR'$_{best}$	99.9	36.9	2.2	3.1	7.3	26.4
LBLR'$_{worst}$	54.8	40.4	1.8	6.2	14.6	28.0

---

[5] As no fixed motif length l is used as input for RTL, we are actually not able to calculate the *RLE* as defined in Sect. 3. To still be able to compare, we used the length for which LBLR' performed best, e.g. $ACP1(l = 200)$.

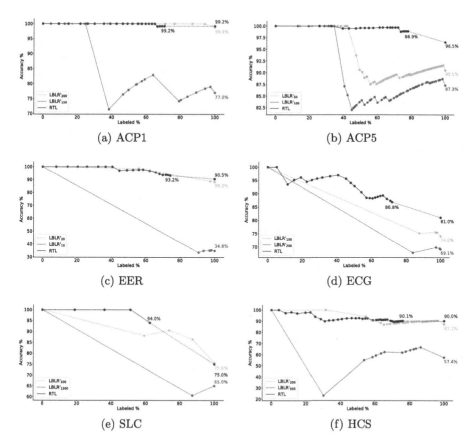

Fig. 2. Comparison between RTL and LBLR'. The parent curve indicates the best performing labeling algorithm concerning the obtained LA and thus label quality. The preferred performance is one with a high labeling quality and low labeling effort, corresponding to a flat curve with a minimal number of dots.

Unlike LBLR, RTL does not return a fully labeled dataset. As stated before, for the purpose of experimental evaluation, we introduced an extra step in the RTL algorithm that automatically labels unlabeled data after termination. The dotted lines in Fig. 2 show that automatically filling the gaps *after* the labeling procedure is terminated, affects the accuracy considerably for most datasets. Whereas ±75% can be labeled robustly by RTL, the so-called *rest-category* seems to require a different approach. These left-overs are unique and cannot be matched based on motif discovery and thus may include e.g. anomalies, novelties, state-changes or noise. Accordingly, we recommend to either not label this, automatically label it as rest-category or to label it manually. Although the latter increases the labeling effort, it may reveal interesting and previously unknown concepts to the user.

To summarize, being independent of fixed-length motifs and automatic labeling, benefits LA. Unfortunately, a higher LA may force a sacrifice with respect to RLE. But with a appreciable reduced RLE, RTL achieved a more robust compromise between the RLE and LA for all considered datasets. Due to this more balanced trade-off, RTL is useful for anyone who wants to efficiently and accurately label time series for TSC tasks in a wide variety of application domains.

6   Discussion

The use of symbolic motif discovery might result in overlooking important details. To remedy this, we introduced the extra *zoom-in* step (Algorithm 1, line 4). To determine the contribution of this extra step, we compared RTL to an adjusted version where line 4 in Algorithm 1 was removed. For all datasets the removal of this line led to a deterioration of LA by 1.4% points ($ACP5$) to 5.0% points (ECG). Thus, this extra step is important with respect to the labeling quality.

The performance of any algorithm depending on SAX, relies on alphabet-size a and PAA-size w. So does RTL.[6] The Matrix Profile used by LBLR is not dependent on such parameters and could be potentially used in future work. However, an extra step – such as using MDL – is needed to find all motifs which are *semantically* the same. Hence, one way or the other, some sort of discretization method is needed to find semantically similar motifs, so that they can be grouped and labeled efficiently.

7   Conclusion and Future Research

Despite the extensive research on TSC, research dedicated to time series labeling is scarce. We demonstrated that the implied user interaction and restriction of fixed motif length hamper LBLR's labeling performance. We presented RTL as an alternative and demonstrated its robustness by comparing the labeling accuracy and relative labeling effort to those of LBLR' on a variety of datasets. With an average accuracy of 93.7% and a significantly reduced labeling effort, the path for TSC tasks in practice is cleared.

The RTL algorithm can be further improved along at least three lines. First, more research should be done on the effect of the PAA-size and alphabet-size on the quality of the motifs and thus labels. Second, the use of e.g. the Euclidean Distance—instead of separate SAX strings—in the zoom-in step could be explored in future research. Finally, in some cases a high-frequency motif could be more relevant than a longer less-frequent motif. In this paper, motifs were selected based on the trade-off between three measures: the similarity, frequency and length of the motif. In other variable-length motif discovery algorithms, the

---

[6] After comparing different values for a and w no significant accuracy changes were obtained. However, more research is needed to fully understand the impact of both parameters on the LA and RLE.

motif is defined using only a similarity or frequency measure, often based on a threshold function. Depending on the application, the right trade-off between measures should be found.

References

1. Chen, Y., Hao, Y., Rakthanmanon, T., Zakaria, J., Hu, B., Keogh, E.: A general framework for never-ending learning from time series streams. Data Min. Knowl. Disc. **29**(6), 1622–1664 (2014). https://doi.org/10.1007/s10618-014-0388-4
2. Dau, H.A., et al.: The UCR time series classification archive, October 2018
3. Esling, P., Agon, C.: Time-series data mining. ACM Comput. Surv. (CSUR) **45**(1), 12 (2012)
4. Gao, Y., Lin, J.: Hime: discovering variable-length motifs in large-scale time series. Knowl. Inf. Syst. 1–30 (2018)
5. Gao, Y., Lin, J., Rangwala, H.: Iterative grammar-based framework for discovering variable-length time series motifs. In: 2017 IEEE International Conference on Data Mining (ICDM), pp. 111–116. IEEE (2017)
6. Hu, B., Chen, Y., Keogh, E.J.: Time series classification under more realistic assumptions. In: Proceedings of the 13th SIAM International Conference on Data Mining, Austin, Texas, USA, 2–4 May 2013, pp. 578–586 (2013). https://doi.org/10.1137/1.9781611972832.64
7. Keogh, E.J., Lin, J., Fu, A.W.: HOT SAX: efficiently finding the most unusual time series subsequence. In: Proceedings of the 5th IEEE International Conference on Data Mining (ICDM 2005), Houston, Texas, USA, 27–30 November 2005, pp. 226–233 (2005). https://doi.org/10.1109/ICDM.2005.79
8. Lin, J., Keogh, E.J., Wei, L., Lonardi, S.: Experiencing SAX: a novel symbolic representation of time series. Data Min. Knowl. Discov. **15**(2), 107–144 (2007). https://doi.org/10.1007/s10618-007-0064-z
9. Madrid, F., Singh, S., Chesnais, Q., Mauck, K., Keogh, E.: Matrix profile xvi: efficient and effective labeling of massive time series archives. In: 2019 IEEE International Conference on Data Science and Advanced Analytics (DSAA), pp. 463–472 (2019)
10. Mueen, A., Chavoshi, N.: Enumeration of time series motifs of all lengths. Knowl. Inf. Syst. **45**(1), 105–132 (2014). https://doi.org/10.1007/s10115-014-0793-4
11. Patel, P., Keogh, E., Lin, J., Lonardi, S.: Mining motifs in massive time series databases. In: 2002 IEEE International Conference on Data Mining, 2002. Proceedings, pp. 370–377. IEEE (2002)
12. Peng, F., Luo, Q., Ni, L.M.: ACTS: an active learning method for time series classification. In: 33rd IEEE International Conference on Data Engineering, ICDE 2017, San Diego, CA, USA, 19–22 April 2017, pp. 175–178 (2017)
13. Souza, V., Rossi, R.G., Batista, G.E., Rezende, S.O.: Unsupervised active learning techniques for labeling training sets: an experimental evaluation on sequential data. Intell. Data Anal. **21**(5), 1061–1095 (2017)
14. Yeh, C.C.M., et al.: Matrix profile i: all pairs similarity joins for time series: a unifying view that includes motifs, discords and shapelets. In: 2016 IEEE 16th International Conference on Data Mining (ICDM), pp. 1317–1322. IEEE (2016)

The Compromise of Data Privacy in Predictive Performance

Tânia Carvalho[1(✉)] and Nuno Moniz[1,2]

[1] Computer Science Department, Faculty of Sciences,
University of Porto, Porto, Portugal
tania.carvalho@fc.up.pt
[2] INESC TEC, Porto, Portugal

Abstract. Privacy-preservation has become an essential concern in many data mining applications since the emergence of legal obligations to protect personal data. Thus, the notion of Privacy-Preserving Data Mining emerged to allow the extraction of knowledge from data without violating the privacy of individuals. Several transformation techniques have been proposed to protect the privacy of individuals. However, their application does not guarantee a null risk of an individual being re-identified. Furthermore, and most importantly, for this paper, the application of such techniques may have a considerable impact on the utility of data and their use in predictive and descriptive tasks. In this paper, we present a study to provide key insights concerning the impact of privacy-preserving techniques in predictive performance. Unlike previous work, our main conclusions point towards a noticeable impact of privacy-preservation techniques in predictive performance.

Keywords: Data privacy · Supervised learning · Re-identification risk · Record linkage

1 Introduction

Privacy-Preserving Data Mining (PPDM) techniques were designed to balance the privacy and utility of data at an acceptable level, in such a way that data mining can still be performed on the protected data accurately. A particular characteristic of PPDM is that data are not released. However, making data more protected may also reduce its utility which provokes an inaccurate extraction of knowledge through data mining [19].

Concerning privacy, de-identification is a procedure which complies with the GDPR (General Data Protection Regulation). This procedure is crucial to prevent revealing the identity of individuals and keeping personal information private. Data must be de-identified so that re-identification, i.e. personal information is linked back to an individual, is not possible. The re-identification of individuals, also known as identity disclosure, can occur by comparing de-identified data with other external data sources, such as public information available on social networks, websites, or other data sets. Commonly, de-identification procedures reduce data granularity to increase privacy. Such a process may result in

© Springer Nature Switzerland AG 2021
P. H. Abreu et al. (Eds.): IDA 2021, LNCS 12695, pp. 426–438, 2021.
https://doi.org/10.1007/978-3-030-74251-5_34

loss of data mining effectiveness: the most popular trade-off between data utility and privacy.

In this paper, we study the impact of applying several transformation techniques to achieve distinct de-identified data sets for further analysis. We also carry out a re-identification risk assessment in each de-identified data sets. Finally, we demonstrate which privacy-preserving technique has more percussion in the performance of a multi-class classification problem.

The main contributions of this work are: i) the comparison of different privacy-preservation techniques and respective privacy level; ii) highlighting the importance of assessing re-identification risk, and iii) an evaluation of the impact of privacy-preservation techniques in predictive performance.

The remainder of this paper is organised as follows. Section 2 describes existing works that are related to this proposal. Section 3 explains in detail the motivation of our work and consequent methodology to solve the problem. Section 4 evaluates our methodology regarding performance under different scenarios and present the experimental analysis. Section 5 concludes the paper.

2 Related Work

Inan et al. [16] proposed a novel approach for building classifiers over de-identified data, in which, each generalised value is associated with statistics as such dot product and square distance, collected from records in the same equivalence class as the generalised value. The authors show different uses of de-identified data sets based on distance functions. They classified de-identified data by modelling de-identified data as uncertain data. The authors conclude that generalisation of values does not significantly degrade performance.

The work of Buratović et al. [3] shows the effects of de-identification on the classification results. To achieve a de-identified data set, they used Samarati's algorithm [23] with attribute generalisation and tuple suppression. The classification results over protected data set and original data set were obtained with the WEKA (Waikato Environment for Knowledge Analysis) [26]. According to the best result, the performance between the two data sets was almost intact.

More recently, Vanichayavisalsakul et al. [24] evaluate the performance of several privacy methods and classification algorithms for protected data. The de-identification process was performed by the ARX tool [21], which needs a privacy method to determine whether a dataset is satisfied by a specific criterion of privacy. To achieve the selected privacy methods, they applied generalisation and suppression on original data. Their results show no significant difference between the performance of the classification algorithms on the original data set and the protected data set.

We verify that previous work does not provide an evaluation of the various types of transformation techniques. Such an evaluation should provide a better understanding of the compromise between data privacy and predictive performance. In this paper, we propose to carry out such an effort.

3   Problem Formulation and Approach

A broad range of privacy-preserving techniques have been suggested to obfuscate personal information in data. However, the resulting de-identified data set might still allow for an intruder to leverage external information, thus obtaining private data about individuals. Beyond that, there is an essential aspect that we should consider: the utility of data after the application of privacy-preserving techniques. The more data we remove about an individual, less useful the data becomes for statistical analysis or other purposes.

The subsequent sections provide a coarse presentation of approaches for handling de-identification, followed by measures to assess the risk of re-identification in de-identified data. Also, we discuss measures to evaluate the utility of the data after the application of privacy-preservation techniques.

3.1   Handling the De-identification

De-identification includes the treatment of direct identifiers, quasi-identifiers (QI) and sensitive attributes. **Direct identifiers**, such as names and social security numbers, must be removed or replaced by pseudonyms. However, when combined, other attributes generate a unique signature, which could allow re-identification of individuals when linked with public data. Such attributes are called **quasi-identifiers**, and some examples are the date of birth, gender, geographical location and profession. **Sensitive information** refers to highly critical attributes, usually protected by law and regulations, for example, religion, sexual orientation, disease and political opinion.

In order to protect such attributes, a wide range of transformation techniques has been proposed in related literature [7,8]. We describe well-known privacy-preserving data transformation techniques as follows.

- **Generalisation** aims to reduce the detail of information. Assuming a data set contains an attribute with the county to which an individual belongs, the idea is to generalise. For example, to group into broader categories combining some counties into districts or to a higher level. In the case of a continuous attribute such as age, we combine it as a range, also known as discretisation.
- **Suppression** of values means that we replace values of an attribute by a missing value (NA) or a unique character (*, ?). Suppression can occur at cell, record or attribute level.
- **Noise** changes the values of original data set by adding or subtracting some random noise.

The implementation of one or more transformation techniques is used in order to achieve a certain privacy degree according to a particular privacy method. One of the most well-known privacy methods and the first proposed in related literature is k-anonymity [23]. It states that k-anonymity is achieved if, for any individual, there are at least k-1 individuals in the data set that share the same properties. More recently, the ϵ-differential privacy method [10] has received much attention. A mechanism satisfies ϵ-differential privacy if the result of differential-private analysis of an individual's information is the same whether or not that information of the individual is included in the input for the analysis. The goal in differential privacy is to create a differentially private mechanism that approximates queries as closely as possible and returns the response given by such a mechanism.

Generalisation and suppression are non-perturbative methods, i.e., reduces the amount of information in the original data, and are the main transformation techniques applied in the k-anonymity method. Noise is a perturbative method which distorts the original data. The ϵ-differential privacy method is achieved by using a mechanism of noise addition.

3.2 Assessing Re-identification Risk

Regardless of the application of transformation techniques, the risk of private information disclosure still exists. Accordingly, it is imperative to assess the risk of re-identification [27]. Besides being a privacy method, we may use k-anonymity to express the re-identifiability of its records [12]. Given k, the number of combinations of a given set of QI in the data set, fk is the frequency of the sample records having the same combination k of QI. If $fk = 1$, the individual has a unique combination of QI values. As such, it is possible to *single out* that individual, which means that she can be re-identified: the rarer a combination of values of the QI, greater the risk of disclosure of the individual's identity.

Record linkage is a strategy often used by intruders to combine de-identified data with external data, which contains private information. In other words, record linkage is useful to identify the presence of the same individual in different data sets [9]. This strategy also can be used to assess the risk of re-identification by comparing a de-identified data set with the original data set.

Although we only focus on re-identification, there are two additional types of disclosure. Attribute disclosure occurs when an intruder determines new characteristics of an individual based on available information in de-identified data. Such disclosure can be achieved even without linking an individual to a specific record. Membership disclosure occurs when an intruder infers some information about an individual not contained in the de-identified data set.

3.3 Data Utility

Privacy-Preserving Data Mining (PPDM) techniques aim to deal with the protection of individual's privacy without sacrificing (or by reducing the impact in) the utility of the data. However, privacy-preservation techniques generally degrade the quality of the data. After the de-identification of data, these are often used in data mining applications. In such a case, the utility of data depends on how well data structures are preserved. In other words, how accurate is the protected data set as a representation of the original data sample.

For a specific application, a utility measure should capture the factors that affect the quality of data. In a classification task, typical metrics used to assess the quality of data mining results include Precision and Recall [18], and FScore [22]. Fletcher et al. [13] provides a thorough description of evaluation metrics in the scope of data mining applications.

4   Experimental Methodology

Based on the description of previous work and the problem scope detailed in the previous section, we now present our experimental study. Such study aims to answer the following research questions.

RQ1 What is the level of privacy when applying privacy-preserving techniques?
RQ2 What is the re-identification risk in the transformed data sets?
RQ3 How do privacy-preserving techniques impact predictive performance?

In the following sections, we present the data used in the experimental study and all related pre-processing steps. Afterwards, we present the methods used, including learning algorithms and respective parameter grids, and evaluation metrics. Finally, we present results and provide subsequent analysis concerning each research question.

4.1   Data Preparation

To accomplish this experiment, we resort to the *Kaggle* platform, a repository of public data. Our research culminated in a compelling use case for our scope: information on NBA (National Basketball Association) players [17]. We extract four data sets. Three of them concern players' game statistics since 1950, and another data set contains details on every injury in the NBA from 2010 to 2018. We divide the first data sets into one data set with personal information, a second data set with game statistics of each player per season and the last data set containing the years that the players are (were) in the NBA. Our goal is to predict whether a player had an injury in a certain year, either minor or severe. In order to achieve such a goal, we have applied the following pre-processing steps.

- We added the first and last years of each players' careers;
- We restricted game statistics to those since 2010;
- We created a new attribute to express the span of players' careers in years;
- We created a new attribute to denote the severity of injuries. Suppose a player did not play more than 15 days due to injury. In that case, we consider it a severe injury, otherwise, a minor injury.
- We added the degree of an injury to the all previous merged data.

After applying these pre-processing steps and the merger of the four data sets, the final data set consists of 3.309 records and 58 attributes. However, several statistical attributes are not necessary for our goal since they are innocuous to privacy and have no relevance for prediction purposes. As such, we do not consider in our study attributes such as true shooting, free throws rate, assists,

Table 1. Details of the NBA data set used including the list of attributes, their data type and a short description.

Attribute	Type	Description
Height	*Numeric*	Player height in centimetres
Weight	*Numeric*	Player weight in pounds
College	*String*	College that the player attended
Born	*Numeric*	Year the player was born
Birth_city	*String*	City where the player was born
Birth_state	*String*	State/Country where the player was born
year_start	*Numeric*	Year the player started playing
year_end	*Numeric*	Year the player ended playing
Year	*Numeric*	Season
Age	*Numeric*	Player's age of the season
NBA_Years	*Numeric*	Years in NBA per season
PER	*Numeric*	Player efficiency rating of the season
G	*Numeric*	Games of the season
GS	*Numeric*	Games started of the season
MP	*Numeric*	Minutes played per game
ORB%	*Numeric*	Offensive rebounds percentage per game
DRB%	*Numeric*	Deffensive rebounds percentage per game
TRB%	*Numeric*	Total rebounds percentage per game
ORB	*Numeric*	Offensive rebounds per game
DRB	*Numeric*	Deffensive rebounds per game
TRB	*Numeric*	Total rebounds per game
PTS	*Numeric*	Points per game
Injury	*Numeric*	Target

steals, blocks, turnovers, among others. In the final data set, we use 23 attributes, detailed in Table 1 along with a brief description.

Figure 1 shows the difference between the three classes of injury status. There are 8.6% of players who had a severe injury between 2010 and 2018. Players with minor injuries correspond to 37%, and 54.4% of the players showed no injury. It is noticeable that the classes are not evenly distributed. However, our goal in this paper is not to maximise predictive performance, but rather to evaluate the impact of privacy-preserving techniques. Accordingly, we did not include the search for methods to tackle the issues raised by imbalanced class distributions.

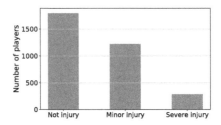

Fig. 1. Distribution of the target attribute.

4.2 Privacy-Preservation

The final data set contains information that, when combined with other sources, may allow the re-identification of players. Then, it is necessary to protect the privacy of each player. Taking into consideration the attributes presented, we test the application of noise in statistical attributes and suppression and generalisation in the remainder attributes. The objective is to construct six new data sets where each of them represents possible combinations of the proposed transformation techniques for this case: *i)* suppression; *ii)* generalisation; *iii)* suppression and generalisation; *iv)* suppression and noise; *v)* generalisation and noise and; *vi)* suppression, generalisation and noise.

So far, we know that noise can be used to achieve ϵ-differential privacy method and suppression and generalisation to achieve k-anonymity. Holohan et al. [15] propose a privacy method, (k, ϵ)-anonymity, that associates both k-anonymity and ϵ-differential privacy. First, we apply k-anonymity to a subset of quasi-identifiers (QI). Then, the ϵ-differential privacy is used in the remaining QI for each equivalence class of the k-anonymous result. An equivalence class consists of all records which have the same combination of QI attribute.

Concerning the application of the privacy-preserving techniques, we initially classified the set of QI into k-QI and ϵ-QI subsets where Table 2 discriminates which attributes are in each subset.

Table 2. Attribute classification for further application of k-anonymity in k-QI, and ϵ-differential privacy in ϵ-QI.

QI	Height, weight, collage, born, birth_city, birth_state, year_start, year_end, Year, Age, NBA_Years, PER, G, GS, MP, ORB%, DRB%, TRB%, ORB, DRB, TRB, PTS
k-**QI**	Height, weight, collage, born, birth_city, birth_state, year_start, year_end, Year, Age, NBA_Years,
ϵ-**QI**	PER, G, GS, MP, ORB%, DRB%, TRB%, ORB, DRB, TRB, PTS

Regarding the application of the suppression technique, in the subset of k-QI, we suppressed the following features: college, city of birth, state of birth, and the first and last year a player's NBA career. In such cases, values in each of the mentioned attributes were replaced by a "*" character.

Remaining attributes in k-QI were used in the application of the generalisation technique. Also, we experimented with a set of parameters to discover which range size is the best to achieve the smallest number of records with $f_k = 1$. For this purpose, we tested the range 3, 5, 10 and 12 in the height and weight attributed, and 3, 5 and 6 in the remaining attributes.

Concerning the application of noise, this was carried out in each equivalence class of the suppressed data set with the Laplace mechanism [11] where the ϵ parameter, which indicates the privacy level, was set to 0.5. The smaller the ϵ, the "noisier" is the data and consequently, a greater privacy guarantee. After, we assess the re-identification risk in each created data set. This procedure was performed with *Python Record Linkage Toolkit* [6], which provides robust tools to automate record linkage. This tool uses a distance function to verify the similarity between two strings. The tool was applied using the default parameter values. For each transformed data set, we compare with the original data set, and we analyse how many records are coincident. These matched records mean that they are at risk and need to be further protected.

4.3   Classification Algorithms

In order to test each transformation technique we have selected four classification algorithms in this experiment, including Random Forest (RF) [14], Bagging [1], XGBoost [4] and Support Vector Machines (SVM) [5]. We use the *Scikit-learn* python library [20] for building the classifiers. Final models for each algorithm are chosen based on a 5-fold cross-validation estimation of evaluation scores. Table 3 details the algorithms and parameter grids used in the experiments.

Table 3. Classification algorithms and respective parameters.

Algorithm	Parameters
RF	n_estimators: {50, 100, 200, 500, 600} max_depth: {4, 6, 8, 10}
Bagging	n_estimators: {50, 100, 200, 500, 600}
XGBoost	n_estimators: {50, 100, 200, 500, 600} max_depth: {4, 6, 8, 10} learning_rate: {0.1, 0.01, 0.001}
SVM	gamma: {1e-2, 1e-3, 13-4, 1e-5} C: {1, 10, 11}

4.4   Evaluation Measures

When evaluating data utility, it is essential to measure how close is the transformed data from the original. Since we have a multi-class classification problem and the three classes in the target attribute are not equally distributed, then traditionally used measures such accuracy are not suitable for this type of problem. For this reason, we used balanced accuracy [2], weighted FScore [22] and weighted AUC (Area Under the ROC Curve) [25]. The balanced accuracy is defined by the average of recall obtained on each class. The weighted FScore calculates the weighted harmonic mean of recall and precision. The weighted AUC performs a weighted average of the values of the true positive rate.

4.5   Results Analysis

In this section, we provide the results and related analysis by answering the research questions mentioned above. After, we present a comparison of our results with the related work above described.

RQ1: What is the level of privacy when applying privacy-preserving techniques? The data set that presents the highest level of privacy is the one combining all transformation techniques tested: suppression, generalisation and noise. If we consider the attributes of k-QI, we can guarantee that 98.46% of players are protected, i.e. the percentage of cases where $f_k > 1$ (not unique combinations). Analysing all attributes simultaneously, we conclude that the data set is fully protected. Suppression, generalisation and both combined presented low privacy level since only subsets of attributes have been transformed and therefore are unique combinations in the three data sets.

RQ2: What is the re-identification risk in the transformed data sets? Figure 2 illustrates a summary of the results of this experiment. For each transformed data set, we assess the re-identification risk presented in the title of each subplot. This percentage corresponds to the records that are *single out*, i.e., the records for which re-identification is possible. We note that re-identification risk is reduced with the noise technique as we are not sure whether or not the correspondence between the transformed data set and the original is correct. Other techniques have a re-identification risk of 100%, which correspond to the matched records with record linkage. This result is because the values of the attributes on the game statistics form unique combinations.

RQ3: How do privacy-preserving techniques impact predictive performance? To capture the impact that transformation techniques have on predictive performance, we represent in each subplot the percentage difference in performance between each technique used and the original data set, where the baseline corresponds to the original data set. The percentage difference values are the average of all iterations from cross-validation.

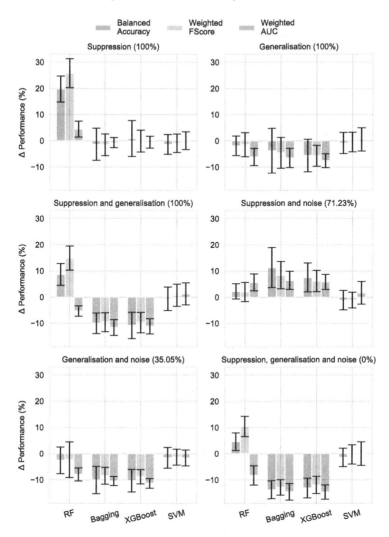

Fig. 2. Percentage difference of performance between each transformation technique and the baseline with the respective percentage of re-identification risk associated to each transformed data set.

According to our results, classification measures with baseline and with transformed data are substantially different. In general, suppression is the technique that shows a smaller percentage difference comparing to the baseline, which means that the attributes suppressed do not have high importance in obtaining accurate predictions. The behaviour of Random Forest (RF) models is because, in suppression, results are more accurate than in the baseline, which is supported by results in Fig. 3. We note that in our results, the generalisation had a negative impact with the Bagging and XGBoost algorithms, specially when combined

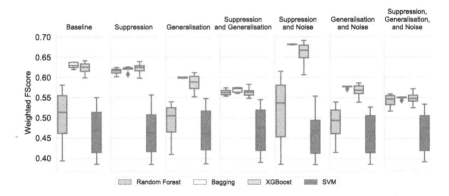

Fig. 3. Weighted FScore values of each classification algorithm for baseline and each transformation technique.

with suppression and noise, which show a higher percentage difference with these algorithms. We also verify that the iterations of cross-validation estimation show high variance between transformation techniques and the baseline.

To evaluate the effectiveness of each transformed data set on the classification task, Fig. 3 shows the weighted FScore values of each classification algorithm for the baseline and all combinations of transformation techniques used. Of the four algorithms tested, SVM models have the worst performance. Concerning transformation techniques, the suppression technique combined with noise presented the best results with the Bagging and XGBoost algorithms. We highlight that this result is an exception compared to the remaining results, as it particularly presents higher performance values than baseline.

Overall, in terms of privacy, the combination of suppression, generalisation and noise presents the best outcome. This data set has a higher privacy level and consequently, lower re-identification risk. However, w.r.t predictive performance was the worse. Bagging and Boosting, the best learning algorithms with baseline data set, presented a lower performance with all transformation techniques.

As a final analysis, we compare our experimental results with conclusions from related work. Innan et al. [16] state that generalisation does not significantly impact predictive performance. The application of the generalisation technique in our study has a negative impact. However, the difference with the baseline is small. Also, contrary to the other results in previous work [3,24], which declares that generalisation and suppression did not degrade the outcome of learning algorithms, our results show that the data set with suppression and generalisation has a negative difference of 10% with the best learning algorithms.

5   Conclusion

Our main goal is to apply several privacy-preserving techniques and evaluate their impact on prediction models' performance. In order to accomplish our purpose, we address three research questions. First, concerning the level of privacy associated with the application of privacy-preserving techniques, we demonstrate that it is possible to guarantee each individual's high privacy level. We obtained the best results when combining suppression, generalisation and noise. We also conclude that the more the data is transformed, the greater the privacy of the individual. Regarding the second research question and the re-identification risk associated with transformation techniques, we demonstrate that it is possible to obtain maximum privacy. However, and regarding the third research question – impact in predictive modelling tasks – results show that the more we protect individuals' privacy, the greater the (negative) impact on the performance of prediction models across various learning algorithms. Finally, despite the limited scope of our work, we stress the importance of our conclusions and the urgency of replicating such a study in a broader scope to allow further insights concerning the interplay between privacy-preserving techniques and models' performance in predictive modelling tasks.

Python code is freely provided at https://github.com/tmcarvalho/NBA. This URL also includes data sets necessary to replicate the experiments in the paper.

Acknowledgements. The work of Tânia Carvalho is supported by Project "POCI-01-0247-FEDER-041435 (Safe Cities)" and financed by the COMPETE 2020. The work of Nuno Moniz is financed by National Funds through the Portuguese funding agency, FCT - Fundaç ao para a Ciência e a Tecnologia within project UID/EEA/50014/2019. This work is also supported by TekPrivacy.

References

1. Breiman, L.: Bagging predictors. Mach. Learn. **24**(2), 123–140 (1996)
2. Brodersen, K.H., Ong, C.S., Stephan, K.E., Buhmann, J.M.: The balanced accuracy and its posterior distribution. In: 2010 20th International Conference on Pattern Recognition, pp. 3121–3124. IEEE (2010)
3. Buratović, I., Miličević, M., Žubrinić, K.: Effects of data anonymization on the data mining results. In: 2012 Proceedings of the 35th International Convention MIPRO, pp. 1619–1623 (2012)
4. Chen, T., Guestrin, C.: Xgboost: A scalable tree boosting system. In: Proceedings of the 22nd ACM International Conference on SIGKDD, pp. 785–794 (2016)
5. Cortes, C., Vapnik, V.: Support-vector networks. Mach. Learn. **20**(3), 273–297 (1995). https://doi.org/10.1007/BF00994018
6. De Bruin, J.: Python Record Linkage Toolkit: A toolkit for record linkage and duplicate detection in Python. Zenodo, December 2019
7. Domingo-Ferrer, J.: A survey of inference control methods for privacy-preserving data mining. In: Aggarwal, C.C., Yu, P.S. (eds.) Privacy-Preserving Data Mining. Advances in Database Systems, vol. 34, pp. 53–80. Springer, Boston (2008). https://doi.org/10.1007/978-0-387-70992-5_3
8. Domingo-Ferrer, J., Sánchez, D., Soria-Comas, J.: Database anonymization: privacy models, data utility, and microaggregation-based inter-model connections. Synth. Lect. Inf. Secur. Priv. Trust **8**(1), 1–136 (2016)
9. Domingo-Ferrer, J., Torra, V.: Distance-based and probabilistic record linkage for re-identification of records with categorical variables, pp. 243–250. Butlletí de lACIA, Associació Catalana dIntelligència Artificial (2002)

10. Dwork, C.: Differential privacy: a survey of results. In: Agrawal, M., Du, D., Duan, Z., Li, A. (eds.) TAMC 2008. LNCS, vol. 4978, pp. 1–19. Springer, Heidelberg (2008). https://doi.org/10.1007/978-3-540-79228-4_1

11. Dwork, C., McSherry, F., Nissim, K., Smith, A.: Calibrating noise to sensitivity in private data analysis. In: Halevi, S., Rabin, T. (eds.) TCC 2006. LNCS, vol. 3876, pp. 265–284. Springer, Heidelberg (2006). https://doi.org/10.1007/11681878_14

12. El Emam, K., Dankar, F.K.: Protecting privacy using k-anonymity. J. Am. Med. Inform. Assoc. **15**(5), 627–637 (2008)

13. Fletcher, S., Islam, M.Z.: Measuring information quality for privacy preserving data mining. Int. J. Comput. Theory Eng. **7**(1), 21 (2015)

14. Ho, T.K.: The random subspace method for constructing decision forests. IEEE Trans. Pattern Anal. Mach. Intell. **20**(8), 832–844 (1998)

15. Holohan, N., Antonatos, S., Braghin, S., Mac Aonghusa, P.: (k, ϵ)-anonymity: k-anonymity with ϵ-differential privacy. arXiv preprint arXiv:1710.01615 (2017)

16. Inan, A., Kantarcioglu, M., Bertino, E.: Using anonymized data for classification. In: 2009 IEEE 25th International Conference on Data Engineering, pp. 429–440. IEEE (2009)

17. Kaggle: NBAplayers stats since 1950 (2018). https://www.kaggle.com/drgilermo/nba-players-stats?select=player_data.csv. Accessed 26 Nov 2020

18. Kent, A., Berry, M.M., Luehrs, F.U., Perry, J.W.: Machine literature searching viii operational criteria for designing information retrieval systems. Am. Documentation **6**(2), 93–101 (1955)

19. Mendes, R., Vilela, J.P.: Privacy-preserving data mining: methods, metrics, and applications. IEEE Access **5**, 10562–10582 (2017)

20. Pedregosa, F., et al.: Scikit-learn: machine learning in python. J. Mach. Learn. Res. **12**, 2825–2830 (2011)

21. Prasser, F., Kohlmayer, F., Lautenschlaeger, R., Kuhn, K.A.: ARX-a comprehensive tool for anonymizing biomedical data. In: AMIA Annual Symposium Proceedings, vol. 2014, p. 984. American Medical Informatics Association (2014)

22. Rijsbergen, C.J.V.: Information Retrieval. Butterworth-Heinemann (1979)

23. Samarati, P., Sweeney, L.: Protecting privacy when disclosing information: k-anonymity and its enforcement through generalization and suppression (1998)

24. Vanichayavisalsakul, P., Piromsopa, K.: An evaluation of anonymized models and ensemble classifiers. In: Proceedings of the 2018 2nd International Conference on Big Data and Internet of Things, pp. 18–22 (2018)

25. Weng, C.G., Poon, J.: A new evaluation measure for imbalanced datasets. In: Proceedings of the 7th Australasian Data Mining Conference, vol. 87, pp. 27–32 (2008)

26. Witten, I.H., Frank, E., Hall, M.A.: Data Mining: Practical Machine Learning Tools and Techniques. Morgan Kaufmann Series in Data Management Systems, 3rd edn. Morgan Kaufmann, Amsterdam (2011)

27. WP29: Opinion 05/2014 on anonymisation techniques (2014). https://www.pdpjournals.com/docs/88197.pdf. Accessed 26 Nov 2020

Efficient Privacy Preserving Distributed K-Means for Non-IID Data

André Brandão[1]($^{\boxtimes}$), Ricardo Mendes[2], and João P. Vilela[1]

[1] CRACS/INESCTEC, CISUC and Department of Computer Science,
Faculty of Sciences, University of Porto, Porto, Portugal
`andrebrandao@ua.pt, jvilela@fc.up.pt`
[2] CISUC, Department of Informatics Engineering, University of Coimbra,
Coimbra, Portugal
`rscmendes@dei.uc.pt`

Abstract. Privacy is becoming a crucial requirement in many machine learning systems. In this paper we introduce an efficient and secure distributed K-Means algorithm, that is robust to non-IID data. The base idea of our proposal consists in each client computing the K-Means algorithm locally, with a variable number of clusters. The server will use the resultant centroids to apply the K-Means algorithm again, discovering the global centroids. To maintain the client's privacy, homomorphic encryption and secure aggregation is used in the process of learning the global centroids. This algorithm is efficient and reduces transmission costs, since only the local centroids are used to find the global centroids. In our experimental evaluation, we demonstrate that our strategy achieves a similar performance to the centralized version even in cases where the data follows an extreme non-IID form.

Keywords: Privacy · Distributed clustering · Federated learning · Homomorphic encryption · Secure aggregation

1 Introduction

Ubiquitous devices allow for ever-growing data collection. This data is useful in machine learning to optimize services and to extract information about the population [17]. For example, sensor data from mobile phones can be used to infer transportation modes [8] or to accurately estimate traffic congestion [23].

One of the techniques to extract information is clustering, where algorithms partition objects into groups in order to find hidden structures in the data [27]. Clustering algorithms belong to the unsupervised learning class, *i.e.*, they can learn from unlabeled data. Labeling datasets is both costly and time consuming [31], therefore clustering plays a crucial role in the machine learning paradigm.

In order to increase the amount and diversity of the data, entities can jointly apply learning algorithms to the combined data. This is also used in the mobile scenario, where each user shares his collected data. Traditionally, in this context, learning is performed in a central trusted server, which receives the data from

© Springer Nature Switzerland AG 2021
P. H. Abreu et al. (Eds.): IDA 2021, LNCS 12695, pp. 439–451, 2021.
https://doi.org/10.1007/978-3-030-74251-5_35

all entities. However, this approach requires data owners to trust the server with their data, thus posing a privacy risk [25]. In order to overcome this issue, distributed privacy preserving mechanisms have been proposed.

Distributed privacy preserving mechanisms can be evaluated in three axis: privacy guarantees, efficiency and robustness to non-IID data. In the context of mobile/crowd-sourcing scenarios, robustness to non-IID data is particularly important, as the clients are the individuals collecting and storing the data. In turn, this data might belong to a single or to a small subset of clusters that may strongly vary between the different clients (non-IID case). This situation can reveal to the clustering server which cluster(s) the client's data belongs to, thus posing a risk to individuals' privacy. For example, in [11] information related to the users' app permission choices were clustered to create privacy profiles, where each user belonged to a single profile. Therefore, in this case, a server would know the privacy preferences of each user.

Existing distributed privacy preserving clustering approaches fall short at either privacy, efficiency and/or robustness to non-IID data. In this paper, we propose a strategy to apply distributed K-Means that, unlike previous work, is efficient, mutually private and robust to non-IID data. To reduce the data that is shared with the server and for robustness against non-IID data, clients compute the K-means locally, with a variable number of clusters, and only the centroids are sent to the server. To preserve privacy, the centroids are encrypted homomorphically, which still allows the server to compute the distance from the local centroids to the global centroids, over encrypted data. The distances are then sent to the clients who, after decryption, assign each local centroid to a global centroid. To update the global centroids in the server, secure aggregation is used, thus keeping the data private. Results show that the proposed strategy achieves a similar performance to the centralized K-means even for non-IID data.

The rest of this paper is organized as follows. Section 2 presents the related work. Section 3 details our proposal and presents the evaluation results, while Sect. 4 concludes this work.

2   Related Work

In this section we revise previous work in clustering and privacy preserving distributed clustering. We identify the advantages and disadvantages of current strategies and compare them according to their efficiency, privacy and robustness to non-IID data.

2.1   K-Means

K-Means [12], is one of the most known and widely used clustering algorithms. The goal of K-Means is to assign each observation to a single cluster minimizing the within-cluster Euclidean distance:

$$C_1^* \ldots C_k^* = \underset{C_1 \ldots C_k}{\operatorname{argmin}} \sum_{k \in K} \sum_{x_i \in C_k} ||x_i - c_k||^2 \tag{1}$$

where K is the set of cluster IDs, C_k is a set of points representing a cluster and c_k is the centroid value, i.e., the mean point for cluster k. The C_i^* are the resulting clusters.

The algorithm works as follows: given a set of k initial centroids $c_1^{(1)}, c_2^{(1)}$, $\ldots, c_k^{(1)}$, the algorithm iteratively executes the following two steps:

Assignment: Assign each observation to the cluster with the nearest mean, with respect to the Euclidean distance.

Update: Compute the new centroids' values:

$$c_i^{(t+1)} = \frac{1}{|C_i^{(t)}|} \sum_{x_p \in C_i^{(t)}} x_p \tag{2}$$

The algorithm repeats these steps until the shift between the new centroids and the previous ones is lower than a specified threshold ϵ, i.e. $||c^{(t+1)} - c^{(t)}|| \leq \epsilon$.

2.2 Privacy Preserving Distributed K-Means

McMahan *et al.* presented in 2017 an efficient strategy to train neural networks from decentralized data [14]. This algorithm, designated by Federated Averaging takes advantage of the local clients' computing power to apply the gradient descent algorithm to the clients' data in their own devices. At each iteration, every client will send the gradient to the server where it is averaged and distributed to every client.

Triebe and Rajagopal joined mini batch K-Means [19] and Federated Averaging to create the **federated K-Means algorithm** [24], where clients share the centroids' position and number of observations per cluster, instead of the gradient. The server applies a weighted average over the centroids' positions based on the cluster size and send back the results to the clients. The main problem with this approach in the context of non-IID data is that averaging points in opposite extremes results in final centroids in the center of the dataset, thus achieving poor performance. Another problem of this strategy is the centroids initialization method. Since we do not have access to the data, we have to randomly select k points from the input space $\mathcal{X}$. However, this method achieves poor performance and may lead to empty clusters [2].

A different approach to privacy preserving clustering is taken by methods that resort to **homomorphic encryption** [10, 26, 28, 30]. This encryption technique allows the clustering to be done over the encrypted data, thus preserving privacy. However, in order for the server to update the global centroids, the clients must send the sum and number of points in each cluster to the server, which can disclose which cluster(s) the clients' data belongs to. Additionally, due to the amount of data that is sent to the server, it allows clients to apply trilateration to find the global centroids [15], thus it is not mutually private. Because all data is encrypted and computations are made over the encrypted data, these approaches are computationally expensive [5].

Another common strategy for private clustering is based on **differential privacy (DP)** [6,13,18,22]. DP consists on adding "statistical noise" that is significant enough to protect client's privacy, but small enough to not affect the model performance. Although this strategy is efficient and robust to non-IID data, it lacks a systematic methodology, due to the challenge of defining the amount of noise, as it highly depends on the dataset [3]. Other problems of differential privacy include the inherent uncertainty in the answer and the fact that the guarantees of immunity to background knowledge attacks are overstated [3]. It has also been shown recently, that DP can increase existing biases and have substantial impacts on the accuracy [4].

An alternative private distributed clustering approach is to select a subset of **local points (representatives)** and apply clustering over them. Soliman *et al.* [21] proposed running the K-Means algorithm locally on each client and using HyperLogLog counters to share the centroids and the approximate number of observations per centroid in a decentralized fashion with the other clients. Then a weighted averaging over all the centroids is done to find the global centroids. Januzaj *et al.* [9] have a similar strategy, where local representatives are extracted on site and then shared with the server, who finally performs a global clustering over the representatives. Both strategies are efficient and robust to non-IID data, but lack privacy. In the first strategy, the clients will know to which cluster(s) the other clients' data belongs to. In the second strategy, partial data, *i.e.* the representatives, is sent to the server.

Finally, two under-looked problems arise in privacy preserving K-Means, when there is no access to the data, which is how to choose the ideal number of clusters and compute the initial centroids. Additionally, because there is no access to the dataset, the typical metrics to evaluate the model cannot be used.

In this paper we present an approach that overcomes the identified issues. Specifically, we propose a K-means algorithm that is efficient, secure and robust to non-IID data. We additionally propose secure inertia, a secure method that allows the estimation of the ideal number of clusters, the creation of the initial centroids and the evaluation of the final model.

3   Efficient Privacy Preserving Distributed K-Means for Non-IID Data

This section details our proposed approach towards an efficient and secure K-Means algorithm that is robust to non-IID data. In Sect. 3.1 we describe our proposed approach and in Sect. 3.2 we present a detailed evaluation of the privacy, efficiency and robustness to non-IID data of our strategy.

3.1   Description

We consider a setup where a set of clients, each possessing its own dataset of N points with two features, aims to cluster their data. In this scenario, we propose a mechanism that allows the clients to cluster their data, alongside the other clients without the server knowing the clients' points. The operation of our proposed mechanism is illustrated via an example in Fig. 1. In the first stage, each client performs Diffie-Hellman Key Exchange so as to agree on a seed with the server. Then, they will compute the sum and number of points in their local dataset. These two statistics will be masked and securely sent to the server using secure aggregation ("Send Masked Statistics" step on Fig. 1). **Secure aggregation** presented by Bonawitz et al. [1] allows the secure sum of vectors using Diffie-Hellman Key Exchange, where the resulting secret will be used as a seed to generate random vectors. These random vectors will be the same for each pair of clients: one of the clients adds the random vector and the other subtracts the vector to their contributions and both send the result to the server. To the server each contribution will be indistinguishable from a random vector. But when the server adds all the contributions, the random vectors cancel out, retaining only the real sum of every client's contribution. Using this strategy the server is able to compute the center point of all clients' datasets. In the example from Fig. 1, $\frac{(28+56,50+58)}{100+200} = (0.28, 0.36)$. To improve the k-Means performance we choose k random points close to the center point as initial centroids. Since the server cannot choose k points from the data (known only to the clients) and choosing random points from the input space would result in a poor performance [2].

While the server is initializing the centroids, the clients will apply the K-Means to their local dataset to generate local clusters. Each client uses the silhouette score to estimate the best number of local clusters as follows. Given the following metrics:

$$a(i) = \frac{\sum_{j \in C_i, i \neq j} d(i,j)}{|C_i| - 1} \qquad b(i) = \min_{k \neq i} \frac{\sum_{j \in C_k} d(i,j)}{|C_k|} \qquad s(i) = \frac{a(i) - b(i)}{max\{a(i), b(i)\}}$$

where C_i is the set of points in cluster i and $d(\cdot)$ is the distance metric. We can interpret $a(i)$ has how well is point i assigned to its cluster and $b(i)$ as the smallest mean dissimilarity of any cluster except C_i. The silhouette score is defined as the mean $s(i)$, over all observations of the local dataset. We compute the silhouette score for $2 \leq k \leq K$, where K is the number of global clusters, defined by the server. Then, the number of clusters for the model with the maximum silhouette score is chosen as the optimal local number of clusters.

The resulting centroids for the local clusters will be sent to the server in a secure way, using homomorphic encryption. **Homomorphic encryption** allows one to perform calculations over encrypted data, in such a way that when the result is decrypted it yields the same result as if the operations were made over unencrypted data. The centroids will be encrypted and sent to the server, that will compute the distances between the encrypted local centroids and the unencrypted global centroids. To calculate the distances between the pairs of points, we will need a schema that is able to subtract scalars from encrypted numbers and multiply an encrypted number by itself. The CKKS schema [20] offers us that possibility. By only providing approximate results, it is more efficient, but still precise enough for machine learning models [20], as we also assess. Even with the encrypted centroids, the server would still be able to known how many clusters each client has. In order to hide this information, each client will always send information about k clusters, by adding random centroids whenever needed. In the example from Fig. 1, the server defined $k = 2$ as the number of clusters and Client B found a single centroid, namely $(0.28, 0.29)$. So, the client is going to send $[c_1 = (0.28, 0.29), c_2 = (0.56, 0.89)]$, where the second centroid is randomly created to deceive the server.

The server computes the squared distance between the encrypted local centroids and every global centroid. The encrypted distances are sent back to the users, who decrypt them and assign each local centroid to a global cluster. Now each client sends to the server the sum and the number of points for each cluster – this information is needed for the server to compute the new centroids (Eq. (2)). In the example from Fig. 1, the resulting statistics are $[((0.28, 0.29), 1), ((0, 0), 0)]$, for client B, where $(0.28, 0.29)$ represents the sum of points in this cluster and 1 the number of points in the cluster. The distances for the random centroid are ignored and both the sum and the number of points are set to zero. Since only the local centroids are sent to the server, this will difficult the trilateration attack, since in order to infer the global centroids from the distances, the client needs to have more points than the number of features [15]. To update the global centroids in the server without revealing the clients' individual statistics, secure aggregation is employed again to send the masked statistics. With these statistics, the server is able to compute the new global centroids' values by dividing the total sum by the total number, just like in Eq. (2). These steps will be

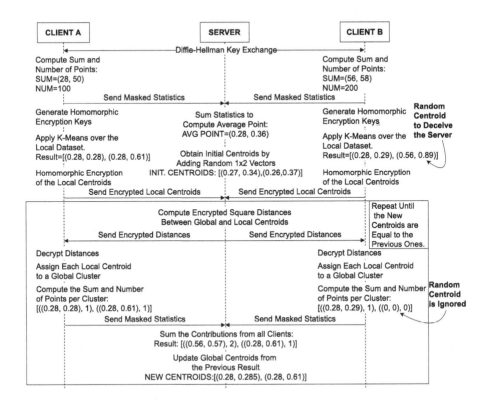

Fig. 1. Sequence diagram (with example) of the proposed algorithm.

repeated until the new centroids are equal to the previous ones or a maximum number of iterations is performed.

3.2   Evaluation

To evaluate this strategy we ran the algorithm through 114 artificial benchmark datasets[1]. To simulate an environment of non-IID data, we created 20 clients, where each has a random number of clusters from 1 to k (depending on the dataset). Every client has a random number of 70 to 90 observations from one cluster and a random number of 1 to 30 observations for each of the remaining clusters, except in the case of only one cluster, with 100 observations from the same cluster. All random numbers are generated from a uniform distribution.

Since we have access to the cluster labels of the benchmark datasets, we used the Adjusted Rand Index (ARI) metric to compare our strategy with the centralized K-Means over the entire dataset [7]. Let K_t be the clustering ground truth and K_p the clustering done by the model. If a is the number of pairs of elements that are in the same set in K_t and K_p and b the number of pairs of elements that are in different sets in K_t and K_p, then

$$\text{RI} = \frac{a+b}{C_2^{n_{\text{samples}}}} \quad (3) \qquad \text{ARI} = \frac{\text{RI} - E[\text{RI}]}{\max(\text{RI}) - E[\text{RI}]} \quad (4)$$

Since the Random Index (RI) in (3) does not guarantee a value close to zero for random label assignments, we resort to the ARI in (4) that counters this effect by subtracting the expected RI. We run the strategy 30 times for each dataset and the one with lowest inertia is chosen. The inertia metric corresponds to the sum of the distances of all points within a cluster to the respective centroid [16]. Each client computes the local inertia and, using secure aggregation, the server obtains the total inertia, without knowing individual contributions. This metric can be used to compare models and allows the server to use the *elbow method* to estimate the best number of clusters in the dataset [29]. We chose the best inertia because our goal is to prove that our strategy can achieve a good performance with few repetitions. Additionally, this procedure replicates a real world scenario where one computes the inertia securely in order to choose the best model. We compared the results of our strategy to the centralized version in terms of efficiency and robustness to non-IID, since the centralized version achieves the best results in these two criteria.

Robustness to Non-IID Data. Figure 2a shows the distribution of the ARI over the 114 datasets of the proposed strategy (orange) versus the centralized K-Means (blue). From this plot, we can see that our strategy and the centralized K-Means have a similar distribution, however our proposal achieves smaller values at the extremes. In fact, our strategy was not able to achieve ARI values above 0.9 in around 10 datasets. However, it also produced fewer ARI values closer to

---

[1] https://github.com/deric/clustering-benchmark.

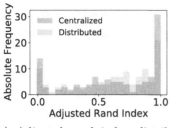
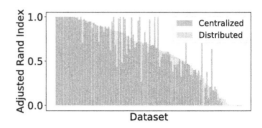

(a) Adjusted rand index distribution.

(b) Adjusted rand index by dataset.

Fig. 2. Adjusted rand index distribution and adjusted rand index by dataset. (Color figure online)

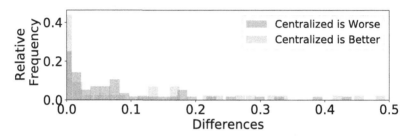

Fig. 3. Adjusted rand index differences.

0 and achieved more ARI values between 0.6 and 0.9. Overall, we can conclude that this strategy is consistent with the centralized version of K-Means.

Figure 2b presents the ARI score for every dataset. The number of datasets for which our approach performed better than the centralized model is 56, worse in 43 and had the same performance in 15 of the 114 datasets. As aforementioned, when the centralized model is better, it is usually better by a larger difference than when the centralized model is worse.

Figure 3 compares the differences between ARI scores when the centralized model is worse than our strategy (blue distribution) and when the centralized model is better than our strategy (orange distribution). We can observe, as previously discussed, that the two distributions are similar. More than 50% of the times, when the centralized model is better, the ARI differences are lower than 0.1 and the same happens when the centralized model is worse. However, we see a more uniform distribution in the interval between 0 and 0.1 when the centralized model is worse, as to when the centralized model is better, where approximately 45% of the times the difference is practically 0.

From Figs. 2 and 3 we conclude that the proposed strategy achieves a similar performance to the centralized K-Means. Specifically, it achieves a better ARI score in more datasets than the centralized version, but the majority of the differences are lower than 0.1. Therefore, our strategy, while decentralized, is robust against non-IID data.

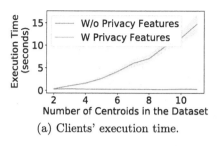
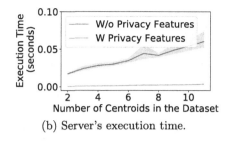

(a) Clients' execution time.   (b) Server's execution time.

Fig. 4. Execution time versus the number of centroids on the clients and server side (95% confidence intervals are shaded). The case with privacy features corresponds to our proposed method.

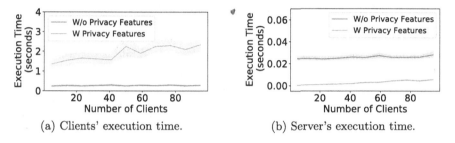

(a) Clients' execution time.   (b) Server's execution time.

Fig. 5. Execution time versus the number of clients on the clients and server side (95% confidence intervals are shaded). The case with privacy features corresponds to our proposed method.

Efficiency. In order to understand the efficiency of our final strategy we compared it to the strategy without privacy features, *i.e.* without secure aggregation and homomorphic encryption. To measure the efficiency, we measured the execution time, without taking into account the network delay, in three dimensions: number of points, number of clusters and number of clients. For each dimension we measured the time spent by the clients and by the server. To facilitate the efficiency evaluation, we assume the server to know how many clusters there are in the dataset. Since the steps executed by the clients are done in parallel, the reported clients' execution time corresponds to the time of the *slowest* client. We trained the model 30 times and in the following figures is presented the mean values and the 95% confidence interval.

In Fig. 4 we present the execution time according to the number of centroids in the dataset. We can observe that for the strategy with privacy features, most of the work is done by the clients (see Fig. 4a). This is expected, since the clients perform local clustering followed by the encryption of the centroids. The server execution time shown in Fig. 4b is much higher without privacy features than with privacy. This result is expected since without privacy features the server needs to apply the full clustering algorithm as opposed to only computing the distances and updating the global centroids. Nevertheless, for the server side, both strategies have a rather low server execution time – below 0.1 s. Thus, the predominant execution time is the clients' time.

In Fig. 5 we present the execution time according to the number of clients. The strategy with privacy takes more time to execute in the client side and slowly increases with the number of clients. Specifically, its execution times are 1 to 2 seconds higher than the strategy without privacy features. This latter strategy has a higher server execution time, but the difference is low, below 0.025, and thus the total execution time is mostly affected by the clients' execution time.

We additionally measured the execution time as a function of the number of points in the dataset. Our results indicate that on both strategies, the execution time is not affected by the number of points in the dataset (between 100 and 50000). On the clients' execution time, the strategy with privacy features takes around 1 s more than the strategy without privacy features. On the server side, this latter strategy takes around 0.025 s more than the strategy with privacy features. We omit these plots due to the lack of space.

Overall, we consider the algorithm to be efficient. While it takes more time than the strategy without privacy features it is only significant when the datasets have many centroids. In this case, our strategy will take longer to execute.

To conclude, our proposal is robust to non-IID data while preserving the privacy of individual contributions, as the server only accesses the encrypted local centroids. Additionally, it is efficient at the expense of a slightly higher execution time, yet within reasonable bounds when compared to the centralized version. In particular, letting n_{pts}, n_{col}, n_{cent} and n_{cli} respectively represent the number of points, coordinates per point, centroids and clients, our method achieves a complexity of $O(n_{cent}^2 \times (n_{pts} \times n_{col} + n_{col}^2 + 1) + n_{pts} \times n_{col})$ for each client and $O(n_{cli} \times n_{cent}(n_{cent} + n_{col}))^2$ for the server. When compared to the strategy without privacy features, with a complexity of $O(n_{pts} \times n_{cent} \times n_{col})$ for each client and $O(n_{cli} \times n_{cent}(n_{cent} \times n_{col}))$ for the server, this confirms that the cost of our scheme lies in the increase of the client execution time, with the server execution time becoming even lower than for the base strategy without privacy.

4   Conclusion

In this paper, we propose a privacy preserving clustering algorithm that is private, efficient and robust to non-IID. As far as we known, there is no method that can fully fulfill the three. Our strategy based on local representatives, homomorphic encryption and secure aggregation is capable of outperforming or matching the centralized version in more than half of the datasets in terms of Adjusted Random Index in a non-IID scenario. In terms of efficiency, the time complexity moves from the server to the clients, yet leading to an overall time complexity within reasonable bounds when compared to the centralized version. Moreover, given the lack of secure metrics to evaluate models in a distributed environment,

---

[2] We assume a constant time complexity for multiplication between the encrypted centroids and the plaintext global centroids, according to [20].

we introduced *secure inertia*, a method to compute the inertia of the model without sharing individual contributions. Our experiments show that our strategy can effectively be made practical in real world settings.

Acknowledgements. The work presented in this paper was carried out in the scope of project COP-MODE, that has received funding from the European Union's Horizon 2020 research and innovation programme under the NGI_TRUST grant agreement no 825618, and the project AIDA: Adaptive, Intelligent and Distributed Assurance Platform (`POCI-01-0247-FEDER-045907`), co-financed by the European Regional Development Fund through the COMPETE2020 program and by the Portuguese Foundation for Science and Technology (FCT) under the CMU Portugal Program. Ricardo Mendes wishes to acknowledge the Portuguese funding institution FCT - Foundation for Science and Technology for supporting his research under the Ph.D. grant SFRH/BD/128599/2017.

References

1. Bonawitz, K., et al.: Practical secure aggregation for privacy-preserving machine learning. In: Proceedings of the 2017 ACM SIGSAC Conference on Computer and Communications Security, pp. 1175–1191 (2017)
2. Celebi, M.E., Kingravi, H.A., Vela, P.A.: A comparative study of efficient initialization methods for the k-means clustering algorithm. Expert Syst. Appl. **40**(1), 200–210 (2013)
3. Clifton, C., Tassa, T.: On syntactic anonymity and differential privacy. In: 2013 IEEE 29th International Conference on Data Engineering Workshops (ICDEW), pp. 88–93. IEEE (2013)
4. Farrand, T., Mireshghallah, F., Singh, S., Trask, A.: Neither private nor fair: impact of data imbalance on utility and fairness in differential privacy. In: Proceedings of the 2020 Workshop on Privacy-Preserving Machine Learning in Practice, pp. 15–19 (2020)
5. Graepel, T., Lauter, K., Naehrig, M.: ML confidential: machine learning on encrypted data. In: Kwon, T., Lee, M.-K., Kwon, D. (eds.) ICISC 2012. LNCS, vol. 7839, pp. 1–21. Springer, Heidelberg (2013). https://doi.org/10.1007/978-3-642-37682-5_1
6. Hu, X., et al.: Privacy-preserving K-means clustering upon negative databases. In: Cheng, L., Leung, A.C.S., Ozawa, S. (eds.) ICONIP 2018. LNCS, vol. 11304, pp. 191–204. Springer, Cham (2018). https://doi.org/10.1007/978-3-030-04212-7_17
7. Hubert, L., Arabie, P.: Comparing partitions. J. Classif. **2**(1), 193–218 (1985)
8. Jahangiri, A., Rakha, H.A.: Applying machine learning techniques to transportation mode recognition using mobile phone sensor data. IEEE Trans. Intell. Transp. Syst. **16**(5), 2406–2417 (2015)
9. Januzaj, E., Kriegel, H.P., Pfeifle, M.: Towards effective and efficient distributed clustering. In: Workshop on Clustering Large Data Sets (ICDM2003), Vol. 60 (2003)
10. Jiang, Z.L., et al.: Efficient two-party privacy-preserving collaborative k-means clustering protocol supporting both storage and computation outsourcing. Inf. Sci. **518**, 168–180 (2020)
11. Liu, B., et al.: Follow my recommendations: a personalized privacy assistant for mobile app permissions. In: Twelfth Symposium on Usable Privacy and Security (SOUPS 2016), pp. 27–41 (2016)

12. Lloyd, S.: Least squares quantization in PCM. IEEE Trans. Inf. Theory **28**(2), 129–137 (1982)
13. Lu, Z., Shen, H.: A convergent differentially private k-means clustering algorithm. In: Yang, Q., Zhou, Z.-H., Gong, Z., Zhang, M.-L., Huang, S.-J. (eds.) PAKDD 2019. LNCS (LNAI), vol. 11439, pp. 612–624. Springer, Cham (2019). https://doi.org/10.1007/978-3-030-16148-4_47
14. McMahan, B., Moore, E., Ramage, D., Hampson, S., Arcas, B.A.: Communication-efficient learning of deep networks from decentralized data. In: International Conference on Artificial Intelligence and Statistics. Proceedings of Machine Learning Research, vol. 54, pp. 1273–1282. PMLR (2017)
15. Navidi, W., Murphy Jr., W.S., Hereman, W.: Statistical methods in surveying by trilateration. Comput. Stat. Data Anal. **27**(2), 209–227 (1998)
16. Palacio-Niño, J., Berzal, F.: Evaluation metrics for unsupervised learning algorithms. arXiv preprint arXiv:1905.05667 (2019)
17. Sarker, I.H., Hoque, M.M., Uddin, M.K., Alsanoosy, T.: Mobile data science and intelligent apps: concepts, AI-based modeling and research directions. Mob. Netw. Appl. 1–19 (2020). https://doi.org/10.1007/s11036-020-01650-z
18. Schellekens, V., Chatalic, A., Houssiau, F., De Montjoye, Y.A., Jacques, L., Gribonval, R.: Differentially private compressive k-means. In: ICASSP 2019–2019 IEEE International Conference on Acoustics, Speech and Signal Processing (ICASSP), pp. 7933–7937. IEEE (2019)
19. Sculley, D.: Web-scale k-means clustering. In: Proceedings of the 19th International Conference on World Wide Web. p. 1177–1178. WWW 2010, Association for Computing Machinery (2010)
20. Microsoft SEAL (release 3.5), Microsoft Research, Redmond, WA (2020)
21. Soliman, A., Girdzijauskas, S., Bouguelia, M.-R., Pashami, S., Nowaczyk, S.: Decentralized and adaptive K-means clustering for non-IID data using hyper-LogLog counters. In: Lauw, H.W., Wong, R.C.-W., Ntoulas, A., Lim, E.-P., Ng, S.-K., Pan, S.J. (eds.) PAKDD 2020. LNCS (LNAI), vol. 12084, pp. 343–355. Springer, Cham (2020). https://doi.org/10.1007/978-3-030-47426-3_27
22. Su, D., Cao, J., Li, N., Bertino, E., Jin, H.: Differentially private k-means clustering. In: Proceedings of the Sixth ACM Conference on Data and Application Security and Privacy, pp. 26–37. ACM (2016)
23. Thiagarajan, A., et al.: Vtrack: accurate, energy-aware road traffic delay estimation using mobile phones. In: Proceedings of the 7th ACM Conference on Embedded Networked Sensor Systems, SenSys 2009, pp. 85–98. Association for Computing Machinery (2009)
24. Triebe, O.J., Rajagopal, R.: Federated K-Means: clustering algorithm and proof of concept (2020)
25. Vaidya, J., Clifton, C.: Privacy-preserving k-means clustering over vertically partitioned data. In: Proceedings of the Ninth ACM SIGKDD International Conference on Knowledge Discovery and Data Mining, pp. 206–215. KDD 2003 (2003)
26. Xing, K., Hu, C., Yu, J., Cheng, X., Zhang, F.: Mutual privacy preserving k-means clustering in social participatory sensing. IEEE Trans. Ind. Inform. **13**(4), 2066–2076 (2017)
27. Xu, R., Wunsch, D.: Survey of clustering algorithms. IEEE Trans. Neural Netw. **16**(3), 645–678 (2005)
28. Yin, H., Zhang, J., Xiong, Y., Huang, X., Deng, T.: PPK-means: achieving privacy-preserving clustering over encrypted multi-dimensional cloud data. Electronics **7**(11), 310 (2018)

29. Yuan, C., Yang, H.: Research on k-value selection method of k-means clustering algorithm. J. Multi. Sci. J. **2**(2), 226–235 (2019)
30. Yuan, J., Tian, Y.: Practical privacy-preserving mapreduce based k-means clustering over large-scale dataset. IEEE Trans. Cloud Comput. **7**(2), 568–579 (2019)
31. Zhang, W., Li, C., Peng, G., Chen, Y., Zhang, Z.: A deep convolutional neural network with new training methods for bearing fault diagnosis under noisy environment and different working load. Mech. Syst. Signal Process. **100**, 439–453 (2018)

Author Index

Printed in the United States
by Baker & Taylor Publisher Services